SECOND EDITION

Effective Teaching Methods

Gary D. Borich
The University of Texas at Austin

Merrill, an imprint of
Macmillan Publishing Company
New York

Maxwell Macmillan Canada
Toronto

Maxwell Macmillan International
New York   Oxford   Singapore   Sydney

Cover photo: George Mattei/Envision
Editor: Linda James Scharp
Developmental Editor: Linda Kauffman Peterson
Production Editor: Jan Mauer
Art Coordinator: Ruth A. Kimpel
Photo Editor: Gail L. Meese
Cover Designer: Robert Vega
Production Buyer: Patricia A. Tonneman
Electronic Publishing Supervisor: Jo Griffith

This book was set in Garamond by Carlisle Communications, Ltd. and was printed and bound by Arcata Graphics/Halliday. The cover was printed by New England Book Components.

Macmillan Publishing Company
866 Third Avenue
New York, NY 10022

Macmillan Publishing Company is part of the Maxwell Communication Group of Companies.

Maxwell Macmillan Canada, Inc.
1200 Eglington Avenue East, Suite 200
Don Mills, Ontario M3C 3N1

Library of Congress Cataloging-in-Publication Data

Borich, Gary D.
    Effective teaching methods / Gary D. Borich.
        p. cm.
    Includes bibliographical references (p.) and indexes.
    ISBN 0-675-22171-4 : $33.95
    1. Teaching.   2. Lesson planning—United States.   I. Title.
LB1025.3.B67   1992
371.1'02—dc20
                                                                91-9500
                                                                CIP

Printing: 3   4   5   6   7   8   9   Year: 3   4   5

Photo credits (all photographs are copyrighted by individuals or companies listed): 18, 69, 107, 202, 285, 300, 313, 322, 429, Andy Brunk/Macmillan; 35, 343, Cleo Freelance Photo; 447, Steve Coffey; 139, 190, Jean Greenwald/Macmillan; 117, Shirley Haley; 56, Jo Hall; 161, Larry Hamill/Macmillan; 44, Bruce Johnson/Macmillan; 262, 443, Lloyd Lemmerman/Macmillan; 24, 127, 179, Macmillan; 293, Frank May; 11, 77, 156, 367, 469, 495, Gail Meese/Macmillan; 330, David Napravnik; 355, 391, 398, 409, David Napravnik/Macmillan; 379, Harvey Phillips; 426, 486, Michael Siluk; 1, 60, 88, 211, 227, 239, 249, 271, 420, 477, Gail Zucker.

On a poster commemorating the late teacher-astronaut Christa McAuliffe appear these words: "I am the future. I teach." This book is about her future, written for those who will take her place.

Although the legacy of a teacher in space could hardly be imagined only a short time ago, it became a reality—if only for a brief moment. Less dramatic but no less startling are the many changes occurring daily in our classrooms and in the practice of teaching. Today's classroom is a far cry from that of only ten years ago, and this meteoric rate of change is unlikely to soon subside.

Microcomputers, competency testing (for students *and* teachers), curriculum reform, new state and federal laws, multicultural classrooms, and new teacher certification and degree requirements are but a few of the factors changing the face of American schools and creating special challenges for you, the beginning teacher. This book has been written to help you prepare to meet these challenges and to discover the opportunities for professional growth and advancement they provide.

To accomplish this, this second edition of *Effective Teaching Methods* has four simple goals. The first is to present effective teaching practices derived from a recent 25-year period of classroom research. In this research, different teaching practices were systematically studied for their effectiveness on learners. The results have made it possible to replace many age-old anecdotal suggestions for "good" teaching with modern, research-based teaching practices that are empirically related to positive outcomes in learners. How to use these teaching practices to become an effective teacher is a major focus of this book.

Second, this text describes these effective teaching practices in a friendly, conversational manner. The language of classrooms is informal, and there is no reason why a book about teachers in classrooms should not use the same language. Therefore, this book talks straight, avoiding complicated phrases, rambling discussions, or pseudoscholarly language. The idea behind each chapter is to get the point across quickly in a friendly and readable style.

The third goal of this book is practicality. Positive prescriptions for your classroom behavior show how you can engage students in the learning process, manage your classroom, and increase student achievement. This book not only tells *what* to do to obtain these results; it also shows *how* to obtain them, illustrating effective teaching practices with concrete examples and entertaining classroom dialogues.

The final goal of this book is to be realistic. Some of the literature on teaching is speculative. However, this book describes what real teachers do in real classrooms and which teaching practices are and are not effective in those classrooms. Nothing in this book is pie-in-the-sky theorizing about effective teaching because most of what is presented results directly from years of research and observation of effective teaching practices in real classrooms.

These, then, are this book's four goals: to provide *research-based* effective teaching practices, presented in a *conversational style*, that are *practical* and *realistic*. Some special features of this book include:

- ☐ Beginning and ending chapters on who an effective teacher is (Chapter 1) and what an effective teacher does in the classroom (Chapter 15).
- ☐ A chapter on understanding the important role of individual differences and cultural diversity—prior achievement, intelligence, self-concept, anxiety, disadvantageness, peer group, home and family life—on student learning needs and classroom achievement (Chapter 2).
- ☐ Two chapters on classroom management, which cover motivation, anticipatory management, and classroom order and discipline (Chapters 11 and 12).
- ☐ Two chapters on teaching strategies that explain how to use direct instructional methods (such as lecture, drill, and practice, and recitation—Chapter 6) and indirect instructional methods (such as group discussion, collaboration, and discovery and problem-solving activities—Chapter 7).
- ☐ A new chapter on self-directed learning and how to use metacognitive techniques, teacher mediation, and the social dialogue of the classroom to help learners control, regulate, and take responsibility for their own learning (Chapter 9).
- ☐ A new chapter on cooperative learning and the collaborative process for productively organizing and managing group and team activities that promote communication skills, self-esteem, and problem-solving and inquiry (Chapter 10).
- ☐ A new chapter on evaluation of student achievement for measuring and interpreting student progress, using teacher-made and standardized tests (Chapter 14).
- ☐ A chapter on teaching methods to use with special types of learners in the regular classroom—slow, gifted, bilingual, and handicapped—who cannot benefit from learning activities and materials that have been designed for the majority (Chapter 13).

Also provided, specifically with you, the student, in mind:

- ☐ End-of-chapter summaries that restate key concepts in an easy-to-follow outline format.
- ☐ End-of-chapter questions for discussion and practice, and keyed answers in Appendix B.

□ Annotated suggested readings at the end of each chapter that highlight or expand major concepts within the chapter.

□ An observation instrument for learning how to "see" effective teaching practices in the classroom, illustrated with example dialogues in Appendix C.

□ A self-report survey instrument for measuring concerns about yourself, the teaching task, and your impact on students (Chapter 3 and Appendix A).

□ A new procedure for organizing unit and lesson plans that lets your students graphically visualize the relationship between lessons and unit (Chapter 5).

Users of the first edition of this book will notice three new chapters that cover self-directed learning, cooperative learning, and classroom measurement and testing. Throughout each of these new chapters, and interspersed through the others, are extensive examples and classroom dialogues that illustrate how each new teaching technique is implemented and embedded within the context of a unit or lesson.

Since publication of the first edition, the author has produced a companion volume, *Observation Skills for Effective Teaching* (Borich, 1990 — also from Macmillan Publishing Co.) to accompany this new edition, either in a preteaching observation experience or as a resource to the present volume.* *Observation Skills for Effective Teaching* provides extensive examples, entertaining and instructional classroom dialogues, and practical observation and recording instruments keyed to and coordinated with the effective teaching methods presented in this text. Together, these texts provide an orderly sequence of learning, as illustrated in the figure on page vi.

Many individuals contributed to the preparation of this book. Not the least are the many professionals whose studies of classroom life have contributed to the effective teacher described in this text. The work of these professionals has made possible an integration and synthesis of effective teaching practices representing a variety of data sources and methodological perspectives. Although I accept responsibility for translations of research into practice that I have made, strengths the reader may see in this approach must be shared with the many individuals who made them possible.

I also wish to acknowledge those teachers who over the years have shared their insights about the teaching process with me. Among these have been teachers in the Austin, Texas Independent School District, especially William B. Travis High School, who provided the opportunity to observe many of the effective teaching methods described herein. For their helpful reviews of the manuscript, I extend gratitude to Linda Curry, Texas A & M University; Carolyn M. Evertson, Vanderbilt; Joseph J. Galbo, California State University–Stanislaus; Shirley McFaul, Lewis University; Deborah L. Norland, University of Minnesota, Morris; Marleen C. Pugach, University of Wisconsin–Milwaukee; Phillip S. Riner, University of Nevada–Las Vegas; Linda Tamura, Pacific University; David A. Wiley, University of Scranton.

---

*An inservice mentoring program for beginning teachers (Borich & Nance, 1990) that incorporates the effective teaching methods and observation skills in both volumes is available from Professional Teachers' Library, 1009 Harwood Pl., Austin, Texas 78704.

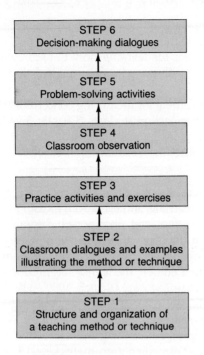

STEP 6
Decision-making dialogues

STEP 5
Problem-solving activities

STEP 4
Classroom observation

STEP 3
Practice activities and exercises

STEP 2
Classroom dialogues and examples
illustrating the method or technique

STEP 1
Structure and organization of
a teaching method or technique

Also, I would like to thank Gerhard Klinzing at the Center for New Learning Methods, University of Tuebingen, West Germany, for his many insights and source documents used in the preparation of this volume, and Lorraine Sheffield for help in preparing the manuscript for publication.

GDB
Austin, Texas

CONTENTS

3
Instructional Goals and Plans 69

4
Instructional Objectives 107

5
Unit and Lesson Planning   139

6
Direct Instruction Strategies   179

12
Classroom Order and Discipline

13
Teaching Special Learners in the Regular Classroom

14
Evaluating Student Achievement

15
Effective Teaching in the Classroom   477

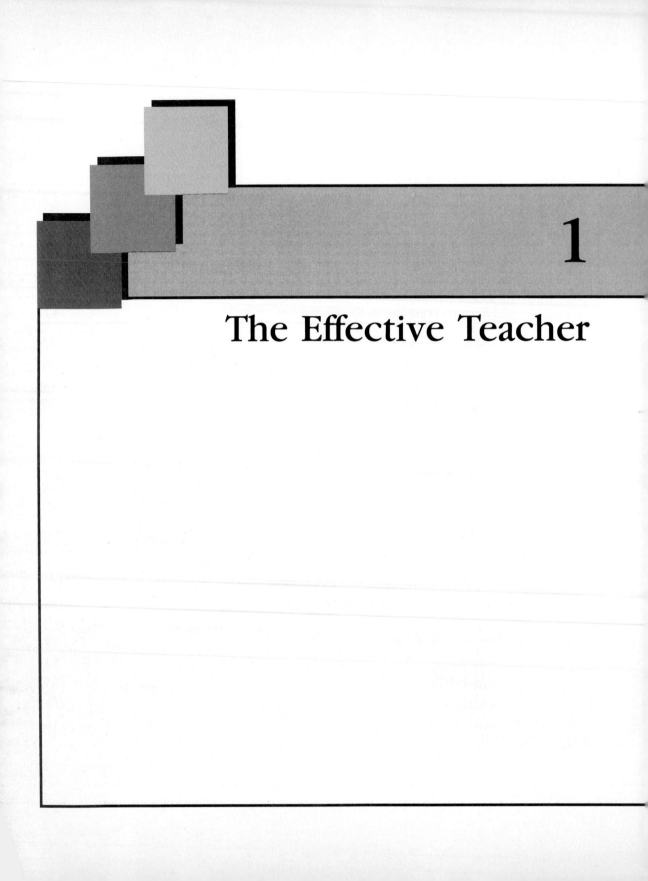

1

The Effective Teacher

What is an effective teacher? How do I become one? How long does it take? These questions have been asked by every teacher, young or old. They are deceptively simple questions, for they have many different answers. Teaching is a complex and difficult task that demands extraordinary abilities. Despite decades of experience and research, one of the most difficult tasks in education today is defining an effective teacher.

This chapter offers no pat definitions of an "effective teacher." Instead, the goal is to introduce you to *practices used by effective teachers*—practices related to positive outcomes in learners. These effective teaching practices do not tell the whole story of what an effective teacher is, but they do form an important foundation to help you understand the chapters that lie ahead and to help you become an effective teacher. Subsequent chapters blend these practices with other activities, such as writing of objectives, lesson planning, teaching strategies, questioning, and classroom management. This will give you a rich and comprehensive picture of an effective teacher and, most importantly, help you become one.

WHAT IS AN EFFECTIVE TEACHER?

The Role-Model Definition

If you had grown up a century ago, you would have been able to answer "What is an effective teacher?" very simply: A good teacher was a good person—a role model who met the community ideal for a good citizen, good parent, and good employee. At that time, teachers were judged primarily on their goodness as people and only secondarily on their behavior in the classroom. They were expected to be honest, hardworking, generous, friendly, and considerate, and to demonstrate these qualities in their classrooms by being authoritative, organized, disciplined, insightful, and dedicated. Practically speaking, this meant that to be effective, all a beginning teacher needed was King Solomon's wisdom, Sigmund Freud's insight, Albert Einstein's knowledge, and Florence Nightingale's dedication!

It soon became evident that this definition of an ideal teacher lacked clear, objective standards of performance that could be consistently applied to all teachers and that could be used to train future teachers.

The Psychological Characteristics Definition

The early role-model approach soon gave way to another, which attempted to identify the **psychological characteristics** of a good teacher: personality characteristics (e.g., achievement-motivation, directness, and flexibility), attitude (motivation to teach, empathy toward children, and commitment), experience (years of teaching, experience in subject taught, and experience with a particular grade level), and aptitude/achievement (scores on ability tests, college grade-point average, and student teaching evaluations).

TABLE 1.1

Commonly studied teacher characteristics

Personality	*Attitude*	*Experience*	*Aptitude/Achievement*
Permissiveness	Motivation to teach	Years of teaching	National Teachers Exam
Dogmatism	Attitude toward children	experience	Graduate Record Exam
Authoritarianism	Attitude toward teaching	Experience in subject	Scholastic Aptitude Test
Achievement-motivation	Attitude toward	taught	1. verbal
Introversion-	authority	Experience in grade	2. quantitative
extroversion	Vocational interest	level taught	Special ability tests,
Abstractness-	Attitude toward self	Workshops attended	(e.g., reasoning
concreteness	(self-concept)	Graduate courses taken	ability, logical ability,
Directness-indirectness	Attitude toward subject	Degrees held	verbal fluency)
Locus of control	taught	Professional papers	Grade-point average
Anxiety		written	1. overall
1. general			2. in major subject
2. teaching			Professional
			recommendations
			Student evaluations of
			teaching effectiveness
			Student teaching
			evaluations

Table 1.1 lists some of these psychological characteristics. Because they have a certain intuitive appeal it is worth noting why they have *not* been useful criteria for defining good teachers.

Personality. Over the years, only a few personality measures have been developed that relate specifically to teaching. Because most personality measures have been designed to record deviant or abnormal behavior in clinical settings, much of what they measure has been of little help in identifying the positive or "normal" behaviors that may be needed to be an effective teacher.

Consequently, the usefulness of many personality tests in predicting a teacher's classroom behavior must be inferred from their more general success in the mental health field. Although certain interpersonal, emotional, and coping behaviors are believed to be required for effective teaching (Levis, 1987), personality tests (especially clinical ones) have provided few insights into the positive social behavior that may be needed for effective teaching.

Attitude. Attitude assessments may be either global (e.g., attitude toward the educational system and the teaching profession) or specific (e.g., attitude toward a particular task, child, or curriculum). In either case, most attempts to measure teacher attitude generally have failed to forecast what a teacher having a particular attitude *actually does in the classroom*. Research generally has shown a low and nonsignificant correspondence between teacher attitude and classroom performance (Walberg, 1986; Jackson, 1968).

Therefore, the use of attitude data for measuring teacher effectiveness has had to rest on the *assumption* that attitudes (such as positive feelings about teaching) are related to other desirable behaviors that are one or more steps removed from the actual teaching process (such as more organized lesson plans or better subject-matter preparation) (Clark & Peterson, 1986). However, defining effective teaching in this manner always will be less direct and credible than observing the actual classroom practices that good teaching is supposed to represent.

Experience.   A listing of a teacher's work experience, such as that requested on a standard job application form, often defines the individual's experience too broadly to be useful in predicting success in a specific classroom setting. Such descriptions typically do not describe experience relevant to performing day-to-day tasks required in a specific classroom, grade level, or subject area.

A teacher's experience with a specific type of curriculum or learner may be more relevant to performance than nonspecific data, such as years of experience, graduate credits earned, or hours of in-service training (Barnes, 1987). The correspondence of such general data to actual classroom performance has been low and nonsignificant because the data by themselves represent only a small piece of a teacher's experience relevant to a particular teaching assignment.

Aptitude and Achievement.   Like experience variables, most aptitude and achievement data do not accurately predict classroom performance. This may surprise you, given our society's emphasis on achievement and intelligence. However, regardless of how these measures are used to predict student performance, the teacher's prior achievement rarely has correlated strongly with classroom performance.

As an example of prior achievement, consider a teacher's college grades. Achieving good grades might indicate a positive attitude and promise good classroom performance. But a relatively narrow spread of scores in course grades and college GPAs typically characterizes the achievement of teachers. Standards set by training institutions usually require teachers to meet some minimum level of achievement. This is usually sufficient to make the small variations in grades among beginning teachers irrelevant to actual performance in the classroom.

To summarize, using psychological characteristics to define a good teacher represented an attempt to measure teacher behavior objectively. But these characteristics often were too remote from the teacher's day-to-day work in the classroom to meaningfully contribute to a definition of a good teacher. Most notably, these definitions excluded the most important and obvious measure of all for determining good teaching: *the performance of the students who are being taught.*

A New Direction

In the last two decades a revolution has occurred in the definitions of good teaching. We have seen that defining good teachers by community ideals proved unrealistic on the job and in the preparation of teachers. We also have seen how teachers' psychological characteristics proved to be poorly related to what teachers actually did in the classroom. This directed researchers to study the impact that specific teacher behaviors had on the specific cognitive and affective behaviors of their students. The term *good teaching* changed to *effective teaching,* and the research focus shifted from studying teachers to studying their effects on students.

These changes have affected the profession of teaching so dramatically that their effects now are felt in the reform of teacher training curricula, in the competency testing of teachers, in the education of teacher trainers, and in textbooks (like this one) on teaching methods. Perhaps most responsible for this change are the new *ways* in which classroom researchers have come to study the nature of teaching. These new ways of studying classroom behavior have made the student and teacher-student interaction the focus of modern definitions of effective teaching.

Linking Teacher Behavior with Student Performance. During the 1970s and 1980s, researchers developed new methods for studying the interactive patterns of teachers and students. The goal was to discover which teacher behaviors promote desirable student performance, such as good grades on classroom tests, higher standardized test scores, better attitudes toward school, and improved problem-solving and thinking skills. But before unveiling the findings of this research and their implications for effective teaching, let's see how the research was performed.

The Research Process. To collect data on the classroom interaction of teachers and students, researchers often used instruments like those shown in Figures 1.1a, 1.1b, and 1.2. These particular instruments, devised by Good and Brophy (1987) for their research on effective teaching in elementary school classrooms, record observations of various student-teacher behaviors. Using the response form in Figure 1.1b, the observer codes both student responses to questions and the teacher's reaction and feedback. For example, in the tenth interchange recorded on this form, a male student fails to answer a question (0), is criticized by the teacher for not answering (− −), and then is given the answer by the teacher (Gives Ans.). Numbers for the interchanges are assigned as they occur, allowing the pattern of question-answer-feedback to be recorded over an entire class period.

In Figure 1.2 the observer codes the student performance behavior being praised by the teacher (perseverance, progress, success, good thinking, etc.). Individual students are identified by assigning each a unique number. This form records not only the praise behavior of the teacher *in relation to* individual student behavior, but also the overall pattern or sequence of action. For example, student "8" is praised three times in a row for "perseverance or effort."

With instruments such as these, a rich and varied picture of classroom activity can be captured over the course of a research study. Obviously, a single observation of a single class would produce too little data to reveal a consistent behavior pattern. However, multiple observation periods extending across different teachers, schools, or school districts can reveal consistent patterns of teacher-student interactions. These patterns of classroom behavior then can be related to student behaviors, such as

FIGURE 1.1a

Coding categories for question-answer-feedback sequences (Good & Brophy, 1987)

Student Sex		
Symbol	Label	Definition
M	Male	The student answering the question is male.
F	Female	The student answering the question is female.
Student Response		
+	Right	The teacher accepts the student's response as correct or satisfactory.
±	Part right	The teacher considers the student's response to be only partially correct or to be correct but incomplete.
−	Wrong	The teacher considers the student's response to be incorrect.
0	No answer	The student makes no response or says he doesn't know (code student's answer here if teacher gives a feedback reaction before he is able to respond).
Teacher Feedback Reaction		
+ +	Praise	Teacher praises student either in words ("fine," "good," "wonderful," "good thinking") or by expressing verbal affirmation in a notably warm, joyous, or excited manner.
+	Affirm	Teacher simply affirms that the student's response is correct (nods, repeats answer, says "Yes," "OK," etc.).
0	No reaction	Teacher makes no response whatever to student's response—he or she simply goes on to something else.
−	Negate	Teacher simply indicates that the student's response is incorrect (shakes head, says "No," "That's not right," "Hm-mm," etc.).
− −	Criticize	Teacher criticizes student, either in words ("You should know better than that," "That doesn't make any sense—you better pay close attention," etc.) or by expressing verbal negation in a frustrated, angry, or disgusted manner.
Gives Ans.	Teacher gives answer	Teacher provides the correct answer for the student.
Ask Other	Teacher asks another student	Teacher redirects the question, asking a different student to try to answer it.
Other Calls	Another student calls out answer	Another student calls out the correct answer, and the teacher acknowledges that it is correct.
Repeat	Repeats question	Teacher repeats the original question, either in its entirety or with a prompt ("Well?" "Do you know?" "What's the answer?").
Clue	Rephrase or clue	Teacher makes original question easier for student to answer by rephrasing it or by giving a clue.
New Ques.	New question	Teacher asks a new question (i.e., a question that calls for a different answer than the original question called for).

FIGURE 1.1b

Coding response form (Good & Brophy, 1987)

Student Sex			Student Response										Teacher Feedback Reaction					
NO.	M	F	+	±	-	0		++	+	0	-	--	Gives Ans.	Ask Other	Other Calls	Repeat	Clue	New Ques.
1		✓	✓															
2	✓		✓			✓			✓									
3	✓			✓														
4	✓		✓					✓	✓									
5	✓	✓	✓														✓	
6	✓		✓		✓			✓				✓						✓
7			✓							✓								
8	✓		✓					✓										
9	✓		✓							✓								
10	✓						✓					✓	✓					
11																		
12																		
13																		
14																		
15																		
-																		
-																		
-																		
-																		

FIGURE 1.2

Coding form for measuring individual praise (Good & Brophy, 1987)

USE: *Whenever the teacher praises an individual student*

PURPOSE: *To see what behaviors the teacher reinforces through praise, and to see how the teacher's praise is distributed among the students*

Behavior Categories	Student Number	Codes
1. Perseverance or effort; worked long or hard	14	1. 3
2. Progress (relative to the past) toward achievement	23	2. 3,4
3. Success (right answer, high score) achievement	6	3. 3
4. Good thinking, good suggestion, good guess, or nice try	18	4. 3
5. Imagination, creativity, originality	8	5. 1
6. Neatness, careful work	8	6. 1
7. Good or compliant behavior, follows rules, pays attention	8	7. 1
8. Thoughtfulness, courtesy, offering to share; prosocial behavior		8.
9. Other (specify)		9.
		10.
NOTES:		11.
		12.
		13.
All answers occurred during social studies discussion.		14.
		15.
Was particularly concerned about #8, a low-achieving male.		16.
		17.
		18.
		19.
		20.
		21.
		22.
		23.
		24.
		25.

performance on end-of-year standardized achievement tests, specially prepared classroom tests, and attitude scales, to determine the effects of teacher-student interaction on student performance.

It was in this manner that patterns of effective classroom teaching began to emerge in studies conducted by different researchers. As in all research, some studies provided contradictory results or found no relationships among certain types of classroom interactions and student outcomes. But many studies found patterns of interaction that consistently produced desirable student outcomes in the form of higher test scores, increased problem-solving skills, improved learning skills, and so on. From these patterns have come our modern definitions of the effective teacher.

Now that you know how the research was conducted, let's look at the teaching behaviors that researchers generally agree contribute to effective teaching, regardless of context. Afterward, we will modify these behaviors and add to them to describe effective teaching at various levels of schooling, in different content areas, and with different student populations.

FIVE KEY BEHAVIORS CONTRIBUTING TO EFFECTIVE TEACHING

Approximately 10 teacher behaviors show promising relationships to desirable student performance, primarily as measured by achievement on classroom and standardized tests. Five of these behaviors have been consistently supported by research studies over the past two decades (Rosenshine, 1971b, 1983; Dunkin & Biddle, 1974; Walberg, 1986; Brophy & Good, 1986; Brophy, 1989). Another five have had some support and appear logically related to effective teaching. The first five we will call **key behaviors**, because they are considered essential for effective teaching. The second five we will call **helping behaviors** that can be used in combinations to implement the key behaviors. The five key behaviors, referred to throughout this text, are:

1. Lesson clarity
2. Instructional variety
3. Task orientation
4. Engagement in the learning process
5. Student success

Lesson Clarity

This key behavior refers to how clear and interpretable a presentation is to the class. Assume for the moment that you are the teacher and ask yourself: Are your points understandable? Are you able to explain concepts clearly so your students are able to follow in a logical step-by-step order? Is your oral delivery to the class clear, audible, intelligible, and free of distracting mannerisms?

One result from research on teacher clarity is that teachers vary considerably on this behavior. Not all teachers are able to communicate clearly and directly to their students without wandering, speaking above students' levels of comprehension, or using speech patterns that impair the clarity of what is being presented. Some indications of a lack of clarity (Land & Smith, 1979; Smith & Land, 1981) are:

- The extent to which a teacher uses vague, ambiguous, or indefinite language ("might probably be," "tends to suggest," "could possibly happen").
- The extent to which a teacher uses overly complicated sentences ("There are many important reasons for the start of World War II but some are more important than others, so let's start with those that are thought to be important but really aren't").
- The extent to which a teacher gives directions that often result in student requests for clarification.

If you teach with a high degree of clarity, you will spend less time going over material. Your questions will be answered correctly the first time, allowing more time for instruction. Clarity is a complex behavior because it is related to many other so-called cognitive behaviors, such as your organization of the content, lesson familiarity, and delivery strategies (whether you use a discussion, recitation, question-and-answer, or small-group format). Nevertheless, research shows that both the *cognitive* clarity and *oral* clarity of presentations vary substantially among teachers. This in turn produces differences in student performance on cognitive tests of achievement (Marx & Walsh, 1988).

Methods will be presented to help you bring clarity to your lessons throughout this text, especially in Chapters 6, 7, and 8.

Instructional Variety

This key behavior refers to the variability or flexibility of delivery during the presentation of a lesson. For example, it includes the planned mixing of different classroom behaviors, such as those measured by the classroom observation instruments shown earlier. Research indicates increased student achievement from the use of variety in instructional materials and techniques, the frequency and variety of reinforcements used, and the types of feedback given to students (Rohrkemper & Corno, 1988; Brophy & Good, 1986; Brophy & Evertson, 1976).

One of the most popular and effective ways of creating variety during instruction is to ask questions. As you will see in Chapter 8, many different types of questions can be asked, and when integrated into the pacing and sequencing of a lesson, they create meaningful variation (Palincsar & Brown, 1989; Gall, 1984). Therefore, the effective teacher needs to know the art of asking questions and how to discriminate among different question formats—fact questions, process questions, convergent questions, divergent questions. (Question types are introduced in Chapter 8 and expanded upon in Chapter 9.)

Another aspect of variety in teaching is perhaps the most obvious: the use of learning materials, equipment, displays, and space in your classroom. The physical texture and visual variety of your classroom can actually encourage student involvement with lesson content. The display of reading materials, use of audio and visual devices, demonstration materials, and the organization of reference materials and learning resources can all contribute to instructional variety. This, in turn, influences student achievement on end-of-unit tests and student engagement in the learning process. For example, some studies found the amount of disruptive behavior to be less in classrooms that had more varied activities and materials (Evertson, Emmer, Sanford, Clements, & Worsham, 1989). Other studies have shown variety to be related to student attention (Lysakowski & Walberg, 1981).

Some ways to incorporate variety into your teaching will be presented in Chapter 6 (direct instruction), Chapter 7 (indirect instruction), and Chapter 10 (cooperative learning and the collaborative process).

Task Orientation

This key behavior refers to how much classroom time the teacher devotes to the task of teaching an academic subject. The more time dedicated to the task of teaching a

The proper use of space and the display of learning materials in the classroom creates a visual texture and variety that encourages students to become involved with lesson content.

specific topic, the greater the opportunity students have to learn. Some task-related questions a teacher must answer are: (1) How much time do I spend lecturing, asking questions, and encouraging students to inquire or think independently? (2) How much time do I spend organizing for teaching and getting my students ready to learn?

These aspects often manifest themselves in the teacher's concern that all material gets presented, learned, and tested, as opposed to a preoccupation with procedural matters or an effort to make all learning "fun." Obviously, all teachers need to prepare their students to learn and want them to enjoy learning. However, most researchers agree that achievement has been higher in classrooms with teachers who spent the majority of their time teaching subject-specific content as opposed to teaching about the process and materials that may be needed to acquire the content. It follows that classrooms in which teacher-student interactions focus more on intellectual content than on process issues (such as how to use materials or classroom rules and procedures) are more likely to have higher rates of achievement (Rosenshine, 1983; Evertson & Emmer, 1982).

Also, teachers who are task-oriented are highly conversant with topics that are likely to appear on departmental tests and end-of-year achievement tests. This is not to say that these teachers "teach to the test." Rather, their classroom instruction parallels the instructional goals and curriculum that guide the construction of tests of student progress.

Task-oriented teachers are goal-oriented. They know what instructional goals they want to achieve in a period of time. They organize instruction around the goals, and stick steadfastly to them even in the midst of student misbehavior, clerical duties, or routine administrative tasks (Emmer, Evertson, Sanford, Clements, & Worsham, 1989). Perhaps most important, a task-oriented teacher has high but realistic expectations of student performance (Evertson, Emmer, Sanford, Clements, & Worsham, 1989). The systematic organization of class content and the use of this organization in the form of well-prepared lesson plans and teaching strategies all are important ingredients of task orientation.

These topics are presented in Chapters 4 and 5, which prepare you to write lesson and unit plans, and in Chapters 6 and 7, which show you how to execute them in your classroom.

Engagement in the Learning Process

This key behavior refers to the amount of learning time devoted to an academic subject. This is one of the most recently researched teacher behaviors related to student achievement. It is related to a teacher's task orientation and to content coverage. A teacher's task orientation should give students the greatest possible opportunity to learn the material to be tested.

For example, notice in Table 1.2 the spectacular results achieved in second-grade reading when the teacher's **task orientation**—or time teaching an academic subject—was increased over a five-week period. Increasing the time devoted to this instructional objective from 4 minutes to 52 minutes a day, over an average of only 25 school days, yielded an increase of 27 percentile points (from 39 to 66) on a standardized achievement test. The researchers who recorded these data indicated that,

TABLE 1.2

Learning time and student achievement: Example from second-grade reading

Reading Score at First Testing (October)		Student Engaged Time in Reading with High Success Rate		Estimated Reading Score, Second Testing (December)	
Raw Score (out of 100)	Percentile	Total Time Over 5 Weeks (Minutes)	Average Daily Time (Minutes)	Raw Score (out of 100)	Percentile
36	50	100	4	37	39
36	50	573	23	43	50
36	50	1300	52	52	66

Note: An average of twenty-five school days occurred between the first and the second testing.

Source: From Charles W. Fisher et al., *Teaching and Learning in the Elementary School: A Summary of the Beginning Teacher Evaluation Study.* Beginning Teacher Evaluation Study Report VII–I. (San Francisco, Calif.: Far West Laboratory for Research and Development, 1978)

although such large increases in instructional time might appear unusual, they actually were achieved by teachers in these elementary school classrooms.

Distinctly different from the amount of instructional time you devote to a topic is the time your students will be *actually engaged* in learning the material. This has been called the engagement rate or the on-task behavior of *students*.

Engagement rate is the percentage of time devoted to learning when the student is actually on-task, engaged with the instructional materials and benefiting from the activities being presented. Even though a teacher may be task-oriented and may provide maximum content coverage, the students may be **disengaged**. This means that they are not actively thinking about, working with, or using what is being presented (Marx & Walsh, 1988; Fisher et al., 1980).

Such disengagement can involve an emotional or mental detachment from the lesson that may or may not be obvious. When students jump out of their seats, talk, read a magazine, or leave for the rest room, they obviously are not engaged in instruction, however clear and thorough the teacher's presentation. Students also can be disengaged in far more subtle ways, such as looking attentive while their thoughts are many miles away. An unpleasant fact of life is that a quarter of a class may be "tuned out" at any one time. Correcting this type of disengagement may be much more difficult, requiring changes in the structure of the task itself and the cognitive demands placed on the learner (Bennett & Desforges, 1988; Doyle, 1983). Strategies for composing tasks and activities that elicit the active participation of your learners are presented in Chapters 6, 7, 8, and 9.

Several research studies have contributed useful data for increasing learning time and, more important, student engagement. From these data, Crawford and others (1978) identified behaviors having potential for increasing learning time, resulting in increased on-task behavior. These behaviors (recently updated by Emmer, Evertson, Sanford, Clements, and Worsham, 1989) have provided these suggestions for teachers to promote student engagement:

1. Set rules that let pupils attend to their personal and procedural needs without obtaining your permission each time.
2. Move around the room to monitor pupils' seatwork and to communicate your awareness of student progress.
3. Ensure that independent assignments are interesting, worthwhile, and easy enough to be completed by each pupil without your direction.
4. Minimize time-consuming activities such as giving directions and organizing the class for instruction by writing the daily schedule on the board. This will ensure that pupils know where to go and what to do.
5. Make abundant use of textbooks, workbooks, and paper-and-pencil activities that are at, or slightly above, a student's current level of functioning.
6. Avoid "timing errors." Act to prevent misbehaviors from occurring or increasing in severity so they do not influence others in the class.

These teaching practices have been extended and updated for small groups and independent seatwork by Anderson, Evertson, & Brophy (1982) and Anderson, Stevens, Prawat, & Nickerson (1988). These and other more specific ways of increasing the engagement rates of students will be explored in Chapters 6, 7, 8, and 9.

Success Rate

This key behavior refers to the rate at which students understand and correctly complete exercises.

A crucial aspect of the research on task orientation and student engagement has been the level of difficulty of the material presented. In these studies, level of difficulty was measured by the rate at which students understood and correctly completed exercises. Three levels of difficulty are:

high success, in which the student understands the task and makes only occasional careless errors,

moderate success, in which the student has partial understanding but makes some substantive errors, or

low success, in which the student does not understand the task at all.

Findings indicate that task orientation and student engagement are closely related to level of difficulty, as measured by success rate. Consistently, instruction that produces a moderate-to-high success rate results in increased achievement, because more content is covered at the learner's current level of understanding. This is especially true for expository or didactic forms of instruction (Fisher et al., 1980). Other research shows that instruction that promotes low error rates (high success) can contribute to increased levels of student self-esteem and to positive attitudes toward the subject matter and the school (Bennett, Desforges, Cockburn, & Wilkinson, 1981).

The average student in a typical classroom spends about half of the time working on tasks that provide the opportunity for high success. But researchers have found that students who spend *more than the average* time in high-success activities—especially during expository or didactic instruction—have higher achievement scores, better retention, and more positive attitudes toward school (Wyne & Stuck, 1982; Brophy & Evertson, 1976).

These findings have led to at least one suggestion that students spend 60–70% of their time on tasks that allow moderate-to-high levels of success. This means spending 60–70% of their time on tasks that allow almost complete understanding with only occasional careless errors the first time through the material, when the material represents content that can be learned most easily through practice and repetition delivered in a direct instruction format. (Rosenshine, 1983; Brophy & Evertson, 1976). (The many forms of direct instruction that can promote moderate-to-high success rates in your classroom will be presented in Chapter 6.)

Moderate-to-high success rates will produce mastery of the lesson content. But they also can provide the foundation for your students to apply learned knowledge in some practical way, such as thinking critically and independently. This has been the unique contribution of strategies for self-directed learning and learning to learn. These strategies encourage learners to derive their own understandings and meanings from lesson content. They also encourage learners to reason, problem solve, and think critically about the content they are learning. By varying the complexity and variety of the tasks provided, such strategies provide opportunities for individual patterns of thinking to emerge through various forms of classroom discussion and dialogue (Duffy & Roehler, 1989; Rohrkemper & Corno, 1988).

Many teachers devote insufficient time to this stage of learning, which is particularly crucial for attaining the goals of problem solving and critical thinking. A key behavior for the effective teacher is organizing and planning instruction that yields moderate-to-high success rates, but then challenges the learner to go beyond the information given. You will discover ways to use moderate-to-high success rates to attain the goals of problem solving and critical thinking in Chapters 7 and 9.

SUMMARY OF KEY BEHAVIORS

The five key behaviors—lesson clarity, instructional variety, task orientation, student engagement, and success rate—are essential for effective teaching. Without the knowledge and skill to present lessons that are clear, that incorporate variety, that are task-oriented, and that actually engage students in the learning process at moderate-to-high rates of success, no teacher can be truly effective in producing desirable patterns of student achievement and attitude. The following chapters present the tools and techniques you will need to use these five key behaviors effectively in your classroom.

Classroom researchers undoubtedly will discover other effective teaching behaviors, and attain a more thorough understanding of those already described. However, for the first time, research has provided a basis for better definitions of effective teaching and for training teachers. As classroom research continues, additions to and modifications of these five key behaviors undoubtedly will be discovered. But today, these five stand as a practical starting point for defining the effective teacher. They are the skeleton on which the remainder of this text will construct the heart, mind, and body of the effective teacher.

You learned earlier that there can be no simple answer to the question, "What is an effective teacher?" As suggested, many behaviors must be orchestrated into *patterns of behavior* for your teaching to be effective. You can see this both in the overlapping relationships among the five key behaviors and the many other behaviors that may be needed to successfully carry out any one or combination of the key behaviors. Identification of only five behaviors is risky because it makes teaching appear deceptively simple. However, as the following sections show, your pattern of teaching behavior must involve much more.

SOME HELPING BEHAVIORS RELATED TO EFFECTIVE TEACHING

To fill out our picture of an effective teacher, more than five general keys to effective teaching are needed. You also need behaviors to help you implement the five key behaviors in your classroom. Let's consider some additional behaviors that can be thought of as catalytic, or helping, behaviors for performing the five key behaviors.

Research findings for helping behaviors, although promising, are not as strong and consistent as those that identified the five key behaviors. There is general agreement on the importance of these helping behaviors, but the research has not been so accommodating as to identify explicitly how these behaviors should be used. Nor has it linked these behaviors to student achievement as strongly as the key five. This is why we suspect that helping behaviors need to be employed *in the context of other behaviors* to be effective, making them catalysts rather than agents unto themselves.

These catalytic behaviors include:

1. Using student ideas and contributions
2. Structuring
3. Questioning
4. Probing
5. Teacher affect

Use of Student Ideas and Contributions

This behavior includes acknowledging, modifying, applying, comparing, and summarizing student responses to promote the goals of a lesson and to encourage student participation. Note how any one of these activities (suggested by Flanders, 1970), could be used in achieving one or more of the five key behaviors:

Acknowledging: using the student's idea by repeating the nouns and logical connectives expressed by him or her (to increase lesson clarity).

Modifying: using the student's idea by rephrasing it or conceptualizing it in your words or another student's words (to create instructional variety).

Applying: using the student's idea to teach an inference or take the next step in a logical analysis of a problem (to increase success rate).

Comparing: taking a student's idea and drawing a relationship between it and ideas expressed earlier by the student (to encourage engagement in the learning process).

Summarizing: using what was said by an individual student or a group of students as a recapitulation or review of concepts taught (to enhance task orientation).

More recently, the use of student ideas and contributions has been extended to reasoning, problem solving, and independent thinking. This has been achieved through teacher-guided dialogue that helps learners restructure what is being learned using their own ideas, experiences, and thought patterns. Teacher-guided dialogue asks the learner not just to respond to textual material, but to internalize its meaning by elaborating, extending, and commenting upon it using the learner's own unique thoughts. In this manner, learners are encouraged to elaborate and communicate the processes by which they are learning, thereby creating their own meanings and understandings of the content.

Use of student ideas and contributions has not demonstrated a strong relationship to student achievement, but it has been observed to significantly increase a student's engagement in the learning process. Thus, it has become a frequently used catalyst for helping achieve that key behavior (Emmer, Evertson, Sanford, Clements, & Worsham, 1989). Consider this brief instructional dialogue that uses student ideas to promote engagement:

TEACHER: Tom, what is the formula for the Pythagorean theorem?
TOM:　　$c^2 = a^2 + b^2$.

At this point the teacher simply could have said "Good!" and gone on to the next question. Instead, this teacher continues:

TEACHER: Let's show that on the board. Here is a triangle; now let's do exactly as Tom said. He said that squaring the altitude, which is *a,* and adding it to the square of the base, which is *b,* should give us the square of the hypotenuse, which is *c.* Carl, would you like to come up and show us how you would find the length of *c,* using the formula Tom just gave us?

CARL: Well, if *a* were equal to 3 and *b* equal to 4, the way I would solve this problem would be to add the squares of both of them together and then find the square root—that would be *c.*

TEACHER: So, we square the 3, square the 4, add them together, and take the square root. This gives us 5, the length of the hypotenuse.

Which of the five ways of using student ideas are in this dialogue? First, by putting Tom's response graphically on the blackboard, this teacher *applied* Tom's answer by taking it to the next step, constructing a proof. Second, by repeating orally what Tom said, the teacher *acknowledged* to the entire class the value of Tom's contribution. And third, by having someone come up to prove the correctness of Tom's response, a *summary* of the concept was provided. All this was accomplished from Tom's simple (and only) utterance, "$c^2 = a^2 + b^2$."

Although the use of student ideas looks simple, it takes skill and planning. Even when your response is unplanned, you must be prepared to seize opportunities to incorporate student ideas into the lesson. In later chapters you'll see how using student ideas can be a catalyst in other ways to performing each of the key teaching behaviors.

Research reveals that student ideas and contributions, especially when used in natural classroom dialogue, are more strongly and consistently related to student engagement than simply approving a student's answer with "Good!" (Brophy, 1981). The standard phrases we use to acknowledge and reward students ("correct," "good," "right") are so overused that they may not convey the reward intended and often fail to contribute to the goals of your instruction.

In our example, the teacher not only *elicited* student ideas but *extended* them to convey lesson content in an alternate or expanded form. This was accomplished when the teacher asked Carl to demonstrate Tom's response for the class. In this

Student ideas and contributions elicited during the naturally occurring dialogue of the classroom add content to a lesson and reinforce previous learning. However, some expressions of the approval of student ideas and contributions, such as "correct," "good," or "right," have become so overused they may no longer convey the reward intended.

manner a student response was used to increase the clarity and variety of the lesson, as well as to promote student engagement. Do you think Tom was pleased by what happened?

We will look at other ways of incorporating student ideas and contributions into your lessons in Chapters 7, 8, and 9.

Structuring

Teacher comments made for the purpose of organizing what is to come, or summarizing what has gone before, are called structuring. Structuring is valuable both before and after an instructional activity. Used prior to an instructional activity or question, structuring is an advance organizer for the students; it aids their understanding and retention of material. Used at the conclusion of an instructional activity or question, structuring reinforces learned content and places it in proper relation to other content. Both forms of structuring are related to student achievement and are useful catalysts for performing the key behaviors (Doenau, 1987; Gage, 1976).

Typically, "before" and "after" structuring takes the following form:

TEACHER (at beginning of lesson): OK, now that we have studied the political and economic climate immediately prior to both World War I and World War II, we will begin to study the political and economic factors that were present during both periods. Most important, however, we will study those political and economic factors that may precede *any* international or world crisis. First, let's see what these two turbulent times had in common.

TEACHER (at end of lesson): So, we have discovered that economic hardship and a feeling of political unrest and insecurity accompanied the periods immediately preceding World War I and World War II. We might conclude from this that conflicts between nations, such as war, sometimes occur when gains in economic improvements and/or territorial security appear from the vantage of at least one nation to outweigh the human and material costs involved in war. Can you think of a very recent time when either of these factors played a role in the behavior of nations?

This sequence illustrates some of the many ways that you can use structuring. One is to signal that a shift in direction or content is about to occur. A clear signal alerts students to the impending change. Without such a signal, students may confuse new content with old, missing the differences. Signals such as, "Now that we have studied the political and economic climate immediately prior to both World War I and World War II, we will begin to study . . ." help students switch gears and provide a perspective that makes new content more meaningful.

Another type of structuring uses emphasis. Can you find a point of emphasis in the previous dialogue? By using the phrase "most important," this teacher alerts students to the knowledge and understanding expected at the conclusion of this activity. This provides students with an *advance organizer* for what is to follow.

In this instance, the students are clued to consider the political and economic factors of war that extend *beyond* the two wars discussed in the lesson. This makes the teacher's final question more meaningful ("Can you think of a very recent time when either of these factors played a role in the behavior of nations?"), because the students have been clued that such a question might be raised and that generalizations beyond the concepts discussed will be expected. Phrases such as "Now this is important," "We will return to this point later," and "Remember this" are called *verbal markers*. They emphasize your most important points.

In addition to verbal markers and advance organizers, the effective teacher organizes a lesson into an activity structure. An *activity structure* is a set of related tasks that differ in cognitive complexity and that to some degree may be placed under the control of the learner. Activity structures (Marx & Walsh, 1988) can be built in many ways (e.g., cooperatively, competitively, independently) to vary the demands they make upon the learner and to give tempo and momentum to a lesson. For the effective teacher, they are an important means for engaging students in the learning process and moving them from simple recall of facts to the higher response levels that require reasoning, critical thinking, and problem-solving behavior (Bennett &

Desforges, 1988; Doyle, 1983). This important means of structuring is expanded in Chapters 8 and 9.

Questioning

Questioning is another important helping behavior. Few other topics have been researched as much as the teacher's use of questions (Gall, 1984; Redfield & Rousseau, 1981; Winne, 1979). One of the most important outcomes of research on questioning has been the distinction between *content* questions and *process* questions, which we'll look at next.

Content Questions. Teachers pose content questions to have the student deal directly with the content taught. An example is when a teacher asks a question to see if students can recall and understand specific material. The correct answer is known well in advance by the teacher. It also has been conveyed directly in class, in the text, or both. Few, if any, interpretations or alternative meanings of the question are possible.

Researchers have used various terms to describe content questions, such as:

Direct: question requires no interpretation or alternative meanings.

Lower-order: question requires the recall only of readily available facts, as opposed to generalizations and inferences.

Convergent: different data sources lead to the same answer.

Closed: question has no possible alternative answers or interpretations.

Fact: question requires the recall only of discrete pieces of well-accepted knowledge.

Here are examples of content-oriented questions:

☐ What was the mechanical breakthrough that gave the cotton gin superiority over all previous machines of its type?
☐ Identify the chemical composition of the atmosphere on the moon.
☐ Define the function of a CPU in a microcomputer.
☐ What are the requirements for entrance to our state university?
☐ Divide the number 47 by the number 6 and then subtract 5.

Research indicates that content-oriented questions are related to student achievement (Armento, 1977). This is not surprising, because some estimates show that up to 80% of the questions asked by teachers refer directly to specific content and have readily discernable, unambiguous "right" answers (Gall, 1984; Brophy & Good, 1974). Perhaps even more important is the well-known fact that approximately the same percentage of test items (and behavioral objectives) are written at the level of recall, knowledge, or fact (Melton, 1978; Davis & Tinsley, 1967). Therefore, test items, behavioral objectives, and most instruction seem to emphasize readily known facts as they are presented in lesson plans, workbooks, and texts.

Chapter 8 has more to say about content questions and the many other types of questions that can increase the variety and behavioral complexity of your lesson plans.

Process Questions.   Not all questions are content questions. There are different purposes for which questions can be asked, with the intent of encouraging different mental processes. To problem solve, to guide, to arouse (e.g., curiosity), to encourage (e.g., creativity), to analyze, to synthesize, and to judge also are relevant and practical goals of instruction that should be reflected in your questioning strategies. For these goals, content is not an end itself, but a means of achieving what some have called "higher order" goals.

Researchers have used various terms to describe process questions, such as:

Indirect: question has various possible interpretations and alternative meanings.

Higher-order: question requires more complex mental processes than simple recall of facts (e.g., making generalizations and inferences).

Divergent: different data sources will lead to different correct answers.

Open: a single correct answer is not expected or even possible.

Concept: question requires the processes of abstraction, generalization, and inference.

Here are examples of process-oriented questions:

□ What were the effects of the invention of the cotton gin on cultural values in the South?
□ From what we know today about the atmosphere on the moon, what type of dwelling would you need to sustain life for one year?
□ Analyze the effect of recent advances in computer technology on the financial life of the family.
□ If you were guaranteed a high-paying job for life *or* a free college education, which would you choose? Explain why.
□ Using examples of your own choosing, compare division with subtraction in ways that illustrate their similar functions.

The relationship between the teacher's use of higher-order (process) questions and student achievement is not as strong as that for lower-order (content) questions (Redfield & Rousseau, 1981). However, with higher-order questions, positive changes in the *thinking patterns* and *problem-solving strategies* of students frequently occur (Martin, 1979). Because the mental processes of analyzing, synthesizing, and decision making are among those most needed in adult life, the occurrence of these processes as a result of higher-order questioning strategies may justify their use, despite the fact that strong relationships have not been found between process questions and student achievement.

Chapter 8 has more on higher-order and lower-order questions.

Probing

Probing refers to teacher statements that encourage students to elaborate upon an answer, either their own or another student's. Probing may take the form of a general question or can include other expressions that *elicit* clarification of an answer, *solicit* additional information about a response, or *redirect* a student's response in a more fruitful direction. Probing often is used to shift a discussion to some higher thought level.

Generally, student achievement is greatest when the eliciting, soliciting, and (if necessary) redirecting occur in cycles. This systematically leads the discussion to a higher level of complexity, as when interrelationships, generalizations, and problem solutions are being sought (Zahorik, 1987; Gage, 1976). In this manner, you may begin a lesson with a simple fact question; then, by eliciting clarification of student responses, soliciting new information, or redirecting an answer, you can move to a higher level involving generalizations, abstractions, and the drawing of inferences.

A typical cycle might occur in the following manner:

TEACHER:	Bobby, what is a scientific experiment?
BOBBY:	Well, it's when you test something.
TEACHER:	But, what do you test?
BOBBY:	Mmm. Something you believe in and want to find out if it's really true.
TEACHER:	What do you mean by that?
MARY:	He means you make a prediction.
TEACHER:	What's another word for "prediction"?
TOM:	Hypothesis. You make a hypothesis, then go into the laboratory to see if it comes true.
TEACHER:	OK. So a scientist makes a prediction or hypothesis and follows up with an experiment to see if it can be made to come true. Then what?
BILLY:	That's the end!
TEACHER:	(No comment for 10 seconds; then...) Is the laboratory like the real world?
DAVID:	The scientist tries to make it like the real world, but it's much smaller, like the greenhouse pictured in our book.
TEACHER:	So what must the scientist do with the findings from the experiment, if they are to be useful? (No one answers, so the teacher continues...) If something important happens in my experiment, wouldn't I argue that what happened could also happen in the real world?
BOBBY:	You mean if it's true in a specific situation it will also be true in a more general situation?
BETTY JO:	That's making a generalization.
TEACHER:	Good. So we see that a scientific investigation usually ends with a generalization. Let's summarize. What three things does a scientific investigation require?
CLASS:	A prediction, an experiment, and a generalization.
TEACHER:	Good work, class.

Can you find the teacher's soliciting, eliciting, and redirecting behaviors in this dialogue? In Chapter 8 you will fully explore dialogues such as this and learn how to produce them, but a few examples should make clear the concept of probing. Notice that all of the ingredients in this teacher's lesson were provided by the class. The concepts of hypothesis, experiment, and generalization were never defined for the class. The students defined these concepts for themselves with only an occasional "OK" or "Good" to let them know they were on track. The teacher's role was limited to eliciting clarification ("What do you mean by that?"), soliciting additional information ("What's another word for it?"), and redirection ("Is the laboratory like the real world?").

The purpose of this cycle of eliciting, soliciting, and redirection presumably was to promote inquiry, or independent discovery of the content of the lesson. Generally, *retention* of material learned has been greater from inquiry teaching than from formal lecturing methods. However, consistent differences in short-term achievement gains have not always occurred (Ryan, 1973).

Teacher Affect

Anyone who has ever been in a classroom where the instructor's presentation was lifeless, static, and without vocal variety can appreciate the common-sense value of affective behavior. However, unlike the behaviors discussed previously, affect cannot be captured in transcripts of teaching behavior or by classroom interaction instruments. Consequently, narrowly focused research instruments often miss a teacher's affective behavior, which may be apparent from a more holistic view of the classroom.

What the instruments miss, the students see clearly. Students are good perceivers of the emotions underlying a teacher's actions, and they often respond accordingly. A teacher who is excited about the subject being taught and shows it by facial expression, voice inflection, gesture, and general movement is more likely to hold the attention of students than one who does not exhibit these behaviors. This is true whether or not teachers consciously perceive these behaviors in themselves.

Students take their cues from such behavioral signs and lower or heighten their engagement with the lesson accordingly. A presentation that is drab and static and that lacks praise, nonverbal approval, and a warm, nurturing, encouraging attitude is a sure formula for putting students to sleep mentally, if not physically. The very presence of this behavior on the part of the teacher is a message to the students that comparable behavior on their part is acceptable.

Enthusiasm is an important aspect of a teacher's affect. Enthusiasm is the teacher's vigor, power, involvement, excitement, and interest during a classroom presentation. We all know that enthusiasm is contagious, but how is it so? Enthusiasm is conveyed to students in many ways, the most common being vocal inflection, gesture, eye contact, and animation. A teacher's enthusiasm is related to student achievement (Bettencourt, Gillett, Gall, & Hull, 1983; Rosenshine, 1970a). It also is believed to be important in promoting student engagement in the learning process.

Obviously, no one can maintain a heightened state of enthusiasm for very long without becoming exhausted emotionally. Nor is this what is meant by enthusiasm. A proper level of enthusiasm is far more subtle, and perhaps that is why it has been so difficult to research. A proper level of enthusiasm involves a delicate balance of vocal inflection, gesturing, eye contact, and movement. It employs each of these behaviors in only moderate ways. *In combination,* these behaviors send to students a unified signal of vigor, involvement, and interest. It is the use of these behaviors in moderation and at the right times that conveys the desired message.

Enthusiasm is an important aspect of a teacher's affect. It is related to student achievement and is believed to be important in promoting student engagement in the learning process. Teachers convey enthusiasm to students in many ways, the most common being vocal inflections, gestures, eye contact, and animation.

Timing and the ability to incorporate these behaviors into a consistent pattern make possible an unspoken behavioral dialogue with students that is every bit as important as your spoken words. Letting students know that you are ready to help them by your warm and encouraging attitude is essential if your enthusiasm is to be taken as an honest and sincere expression of your true feelings.

THE NEED FOR MULTIPLE DEFINITIONS

You may have noticed this book's use of the plural when discussing *definitions* of effective teaching. There can be no *single* definition of the effective teacher because there is no *simple* definition. There must be multiple definitions because effective teaching varies with the age of the student population (elementary, junior high, or secondary), the subject matter (reading vs. math), and even the background characteristics of the students (high vs. low socioeconomic status). These factors produce multiple definitions of effective teaching, each of which applies to a particular teaching context, thereby defining effective teaching more accurately.

Herein lies one of the major problems with earlier attempts to define effective teaching by describing ideal types or by describing a teacher's personality, attitude, experience, achievement, and aptitude. These attempts failed to consider (or even acknowledge) that *different* teaching contexts require *different* teaching behaviors. The complexity and difficulty of learning to teach arises from the complexity of the varied decision-making contexts in which teaching must occur. Thus, any single definition of effective teaching would be simplistic and inaccurate because of its insensitivity to the different learners, curricula, grade levels, and instructional materials with which teaching and learning must take place.

Now let's turn to the importance of certain behaviors in several different teaching contexts.

EFFECTIVENESS INDICATOR DIFFERENCES ACROSS SES AND CONTENT

In addition to the teaching behaviors that have elicited achievement across a wide variety of students and content, researchers have uncovered other behaviors of special importance to certain types of students and content. Two subareas of findings having the most consistent results are the teaching of low- and high-socioeconomic status (SES) students and the teaching of reading and mathematics.

Teaching Low-SES and High-SES Students

The phrase *socioeconomic status* can mean many different things, but generally it is an approximate index of one's income and education level. For the classroom researcher, the SES of a student is determined directly by the income and education of his or her parents, or indirectly by the nature of the school the student attends.

Some schools are in impoverished areas where the income and education level of the community are low, whereas other schools are located in more affluent communities. Many schools in impoverished areas qualify for special financial assistance from the federal government, based upon the median income of their students' parents. Researchers consider these "Chapter I" schools to be those where the majority of students come from low-SES homes, are disadvantaged, and/or are "at risk" of dropping out of school.

Because low-SES and high-SES students are facts of life that are likely to exist for some time, classroom researchers have determined what teacher behaviors promote the most achievement in these two types of students. Brophy and Evertson (1976), using a sample of elementary school classrooms, were among the first to provide suggestions for teaching these two types of students. Many of their suggestions have been confirmed by subsequent research and practice (Hill, 1989). A few of the most important teaching behaviors for these two groups are summarized in Table 1.3.

Notice in Table 1.3 that teacher affect seems to be particularly important in low-SES classrooms. Also, notice that some of these teaching behaviors received little or no mention in our preceding discussions, because those discussions applied generally to students representing the full range of SES. Four of the behaviors shown for low-SES classrooms (student responses, overteaching/overlearning, classroom interaction, and individualization) can be seen as special ways of creating student engagement at high rates of success. This presents a particular challenge when teaching slow learners who may be inattentive, disinterested, and "at risk."

Also, frequently correcting wrong answers in the absence of warmth or encouragement could be construed as a personal criticism by the low-SES student, who

TABLE 1.3
Important teaching behaviors for low-SES and high-SES students

	Findings for Low-SES Pupils
Teacher Affect	Be warm and encouraging; let students know that help is available.
Student Responses	Elicit response from the student each time a question is asked before moving to the next student or question.
Overteaching/ Overlearning	Present material in small pieces, at a slow pace, with opportunity for practice.
Classroom Interaction	Stress factual knowledge. Monitor student progress. Minimize interruptions by maintaining smooth flow from one activity to another. Help student who needs help immediately.
Individualization	Supplement standard curriculum with specialized material to meet the needs of individual students.
	Findings for High-SES Pupils
Praise and Criticism	Correct poor answers immediately when student fails to perform.
Individualization	Ask questions that require associations, generalizations, and inferences. Supplement curriculum with challenging material. Assign homework and/or extended assignments.
Classroom Management	Be Flexible. Let students initiate teacher-student interaction. Encourage students to reason out correct answer.
Verbal Activities	Actively engage students in verbal questions and answers.

Based on research by Brophy & Evertson (1976) and Good, Ebmeier, & Beckerman (1978).

already may have a poor self-concept. Therefore, feedback that could be construed as criticism may need to occur in the context of a consistently warmer and more encouraging environment than is needed for the high-SES learner. Also, behaviors such as unstructured discussion and the simultaneous interaction among students, which can make classroom management and discipline with low-SES groups sometimes difficult, may be employed with greater success and frequency in the high-SES classroom.

Because much of the research on SES has been conducted in elementary classrooms, it is as yet uncertain to what extent these teaching behaviors apply to the secondary classroom. However, many of the learning characteristics of high-SES and low-SES students appear to be similar across these school contexts. Therefore, your success as a teacher in a predominately low-SES or high-SES classroom may depend on your ability to distinguish and execute the different behaviors in Table 1.3.

These and other teaching practices for special types of learners, including the less-able, gifted, handicapped, and bilingual, will be discussed in Chapter 13.

Teaching Reading and Mathematics

Another set of findings pertain to the different teaching behaviors that distinguish reading from mathematics instruction (Good & Grouws, 1979; Brophy & Evertson, 1976). Although not all teachers will teach either reading or mathematics, this set of findings may be generalized to some extent to other types of content that are similar in form and structure.

For example, social studies, history, and language instruction all have high reading content and share some structural features with reading. General science, biology, physics, and chemistry are similar to the science of mathematics in that concepts, principles, and laws all play a prominent role. Also, visual forms and symbolic expressions are at least as important to understanding science subjects as is the written word. Therefore, some cautious generalizations may be made about the teaching behaviors important for reading and mathematics instruction and for subjects similar to each.

Some important findings are summarized in Table 1.4. Notice the two different approaches implied by the behaviors listed. For mathematics instruction, a formal, direct approach appears to be most effective, especially when teaching the basics or fundamentals. This approach includes maintaining a high degree of structure through close adherence to texts, workbooks, and programmed texts. It also maximizes instructional coverage by teaching to the full class as much as possible, minimizing independent work that could diminish engaged learning time. On the other hand, reading instruction allows a more interactive and indirect approach, using more classroom discussions and question-and-answer sessions.

These approaches, however, are not mutually exclusive. What the research shows is that, in general and *over time,* a more formal, direct instructional approach during mathematics *tends* to influence student achievement positively more than would, say, an inquiry approach. For reading, the reverse appears to be true; an explorative, interactive approach that encourages the use of classroom discussion and student ideas *tends* to produce better student achievement over time.

TABLE 1.4

Important teaching behaviors for reading and mathematics instruction

	Findings for Reading Instruction
Instructional Activity	Devote considerable time to discussing, explaining, questioning, and stimulating cognitive processes during reading instruction.
Interactive Technique	Employ specific cues and questions that require the student to attempt a response during reading instruction.
Questions	Employ thought-provoking questions during reading instruction.
	Findings for Mathematics Instruction
Textbooks and Programmed Workbooks	Use textbooks and programmed workbooks during mathematics instruction that foster task persistence.
Instructional Content	Maximize coverage of instructional content per unit of time during mathematics instruction.
Instructional Organization	Maximize group work during mathematics instruction. Minimize independent work during mathematics instruction, especially that which may interfere with on-task behavior.

Based on research by Brophy & Evertson (1976) and Good & Grouws (1979).

An important point is that the different approaches represent *degrees of emphasis,* and not exclusive strategies. Clearly, teaching mathematics sometimes requires an inquiry approach, just as reading sometimes requires a lecture approach. More important than either of these approaches or the behaviors that represent them is the ability of the teacher to be flexible. The teacher must sense when a change from one emphasis to another is necessary, regardless of the content being taught (Marx and Peterson, 1981).

Chapter 2 presents more about the learners for whom these types of decisions must be made.

REVIEW OF SOME IMPORTANT TEACHER EFFECTIVENESS INDICATORS

If this chapter were reduced to simple advice for you to improve your teaching, the result would be a return to a simplistic and flawed definition of an effective teacher. However, if you ask for some indicators of teaching effectiveness that have demonstrated importance in improving student achievement, the following list will help. These are some of the general indicators of effective teaching that are currently supported by the research literature. They are *indicators* of effective teaching that might be seen if you observed over considerable time. These indicators will be used in the chapters ahead to introduce specific instructional practices that will help you create these same behaviors in your own classroom.

The effective teacher:

- ☐ Takes personal responsibility for students' learning and has *positive expectations* for every learner.
- ☐ *Matches* the difficulty of the lesson with the ability level of the students and *varies* the difficulty when necessary to attain moderate-to-high success rates.
- ☐ Gives students the *opportunity to practice* newly learned concepts and to receive timely feedback on their performance.
- ☐ *Maximizes instructional time* to increase content coverage and to give students the greatest opportunity to learn.
- ☐ Provides direction and control of student learning through *questioning, structuring,* and *probing.*
- ☐ Uses a *variety of instructional materials and verbal and visual aids* to foster use of student ideas and engagement in the learning process.
- ☐ *Elicits responses* from students each time a question is asked before moving to the next student or question.
- ☐ Presents material in *small steps* with opportunities for practice.
- ☐ Encourages students to *reason out* and *elaborate upon* the correct answer.
- ☐ Engages students in *verbal questions and answers.*
- ☐ Uses naturally occurring *classroom dialogue* to get students to *elaborate, extend,* and *comment on* the content being learned.
- ☐ Gradually *shifts some of the responsibility for learning to the students—* encouraging *independent thinking, problem solving,* and *decision making.*
- ☐ *Provides* learners with *mental strategies* for organizing and learning the content being taught.

So there is a powerful list of some indicators of the effective teacher. At this point, you might think that an effective teacher simply is one who has mastered all of the key behaviors and helping behaviors. But teaching involves more than a knowledge of how to perform *individual* behaviors. Much like an artist who blends color and texture into a painting to produce a coherent impression, so must the effective teacher *blend* individual behaviors to promote student achievement. This requires orchestration and integration of the key and helping behaviors into meaningful patterns and rhythms that can achieve the goals of instruction.

The truly effective teacher knows how to execute individual behaviors with a larger purpose in mind. This larger purpose always requires placing behaviors side by side in ways that accumulate to create an effect greater than can be achieved by any single behavior or small set of them. This is why teaching involves a sense of timing, sequencing, and pacing that cannot be conveyed by any list of behaviors. It is the behaviors that connect these behaviors *together* that are so important to the effective teacher, and it is the combination of curriculum, learning objectives, instructional materials, and learners that provides the decision-making context for the proper connection. Considerable attention will be devoted to this important decision-making context in the chapters ahead.

This chapter has presented some key and catalytic behaviors for becoming an effective teacher. These are not all of what the effective teacher is or does, but they are an important basis—perhaps the most valid basis—for beginning to understand the effective teacher. For us they form the backbone and skeleton of an effective teacher. In the chapters ahead we will assemble the remainder of this complex person called the effective teacher.

As you have seen, the major teaching goals representing effective teaching are lesson clarity, instructional variety, task orientation, student engagement in the learning process, and student success. Some of the more specific means of achieving these goals have included the use of student ideas and contributions, structuring, questioning, probing, and teacher affect. The remaining chapters present teaching practices and decisions that can help you orchestrate these components into patterns that will create a lasting impression on your students. It is to this important task that we now turn.

SUMMING UP

This chapter introduced you to definitions of effective teaching and key behaviors that help achieve it. Its main points were:

1. Early definitions of effective teaching focused primarily on a teacher's goodness as a person and only secondarily on his or her behavior in the classroom.
2. The psychological characteristics of a teacher—personality, attitude, experience, achievement, and aptitude—do not relate strongly to the teacher's behavior in the classroom.
3. Most modern definitions of effective teaching identify patterns of teacher-student interaction in the classroom that influence the cognitive and affective performance of students.
4. Classroom interaction analysis is a research methodology in which the verbal interaction patterns of teachers and students are systematically observed, recorded, and related to student performance.
5. Five key behaviors for effective teaching and some indicators pertaining to them are:
   - Lesson clarity: logical, step-by-step order, clear and audible delivery free of distracting mannerisms.
   - Instructional variety: variability in instructional materials, questioning, types of feedback, and teaching strategies.

- Task orientation: achievement (content) orientation as opposed to process orientation, maximum content coverage, and time devoted to instruction.
- Engagement: maintaining on-task behavior, limiting opportunities for distraction, and getting students to work on, think through, and inquire about the content.
- Success rate: 60–70% of time spent on tasks that afford moderate-to-high levels of success, especially during expository or didactic instruction.
6. Five helping behaviors for effective teaching and some indicators pertaining to them are:
   - Use of student ideas and contributions: using student responses to foster the goals of the lesson, and getting students to elaborate on and extend learned content using their own ideas, experiences, and thought patterns.
   - Structuring: providing advance organizers and mental strategies at the beginning of a lesson and creating activity structures with varied demands.
   - Questioning: using both content (direct) and process (indirect) questions to convey facts and to encourage inquiry and problem solving.
   - Probing: eliciting clarification, soliciting additional information, and redirecting when needed.
   - Enthusiasm: exhibiting vigor, involvement, excitement, and interest during classroom presen-

tations through vocal inflection, gesturing, eye contact, and animation.

7. The key behaviors appear to be consistently effective across all or most teaching contexts.

8. Other teaching behaviors, such as use of student ideas and contributions, structuring, and question-ing, may be more important with some learners and objectives than with others.

9. Effective teaching involves the orchestration and integration of key and helping behaviors into meaningful patterns to achieve specified goals.

FOR DISCUSSION AND PRACTICE

*1. In the following list, place the number *1* beside those indicators that most likely would appear in early definitions of effective teaching, based on the characteristics of a "good" person. Place the number *2* beside those indicators that most likely would appear in later definitions of effective teaching, based on the psychological characteristics of teachers. Place the number *3* beside those indicators most likely to appear in modern definitions of effective teaching, based on the interaction patterns of teachers and students.

_____ is always on time for work

_____ is intelligent

_____ stays after class to help students

_____ works well with those in authority

_____ has plenty of experience at his or her grade level

_____ varies higher-level with lower-level questions

_____ likes his/her job

_____ uses attention-getting devices to engage students in the learning task

_____ is open to criticism

_____ shows vitality when presenting

_____ has worked with difficult students before

_____ always allows students to experience moderate-to-high levels of success

_____ matches the class content closely with the curriculum guide

2. In your opinion, which of the following catalytic behaviors on the right would be *most* helpful in implementing the key behaviors on the left? (The catalytic behaviors may be used more than once across key behaviors, and more than a single catalytic behavior may be used for a given key behavior.) Compare your results with those of another and discuss the reasons for any differences.

Lesson clarity _____	1. student ideas
Instructional variety _____	2. structuring
Task orientation _____	3. questioning
Engagement in the learning task _____	4. probing
	5. enthusiasm
Success rate _____	

*3. Using Table 1.3, identify one way in which you would implement each of the following behaviors across high-SES and low-SES pupils.

Behavior	High-SES	Low-SES
Individualization		
Teacher affect		
Overteaching/ overlearning		
Classroom interaction		

4. Which two teaching effectiveness behaviors would you emphasize if you were teaching fifth-grade mathematics? Which two would you emphasize when teaching fifth-grade reading? Justify your choices from the summary research tables in this chapter.

5. Indicate your perceived strengths in exhibiting the five key and five catalytic behaviors, using the following technique. First, notice the number assigned to each of the key behaviors.

1 lesson clarity
2 instructional variety
3 task orientation
4 engagement in the learning process
5 success rate

Now, for each of the following rows of numbers listed, circle the number representing the key behavior in which you perceive yourself to have the greater strength.

1 versus 2	2 versus 4
1 versus 3	2 versus 5
1 versus 4	3 versus 4
1 versus 5	3 versus 5
2 versus 3	4 versus 5

Count up how many times you circled a 1, how many times you circled a 2, a 3, etc., and place the frequencies on the following lines.

1. _____
2. _____
3. _____
4. _____
5. _____

Your perceived greatest strength is the key behavior having the highest frequency. Your perceived least strength is the key behavior with the lowest frequency. In subsequent chapters, underscore material related to your perceived least strength and note the suggested readings related to it.

6. Repeat the paired comparison technique in the same manner for the five catalytic behaviors.

1 use of student ideas
2 structuring
3 questioning
4 probing
5 enthusiasm

1 versus 2	2 versus 4
1 versus 3	2 versus 5
1 versus 4	3 versus 4
1 versus 5	3 versus 5
2 versus 3	4 versus 5

1. _____
2. _____
3. _____
4. _____
5. _____

7. Recall a particularly good teacher you had during your high-school years—and a particularly poor one. Try to form a mental image of each one. Now rate each of them on the five key behaviors in the following table. Use *1* to indicate strength in that behavior, *2* to indicate average performance, and *3* to indicate weakness in that behavior. Are the behavioral profiles of the two teachers different? How?

Behavior	Teacher X (good)	Teacher Y (poor)
Lesson clarity		
Instructional variety		
Task orientation		
Engagement in the learning process		
Success rates		

8. Now do the same for the five helping behaviors, using the same two teachers. Is the pattern the same? What differences in ratings, if any, do you find across key and catalytic behaviors for the same teacher? How would you account for any differences that occurred?

_____

*Answers to asterisked questions (*) in this and the other chapters are in Appendix B.

SUGGESTED READINGS

Anderson, L. (1987). Opportunity to learn. In M. J. Dunkin (Ed.), *International encyclopedia of teaching and teacher education*. New York: Pergamon.
A brief and authoritative introduction to the key behavior of engagement in the learning process.

Bennett, N., & Desforges, C. (1988). Matching classroom tasks to students' attainments. *The Elementary School Journal, 88*, 221–224.
Shows how activities and tasks can be altered to vary the cognitive demands placed on learners.

Borich, G. (1977). *The appraisal of teaching: Concepts and process*. Reading, MA: Addison-Wesley.

Illustrates different methods and systems that can be used for evaluating the performance of teachers and addresses some of the measurement issues related to conducting a valid appraisal of a teacher's performance.

Borich, G. (1979). Implications for developing teacher competencies from process-product studies. *Journal of Teacher Education, 30,* 77–86.

Reviews research results of five major classroom observation studies (using classroom interaction analysis) for the purpose of identifying and summarizing effective teaching practices.

Borich, G., & Nance, D. (1990). *The effective teacher program.* Professional Teachers' Library, 1009 Harwood Pl., Austin, TX 78704.

Twenty-seven activity booklets for the beginning teacher, containing extensive examples, entertaining classroom dialogues, and practical observation instruments for effective teaching, keyed to this and its companion volume.

Borich, G. (1992). *Clearly outstanding: Making each day count in your classroom.* Boston: Allyn & Bacon.

A self-improvement guide for how to be effective during your very first year of teaching—new teaching ideas and directions for today's classroom teacher.

Brophy, J., & Evertson, C. (1976). *Learning from teaching: A developmental perspective.* Boston: Allyn & Bacon.

A very readable summary of an extensive classroom research study that contributed much to our modern definitions of effective teaching.

Brophy, J., & Good, T. (1986). Teacher behavior and student achievement. In M. C. Wittrock (Ed.), *Handbook of research on teaching* (3rd ed.). New York: Macmillan.

An authoritative review of the major findings of teacher effectiveness research over the past 25 years. Due to this article's length and wealth of information, it is helpful to divide it into sections that interest you most and read it over time.

Dunkin, M., & Biddle, B. (1974). *The study of teaching.* New York: Holt, Rinehart & Winston.

An extensive and thorough book reviewing all relevant research on teaching effectiveness. Many easy-to-follow tables summarize research results for many specific teaching behaviors (e.g., lesson clarity), which still reflect many of today's more recent findings.

Fisher, C., Berliner, D., Filby, N., Marliave, R., Cahen, L., & Dishaw, M. (1980). Teaching behaviors, academic learning time and student achievement: An overview. In C. Denham & A. Lieberman (Eds.), *Time to learn.* Washington: National Institute of Education.

A concise and readable summary of much of the important research on task orientation and engagement in the learning process.

Good, T. (1979). Teacher effectiveness in the elementary school. *Journal of Teacher Education, 30,* 52–64.

A summary of effective teaching behaviors for the elementary school teacher, derived from classroom research.

Land, M. (1987). Vagueness and clarity. In M. J. Dunkin (Ed.), *International encyclopedia of teaching and teacher education* (pp. 292–397). New York: Pergamon.

A good overview of the dimensions of teacher clarity and the empirical support for the importance of this key behavior.

Palincsar, A., & Brown, A. (1989). Classroom dialogues to promote self-regulated comprehension. In J. Brophy (Ed.), *Advances in research on teaching* (Vol. 1, pp. 35–62). Greenwich, CT: JAI Press.

Illustrates the use of classroom discussion and dialogue to promote higher-order thought process.

Rosenshine, B., & Stevens, R. (1986). Teaching functions. In M. C. Wittrock (Ed.), *Handbook of research on training* (3rd ed., pp. 376–391). New York: Macmillan.

Summarizes some of the more generally applicable findings from recent research on teaching effectiveness, with particular emphasis on those teaching functions related to student achievement. Can be used as a short summary of the Brophy and Good article.

2

Understanding
Your Students

Chapter 1 explained that teaching is not simply the transmission of knowledge from teacher to learner but rather is the *interaction* of teacher with learner. For this reason, effective teaching practices are always defined by *who* is being taught and under *what* conditions (curriculum, learning objectives, instructional materials, and learners). This idea appeared in Chapter 1: some teaching behaviors are more effective with some types of learners (high-SES vs. low-SES) and content (math vs. reading) than with others. This chapter discusses the decisions you must make about *whom* you will teach. In subsequent chapters, we will consider the decisions you must make about *what* and *how* you will teach.

It was not so long ago that some teachers thought of their students as blank slates onto which they were to transfer knowledge, skills, and understanding. They perceived their task to be the skilled transmission of appropriate grade-level content as it appeared in texts, curriculum guides, workbooks, and the academic disciplines. Students were viewed as empty vessels into which the teacher poured the contents of the day's lesson.

You can see how contradictions arose from such a simplistic definition of teaching and learning. For example, this definition could not explain why some "bright" students get poor grades and some "dull" students get good grades. Nor could it explain why some students want to learn while others do not even want to come to school; why some students do extra homework while others do none at all; or why some students have attitudes conducive to learning while others talk harshly to their peers about the value of schooling.

These are just some of the individual differences existing in every classroom; they will influence the outcome of your teaching, regardless of how adept you may be at transmitting content. Your transmission of knowledge onto the blank slate will be interrupted by more than a few of these individual differences.

Becoming an effective teacher includes not only learning to be knowledgeable about content and how to teach it, but also *how to adjust both content and teaching practices to the individual differences that exist among learners*. Your understanding of how individual differences affect learning will determine the degree of success you achieve with your teaching objectives. This chapter contains some important facts about the psychology of learners that will help you understand and appreciate the many differences in human behavior that exist within every classroom.

WHY PAY ATTENTION TO INDIVIDUAL DIFFERENCES?

Any observer in any classroom quickly notices that schoolchildren vary in intelligence, achievement, personality, interests, creativity, self-discipline, and many other ways. Of what consequence is such an obvious observation to you? After all, you must teach all the students assigned to you, regardless of their differences.

There are two reasons for being aware of individual differences among learners in a classroom:

1. By recognizing individual differences, you may be able to match or adapt your instructional method to the individual learning needs of your stu-

dents. Within the same class you may be able to use different instructional approaches with different groups that have different learning needs.

2. Even when you cannot use different instructional approaches with different groups, it still is important to understand the powerful effect that individual differences can have on learning outcomes. When counseling students and consulting with parents about the achievement and competencies of those who have difficulty learning or who are learning above expectations, you will need to convey the reasons for the behavior you are describing. Understanding your students' behavior provides perspective for parents, counselors, and other teachers when they wonder why Johnny is not learning, why Mary learns without studying, or why Betty does not even want to learn.

Understanding individual differences among learners will enable you to adapt instructional methods to their needs. For example, information about intelligence, achievement, personality, and interests may be used to select the most appropriate teaching style or method for a given instructional objective. Researchers are discovering many content areas and individual differences where the application of different instructional strategies to different types of learners has significantly improved their performance (Corno & Snow, 1986; Cronbach & Snow, 1977).

In one instance, student-centered *discussions* were found to significantly improve the achievement of highly anxious students, while teacher-centered *lecture* classes significantly improved achievement among low-anxiety students (Dowaliby & Schumer, 1973). These results were explained by the more informal, nurturing climate accompanying the student-centered discussion, which allowed the highly anxious students to focus more intently on the content, resulting in greater learning. In contrast, the low-anxiety students achieved better under the more efficient direct-lecture approach in which greater content coverage was achieved.

In another example involving the teaching of reading, the *linguistic* approach resulted in higher vocabulary achievement for students *high* in auditory ability, while the *whole-word* approach was more effective for students *low* in auditory ability (Stallings & Keepes, 1970). Achievement was maximized when the instructional method favored the learners' natural abilities. In this case, those who learned best by *seeing* benefited from the whole-word approach, while the auditory approach was better for those who learned best by *hearing*.

Adaptive Teaching

The general approach to achieving a common instructional goal with learners whose prior achievement, aptitude, or learning styles differ widely is called **adaptive teaching**. Adaptive teaching techniques apply different instructional strategies to different groups of learners so that the natural diversity prevailing in the classroom does not prevent any learner from reaching the common goal. Two approaches to adaptive teaching have been reported to be effective (Corno & Snow, 1986). They are the remediation approach and the compensatory approach.

The Remediation Approach.   The **remediation approach** provides the learner with the prerequisite knowledge, skill, or behavior needed to benefit from the planned instruction. For example, in the first research example cited (discussion vs. lecture), you might first attempt to lower the anxiety of the high-anxious group, so that the lecture method could equally benefit all students. In the second example (linguistic vs. whole-word), you might attempt to raise the auditory (listening) skills of those who are deficient in them so that both groups could profit equally from the linguistic approach (which, due to limitations in time and materials, may be the only method available).

The remediation approach to adaptive teaching will be successful to the extent that the desired prerequisite information, skill, or behavior to overcome a deficiency can be taught within a reasonable period of time. However, this often is not possible or represents an inefficient use of classroom time, and the compensatory approach to adaptive teaching must be taken.

The Compensatory Approach.   The **compensatory approach** chooses an instructional method to circumvent or compensate for deficiencies in information, skills, or ability known to exist among learners. With this approach to adaptive teaching, content presentation is altered to circumvent a fundamental weakness or deficiency. This is done by using alternate modalities (e.g., pictures vs. words) or by supplementing content with additional learning resources (games and simulations) and activities (group discussions, hands-on experiences). This may involve modifying the instructional technique to compensate for known deficiencies and to use known strengths. Techniques include the visual representation of content, using more flexible instructional presentations (films, pictures, illustrations), or shifting to alternate instructional formats (self-paced texts, simulations, experience-oriented workbooks).

For example, students who are poor at reading comprehension and lack a technical math vocabulary might be taught a geometry unit almost exclusively by visual handouts. Portraying each theorem and axiom graphically emphasizes the visual modality. Other students having an adequate reading comprehension and vocabulary level might skip this more time-consuming approach and proceed by learning the same theorems and axioms from a highly verbalized text, thereby emphasizing the verbal modality.

Benefits of Adaptive Teaching.   Notice that adaptive teaching goes beyond the simpler process of ability grouping, in which students are divided into slow and fast learners and then presented approximately the same material at different rates. Some research suggests that differences in academic performance between high and low achievers may actually *increase* with the use of ability grouping, creating a loss of self-esteem and motivation for the low group (Good & Stipek, 1983).

Adaptive teaching, on the other hand, works to achieve the common goal with all students, regardless of their individual differences. It does so either by remediation (building up the knowledge, skills, or abilities required to profit from the planned instruction) or by compensation (circumventing known weaknesses by avoiding instructional methods/materials that rely on abilities that may be less well developed).

Therefore, adaptive teaching requires an understanding of your students' learning abilities and the alternative instructional methods that can maximize their strongest receptive modalities (e.g., visual vs. auditory).

The chapters ahead provide a menu of such strategies from which to choose. Some of the most promising instructional alternatives in adaptive teaching include:

> High/low vividness of materials
>
> Inductive/expository presentation
>
> Rule-example/example-rule ordering
>
> Inductive/deductive presentation
>
> Teacher-centered/student-centered presentation
>
> Structured/unstructured teaching methods
>
> Lecture/student presentation
>
> Group phonics/individualized phonics instruction
>
> Presence/absence of advance organizers
>
> Programmed/conventional instruction

Each of these teaching methods or presentation styles is more effective for some types of learners than others (Rohrkemper & Corno, 1988; Cronbach & Snow, 1977). This suggests their potential for adaptive teaching. Curriculum texts in your specific teaching area can help identify the learners for whom each alternative is most effective and appropriate in achieving your instructional goals.

The research literature offers many examples of specific content areas in which a particular instructional method—in association with a particular student characteristic—has enhanced student performance. However, common sense and classroom experience will suggest many other ways in which you can alter teaching to fit the individual needs of your students. By knowing your students and having a variety of instructional methods available, you can adjust instruction to learning needs with one of the two methods of adaptive teaching.

This requires your conviction that there may be no single, best method of teaching that can be equally successful with all of your students. To become an effective teacher, you must know the aptitude, achievement, and learning styles of your students so you can choose the most appropriate teaching approaches. This chapter contains some of the important aptitude, achievement, personality, peer, and family characteristics of your students that can affect both their learning and your teaching.

THE EFFECTS OF GENERAL INTELLIGENCE ON LEARNING

One thing everyone remembers about elementary school is how some students seemed to learn so easily, while others had to work so hard. In high school there was an even greater range of "smartness." In a practical sense, we associate the terms *smart, bright, ability to solve problems, learn quickly,* and *figure things out* with intelligence. Both in the classroom and in life it is obvious that some have more intelligence than others. This observation often has been a source of anxiety, concern, and jealousy among learners. Perhaps because the topic of intelligence can so easily elicit emotions like these, it is the most talked about and least understood aspect of student behavior.

One of the greatest misunderstandings that teachers, parents, and school administrators have about intelligence is that it is a single, unified dimension. Such a belief is often expressed by the use of word pairs such as *slow/fast, smart/dumb, bright/dull* when referring to different kinds of learners. These phrases indicate that a student is *either* fast *or* slow, *either* bright *or* dull, *either* smart *or* dumb, when in fact, each of us (regardless of our intelligence) is *all* of these at one time or another. On a particular task of a certain nature, you may appear to be "slow and dull," but given another task requiring different abilities, you may be "fast and bright." How do such vast differences occur within a single individual?

Everyone knows from personal experience in school, hobbies, sports, and interpersonal relationships that degree of intelligence depends on the *circumstances* and *conditions* under which the intelligence is exhibited. Observations such as these have led researchers to study and identify more than one kind of intelligence. This relatively new way of looking at intelligence has led to a better understanding of classic contradictions like why Carlos is good in vocabulary but not in mathematics, why Angela is generally good in social studies but specifically bad at reading maps, or why Betty is good at analyzing the reasons behind historical events but poor at memorizing the names and dates that go along with them. Each of these seemingly contradictory behaviors can be explained by the special abilities required by each task. It is these special abilities, in which we all differ, that will be the most useful for understanding the learning behavior of your students.

You should be aware of some controversial issues on the use of general intelligence tests when discussing "intelligence" with parents, other teachers, and school administrators. These issues often strongly divide individuals into two camps, known as the environmentalist position and the hereditarian position.

The Environmentalist Position

The **environmentalist** position criticizes the use of general IQ tests in the schools in the belief that they are culturally biased. Environmentalists believe that differences in IQ scores among groups such as blacks, Hispanics, and whites can be attributed largely to social class or environmental differences. They reason that some groups of students, particularly minorities, may come from impoverished home environments in which the verbal skills generally required to do well on intelligence tests are not practiced. Therefore, a significant part of minority-student scores on any IQ test represents the environment in which they grew up and not their true intelligence.

Environmentalists conclude (and some research supports) that the effect of home environment is at least as important as heredity in contributing to one's IQ (Bloom, 1981; Smilansky, 1979). This group believes that intelligence tests are biased in favor of the white middle class, who generally provide their children with more intense patterns of verbal interaction, greater reinforcement for learning, more learning resources, and better physical health during the critical preschool years in which cognitive growth is fastest.

The Hereditarian Position

The **hereditarian** position concludes that heredity rather than environment is the major factor determining intelligence. Hereditarians base their beliefs on the research and writings of Arthur Jensen (1969). They believe that not all children have the same potential for developing the same mental abilities. They contend that efforts such as compensatory education programs to make up for environmental disadvantages in the early elementary grades through remediation can have only limited success because the origin of the difference is genetic and not environmental.

Specific vs. General Intelligence

Common sense tells us there is some truth in *both* arguments. However, despite how parents, fellow teachers, and even your own students may feel, these issues are highly dependent on the notion of *general* intelligence. They become less relevant in the context of specific abilities. General intelligence tests are not very predictive of anything other than school grades, whereas specific abilities tend to predict not only school grades but also more important real-life behaviors that school grades are supposed to represent. For example, tests of general intelligence do not predict success as a salesman, factory worker, carpenter, or teacher, because they measure few of the abilities required for success in these occupations.

Specific and not general abilities ultimately are responsible for success in the real world, so general intelligence test scores are not constructive for planning instruction, selecting classroom groups, and counseling students and parents about performance deficiencies. Knowing your learners' *specific* strengths and weaknesses and altering your instructional goals and activities accordingly will contribute far more to your effective teaching than will categorizing your students' performances in ways that indicate only their *general* intelligence.

THE EFFECTS OF SPECIFIC ABILITIES ON LEARNING

Specific definitions of intelligence and the behaviors they represent commonly are called **aptitudes** or **factors**. As a teacher, you are unlikely to measure aptitudes in your classroom, but you need to know of their influence on the performance of your students. Your students may already have been aptitude-tested in a districtwide testing program, or you can ask the school counselor or psychologist to measure a specific aptitude to find the source of a specific learning problem. Your acquaintance with the division of general intelligence into specific aptitudes will help you see how a learner's abilities in specific areas can directly affect the degree of learning that takes place.

Thurstone's Specialized Abilities

Some of the many specialized abilities that have been reliably measured include *verbal comprehension, general reasoning, memory, use of numbers, psychomotor speed, spatial relations,* and *word fluency*. This list of abilities resulted from the work of L. L. Thurstone (1947). Instead of reinforcing the idea of a single IQ score, Thurstone's work led to the development of seven different IQs, each measured by a separate test. In this manner the concept of general intelligence was factored into component parts; it had the obvious advantage that a specific score for a given factor could be related to certain types of learning requirements.

Some learning activities require a high degree of memory, such as memorizing long lists of words in preparation for a spelling bee or a vocabulary test. Likewise, spatial relations, use of numbers, and general reasoning ability are essential for high levels of performance in mathematics. Such differences in aptitude are far more useful than general intelligence in explaining to parents why Johnny can get excellent scores on math tests that emphasize number problems (12 + 2 × 6 =) but poor scores on math tests that emphasize word problems (If Bob rows 4 mph against a current flowing 2 mph, how long will it take him to row 16 miles?). Such apparent contradictions become more understandable in the light of specific aptitudes.

While Thurstone's dimensions were among the earliest, other researchers have found still more specific components within them. For example, some content specialists in reading identify no fewer than nine verbal comprehension factors, which indicate ability to:

Know word meanings

See contextual meaning

See organization

Follow thought patterns

Find specifics

Express ideas

Draw inferences

Identify literary devices

Determine a writer's purpose

In other words, a learner's general performance in reading may be affected by any one or a combination of these specific abilities. This and similar lists point up a most interesting and controversial aspect of identifying the specific aptitudes that underlie general intelligence: once aptitudes such as memory, use of numbers, reasoning, verbal comprehension, etc. are defined by their underlying factors, is it possible to *teach* these so-called components of intelligence?

Hereditarians say that intelligence is not teachable, but it seems logical that, with proper instruction, a learner could be taught to draw inferences, find specifics, and determine a writer's purpose. As general components of intelligence, such as those defined by Thurstone, become divided into smaller and more specific aptitudes, the general concept of intelligence has become "demystified." At least some elements of intelligence depend upon achievement in certain areas that *can* be influenced by instruction. Therefore, another advantage of the multidimensional approach to intelligence is that some specific deficiencies once thought to be unalterable can be remedied by instruction.

Sternberg's Theory of Intelligence

One of the most recent conceptions of specialized abilities comes from R. Sternberg (1986). He believes that intelligence, as defined by its components, can be altered through instruction. Sternberg's work has been important in forming new definitions of intelligence that allow for intellectual traits, previously believed to be inherited and unalterable, to be improved through instruction. Further, Sternberg suggests not only that intelligence can be taught but that the classroom is the logical place to teach it.

Let's look more closely at the theory from which this fascinating claim is made. Sternberg's theory of intelligence is called *triarchic* because it consists of three parts: the individual's internal world, how the individual acquires intelligence, and the individual's external world.

1 — The Individual's Internal World. The first part of Sternberg's theory relates to the individual's internal world that governs thinking. Three kinds of mental processes occur, instrumental in (1) planning what things to do, (2) how to learn to do them, and (3) how to actually perform them. The first of these processes is used in planning, monitoring, and evaluating the performance of a task. In essence, this is an "executive" component that tells all other components of our intelligence what to do, like the boss who gives directions but who does none of the work. Hence, this component's role is purely administrative.

A second component of this internal world of intelligence governs behavior in actual task performance. This component controls the various strategies used in solving problems. For example, one strategy is to guide you to the most relevant details of a problem and steer you away from the irrelevant. Thus, individuals can become more or less intelligent by learning which details need attention and which to ignore.

A third component of this internal world of intelligence governs what previously acquired knowledge we bring to a problem. It is here that Sternberg's theory differs most from other concepts of intelligence. In his view, the innate and less alterable characteristics of memory, manipulating symbols, or mental speed are not particularly important to intelligence. Instead, he sees the *previously acquired knowledge* that one brings to problem-solving as more important to thinking intelligently.

Sternberg points out that one of the biggest differences between "experts" and "nonexperts" in the real world is not the mental processes they use in performing a task, but their previously acquired knowledge. The task in explaining intelligence or "expertness," then, is to understand how experts acquire needed information, when

Some aspects of the age-old concept of intelligence, once thought to be unalterable, now may be taught in the classroom.

nonexperts seemingly fail to acquire it. This notion leads to the second part of Sternberg's triarchic theory.

2—How the Individual Acquires Intelligence. Sternberg proposes that intelligence is the ability to learn and to think using previously discovered patterns and relationships to solve new problems in unfamiliar contexts. By experiencing many novel tasks and conditions early in life, we discover the patterns and relationships that tell us how to solve new problems with which we may be totally unfamiliar. In other words, the greater our experience in facing unique and novel conditions, the more we grow and can adapt to the changing conditions around us.

Sternberg suggests that confronting novel tasks and situations and learning to deal with them is one of the most important instructional goals in learning intelligent behavior. His writings provide many practical exercises and examples of how to become facile at learning to deal with novel tasks and situations that provide the patterns and relationships with which to enhance our intelligence.

3—The Individual's External World.   The third part of Sternberg's theory relates intelligence to the external world of the individual. This is where an individual's intelligence shows most and can be altered quickest. This part of intelligence is governed by how well one learns to adapt to the environment (changes his or her way of doing things to fit the world), to select from the environment (avoid unfamiliar things and choose familiar and comfortable ones), and to shape the environment (change it to fit a personal way of doing things). Thus, "intelligent" people *learn* to adapt, select, and shape their environment better and faster than do "less intelligent" people. Therefore, perhaps the most important aspect of Sternberg's theory is that intelligence results as much from how people learn to *cope* with the world around them as it results from the internal mental processes with which they are born (e.g., memory, symbol manipulation, mental speed).

This notion of coping is expressed by 20 characteristics that Sternberg suggests often impede intelligent behavior and, therefore, are often found in the "unintelligent" or the "nonexpert." Sternberg's 20 impediments are:

Lack of motivation

Lack of impulse control

Lack of perseverance

Using the wrong abilities

Inability to translate thought into action

Lack of a product orientation

Inability to complete tasks and to follow through

Failure to initiate

Fear of failure

Procrastination

Misattribution of blame

Excessive self-pity

Excessive dependency

Wallowing in personal difficulties

Distractibility and lack of concentration

Spreading oneself too thin

Inability to delay gratification

Inability or unwillingness to see the forest for the trees

Lack of balance between critical thinking and creative thinking

Too little or too much self-confidence

From these 20 impediments to intelligent thinking, you can see why Sternberg believes many aspects of intelligence can and should be taught and why the classroom may be a logical place to convey the attitudes and behaviors that can help learners avoid these impediments to intelligent behavior.

THE EFFECTS OF PRIOR ACHIEVEMENT ON LEARNING

Closely related to Sternberg's notion of intelligence are the prior knowledge and skills of your learners—specifically, their task-relevant knowledge and skills. *Task relevant* means those facts, skills, and understandings that must be taught if subsequent learning is to occur. Mastery of these behaviors makes possible future learning. Thus, their identification is important not only in planning instruction but also in accounting for why learning does not occur in some situations and for some students.

These task-relevant facts, skills, and understandings come in various shapes and sizes. In each content area they are part of the logical progression of ideas with which a lesson is conveyed. For example, various orders of reasoning may be used—general-to-detailed, simple-to-complex, abstract-to-concrete, or conceptual-to-procedural. These logical progressions are *learning structures* that identify at each step those behaviors needed before new learning can take place (e.g., procedures must come before concepts, and simple facts must come before complex details).

Chapters 6, 7, and 8 present more about the many logical progressions with which teaching can be structured, but for now it is important to appreciate that many task-relevant prior learnings are embedded within these progressions. It is upon these that the final outcomes of a lesson or unit depend. This point is illustrated in Figure 2.1 for an instructional unit on government and Figure 2.2 for a unit on writing skills. Regardless of the type of progression that may apply in a specific instance, notice that a breakdown in the flow of learning at almost any point will prevent learning from taking place at any subsequent point. Failure to attain concepts at higher levels in the instructional plan, therefore, may not indicate a lack of ability or specialized aptitude but a failure to adequately grasp *task-relevant prior behaviors*.

FIGURE 2.1
Organization of content indicating a logical progression for a unit on government

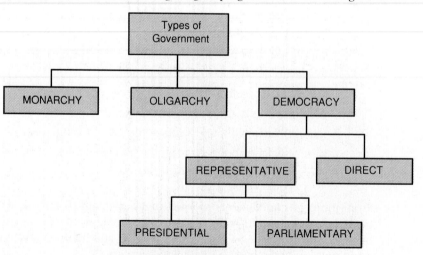

FIGURE 2.2
Organization of content indicating a logical progression for a unit on writing skills

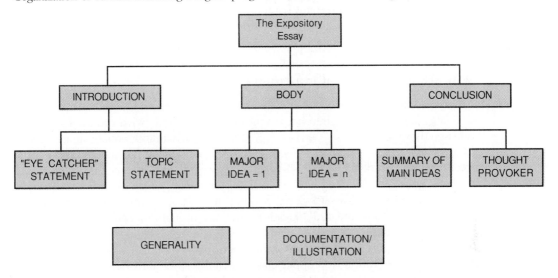

Chapter 5 indicates how to plan instructional units using different types of "learning structures." Chapters 7, 8, and 9 present some of the many classroom activities with which these learning structures can be taught.

THE EFFECTS OF HOME AND FAMILY ON LEARNING

It is well known that a close relationship exists between social class and educational achievement. The effect of socioeconomic status (SES) on achievement has been so pronounced in some instances that it has lead to identifying different teaching behaviors for high-SES and low-SES students, as noted in Chapter 1. Traditionally, students from lower-class and lower middle-class families have not performed as well on standardized achievement tests as have students from middle-class and upper-class families. Some of this difference is related to possible differences in the IQ test scores of these groups. However, differences in IQ scores that are unrelated to occupational success are one thing, but differences in the achievement of basic language and mathematics skills are quite another. These latter differences are so pertinent to success that they are immediate cause for concern.

In this regard, observers have noted the close relationship among social class, race/ethnicity, and school achievement (Sleeter & Grant, 1986; National Center for Education Statistics, 1980). Their studies generally conclude that most differences in educational achievement occurring by race and ethnicity can be accounted for by social class, *even after the lower socioeconomic status of minority groups is considered* (Levine & Havinghurst, 1984). In other words, if you know the socioeconomic status of a group of students, you can predict their achievement with reasonable accuracy. Information about their racial and ethnic group does little to improve the prediction. This indicates the powerful effect social class can have upon the behavior of your students. You will see in Chapters 11 and 12 that this effect can extend to the affective and emotional makeup of your students as well as to their cognitive achievement.

Why SES Is So Important in Learning

It is now appropriate to ask, "What is it about one's socioeconomic status that creates such large and important differences in the classroom?" and "What can I, a teacher, do to lessen these differences?" Obviously, if SES plays such an influential role in student achievement, it must stand for something more specific than income and the educational level of parents. Research shows that associated with income and educational level are a number of more meaningful characteristics in which the home and family lives of high-SES and low-SES families differ. It is these characteristics—which are indirect results of income and education—that are thought to influence the achievement of schoolchildren.

One important characteristic that seems to distinguish lower-class children from those in the middle and upper class is that the latter are more likely to acquire knowledge of the world *outside* their home and neighborhood (Hunt, 1979). Through greater access to books, magazines, social networks, cultural events, and other families that value these learning resources, middle-class and upper-class students develop their reading and speaking abilities more rapidly. This, in combination with parental teaching (which tends to use the formal or elaborated language that trains the child to think independently of the specific communication context), may give the middle-class and upper-class student an advantage at the start of school.

This contrasts with children who come from lower-class homes where values and attitudes may emphasize obedience and conformity rather than independent thinking. Researchers who have studied low-SES families report that they generally are more likely than middle-SES and high-SES families to emphasize physical punishment rather than reasoning and to encourage rote learning (memorization, recall of facts, etc.) rather than independent, self-directed learning (Newson & Newson, 1976).

And why do these differences exist between lower-SES and higher-SES learners? Contributing to the problem of the low-SES learner is the fact that 70% of working-age mothers of disadvantaged students must work. This leaves at least four million latchkey children of school age home alone (Hodgkinson, 1988). In the last 30 years, the composition of the family has undergone a dramatic change. The traditional family unit is no longer the rule, but the exception. As recently as 1955, more than 60% of American families were traditional: a working father and a mother who kept the house and took care of the children. Only 10% of today's families represent the traditional family of past generations. The Internal Revenue Service currently recognizes no fewer than 13 variations of the family. Today's family is more likely to be a dual-career family, a single parent family, a stepfamily, or a family that has moved an average of 14 times. All of these conditions affect the fabric of the family and the development of the school-age learners within it.

By some estimates, 50% of the children born in 1983 will live in a single-parent household in which the only adult is gone 12 hours a day. Under these conditions, the adult has little time to provide the model of self-discipline, motivation, and good study habits that is important to school-age learners. And, despite increases in the number of working mothers, the real income of the typical family with school-age children has actually fallen. The U.S. government reports that over one million children today have a higher poverty rate than at any other time since it began collecting data. Fewer involved parents, more distracting lifestyles, greater job and occupational stress, and the increased rate of divorce all have contributed to the growing number of disadvantaged and lower-SES learners. Levin (1986) has estimated that educationally disadvantaged youth now comprise about one-third of all school-age children.

The Teacher's Role in Improving Lower-SES Achievement

The classroom is the logical place to begin the process of reducing some of the achievement differences that have been noted between lower-SES and middle/upper-SES students. Many formal interventions are trying to reduce the differences, from preschools to federally funded compensatory education programs. However, these interventions and programs have not made, and are not likely to make, a major impact on achievement differences among various groups of students who have highly divergent home and family lifestyles.

This leaves you, the classroom teacher, to deal with these differences as a daily fact of life. The difficulty of planning instruction in the midst of these differences can be overstated, because differences *within* the behavior of low-SES students actually can be greater than differences *between* low-SES and middle-SES students. However, even admitting that the variation in behavior within a group may sometimes exceed the variability between groups, the general tendencies are clear: the home and family backgrounds of lower-SES and higher-SES students differentially prepare them for school. For you, the effective teacher, the task becomes one of planning instruction around these differences in ways that reduce them as much as possible.

This means various things in various classrooms, depending upon the nature of the differences. However, regardless of classroom content and grade level, several important attitudes will make the differences more open to influence by an instructional approach. One of these attitudes is willingness to incorporate a variety of audiovisual aids and exploratory materials into your lesson, thus requiring alternative modalities of your students (e.g., sight vs. sound). You can plan these as part of a lesson or as supplementary materials for those who need alternative ways of learning.

Another attitude you can adopt for reducing achievement differences due to social class is to have high expectations for your students, and to reward them for intellectual accomplishments. Neither of these behaviors may be present in lower-SES homes. Your role in providing support and encouragement could be instrumental in getting students to realize that someone cares about them.

Also, you can help students expand their vocabularies and quality of language by providing them access to newspapers, periodicals, and popular books. In some cases the classroom will be the only place where students can come in contact with these language sources. Emphasizing correct word usage and correcting incorrect linguistic patterns—while respecting the learner's dialect or "street language"—also can help reduce differences in the verbal performance. Correcting without criticizing or embarrassing a student is an art, but one for which there is no substitute in a classroom having diverse language differences. Curriculum specialists generally agree that alternative linguistic forms, such as street language and dialects, can be used effectively as an intermediate or transitional device for moving students to standard English (Green, 1983).

Finally, you as an effective teacher must have an attitude that seeks opportunities for getting lower-SES students to talk about their experiences. One of the most significant differences among students coming from different social classes is that lower-SES students have poorer self-concepts than higher-SES students. Getting students to talk about personal experiences and using these to help attain instructional goals has a double effect. It promotes student cooperation and interest while showing them that someone—you—thinks they have something worthwhile to say. Strategies for accomplishing this will be presented in Chapters 9 and 10.

Each of these attitudes, rather than having the lofty goal of changing students' behavior, has the more realistic goal of getting them *ready to learn*. Perhaps the most beneficial attitude of all is recognizing that, while neither you nor any other single teacher can overcome the powerful influences of family and home life, you can create a readiness to learn. And this is the first step in reducing achievement differences that are attributable to social class.

THE EFFECTS OF PERSONALITY ON LEARNING

Preceding sections discussed the potential influence on learning of students' general intelligence, specific aptitude, task-relevant prior achievement, and home life. In this section your students' personalities will be added to this equation.

When words such as *trustworthy, creative, independent, anxious, cheerful, authoritarian,* or *aggressive* are used to describe a student, they refer to an aspect of that student's personality. **Personality** is the integration of one's traits, motives, beliefs, and abilities, including emotional responses, character, and even morals. The notion of personality is indeed broad and, according to some authors, even subsumes intelligence and specialized abilities. It is not necessary to take so broad a view of personality here because not every part of what is considered to be personality is equally applicable to classroom learning. On the other hand, several aspects of personality are so important to learning that learning probably could not occur without them. These aspects of personality are called traits.

Traits are enduring aspects of a person's behavior that are consistent across a wide variety of settings. Traits are not specific to subject matter content, grade level, or instructional objective, as are aptitude and achievement. However, this does not mean that variations in content, grade level, and objectives are unimportant to personality. In fact, many things within an environment, such as a classroom, can trigger some personality traits and not others. Some parts of personalities lie dormant until stimulated to action by some particular perception of the world. This is the reason teachers often are dismayed to hear, for example, that an aggressive and verbally abusive child in fifth-period social studies is shy and cooperative in someone else's seventh-period mathematics. It also is the reason that some students and teachers may never quite see eye to eye. Fortunately, such personality conflicts are rare, but they can be devastating to classroom rapport if left to smolder beneath the surface.

Erikson's Crises of the School Years

Some psychologists believe that different personality aspects dominate at certain periods of our lives. For example, Erikson (1968), who developed a theory on how we form our personalities, hypothesized eight different stages of personality growth between infancy and old age that he called "crises." Three of these stages occur during the school years:

1. The crisis of accomplishment versus inferiority, which occurs sometime during the elementary school years.
2. The crisis of identity versus confusion, which occurs sometime during the adolescent or high school years.
3. The crisis of intimacy versus isolation, which occurs in early adulthood.

During the first crisis of accomplishment versus inferiority, the student seeks ways of producing products or accomplishments that are respected by others. In this manner the child creates a feeling of worth to dispel feelings of inferiority or inadequacy that result from competing in a world where adults appear confident and competent. At first such accomplishments may take the easiest course—being good at sports, being good in school, or being helpful at home. For the teacher this is a particularly challenging time, because student engagement at high rates of success is needed to keep some feelings of worth focused in the classroom. Seeing that every student has some successful experiences in the classroom can be an important vehicle for helping students through this crisis.

Erikson's second crisis during the school years is precipitated by the student's need to come to an understanding of self—to find his or her identity, the "real me." One's sex, race, ethnicity, religion, and physical attractiveness can play important roles in producing—or failing to produce—a consistent and acceptable self-image. This is a process of accepting oneself as one truly is apart from illusions, made-up images, and exaggerations.

The process can be painstakingly slow as illusions are stripped away and replaced by realistic conceptions formed by cruel experiences with the real world. Remember the person who spurned your affections and the hours you spent wondering why? As an effective teacher, you must realize that extreme, rapid fluctuations in a student's behavior may be a signal that this turbulent process is taking place. During this crisis, students sometimes try out different personalities, taking on all the accoutrements of a particular persona (for example, the "jock," "preppie," "socialite," "Casanova," "model," "tough guy," "feminist").

A strict task orientation can help reduce, or at least control, the emotional temperature of a classroom, which may have during these times the fictitious quality of a movie set more than a place for learning. The effective teacher not only understands and empathizes with the conflicting emotions of students at this stage, but also provides the structure and realism needed to help resolve the crisis.

Erikson's third crisis during the school years is that of giving up part of one's identity to develop close and intimate relationships with others. For some, this stage may occur after the high school years, but for most its roots are in high school. Forming relationships, especially with the opposite sex, may be one of the most important and traumatic experiences of school. For some students it may represent the only reason for coming to school. It is not unusual for students during this crisis to form emotional relationships with their teachers as well, especially when relationships with their peers are thwarted due to differences in maturity, attractiveness, interests, or even physical size. There are no simple ways to deal with these emotions. Be aware of their occurrence, try to cushion their impact on the student, and try to channel the student's emotions productively.

Personality differences due to anxiety, motivation, and self-concept are important in all three of the crises. Hardly a day goes by when differences from these sources are not observed. Researchers have confirmed the significant influence of each of these three characteristics on learning, their close relationship to one another, and differences among them across social classes.

Anxiety

Everyone finds anxiety uncomfortable, if only because of its debilitating effect on getting things done. Anxiety about something makes even the simplest tasks seem difficult. One feels threatened, fearful of the unknown, and generally tense. Among your acquaintances, and perhaps within yourself, you have observed (perhaps not consciously) at least two types of anxiety. They are called state anxiety and trait anxiety.

State Anxiety. **State anxiety** (Spielberger, 1966) is an experience of fear or threat related to a particular environmental situation. A common example is the anxiety felt before taking a test. This represents a state or condition that is *momentary* and produced by some specific stimulus in the environment (a test, a report card, a speech before the class, a first date). Levels of state anxiety vary with different environmental stimuli. However, given the right stimulus, this anxiety can occur at any time.

There is a positive side to state anxiety: some is necessary for learning. Without some fear of injury in a poorly executed lab experiment, Johnny may not be cautious enough to avoid the danger. Without fearing the negative consequences of a failing grade, Mary may not do the extra preparation required for a passing grade. Without fear of doing poorly in front of his peers, Billy may not organize his speech very well. Therefore, some state anxiety is important to instructional goals. Devices such as grades, report cards, and assignments are generally sufficient to provide the level of state anxiety necessary to motivate one to respond properly.

However, some danger exists when high levels of state anxiety occur. This can happen when devices like grades, report cards, and assignments are perceived by students as being more significant than they are, thus unintentionally producing high levels of anxiety. In these instances anxiety levels may reach extremes and the student can become nearly immobilized by fear of failure. For example, a student may believe that a "C" on an exam will prevent him or her from entering college, or that doing poorly on a speech will prevent a career requiring oratory ability, or that failing an assignment is a prelude to failing the course. In such instances students perceive the stimulus *out of its proper context*. The consequences can lead to responses such as studying to exhaustion, skipping class the day of the traumatic event, plagiarizing an assignment, or symptoms of illness such as a headache or upset stomach.

There are things that you, the effective teacher, can do to prevent extreme levels of state anxiety. Communicate clearly and directly the exact value—level of importance—to be placed upon each test, product, or assignment *before* it is given (Emmer, Evertson, Sanford, Clements, & Worsham, 1989). Also, provide a variety of tests and assignments for the explicit purpose of creating as large a context as possible; that way, any *single* test, product, or assignment becomes a relatively small part of the total. Reducing students' tendency to exaggerate the significance of any single outcome helps lower state anxiety.

Trait Anxiety. A second type of anxiety found among some students is a general disposition to feel threatened by a wide range of conditions perceived to be harmful. This type of anxiety has been labeled **trait anxiety**, indicating its stability over time. No single stimulus, such as a grade or assignment, can be identified as the source of the anxiety. It results instead from many ill-defined sources. Unlike state anxiety, which all students experience to some degree, this type of anxiety tends *not to fluctuate* within individuals. It exists in different amounts from person to person. In sum, this type of anxiety is a fairly stable characteristic of one's personality, with different individuals having different amounts of it.

High levels of trait anxiety seem to go with high motivation and the need to achieve. But, like state anxiety, extremely high levels can be immobilizing, especially when the need to achieve is guided more by a fear of failure (shame, ridicule by peers, punishment from parents) rather than by a wish to do well. When fear of failure is the primary motive among high-anxiety students, more assignments may be completed with more accuracy, but they will be completed in a mechanical, perfunctory way allowing for little more than the most obvious and expected learning outcomes.

Research shows that when motivation to do well among high-anxiety students is guided more by a desire to do well (e.g., to "produce a perfect product," "create the spectacular," "gain the respect of others," "tackle the impossible") rather than by a fear of failure, more work is accomplished toward a given end in less time and in ways that engage students in discovery types of learning experiences that result in more creative outcomes (Weiner, 1972).

This suggests that one of your tasks as an effective teacher is to control the learning conditions of high-anxiety students. High *state* anxiety requires careful instructions, practice test sessions, and information about the larger context to help lower the anxiety to where it works for, not against, the student. In the case of high *trait* anxiety, conveying a feeling of warmth, encouragement, and support prior to the assignment can turn fears of failure into more productive motives involving a desire to do well. Structuring the assignment in ways that provide for a *range of acceptable responses* serves to focus the high-anxiety student on an attainable end product and away from general fears of being unable to achieve an acceptable level of performance.

Self-Concept

A third aspect of personality relevant to Erikson's three crises is self-concept. Self-concept grows out of interactions with significant others, such as parents, teachers, and peers, during growing up. Significant others act as mirrors for our behavior. That is, they reflect the images we create of ourselves, sometimes in modified and revised form. When the image that is returned looks good, is acceptable to others, and is consistent with what we want it to be, a positive self-concept is formed. When the reflected image does not look good, is unacceptable to others, and is inconsistent with our beliefs about ourselves, a less favorable self-concept is formed.

The formation of self-concept is perhaps one of the most fascinating aspects of personality. It has captured the attention of many psychologists and researchers who have studied the relationship of self-concept to student achievement. The research thus far is sketchy and focuses only upon certain grades and subjects. However, some early evidence indicates that a positive self-concept may be related to better achievement. For example, a strong relationship has been found between poor self-concept and reading disability in the third grade (Bodwin, 1957). A moderate relationship was discerned between self-concept and achievement in the seventh grade (Brookover, Paterson, & Thomas, 1962).

The most recent reviews of the self-concept literature generally report modest but consistent relationships to school achievement (Hansford & Hattie, 1982; Kash & Borich, 1978). This research has been taken as an encouraging sign that a student's concept of self can affect the extent to which he or she *becomes actively engaged in the process of learning,* even if it is not always strongly related to scores on tests of academic performance.

Does a positive self-concept promote achievement? Or does achievement promote a positive self-concept? We don't know. However, the intuitive value of having a positive self-concept is so pervasive in our culture that the order of the relationship may not be all that important. An increase in self-concept is believed to have positive results on behavior, either directly on school achievement or indirectly on one's ability to relate to others, to cope with the problems of daily life, and ultimately to be successful in a career or occupation.

Such important outcomes are not measured by tests of academic achievement. However, good performance on school tests might improve one's self-concept. This, in turn, could influence the other important life outcomes. This is reason enough for engaging students in the learning process at moderate-to-high rates of success: to provide a mirror with a positive image. It also is one reason why high rates of success are so important to low-SES students. It is these students who have been found to have the poorest self-concepts and whose home life provides few opportunities for improving them.

The crucial question asked by every student in the process of forming a self-concept is "How am I being perceived?" In the school environment, this reflected self-image is derived most often from direct, personal interaction with you, the teacher. As a teacher it is your task to be sensitive to and understanding of the impact of the images you are reflecting to students by your words and deeds.

Clearly, you will not always want to reflect what your students believe about themselves. On the other hand, consider that any image you send back by interactions and performance evaluations may have implications far beyond the time when you deliver the message. The message you reflect may contribute to the ever-growing complement of data used by each of your students to form the self-concept they will "wear" for years to come.

Finally, it is not a question of *whether* you will influence the self-concept of your students, but *how*. You will have this influence, at least for some students, whether you know it or not. Thus, it is the *quality* of your performance in this role that counts. Good performance on your part begins with your awareness of your own self-concept and its influence in the formation of self-concepts in your students. Your positive self-concept encourages good self-concepts in your students if you allow a warm and encouraging attitude to come through in words and actions. It continues with your realization that students are identical in some respects, are similar to each other in other respects, and are unique in still other respects.

Your performance as an effective teacher—as a significant other—is always guided by a belief in the inherent value of the unique talents and contributions of each individual student. The secret to improving students' self-concepts lies in the process of finding and reflecting back to students the value of their unique talents.

THE EFFECTS OF THE PEER GROUP ON LEARNING

One of the most powerful but least noted influences on a student's behavior is the peer group. Often considered as the source of a "hidden curriculum," the peer group can influence and even teach students how to behave in class, study for tests, converse with teachers and school administrators, and can contribute to the success or failure of performance in school in many other ways. From the play group in the elementary school to the teenage clique in high school, a student learns from peers how to behave in ways that are acceptable and that will establish status in the eyes of others. Establishing such status reflects group approval, which promotes a good self-concept.

The power of the peer group in influencing individual student behavior stems from the fact that it is the *voluntary* submission of one's will to some larger cause. Teachers and parents must beg, plead, punish, reward, and cajole to exact appropriate behavior from their students, sons, and daughters. But peer groups need not engage in any of these behaviors to obtain a high level of conformity to often unstated and abstract principles of behavior. Trendy school fashions, new slang words, places to "hang out," acceptable social mates, and respected forms of out-of-school activities are communicated and learned to perfection without lesson plans, texts, or even direct verbalization. Instead, these and other behaviors are transmitted by willing "expressors" and received indirectly by "receptors" who anxiously wish to maintain membership in or gain acceptance to a particular peer group.

The power of the peer group to influence the behavior of others was underscored in a 1984 survey by John Goodlad of more than 17,000 junior high and senior high students in 1000 classrooms across the United States. In Goodlad's survey, each student was asked "What is the *one* best thing about this school?" The most frequent response, "my friends," occurred more than twice as often as any other. Teachers were mentioned least often.

Friendship patterns often are created through peer groups and sometimes are adhered to with strong commitments of loyalty, protection, and mutual benefit. These commitments can create individual peer cultures or even gangs within a school. Such cultures can rival the academic commitments made in the classroom and frequently supersede them in importance. Studying for a test or completing homework

Friendship patterns in the classroom often are created through peer groups that exhibit strong commitments of loyalty, protection, and mutual benefit. The importance of peer group characteristics lies with their power to create, promote, and reinforce behaviors that can be conducive or disruptive to the goals of the classroom.

frequently may be sacrificed for the benefit of the peer group. Peer groups can form on the basis of many different individual differences, such as intelligence, achievement, personality, home life, physical appearance, and personal and social interests. But they commonly result from complex combinations of these that are not always discernable to outsiders and sometimes not even to those within the peer group (Epstein & Karweit, 1983).

The importance of peer-group characteristics in the classroom lies in the extent to which they can create, promote, and reinforce behaviors that are disruptive to teaching objectives. More specifically, to what extent can the hidden rules, regulations, and rituals often required by a peer group affect a member's engagement with the learning process?

Some peer groups can promote an increased activity in the learning process. When intelligence, a high need to achieve, and acceptance of responsibility are the basis of a peer group, it well may promote sharp competition and a conformity among its members to achieve in accord with the highest academic standards. Membership in the National Honor Society, ambition to enroll in college, and a desire to pursue certain types of careers sometimes are the "glue" that holds such peer groups together.

However, combinations of individual differences also can combine to promote two problem types (Lightfoot, 1983). One is passive learners, in which bare minimum effort is the desired standard (nothing extra is volunteered). The other is troublemakers whose willingness to disrupt, intimidate, and provoke is reinforced and accorded special tribute by peer-group members. The latter type, in contrast with the passive learner who simply is not motivated or successful in school, actually fights against the conformity and routine demands of the classroom by waging a surreptitious war in which all authority figures become targets.

Teachers can have little influence in the formation of peer groups, particularly the troublemaking type. But here are several approaches you can employ to help dissipate peer-group influence in your classroom:

1. *Rearrange potentially disruptive peer groups into more heterogeneous groups* in terms of characteristics and interests. Perhaps you can arrange with the school counselor to send some members to other classes in return for an equal number of students.

2. *Divide peer-group members among other peer groups within your own classroom.* Such a division could be part of a process in which different subgroups are assigned different activities, or potentially disruptive peer-group members are assigned to different parts of the classroom.

3. *Stress group work* in which members are from different peer groups. This lessens disruptive behavior, especially when equal numbers of actively engaged learners are assigned to the disruptive group. When different types of individuals are assigned to work cooperatively, group dynamics predict that group behavior will approach a middle ground, preventing members from executing extreme behaviors.

4. *Assign older students to interact with and supervise younger students in a peer-tutoring situation.* This cross-age tutoring can increase pressure for prosocial behavior and reduce pressure for antisocial behavior.

Chapter 10 offers more about effective teaching practices for cooperative learning. Chapter 13 presents effective teaching practices for special types of learners.

THE EFFECTS OF SOCIAL CONTEXT ON LEARNING

Closely associated with the effects of the peer group on learning is the influence of the social context in which your learners live. Among the influences upon learners the social context provides are media, sexual pressure, drugs, cars, and jobs.

A study by the American Association of School Administrators (1988) estimated that a typical year of prime-time television viewing included over 20,000 scenes of suggested sexual intercourse, sexual comment, and innuendo between unmarried partners. That is outdated by today's sexual standard, and some statistics now indicate that television transmits over 65,000 such sexual messages each year. And these estimates do not include the explicit sexual conduct that has become commonplace on the big screen, which is attended by the typical teen an average of once every other week. In a 1986 Harris and Associates poll conducted for The Planned Parenthood Federation of America, large numbers of teens told researchers they believe that television gives a realistic picture of sexually transmitted diseases (45%), pregnancy and the consequences of sex (41%), family planning to prevent pregnancy (28%), and people making love (24%).

Although relationships between the media and teenage sex may be speculative, statistics reveal that teenage sex translates into teenage pregnancy in a fairly direct way. Of every 100 children born today, 12 will be born out of wedlock. Of the children born out of wedlock, 50% are from teenage mothers. Facts about teen pregnancy acquired by the Children's Defense Fund (1986, 1988), National Research Council (1987), and The Alan Guttmacher Institute (1986) indicate that:

☐ More than one million teens become pregnant each year—that's 1 of every 10. Nearly 30,000 of these are under the age of 15.

☐ Before leaving high school, one in four girls will experience pregnancy.

☐ Half the teenagers who become parents before they are 18 will not receive a high school diploma by the time they are in their twenties.

☐ A study in one major city found that the suicide rate of teenage mothers is seven times higher than for other teenagers.

☐ Teens most likely to become pregnant are also those least able to cope with it: teens who are young, live in urban centers, are poor, whose parents have limited educations, who live with only one parent, and who have poor academic skills.

☐ Teenage girls with poor academic skills are five times as likely to become mothers before the age of 16 as are teenagers with average or above average skills in high school.

Teenage pregnancy combines the themes of poverty, poor academic skills, low self-esteem, and a single-parent household or one that has experienced divorce or separation. On the other hand, some evidence suggests that teens who feel positive about themselves, have good academic records, are involved in sports or other extracurricular activities, and come from two-parent households are the least likely to become teenage parents (American Association of School Administrators, 1988).

Another factor that may affect your learners is the prevalence of drugs in the school environment. There is now major agreement that drugs play a pervasive role in school. Research by the U.S. Department of Education in 1986 suggests that drug use among children may be 10 times more prevalent than previously suspected. They report that:

- ☐ The U.S. has the highest rate of teenage drug use of any industrialized nation.
- ☐ 61% of high school seniors in the U.S. have used drugs.
- ☐ 57% of students buy most of their drugs at school.
- ☐ 33% of high school seniors who have used marijuana report having used it at school.
- ☐ 66% of high school seniors who have used amphetamines report having taken them at school.

Experts have long agreed that drug use creates a psychological dependence or bonding with the drug that can have deleterious effects on school performance. In addition, more than half of all adolescent suicides are suspected to be drug related. Drug use has been unmistakably tied to:

- ☐ Erosion of the self-discipline and motivation required for learning.
- ☐ Truancy and dropping out of school.
- ☐ Crime and misconduct that disrupt an orderly and safe atmosphere conducive to learning.

The influence of media and drugs on the personal and academic lives of some learners is significant. But, for the secondary school learner, the influence of cars and jobs must be added to this equation. Oftentimes, cars and jobs are synonymous in the life of a teen, for with the automobile comes the job to pay for it and its fuel, insurance, and upkeep. The companion ingredients of car and job may represent the glue that gives all other sources of social distraction their significant and unabating influence.

A car and a job after school (and sometimes before school) can compete mightily with the less inviting aspects of the classroom. Unfortunately, the effects of owning a car can be masked everywhere but in a classroom. The classroom requires not just the presence of a recuperating warm body, but a body that is alert, mentally active, and willing to submit to the cognitive demands of learning.

This oftentimes is too much for a working student whose schedule sandwiches school between job, peers, and courtship. For some of your learners, school will be a place to rest and replenish their energy before the scheduled onslaught of activity begins at the end of the school day. Needless to say, this makes the span of

Drug use creates a psychological dependence or bonding with the drug that has been related to an erosion of the self-discipline required for learning as well as truancy, dropping out, and crime. More than half of all adolescent suicides are suspected to be drug related.

individual differences within a classroom even larger, because only some learners will be ready and willing to learn. In other words, on some days, some potential learners may not be teachable under *any* circumstances—an unfortunate fact of the complex social environment in which we live.

There are no simple methods to combat the debilitating effects the social environment may have upon some of your students. However, your early awareness of the behavioral signs of learners in trouble is essential for school programs and social agencies to intervene effectively. The important first step toward providing assistance is to acknowledge that these problems will occur among some of your learners.

It also is necessary that you know about school and community programs that aid students who are experiencing substance abuse, pregnancy, divorce, and/or adult responsibilities that may be incompatible with school. Your knowledge can direct students to programs and services that can help them. Above all, your cooperation and a good working relationship with other school professionals (e.g., psychologist, counselor, nurse, social worker) is critical to helping troubled learners return to the state of readiness and self-discipline they must have to benefit from the goals of your classroom.

SCHOOLS, NEIGHBORHOODS, SUBCULTURES, AND THE LEARNING ENVIRONMENT

There is no question that your students' individual differences in intelligence, achievement, personality, home life, peer group, and social context can dramatically impact teaching methods and learning results. So, why place such diverse students in the same classroom? Would it not be more efficient to segregate students by intelligence and achievement level, personality type, degree of disadvantage due to home life, or even according to the most advantageous peer group? The result of such grouping might be quite astounding, if it were tried.

It is difficult to imagine life in such a segregated environment, for we live, work, and play in a world that is complex and diverse. However, our forefathers seriously considered this very question. Their answer is in the first 10 amendments to the U.S. Constitution, known as the Bill of Rights, which gives every citizen the unqualified right to "life, liberty, and the pursuit of happiness." This constitutional guarantee specifically precludes any attempt to advance a single group at the expense of any other group. It even precludes segregating groups when "separate but equal" treatment is accorded them, because even the labeling of groups as "different" implies inequality, regardless of the motives for forming them.

These are important constitutional implications for the American classroom. They promote an environment that not only tolerates differences among individuals but also is conducive to integrating diverse individuals. This constitutional implication has been called the "pluralistic ideal."

The Pluralistic Ideal

The pluralistic ideal has become a guide at national and state levels for making our most important societal decisions on housing, job opportunities, college and professional school admissions, transportation, elementary and secondary education, and the dispersal of public services. What is not always evident is that the pluralistic ideal also provides the rationale for the composition of our neighborhoods, schools, and classrooms. And it is not limited to cultural and minority issues; it extends to the integration and mixture of all types of individuals, including those marked by the individual differences discussed in this chapter.

It is important to note why the pluralistic ideal has become an insightful constitutional legacy. The pluralistic ideal has two advantages that our forefathers recognized. First is the realization that our country is and always will be a melting pot of enormous diversity. Second is the need for such diversity.

The Melting Pot.   America's diversity two centuries ago resulted from the varied nationalities and religious persuasions that contributed to our general culture. It later was enriched by different ethnic groups and most recently by increasingly diverse lifestyles, politics, dress, and values.

With all this diversity, clearly a cultural core would be difficult as a common ground from which to govern all the people. The role of our pluralistic ideal was to acculturate and to socialize vastly different groups to a general core of values that could provide the framework of a government. The means of accomplishing this was our Constitution. It promotes the integration and mixing of all individuals in the land, regardless of how different they are. The Constitution makes illegal the segregation of individuals into any group that, by labeling or any other means, would limit their life, liberty, and the pursuit of happiness, or deny maximum individual development. The Constitution encourages and promotes the establishment of a core culture to which all individuals adhere, regardless of their personal values and cultural preference.

By having to work, live, and play with diverse individuals—at least in our public lives—we have established a common cultural heritage. This heritage has rules (e.g., paying taxes), loyalties (going to war), rituals (observing specified holidays), and laws (respecting the rights of others). We all have come to accept these, regardless of our differences.

The Need for Diversity.   A second insight reflected in the pluralistic ideal was the shared realization that, in a world complicated by such social and technological problems as pollution, disease, illiteracy, and congestion, we need divergent viewpoints, different abilities, and diverse values to address these problems. No single set of skills, attitudes, temperament, personality, or aptitude can provide all that is needed to solve our problems.

By allowing and encouraging this diversity in human potential, our country has possessed for the better part of its history the most enviable work force in the world. It has been responsible for impressive breakthroughs in medicine, electronics, energy, and aerospace, and highly creative approaches to problems in health, education, and the behavioral sciences. This has been accomplished as a result of, not in spite of, the cultural diversity and differences that flourish in our communities, schools, and classrooms. This flourishing diversity directly results from the pluralistic ideal.

Your Role in the Pluralistic Ideal.   To continue this success, you as an effective teacher must carry on the pluralistic ideal by respecting and accepting the diversity of human potential that lies within your classroom, and every classroom. Even more important, you must fully develop such potential if the pluralistic ideal is to serve us in the future as it has in the past. Your flexibility in teaching allows for adapting instruction to students' group-related learning styles, using different instructional approaches in teaching students of differing ethnic and racial backgrounds, and adapting instruction to the concerns and needs of the community. Above all, your teaching strategies must emphasize the importance of all students working cooperatively with their peers and with their teachers. In the chapters ahead we will explore many ways of accomplishing these important goals.

A FINAL WORD

This chapter discussed individual differences that affect learning and determine the degree of success in teaching different types of learners. Individual differences are many and their apparent influence on the learning process is great. Your teaching will be successful to the extent that you (1) become acquainted with the individual differences operating in your classroom and (2) can adapt your teaching style to accommodate these differences.

You have seen in this chapter the considerable influence on learning exerted by your students' aptitudes, prior achievements, personalities, home lives, peer groups, and social contexts. Your students are far from being blank slates onto which you impart knowledge and understanding of your subject matter. On the contrary, your students, with all of their individual differences, are an active force in determining your success at transmitting your knowledge and understanding. In other words, not only your own behavior but also that of your students will affect how successfully you can execute the key teaching behaviors of lesson clarity, instructional variety, task orientation, engagement in the learning process, and student success.

SUMMING UP

This chapter introduced the diversity of students found in classrooms and how this diversity must be acknowledged in your teaching methods. Its main points were:

1. Early conceptions of teaching viewed students as empty vessels into which the teacher poured the content of the day's lesson. These conceptions failed to consider the effect of individual differences on learning.

2. A knowledge of the individual differences among learners is important (a) to adapt instructional methods to individual learning needs and (b) to understand and place in perspective the reasons behind the school performance of individual learners.

3. One misunderstanding that some teachers and parents have about intelligence, or IQ, is that it is a single, unified dimension.

4. Specific aptitudes or factors of intelligence are more predictive of success in school and specific occupations than is general intelligence.

5. Knowing your learners' specific strengths and weaknesses and altering instructional goals and methods accordingly will contribute to greater learning than will categorizing and teaching your students according to their general intelligence.

6. Task-relevant prior learning represents the facts, skills, and understandings that must be taught if subsequent learning is to occur. Mastery of task-relevant prior learning often is required for subsequent learning to take place.

7. Traditionally, students from lower-class and lower middle-class families have not performed as well on standardized achievement tests as students from middle-class and upper-class families. Most of the differences in educational achievement that occur by race and ethnicity can be accounted for by social class.

8. An important characteristic that distinguishes lower-class children from middle-class and upper-class children is that the latter more rapidly

acquire knowledge of the world outside their homes and neighborhoods.

9. Low-SES families are more likely than middle-SES and high-SES families (a) to emphasize physical punishment rather than reasoning and (b) to encourage rote learning (memorization, recall of facts, etc.) rather than independent, self-directed learning.

10. Some instructional strategies to meet the learning needs of low-SES students include (a) use a variety of audiovisual and exploratory materials that require alternate modalities (e.g., sight vs. sound), (b) have high expectations and reward intellectual accomplishments, (c) emphasize correct word usage and correct linguistic patterns, and (d) get students to talk about personal experiences to improve their self-concepts.

11. Erikson's (1968) three crises during the school years are: (a) accomplishment versus inferiority, occurring during the elementary school years; (b) identity versus confusion, occurring during the adolescent or high school years; and (c) intimacy versus isolation, occurring in early adulthood.

12. State anxiety is a temporary condition produced by some specific stimulus in the environment, such as a test.

13. Some state anxiety is necessary for learning; grades, report cards, and assignments generally provide proper levels of state anxiety to motivate students to engage in the learning process.

14. Extreme levels of state anxiety can be avoided by putting in perspective the value (importance) of a specific assignment compared to other assignments, and by creating a large total context of assignments.

15. Trait anxiety is stable within individuals over time but varies among individuals. It is produced by a wide range of ill-defined conditions perceived by an individual to be harmful.

16. High levels of trait anxiety are associated with high motivation and a need to achieve, but extreme levels are associated with an intense fear of failure that dampens creativity and results in perfunctory, mechanical responses.

17. Extreme levels of trait anxiety sometimes can be avoided by making a range of alternative responses acceptable for a given assignment.

18. Self-concept has only a modest relationship to school achievement but has a strong relationship to active engagement in the learning process and success in one's career or occupation.

19. You can improve students' concept of self by finding and reflecting back to them the value of their unique talents.

20. Peer groups are an influential source of learners' behavior both in and out of the classroom. When their effects are negative, they may be dissipated by placing the members of potentially disruptive peer groups into more heterogeneous groups and assigning cooperative work assignments within the groups.

21. The debilitating effects of substance abuse, pregnancy, divorce, and adult responsibilities can be mitigated by (a) an awareness that these problems often occur in classrooms and (b) a knowledge of and cooperation with other school professionals who assist and direct troubled learners to programs and agencies that can help.

22. The pluralistic ideal describes the bringing together of diverse individuals so that (a) a common core of values can be established to provide the framework for a system of cooperation and government and (b) the unique and individual talents of individuals can be applied to solving the problems common to all.

FOR DISCUSSION AND PRACTICE

*1. In what two ways might you use your knowledge of the individual differences in your classroom to become a more effective teacher?

*2. Given the following list of learners, what types of instructional strategies might you emphasize for each type to meet their learning needs?

high-state anxiety

low auditory ability

gifted

low SES

poor self-concept

high-trait anxiety

unassertive, overassertive, and aggressive

disruptive peer group

3. Describe briefly the environmentalist and hereditarian positions concerning the use of general IQ tests in schools. Devise a counterargument you could use in responding to an argument from an extremist in each camp.

4. Explain the role that socioeconomic status (SES) is believed to play in influencing the score one might attain on a test of general intelligence. If behaviors solely related to SES could be eliminated, how might differences in the tested IQ among subgroups of learners change?

5. Identify aptitudes or factors that are likely to be more predictive than general IQ of success in selected school subjects and occupations.

6. For each of the following, give an example of a school subject or content area in which you might expect a high score on an aptitude test to predict a high score on a test of subject-matter achievement.

Aptitude	School Subject or Content Area
verbal comprehension	_____
general reasoning	_____
memory	_____
use of numbers	_____
psychomotor speed	_____
spatial relations	_____
word fluency	_____

7. Give an example of task-relevant prior knowledge that might be required before each of the following instructional objectives could be taught successfully.
   a. Adding two-digit numbers
   b. Reading latitude and longitude from a map
   c. Writing a four-sentence paragraph
   d. Seeing an amoeba under a microscope
   e. Correctly pronouncing a new two-syllable word
   f. Understanding how the executive branch of government works

   g. Playing ten minutes of basketball without committing a foul
   h. Responding correctly to a fire alarm
   i. Solving the equation
      $c^2 = a^2 + b^2$
   j. Punctuating two independent clauses

8. What might be some of the home-life characteristics of low-SES students that make them consistently score lower than high-SES students on standardized achievement tests? What are some teaching practices that might shrink differences in standardized achievement due to SES?

*9. Identify one approach that might be used to improve the poor self-concept of a low-SES student.

*10. Which indicators best represent state anxiety and which best represent trait anxiety?
   a. Looks scared and exhausted before a test
   b. Becomes nervous whenever asked about where he lives
   c. Continuously combs hair and puts on makeup
   d. Has an incessant drive to get into college
   e. Skips school whenever an oral presentation is required
   f. Never fails to complete an extra credit assignment
   g. Always boasts and exaggerates about the number of girls he dates
   h. Copies others' homework often
   i. Wants to become the most respected athlete in the school
   j. Never brings home papers that have received a grade lower than "A"

*11. Identify two reasons why it is important to promote a positive self-concept, even though its relationship to tests of academic achievement may not be strong.

*12. Identify two methods for dealing with a disruptive peer group in your classroom.

13. Explain what steps you would take after suspecting one of your learners is experiencing the effects of substance abuse.

14. Explain in your own words what is meant by "pluralistic ideal." What are some signs in a typical school that show the commitment made by our country, its people, and its government toward this ideal?

---

*Answers to asterisked questions (*) in this and the other chapters are in Appendix B.

SUGGESTED READINGS

Bloom, B. (1981). *All our children learning.* New York: McGraw-Hill.

Shows how learning differences can be greatly reduced with appropriate environmental and instructional conditions.

Epstein, J., & Karweit, N. (Eds.). (1983). *Friendship in school.* New York: Academic Press.

A compilation of different views and school descriptions that vividly portray the peer-group culture comprising the "hidden curriculum."

Good, T., & Stipek, D. (1983). Individual differences in the classroom: A psychological perspective. In G. D. Fenstermacher & J. I. Goodlad (Eds.), *Individual differences and the common curriculum* (82d yearbook of the National Society for the Study of Education, Part 2). Chicago: University of Chicago Press.

A review of the many different types of individual differences in the classroom and their known or hypothesized effect on student achievement.

Hill, H. (1989). *Effective strategies for teaching minority students.* Bloomington, IN: National Educational Service.

A guide to successfully teaching minority youth and developing cultural sensitivity that promotes learning and achievement.

Kash, M., & Borich, G. (1978). *Teacher behavior and pupil self-concept.* Reading, MA: Addison-Wesley.

Illustrates five separate dimensions of self-concept using autobiographical quotations from well-known individuals, and reviews the most current research relating to these divisions of the self-concept.

Labov, W. (1972). Academic ignorance and black intelligence. *Atlantic Monthly, 229*(6), 59–67.

Dispels the myth that there are any meaningful intellectual differences among the races.

McClelland, D. C. (1973). Testing for competence rather than for "intelligence." *American Psychologist, 28,* 1–14.

A case against general intelligence and for the measurement of specific skills related to success in school and in the workplace.

Sinclair, K. (1987). Students' affective characteristics. In M. J. Dunkin (Ed.), *International encyclopedia of teaching and teacher education.* New York: Pergamon.

An interesting article on the complex social and emotional behaviors of school learners and their potential effects in the classroom.

Steinberg, R. H. (1983). Reasoning, problem solving and intelligence. In R. J. Sternberg (Ed.), *Handbook of human intelligence.* New York: Cambridge University Press.

One of the most authoritative sources on new ways of defining and teaching intelligence.

Wang, M., & Lindvall, C. (1984). Individual differences and school learning environments. *Review of Research in Education, 11,* 161–225.

A summary of some of the most recent research on the individual differences of learners and the effect on what is learned.

3

Instructional
Goals and Plans

Chapters 1 and 2 introduced some behaviors expected of you as a teacher and some individual differences you can expect among your students. This chapter combines these two topics and shows how to organize your thinking about whom, what, and how you will teach. We'll look at how goals are formulated, where they come from, and the important relationship between goals and planning. First, let's consider the distinction among aims, goals, and objectives and their use in instructional planning.

AIMS, GOALS, AND OBJECTIVES

The words "aims," "goals," and "objectives" often are used interchangeably without recognizing their different, albeit related, meanings. **Aims** are general expressions of values that provide a sense of direction. They are broad enough to be acceptable to large numbers of individuals, such as "the taxpayers," "parents," or "the American people." Common examples of aims are:

Every citizen should be prepared to work in a technological world.

Every adult should be functionally literate.

Every American should be able to vote as an informed citizen in a democratic society.

Aims such as these are important in expressing values and communicating societal concerns with which many individuals can agree. However, aims are so broad and general that their implementation is difficult. To be useful, aims often require greater specification in the form of goals and objectives.

Goals, like aims, provide a sense of direction, but they are more specific. Goals relate a general aim to some specific aspect of the curriculum. The three aims stated previously could be converted to goals like these:

Students should understand the use of the microcomputer.

Students should be able to read and write well enough to become gainfully employed.

Students should know how to choose a candidate and vote in an election.

Goals bring aims down to earth by connecting them to some tangible aspect of the curriculum (e.g., computer literacy, language instruction, or a unit on local government). Although goals are more specific than aims, they always are derived in ways that contribute to realizing the aims. Goals often are formulated at the national or state level by specially convened groups—legislators, panels of informed citizens, and curriculum specialists—charged with establishing school curricula.

Common sources from which goals can be derived are:

School district reports and policies

Faculty handbooks

National curriculum commissions

Blue ribbon committee reports

State boards of education

National teacher groups and associations

Textbook committees

Curriculum guides

Courses of study, texts

Needs assessment reports

Objectives carry this process one step further by describing the *specific behavior* the learner is to attain, the *conditions* under which the behavior must be demonstrated, and the *proficiency level* at which the behavior is to be performed. The three previously stated goals could be converted to objectives like these:

☐ Students will, using their own choice of microcomputer, produce an edited two-page manuscript free of typographical errors in 15 minutes or less.

☐ Students will, at the end of the 12th grade, be able to write a 500-word essay with no more than two grammatical and punctuation errors and to read newspapers and magazines with no errors in comprehension.

☐ Students will, at the end of an eighth-grade unit on government, participate in a mock election by choosing a candidate from the prescribed list and giving three reasons for their choice.

Objectives like these often are included in curriculum guides and teacher's manuals that accompany textbooks and workbooks. Unfortunately, objectives are not always well written and do not always fit a particular class of students or the way you may choose to structure the content you are teaching. Often, you must formulate objectives or rewrite them to fit individual students, the instructional goals of your school district, and your organization of content.

Table 3.1 summarizes distinctions among aims, goals, and objectives.

THE FLOW OF AIMS TO GOALS

How societal aims are to be achieved is purposely left vague, to allow professionals the greatest flexibility in translating aims into goals and objectives. Goals are an important link between aims and objectives because they specify *areas of the curriculum*. Goals thus help make the aims implementable. Flexibility is left to other education professionals to specify the *exact behaviors, conditions, and proficiencies* required to achieve the goals within a particular school context. These professionals include teachers, principals, and school administrators. Their knowledge of the classroom, school, and school district ensures that the translation of goals to objectives is feasible, practical, and serves local needs.

Translation of aims into goals and objectives must respond to societal needs and values. This is essential because education costs are borne by all in our society. If a superintendent or school board implements goals too far removed from societal aims—too different from what the community wants, needs, and values—then the superintendent may be out of a job, and the school board may not be reelected. Often it is mistakenly believed that only school administrators are responsible for the cur-

TABLE 3.1
Aims, goals, and objectives

Category	Description	Examples
Aims	Broad statements of very general outcomes that 1. do not include specific levels of performance 2. do not identify specific areas of the curriculum 3. tend to change infrequently and in response to societal pressure	Become a good citizen Be competent in the basic skills areas Be creative Learn problem solving Appreciate art Develop high-level thinking skills
Goals	More narrowly defined statements of outcomes that 1. apply to specific curricula 2. may be formulated on an annual basis 3. are developed by program coordinators, principals, and other school administrators	Students receiving the new reading program should realize achievement gains on the Iowa Test of Basic Skills.
Objectives	Specific statements of learner behavior or outcomes that state the conditions under which the behavior is to be exhibited (e.g., given a list of 25 vocabulary words at the 8th-grade level) and the proficiency to be attained (e.g., the student will correctly provide synonyms for 20 out of the 25). These behaviors are expected to be attained at the end of a specified time of instruction.	By Friday, the students will be able to recite the names of the months in order. The student will be able to take apart and reassemble correctly a one-barrel carburetor with the tools provided within 45 minutes.

riculum in a school. They are responsible for *implementing* the curriculum, but ultimately the local public and citizens within a state control the aims of schooling upon which are based the goals and objectives of a curriculum.

Figure 3.1 illustrates how public concerns reach the classroom. This process also can be viewed as a funneling or narrowing of focus (Figure 3.2) in which the general aims of society gradually are translated into specific and manageable objectives for instruction. Two things of particular importance to you, the classroom teacher, are apparent from these illustrations.

First, *objectives must relate closely to the goals* and reasonably closely to the aims from which they are derived. Thus, to write objectives, you must be knowledgeable about the goals they represent. Forming objectives without knowing the goals or aims places you in the precarious situation of not being able to *justify* your objectives

FIGURE 3.1

Back to basics: The flow of aims to objectives

From Educational Testing and Measurement: *Classroom Application and Practice,* 3rd ed. by Tom
Kubiszyn and Gary Borich. Reprinted by permission of HarperCollins Publishers.

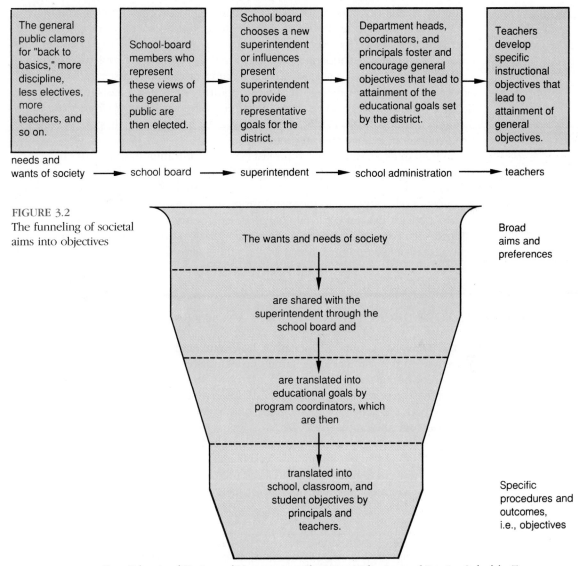

FIGURE 3.2

The funneling of societal
aims into objectives

From Educational Testing and Measurement: *Classroom Application and Practice,* 3rd ed. by Tom
Kubiszyn and Gary Borich. Reprinted by permission of HarperCollins Publishers.

to parents, the community, school administrators, and students. Your most valuable
resource for preparing objectives based on community values is your adopted textbook and curriculum guide, plus the previously mentioned sources from which goals
are commonly derived.

The second aspect of translating aims into objectives is the importance of local community prerogatives. While local community values and needs often represent the values and needs of the general public at the state and national level, they may not always be identical. School boards and local citizens have the right and responsibility to establish a curriculum that is sensitive to the needs of their community.

State-adopted textbooks and curriculum guides generally are chosen to reflect local priorities. However, these publications often must be expanded and enhanced by individual school districts in response to (1) specific problems and opportunities (e.g., the need to teach remedial reading, advanced courses in mathematics, or English as a second language), (2) areas requiring special emphasis (e.g., computer literacy, critical thinking skills, or multicultural awareness), and (3) immediate priorities representing the socio-emotional needs of the learner (e.g., dropout prevention, drug education, and suicide prevention).

As an effective teacher, you must be aware of community priorities that could require local interpretation of state-mandated curricula or general societal concerns and values. These community priorities often appear in press reports and television accounts of school issues, in the platforms of school board candidates, and in school district policies that reflect local concerns. As an effective teacher you may have to address such issues as declining scores on standardized achievement tests, increasing school dropout rate, unmet needs of the gifted and talented, or moral and ethical issues within the context of your regular instruction.

SOCIETAL GOALS FOR EDUCATION IN THE 1980s AND 1990s

In the previous section we looked at how aims and goals justify your classroom objectives. At the national level, some important aims and goals have emerged from policy reports that call for reform and improvement of our entire educational system. Five of these reports, issued during the 1980s, have been particularly instrumental in revising both elementary and secondary school curricula and in setting the direction of curriculum reform for the 1990s.*

These reports were stimulated in part by a growing disenchantment with the quality of public school education voiced by many segments of our society, including parents, taxpayers, legislators, business and military leaders, and some teacher groups. This disenchantment was not limited to matters of curriculum. It extended to the

---

*The reports are: (1) The College Board, (1983), *Academic preparation for college: What students need to know and be able to do*, New York: Author; (2) Education Commission of the States, Task Force on Education for Economic Growth, (1983), *Action for excellence: Comprehensive plan to improve our nation's schools*, Denver: Author; (3) National Commission on Excellence in Education, (1983), *A nation at risk: The imperative for educational reform*, Washington: U.S. Department of Education; (4) U.S. National Science Board, Commission on Precollege Education in Mathematics, Science, and Technology, (1983), *Educating Americans for the 21st century: A plan of action for improving mathematics, science and technology education for all American elementary and secondary students so that their achievement is the best in the world by 1995*, Washington: National Science Foundation; and (5) Twentieth Century Fund Task Force on Federal Elementary and Secondary Education Policy, (1983), *Making the grade: A report of the task force*. New York: The Fund.

quality of teaching, leading in some cases to recommendations for teacher competency testing and new requirements for certification. Each of the five reports registered its own concerns, but together they expressed a consensus about what was wrong with American education and what to do about it.

For example, all five reports generally agreed that our schools needed a back-to-basics approach. They saw as essential a strengthening of curricula in math, science, English, foreign languages, and social studies. Also, high technology was represented by a call for more computer science and computer literacy, both as separate courses and as adjuncts to other courses. The reports called for renewed effort in teaching higher-order thinking skills, including the teaching of concepts, problem solving, and creativity (as opposed to rote memorization and parroting of facts, lists, names, and dates that are divorced from a larger problem-solving context).

Not surprisingly, all the reports recommended increasing both grading standards and the number of required core courses (as opposed to elective courses), especially at the secondary level. This recommendation went hand in hand with the suggestion that colleges raise their admission requirements by requiring more course work in core subjects, especially math and foreign languages.

Most of the reports recommended increasing school hours and homework time. For example, one report suggested a minimum seven-hour school day (some schools have fewer than six hours) and a 200-day school year (many have a 180-day year). Presumably, students would spend more time actively engaged in the learning process if they took more courses and spent more time in school. Time spent on extracurricular and other noninstructional activities was to be reduced accordingly, as would administrative interruptions. These recommendations foreshadowed a tough new policy in which many school districts went on record as wanting to reverse the more flexible curriculum, grading standards, and school management style of the 1960s and 1970s.

The recommendations in these reports were from blue ribbon committees of informed citizens who were far enough removed from the day-to-day workings of education that they could gain fresh insights into the problems of our nation's schools. For example, by taking a broad view of our educational establishment, these committees noted that:

1. During the 1960s and 1970s, many elective and remedial courses replaced core courses in mathematics, science, English, and foreign language.
2. Students in the 1960s and 1970s were assigned less homework than their counterparts in earlier times.
3. Scores on many standardized achievement tests declined, particularly in math and reading. [Today, these scores appear to be increasing, perhaps due to the enactment of some of these reforms.]
4. Requirements for graduation became lower over the years; fewer students took advanced math, science, and foreign languages.
5. Proficiency in the basic skills of reading, writing, and arithmetic were at an all-time low; many new business employees and military recruits required training in the fundamentals of reading, writing, and mathematics.

At the core of the five reports was the perception that our schools had lost sight of their role in teaching students *how to think*. Traditionally, this was accomplished through the core curriculum (English, math, science, foreign languages, and social studies). However, with fewer advanced offerings in these areas and with so much time being spent in remedial activities, teaching children how to think may have been seriously curtailed. These reports suggested that the schools must reverse this trend by requiring students to study both the basic core and more advanced areas. Such instruction would require more homework, higher testing and grading standards, and higher-order thinking skills. Mastering these thinking skills (problem solving, concept learning, decision making, and making value judgments) is important because they are required both in the working world and in advanced education and training.

Here are some of the major goals contained in these recommendations:

Students should be trained to live and function in a technological world.

Students should possess minimum competencies in reading, writing, and mathematics.

Students should possess high-order thinking, conceptual, and problem-solving skills.

Students should be required to enroll in all the core subjects each school year, to the extent of their abilities.

Students should be trained to work independently and to complete assignments without direct supervision.

Students should improve school attendance and stay in school longer each day and year.

Students should be given more tests that require problem-solving skills and higher grading standards.

Although other goals can be derived from these reports, the preceding list exemplifies how a broad national consensus can affect the formulation of goals and objectives for some time. Corresponding objectives still are being written—by state education agencies, school districts, curriculum specialists, and classroom teachers—to tie these goals to specific areas of the school curriculum.

Chapter 4 shows how such goals can be converted into objectives for implementation in your classroom. Chapters 6, 7, and 8 present teaching strategies that can help you address the specific goals in these reports.

INPUTS TO THE PLANNING PROCESS

You are now ready to consider planning and its relationship to decisions you make in the classroom. Planning is the process of deciding what and how your students should learn. Teachers make one such decision on the average of every two minutes while they are teaching, according to an estimate by Clark and Peterson (1986). However,

An important recommendation for curriculum reform in the 1990s is that learners be better trained to work independently and to attain more high-level thinking, conceptual, and problem-solving skills.

these "in-flight" decisions (McNair, 1978–1979) are only part of the decision-making process. Teachers also make many other decisions involving priorities and judgments about the form and content of instruction.

For example, how much lecturing, questioning, discussing, and testing are you going to do? How much material will you cover for a specific topic? How in-depth will your instruction be? The first question requires a planning decision on the *form* or style of teaching. The other two questions require decisions on the *content* of instruction. You will make many decisions on both form and content before, during, and after teaching a lesson. Planning is the systematic process that helps you decide issues of form and content and helps you set priorities.

Although preparing lesson plans is closely linked to objectives, planning begins with your knowledge of aims and goals, acquired from sources such as blue ribbon reports, textbooks, curriculum guides, and school district policies. Planning also begins from your knowledge of the learner, of the subject matter to be taught, and of teaching methods. Your keys to the planning process are gathering information and systematically recording data in these areas.

In the previous section you saw the importance of aims and goals. Now let's consider the three other inputs to planning: knowledge of the learner, knowledge of the subject matter, and knowledge of teaching methods.

Knowledge of the Learner

Chapter 2 showed the importance of acquainting yourself with learners' needs and individual differences. In fact, in a review of six research studies on planning, teachers were found to spend more of their planning time on learner characteristics (an average of 43%) than on any other area (Clark and Peterson, 1986). Recall the major characteristics of students: intelligence and achievement, personality (anxiety, motivation, and self-concept), home life and extent of disadvantagedness, and peer-group influence. These are windows through which you "see" special learning needs. They also are the psychological characteristics that reflect how ready your students are to learn, telling you at what level to begin your instruction.

Planning with respect to learners includes consciously noting their characteristics in these areas and recording significant departures from what might be expected within the traditional curriculum. These departures can signal special learning needs that require you to select content, materials, objectives, and methods that match your students' characteristics. These inputs are instrumental in helping you organize, select, sequence, and allocate time to various topics of instruction.

Knowledge of Subject Matter

A second primary input to planning is your knowledge of your academic discipline and grade level. As a student, you have spent much time and effort becoming knowledgeable in the subjects you will teach. You also have learned a subtle yet important aspect of your discipline, perhaps without realizing it. You have observed and absorbed valuable information about how textbook authors, your instructors, and subject-matter specialists *organize* concepts in your teaching area. This includes how parts relate to the whole, how content is prioritized, how transitions are made between topics, and which themes are major or minor.

Figure 3.3 illustrates three of the many content organizations you can use in lesson and unit planning. Such organizations are used by teachers, curriculum specialists, and textbook authors to make learning easier, more orderly, and more conducive to retention and later use (Clark & Yinger, 1979). These organization schemes usually are spelled out by subject matter specialists in textbooks, instructional mate-

FIGURE 3.3

Some ways of organizing content

From *Instructional Design Theories and Models: An Overview of Their Current Status* (p. 345) by C. Reigeluth, 1983, Hillsdale, NJ: Lawrence Erlbaum Associates, Inc. Copyright © 1983 by Lawrence Erlbaum Associates, Inc. Reprinted by permission.

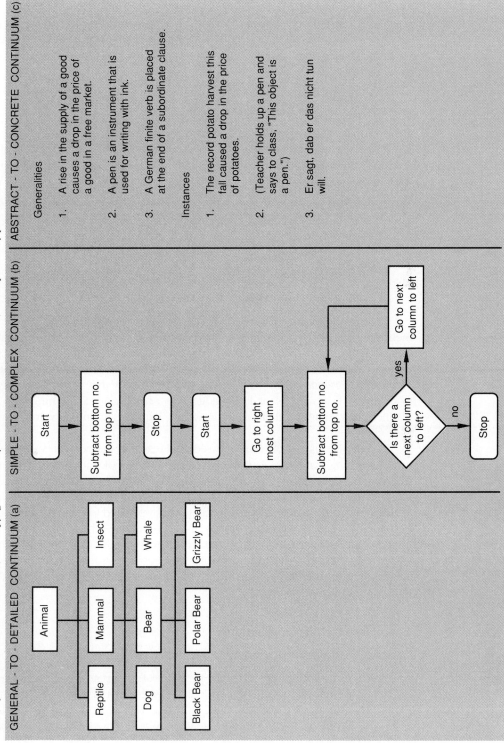

GENERAL - TO - DETAILED CONTINUUM (a)

SIMPLE - TO - COMPLEX CONTINUUM (b)

ABSTRACT - TO - CONCRETE CONTINUUM (c)

Generalities

1. A rise in the supply of a good causes a drop in the price of a good in a free market.

2. A pen is an instrument that is used for writing with ink.

3. A German finite verb is placed at the end of a subordinate clause.

Instances

1. The record potato harvest this fall caused a drop in the price of potatoes.

2. (Teacher holds up a pen and says to class, "This object is a pen.")

3. Er sagt, dab er das nicht tun will.

rials, and curriculum guides. Deriving your content organization—or learning structure—from these sources, along with your content knowledge, is instrumental in selecting, sequencing, and allocating time to instruction (Clark & Elmore, 1981; Smith & Sendelback, 1979).

Knowledge of Teaching Methods

A third input to the planning process is your knowledge of teaching methods (presented in subsequent chapters). With this knowledge comes an awareness of different teaching strategies with which you can implement the key and helping behaviors introduced in Chapter 1. Also included under teaching methods are your decisions about:

appropriate pacing or tempo (e.g., the speed at which you introduce new material),

mode of presentation (e.g., lecture vs. group discussion),

class arrangement (e.g., small groups, full class, independent study), and

classroom management (e.g., raise hand, speak out).

Included in the planning process is your careful consideration of these dimensions and how to interweave them during content presentation. Teaching requires combinations of activities and the orchestration of both key and helping behaviors. Therefore, your teaching must be planned with strategies that provide *connections, relationships, transitions,* and *sequences* that form a coherent whole from the individual bits of knowledge you present. Your teaching also must be planned with strategies that add momentum, expectancy, and forward movement to your classroom.

Another aspect of your knowledge of teaching methods is your selection and use of teaching materials. Your decisions about textbooks and curriculum materials, workbooks, films, tests, and reference works are crucial to planning. Therefore, you need to identify and record the materials and communication media that may be useful in meeting your instructional goals. Also, you need to connect specific learning objectives to specific media and materials to preorganize the teaching task and make lesson planning faster and easier. You will grow more familiar with available media and materials as you gain experience in your subject area or grade level. Recording alternative texts, workbooks, media, references, and tests as you encounter them is an important aspect of planning.

Summary of Inputs to Planning

To recap, the four primary inputs to the planning process are:

1. Aims and goals, reflected by national and state policies and legislation, school district curriculum guides, and adopted textbooks and materials.
2. Learner characteristics and individual differences, reflected by student aptitude and achievement, personality traits (anxiety level, motivation, and

self-concept), home life and extent of disadvantagedness, and peer influences in school and neighborhood.

3. Knowledge of academic discipline and grade-level curriculum, reflected by content organization (such as general-to-detailed, simple-to-complex, abstract-to-concrete), ordering of priorities (such as connections and transitions among and between parts), major and minor themes (such as most important/least important), and content-specific facts, rules, concepts, and abstractions.

4. Knowledge of teaching methods, reflected by key and helping behaviors (such as lesson clarity, instructional variety, task orientation, and student engagement in the learning process at moderate-to-high rates of success), pacing, mode of presentation, class arrangement, classroom management, and selection and use of textbooks, media, and materials.

Reflection, observation, and data collection in each of these four areas will be required before you can prepare lesson plans. This is the *process* of planning. The effective teacher actively collects information pertaining to all four inputs, typically using observation/data collection for determining aims, goals, and learner characteristics, and study/review for acquiring knowledge about an academic discipline and teaching methods. As you have seen, these inputs provide an important framework for formulating your lesson objectives and teaching strategies.

DECISION MAKING AND TACIT UNDERSTANDING

As a beginning teacher, you probably regard your content and method knowledge as hard-won during four long years of schooling. To be sure, it is—but you've only just begun. Your knowledge in content and methods will change with the *interaction* of "book learning" and classroom experience. Expect your classroom experiences to change the way you organize and prioritize content, your instructional style, your questioning strategies, mode of presentation, and even the content you teach and how you present it. These experiences and their effect on your thinking also are inputs for planning. As part of this process, be aware of—and accept—the changes occurring in your thoughts and feelings from day-to-day classroom experiences.

These changes result from what is called *tacit,* or personal, knowledge (Elbaz, 1981; Polanyi, 1958). This knowledge represents "what works" or "best practices" discovered through *experience.* Through everyday experiences we all compile vast amounts of tacit knowledge that guide our actions as effectively as knowledge from books and formal instruction. Acting upon your tacit knowledge adds to the quality of your planning and decision making by bringing variety and flexibility to your lessons. Tacit knowledge makes planning less rigid and may from time to time add fresh insights to your behavior, which can become stale and outdated through habit or routine.

Effective teachers use their day-to-day experiences in the classroom as yet another input to planning, just as they use more formally acquired knowledge. Incorporating into lesson planning those practices tacitly acquired from day-to-day ex-periences will give your teaching the variety, flexibility, and creativity it deserves. Thus we add this fifth input to the planning process, shown in Figure 3.4.

STEPS IN THE PLANNING PROCESS

You have seen that planning includes gathering and recording information for five inputs to the process. Recall that the five inputs are aims and goals, knowledge of learner characteristics, knowledge of subject matter, knowledge of teaching methods, and tacit knowledge acquired from your day-to-day classroom experience. Each is a step in the planning process for which decisions must be made. For example:

1. Which aims and goals from among the many should I try to achieve?
2. To which learner needs should I direct my instruction?
3. What should I teach, and in what ways can I structure the content to produce maximum learning in minimum time? (For example, establish sequences, make transitions, highlight important points, interweave themes.)
4. How can I orchestrate various teaching methods to meet my objectives? (For example, questioning strategies, testing, class organization.)
5. What instructional media and materials should I use to present the content and to test whether it has been learned?
6. On what basis should I revise my instruction?

For each question there are many alternatives. Selecting an instructional goal, determining to which learner characteristics instruction will be directed, organizing content for maximum learning and retention, selecting instructional methods and

FIGURE 3.4
Inputs to the planning
process

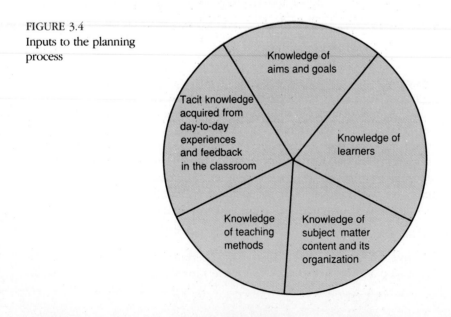

materials, and revising your instruction—all require planning skills that must reduce the alternatives to the most practical and effective ones. These planning skills include the ability to generate alternatives, to recognize value assumptions contained in the choice of alternatives, and to extend or change previously chosen alternatives when needed. Consider how these skills can be used as an organizing framework for planning and, as is explained in a later chapter, as the basis for writing lesson plans.

As mentioned, planning begins with a broad aim and ends in a specific course of action expressed as an objective. Between the beginning and end, planning generates and distinguishes among alternative courses of action, recognizes the values implied by each course of action, and when necessary revises the alternatives chosen.

GENERATING ALTERNATIVES

Generating alternative courses of action is one of the first steps in good planning. For example, you must (1) choose among different instructional goals to select the learner characteristics to which your instruction will be tailored, (2) organize the content, and (3) select teaching methods and instructional materials. Each of these tasks requires choices. Some possibilities can be eliminated due to their impracticality for a specific set of learners, lack of resources, or the time required. Others will stand out as viable alternatives for certain learning needs.

The first step in planning, then, is to describe alternative courses of action and determine what is practical considering the content, learning needs, time, and resources. Here are example alternatives:

1. Possible instructional goals (from curriculum guide and textbook):
   - ☐ Teach facts regarding . . .
   - ☐ Teach appreciation of . . .
   - ☐ Teach analytical thinking in . . .
   - ☐ Teach how to make decisions about . . .
2. Possible learning needs (from previous testing, prior classroom assignments, and informal observation):
   - ☐ Remediate deficiencies
   - ☐ Improve problem solving
   - ☐ Acquire new skills
3. Possible content organizations (from curriculum guide, text, subject-matter references, and tacit knowledge):
   - ☐ Simple-to-complex ordering
   - ☐ Most-interesting-to-least-interesting ordering
   - ☐ First-step-to-last-step ordering
   - ☐ General-to-specific ordering
4. Possible methods (from knowledge of teaching methods):
   - ☐ Independent, programmed learning
   - ☐ Question and answer
   - ☐ Small-group discussion
   - ☐ Lecture and recitation

Taken together, these alternatives are examples of the complex decisions involving goals, learners, content, and methods that you must make prior to nearly every lesson plan. The alternatives under each planning input depend on what is practical and feasible for your learners and the subject. What is practical and feasible depends on your goal, time available for instruction, student characteristics, and available resources (workbooks, media, and tests) to assist in formulating the instruction.

For this lesson, four different goals appear possible, three different learning needs have been identified, four organizational patterns seem applicable to the goals, and four instructional methods or combinations have been selected as possibilities. It is important to note the sources of these alternatives:

- Alternatives for goals come from external sources, such as curriculum guides and adopted textbooks, indicating desirable aims and goals.
- Alternatives for learners come from student test data, prior student performance on exercises and assignments, and informal observations of the learning needs of students in your classroom.
- Alternatives for content organization come from review of and familiarity with the subject matter and its organization.
- Alternatives for methods come from texts, coursework, inservice training, and classroom experience, from which you have gained a knowledge of teaching.

RECOGNIZING VALUE ASSUMPTIONS

Considering data from the four planning process inputs will suggest specific alternatives under each category. Then, you must match up goals, learning needs, organization, and methods. Match goals with learning needs, and then tie them to a specific organizational pattern and instructional arrangement to make the best "goal–learning need–organization–method" match. For example, a reasonable match might be the teaching of facts (goal) to remediate deficiencies (learning need) using simple-to-complex ordering (organization) in small groups (method). Another might be teaching skills (goal) to improve problem-solving performance on weekly quizzes (learning need) using general-to-specific ordering (organization) in a discussion format (method).

Clearly, you can't achieve all possible goals, meet all learning needs, or use every organization and method. The point of this planning phase is to *lay out the possibilities,* not to see that all of them are achieved. Time and resources available in any one classroom will preclude such a broad approach to instruction. On the other hand, laying out the possibilities in accord with the four planning process inputs permits a practical matching of alternatives at the time of lesson planning. This lets you *prioritize* different goal–learning need–organization–method matches, so you can pursue them in priority order over longer periods as time and resources permit.

One of the most important results of prioritizing your goal–learning need–organization–method matches is that you will recognize the *value assumptions* that such ordering implies. For example, if your highest priority is teaching analytical skills to improve problem solving using most-complex-to-least-complex organization in a lecture format, this implies that time and resources may not be available to teach the facts needed to remove existing deficiencies. When you recognize the values implied by your choices, and their conflict with other value sources such as those of the school and community, you may reconsider your selection and might divide your time and resources more evenly among various matches.

This part of the planning process is successful to the extent that it makes you consider and reconsider *all practical and available instructional alternatives*. Matching and prioritizing are planning activities that encourage (ideally, force) you to actively consider the values, implications, and consequences of your decisions. Recognizing the values implied by a choice is a powerful means of promoting thoughtful planning.

ALTERNATIVES

You need not identify all instructional alternatives during the planning process. You also can choose alternatives based upon feedback you receive. In other words, you can use the tacit knowledge acquired through day-to-day experience with your learners. Suppose that you selected a particular goal–learning need–organization–method match to achieve a certain end (e.g., improved basic skills, greater problem-solving ability, more creativity). If feedback from work samples, tests, and class performance indicates the intended result is not being attained, that means the match is not a useful means to achieving the behavior. Alter it to establish a tighter, more observable connection between the match and the end result. Shift to other learning needs, organizational patterns, or teaching methods to adjust the match and improve the outcome.

It is important to remember that feedback from the observation and measurement of learners is another equally important input to the planning process. Sensitivity to these data provides your best means of monitoring the consequences of your instructional decisions, and the most effective means of revising them. This planning process is shown in Figure 3.5.

PLANNING TO ELIMINATE BIAS

Planning to eliminate bias in classroom teaching can be one of the most significant aspects of becoming an effective teacher. Researchers recently have brought to our attention that, consciously or unconsciously, everyone has biases of one kind or another (Gage & Berliner, 1984). When applied in ways that affect only your own behavior and not that of others, we use the word *preference* instead of *bias*. Preferences are the harmless results of values manifest in choosing clothing, cars, music, etc.

Biases, on the other hand, are not harmless; they can injure the personal growth and well being of others. The fact that many biases are covert and unconscious

FIGURE 3.5
Stages of the planning process

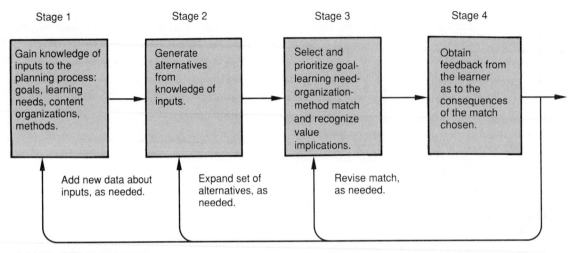

makes them even more devastating and difficult to control, especially in a culturally diverse classroom. Your biases, if left unchecked, can significantly affect the growth and development of learners. As the previous section showed, one purpose of planning is to raise to a conscious level the thoughts, feelings, and understandings that you may have acquired tacitly or informally. You also can use this process to become aware of biases that influence how and what you teach.

Biases in Labeling and Grouping

A particularly alarming case of bias was uncovered by Rist (1970) when he studied a single class of ghetto students from kindergarten through second grade. Rist observed that from the time these students entered kindergarten, they were divided into three groups—"tigers," "cardinals," and "clowns"—each seated at a different table. Initial placement into these groups in kindergarten was made by the teacher according to SES, using information from registration forms and from interviews with mothers and social workers. The highest status children, called tigers, were seated closest to the teacher and quickly labeled "fast learners." The lowest status children, called clowns, were farthest removed from the teacher and quickly were led to believe they were "slow learners."

In reality, each of the three groups had a mixture of slow and fast learners; but the slow learners seated farthest from the teacher seldom got the opportunity to interact with her, while those closest to the teacher frequently received attention. Before long the abilities of each group were taken as fact rather than as creations of the teacher, so much so that it was increasingly difficult for the "clowns" to be considered other than slow by their teachers in the following grades.

At no time did the teacher seem to be aware that the arrangement was biased or that seating certain students consistently in the back of the room would reduce their contact with her. Thus, this teacher's bias became a self-fulfilling prophecy that extended even to subsequent grades and classes—all as a result of biased labeling during the early years of schooling.

Many other examples of teacher biases have been catalogued. For example, Brophy and Good (1974) summarize how teachers sometimes respond unequally to high and low achievers by communicating low expectations and thereby accepting, and unintentionally encouraging, a low level of performance among some students. Brophy and Good identified the following areas in which some teachers responded differently toward low and high achievers:

□ Wait less time for lows to answer.
□ Give lows the answer after their slightest hesitation.
□ Praise marginal or inaccurate answers of lows.
□ Criticize lows more frequently for having the wrong answer.
□ Praise lows less when the right answer is given.
□ Do not give feedback to lows as to why an answer is incorrect.
□ Pay attention to (e.g., smile at) and call on lows less.
□ Seat lows farther from the teacher.
□ Allow lows to "give up" more.

Generally, these findings confirm that teachers usually do not compensate for differences between high and low achievers in allowing more response opportunities and more teacher contact for the latter.

Biases in Interacting

Other types of bias can affect interactions with students. For example, Gage and Berliner (1984) identified several biased ways in which teachers interact with their students and then analyzed the extent to which experienced teachers actually exhibited these biases in their classrooms. Their biases included interacting with or calling on students disproportionately in these ways:

Seated in front half of class vs. seated in back half of class

Nicer-looking students vs. average-looking students

More-able students vs. less-able students

Nonminority group members vs. minority group members

Gage and Berliner calculated the number of student-teacher interactions that would be expected by chance for these classifications, and then from observation determined the actual number of interactions that occurred. Somewhat surprisingly, their results indicate that *every* teacher showed some bias in these categories. In other words, every teacher favored at least one student classification over another by nam-

Bias in interacting with students can routinely occur when potential sources of bias are not identified beforehand and steps are not taken to avoid them. For example, calling on some students more than others is an open message that some are less desirable and less worthy than others, regardless of how unintentional the bias may be.

ing, calling on, requiring information from, and otherwise interacting with those in some classification disproportionally to those not in that classification.

Such biases may be meaningless over a single class period but can have significant and long-lasting emotional impact on students if continued throughout weeks, months, or the entire school year. The accumulated effect of systematic bias in a classroom is an open message to some students that they are less desirable and less worthy of attention than others, regardless of how unintentional the bias may be. If the message is received, and it surely will be, the result is change in motivation, self-concept, and even anxiety level of some students in ways that impede their development and learning.

Biases Regarding Ethnicity

Bias in the way a teacher interacts with students is undesirable in any form, but it is particularly distasteful when it pertains to students' ethnicity. As we saw in Chapter 2, our nation as well as our educational system is based on the pluralistic ideal and respect for individual differences of all types. This means that our classrooms become one of the most—some would say *the* most—important showplaces of our democratic values. It is disturbing that researchers report frequent ethnic bias during student-teacher interactions in classrooms that combine blacks, Hispanics, Asians, and whites.

In one study of interactions between teachers and Anglo-American and Mexican-American students in 429 classrooms in the American Southwest, interaction frequency consistently favored Anglos in teacher questioning, positive responses, use of student ideas, and praise and encouragement (Civil Rights Commission, 1973). Reverse bias also has been observed between blacks and Anglos in inner-city schools, where student-teacher interaction bias favors the black majority. Regardless of the direction, biases must be brought to a conscious level and controlled through the planning process.

Gage & Berliner (1984) make these suggestions for planning to control bias:

1. Spread your interactions as evenly as possible across student categories by deciding in advance which students to call on. Because the many classifications of potential bias are cumbersome to deal with, choose one or two bias categories you know or suspect you are most vulnerable to.
2. If you are giving special assignments to only some of your students, choose the students randomly. Place all of your students' names in a jar and have one student draw the names of individuals needed for the special assignment. This protects you from inadvertently choosing the same students repeatedly and conveying the impression that you have "pets."
3. Try consciously pairing opposites in what you believe to be your area of bias—for example, pair minority with nonminority, more-able with less-able, easy to work with and difficult to work with, etc. In this manner, when you interact with one member of the pair you are reminded to interact with the other. Occasionally change one member of the pair so that your pairing does not become obvious to the class.
4. When you discover a bias, you might develop a code to remind you of the bias and then embed it within your class notes, text, or lesson plan at appropriate intervals. For example, should you discover you systematically favor more-able (MA) students over less-able (LA) students, place the code LA on the margins of your exercise, to remind you to choose a less-able student for the next response.

Although these suggestions are for controlling bias during instruction, the *planning process* is the proper vehicle for identifying potential biases *before they occur* and planning to deal with them. If you don't consider bias during this phase of your preparation to teach, you probably won't deal with it during any later phase.

A HIERARCHY OF PLANNING NEEDS

When you face the planning process for the first time, you will recognize that some aspects of teaching concern you more than others. If you are a typical beginning teacher, you will at first focus on your own survival and only later on the teaching task and your students. For example, Fuller (1969) found that during the early, middle, and late phases of student teaching, students expressed a shift in their teaching concerns. A focus upon oneself (Do my students really like me? Will I do well when my supervisor is present?) shifted to concerns that emphasized the teaching task (Are there sufficient instructional materials? Is there time to cover all the topics?) and to concerns that emphasized students' needs (Are they learning? How does what I do affect their social and emotional development?). Fuller's three stages of teacher concerns are summarized in Figure 3.6.

Some typical concerns during each stage are:

1. Self concerns
   □ Whether the students really like the teacher or not.
   □ Feeling under pressure too much of the time.
   □ Doing well when a supervisor is present.
2. Instructional (task) concerns
   □ Lack of freedom to initiate innovative instructional ideas.
   □ The nature and quality of instructional materials.
   □ Adequately presenting all of the material.
3. Student needs (impact) concerns
   □ Increasing students' feelings of accomplishment.
   □ Recognizing social and emotional needs of students.
   □ Challenging unmotivated students.

Fuller speculated that concerns for self, task, and student are natural stages through which most teachers pass, representing a developmental pattern extending over months and even years of a teacher's career. Some teachers may pass through these stages faster than others and at different intensity levels, but Fuller suggested that almost every teacher will experience them. The most effective and experienced teachers will express *student-centered concerns at a high level of commitment*.

Fuller's "concerns theory" has several other interesting implications. A teacher might return to an earlier stage of concern—move from a concern for stu-

FIGURE 3.6
Hierarchy of planning needs

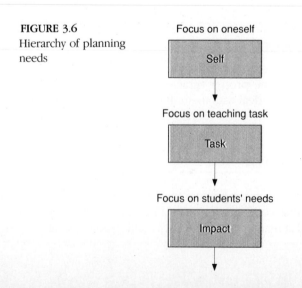

Focus on oneself

Self

Focus on teaching task

Task

Focus on students' needs

Impact

dents *back* to a concern for task as a result of having to teach a new grade or subject, or move from a concern for task *back* to a concern for self as a result of having to teach different and unfamiliar students. The second time spent in a stage might be expected to be shorter than the first. Finally, the three stages of concern need not be exclusive of one another. A teacher could have concerns predominately in one area while still having concerns at lesser levels of intensity in the other stages.

The implications of Fuller's data also provide interesting recommendations for teacher training (Borich, 1990, 1992; Borich & Nance, 1990). If the beginning teacher is preoccupied with concerns of personal adequacy and survival, which appears to be true even to the casual observer, instruction addressing these concerns might be presented very early in teacher training. Concerns such as "Can I control the class?" would be addressed at the beginning, perhaps through early teaching and practicing of classroom management techniques.

With survival concerns addressed, concerns about the teaching task (instructional design, methods of presenting subject matter, tailoring content to individual needs) would be covered next, perhaps through lesson planning and microteaching exercises. Finally, concerns about the teacher's impact upon students (producing learning outcomes, assessing achievement, determining one's contribution to student behavior) would be addressed, perhaps through courses in measurement, observation, and practice teaching.

Based on the work of Fuller (1969), Borich (1992) with J. Rogan constructed a 45-item self-reporting instrument for assessing the stages of concern with which a teacher most strongly identifies. The list in this section includes examples from the instrument, which appears in full in Appendix A. This instrument has been administered to both preservice and inservice teachers in a number of studies. From these data it was possible to construct a hierarchy of planning needs based upon the three stages of the concerns model. This hierarchy suggests the concerns of beginning teachers that might be addressed in each of the three stages and lists options to reduce high levels of concern. The hierarchy appears in Table 3.2 within a planning framework suggested by Morine (1973).

Using the Teacher Concerns Checklist (Appendix A), rank your own level of concern from high (totally preoccupied) to low (not concerned) in each of the three stages and then determine which stage of concern you identify with most closely. Then consult the suggestions in Table 3.2 for those items that most concern you.

TABLE 3.2
Planning aids for three stages of concerns using selected items from the Teacher Concerns Checklist (Appendix A)

Stage	Concern	Generating an Approach	Recognizing the Value Assumptions	Altering or Extending the Approach
SELF	Whether the students really like me	Construct a simple attitude instrument to measure your student's attitudes toward your organization, clarity, and fairness at the end of a major unit. Then try altering your instructional procedures in the areas in which you were rated the lowest until some improvement can be noted. If possible, compare your results with those of another student teacher using the same instrument.	You may want to value your own intuition more than your students' opinions, which may be influenced by factors unrelated to you or your teaching. Keep in mind that some students will be chronic complainers while others are forever silent. Your own instincts may be the best guide to whether your students like you.	Many times the most honest and helpful responses as to how well you are doing are acquired informally rather than from evaluation instruments. Choose a few students of high, average, and low ability and find out how you are doing by asking them the things they thought were the easiest to learn and why, and the things that were the most difficult to learn and why.
	Feeling under pressure too much of the time	Organize your planning time so that a specified amount of time is allotted for planning and organizing each major instructional activity you have responsibility for. Allot more time to your hardest subjects, less to your easiest. Then stick to your schedule.	Feeling some pressure is normal and may even make you perform better by forcing you to "rise to the occasion" when special demands are being placed upon you.	Rotate from lecturing, to question and answer, to assigning seatwork on alternate days or periods thereby reducing the type and amount of planning you must do each day.
	Doing well when a supervisor is present	Ask your supervisor if your first observation can be in a more informal instructional activity, such as tutoring, working with small groups, or	Most supervisors are aware of your anxiety during your first few observations and take this into account in evaluating your performance.	Practice performing three specific instructional activities that are among the most often used in your classroom (e.g., probing, asking a

TABLE 3.2, *continued*

Stage	Concern	Generating an Approach	Recognizing the Value Assumptions	Altering or Extending the Approach
SELF		cooperatively teaching with the classroom teacher.		higher-level question, using media to illustrate a point). Then use them at the time you are being observed.
	Clarifying the limits of my authority and responsibility	Ask your supervisor what is expected at your school, and then ask the classroom teacher. Consider all of what both say as the limits of your authority and responsibility.	Often times the limits of behavior can only be defined as a result of trial and error. Increasing in *small degrees* your authority and responsibility over your instructional decisions until a problem is noted is one way to define these limits in concrete ways.	Observe in other classrooms and especially in the classrooms of other student teachers in your department to gain a sense as to how much authority and responsibility is expected.
	Feeling more adequate as a teacher	Recall past microteaching experiences, exercises, or simulations in which you were judged adequate by external standards. Use your performance during these experiences as a baseline for your performance now. Devote time in your classroom to fine tuning these already acquired skills.	Few teachers, even those who are experienced, rarely feel completely adequate, regardless of outward signs to the contrary. The intensity and complexity of the teaching task separates it from most other occupations and makes perfection an unattainable goal for most, if not all, teachers.	Identify those areas in which you have signs you are less adequate than desired. Seek specific references and materials that address those areas and observe other teachers for their behavior in these areas. Then practice what you have learned in small-group settings.
	Being accepted and respected by professional persons	To become a meaningful part of your school, not just another student teacher, accept responsibilities	Student teachers and beginning teachers are, in general, accepted and respected less as a result of their	Let your skills and personality be known outside of your classroom by becoming familar with the members of

TABLE 3.2, *continued*

Stage	Concern	Generating an Approach	Recognizing the Value Assumptions	Altering or Extending the Approach
SELF		beyond those you are specifically assigned. With the permission and cooperation of the classroom teacher, try innovative ideas even when they require extra or difficult planning. Include the classroom teacher in the planning of these ideas from the very start.	newness and transient nature in the school than are older, more experienced teachers. *Complete* acceptance and respect results from the acquaintance of others with you over time, which may not be sufficient during your student teaching experience.	the various teacher organizations represented at your school, working voluntarily with other teachers who sponsor clubs and activities in which you have an interest, and attending sports functions that are important to your students. The first step of being accepted and respected is being involved.
TASK	The nature and quality of instructional materials	Catalogue the materials available to you along with the advantages and disadvantages of each. Specifically, note those for which the disadvantages outweigh the advantages and show this to the classroom teacher for possible alternatives.	Inadequate materials do not always translate into inadequate learning, and sometimes may be a result of personal preferences, not inadequate or poor design. How materials are used and what they are supplemented with often can reduce inadequacies.	Pair weak or inadequate materials with other more adequate resources which might compensate, in part, for their poor coverage, accuracy, or difficulty level.
	Maintaining the appropriate degree of class control	Establish specific classroom rules in all important areas, e.g., speaking out, leaving seats, leaving room, talking, neatness, etc. prior to your first teaching day. Hand out and/or display these rules prominently in your classroom.	The amount of class control that is desirable will change according to your objectives and instructional activities. While the teacher must always be in control, there is a degree of control which can be chosen by the	Anticipate and carefully structure in advance those activities that may cause discipline problems, such as discussion sessions, question and answer periods, problem solving exercises— especially those requiring more

TABLE 3.2, *continued*

Stage	Concern	Generating an Approach	Recognizing the Value Assumptions	Altering or Extending the Approach
TASK			teacher for a specific objective, such as when students are to explore and discover in small groups versus listening to you lecture.	student talk.
	Being fair and impartial	Establish your grading standards *before* grading tests and evaluating papers, and stick to it. If changes in your standards seem called for, make them starting on the *next* test or paper, not on the present test or exam.	Oftentimes, concern with being fair and impartial leads to too low a grading standard and over-reactions to student complaints. Your own intuition as to your fairness and impartiality may be the best guide—not the opinions of others.	After important tests and papers, ask students if they believe the grade they received accurately represented their knowledge and effort. Use this information and your own judgment to decide if your grading standards or procedures need changing.
	Work with too many students each day	For large classes, vary your instructional procedures each day, e.g., from lectures one day to discussion or question and answer the next. For small groups and tutorials combine similar groups or individuals into a single group and employ peer teaching when possible.	Working with fewer actual students each day, that is, having a reduced class load, may not make instruction easier, since small classes often require more attention to individual needs and can represent a student mix that can be as difficult or more difficult to teach than a larger class.	Identify those in your class who are most in need of special attention. Then, attend to the special learning needs of these individuals, giving special attention to others as time permits and allowing those who are capable to work independently when possible.
	Insufficient time for class preparation	Reserve the first 10 minutes of each class for a review of previous concepts and the last 10 minutes for a	Rarely is there a teacher who has sufficient time for preparation. The fact that teachers generally are not	Use a variety of teaching techniques that make students more responsible for their own learning, such as question-

TABLE 3.2, *continued*

Stage	Concern	*Generating an Approach*	*Recognizing the Value Assumptions*	*Altering or Extending the Approach*
TASK		summary of what was just covered. This should reduce the amount of new planning you will have to do each day, while still providing needed instruction and review.	provided sufficient time to prepare during the school day should encourage you to plan as efficiently as possible but not feel guilty for an instructional arrangement that does not include the provision for adequate preparation.	and-answer groups, small-group discussion, research assignments, and seatwork employing exercises and self-instructional workbooks.
	Adequately presenting all of the material	Rearrange content in workbooks and texts so that conceptually similar content is taught at the same time. Emphasizing concepts more than facts will give your students the tools to learn whatever content was not covered on their own at a later time.	This is an often-expressed concern of teachers both experienced and inexperienced. Having the concern itself does not necessarily mean, however, that sufficient material will not be adequately presented. Much of the work of teaching involves making compromises in the use of teaching time and content covered. The nature of the compromise is more important than the fact that a compromise must be made.	Individualize content coverage to the extent possible by providing self-instructional materials and teaching activities at your students' current level of functioning. Ability groups can be formed which avoid unnecessary or unproductive content coverage that may be too easy or too hard for some students.
	The wide diversity of student ethnic and socioeconomic backgrounds	Determine the range of ability in your classroom from standardized achievement scores and ability measures	Diversity of ethnic and socioeconomic backgrounds does not necessarily imply that teaching and learning will be	Use ability grouping based upon prior achievement, motivation, and individual strengths to create

TABLE 3.2, *continued*

Stage	Concern	Generating an Approach	Recognizing the Value Assumptions	Altering or Extending the Approach
TASK		recorded on school records. Note from these data if placement changes to higher or lower classes would be in the best interest of the student. Where such changes conform with school policies, refer appropriate students to a school counselor.	more difficult. These are outward signs that may or may not indicate diverse learning needs. Your experience with and the achievement of specific students must determine exactly how diverse the instructional needs are in your classroom.	homogeneous subgroups to which specific materials and objectives can be directed.
	Increasing students' feeling of accomplishment	Use a flexible system of reward and feedback that adjusts your standards and expectations to the students' current level of functioning. In this manner gain or growth from a baseline of each student's own behavior can be used as a source of praise and accomplishment regardless of how the student performs against an objective class standard.	Reward and reinforcement to be meaningful must actually be earned. Simply bestowing undeserved or unearned praise on a student may actually lessen a student's feeling of accomplishment by drawing attention to the fact that something was said that was known to be untrue.	Each week choose a few students from your class to congratulate on having done well by writing them a note on which you identify the work or deed being praised. Singling different students out in this manner over time can often increase the feeling of accomplishment of your entire class.
IMPACT	Diagnosing student learning problems	Assign ample exercises and seatwork activities during the first few days and weeks of school in order to obtain a reasonable sample of your students' performance with	Diagnosing the learning problems of individual students may be beyond the scope and even expertise of most teachers. Although learning problems at the class level must be dealt with	Choose students with the most severe learning problems and arrange a learning center where the students can go to obtain special reference material, media, exercises, and peer

TABLE 3.2, *continued*

Stage	Concern	Generating an Approach	Recognizing the Value Assumptions	Altering or Extending the Approach
IMPACT		respect to grade-level expectations. Large discrepancies should be brought to the attention of the school counselor. Smaller discrepancies can be your individualized agenda for working with these students the remainder of the year.	through your lesson planning, diagnosing the special learning needs of individual students may not be practical in the average classroom and such needs when obvious may best be dealt with by bringing them to the attention of the counselor, special educators, or school administrators.	tutoring geared to their special problems. Their work at the center can also be used to further diagnose their learning problem.
	Challenging unmotivated students	At the beginning of the year record each student's personal interests and unique experiences. Where possible, select materials and assignments for poorly motivated students that match their interests and experiences.	Some students may remain unmotivated regardless of what is done to accommodate their interests in the classroom. For these students the reasons for their lack of motivation may lie outside your classroom and out of your control.	Choose learning materials for unmotivated students that are visually oriented and concrete in nature. Allow them more flexibility to substitute these materials for regular school curricula.
	Whether students apply what they learn	At the end of each major unit of instruction include a real-world problem-solving exercise whose solution calls for the practical application of some of the concepts you have taught.	Oftentimes being able to successfully apply what one "knows" requires extensive interactions with problems in the real world. While school must help prepare individuals for the real world, being able to actually apply school concepts with efficiency and proficiency must, in part, be the result of	Assign action research projects, experiments, demonstrations, and fieldwork to help relate classroom learning to the types of problem-solving contexts in which this learning will be most likely used.

TABLE 3.2, *continued*

Stage	Concern	Generating an Approach	Recognizing the Value Assumptions	Altering or Extending the Approach
IMPACT			experience outside the domain and control of any one classroom.	
	Slow progress of certain students	When slow progress persists, test to see if remediation is indicated and, if so, assign remedial work in place of regular school assignments until some progress is made.	Slow progress is a fact of life for some students, calling for patience and understanding from the teacher. Slow progress, if it persists, may require a lowering of standards so that what was once considered slow for a particular student may now be considered acceptable.	Examine the alternative modes of instruction that may exist in your school, such as a "low ability" track, remedial programs, or federally-funded districtwide programs that provide special instruction or materials for slow learners. Use these when the problems of the learner match the objectives of the program.
	Helping students to value learning	Relate learning to real-world accomplishments wherever possible, indicating the cause and effect relationship between them. Use examples that support the fact that knowledge, in a sense, is "power" by indicating the knowledge of individuals that preceded and made possible modern-day inventions, discoveries, and personal successes.	To value is to have a deep and unwavering belief in something. Such a belief comes from many different experiences over years of someone's life. School is only one context in which the value of learning can and should be taught. Others are the home, workplace, and community.	Incorporate into your planning ways in which learning can be made fun, exciting, or unusual. Games, simulations, and group projects, for example, can encourage students to value learning for its own sake if they are planned in a way that leads to discoveries within oneself and a greater understanding of self.
	Recognizing the social and emotional needs of students	Social and emotional needs in the classroom are rarely	Practically all students have social and emotional	A warm and nurturing attitude toward your students

TABLE 3.2, *concluded*

Stage	Concern	Generating an Approach	Recognizing the Value Assumptions	Altering or Extending the Approach
IMPACT		indicated by major episodes or events but rather are often marked by seemingly inconsequential forms of behavior that communicate a larger message. Follow up unusual expressions of need or distress through observation and direct student contact to determine if a social or emotional need is being expressed that hinders the learning process.	needs, only some of which will be debilitating to the learning process. Although social and emotional needs are important to recognize, seldom can they be met in the instructional context of the classroom.	can reduce some of their most important emotional needs by providing a climate of acceptance, security, and understanding in which learning can occur.

A FINAL WORD

Earlier in this chapter the important distinction was made between the process of planning and the process of writing lesson plans. Planning would be sterile and ineffective if it did not culminate in lesson plans. It is equally true that lesson plans would be sterile and ineffective if not preceded by consideration of goals, learning needs, organization, and teaching methods. This chapter has presented some of the data sources for these inputs and ways in which possibilities can be generated and matched to form the basis for a lesson or unit plan. Without an awareness of these alternatives, created through deliberation of all inputs to the planning process, the resulting lesson plans would have no rational structure.

The next chapter presents one other crucial link in the development of lesson plans—*objectives*. Objectives are a critical link between the planning concepts discussed in this chapter and preparation of lesson plans to be addressed in Chapter 5. Recall that aims and goals are useful inputs to the planning process, but they are far too general to use in preparing lesson plans. They do not indicate how to carry out an alternate course of action or how to determine whether the alternate course was effective. This is the role of objectives, for they identify the specific behaviors, the conditions under which the behaviors are to be achieved, and the level of proficiency at which the behaviors are to be performed.

SUMMING UP

This chapter introduced aims and goals, recent educational reform, the planning process and its inputs, how to handle bias, and the three concerns of self, task, and students. The main points were:

1. The words *aims, goals,* and *objectives* often are used interchangeably but have different meanings.

2. Aims are expressions of societal values that are broad enough to be acceptable to large numbers of individuals.

3. Goals bring aims down to earth by connecting them to some tangible aspect of the school curriculum.

4. Objectives are more specific than goals; they describe the specific behavior a learner is to attain, the conditions under which the behavior must be demonstrated, and the proficiency level at which the behavior is to be performed.

5. Aims are translated into goals and goals into objectives by a process of funneling or narrowing.

6. Local community prerogatives can expand or enhance societal aims and may establish a curriculum sensitive to the learning needs of a particular community.

7. With the publication of five specially commissioned reports, American education began a period of reform that called for:
   □ Strengthening of the curriculum in math, science, English, foreign language, and social studies.
   □ Renewed effort to teach higher-order thinking skills.
   □ Raising school grading standards.
   □ Raising college admission standards.
   □ More work in the core subjects, especially math and foreign language.

8. Planning is the process of deciding what and how teachers want their students to learn. The preparation of lesson plans, often confused with the planning process, is the *result* of this process.

9. The process of planning structures and prioritizes behavior so that only the most effective teaching behaviors are employed for attaining a given objective, providing maximum instruction in minimum time.

10. The five primary inputs to the planning process are:
    □ Aims and goals
    □ Learner characteristics and individual differences
    □ Knowledge of academic discipline and grade-level content
    □ Knowledge of teaching methods
    □ Tacit knowledge acquired from day-to-day experience in the classroom.

11. Knowledge of aims and goals is reflected by national and state policies and legislation, school curriculum guides, and adopted texts.

12. Knowledge of learner characteristics and individual differences is reflected by student aptitude and achievement data; student anxiety, motivation, and self-concept levels; home life indicators; and peer-group influences.

13. Knowledge of academic discipline and grade-level content is reflected by a knowledge of content and its organization.

14. Knowledge of teaching methods is reflected by the key and catalytic behaviors for effective teaching, teaching strategies that encompass these behaviors, classroom management techniques, and use and selection of instructional media and materials.

15. Tacit knowledge is knowledge derived from feedback received from learners about the success of your instruction. Tacit knowledge is useful in the planning process for revising teaching practices and making the planning process less rigid.

16. To be effective, the planning process must generate and distinguish among alternative courses of action, recognize the values implied by each course of action, and revise the alternative courses of action as needed.

17. Generating and distinguishing among alternative courses of action means identifying the different goals, learners, content organization, and teaching methods that may be relevant to the classroom.

18. Recognizing the values implied by each course of action means examining various goal–learning need–organization–method matches for their practicality and conflict with school and community priorities.

19. Revising the alternatives chosen means altering the goal–learning need–organization–method match based on feedback about its effectiveness in the classroom.

20. Almost every teacher shows some type of bias in interacting with students. Bias may be avoided by:
    - ☐ Consciously spreading interactions across categories of students toward whom you have identified bias.
    - ☐ Randomly selecting students for special assignments.
    - ☐ Covertly pairing students who are opposite in your category of bias and then interacting with both members of the pair.
    - ☐ Coding class notes to remind yourself to call on students toward whom you may be biased.

21. Most teachers express concerns related to self (e.g., Do students like me?), related to the teaching task (Is my coverage of content adequate?), and related to their impact on students (Are the students learning?). The three concerns of self, task, and student appear to be natural stages through which most teachers pass (and occasionally revisit), representing a developmental pattern extending over months and even years of a teacher's career.

FOR DISCUSSION AND PRACTICE

*1. Distinguish aims from goals by placing an *a* to the left of each aim and a *g* to the left of each goal.

_____ To be able to live in a technological world

_____ To know how to add, subtract, multiply, and divide

_____ To appreciate the arts, both nationally and internationally

_____ To know the historical reasons for World War II

_____ To work together cooperatively

_____ To know parliamentary procedure

_____ To be able to read a popular magazine

_____ To experience literature from around the world

_____ To understand the rudiments of health and hygiene

_____ To know how to swing a tennis racket

2. Select one of the aims identified in the previous question, (1) translate it into a goal, and (2) translate that goal into an objective. Make sure your objective is responsive to the aim from which it was derived.

3. In your own words, indicate some of the differences you see among aims, goals, and objectives. How are they the same?

4. Give an example of a local community prerogative that might be used to expand or enhance statewide curriculum goals in communities having these characteristics:

    a. The average standardized grade equivalent reading achievement in the fourth grade is 2.7.
    b. The average IQ is 117.
    c. The dropout rate in high school last year was 42%.
    d. One out of 10 adults in the surrounding community is believed to have received treatment for substance abuse in the past year.
    e. The teen suicide rate is among the highest in the state.
    f. The school sits within a stone's throw of the world's top three computer manufacturers.
    g. Many students who want to go to the state college cannot get in because their SAT math scores are too low.

*5. Name five recommendations for the reform of American education shared by most of the national policy reports issued in 1983.

*6. If you had to sum up in a single phrase the most general and agreed-upon problem with our schools as seen by the authors of the policy reports of 1983, what would it be?

7. Identify five changes that you now see being implemented in our schools as a result of the national policy reports and of local and state efforts to reform school curricula. Which, if any, do you *not* agree with, and why?

8. In your own words, how would you convince another teacher (who disagrees with you) that lesson plans are the *result* of the planning process, and are not the process itself? What improve-

ments in the other teacher's performance might result from seeing the planning process as different from plan making (preparing lesson plans)?

*9. What are the five inputs to the planning process? Where can you get information about each?

10. If tacit, or personal, knowledge is known only through experience and cannot be found in the pages of a textbook or in a college lecture, what are examples of tacitly acquired knowledge that you might have at the end of your first full day of teaching?

11. For a particular lesson at your grade level or in your content area, construct a list of alternative goals, learning needs, ways of organizing the content, and teaching methods. Choose one alternative from each category to create a goal—learning need—organization—method match that you feel should be of highest priority in your classroom or that you would most like to teach. Now construct another match of highest priority (which may use some of the same alternatives). Construct a third match, if possible.

12. Consider the two or three matches you constructed for the previous question. What educational values did you assume were important when choosing your highest priority match? What educational values did you assume were important when choosing your next-highest priority match?

*13. Gage and Berliner (1984) identify a number of ways in which your interactions with students can be biased. Name four and then add one of your own that is not mentioned by Gage and Berliner.

*14. Identify four procedures for reducing or eliminating the biases you may have when interacting with your students.

*15. Name Fuller's three stages of concern and give an original example of a concern *you* have in each of the three areas.

16. Complete The Teacher Concerns Checklist in Appendix A according to the instructions provided. After completing the checklist, calculate your average score within each of the three categories using the key provided to determine the relative intensity of your concerns in each of these three areas. How does your score in each of the three areas compare with the average of the class?

*17. Teachers A, B, C, and D have the following profile of scores on The Teacher Concerns Checklist.

	Self	*Task*	*Impact*
Teacher A	low	medium	high
Teacher B	high	medium	low
Teacher C	low	medium	high
Teacher D	high	low	high

One teacher has been teaching for 4 months, another has taught the same subject in the same school for 8 years, another has taught in the same school for 11 years but just recently has been assigned to teach a subject he never taught before, and the fourth teacher has taught in the same school for 6 years but recently was declared "surplus" and reassigned to the same subject in an inner city vocational school. Which teacher most likely would have which profile, according to Fuller's concerns theory?

18. Using ideas from Fuller's concerns theory, how might you rearrange the course you are now taking? How might you extend your ideas to the design of a new undergraduate teacher training curriculum?

---

*Answers to asterisked questions (*) in this and the other chapters are in Appendix B.

SUGGESTED READINGS

Clark, C., & Yinger, R. (1979). Teachers' thinking. In P. L. Peterson & H. J. Walberg (Eds.), *Research on teaching*. Berkeley, CA: McCutchan.
This article contains many good examples of how teachers' thinking influences planning and instruction.

Joyce, B., Hersch, R., & McKibbin, M. (1983). *The structure of school improvement*. New York: Longman. *Some constructive suggestions on how to improve American education based on many of the same insights reported in the national policy reports of 1983.*

McCutcheon, G. (1980). How do elementary school teachers plan? The nature of planning and influences on it. *Elementary School Journal, 81,* 4–23.
An informative guide for elementary teachers on how to plan and what forces influence the planning process.

Morine-Dershimer, G. (1978–1979). Planning and classroom reality: An in-depth look. *Educational Research Quarterly, 3*(4), 83–99.
This article examines the relationship between teacher planning and content organization.

National Commission on Excellence in Education. (1983). *A nation at risk: The imperative for educational reform.* Washington: U.S. Department of Education.
The premiere and most-talked-about policy report of 1983, detailing many critical insights and an agenda for reforming American education to the end of the century.

Shavelson, R. (1987). Planning. In M. J. Dunkin (Ed.), *International encyclopedia of teaching and teacher education.* New York: Pergamon.
An overview of teacher planning and its relationship to effective teaching.

Yinger, R. (1979). Routines in teacher planning. *Theory into Practice, 18,* 163–169.
Some typical scenarios describing how teachers plan and what factors influence what they plan.

Zahorik, J. (1975). Teacher's planning models. *Educational Leadership, 33,* 134–139.
Describes several practical approaches to lesson and unit planning, from the teacher's perspective.

Instructional Objectives

In Chapter 3 we noted the strength of aims and goals: they provide a general direction for curriculum development, state and national mandates, and local school district policies. However, aims and goals have weaknesses. They are not necessarily tied to a specific curriculum, they do not provide strategies for attaining a result, and they do not provide a means for knowing when that result has been achieved. In this chapter you will learn how you, the classroom teacher, play an active role in translating aims and goals into specific classroom strategies and outcomes.

THE PURPOSE OF OBJECTIVES

Objectives help you plan and organize instruction in ways that save time, avoid redundancy, and ensure that critical learning needs are addressed. Objectives set a clear course and level of performance both for you and your students. Good objectives are fundamental communication—they simply tell everyone what to expect. Unfortunately, some teachers waste a lot of time because they lack clear objectives for themselves or their students. These teachers do not know where they are going with their instruction and so cannot know when, or even if, they have reached their desired destination. Objectives not only tie classroom activities to desired goals at the district, state, and national levels; they also bring specificity and concreteness to classroom activities.

Objectives have two practical purposes. The first is to tie general aims and goals to specific classroom strategies that will achieve those aims and goals. The second is to express teaching strategies in a format that allows you to measure their effects upon your learners. The format that allows measurement of learning is the *behavioral objective*.

What Does "Behavioral" Mean?

When the word **behavioral** precedes the word *objective,* the learning is being defined as a change in *observable* behavior. Behavioral objective means that learning is being defined as a change in the learner's *observable* behavior. Therefore, the writing of behavioral objectives requires that the behavior being addressed be observable and measurable (with a test, attitude survey, checklist, etc.). Covert or mentalistic activities occurring in the seclusion of your learners' minds are not observable and thus cannot be the focus of a behavioral objective. (Of course, unobservable activities, such as the creation of mental images or rehearsing a response subvocally, can precede learning, but they *cannot constitute evidence that learning has occurred,* because they cannot be directly observed.)

Further, the behavior must be observable over a period of time during which specifiable content, teaching strategies, and instructional media (e.g., films, homework exercises, texts) have been used. This effectively limits a behavioral objective to a time frame consistent with the logical divisions used in school curricula, such as lessons, chapters, units, and grading periods. Feedback from behavioral objectives (e.g., tests, work samples, and student observation) provides data for monitoring the consequence of your instructional strategy and for revising the goal–learning need–organization–method match.

Where Did the Notion of Objectives Come From?

Historically, the idea of an educational objective can be traced to the early part of the century when Tyler (1934) first conceived of the need for goal-directed statements for teachers. He observed that teachers were concerned far more with the content of instruction (what to teach) than with what the student should be able to do with the content (i.e., whether it could be applied in some meaningful context).

Tyler also noticed implicitly what Fuller later conceptualized (1969) as the stages of concern through which teachers move, starting with concerns for self (Can I make it through the day?), to concerns for task (What will I teach next?), and finally to concerns for students (Are they learning what I teach?). Recall from Chapter 3 Fuller's observation that beginning teachers, particularly those in their first weeks and months of teaching, are preoccupied with concerns for self to the exclusion of concerns for their impact upon students. This has been borne out more recently; the average planning time devoted to goals and objectives in four separate studies ranged from only 2.7% to 13.9% (Clark & Peterson, 1986). These short times indicate that relatively little attention is being focused on student outcomes.

To help teachers shift concern to their impact on students, Tyler developed the idea of behavioral objectives, which subsequently has been expanded by a number of educators. In this chapter you will see how behavioral objectives can be used to help you better plan and prepare your lessons.

What Are the Dangers of Not Having Objectives?

The most important factor in the lack of lesson clarity and lack of task orientation among beginning teachers may be their *inability to specify the learning outcomes* from instruction (Rosenshine, 1983). If student outcomes are ignored, your planning may not go beyond a concern for yourself or the teaching task, and learning either will not occur or will occur in undesirable ways.

The danger is twofold when planning does not go beyond a concern for self or for the teaching task. The first danger is that any and all organizational patterns and teaching methods become equally desirable to the teacher. The second danger is that any and all forms of learning outcomes become equally desirable to the students. The result may be a teacher who is teaching on one "frequency" and students who are listening on another. The teacher may, for example, be organizing the content and selecting teaching strategies in ways that promote problem solving, but the students are receiving the instruction with the intent of parroting names, dates, and facts devoid of any problem-solving context.

If you do not specify objectives, students cannot be sure what is expected of them—you have not told them the extent to which they must be able to perform the behaviors you are teaching. This is why a goal–learning need–organization–method match is so important for planning instruction. Learning outcomes expressed as specific objectives must be tightly coupled to specific learning needs, content organization, and teaching methods to ensure that efficient and effective instruction occurs. You can see that objectives which express the desired outcomes provide a means for evaluating the goal–learning need–organization–method match chosen and for revising it as needed.

Aside from the role of objectives in directing instructional decisions during lesson planning, they may be the single best way of shifting from a concern for self and task to a concern for your impact on students and your focus on the learner. Objectives are a key to reaching your highest and most mature level of professional performance.

AN OVERVIEW OF BEHAVIORAL OBJECTIVES

The goal of this chapter is to show you how to prepare useful objectives as painlessly as possible. Simply put, behavioral objectives have three purposes:

- ☐ They focus instruction on a specific goal that has an observable outcome (a learning outcome).
- ☐ They identify the conditions under which learning can be expected to occur (e.g., with what materials, texts, and facilities and in what period of time).
- ☐ They specify the criterion level—the amount of behavior that can be expected from the instruction under the specified conditions.

Before considering the actual written form of behavioral objectives, we must explore these three purposes in more detail.

Specifying the Learning Outcomes

The first purpose of behavioral objectives is to identify an observable learning outcome. Recall that for an objective to be behavioral, it must be observable. It also must be measurable so you can determine whether the behavior is present, partially present, or absent. The key to identifying an observable outcome is your choice of words to describe the goal.

Word choice is tricky because words have so many connotations. The endless puns used in our culture are humorous illustrations of this: Does "well-rounded person" mean broadly educated or well fed? Another illustration is the way that foreigners sometimes use words literally without awareness of subtle connotations. Words can express a concept not only accurately or inaccurately, but also specifically or vaguely. It is vague usage that gives us the most trouble in writing behavioral objectives.

In a behavioral objective, learning outcomes must be expressed very directly, concretely, and observably, unlike the way behaviors usually are described in the popular press, television, and even some textbooks. If you took these everyday sources as a guide for writing the behavioral expressions needed in the classroom, you would quickly find that they could not be easily observed and thus could not be measured either. For example, we often hear these expressions as desirable goals:

mentally healthy citizens

well-rounded individuals

self-actualized schoolchildren

informed adults

literate populace

But, what do *mentally healthy, well-rounded, self-actualized, informed,* and *literate* actually mean? If you asked a large number of people to define these terms, you would receive quite an assortment of responses. These diverse responses would have widely divergent implications for how to achieve each desired behavior and for observing its attainment. The reason, of course, is that the words are vague and open to many interpretations. Imagine the confusion such vagueness could cause in your classroom if your objective for the first grading period were simply to make the class *informed* about the content or to make them *high achievers*. Johnny's parents would have one interpretation of "informed," and Betty's parents would have quite another. One hopes they both do not show up on parent-teacher night! Also, you might mean one thing by *high achievers,* but your principal might mean another.

The point is that vague behavioral language quickly becomes a problem for the one who is accountable for bringing about the behavior in question—that's you. This is why vague language is gotten away with in the press and everyday conversation—those who write or speak it are, unlike teachers, seldom accountable for having to produce the behaviors described. Needless to say, school boards, school administrators, parents, and taxpayers may call to account those who use vague or general language to describe the behavioral outcomes for which they are responsible.

To avoid this problem, write behavioral outcomes in precise language that makes observation and measurement specific and noncontroversial. Do so by exchanging such popular but vague expressions as *mentally healthy, well-rounded, self-actualized, informed,* and *literate* with expressions that show *specifically what the individual must do* to show mental health, well-roundedness, self-actualization, and so on. The task is not easy, because these expressions are so broad that the behaviors required to exhibit the attribute of mental health, for example, are quite extensive (from staying out of a mental institution, to passing psychological tests, to getting along with family and friends, and so on). This is one reason why such expressions are unsuited for behavioral objectives, because the behavior indicated could be expected only after a long period of time unrelated to any specific curriculum, teaching strategy, or instructional program.

A solution is to choose behavioral expressions from a *list of action verbs* that have widely accepted meanings. These action verbs also allow easy identification of the operations necessary for displaying the behavior. For example, instead of expecting students to be informed or literate in a certain subject, a teacher expects them to:

differentiate between . . .

identify outcomes of . . .

solve a problem in . . .

compare and contrast . . .

Such action verbs truly point toward the goal of being informed or literate by stating specific, observable behaviors that represent the general intent.

Notice that nothing has yet been said about grading or determining the acceptability of the differentiation, identification, problem solving, and comparing and contrasting. But we are now much closer to specifying the type of evidence that can be used to determine whether the objective has been achieved.

Although a behavioral objective should include an action verb that specifies a learning outcome, not all action verbs are suitable for specifying learning outcomes. Some are better suited to specifying *learning activities*. Unfortunately, learning outcomes often are confused with learning activities. For example, which of the following examples represents learning *outcomes* and which represents learning *activities?*

1. The child will identify pictures of words that sound alike.
2. The child will demonstrate an appreciation of poetry.
3. The student will subtract one-digit numbers.
4. The student will show a knowledge of punctuation.
5. The student will practice the multiplication tables.
6. The student will sing the "Star-Spangled Banner."

In the first four objectives, the action words *identify, demonstrate, subtract,* and *show* all point to outcomes—end products of instructional units. However, the action word in the fifth example, *practice,* is only a learning activity; it is not an end in itself and only can work toward a learning outcome. The sixth objective is more ambiguous. Is *sing* an outcome or an activity? It is hard to say without more information. If the goal is to have a stage-frightened student sing in public, then it is a learning outcome. However, if singing is only practice for a later performance, it is a learning activity.

The following examples differentiate between verbs used for learning outcomes and verbs used for learning activities:

Learning Outcomes (Ends)	Learning Activities (Means)
identify	study
recall	watch
list	listen
write	read

Behavioral objectives must include the end product, because you must use this end product in choosing instructional procedures and evaluating the goal–learning need–organization–method match.

Identifying the Conditions

The second purpose for writing behavioral objectives is to identify specific conditions under which learning will occur. If the observable learning outcome can be achieved only through use of particular materials, equipment, tools, or other resources, you must state these conditions in the objective. Here are examples of objectives that clearly state conditions:

□ Using examples from short stories by John Steinbeck and Mark Twain, differentiate between naturalism and realism in American literature.
□ Using the map of strategic resources handed out in class, identify the economic conditions in the South resulting from the Civil War.
□ Using an electronic calculator, solve problems involving the addition of two-digit signed numbers.
□ Using pictures of fourteenth-to-eighteenth-century Gothic and Baroque European cathedrals, compare and contrast the styles of architecture.

If the conditions are obvious, they need not be specified, for they add nothing critical. For example, it is not necessary to specify "Using a writing instrument and paper, write a short story." On the other hand, when conditions can focus learning in specific ways, eliminating some areas of study and including others, the statement of conditions can be critical to attaining the objective, and you must include it. For example, imagine that a student will be tested on the behavior indicated in the first objective in the preceding list, but without the condition indicated. Differentiating naturalism from realism without reference to concrete examples in the writings of specific authors who represent these styles will produce a more general, less structured response. Also, if students are told the conditions, they can focus their studying on the precise behavior called for (in this case, applying already learned definitions of naturalistic and realistic styles to specific examples, as opposed to parroting general distinctions between the styles).

Note also that without a statement of conditions to focus instruction, different students easily can assume different conditions. In the absence of concrete examples, some students might prepare by studying the *philosophical differences* between the two styles of writing; others might focus their study on being able to *apply their knowledge* to examples in the literature. And, because objectives form the basis for tests, the tests might be more fair to some students than others simply on the basis of assumptions students must make if you fail to state conditions.

Notice in the other preceding examples that learning can take on quite a different meaning, depending on whether students study and practice with or without use of a map, a calculator, and pictures of cathedrals. You can see clearly that teaching and learning become more structured and resources become more organized when conditions are stated as part of the objectives. Also—perhaps most important for good relations with students—objectives that specify conditions lead to tests that are fairer. Proper statement of the conditions of learning is one of the most important ingredients for achieving the key behaviors of lesson clarity and a moderate-to-high rate of student success.

Conditional statements within a behavioral objective can be singular or multiple. It is possible, and sometimes necessary, to have two or even three conditional statements in an objective to focus the learning. Although too many conditions attached to an objective can narrow learning to irrelevant details, multiple conditions often are important adjuncts to improving the clarity of the behavior desired and the organization and preparation of instructional resources. Here are examples of multiple conditions, indicated by italics:

- ☐ Using a centigrade *thermometer,* measure the temperature of two liters of *water* at a depth of 25 centimeters.
- ☐ Using a *compass, ruler,* and *protractor,* draw three conic sections of different sizes and three triangles of different types.
- ☐ Using four grams of *sodium carbonate* and four grams of *sodium bicarbonate,* indicate their different reactions in H_2O.
- ☐ *Within 15 minutes* and using the *reference books* provided, find the formulae for wattage, voltage, amperage, and resistance.
- ☐ Using a *microcomputer* with word processing capability, correct the spelling and punctuation errors on a *two-page manuscript* in 20 minutes or less.

It is important not to add so many conditions that learning is reduced to some trivial detail. It also is important to choose conditions that are realistic. Setting extremely short time periods in which a behavior is to be acquired or requiring the use of complicated equipment or resources not generally available places unrealistic restrictions on learning and promotes learning that is not generalizable to the real world. The idea behind stating conditions, especially multiple conditions, is not to complicate the behavior but rather to make it more natural and *close to the conditions under which the behavior will have to be performed in the real world* and in subsequent instruction. Always check the conditions specified to see if they are those under which the behavior is *most likely to be performed outside the classroom or in subsequent instruction.*

Stating Criterion Levels

The third purpose of a behavioral objective is to state the level of performance that must be attained to meet the objective. Recall that one of the most important reasons for translating goals into objectives is to provide some way of determining whether the behavior implied by the goal has been attained. Part of this purpose is accomplished by being specific about the behavior desired (e.g., "differentiate between" instead of "inform," and "identify outcomes of" rather than "educate"). Another part is accomplished by stating the conditions under which learning is expected to occur. Specifying the outcome and conditions reveals the procedures necessary for the behavior to be observed.

However, one important element is missing. You also must specify *how much* of the behavior is required for you to consider the objective to be attained. This element of objective writing is the **criterion level**. It is the level or degree of performance desired or the level of proficiency that will satisfy you that the objective has been met.

Setting criterion levels is one of the most misunderstood aspects of objective writing. At the root of this misunderstanding is failure to recognize that criterion or proficiency levels are value judgments, or educated guesses, as to what performance level is required for adequately performing the behavior in some later setting. The mistaken assumption is often made that a single "correct" level of proficiency exists and that once established it must forever remain in its original form.

Criterion levels should be viewed as educated guesses about the degree of proficiency needed to adequately perform the behavior in the next grade, another instructional setting, or the world outside the classroom. Most important to the setting of criterion levels, then, is their periodic *adjustment* upward or downward to conform with knowledge of how well the students are able to perform the behavior in contexts beyond your classroom. This means that observing your students in other subjects and class periods, as well as observing other students in other grades and classes, is a necessary part of establishing nonarbitrary criterion levels.

Often, criterion levels are set to establish a benchmark for testing whether an objective has been met, without recognizing that this level may be irrelevant for any subsequent learning task or instructional setting. To avoid this, always consider criterion levels to be adjustable and dependent on continual evaluation of how well students can *adequately use the behavior in contexts beyond your classroom*.

Proficiency levels come in many sizes and shapes. For example, they can be stated as:

Number of items correct on a test.

Number of consecutive items correct (or consecutive errorless performances).

Essential features included (as in an essay question or paper).

Completion within a prescribed time limit (where speed of performance is important).

Completion with a certain degree of accuracy.

Earlier in this chapter, several objectives were shown. The first objective was "Using short stories by John Steinbeck and Mark Twain, differentiate between naturalism and realism in American literature." Is a criterion level stated? (Remember, a criterion level establishes the degree of behavior required for the objective to be met. This level is the *minimum proficiency that must be exhibited*.) How would the teacher know if a minimum level of differentiation has been demonstrated by a student's written response to this objective? With only the information given, it would be difficult and quite arbitrary, because no criterion level of performance is stated. Now, add a criterion to this objective:

☐ Using short stories by John Steinbeck and Mark Twain, differentiate between naturalism and realism by selecting four passages from each author that illustrate differences in these writing styles.

Now there is a basis for evaluating the objective. The newly added criterion level includes the identification of differences illustrated over four passages. This particular way of expressing a criterion level is fairly complex; it requires considerable skill in applying learned information in different contexts and allows for flexibility in the range of responses that are acceptable. This type of objective is sometimes called an **expressive objective** (Eisner, 1969) because it allows for a variety of correct responses or for the student to express himself or herself in a variety of forms for which there is not any *single* correct answer. The amount of expressiveness in a response allowed by an objective is always a matter of degree. In other words, objectives can have more- or less-rigid criterion levels.

Consider another example:

☐ Using an electronic calculator, the student will solve problems involving the addition of two-digit signed numbers.

Is there a stated criterion level for this objective? No. There is no unambiguous basis for deciding whether Mary met the objective and Bobby did not. Now, add a criterion level:

☐ Using an electronic calculator, the student will correctly solve 8 out of 10 problems involving the addition of two-digit signed numbers.

This objective now precisely identifies the minimum proficiency that must be observed to conclude that the desired behavior has been attained. Unlike the first objective, little flexibility is allowed in the required response (except that more than 8 out of 10 could be solved correctly). Notice that far less expression is possible in answering a question about mathematics than about literature; the former is more highly structured and more rigid in terms of possible responses. Notice also that this more-structured approach to an acceptable response fits well with the nature of this particular objective, while the less-structured approach fits well with the previous objective (differentiating between naturalism and realism).

Both of these objectives illustrate that the expressiveness of an objective is established by how you set an acceptable criterion. Also, the level of expressiveness that fits best often is a function of the objective itself—how many correct answers are possible. Different types of criterion behaviors will be discussed shortly, but for now keep in mind that you must establish the degree of expressiveness allowed, and that proficiency level is alterable at any time. These two considerations—level of proficiency and expressiveness—are under your control. Continually reevaluate them and adjust them as you gain experience regarding the level and quality of the students' responses.

Here are some of the earlier objectives with criterion levels added in brackets (or italicized where a criterion already was included):

☐ Using a centigrade thermometer, measure the temperature of two liters of water at a depth of 25 centimeters [to within one degree accuracy].
☐ Using a compass, ruler, and protractor, draw *three* conic sections of *different sizes* and *three* triangles of *different types*.

One essential ingredient of a well-written objective is that it identifies the proficiency level that must be displayed for the desired behavior to be achieved. Objectives can have either more rigid or less rigid levels of proficiency, the latter allowing for more flexibility in the response of the student.

☐ Using four grams of sodium carbonate and four grams of sodium bicarbonate, indicate their different reactions with H_2O [by testing the alkalinity of the H_2O and reporting results in parts per million (PPM)].

☐ Within 15 minutes and using the reference books provided, find [and write correctly] the formulae for wattage, voltage, amperage, and resistance.

☐ Using a microcomputer with word-processing capability, correct the spelling and punctuation errors for a two-page manuscript in *20 minutes* [with 100% accuracy].

These examples illustrate well-written behavioral objectives.

You have seen how to specify learning outcomes, state conditions for learning, and establish criterion levels. These are the three most important ingredients of well-written behavioral objectives. Before moving to the next topic, there is one more point to know about preparing well-written objectives.

Keeping Objectives Simple

Teachers often make the mistake of being too sophisticated in measuring learning outcomes. As a result, they resort to indirect or unnecessarily complex methods of measurement. If you want to know whether Johnny can write his name, ask him to write his name—but not while blindfolded! Resist the temptation to be tricky. Consider these examples:

☐ The student will show his or her ability to recall characters of the book *Tom Sawyer* by painting a picture of each.

☐ Discriminate between a telephone and television by drawing an electrical diagram of each.

☐ Demonstrate that you understand how to use an encyclopedia index by listing the page on which a given subject can be found in the *Encyclopedia Britannica*.

In the first example, painting a picture surely would allow you to determine whether the students can recall the characters in *Tom Sawyer,* but is there an easier (and less time consuming) way to measure recall? How about asking the students simply to list the characters? If the objective is to determine recall, listing is sufficient. For the second example, how about presenting students with two illustrations, one of a telephone, the other of a television, and simply ask them to tell (verbally or in writing) which is which?

The third example is on target. The task required is a simple and efficient way of measuring whether someone can use an encyclopedia index.

You must practice writing objectives on your own. Return to the examples in this chapter if you need help, as they are useful models. Be sure to include the three components in every objective you write: (a) observable learning outcome, (b) conditions, and (c) criterion level. Once you have written a behavioral objective, always analyze it to make sure that these three essential components are included.

THE COGNITIVE, AFFECTIVE, AND PSYCHOMOTOR DOMAINS

You might have noticed that some of the example objectives shown earlier in this chapter have illustrated vastly different types of behavior. For example, compare the behaviors called for in these objectives:

☐ Using short stories by John Steinbeck and Mark Twain, differentiate between naturalism and realism by selecting four passages from each author that illustrate differences in these writing styles.

☐ Using a centigrade thermometer, measure the temperature of two liters of water at a depth of 25 centimeters to within one degree accuracy.

Intuition tells us that the behaviors called for require quite different preparation and study to attain. Common sense suggests that the study and preparation to achieve each objective would take the student in different directions.

In the former objective, study and practice would focus on analysis— identifying the key aspects of naturalism and realism and explaining relationships between them, noting their similarities and differences and the application of these ideas to actual examples of the writings of a naturalist and a realist. Contrast this complicated process with how one might study to acquire the behavior in the second objective. Here the study and practice might consist simply of learning to accurately perceive distances between the markings on a centigrade scale. Such practice might be limited to training one's eyes to count spaces between the gradations and then assigning the appropriate number to represent temperature in degrees centigrade.

Note also the difference in study and preparation time required to achieve these two different objectives: the second could be learned in minutes, but the other might take hours, days, or even weeks. These different objectives represent only two examples of the variety of behavioral outcomes possible in your classroom.

Objectives can require vastly different levels not only of cognitive complexity but of affective and psychomotor complexity as well. The following section introduces behaviors at different levels of complexity for which behavioral objectives can be prepared. For convenience, these are organized into *cognitive* behaviors (development of intellectual abilities and skills), *affective* behaviors (development of attitudes, beliefs, and values), and *psychomotor* behaviors (coordination of physical movements and bodily performances).

The Cognitive Domain

Bloom, Englehart, Hill, Furst, and Krathwohl (1956) devised a method for categorizing objectives according to cognitive complexity. They delineate six levels of cognitive complexity, ranging from the knowledge level (least complex) to the evaluation level (most complex). As illustrated in Figure 4.1, they presume the levels to be hierarchical—higher-level objectives are assumed to include, and to be dependent on, lower-level cognitive skills.

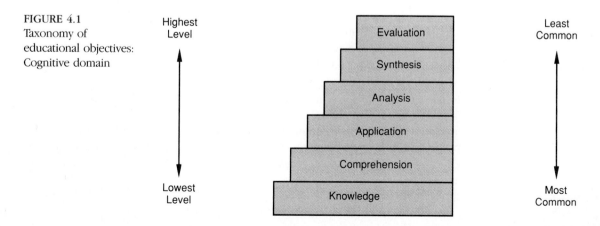

FIGURE 4.1
Taxonomy of
educational objectives:
Cognitive domain

Highest Level / Lowest Level

Evaluation
Synthesis
Analysis
Application
Comprehension
Knowledge

Least Common / Most Common

Each level—knowledge, comprehension, application, analysis, synthesis, and evaluation—has different characteristics and is described in the following sections with examples of action verbs that represent each level.

Knowledge.   Objectives at the knowledge level require your students to remember or recall information such as facts, terminology, problem-solving strategies, and rules. Some action verbs that describe learning outcomes at the knowledge level are:

define	list	recall
describe	match	recite
identify	name	select
label	outline	state

Here are example knowledge objectives that use these verbs:

- ☐ The student will recall the four major food groups, without error, by Friday.
- ☐ From memory, the student will match United States generals with their most famous battles, with 80% accuracy.

Comprehension.   Objectives at this level require some degree of understanding. Students are expected to be able to change the form of a communication; translate; restate what has been read; see connections or relationships among parts of a communication (interpretation); or draw conclusions or see consequences from information (inference). Some action verbs that describe learning outcomes at the comprehension level are:

convert	estimate	infer
defend	explain	paraphrase
discriminate	extend	predict
distinguish	generalize	summarize

Here are example comprehension objectives that use these verbs:

- ☐ By the end of the semester, the student will summarize the main events of a story in grammatically correct English.
- ☐ The student will discriminate between the *realists* and the *naturalists,* citing examples from the readings.

Application.   Objectives written at this level require the student to use previously acquired information in a setting other than the one in which it was learned. Application objectives differ from comprehension objectives in that application requires the presentation of a problem in a different and often applied context. Thus, the student can rely on neither the *content* nor the *context* in which the original learning occurred to solve the problem. Some action verbs that describe learning outcomes at the application level are:

change	modify	relate
compute	operate	solve
demonstrate	organize	transfer
develop	prepare	use

Here are example application objectives that use these or similar verbs:

☐ On Monday, the student will demonstrate for the class an application to real life of the law of conservation of energy.

☐ Given fractions not covered in class, the student will multiply them on paper with 85% accuracy.

Analysis. Objectives written at the analysis level require the student to identify logical errors (e.g., point out a contradiction or an erroneous inference) or to differentiate among facts, opinions, assumptions, hypotheses, and conclusions. At the analysis level students are expected to draw relationships among ideas and to compare and contrast. Some action verbs that describe learning outcomes at the analysis level are:

break down	distinguish	point out
deduce	illustrate	relate
diagram	infer	separate out
differentiate	outline	subdivide

Here are example analysis objectives that use these verbs:

☐ Given a presidential speech, the student will be able to point out the positions that attack an individual rather than that individual's program.

☐ Given absurd statements (e.g.: A man had flu twice. The first time it killed him. The second time he got well quickly.), the student will be able to point out the contradiction.

Synthesis. Objectives written at the synthesis level require the student to produce something unique or original. At the synthesis level students are expected to solve some unfamiliar problem in a unique way or to combine parts to form a unique or novel solution. Some action verbs that describe learning outcomes at the synthesis level are:

categorize	create	formulate
compile	design	predict
compose	devise	produce

Here are example synthesis objectives that use these or similar verbs:

☐ Given a short story, the student will write a different but plausible ending.

☐ Given a problem to be solved, the student will design on paper a scientific experiment to address the problem.

Evaluation.   Objectives written at this level require the student to form judgments and make decisions about the value of methods, ideas, people, or products that have a specific purpose. Students are expected to state the bases for their judgments (e.g., the external criteria or principles they drew upon to reach their conclusions). Some action verbs that describe learning outcomes at the evaluation level are:

appraise	criticize	justify
compare	defend	support
contrast	judge	validate

Here are example evaluation objectives that use these verbs:

☐ Given a previously unread paragraph, the student will judge its value according to the five criteria discussed in class.
☐ Given a description of a country's economic system, the student will defend it, basing arguments on principles of democracy.

The Affective Domain

Another method of categorizing objectives was devised by Krathwohl, Bloom, and Masia (1964). This taxonomy delineates five levels of affective complexity ranging from the receiving level (least complex) to the characterization level (most complex). As in the cognitive domain, these levels are presumed to be hierarchical—higher-level objectives are assumed to include and be dependent upon lower-level affective skills (Figure 4.2). As one moves up the hierarchy, more involvement, commitment, and reliance on one's own self occurs, as opposed to having one's feelings, attitudes, and values dictated by outside sources.

For each level of the affective domain—receiving, responding, valuing, organization, and characterization—the following sections contain some examples of action verbs indicating each level.

Receiving.   Objectives at the receiving level require the student to be aware of, or to passively attend to, certain phenomena and stimuli. At this level students are expected

FIGURE 4.2
Taxonomy of
educational objectives:
Affective domain

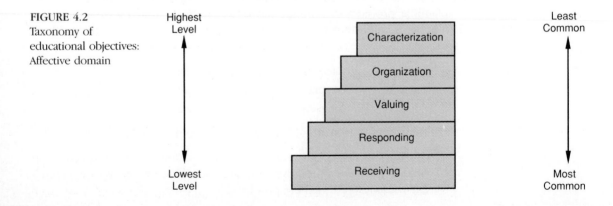

simply to listen or be attentive. Some action verbs that describe outcomes at the receiving level are:

attend	discern	look
be aware	hear	notice
control	listen	share

Here are example receiving objectives that use these verbs:

☐ The student will be able to notice a change from small-group discussion to large-group lecture by following the lead of others in the class.
☐ The student will be able to listen to all of a Mozart concerto without leaving his or her seat.

Responding. Objectives at the responding level require the student to comply with given expectations by attending or reacting to certain stimuli. Students are expected to obey, participate, or respond willingly when asked or directed to do something. Some action verbs that describe outcomes at the responding level are:

applaud	follow	play
comply	obey	practice
discuss	participate	volunteer

Here are example responding objectives that use these verbs:

☐ The student will follow the directions given in the book without argument when asked to do so.
☐ The student will practice a musical instrument when asked to do so.

Valuing. Objectives at the valuing level require the student to display behavior consistent with a single belief or attitude in situations where he or she is neither forced nor asked to comply. Students are expected to demonstrate a preference or display a high degree of certainty and conviction. Some action verbs that describe outcomes at the valuing level are:

act	debate	help
argue	display	organize
convince	express	prefer

Here are example valuing objectives that use these verbs:

☐ The student will express an opinion about nuclear disarmament whenever national events raise the issue.
☐ The student will display an opinion about the elimination of pornography whenever discussing social issues.

Organization. Objectives at the organization level require a commitment to a set of values. This level of the affective domain involves (1) forming a reason why one values certain things and not others, and (2) making appropriate choices between things that are and are not valued. Students are expected to organize their likes and preferences into a value system and then decide which ones will be dominant. Some action verbs that describe outcomes at the organization level are:

abstract	decide	select
balance	define	systematize
compare	formulate	theorize

Here are example organization objectives that use these verbs:

☐ The student will be able to compare alternatives to the death penalty and decide which ones are compatible with his or her beliefs.
☐ The student will be able to formulate the reasons why she or he supports civil rights legislation and will be able to identify legislation that does not support her or his beliefs.

Characterization. Objectives at the characterization level require that all behavior displayed by the student be consistent with his or her values. At this level the student not only has acquired the behaviors at all previous levels but also has integrated his or her values into a system representing a complete and pervasive philosophy which never allows expressions that are out of character with these values. Evaluations of this level of behavior involve the extent to which the student has developed a consistent philosophy of life (e.g., exhibits respect for the worth and dignity of human beings in all situations). Some action verbs that describe outcomes at this level are:

avoid	internalize	resist
display	manage	resolve
exhibit	require	revise

Some example objectives are:

☐ The student will exhibit a helping and caring attitude toward handicapped students by assisting with their mobility both in and out of classrooms.
☐ The student will display a scientific attitude by stating and then testing hypotheses whenever the choice of alternatives is unclear.

The Psychomotor Domain

A third method of categorizing objectives has been devised by Harrow (1969). This taxonomy delineates five levels of psychomotor complexity ranging from the imitation level (least complex) to the naturalization level (most complex). Figure 4.3 illustrates the hierarchical arrangement of the psychomotor domain levels. These behaviors place primary emphasis on neuromuscular skills involving various degrees of physical dexterity. As behaviors in the taxonomy move from least to most complex, behavior changes from gross to fine motor skills.

FIGURE 4.3
Taxonomy of
educational objectives:
Psychomotor domain

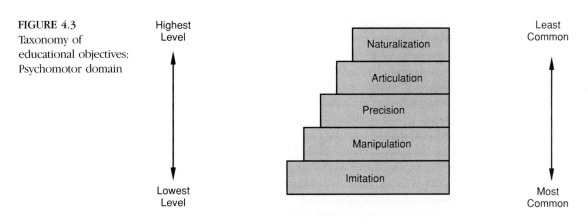

Each of the levels—imitation, manipulation, precision, articulation, and naturalization—has different characteristics and is described in the following sections with examples of action verbs that represent each level.

Imitation. Objectives at this level require that the student be exposed to an observable action and then overtly imitate it, such as when an instructor demonstrates the use of a microscope by placing a slide on the specimen tray. Performance at this level usually lacks neuromuscular coordination (e.g., the slide may hit the side of the tray or be improperly aligned beneath the lens). Thus the behavior generally is crude and imperfect. At this level students are expected to observe and be able to repeat (although imperfectly) the action being visually demonstrated. Some action verbs that describe outcomes at this level are:

align	grasp	repeat
balance	hold	rest (on)
follow	place	step (here)

Here are example imitation objectives that use these or similar verbs:

☐ After being shown a safe method for heating a beaker of water to boiling temperature, the student will be able to repeat the action.
☐ After being shown a freehand drawing of a parallelogram, the student will be able to reproduce the drawing.

Manipulation. Objectives at this level require the student to perform selected actions from written or verbal directions without the aid of a visual model or direct observation, as in the previous (imitation) level. Students are expected to complete the action from reading or listening to instructions, although the behavior still may be performed crudely and without neuromuscular coordination. Useful expressions to describe outcomes at the manipulation level are the same as at the imitation level, using the same action verbs, except they are performed from spoken or written instructions.

Here are example manipulation objectives:

☐ Based on the picture provided in the textbook, type a salutation to a prospective employer using the format shown.
☐ With the instructions on the handout in front of you, practice focusing your microscope until the outline of the specimen can be seen.

Precision.   Objectives at this level require the student to perform an action independent of either a visual model or a written set of directions. Proficiency in reproducing the action at this level reaches a higher level of refinement. Accuracy, proportion, balance, and exactness in performance accompany the action. Students are expected to reproduce the action with control and to reduce errors to a minimum. Expressions that describe outcomes at this level include performing the behavior:

accurately	independently	with control
errorlessly	proficiently	with balance

Here are example precision objectives:

☐ The student will be able to accurately place the specimen on the microscope tray and use the high-power focus with proficiency as determined by the correct identification of three out of four easily recognizable objects.
☐ The student will be able to balance a light pen sufficiently to place it against the computer screen to identify misspelled words.

Articulation.   Objectives at this level require the student to display coordination of a series of related acts by establishing the appropriate sequence and performing the acts accurately, with control as well as with speed and timing. Expressions that describe outcomes at this level include performing the behaviors with:

confidence	integration	speed
coordination	proportion	stability
harmony	smoothness	timing

Here are example articulation objectives:

☐ Students will be able to write all the letters of the alphabet, displaying the appropriate proportion between upper case and lower case, in 10 minutes.
☐ Students will be able to accurately complete 10 simple arithmetic problems on a hand-held electronic calculator quickly and smoothly within 90 seconds.

Naturalization.   Objectives at this level require a high level of proficiency in the skill or performance being taught. At this level the behavior is performed with the least expenditure of energy and becomes routine, automatic, and spontaneous. Students are expected to repeat the behavior naturally and effortlessly time and again. Some expressions that describe this level of behavior are:

automatically	professionally	with ease
effortlessly	routinely	with perfection
naturally	spontaneously	with poise

Here are example naturalization objectives:

☐ At the end of the semester, students will be able to write routinely all the letters of the alphabet and all the numbers up to 100 each time requested.
☐ After the first grading period, students will be able to automatically draw correct isosceles, equilateral, and right triangles, without the aid of a template, for each homework assignment that requires this task.

Objectives that require a high level of proficiency in the psychomotor domain expect the learner to repeat the behavior naturally and effortlessly time and again.

CREATING A CONTENT-BY-BEHAVIOR
BLUEPRINT WITH TEACHING OBJECTIVES

We have devoted a good deal of time to writing and analyzing objectives. It also is necessary to spend time on a technique that reminds you to write objectives at different levels. This technique is the **content-by-behavior blueprint**. Much like a blueprint used to guide the construction of a new building, the content-by-behavior blueprint guides your unit and lesson planning.

The blueprint for a building ensures that the builder will not overlook essential details. Similarly, the content-by-behavior blueprint ensures that you will not overlook details essential to good teaching. Specifically, it ensures that your lessons will address all the content areas covered in the curriculum guide and text, and all the behaviors that represent important learning needs.

Table 4.1 illustrates a content-by-behavior blueprint for a unit in secondary school mathematics. Consider each component of the blueprint. Once you see how the components are interrelated, the significance of a content-by-behavior blueprint becomes clear. Always assemble such a blueprint before you actually begin teaching a unit.

Content Outline Portion of Blueprint

The content outline lists the topic areas to be taught; these are usually found in the curriculum guide and adopted text. It is for these topical areas that you will write objectives and test items. Generally, one objective is written for each topic area. Keep the number of topic areas to a manageable number within any single blueprint—otherwise, the number of objectives for unit plans, lesson plans, and tests will be too large.

Behavior Categories Portion of Blueprint

These categories serve as a reminder or a check on the behavioral complexity of your instruction. In the cells under each category in Table 4.1, you can report the number of test items needed to cover a particular area. Obviously, some units will contain objectives that do not go beyond the comprehension or application level. However, depending on the content outline, you might want to incorporate behaviors at higher (or lower) levels into your instruction and tests.

In summary, the information in Table 4.1 indicates:

the content and behaviors for which objectives are to be written;

whether the instruction reflects a balanced picture of what is to be taught; and

whether instruction will be planned for all topics and objectives specified in the curriculum and text.

Seldom can a perfectly balanced blueprint that incorporates all levels of behavior for each content area be attained—nor is such a balance always desirable.

However, the little extra time required to construct such a blueprint for instruction often is repaid. It can suggest levels of behavioral complexity that were not originally planned but which can and should be incorporated into the unit and lesson plan.

A content-by-behavior blueprint also is essential to good test construction, ensuring that your tests include a variety of items that tap different levels of behavioral complexity. In Chapter 14, you will see how the content-by-behavior blueprint is used for constructing test items.

With a content-by-behavior blueprint you avoid not only spotty instruction but also the necessity of going back to teach concepts needed for subsequent learning, concepts that you missed in previous lesson plans. You also will feel satisfaction from constructing a framework to use in creating fair and representative tests for the objectives you have taught.

SOME MISUNDERSTANDINGS ABOUT BEHAVIORAL OBJECTIVES

You should be aware of several misconceptions that unfortunately have grown up around behaviors associated with the cognitive, affective, and psychomotor domains. These misconceptions are the understandable results of categorizing behaviors in minute detail, in hopes of being useful and appealing to teachers. However, such detail makes it harder to see the forest for the trees. When behavior is divided into so many appealing bits and chunks, it is easy to lose sight of the larger concepts.

Are Some Behaviors More Desirable Than Others?

One misconception that often results from study of the cognitive, affective, and psychomotor domains is that the simple-to-complex ordering of behavior within each of these domains also represents an ordering from least to most *desirable*. Some believe that simple behaviors, like the recall of facts and dates, are less desirable than more complex behaviors requiring the cognitive operations of analysis, synthesis, and decision making. However, the behaviors within the cognitive, affective, and psychomotor domains do not imply desirability, because many lower-order behaviors (such as memorizing facts) must be learned before higher-order behaviors can even be attempted.

Some teachers pride themselves on preparing objectives almost exclusively at the highest levels of cognitive complexity; they do not recognize that objectives at a lower order of complexity always will be required for some students to stay actively engaged in the learning process with moderate-to-high rates of success. Without adequate instruction in the simpler behaviors, students will not be actively engaged when behaviors of greater complexity are taught. In this case, neither task-relevant prior knowledge nor skills necessary for acquiring more complex behaviors will have been taught. This may cause high failure rates and predictably less active engagement in the learning process.

One of the most important uses of the taxonomies of behavior we have presented is to provide you with a menu of behaviors at different levels of complexity

TABLE 4.1
Context-by-behavior blueprint for secondary school mathematics

Behavior Categories

CONTENT OUTLINE	A. Knowledge			B. Comprehension					C. Application				D. Analysis				
	A.1 Ability to list specific facts	A.2 Ability to define terminology	A.3 Ability to state algorithms	B.1 Ability to summarize	B.2 Ability to distinguish principles, rules, and generalizations	B.3 Ability to infer mathematical structure	B.4 Ability to extend problem elements from one mode to another	B.5 Ability to defend a line of reasoning	C.1 Ability to solve routine problems	C.2 Ability to develop comparisons	C.3 Ability to operate on data	C.4 Ability to organize patterns, isomorphisms, and symmetries	D.1 Ability to separate out nonroutine problems	D.2 Ability to decide relationships	D.3 Ability to illustrate proofs	D.4 Ability to break down proofs	D.5 Ability to outline generalizations
Number systems																	
1.1 Whole numbers																	
1.2 Integers																	
1.3 Rational numbers																	
1.4 Real numbers																	
1.5 Complex numbers																	
1.6 Finite number systems																	
1.7 Matrices and determinants																	
1.8 Probability																	
1.9 Numeration systems																	
Algebra																	
2.1 Algebraic expressions																	

TABLE 4.1, *concluded*

Behavior Categories

CONTENT OUTLINE	A. Knowledge			B. Comprehension					C. Application				D. Analysis				
	A.1 Ability to list specific facts	A.2 Ability to define terminology	A.3 Ability to state algorithms	B.1 Ability to summarize	B.2 Ability to distinguish principles, rules, and generalizations	B.3 Ability to infer mathematical structure	B.4 Ability to extend problem elements from one mode to another	B.5 Ability to defend a line of reasoning	C.1 Ability to solve routine problems	C.2 Ability to develop comparisons	C.3 Ability to operate on data	C.4 Ability to organize patterns, isomorphisms, and symmetries	D.1 Ability to separate out nonroutine problems	D.2 Ability to decide relationships	D.3 Ability to illustrate proofs	D.4 Ability to break down proofs	D.5 Ability to outline generalizations
2.2 Algebraic sentence																	
2.3 Relations and functions																	
Geometry																	
3.1 Measurement																	
3.2 Geometric phenomena																	
3.3 Formal reasoning																	
3.4 Coordinate systems and graphs																	

131

from which to choose. As with any good diet, variety and proper proportion are the keys to good results.

Are Less Complex Behaviors Easier to Teach?

Another misconception about behaviors in the cognitive, affective, and psychomotor domains is that behaviors of less complexity (e.g., the recall of facts) are easier to teach than behaviors of greater complexity (e.g., problem solving). This is an appealing argument because intuition and common sense indicate that this should be so. After all, complexity—especially cognitive complexity—often has been associated with greater difficulty, greater amounts of study time, and more extensive instructional resources.

Although simpler behaviors may be easier to teach some of the time, it often is just the opposite. For example, consider the elaborate study card and mnemonic system that might be needed to recall the periodic table of chemical elements, as opposed to the simple visual demonstration of an experiment to promote problem-solving activity. In this case, the so-called less complex behavior requires greater time and instructional resources. Also, whether a behavior is easier or harder to teach always will depend on the ability level, motivation, discipline, and prior achievement of the students. It is quite possible that the teaching of dull but important facts to less-able, poorly motivated students will be considerably more difficult than demonstrating the practical application of those facts to the same students.

These examples point out that errors of judgment can easily be made by automatically assuming that lower-order, less complex behaviors necessarily require little preparation, fewer instructional resources, and less teaching time than do higher-order, more complex behaviors. The ease with which a behavior can be taught is not synonymous with the level of the behavior in the taxonomy (i.e., lower or higher). These designations refer to the *actions required of the student and not the complexity of the activities required of the teacher to produce the behavior*.

Are Cognitive, Affective, and Psychomotor Behaviors Mutually Exclusive?

Finally, categorizing behaviors into cognitive, affective, and psychomotor domains does not mean that behaviors listed in one domain are mutually exclusive of those listed in other domains. For example, it is inconceivable that we could think without feeling about what we are thinking, or that we could feel or have a reaction devoid of cognition. Also, much thinking involves physical movements and bodily performances that require psychomotor skills and abilities. For example, conducting a laboratory experiment requires not only thought but pouring from one test tube to another, safely igniting a Bunsen burner, adjusting a microscope correctly, etc.

It is convenient for an objective to contain behavior from only one of the three domains at a time. But keep in mind that one or more behaviors from the other domains also may be required for the behavior to occur—for example, a good attitude is required for the memorization of facts to occur. This is one of the best reasons for preparing objectives in all three domains: it is evidence of your awareness of the close and necessary relationship among cognitive, affective, and psychomotor behaviors.

To sum up, keep in mind the following cautions when using and writing behavioral objectives:

☐ Behaviors listed within the cognitive, affective, and psychomotor domains do not imply that some behaviors will be more or less desirable in your classroom than others.

☐ Less complex behaviors within the cognitive, affective, and psychomotor domains do not imply that less teacher preparation, fewer instructional resources, or less teaching time will be required than for more complex behaviors.

☐ Although objectives usually contain behaviors from only one of the three domains, one or more behaviors from the other domains may also be required for the behavior to occur.

THE CULTURAL ROOTS OF OBJECTIVES

You should know that the source of objectives often is questioned by parents, community members, and students. As noted, the technical process of writing objectives sometimes can obscure the forest because of the trees, i.e., prevent you from recognizing the obvious because you were working so hard to produce objectives in the correct technical form. Therefore, typical teachers' responses about the source of objectives include "from textbooks," "from curriculum guides," or "from department policies."

These answers are technically correct but miss the fundamental point, which is that objectives have roots much deeper than any single text, curriculum guide, or set of policies. These roots lie in the educational values we espouse as a nation. While parents, students, and other teachers may argue with the text used, the curriculum guide followed, or the department policies accepted, it is quite another thing to take exception to the values we share as a nation and that were created by many different interest groups over many years of thoughtful deliberation.

Texts, curricula, and policies are interpretations of these values shared at the broadest national level and translated into practice through goals and objectives. Texts, curriculum guides, and school district policies can no more create objectives than they can create values. Goals and their objectives are carefully created to reflect our values from sources such as curriculum reform committees, state and national legislative mandates, and national educational policies. This is why you must have a knowledge of these ultimate sources from which you have derived your objectives, or else you may continually be caught in the position of justifying a particular text, curriculum, or policy to parents, students, and peers—some of whom will always disagree with you. Reference to any one text, curriculum, or policy can never prove that Johnny should appreciate art or that Mary should know how to solve an equation.

On the other hand, our *values,* as indicated by curriculum reform committees, state and national mandates, and national educational policies, can provide appropriate and adequate justification for intended learning outcomes. Attention to these values as reported by the press, professional papers and books, curriculum committees, and national teacher groups is as important to teaching as the objectives you write.

SUMMING UP

This chapter introduced instructional objectives. Its main points were:

1. Objectives have two purposes: (a) to tie general aims and goals to specific classroom strategies that will achieve those aims and goals, and (b) to express teaching strategies in a format that allows you to measure their effects upon your learners.

2. When the word *behavioral* precedes the word *objective,* the learning is being defined as a change in *observable* behavior that can be *measured* within a *specified period of time*.

3. The need for behavioral objectives stems from a natural preoccupation with concerns for self and task, sometimes to the exclusion of concerns for the impact on students.

4. Objectives that express the desired outcomes provide the means for evaluating the chosen goal–learning need–organization–method match.

5. Simply put, behavioral objectives:
   □ Focus instruction on a specific goal whose outcomes can be observed.
   □ Identify the conditions under which learning can be expected to occur.
   □ Specify the level or amount of behavior that can be expected from the instruction under the conditions specified.

6. Action verbs help operationalize the learning outcome expected from an objective and identify exactly what the learner must do to achieve the outcome.

7. The outcome specified in a behavioral objective should be expressed as an end (e.g., to identify, recall, list) and not as a means (e.g., to study, watch, listen).

8. If the observable learning outcome is to take place with particular materials, equipment, tools, or other resources, these conditions must be stated explicitly in the objective.

9. Conditional statements within a behavioral objective can be singular (one condition) or multiple (more than one condition).

10. Conditions should match those under which the behavior will be performed in the real world.

11. A proficiency level is the minimum degree of performance that will satisfy you that the objective has been met.

12. Proficiency levels represent value judgments, or educated guesses, as to what level of performance will be required for adequately performing the behavior in some later setting beyond your classroom.

13. The expressiveness of an objective refers to the amount of flexibility allowed in a response. Less expressive objectives may call for only a single right answer, whereas more expressive objectives allow for less structured and more flexible responses. The expressiveness allowed is always a matter of degree.

14. "Complexity" of a behavior in the cognitive, affective, or psychomotor domain pertains to the operations required of the student to produce the behavior, not to the complexity of the teaching activities required.

15. Behaviors in the cognitive domain, from least to most complex, are knowledge, comprehension, application, analysis, synthesis, and evaluation.

16. Behaviors in the affective domain, from least to most complex, are receiving, responding, valuing, organization, and characterization.

17. Behaviors in the psychomotor domain, from least to most complex, are imitation, manipulation, precision, articulation, and naturalization.

18. A content-by-behavior blueprint is a graphic device for ensuring that the lesson and tests adequately address and provide a balanced coverage of (a) all the content areas identified in the cur-

riculum guide, and (b) all the important cognitive, affective, and psychomotor behaviors.

19. Behavioral objectives have their roots in the educational values we espouse as a nation. Texts, curricula, and department and school policies are interpretations of these values shared at the broadest national level and translated into practice through behavioral objectives.

20. Three important cautions in using the taxonomies of behavioral objectives are:

☐ No behavior specified is necessarily more or less desirable than any other.

☐ Less complex behaviors are not necessarily easier to teach, less time consuming, or dependent on fewer resources than are more complex behaviors.

☐ Behavior in one domain may require one or more behaviors in other domains to be achieved.

FOR DISCUSSION AND PRACTICE

*1. Identify the two general purposes for preparing behavioral objectives. If you could choose only one of these purposes, which would be more important to you? Why?

*2. Explain what three things the word *behavioral* implies when it appears before the word *objectives*.

*3. Identify the three components of a well-written behavioral objective and give one example of each component.

*4. Historically, why did the concept of behavioral objectives emerge?

*5. Why are action verbs necessary in translating goals such as *mentally healthy citizens, well-rounded individuals* and *self-actualized school-children* into behavioral outcomes?

*6. Distinguish learning outcomes (ends) from learning activities (means) by placing an *O* or *A* beside the following expressions:

_____ working on a car radio

_____ adding signed numbers correctly

_____ practicing the violin

_____ playing basketball

_____ using a microscope

_____ identifying an amoeba

_____ naming the seven parts of speech

_____ punctuating an essay correctly

*7. Define a *condition* in a behavioral objective. Give three examples.

*8. How can the specification of conditions help students study and prepare for tests?

*9. In trying to decide upon what condition(s) to include in a behavioral objective, what single most important consideration should guide your selection?

*10. What is the definition of *criterion level* in a behavioral objective? Give three examples.

11. Provide examples of two behavioral objectives that differ in the degree of expressiveness they allow.

*12. Column A contains objectives. Column B contains levels of cognitive behavior. Match the levels in Column B with the most appropriate objective in Column A. Column B levels can be used more than once.

Column A	Column B
_____ 1. Given a two-page essay, the student can distinguish the assumptions basic to the author's position.	a. knowledge b. comprehension c. application d. analysis e. synthesis f. evaluation
_____ 2. The student will correctly spell the word *mountain*.	
_____ 3. The student will convert the following English passage into Spanish.	

Column A

_____ 4. The student will compose new pieces of prose and poetry according to the classification system emphasized in lecture.

_____ 5. Given a sinking passenger ship with 19 of its 20 lifeboats destroyed, the captain will decide, based on his perceptions of their potential worth to society, who is to be placed on the last lifeboat.

Column B

a. knowledge
b. comprehension
c. application
d. analysis
e. synthesis
f. evaluation

13. Make up two objectives for each of the knowledge, comprehension, application, analysis, synthesis, and evaluation levels of the taxonomy of cognitive objectives. Select verbs for each level from the lists provided in the chapter. Try to make your objectives cover the same subject.

14. Exchange the objectives you have just written with a classmate. Have the classmate check each objective for (a) an observable behavior, (b) any special conditions under which the behavior must be displayed, and (c) a performance level considered sufficient to demonstrate mastery. Revise your objectives if necessary.

*15. A parent calls to tell you that, after a long talk with her son, she disapproves of the objectives you have written for health education—particularly those referring to the anatomy of the human body—but which you have taken almost verbatim from the teachers' guide to the adopted textbook. Compose a response to this parent that shows your understanding of the roots of objectives and justifies your decision to teach these objectives.

---

*Answers to asterisked questions (*) in this and the other chapters are in Appendix B.

SUGGESTED READINGS

Deno, S., & Jenkins, J. (1969). On the "behaviorality" of behavioral objectives. *Psychology in the Schools, 6,* 18–24.
A thorough accounting of what the "behavioral" in behavioral objectives really means.

Duchastel, P., & Merrill, P. (1973). The effects of behavioral objectives on learning: A review of empirical studies. *Review of Educational Research, 43,* 53–69.
A comprehensive review of research evidence that both supports and fails to support the effects of objectives on student learning.

Gagné, R. (1972). Behavioral objectives? Yes! *Educational Leadership, 29,* 304–306.
The case for behavioral objectives, articulately expressed by an eminent scholar who has contributed much to the concept.

Gagné, R. (1977). Analysis of objectives. In L. J. Briggs (Ed.), *Instructional design: Principles and application.* Englewood Cliffs, NJ: Educational Technology Publications.
A closer look at objectives from the field of psychology—an alternative to the taxonomic approach provided in this chapter.

Grondlund, N. (1985). *Measurement and evaluation in teaching.* New York: Macmillan.
This text contains several excellent chapters on the many possible types of objectives and how to put them to use in your classroom.

Kneller, G. (1972). Behavioral objectives? No! *Educational Leadership, 29,* 397–400.
The case against behavioral objectives, expressing the pitfalls and problems with their indiscriminate use.

Kubiszyn, T., & Borich, G. (1990). *Educational testing and measurement: Classroom application and practice* (3rd ed.). Glenview, IL: Scott, Foresman. *A practical text including chapters on instructional goals and objectives, measuring learning outcomes, and writing essay and objective test items.*

Mager, R. (1975). *Preparing instructional objectives* (2nd ed.). Palo Alto, CA: Fearon Publishers. *The first and most popular book on how to write objectives; written for the teacher and school administrator.*

Melton, R. (1978). Resolution of conflicting claims concerning the effect of behavioral objectives on student learning. *Review of Educational Research, 48,* 291–302. *An attempt to resolve the dilemma of why some researchers have found positive effects on student learning with the use of objectives while others have not.*

Popham, W. (1981). *Modern educational measurement.* Englewood Cliffs, NJ: Prentice-Hall. *Contains several chapters that cogently state the case for the use of objectives in the schools—widely read and often referenced.*

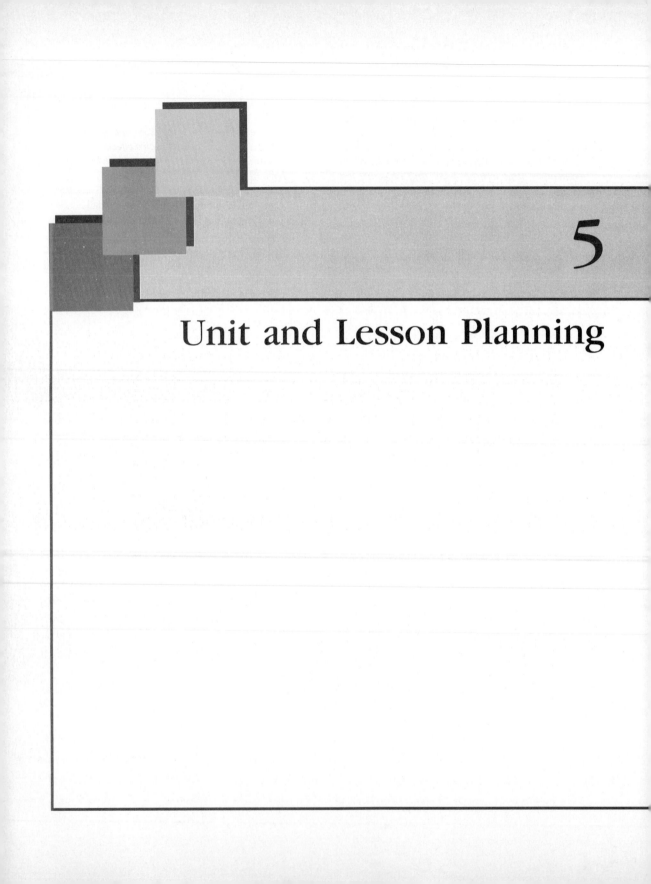

5

Unit and Lesson Planning

In Chapter 3 we noted that, before you can prepare a lesson plan, you must decide on instructional goals, learning needs, content, and methods. These prelesson planning decisions are crucial for developing effective lesson plans, because they give structure to lesson planning and tie it to important sources of societal and professional values. In this chapter, unit and lesson plans are presented as tools for tying these values to the classroom learning needs and the school curriculum. Before discussing how to prepare unit and lesson plans, however, let us review the inputs to the planning process that were covered in Chapter 3 (Figure 5.1).

These inputs represent the first part of a three-stage process that includes (a) prelesson planning (Figure 5.1), (b) actual preparation of lesson plans, and (c) evaluation of lesson plans. In the prelesson planning stage covered in Chapter 3, you learned of an approach for organizing your instructional planning according to the inputs shown in Figure 5.1. In this chapter you will learn specific ways to use these inputs to build unit and lesson plans. In Chapter 14 you will learn how to evaluate the success of your lessons with learners.

UNIT AND LESSON PLANS

The important process of unit and lesson planning begins with implementing the five planning inputs (Figure 5.1). This stage of the planning process takes a **system perspective,** meaning that your lessons will be part of a larger system of interrelated learning, called a unit.

The word *system* brings to mind phrases like *school system, mental health system,* and *legal system.* Schools, mental health services, and criminal justice agencies are supposed to work as systems. This means that their component parts, departments, and branches are to interrelate and build toward some unified concept: an educated

FIGURE 5.1
Inputs to the planning
process

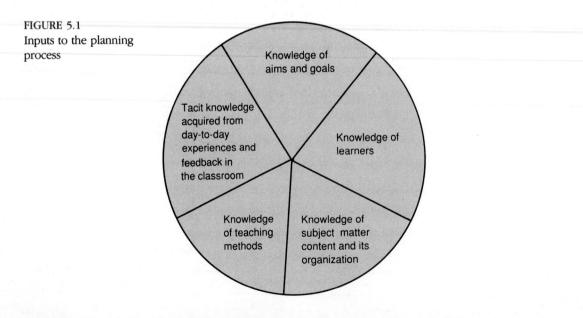

adult, a mentally healthy individual, a rehabilitated offender. For example, in a school system, discrete facts, skills, and understandings learned by the completion of sixth grade not only are important in themselves but also are important for successful completion of seventh grade. This, in turn, is important for completion of eighth grade, and so on through the educational system until the high school graduate has many of the facts, skills, and understandings necessary for adult living.

Notice that these skills, facts, and understandings are not acquired from twelfth-grade instruction alone but are *accumulated* through the entire schooling process, which is a sequence of many different learning activities. At no one point or time could it be said that Johnny's education was complete (not even at grade twelve); nor could Mary's facts at grade seven, Bobby's skills at grade ten, and Betty Jo's understandings at grade twelve be added together to define an educated adult. This illustrates not only how dependent a system outcome is upon the outcomes of all its component parts, but also the importance of the relationship among its parts.

The strength of a system is that "the whole is greater than the sum of its parts." But how can anything be more than the sum of its parts? Can a unit of instruction comprised of individual lessons ever add up to anything more than the sum of the individual lessons? This sounds like getting something for nothing, a concept that does not ring true. But, if the system of individual lessons really does produce outcomes in learners that are greater than the sum of the outcomes of the individual lessons, then there must be a missing ingredient that we haven't mentioned.

That missing ingredient is *the relationship among the individual lessons*. This relationship must allow the outcome of one lesson to build upon the outcomes of preceding lessons. Knowledge, skills, and understanding evolve gradually through the joint contribution of many lessons arranged sequentially to build more and more complex outcomes. It is this invisible but all-important relationship among the parts of a system, or instructional unit, that allows the unit outcomes to be greater than the sum of the lesson outcomes.

This does not mean that anything labeled a system or an instructional unit necessarily will achieve outcomes greater than the sum of its parts. If the relationship among parts of the system or instructional unit is not painstakingly planned to ensure that earlier lessons become building blocks for more complex later lessons, a true system will not exist. Instead, only a mixture of bits and pieces bound together by some common unit title may exist, like the accumulation of junk in an attic or in the glove compartment of a car. Nothing works in harmony with anything else to produce a coherent whole or a unified concept. One of the goals of this chapter is to provide concepts and tools to help your individual lessons add up to more than the sum of their individual outcomes.

Of considerable importance is the relationship of your district's curriculum guide to your unit and lesson plans. *Units* generally extend over an instructional time period of two to six weeks. They usually correspond to well-defined topics in the curriculum guide. *Lessons,* on the other hand, are considerably shorter, spanning a single class period or occasionally two or three periods. Because lessons are relatively short, they are harder to associate with a particular segment of a curriculum guide. This means that you can expect unit content to be fairly well structured and defined but lesson content to be much less detailed.

This is as it should be, because the arrangement of day-to-day content in the classroom must be flexible to meet individual student needs, your instructional preferences, and special priorities and initiatives in the school and district. So, although the overall picture at the unit level may be clear from the district's curriculum guide, at the lesson level you must apply considerable independent thought, organization, and judgment. Figure 5.2 illustrates the flow of teaching content from the state level to the classroom.

MAKING PLANNING DECISIONS

Unit planning begins with an understanding of the alternative goals, learning needs, content, and methods which are involved in writing lesson plans. These inputs to the learning process result from prelesson planning, in which you consult sources of societal and professional values, and select as relevant certain goals, learning needs, content, and methods. This selection is made in part by the curriculum adopted by your school district, because both societal and professional values were instrumental in curriculum selection.

However, the entire job of determining goals, learning needs, and content has not been completed by this selection process. You must decide the relative degree of emphasis to place upon these goals, and determine toward what learning needs and what area of content the goals are directed. Let us look closer at several types of decisions you will have to make pertaining to goals, learners, and content.

Goals

Curriculum guides at the grade, department, and school district level usually clearly specify what content must be covered in what period of time. But they may be far less clear about the specific behaviors that students are expected to acquire. For example, an excerpt from a curriculum guide for English language instruction might take this form:

I. Writing concepts and skills. The student shall be provided opportunities to learn:
   A. The composing process.
   B. Descriptive, narrative, and expository paragraphs.
   C. Multiple paragraph compositions.
   D. Persuasive discourse.
   E. Meanings and uses of colloquialism, slang, idiom, and jargon.

Or for a life-science curriculum:

I. Life science. The student shall be provided the opportunity to learn:
   A. Skills in acquiring data through the senses.
   B. Classification skills in ordering and sequencing data.
   C. Oral and written communication of data in appropriate form.
   D. Concepts and skills of measurement using relationships and standards.
   E. Drawing logical inferences, predicting outcomes, and forming generalized statements.

FIGURE 5.2
Flow of teaching content
from the state level to
the classroom level

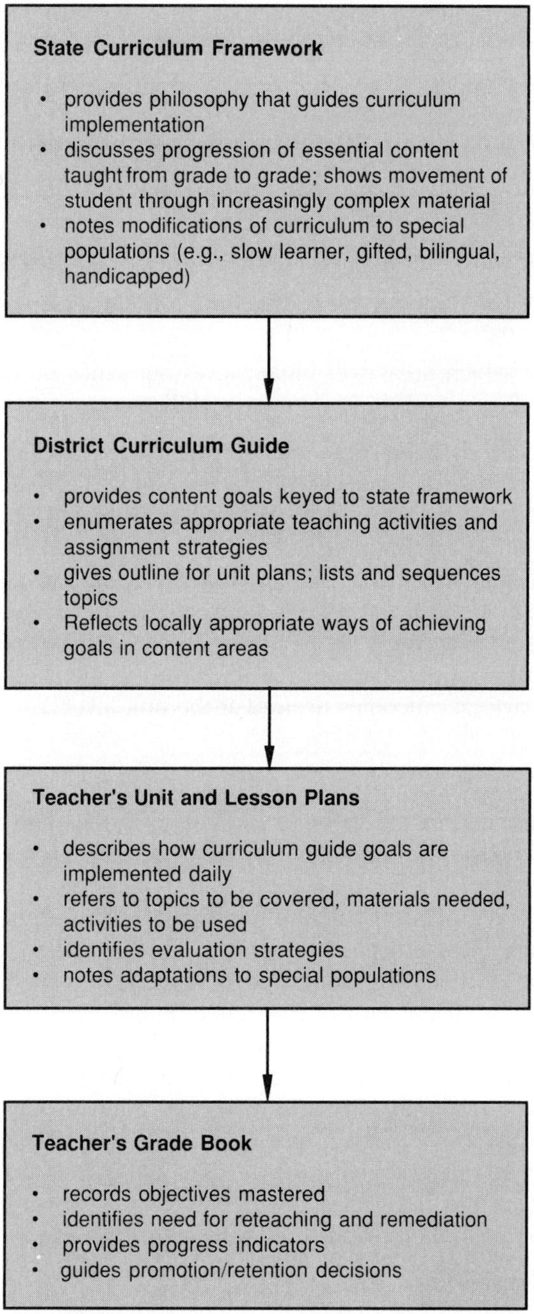

State Curriculum Framework

- provides philosophy that guides curriculum implementation
- discusses progression of essential content taught from grade to grade; shows movement of student through increasingly complex material
- notes modifications of curriculum to special populations (e.g., slow learner, gifted, bilingual, handicapped)

District Curriculum Guide

- provides content goals keyed to state framework
- enumerates appropriate teaching activities and assignment strategies
- gives outline for unit plans; lists and sequences topics
- Reflects locally appropriate ways of achieving goals in content areas

Teacher's Unit and Lesson Plans

- describes how curriculum guide goals are implemented daily
- refers to topics to be covered, materials needed, activities to be used
- identifies evaluation strategies
- notes adaptations to special populations

Teacher's Grade Book

- records objectives mastered
- identifies need for reteaching and remediation
- provides progress indicators
- guides promotion/retention decisions

Notice in these excerpts the specificity at which the content is identified (e.g., the composing process; descriptive, narrative, and expository paragraphs; multiple paragraph composition). In contrast, note the lack of clarity concerning the *level of behavioral complexity* to which the instruction should be directed. This is typical of many curriculum guides. Recalling the taxonomy of behavior in the cognitive domain (Chapter 4), you might ask:

For which of these content areas will the simple recall of facts be sufficient?

For which areas will comprehension of those facts be required?

For which areas will application be expected of what the student comprehends?

For which areas will higher-level outcomes be desired, involving analysis, synthesis, and decision-making skills?

Decisions made about goals often involve (1) selecting the level of behavioral complexity for which teachers will prepare an instructional unit or lesson and (2) the level at which they will expect student outcomes and test for them. The flexibility afforded by most curriculum guides in selecting the behavioral level to which instruction can be directed often is both purposeful and advantageous for you. For the curriculum guide to be adapted to the realities of your classroom, a wide latitude of expected outcomes must be possible. These depend upon the unique behavioral characteristics of your students, the time you can devote to a specific topic, and the overall behavioral outcomes desired at the unit level.

Learners

The primary reason that curriculum guides, textbooks, and even some workbooks are flexible in behavioral complexity—or allow for different activities at different levels of behavioral complexity—is so you can adapt your behavioral expectations for learners to their learning needs. Chapter 2 presented several categories of individual differences that are characteristic of students in the classroom. These include differences in intelligence, prior achievement, anxiety, self-concept, motivation, and degree of disadvantagedness. These factors can reflect entire classrooms as well as individuals. Other categories of learners—slow, bilingual, gifted, and handicapped—add even greater diversity to the classroom. They may create the need for subgroups that require instruction individually or in special-ability groups.

The effective teacher remains flexible when choosing the behavioral complexity of unit or lesson goals. For this area of decision making, the information you need to adapt the behavioral complexity of the instruction to the needs of your learners will be in their test results, oral performances, practice exercises, and homework.

Content

Perhaps foremost in the mind of beginning teachers is the content to be taught. Your content decisions appear easy inasmuch as textbooks, workbooks, and curriculum guides were selected long before your first day in the classroom. Indeed, as you saw in the excerpts from the curriculum guide, content often is designated in great detail. Textbooks and workbooks carry this detail one step further by offering activities and exercises that further define and expand the content in the curriculum guide. From this perspective it appears that all of the content has been handed to you, if not on a silver platter, then surely in readily accessible and highly organized tests, workbooks, and curriculum materials.

Although every teacher might wish this were true, most quickly realize that as many decisions must be made about content, or what to teach, as about behavioral goals and learning needs. You quickly come to realize that adopted texts, workbooks, and even detailed curriculum guides identify the content but do not select, organize, and sequence that content *according to the needs of your learners*. For this task you must be capable of selecting from among textbook and curriculum guide content and sometimes expanding upon it to strengthen the relationship among behavioral goals, learner needs, and required content.

Thus, the content you present cannot be decided until you have addressed the complexity level of the desired behavioral outcome (e.g., knowledge, comprehension, application) and your learners' characteristics (e.g., level of achievement, motivation, cultural diversity). Although textbook and curriculum guides indicate the content coverage to strive for, the effective teacher knows that this content must be *selected from* for some behavioral goals and learners and *added to* for other goals and learners to engage students in the learning process at the *most appropriate level of behavioral complexity*.

ORGANIZATION

Chapter 3 provided brief examples of content organization. They showed ways to sequence content into a learning structure (e.g., simple-to-complex, abstract-to-concrete, general-to-detailed, etc.). However arranged, content must contribute to your instructional goals. Establishing content sequence is one of the most troublesome planning decisions for beginning teachers because the lesson sequence is largely responsible for achieving unit outcomes. In other words, how the lessons are interrelated is important to the achievement of higher levels of cognitive, affective, and psychomotor complexity at the unit level.

These higher levels of behavior (analysis, synthesis, evaluation; value, organization, characterization; precision, articulation, naturalization) can rarely if ever be achieved in a single lesson. Thus, lessons must be placed within a unit (system) in which individual lessons successively build upon previously taught behaviors to achieve these higher-order behaviors. This is why your structuring and sequencing of content is so important to unit planning: without it, behavioral outcomes at the unit's end probably would be no different than the outcomes achieved at the completion of each single lesson. Unlike junk in the attic or the glove compartment of your car, units must have a coherent, unified theme that rises above the cognitive, affective, and psychomotor complexity of any single lesson.

We have spoken as though organization and sequencing of content is only a matter of personal preference, perhaps when one's teaching style dictates a simple-to-complex organization as a matter of habit or tradition. As noted, however, the content organization must be selected with regard to goals and learners. For example, one reason for choosing a concrete-to-abstract content organization might be to achieve outcomes at a high level of behavioral complexity (application, analysis, and synthesis) with less-able learners. The reasoning behind this choice might be that, because more difficult behaviors are expected at the conclusion of the unit, the most concrete content should be presented first. Thus, learners can reacquire the basics and maintain an interest in moving deeper into the topic. In this case, the unit goal and the learner each play a role in selecting a particular organization. This illustrates how decisions about the behavioral complexity of goals and learners depend upon teachers' knowledge of their own classrooms.

As noted in Figure 5.1, choosing a teaching method is yet another important decision area in the planning process. Chapters 6–13 are devoted exclusively to helping you acquire these methods.

MAKING UNIT PLANS

A Chinese proverb says that "a picture is worth a thousand words." Here we apply this idea to unit planning by showing how to create a visual blueprint of a unit. While this visual device cannot substitute for a written description or outline of what you plan to teach, it is an effective means of organizing your thinking—i.e., planning. Scientists, administrators, engineers, and business executives long have known the value of visuals in the form of flow charts, organization charts, blueprints, technical diagrams, and even "doodles" to convey the essence of a concept, if not the details. From the beginning, teachers have used this basic method, too. Pictures not only communicate the results of planning but are useful during that process, because they help to select, organize, order, evaluate, and revise the substance of unit plans.

Although teaching parallels many other fields by using visual devices in planning, in many ways teaching is a unique profession. Unlike business, education's product does not roll off an assembly line, nor does education build its product with the mathematical laws and physical substances used by the scientist and engineer. Consequently, your visual blueprints differ from those of others, but at the same time must reflect the qualities that have made pictures so important to planning in these other professions. You already have been introduced to two of these qualities: the concept of *hierarchy,* which shows the relationship of parts to the whole (lessons to unit), and the concept of *task-relevant prior knowledge,* which shows the necessity for a certain order of events (lesson sequence).* Both concepts are put to work in creating a visual picture of a unit; such a picture can both stimulate and organize your thoughts and communicate the results to others in an easy-to-follow graphic format.

---

*The phrase *task-relevant prior knowledge* applies to outcomes at any level of behavioral complexity.

There are two simple methods used in drawing a picture of a planned unit. The first is to diagram how the teaching goal is divided into specific teaching activities. The second is to show the sequence of the activities and how lesson outcomes build upon one another to achieve a unit goal. Let us look at these two methods in detail.

Diagraming Specific Teaching Activities

A teaching activity usually is described by indicating the content to be taught and the outcome that is expected. General teaching activities and outcomes tend to serve as unit objectives, while specific teaching activities and outcomes tend to serve as lesson objectives. General teaching activities and outcomes always require you to identify more specific activities and outcomes to show *how the more generally stated activities and outcomes are achieved*. In other words, any goal at the unit level can be broken into its component parts at the lesson level. Those component parts represent everything that is important for attaining the goal. This idea is illustrated in Figure 5.3.

Notice that Figure 5.3 has three levels. For now, focus on the top and bottom levels. The top shows the unit's general intent, which is derived from the curriculum guide and adopted textbook, which in turn are based upon societal, state, or locally stated goals. The bottom row shows unit content, expressed at a level specific enough to prepare individual lessons. Notice that, in the judgment of this unit planner, ending

FIGURE 5.3

Example of a hierarchy of reading content at different levels of specificity

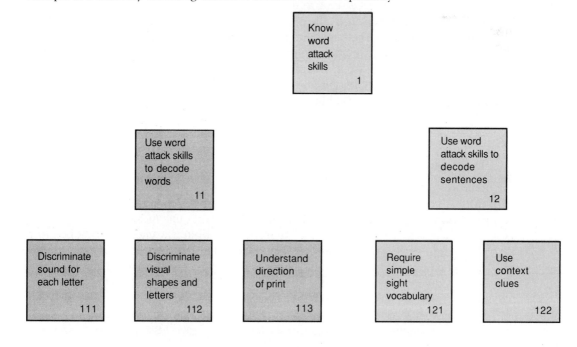

the plan at a more detailed level than boxes 111, 112, and 113 would result in content sized for less than one lesson; beginning the plan with content at a more general level than box 1 (top) would result in content sized too big for one unit.

This unit plan ends with bite-sized chunks that together exhaust the content specified at the higher levels. Just as in the story of Goldilocks and the three bears, the bottom of the unit plan hierarchy must end with the portion of content being served up as "not too big and not too small, but just right." How can you know whether you have achieved the right size and balance for a single lesson? Experience and judgment are the best guides, although logical divisions within the curriculum guide and text are helpful too.

The second level of Figure 5.3 is simply a logical means of getting from the general unit goal to specific lesson content. It is an intermediate thinking process that produces the lower level of just-right-sized pieces. How many intermediate levels should you have? There is no magic number; this depends on how broadly the initial goal is stated and the number of steps needed to produce content in just the right amounts for individual lesson plans.

In some cases, the route from unit to lesson content can be very direct (two levels), while in other instances several levels may have to be worked through before arriving at lesson-sized chunks. If you have trouble getting sufficiently specific for lesson-sized content, you may need to revise the unit goal by dividing it into two or more subgoals and beginning a new hierarchy from each subgoal. This was done in Figure 5.3, where one subgoal is shaded (representing word-specific content), and the other is unshaded (representing sentence-specific content). Starting at such a high level of generality, the unit planner had to devise two units of instruction.

Notice that this is done in the same way that you create an outline, beginning with Roman numerals (I, II, III, etc.), their subdivisions (A, B, C, etc.), and perhaps further subdivisions. The initial statement of unit content (top box) often turns out to be more comprehensive than you expected, representing a whole domain or cluster of units. This was the case in Figure 5.3; what initially was seen as an individual lesson turned out to be a whole unit.

This process of building a content hierarchy will guide you in making the important distinction between unit and lesson content; this prevents many false starts in lesson planning.

Diagraming the Sequence of Activities

Our first diagraming method simply used boxes to picture areas of content—instructional goals—at various levels of generality. The second method, equally simple, shows sequence among lessons and how lesson outcomes can build upon one another to achieve a unit goal. For Figure 5.4, we arbitrarily chose the first box from the second level of the hierarchy in Figure 5.3. The procedure is to first indicate the intended unit outcome with an arrow from the top box, as shown in Figure 5.4. Next, identify the intended outcomes at the lesson level. If a certain order is important, draw it to so indicate, as we have done in Figure 5.4.

This second method of diagraming unit plans connects the content of the lessons, using the behavioral outcomes implied for each lesson. The outcome of all

FIGURE 5.4

A unit plan showing a sequence among lessons

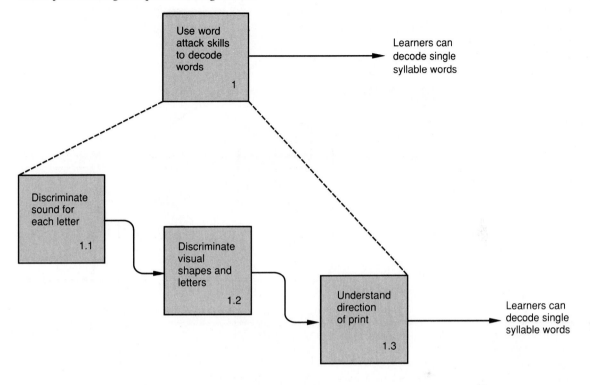

the lessons *taken together* must be the same as the unit outcome. This always is true, whether or not the sequence is important. In some instances the sequence of lessons can be arbitrary (Figure 5.5a), while for others only a partial sequence need be maintained (Figure 5.5b).

The second method recognizes how previous lessons can constrain or modify the outcomes of subsequent lessons. It encourages you to use sequence, building upon previously taught learning to produce more behaviorally complex outcomes at the unit level. This is essential, for if lesson outcomes are not connected in any way, it is unlikely that the unit outcome will be at any higher level of cognitive, affective, or psychomotor complexity than the individual lessons.

This was our earlier point about the "whole being greater than the sum of its parts." The *whole* is the unit, and the *parts* are the lessons. An effective unit, therefore, is one that uses the relationship among lessons and their cumulative effect to achieve unit outcomes at higher levels of complexity. Behaviors at these more complex levels represent the learning of concepts, the application of facts and understandings to real-world problem solving, and the ability to make value judgments. These are the most sought and frequently used behaviors in adult life. As an effective teacher, you should plan the interrelationships among lessons in a way that encourages these behaviors to emerge at the unit level.

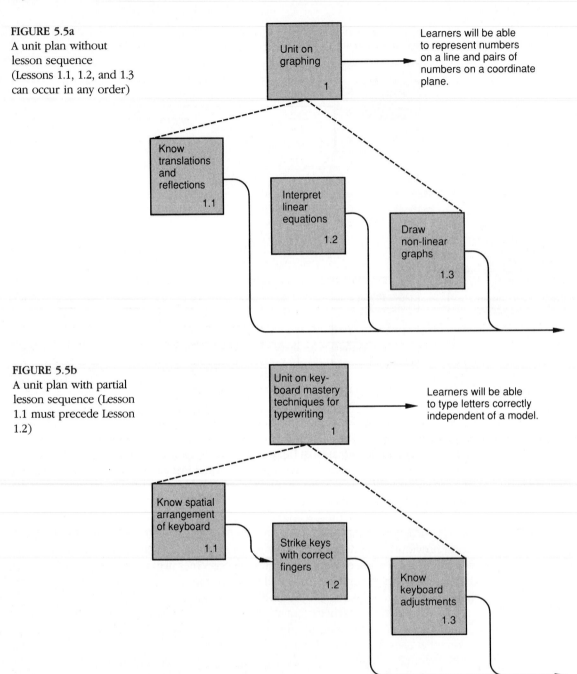

FIGURE 5.5a
A unit plan without
lesson sequence
(Lessons 1.1, 1.2, and 1.3
can occur in any order)

Unit on
graphing

1

Learners will be able
to represent numbers
on a line and pairs of
numbers on a coordinate
plane.

Know
translations
and
reflections

1.1

Interpret
linear
equations

1.2

Draw
non-linear
graphs

1.3

FIGURE 5.5b
A unit plan with partial
lesson sequence (Lesson
1.1 must precede Lesson
1.2)

Unit on key-
board mastery
techniques for
typewriting

1

Learners will be able
to type letters correctly
independent of a model.

Know spatial
arrangement
of keyboard

1.1

Strike keys
with correct
fingers

1.2

Know
keyboard
adjustments

1.3

You can see that diagraming whole units has several advantages. Seeing a lesson in context with other lessons that share the same purpose at the unit level focuses your attention upon the importance of task-relevant prior knowledge to lesson success. Recall that if prerequisite knowledge and skills relevant to the lesson have been inadequately acquired (or not at all), the lesson objective cannot be attained. Thus, some prior lessons may be expressly planned to match subsequent lessons to the learner's current level of functioning. One purpose of simultaneously seeing lessons within a unit plan is to determine whether all task-relevant prior knowledge required by each lesson has been provided by the unit plan. Because unit plans precede lesson plans, overlooked lessons and objectives prerequisite to later lessons can be added easily to the unit plan.

The Written Unit Plan

Planning units graphically is very helpful in organizing, sequencing, and arriving at bite-sized pieces of content at the lesson level. Still, you must write a description that will communicate details of the unit to others (and to remind yourself) at a later time. When you have completed graphically organizing, sequencing, and sizing your units, write down the details needed for presenting them to students at a later time.

One format for a written version of a unit plan appears in Figure 5.6. This format, suggested by Kim and Kellough (1978), divides a written unit plan into its (a) main purpose, (b) behavioral objectives, (c) content, (d) procedures and activities, (e) instructional aids or resources, and (f) evaluation methods. To this written plan attach the visual blueprint to indicate at a glance the organization, sequence, and sizing of the unit and to provide both an introduction and overview of the written details.

Finally, in the example unit plan, notice that both objectives and individual learners progress from the lower levels of cognitive and psychomotor complexity (comprehension, application, imitation) to the higher levels (analysis, synthesis, precision). This illustrates that early lessons in the unit can be used as building blocks for higher levels of behavioral complexity at the end.

MAKING LESSON PLANS

Up to this point we have emphasized:

1. Classifying unit outcomes at a higher level of behavioral complexity than lesson outcomes, by using one of the three taxonomies presented in Chapter 4.
2. Deriving lesson content from unit outcomes in bite-sized chunks suitable for presentation in one or two instructional periods.
3. Planning these bite-sized pieces sequentially so that outcomes of previously taught lessons are instrumental in achieving the outcomes of subsequent lessons.
4. Rearranging or adding lesson content where necessary to provide the task-relevant prior knowledge required for subsequent learning.

FIGURE 5.6 Example unit plan
From *Curriculum Planning: A Ten-Step Process* by W. Zenger and S. Zenger, 1982, Palo Alto, CA: R and E
Research Associates. Copyright © 1982 by R and E Research Associates. Reprints by permission.

Grade: 10
Unit Topic: Pizza with Yeast Dough Crust
Course/Subject: Contemporary Home Economics
Approximate Time Required: One week

1. Main Purpose of the Unit: The purpose of this unit is to acquaint the students with the principles of making yeast dough by making pizza. The historical background, nutritional value, and variations of pizza will also be covered.
2. Behavioral Objectives
   The student will be able to:
   A. Describe the functions of each of the ingredients in yeast dough. (Cognitive-knowledge)
   B. Explain the steps in preparing yeast dough. (Cognitive-comprehension)
   C. Make a yeast dough for a pizza crust. (Cognitive-application and psychomotor-imitation)
   D. State briefly the history of pizza. (Cognitive-knowledge)
   E. Match the ingredients in pizza to the food groups they represent. (Cognitive-knowledge)
   F. Classify and give examples of different types of pizza. (Cognitive-analysis)
   G. Create and bake a pizza of their choice. (Cognitive-synthesis and psychomotor-precision)
3. Content Outline
   A. Essential ingredients in yeast dough
      (1) Flour
      (2) Yeast
      (3) Liquid
      (4) Sugar
      (5) Salt
   B. Non-essential ingredients
      (1) Fats
      (2) Eggs
      (3) Other, such as fruit and nuts
   C. Preparing yeast dough
      (1) Mixing
      (2) Kneading
      (3) Rising (fermenting)
      (4) Punching down
      (5) Shaping
      (6) Baking

D. History of pizza
   (1) First pizza was from Naples.
   (2) Pizza is an Italian word meaning pie.
   (3) Originally eaten by the poor, pizza was also enjoyed by royalty.
   (4) Italian immigrants brought pizza to the United States in the late 1800s.
E. Types of pizza
   (1) Neapolitan
   (2) Sicilian
   (3) Pizza Rustica
   (4) Pizza de Polenta
F. Nutritional value of pizza
   (1) Nutritious meal or snack
   (2) Can contain all four food groups
   (3) One serving of cheese pizza contains:
      (a) Protein
      (b) Vitamins
      (c) Minerals
G. Making a pizza
   (1) Prepare dough
   (2) Roll out dough
   (3) Transfer to pan
   (4) Spread sauce
   (5) Top as desired
   (6) Bake
4. Procedures and Activities
   A. Informal lecture
   B. Discussion
   C. Demonstration of mixing and kneading dough
   D. Filmstrip on pizza
   E. Education game (Pizzeria): Each time a student answers correctly a question about yeast dough or pizza, he gets a part of a paper pizza. The first to collect a complete pizza wins.
   F. Cooking lab
5. Instructional Aids or Resources
   A. Test: *Guide to Modern Meals* (Webster, McGraw-Hill, 1970)
   B. Filmstrip: *Pizza, Pizza* 10 minutes
   C. *Pizza, Pizza* booklets by Chef Boyardee
   D. Eduational game (Pizzeria)
   E. *Bake-it-easy Yeast Book* by Fleischmann's Yeast
   F. Poster (showing different kinds of pizza from Pizza Hut)
6. Evaluation
   A. Unit test
   B. Lab performance

If lessons are planned with no conception of a higher-level unit outcome, student attention will fall exclusively on each individual lesson without considering the relationship among the lessons. This relationship will appear deceptively unimportant until it becomes apparent (often too late) that your lessons seem to pull students first in one direction (e.g., knowledge acquisition) and then abruptly in another (e.g., problem solving) without intermediate instruction to guide them in the transition. The end result of such a conglomeration of isolated lesson outcomes may be confusion, anxiety, and distrust on the part of the students, regardless of how meticulously you prepared the lessons and how effective they are in accomplishing their stated—but isolated—outcomes. Because outcomes at higher levels of behavioral complexity rarely can be attained within the time frame of a single lesson, they must be achieved in the context of unit plans.

Before actually writing out a lesson plan, there are three preliminary considerations necessary for your unit plan to flow smoothly: (1) determining where to start, (2) providing for student diversity, and (3) mastery learning and relearning. These preliminaries are discussed in the following sections.

Determining Where to Start

Perhaps most perplexing to new teachers is deciding the level of behavioral complexity at which a lesson should begin. Do you always begin by teaching facts (i.e., instilling knowledge), or can you begin with activities at the application level, or even at the synthesis and decision-making levels? Both alternatives are possible, but each makes different assumptions about the behavioral characteristics of the students and the sequence of lessons that has gone before.

Beginning a lesson or a sequence of lessons at the knowledge level (e.g., to list, to recall, to recite, etc.) assumes that the topic is mostly new material. Such a lesson usually occurs at the beginning of a sequence that will progressively build this knowledge toward more complex behaviors—perhaps ending at the application, synthesis, or evaluation level. When no task-relevant prior knowledge is required, the starting point for the lesson often is at the knowledge or comprehension level. When some task-relevant prior knowledge is required, lessons can begin at higher levels of behavioral complexity. Notice from the list of objectives in Figure 5.6 that each lesson having an outcome at a higher level of behavioral complexity is preceded by a lesson at some lower level. The complexity level with which the lesson starts depends upon where it falls in the sequence.

Typically, unit plans should instill a range of behaviors and end with a higher level of behavioral complexity than they begin with. Some units might begin at the application level and end at a higher level if a previous unit has provided the task-relevant prior knowledge and understandings required. It also is possible, and feasible in some content areas, to progress from one behavioral level to another within a single lesson. This becomes increasingly difficult when the lessons start at higher levels of behavioral complexity, but it is possible and often desirable to move from knowledge to comprehension and even to application activities within a single lesson. This is illustrated in the flow of behaviors for the following third-grade social studies lesson.

Unit Title: Local, State, and National Geography
Lesson Title: Local Geography
Behaviors:

- ☐ Student will know geographical location of community relative to state and nation (knowledge).
- ☐ Student will be able to describe physical features of community (comprehension).
- ☐ Student will be able to locate community on map and globe (application).
- ☐ Student will be able to discuss how the community is similar to and different from other communities (analysis).

In this lesson a comprehensive span of behaviors is required in relatively brief time (a single lesson) by using objects already known to the students (their own community; map; globe) and by dovetailing one behavior into another so that each new activity is a continuation of the preceding one. When a transition across behavioral levels is planned within a single lesson, the necessary question before each new level of complexity is "Have I provided all the required task-relevant prior knowledge?" Only when you can answer "Yes" will the lesson be directed at the students' current level of understanding, and only then can students attain the unit objective.

Providing for Student Diversity

A second consideration before writing a lesson plan is the extent to which the lesson provides for student diversity. Thus far, we have considered all the students within a class to be identical, sharing the same behavioral characteristics and task-relevant prior knowledge. Of course, diversity is the rule in any classroom, and in Chapter 2 we presented some of the varieties of students that you are likely to encounter.

Regardless of where you position the entry level of a lesson, some students will be above it and other students will be below it. Much of the work of unit and lesson planning is playing a game of averages in which you attempt to provide *most* of the instruction at the current level of functioning of *most* of the learners. Unless an entire course of study is individualized (sometimes the case with programmed and computer-assisted instruction curricula), most instruction must be directed at the "average" learner in your classroom.

However, there are some procedures that can supplement the game of averages. They are presented in the following subsections on ability grouping, peer tutoring, learning centers, review and follow-up materials, games and simulations, teams and group activities, and mastery learning and relearning. Before you begin the lesson plan, you must decide to what extent these alternatives are required by the diversity in your class and your instructional goals. These and other alternatives are detailed in Chapters 8 and 9, but for now the following overviews will suggest some of your options for individualizing instruction.

Ability Grouping. A class can be subdivided by intellectual skills required to grasp the content. The more-able students can read ahead and work independently on advanced exercises while the lesson is directed to the average and less-able learner. Lesson plans, objectives, activities, instructional materials, and tests can be divided into two or more appropriate parts.

Peer Tutoring.   Your lesson plan can contain a minimum of discourse and a maximum of independent work by your students. For example, each more-able student might be assigned to help a less-able student who lacks task-relevant prior knowledge. Because each student in need would require different amounts and levels of remediation, the peer tutor would begin at the student's current level of understanding and bring it to the level required for the next lesson.

Learning Centers.   Some types of students may profit more from working at learning centers than from listening to a lecture. When a learning center contains media, supplemental resources, and exercises directly related to your lesson content, include them as an integral part of your lesson plan. These centers can help individualize a lesson for those students who lack the prerequisite knowledge or skills.

Review and Follow-up Materials.   The lesson may begin with a review of the task-relevant prior knowledge required. A quick summary, together with supplementary handouts in which the required information can be looked up as needed, may be sufficient to bring some students to the required level while not boring others for whom the review may be redundant. The key to this technique is careful preparation of the handout covering the most critically needed prerequisite knowledge. This lets you limit your review to the barest essentials, involving the least amount of time.

Games and Simulations.   These can be used either cooperatively or independently by students who may require an alternative means of attaining your classroom objectives. Lessons may begin with whole-class instruction and, depending on interests and abilities, students can be directed to games and simulations singly or in groups to receive hands-on experiences that may remediate or enrich skills taught during full-class instruction.

Teams and Group Activities.   Sometimes students can benefit from learning together while working on specialized tasks. Such team and group activities can be an important addition to a lesson plan. These activities can teach students collaborative and communication skills that enhance lesson objectives and individual strengths, preparing them to acquire the outcomes of subsequent, more advanced unit objectives.

These are some of the ways your lesson plan can provide for diverse learning needs among your students. We will return for a closer look at them in the chapters ahead.

Mastery Learning and Relearning

The third consideration preliminary to writing your lesson plan is the level of proficiency expected of your students at the end of the lesson. This relates to alternatives

Learning centers containing media, supplemental resources, demonstration materials, and exercises can help individualize a lesson for those who may lack the prerequisite knowledge or skills required at the beginning of the lesson. The use of a learning center should be indicated in the lesson plan whenever applicable.

for individualized instruction, because those alternatives often are implemented to foster mastery learning (Block, 1987). **Mastery learning** requires that each student display a high level—if not complete proficiency—of each intended outcome before he or she can receive instruction at the next-higher level. If mastery learning is desired, each lesson must be designed with that end in mind. Notice that a sequence of lessons in a least-to-most complex or concrete-to-abstract ordering requires proficiency at some lower level before an outcome at a higher level can be attained. If such a sequence comprises a unit plan, some lessons will provide the task-relevant prior knowledge needed to attain the outcomes of subsequent lessons.

When units are planned in such a manner, mastery learning becomes an indispensable tool for obtaining unit outcomes. This is why some provision for mastery learning must be made for each lesson that provides critical task-relevant prior knowledge for subsequent lessons. Most frequently, provision for mastery learning takes the form of individualized and self-directed instruction. In the following chapter and in Chapter 9, specific techniques are presented for individualized and self-directed instruction.

EVENTS OF INSTRUCTION

After you have determined where to start the lesson, and how much it must provide for diverse learning needs, and whether mastery learning is required, you are ready to start planning the lesson. In this process you specify the key events that occur during the lesson—and for which you alone are responsible. By placing the responsibility on you for providing these events, we distinguish between *teaching* and *learning*. Learning refers to the internal events that go on in the heads of your learners; learning is the end product of the external teaching events you provide.

The sequence of steps in lesson planning assumes that the instructional events you plan must influence events in the heads of the learners. It is not unusual for teaching to be unrelated to learning, as when teachers teach and students listen, but nothing "sinks in." The process of getting instructional events to sink in is one of planning an instructional sequence that fosters a close relationship between the external events of instruction and the internal events of learning, *actively engaging the learners in the learning process.*

You can achieve this tightly knit relationship between teaching and learning by following a sequence of seven instructional events suggested by Gagné and Briggs (1979). They include the most relevant parts of other models of lesson preparation (Hunter, 1982). Although not all of these events are applicable to every lesson, they provide a basis—or menu—from which many different lesson plans can be formulated. The seven instructional events are:

1. Gaining attention
2. Informing the learner of the objective
3. Stimulating recall of prerequisite learning
4. Presenting the stimulus material
5. Eliciting the desired behavior
6. Providing feedback
7. Assessing the behavior

Describing instructional events using each of these seven areas is the heart of the lesson-writing process. Let's consider the types of instructional events that each entails and how to relate each to the internal processes of learning to actively engage your students in the learning process.

1. Gaining Attention

Without students' attention, nothing in the lesson will be heard, let alone actively engage them in the learning process. Thus each lesson plan begins with an instructional event to engage the students' interest, curiosity, and attention. In some classes this will mean raising their attention from complete disengagement to where their vision and hearing are receptive. In other classes this will mean raising their attention from an already receptive mode to a higher level of curiosity, interest, and attention.

The intensity of your attention-gaining event will depend upon the starting point of the learners. A less-able fifth-period class that meets after lunch may require a more dramatic attention-gaining event than will a bright and eager first-period class. You must be aware of students' characteristics in this regard to find the right event for gaining their attention.

One of the most common attention-gaining devices is to *relate the content to the students' interests* or to *arouse their curiosity*. Often this can be accomplished by asking questions, such as:

> Have you ever wondered how we got the word "horsepower"? Who would like to guess? (from a lesson on energy)

> Can anyone think of a popular automobile with the name of a Greek god? (from an introductory lesson on mythology)

> Have you ever wondered how some creatures can live both in the water and on land? (from a lesson on amphibious animals)

These questions, called *openers,* are designed not to have any single correct answer or even to accurately reflect the fine details of what is to follow. Instead they *amuse, stimulate, or even bewilder* students so that they become receptive to the content and questions that follow. Some other good openers are:

> Why do some scientists think that traveling to the planets will make the space traveler younger? (from a lesson in physics)

> Why do we have the word i-t-s and another word i-t-apostrophe-s? (from a lesson in punctuation)

> Why do you think the Greek empire collapsed when it was at its strongest? (from a lesson in world history)

> Why is the dollar worth more today in Mexico than in Switzerland? (from a lesson in economics)

> Why do you think some eloquent lawyers become disliked by the juries they speak to? (from a lesson in public speaking)

Another useful technique for gaining students' attention is to present:

☐ an apparent *contradiction*:

Why do we illustrate water using the color blue when water is really clear?

☐ or a seeming *inconsistency* in real life:

Why do some lower forms of animal life live longer than human beings?

☐ or something that at first appears to be *illogical*:

Why must something go backward every time something else goes forward?

For example, introducing a lesson in signed numbers by informing your learners that the multiplication of two negative numbers always results in a positive product may puzzle them, but it can arouse their curiosity about how two negatives could ever result in something positive. You could continue by explaining the mathematical rules behind this apparent contradiction.

Some other opening questions designed to make learners curious and more ready to learn are:

Do any of you think that, with just your own eyes, you can see an amoeba? (from a biology lesson)

How do you think the Grand Canyon was formed? (from a lesson in physical geography)

What occupations use numbers instead of words? (from a math lesson)

On the average, how many spelling mistakes do you think occur each day in a large metropolitan newspaper? (from a spelling lesson)

When is the value of paper greater than its own worth? (from a lesson in economics).

Diagrams, pictures, illustrations, scale models, and films are other attention-getting aids. Use these devices to appeal to your learners' sense of vision while your oral presentation appeals to their sense of hearing. Graphics or visuals are particularly effective openers with less-able students who are known to be more oriented and responsive to visual than auditory presentations. A visual opener can include samples of materials for the day's lesson so that students can touch them before the lesson begins. A visual opener also can show equipment you will use during the lesson (e.g., scales, meters).

2. Informing the Learner of the Objective

Once the learner's attention has been gained, you must activate the internal processes of learning in ways that correspond to the content. Just because your learners have been turned on with some attention-getting device does not mean they will be tuned to the wavelength at which you present the lesson. You need to tell them the channel on which the lesson is transmitted. The most effective way to focus learners' receptivity is to inform them of the degree of complexity of the behavioral outcome they are expected to attain by the end of the lesson. You can do this by telling them early in the lesson or unit how they will be examined or expected to show competence in the subject matter. For example, such expectations might include:

- □ Remember the four definitions of *power* that will be presented (science).
- □ Be able to express ownership orally in a sentence to the class (English).
- □ Identify correctly a mystery specimen of lower animal life using the microscope (life science).
- □ State their true feelings about the laws dealing with pornography (social studies).

Such statements allow learners to know when they have attained the expected level of behavior and to become selective in how to use and remember the lesson information. If your students know they will be expected to recall four definitions of power at the end of your lesson on energy, then they know to focus their search, retrieval, and retention processes *during the lesson* on the definitions or categories of power you present.

Informing learners of your objective helps them organize their thinking in advance of the lesson by providing mental "hooks" on which to hang the key points. This activates the learning process and focuses it on obtaining the required behavioral outcome.

The key to the success of this instructional event is to communicate your objective clearly. Therefore, choose your words with your learners' vocabulary and language level in mind, and record what you tell them as a reminder in this second part of your lesson plan. The best way to communicate your objective is to provide examples of tasks that you expect your students to be able to perform after the lesson. This effectively translates the action verb associated with a level of behavioral complexity into some ways this behavior might be measured on tests, in class discussions, and in question-and-answer sessions.

For example, you might write on the blackboard the following examples of expected behavior at the beginning of a unit on lower forms of animal life, and then checkmark the ones that most apply at the start of each day's lesson:

Define an amoeba.

Draw the cellular structure of an amoeba.

Explain the reproduction cycle of an amoeba.

Using a microscope, properly distinguish an amoeba from other single-celled animals.

Notice that these behavioral outcomes range from recounting a fact to making decisions and judgments in a real biological environment. Without knowing in advance at which of these levels they are expected to perform, your learners will have no way of selecting and focusing their attention on those parts of the instruction leading to the desired behavior. This is not to say that they should ignore other aspects of the presentation, but students can now see the other aspects as tools or means for gaining the highest level of behavior required, and not as ends in themselves.

3. Stimulating Recall of Prerequisite Learning

Before you can proceed with the new lesson content, one final preliminary instructional event is needed. Because learning cannot occur in a vacuum, the necessary task-relevant prior information must be retrieved and made ready for use. This calls for some method of reviewing, summarizing, restating, or otherwise stimulating the key concepts acquired in previous lessons. This information is instrumental for achieving the level of behavioral complexity intended in the present lesson.

If a goal is to have learners use a microscope to properly distinguish an amoeba from other single-celled animals, it is clear that previously acquired facts, concepts, and skills are relevant to this new task. Definitions of single-celled animals, unique characteristics of an amoeba that make it distinguishable from other one-

Before the actual presentation of new content begins, the necessary task-relevant prior information must be retrieved and made ready for use. This can be accomplished by reviewing, summarizing, and restating, stimulating into action the key concepts acquired in previous lessons.

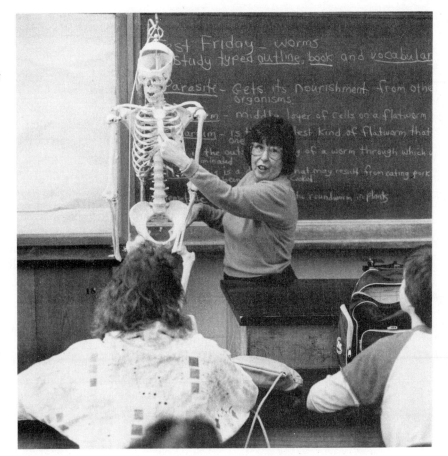

celled animals, and skill in using the microscope are among the task-relevant prior knowledge that greatly influences attainment of the outcome.

One purpose of a unit plan is to provide an instruction sequence in which lessons are explicitly planned to provide all prerequisite information. However, this will not be sufficient when key prerequisite lessons are separated by intervening ones or when the content of these earlier lessons will be used in new ways. Stimulate recall of task-relevant prior information at the beginning of the lesson to bring this information to the immediate attention of the learners. This will make the instructional context more conducive to combining of old and new facts, concepts, and skills. It is this mixing of previous learning with new learning that leads to a higher level of behavioral complexity.

Helping students retrieve earlier information requires condensing the key aspects into brief, easily understood form. Obviously, it is not practical to summarize all of it in a few minutes. You need to use thought-provoking and stimulating techniques to focus upon sizable amounts of prior learning, but without reviewing all the content that was previously covered or that is needed for the new learning. Questions can help your students recall the most significant and memorable parts of earlier lessons:

> Do you remember why Johnny couldn't see the amoeba in the microscope? (it was on low magnification instead of high)

> Do you remember Betty Jo's humorous attempt to relate the reproduction cycle of an amoeba to that of human beings? (she had equated cell division with waking up one morning to find a new baby in the family)

> Do you remember the three-color picture Bobby drew of the cellular structure of an amoeba? (everyone had commented on how lifelike the picture was)

Such questions help students retrieve task-relevant prior learning—not by summarizing that learning, but by tapping into a single *mental image* that recalls that learning. Once the image has been retrieved, students can turn it on and off at will to search for details that may be nestled within it, achieving still greater recall. Describing how to stimulate the recall of prerequisite learning, then, is the third entry in your lesson plan.

4. Presenting the Stimulus Material

This is the heart of the lesson plan. This component may seem to require little explanation, but several important considerations often go unnoticed—the form of presentation used, selectivity, and variety. These are described in the following sections.

The Form of Presentation.   Present the lesson content in the *same form and mode* that will be used by learners on tests, in class assignments, and in the real world. For example, if students are to fully understand signed numbers, they must be given examples using both single-digit and multiple-digit numbers in various formats.

Also, remember to change any *irrelevant* aspects of the learning stimulus as often as possible, and in as many different ways as possible, so that students will learn which dimensions of the problem are irrelevant. This prevents learning an objective under only one condition but not under others that may be encountered in subsequent lessons, grades, and courses. Some examples of changing the irrelevant aspects of a learning stimulus include:

□ In math, show both stacked format and line format:

$$-2 \text{ as well as } -2 + 5 =$$
$$\underline{+5}$$

□ Introduce learners to examples of proper punctuation by using popular magazines and newspapers as well as the text and workbook (English or a foreign language).

- ☐ Show how the laws of electricity apply to lightning during a thunderstorm as well as to electrical circuitry in the laboratory (science).
- ☐ Relate rules of social behavior found among humans to those often found among animals (social studies).
- ☐ Compare the central processing unit in a microcomputer to the executive processes in the human brain (computer science).
- ☐ Show how the reasons for a particular war also can be applied to other conflicts hundreds of years earlier (history).

In each of these examples the lesson designer is changing the irrelevant dimensions of the objective by applying key lesson ideas in different contexts. As a result, learners are more likely (a) to focus upon correct mathematical operations and not the format of the problem, (b) to notice improper punctuation when it appears in a slick or popular publication, (c) to understand the universality of physical laws governing electricity, (d) to not think that social behavior is a uniquely human phenomenon, (e) to not confuse the wonders of data processing with the hardware and equipment that only sometimes are needed to perform it, and (f) to understand that some reasons for conflict, war, and hostility are general as well as specific.

Selectivity. A second consideration is presenting instructional stimuli to foster selective perception of the content presented. Not everything in a text, workbook, film, lecture, or on the chalkboard is of equal importance to the day's objective. Consequently, highlighting key aspects of the text and workbook provides important guidance for helping students selectively perceive and retain the main parts of your lesson. Examples of such highlighting include verbally emphasizing the importance of certain events; telling students what to look for in a film (even stopping it to reinforce an idea if need be); emphasizing key words on the chalkboard with underlining, circling, or color; and using verbal markers ("This is important . . .," "Notice the relevance of this . . .," "You'll need this information later . . .").

The Importance of Variety. A key behavior of the effective teacher described in Chapter 1 is instructional variety. Gaining students' attention at the start of the lesson is one thing, but keeping their attention is quite another. Variety in the modalities of instruction (e.g., visual, oral, tactile) or some combination of instructional procedures (large group lecture, question and answer, small group discussion) stimulates student thinking and interest. Shifting from visually dominated instruction to orally dominated instruction (or using both simultaneously) and breaking a lesson into several instructional arrangements (e.g., a lecture followed by question and answer) is important.

Planning these occasional changes in modality and procedure presents the lesson in varied contexts, giving learners the opportunity to grasp material in several different ways, according to their individual learning styles. Such changes also give students the opportunity to see previously learned material used in different ways. This reinforces learned material better than simply restating it in the same mode and form. It also encourages learners to extend or expand material according to the new mode or procedure being used. For example, material learned in a lecture may be pushed to its limit in a question-and-answer period when the learner answers a question and finds out that previous understandings were partly incorrect due to the limited context in which they were learned.

Quite apart from the well-known fact that instructional variety helps keep students attentive and actively engaged in the learning process, it also offers them an individualized learning experience and tests their previous understanding.

Your lesson plans can divide presentation of content into three parts representing (a) the content to be taught, (b) the modalities through which content is transmitted (e.g., oral, visual, tactile), and (c) the procedures used to convey the content (e.g., lecture, small group, question and answer).

5. Eliciting the Desired Behavior

After presentation of the stimulus material, provide learners an opportunity to show whether they can perform the behaviors at the intended level of complexity. Learning cannot occur effectively in a passive environment—one that lacks activities to engage the learner in the learning process at moderate-to-high rates of success. Active engagement in the learning process at an appropriate level of difficulty must be a goal of every lesson, because without it little or no learning occurs.

Such engagement can be accomplished in many ways. It may even occur spontaneously as a result of getting your students' attention, informing them of the objectives, stimulating the recall of prerequisite learning, and presenting the stimulus material—but you cannot count on it! Active engagement, especially at an appropriate level of difficulty, is a slippery concept. If left to chance, it rarely occurs to the extent required for significant learning. While all of the instructional events presented thus far are required to actively engage your learners, they cannot guarantee engagement. Therefore, a fifth instructional event is needed; when added to a lesson plan it encourages and guides learners through a process that can be expected to produce the behavior intended.

This fifth event—eliciting the desired behavior—differs from the four preceding ones in that it seeks the individual's covert and personal engagement in the learning process. Each learner must be placed in a position of grappling in a trial-and-error fashion with summarizing, paraphrasing, applying, or solving a problem involving the lesson content. It is not important that the behavior be produced at this stage in a recognizable form, as long as the activity provided stimulates an *attempt to produce the intended behavior*. This activity encourages the learner to *organize a response* that meets the level of behavioral complexity stated when the student is informed of the objective.

The primary ways of staging this instructional event include workbooks, handouts, textbook study questions, verbal and written exercises, and questions that have students apply what was learned, if only in the privacy of their minds. The idea is to pose a classroom activity that encourages students to use the material in a nonevaluative atmosphere, as close in time as possible to presentation of new material. Sometimes such activities can be inserted throughout the lesson at the end of each new chunk of information, which also adds variety. In other instances, these activities occur near the end of presenting the new material.

Either way, the eliciting activity is brief, nonevaluative, and focused exclusively on posing a condition for which the learner must organize a response (such as a question, problem, or exercise). This response may be written, oral, or subvocal (the students respond in their own minds). Eliciting activities can be as simple as your posing a question anywhere in a lesson, or as complex as a problem exercise completed in a workbook at lesson's end. The main attribute is that these activities be *nonevaluative,* to encourage a response unhampered by the anxiety and conservative response patterns that generally occur during testing. Rosenshine and Stevens (1986) suggest additional ways of eliciting the desired behavior:

☐ Preparing a large number of oral questions beforehand.

☐ Asking many brief questions on main points, on supplementary points, and on the process being taught.

☐ Calling on students whose hands are not raised in addition to those who volunteer.

☐ Asking students to summarize a rule or process in their own words.

☐ Having all students write their answers (on paper or the chalkboard) while you circulate.

☐ Having all students write their answers and check them with a neighbor (this is frequently used with older students).

☐ At the end of a lecture/discussion (especially with older students), writing the main points on the chalkboard and then having the class meet in groups to summarize the main points to each other.

6. Providing Feedback

The sixth instructional event is closely connected in time and substance to the fifth one (eliciting activity). Eliciting activity promotes learning to the extent that learners understand the correctness of their responses. The response itself must be an individual attempt to recall, summarize, paraphrase, apply, or problem-solve with the new learning, but the feedback that should immediately follow can be directed to the entire class. For example, you may want to reveal an individual's answer to the question or to hold up to the class another student's answer for comparison.

However, we just stated in the previous section that the main attribute of eliciting activities is that they are nonevaluative. You must be careful to respond to a wrong answer encouragingly, to maintain the nonevaluative flavor of the eliciting activity. Responses such as "That's a good try," or "That's not quite what I'm looking for," or "Keep thinking" can switch the focus to more useful responses without penalizing students for responding.

Ways of confirming a correct response are to read aloud the correct answers from a workbook, or provide a handout with the correct answers, or provide a copy of the exercise with correct answers penciled in. You could use a transparency to pose the eliciting activity and then record volunteered answers. If students are working silently at their seats, you might walk about the room, using a simple nod and smile to indicate the correctness of an individual performance or to encourage the revision of a wrong response. This part of the lesson plan, then, should include the means by which feedback will be given learners about their responses. These and some additional ways of providing feedback are summarized in Table 5.1.

7. Assessing the Behavior

Note that you do not have to provide all eliciting activities and feedback within a single instructional period. There are other ways to engage the student in the learning process, encourage the creation of a product, and organize a response. These include tests and homework problems that are returned the next day, or extended assignments that are returned days or weeks later (essays and research papers). However, tests, essays, term papers, and projects result from several individual lessons and therefore are considerably larger than the elicitation activities discussed thus far. These larger activities are particularly valuable for eliciting more complex behavior than could be expected at the end of any single lesson and for evaluating how well behaviors are performed.

This final instructional event specifies what activity you will use to evaluate the behavior. As we have seen, eliciting activities can be immediate or delayed (an oral question vs. a research paper), and evaluative or nonevaluative. The fifth event described an immediate and nonevaluative eliciting activity. But for this instructional event—assessing the behavior—you will describe a *delayed* eliciting activity that is primarily *evaluative*.

Evaluative eliciting activities such as tests, research papers, and graded homework sometimes are disadvantageous at the earlier stages of learning because they limit risk-taking—or exploratory—behavior and because their feedback lacks immediacy. Both factors can be counterproductive to learning when the instructional goal is to get learners to respond for the first time. Consequently, do not use a delayed

TABLE 5.1
Some methods of providing feedback

Individual students	*Small Groups*	*Class*
Nod while walking past	Sit with group and discuss answers	Place answers on a transparency
Point to correct answer in workbook or text	Have one group critique another group's answers	Provide answers on a handout
Show student the answer key	Give each group the answer key when finished	Read answers aloud
Place check alongside incorrect answers	Assign one group member the task of checking the answers of other group members	Place answers on the chalkboard
Have students grade each others' papers by using the text, or assign references as a guide		Have selected students read their answers aloud
		Have students grade each others' papers as you give answers

eliciting activity to the exclusion of immediate and nonevaluative eliciting activities earlier in the lesson plan.

The seventh instructional event for your lesson plan is the means by which you will provide a delayed eliciting behavior for evaluation. The means can include:

Tests and quizzes

Homework exercises

In-class workbook assignments

Performance evaluations

Lab assignments

Oral presentations

Extended essays

Research papers

EXAMPLE LESSON PLANS

We are now ready to place these seven instructional events into a brief but effective lesson plan. To be both practical and effective, lesson plans must be short and yet provide all the ingredients needed to deliver the lesson. Following are some example plans on various subjects and grade levels that show how easy lesson planning can be when the task is organized by the seven critical events.

First, title the lesson to indicate the content. Include a lesson number that references the lesson back to its unit plan. Observe in Figure 5.3 the numbers in the lower right corners of each lesson (box) in the unit blueprint; these numbers tie each lesson to its larger content domain. As multiple lessons are developed for a single unit, these numbers become a ready reference that show how the lessons contribute to a unit outcome at a higher level of complexity. Here is the format of a typical lesson for beginning readers:

Unit Title: Reading: Word Attack Skills

Lesson Title: Sound Discrimination, Letters of the Alphabet—Lesson 2.1

This indicates the general content of the lesson and its placement in a unit on word attack skills. The lesson identifier, 2.1, indicates that this lesson is the first one in Unit 2. It would appear on the graphic unit plan as indicated in Figure 5.7.

Next appears the elaboration of each of the seven instructional events for delivering this lesson to students.

1. Gaining attention   Play an audiotape of a voice articulating the sounds.

This instructional event gains student attention and focuses them on what is to be presented. Whatever device or procedure you use should not only gain their attention but also motivate their continued concentration well into the lesson. Keep in mind that students, especially young ones, have trouble picking up subtle transitions in classroom activities. Often their attention is steadfastly on what has immediately preceded the lesson, and they are reluctant to change focus unless something new, interesting, or exciting is on the horizon.

FIGURE 5.7

The relationship between lessons, units, and a course or domain

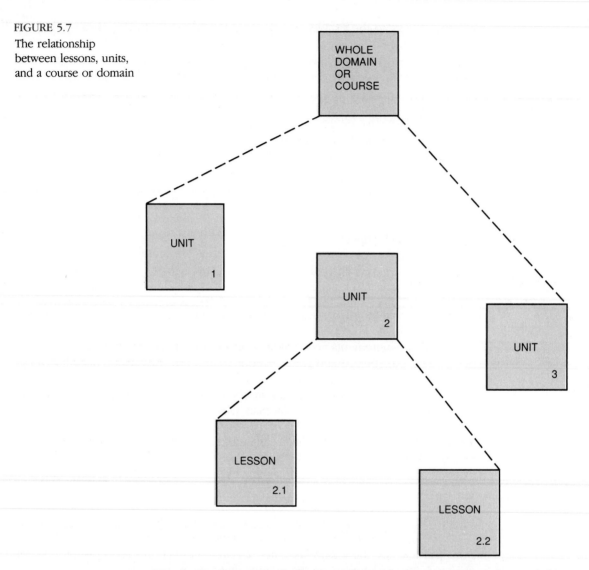

Visual or auditory stimuli often are effective as attention-getters, because their ability to penetrate the senses exceeds that of more neutral stimuli like written words, verbal expressions, or pronouncements. Changing sensory modalities from listening to looking (or vice versa) often provides the incentive necessary to more selectively perceive and receive the message about to be communicated.

2. Informing the learner of the objective   When the tape is finished, indicate that by the end of the lesson students will be expected to repeat the vowel sounds out loud, independently of the tape.

This instructional event translates the behavioral objective for the lesson into a form that is meaningful to students. In this example, the transfer of information from one modality (listening) to another (speaking) is sought, indicating that the objective for this lesson is written at the comprehension level of the cognitive domain. The attention-getting device should be chosen to lead into the objective for the lesson. Simply clapping one's hands to gain attention, followed by conveying the objective of the lesson, is not as effective as having the objective actually *contained within* or *reflected by* the attention-getting procedure.

In this case, the audiotape was directly related to the lesson's content, allowing these two instructional events to work together to produce a unified theme, enhancing the learners' attention. Other simple but effective attention getters that easily can be made to reflect the lesson objective are a picture or chart, a question on the chalkboard, or a demonstration derived directly from lesson content.

3. Stimulating recall of prerequisite learning	Show how each vowel sound is produced by the correct positioning of the mouth and lips.

Identifying and successfully communicating task-relevant prior knowledge to students is critical to attaining the lesson objective. Unless you paraphrase, summarize, or otherwise review this information, at least some students will be unable to comprehend the information to be conveyed. Among the most frequent reasons that learners are unable to attain lesson outcomes is that they lack the outcomes of previously taught lessons that are necessary for subsequent learning.

Prerequisite content must be recalled or stimulated into action for it to play a meaningful role in acquiring new learning. Most lessons require some previous facts, understandings, or skills, and these should be recalled and identified at this step of the lesson plan. You can achieve this by touching on the high points of this prior learning.

4. Presenting the stimulus material	Say each vowel sound and then have the class repeat it twice, pointing to a chart of the position of the mouth and lips during the articulation of each vowel sound. Do the most commonly used vowels first.

You may feel that this is the heart of the lesson. You are partly right, except that there are six other hearts, each of which could entail as much effort in planning and instructional time as this event does. Beginning teachers tend to pack their lessons almost entirely with new stimulus material. They devote far less effort to gaining attention, to informing the learner of the objective, to recalling prerequisite learning, and to other instructional events that must follow the presentation of new material.

Obviously the presentation of new material is indispensable, but it need not always encompass most (or even a large portion) of the lesson. The result of devoting a large portion of the lesson to new material, exclusive of the other instructional events, is that the lesson is likely to present content in pieces too big for learners to grasp. This often results in considerable reteaching during subsequent lessons and ultimately less content coverage at the end of a unit.

Although the presentation of new stimulus material is an important part of most lessons, it does not always have to comprise the majority of instructional time. Just as the first three instructional events must come before the presentation of new material for this material to be meaningful, the next three instructional events will make clear that this new stimulus material must itself be a stimulus for something more to come.

5. Eliciting the desired behavior   Have students silently practice forming correct mouth and lip positions for each vowel sound, following the pictures in their workbooks.

For this instructional event the learner is given guidance in how to perform the behavior and an opportunity to practice it—two activities that must go hand in hand. Eliciting the desired behavior without providing the opportunity to practice it can cancel out the positive effect of this instructional event. Here, the new stimulus material described in the previous event can be presented in some different form with an opportunity to practice the behavior in as nonthreatening, nonevaluative an atmosphere as possible.

Grading or performance evaluations should not be part of the performance being elicited in this instructional event, because spontaneity, freedom to make mistakes, and an opportunity for immediate feedback are the goals. You should provide an opportunity for independently practicing or applying the new stimulus material presented in the previous event along with any graphic or verbal aids that contain key portions of the stimulus material.

6. Providing feedback   Randomly choose students to recite the vowel sounds; correct their errors to demonstrate to the class the desired sound.

Feedback should be integrally related to the eliciting activity. A short time between performance and feedback has long been thought to be an essential element of learning; the closer the correspondence between a performance and feedback, the more quickly learning will occur.

Feedback either can be integrated with eliciting the desired behavior, or it can be a subsequent separate activity. In the previous example of an eliciting activity (i.e., the fifth instructional event), feedback was not provided; learners had no way of knowing the correctness of their behavior (mouth and lip movements). Pictures in the text guided the behavior, but because students could not see themselves, they could not determine the accuracy of their responses. In such a case, feedback would have to follow the eliciting activity. The eliciting activity, however, easily could have included feedback—for example, the student could recite a vowel sound and you could immediately report its accuracy. The correspondence of an eliciting activity and feedback is always a matter of degree, but these two events should take place as closely in time as possible.

7. Assessing the behavior   This lesson objective is assessed as part of the unit test on word attack skills and from exercises completed in the workbook.

Few lesson objectives are assessed by individual lesson tests. Amounts of content larger than that contained in a single lesson usually are necessary to make tests efficient and practical. However, it is important to indicate which unit or subunit tests cover the lesson content and what individual means, other than formal tests, will be used to grade the behaviors.

This entry on the lesson plan will remind you to include the lesson's content on subsequent tests or to find other means of checking learners' attainment of it. Some assessment method always should be designed into a lesson plan (tests, workbook exercises, homework, handouts, worksheets, oral responses, etc.). This information provides important feedback about students' readiness for new stimulus material and possible reasons for poor performance in later lessons for which the current material is prerequisite.

Table 5.2 presents the *approximate* amount of time during a hypothetical 50-minute class period that you might devote to each instructional event. Some periods will differ considerably from these amounts of time, such as when the entire lesson is devoted to a review or when recall of prior learning and assessing behavior is not relevant to the day's lesson. Keep in mind that experience, familiarity with content, and common sense always are your best guides for the percentage of time to devote to each instructional event.

From Table 5.2 it is apparent that when you emphasize one instructional event, another must be deemphasized; tradeoffs always are necessary. Although every teacher would like to have more (or less) time than allotted for an instructional period, decisions must be made that fit a lesson into the available time frame. Table 5.2 indicates some of the ways this might be done when planning a typical lesson.

We conclude with several additional lesson plans that illustrate the seven instructional events in other content areas and grade levels.

TABLE 5.2
Approximate distribution of instructional time across instructional events for a hypothetical 50-minute lesson

Instructional event	Ranges in minutes	Ranges in percentages of time
Gaining attention	1–5	2–10
Informing learners of the objective	1–3	2–6
Stimulating recall of prerequisite learning	5–10	10–20
Presenting the stimulus material	10–20	20–40
Eliciting the desired behavior	10–20	20–40
Providing feedback	5–10	10–20
Assessing behavior	0–10	0–20

Unit Title: United States History (Early Beginning through Reconstruction)
Lesson Title: Causes of the Civil War—Lesson 2.3

1. Gaining attention	Show the following list of wars on a transparency: French and Indian War 1754–1769 Revolutionary War 1775–1781 Civil War 1861–1865 World War I 1914–1918 World War II 1941–1945 Korean War 1950–1953 Vietnam War 1965–1975
2. Informing the learner of the objective	Learners will be expected to know the causes of the Civil War and to show that those causes also can apply to at least one of the wars listed on the transparency.
3. Stimulating recall of prerequisite learning	Briefly review the causes of both the French and Indian War and the Revolutionary War as covered in Lessons 2.1 and 2.2.
4. Presenting the stimulus material	(a) Summarize major events leading to the Civil War: —rise of sectionalism —labor-intensive economy —lack of diversification (b) Identify significant individuals during the Civil War and their roles: —Lincoln —Lee —Davis —Grant (c) Describe four general causes of war and explain which are most relevant to the Civil War: —economic (to profit) —political (to control) —social (to influence) —military (to protect)
5. Eliciting the desired behavior	Ask the class to identify which of the four causes is most relevant to the major events leading up to the Civil War.
6. Providing feedback	Ask for student answers and indicate plausibility of the volunteered responses.
7. Assessing the behavior	Assign as homework a one-page essay assessing the relative importance of the four causes for one of the wars listed on the transparency.

Unit Title: Writing Concepts and Skills
Lesson Title: Descriptive, Narrative, and Expository Paragraphs—Lesson 1.3

1. Gaining attention	Read examples of short descriptive, narrative, and expository paragraphs from Sunday's newspaper.
2. Informing the learner of the objective	Students will be able to discriminate among descriptive, narrative, and expository paragraphs from a list of written examples in the popular press.
3. Stimulating recall of prerequisite learning	Review the meanings of the words *description, narration,* and *exposition* as they are used in everyday language.
4. Presenting the stimulus material	Using a headline from Sunday's newspaper, give examples of how this story could be reported by description, narration, and exposition.
5. Eliciting the desired behavior	Take another front-page story from Sunday's newspaper and ask students to write a paragraph relating the story in descriptive, narrative, or expository form, whichever they prefer.
6. Providing feedback	Call on individuals to read their paragraphs, checking each against the type of paragraph he or she intended to write.
7. Assessing the behavior	Provide multiple choice examples of each form of writing on the unit test. Have students revise their paragraphs as needed and turn in as homework the following day.

Unit Title: Consumer Mathematics
Lesson Title: Operations and Properties of Ratio, Proportion, and Percentage— Lesson 3.3

1. Gaining attention	Display so all can see: (a) can of diet soft drink (b) one-pound package of spaghetti (c) box of breakfast cereal
2. Informing the learner of the objective	Learners will be expected to know how to determine ratios, proportions, and percentages from the information on labels of popular food products.
3. Stimulating recall of prerequisite learning	Review the definitions of *ratio, proportion,* and *percentage* from the math workbook.
4. Presenting the stimulus material	Place the information from the soft-drink label on a transparency and ask students to identify the percentage of sodium.

5. Eliciting the desired behavior	Write on the board the list of ingredients given on the cereal box; ask students to determine (a) the percentage of daily allowance of protein, (b) the proportion of daily allowance of Vitamin A, and (c) the ratio of protein to carbohydrates.
6. Providing feedback	Using the information on the board, point to the correct answer for a and b and show how to find the appropriate numerator and denominator for c from the ingredients on the label.
7. Assessing the behavior	Provide on the weekly quiz five problems covering ratios (two problems), proportions (two problems), and percentages (one problem) using labels from other consumer products.

Unit Title: Manipulative Laboratory Skills
Lesson Title: Use of the Microscope—Lesson 1.1

1. Gaining attention	Show the first five minutes of a film about making a lens.
2. Informing the learner of the objective	Learners will be expected to be able to focus correctly a specimen of one-celled animal life, using both high and low magnification.
3. Stimulating recall of prerequisite learning	Review procedures for selecting a slide from the one-celled specimen collection and mounting it on the specimen tray of the microscope.
4. Presenting the stimulus material	Using a student in front of the class as a demonstrator, help position his or her posture and hands on the microscope. Gently bend body and hands until the correct posture results. Demonstrate the position of the eyes and show clockwise and counterclockwise rotation of low and then high magnification adjustment.
5. Eliciting the desired behavior	Have each student obtain a specimen slide, mount it on a microscope and focus on low magnification. Randomly check microscopes, correcting slide, positions, and focus as needed with student observing. Repeat for high magnification.
6. Providing feedback	Feedback has been provided in the context of the eliciting activity (step 5) to increase immediacy of the feedback. Also, refer students to the text for examples of focused and unfocused specimens.
7. Assessing the behavior	At the completion of the unit, students will be assessed during a practical lab exam requiring the correct mounting and identification of three unknown specimens using the microscope.

SUMMING UP

This chapter introduced you to unit and lesson planning. Its main points were:

1. A unit of instruction may be thought of as a "system"; individual lessons within the unit are its component parts.

2. The concept of *hierarchy* tells us the relationship of parts to the whole (in this case, lessons to units) and the concept of *task-relevant prior knowledge* tells us what must come before what in a sequence of events (lesson sequence). Systems thinking draws our attention to the relationship among parts of varying sizes to see what lessons make up what units, what units make up what content domains, and what content domains make up what grades and subjects.

3. Three primary activities within the planning process are establishing instructional goals, identifying the type of learner to which your instruction is directed, and selecting and organizing content.

4. Any goal at the unit level can be broken into its component parts at the lesson level; these parts represent everything that is important for attaining the unit goal.

5. The two purposes of unit planning are (a) to convert generally stated activities and outcomes into specific objectives and lessons, and (b) to provide a picture of long-term goals.

6. Lesson outcomes are the means by which unit goals are achieved.

7. In the graphic approach to lesson planning, boxes illustrate areas of content, or instructional goals, at various levels of generality. Lines and arrows indicate sequences among lessons and how outcomes of lessons build upon one another to achieve a unit goal.

8. A graphic representation of a unit plan may specify that every lesson must be taught in a specific sequence or that lessons may be taught in any order. In some unit plans, the ordering of lessons may be unimportant.

9. The bottom of a unit plan hierarchy represents content suitably sized for the preparation of individual lessons.

10. An effective unit uses the relationship between individual lessons and their cumulative effects to achieve outcomes at higher levels of behavioral complexity, which may include the learning of concepts, the application of facts and understandings to real-world problem solving, and the ability to make value judgments.

11. One purpose of seeing a whole unit at a glance in a graphic format is to determine if all necessary task-relevant prior knowledge required by each lesson has been provided by the unit plan.

12. The three activities of unit planning are:
    - Classifying unit outcomes at a higher level of behavioral complexity than lesson outcomes by using one or more taxonomies of behavior.
    - Planning the instructional sequence so that the outcomes of previously taught lessons are instrumental in achieving the outcomes of subsequent lessons.
    - Rearranging or adding lesson content where necessary to provide task-relevant prior knowledge where needed.

13. Before starting the preparation of a lesson plan, you must determine the behavioral complexity level of the lesson (e.g., knowledge, application, evaluation), to what extent provisions for student diversity must accompany the lesson plan (e.g., ability grouping, peer tutoring, learning centers, specialized handouts, cooperative groups), and what level of proficiency you expect of students at the end of the lesson (e.g., whether mastery learning is required).

14. *Learning* refers to internal events in the heads of learners that result from external teaching events you provide. Hence, the words *teaching* and *learning* refer to two different but related sets of activities.

15. The external events that can be specified in a lesson plan are:
    - Gaining attention
    - Informing the learner of the objective
    - Stimulating recall of prerequisite learning
    - Presenting the stimulus material
    - Eliciting the desired behavior
    - Providing feedback
    - Assessing the behavior

16. Gaining attention involves gaining your students' interest in what you will present and getting them to switch to the appropriate modality for the coming lesson.

17. Informing learners of the objective also involves informing them of the complexity of the behavior expected at the end of the lesson.
18. Stimulating recall of prerequisite learning is reviewing task-relevant prior information required by the lesson.
19. Presenting the stimulus material is delivering the desired content in a manner conducive to the modality in which it is to be received, using procedures that stimulate thought processing and maintain interest.

20. Eliciting the desired behavior gets learners to produce the intended behavior by organizing a response corresponding with the level of complexity of the stated objective.
21. Providing feedback tells the learner the accuracy of his or her elicited response in a nonthreatening, nonevaluative atmosphere.
22. Assessing the behavior evaluates the learner's performance with tests, homework, and extended assignments.

FOR DISCUSSION AND PRACTICE

*1. Identify the five inputs to the planning process from which the preparation of lesson plans proceeds.
*2. How can a unit outcome be more than the sum of individual lesson outcomes?
*3. Explain in your own words how the concepts of hierarchy and task-relevant prior knowledge are used in unit planning.
*4. How are the concepts of *hierarchy* and *task-relevant prior learning* related?
*5. Name the levels of behavioral complexity in each of the three domains (cognitive, affective, and psychomotor) that generally would be most suitable for a unit outcome.
*6. How are the boxes further down on a graphic unit plan different than the boxes higher up?
7. Graphically portray a three-lesson unit in which the sequence of lessons is critical to achieving the unit outcome. Then, portray another three-lesson unit in which the lesson sequence is unimportant. Be sure to draw the lesson outcomes for each unit to properly reflect the unit outcome.
*8. Explain why a graphic unit plan that began with a very broad and encompassing outcome (e.g., understanding poetry) would have more intermediate levels represented in it than a unit plan that began with a very narrow and specific outcome (e.g., understanding poetic meter).
*9. Identify some ways of providing for student diversity in the context of a lesson plan.

*10. Explain what is meant by mastery learning and its relationship to task-relevant prior knowledge.
*11. Name the seven events of instruction that can be described in a lesson plan. Give a specific example of how you would implement each one in a lesson of your own choosing.
*12. Identify the instructional event(s) for which the key behavior of *instructional variety* would be most important.
*13. Identify the instructional event(s) for which the key behavior of *student success* would be most important.
*14. Identify the instructional event(s) for which the key behavior of *engagement in the learning process* would be most important.
*15. Indicate how the instructional events of (a) providing feedback and (b) assessing behavior differ according to the evaluative nature of the feedback provided and the immediacy with which the feedback is given.
16. Following the form of the examples provided in this chapter, prepare a lesson plan for a topic in your major or preferred teaching area and another in your minor teaching area. Include the approximate number of minutes you expect to devote to each event out of a 50-minute class period.

---

*Answers to asterisked questions (*) in this and the other chapters are in Appendix B.

Block, J. (1987). Mastery learning models. In M. J. Dunkin (Ed.), *International encyclopedia of teaching and teaching education*. New York: Pergamon.
An excellent article on how to achieve mastery learning and what this important concept means for effective teaching.

Briggs, L. (Ed.). (1977). *Instructional design: Principles and applications*. Englewood Cliffs, NJ: Educational Technology Publications.
A practical text on how to plan, design, and implement instruction at the lesson and unit levels.

Clark, C., & Yinger, R. (1979). *Three studies of teacher planning* (Research Series No. 55). East Lansing: Michigan State University, Institute for Research on Teaching. (Available by writing the Institute in East Lansing, MI 48824)
A report on the results of three research studies which related the planning activities of teachers to observable changes in teachers in the classroom.

Dunkin, M. J. (1987). Lesson formats. In M. J. Dunkin (Ed.), *International encyclopedia of teaching and teacher education*. New York: Pergamon.

A sampling of the many varieties of and ways to prepare lesson plans.

Gagné, R., & Briggs, L. (1979). *Principles of instructional design*. New York: Holt, Rinehart & Winston.
A thorough and authoritative text on the design of instruction from a psychological perspective.

Kim, E., & Kellough, R. (1978). *A resource guide for secondary teaching* (2nd ed.). New York: Macmillan.
A practical guide with models for writing unit and lesson plans at the secondary level.

Pratt, D. (1980). *Curriculum, design and development*. New York: Harcourt, Brace, Jovanovich.
An introductory text on how to design classroom instruction using many of the concepts presented in this chapter.

Saylor, G., Alexander, W., & Lewis, A. (1981). *A curriculum planning for better teaching and learning* (4th ed.). Chicago: Holt, Rinehart and Winston.
A companion volume to the previous one that relates lesson planning to unit planning to produce an integrated sequence of instruction.

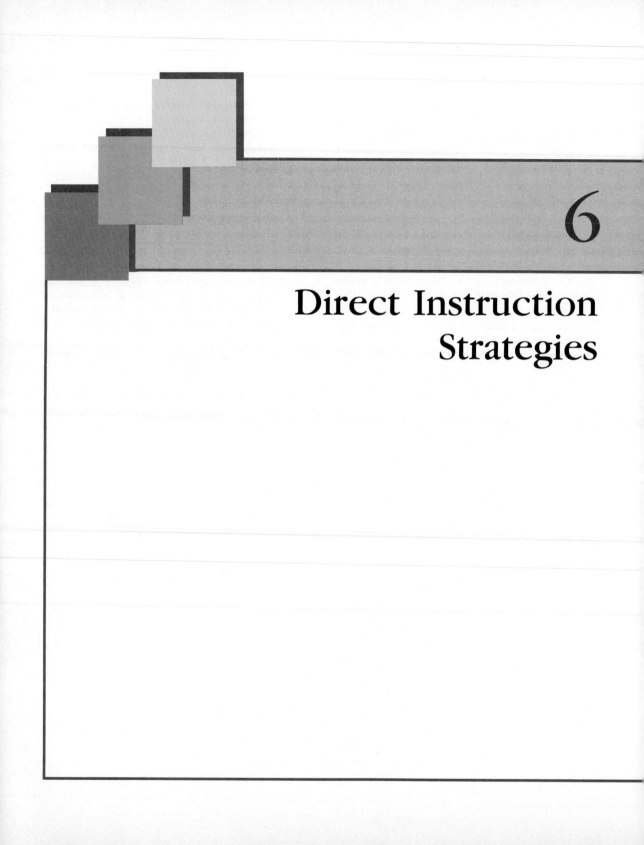

6

Direct Instruction
Strategies

The previous chapter presented seven instructional events that form the skeletal structure of a lesson plan:

1. Gaining attention
2. Informing the learner of the objective
3. Stimulating recall of prerequisite learning
4. Presenting the stimulus material
5. Eliciting the desired behavior
6. Providing feedback
7. Assessing the behavior.

To add flesh to this skeleton, this and subsequent chapters present different instructional strategies by which these seven events can be carried out with ease and perfection. This chapter presents strategies for direct teaching that include explanations, examples, review, practice, and feedback in the context of a lecture format. The next chapter presents strategies for indirect teaching that include guided questions, inductive and deductive logic, student ideas, and group discussion in an inquiry or problem-solving format. Subsequent chapters show how you can use the ideas in both chapters to teach your learners to direct, control, and regulate their own learning and to learn cooperatively with others.

Have you ever wondered why some teachers are more interesting than others? This is an ageless phenomenon, well known to anyone who has spent time in school. Students cannot wait to attend the classes of some teachers, but dread attending the classes of others. Interesting teachers often are described with phrases such as "more intelligent," "has a better personality," and "is warmer and friendlier." Although these qualities may be present in teachers judged to be the most interesting, they are not the only reasons that a teacher can be interesting.

It may surprise you that one of the most important factors in how interesting teachers are to their students is their use of the key behavior *instructional variety*. In a study of experienced and inexperienced teachers (Emmer, Evertson, & Anderson, 1980), experienced teachers who showed flexibility and variety in their instructional strategies were found to be more interesting than inexperienced teachers who had no knowledge of alternative teaching strategies.

Knowledge of a variety of instructional strategies and the flexibility to change them both within and among lessons are two of the greatest assets a teacher can have (McNair, 1978–1979). Without variety and flexibility to capture the interest and attention of students, it is unlikely that any other key behavior, however well executed, will have an effect on them. This chapter provides a variety of teaching strategies you can use to compose lesson plans and to create and maintain an atmosphere of interest and variety in your classroom.

CATEGORIES OF TEACHING AND LEARNING

Just as the carpenter, electrician, and plumber must select the proper tool for a specific task, you must select the proper instructional strategy for a learning outcome.

To help determine your choice of strategies, here are two broad classifications of learning outcomes:

> Type 1. Facts, rules, and action sequences.
>
> Type 2. Concepts, patterns, and abstractions.

Type 1 outcomes often represent behaviors at lower levels of complexity in the cognitive, affective, and psychomotor domains. As discussed in Chapter 4, these include the knowledge, comprehension, and application levels of the cognitive domain; the awareness, responding, and valuing levels of the affective domain; and the imitation, manipulation, and precision levels of the psychomotor domain.

Type 2 outcomes, on the other hand, frequently represent behaviors at the higher levels of complexity in these domains. They include objectives at the analysis, synthesis, and evaluation levels of the cognitive domain; the organization and characterization levels of the affective domain; and the articulation and naturalization levels of the psychomotor domain.

These are fairly broad distinctions that can overlap, but they are useful guides in selecting an instructional strategy to maximize learning when the objectives include facts, rules, and action sequences or concepts, patterns, and abstractions. Some important differences between instructional goals requiring these two types of learning are shown in Table 6.1.

Notice across the left and right columns of Table 6.1 that two types of learning are being required. In the left column, Type 1 tasks require combining facts and rules at the knowledge and comprehension level into a sequence of actions that could be learned by observation, rote repetition, and practice. Students can learn the "right answers" by memorizing and practicing behaviors that you model.

In the right column, a quite different learning type is called for. The "right answers" are not so closely connected to facts, rules, or action sequences that can be memorized and practiced in some limited context. Something more is needed to help the learner go beyond the facts, rules, or sequences to create, synthesize, and ultimately identify and recognize an answer that cannot be easily modeled or memorized. The missing link involves learning an abstraction called a *concept*.

For example, to learn the *concept* of a frog involves learning the essential characteristics that make an organism a frog, as distinguished from closely similar animals (e.g., a green chameleon). In other words, the learner needs to know not only the characteristics that all frogs have (e.g., green color, four legs, eats insects, amphibious) but also what characteristics distinguish frogs from other animals. If we classified frogs only on the characteristics of being green, having four legs, eating insects, and being amphibious, some turtles could be misidentified as frogs. Another category of knowledge must be learned that contains characteristics that separate frogs from similar animals (e.g., frogs have soft bodies, moist skin, strong hind limbs, and do not change color).

Notice that to properly classify a frog among other animals that may look like one, both *nonessential* and *essential* frog attributes need to be learned. The nonessential attributes can be learned only by studying nonexamples, thus allowing learners to eliminate characteristics that are not unique to frogs. Finally, as the learner gains

TABLE 6.1
Some instructional goals requiring Type 1 and Type 2 behaviors

Type 1: Goals requiring facts, rules, and sequences	*Type 2: Goals requiring concepts, patterns, and abstractions*
1. IF	BUT IF
GOAL is to keep ANIMAL alive	GOAL is to recognize and
and ANIMAL has four legs	identify frogs
and ANIMAL is green	and ANIMAL has four legs
and ANIMAL is slimy	and ANIMAL is green
and ANIMAL is size of fist	and ANIMAL is slimy
	and ANIMAL is size of fist
THEN TEACH HOW TO	THEN TEACH HOW TO
Put ANIMAL near water, catch flies and feed ANIMAL flies	Classify ANIMAL as a frog
2. IF	BUT IF
GOAL is to combine two SENTENCES	GOAL is to recognize and identify contrasts
and there are two IDEAS in the SENTENCES	and there are two IDEAS
and the IDEA in one SENTENCE is different from the IDEA in the other SENTENCE on one DIMENSION	and one IDEA is different from other IDEA on one DIMENSION
THEN TEACH HOW TO	THEN TEACH HOW TO
Remove period from end of first SENTENCE and put comma at end of first SENTENCE and write *but* after comma and write second SENTENCE after *but*	Classify pair of IDEAS as a contrast
3. IF	BUT IF
GOAL is to plot a linear EQUATION and the EQUATION has the form $y = a + bX$	GOAL is to recognize and identify EQUATIONS of the form $y = a + bX$
THEN TEACH HOW TO	THEN TEACH HOW TO
Put POINT 1 at a on y axis and count 1 to the right from POINT 1 and go up whatever number b is and put POINT 2 there and draw LINE through POINT 1 and POINT 2	Classify EQUATIONS that describe a straight line

From THE COGNITIVE PSYCHOLOGY OF SCHOOL LEARNING by Ellen D. Gagné. Copyright © 1985 by Ellen D. Gagné. Adapted by permission of HarperCollins Publishers.

more practice with both examples and nonexamples, the concept of a frog emerges as a tightly woven combination of characteristics (Figure 6.1). Now the learner is able to disregard superficial characteristics such as color and to focus on characteristics that are unique to frogs. Given pictures of various toads, chameleons, turtles, snakes, and so on, the student learns to identify correctly those that are frogs.

FIGURE 6.1
Learning the concept of
a frog

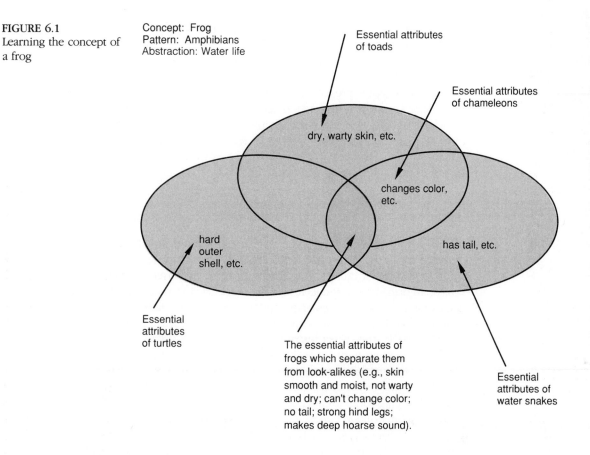

Concept: Frog
Pattern: Amphibians
Abstraction: Water life

Essential attributes
of toads

Essential attributes
of chameleons

dry, warty skin, etc.

changes color,
etc.

hard
outer
shell, etc.

has tail, etc.

Essential
attributes
of turtles

The essential attributes of
frogs which separate them
from look-alikes (e.g., skin
smooth and moist, not warty
and dry; can't change color;
no tail; strong hind legs;
makes deep hoarse sound).

Essential
attributes of
water snakes

At this point the learner has discovered at least some of the essential attributes of a frog and has formed an initial concept. Notice how different this teach-
ing/learning process is from simply having Johnny repeat some recently memorized
facts about frogs: "Frogs are green, have four legs, eat insects, and can swim." This
response does not tell you whether Johnny has the concept of a frog, or a pattern of
which frogs are a part (e.g., amphibian), or even the most general and abstract frog
characteristics (e.g., "water life"). Even if Johnny learns the considerably more complex task of how to care for frogs, he still has not learned the *concept* of a frog. He has
grasped only how to arrange a constellation of facts (and perhaps other concepts) into
an action sequence (Table 6.1).

The preceding demonstrates how the processes used to learn facts, rules, and
action sequences are different from those used to learn concepts, patterns, and abstractions. And just as different processes are involved in such learning, so are different instructional strategies needed to teach these outcomes. We most commonly teach
facts, rules, and action sequences using strategies that emphasize knowledge acquisition. We most commonly teach concepts, patterns, and abstractions using strategies
that emphasize inquiry or problem solving. These follow distinctions suggested by

R. M. Gagné (1977), J. R. Anderson (1980), and E. Gagné (1985), whose writings have highlighted the different instructional strategies required by these two types of learning.

Knowledge acquisition and inquiry are different types of learning outcomes, so each of them must be linked with the specific strategies most likely to produce them. This chapter presents a group of strategies for teaching knowledge acquisition involving facts, rules, and action sequences. The next chapter presents strategies for teaching inquiry and problem solving involving concepts, patterns, and abstractions. In subsequent chapters, both types of learning are combined to show how together they can build additional teaching strategies to help your learners solve problems, think critically, and work cooperatively.

INTRODUCTION TO DIRECT INSTRUCTION STRATEGIES

The teaching of facts, rules, and action sequences is most efficiently achieved through a process called the **direct instruction model**. Direct instruction, sometimes synonymous with expository or didactic teaching, is a *teacher-centered* strategy in which you are the major information provider. In the direct instruction model, your role is to pass facts, rules, or action sequences on to students in the most direct way possible. This usually takes the form of a lecture with explanations, examples, and opportunities for practice and feedback. The direct instruction lecture is a multifaceted presentation requiring not only large amounts of verbal lecture but also teacher-student interactions involving questions and answers, review and practice, and the correction of student errors.

In the direct instruction model, the concept of a lecture in the elementary and secondary classroom differs considerably from the concept of a lecture that you might acquire from college experience. The typical one-hour college lecture rarely will be suitable for your classroom, because your learners' attention spans, interest levels, and motivation will not be the same as your own. Therefore, the "lecture" as presented here is neither a lengthy (and boring) monologue nor an open, free-wheeling discussion of problems that interest the student. Instead, it is a quickly paced, highly organized set of interchanges that you control, focusing exclusively on acquiring a limited set of predetermined facts, rules, or action sequences.

Rosenshine and Stevens (1986) have equated this type of lecture with that of an effective demonstration in which:

1. You clearly present goals and main points by:
   a. Stating goals or objectives of the presentation beforehand.
   b. Focusing on one thought (point, direction) at a time.
   c. Avoiding digressions.
   d. Avoiding ambiguous phrases and pronouns.
2. You present content sequentially by:
   a. Presenting material in small steps.
   b. Organizing and presenting material so that one point is mastered before the next point is given.
   c. Giving explicit, step-by-step directions.
   d. Presenting an outline when the material is complex.

3. You are specific and concrete by:
   a. Modeling the skill or process (when appropriate).
   b. Giving detailed and redundant explanations for difficult points.
   c. Providing students with concrete and varied examples.
4. You check for students' understanding by:
   a. Being sure that students understand one point before proceeding to the next.
   b. Asking students questions to monitor their comprehension of what has been presented.
   c. Having students summarize the main points in their own words.
   d. Reteaching the parts that students have difficulty comprehending—either through further teaching, explanation or by students tutoring each other.

The examples that appear later illustrate this type of lecture. For now, note the following action verbs that correspond to the objectives most suited for direct instruction:

Cognitive objectives	Affective objectives	Psychomotor objectives
to recall	to listen	to repeat
to describe	to attend	to follow
to list	to be aware	to place
to summarize	to comply	to perform accurately
to paraphrase	to follow	to perform independently
to distinguish	to obey	to perform proficiently
to use	to display	to perform with speed
to organize	to express	to perform with coordination
to demonstrate	to prefer	to perform with timing

These outcomes are learned through application of facts, rules, and action sequences that usually can be taught in a single lesson. You can most easily and directly test them with multiple choice, listing, matching, and fill-in exercises. Test items would call for the listing of memorized names, dates, and other facts; summarizing or paraphrasing of learned facts, rules, or sequences; or connecting together and applying learned facts, rules, and sequences in a context slightly different than the one in which it was learned.

Both Rosenshine (1983) and Good (1979) have identified this type of learning as what results from direct instruction or "active teaching." This type of instruction most often is characterized by:

full-class instruction (as opposed to small group);

organization of learning around questions you pose;

provision of detailed and redundant practice;

presenting material so that one new fact, rule, or sequence is mastered before the next fact, rule, or sequence is presented; and

formal arrangement of the classroom to maximize drill and practice.

Table 6.2 presents some teacher behaviors most commonly associated with the direct instruction model. You can see that from these behaviors that a large share of teaching time is likely to be devoted to direct instruction, i.e., to providing information directly to students via lecture interspersed with explanations, examples, practice, and feedback.

Whether lecturing, explaining, pointing out relationships, giving examples, or correcting errors, there is much to say for using strategies that follow the direct instruction model. Research indicates that direct instruction functions (Table 6.2) and the teaching behaviors that comprise them (e.g., teacher reviews previous day's work, teacher provides feedback and corrections, teacher provides for student practice) are among the teaching functions that correlate highest with student achievement (Anderson, Evertson, & Brophy, 1982; Becker, 1977).

TABLE 6.2

Some direct instruction functions

---

1. Daily review, checking previous day's work, and reteaching (if necessary):
   Checking homework
   Reteaching areas where there were student errors
2. Presenting and structuring new content:
   Provide overview
   Proceed in small steps (if necessary), but at a rapid pace
   If necessary, give detailed or redundant instructions and explanations
   New skills are phased in while old skills are being measured
3. Guided student practice:
   High frequency of questions and overt student practice (from teacher and materials)
   Prompts are provided during initial learning (when appropriate)
   All students have a chance to respond and receive feedback
   Teacher *checks for understanding* by evaluating student responses
   Continue practice until students are firm
   Success rate of 80% or higher during initial learning
4. Feedback and correctives (and recycling of instruction, if necessary):
   Feedback to students, particularly when they are correct but hesitant
   Student errors provide feedback to the teacher that corrections and/or reteaching is necessary
   Corrections by simplifying question, giving clues, explaining or reviewing steps, or reteaching last steps
   When necessary, reteach using smaller steps
5. Independent practice so that student responses are firm and automatic:
   Seatwork
   Unitization and automaticity (practice to overlearning)
   Need for procedure to ensure student engagement during seatwork (i.e., teacher or aide monitoring)
   95% correct or higher
6. Weekly and monthly reviews:
   Reteaching, if necessary

From "Teaching Functions in Instructional Programs" by B. Rosenshine, 1983, *Elementary School Journal, 83*, p. 338. Reprinted by permission of the University of Chicago. Copyright © 1986 by the University of Chicago. All rights reserved.

WHEN IS DIRECT INSTRUCTION APPROPRIATE?

When direct instruction strategies are used for the proper purpose, with the appropriate content, and at the right time, they are important adjuncts to a teaching strategy menu. Most of these strategies are at their best when your purpose is to disseminate information that is not readily available from texts or workbooks in appropriately sized pieces. If such information were available, your students might well learn the material from these sources independently, with only introductory or structuring comments provided by you. However, when you must partition, subdivide, and translate textbook and workbook material into a more digestible form before it can be understood by your students, a direct instruction lecture is appropriate.

Another time for direct instruction strategies is when you wish to arouse or heighten student interest. Students often fail to complete textbook readings and exercises in the mistaken belief that the chapter is boring, is not worth their effort, or presents material already learned. Your active participation in the presentation of content can change such misperceptions by mixing interesting supplemental or introductory information with the "dry" facts, by showing their application to future schoolwork or world events, and by illustrating with questions and answers that the material is neither easy nor previously mastered. Your direct involvement in presenting content provides the human element that may be necessary for learning to occur in many of your students.

Finally, direct instruction strategies are indispensable for achieving content mastery and overlearning of fundamental facts, rules, and action sequences that may be essential to subsequent learning (Anderson & Block, 1987). The degree of learning that occurs is directly related to the time a student is actively engaged in the learning process. Therefore, efficient use of class time and active student practice of content are important ingredients of mastery learning.

These two goals in the mastery learning concept are achieved by an instructional sequence of review, presenting new content, practice, feedback, and reteaching. These repetitive cycles compose nearly all of the instructional time scheduled for a lesson. Many of the examples in this chapter illustrate this type of instructional sequence. When the content to be taught represents task-relevant prior knowledge for subsequent learning, mastery learning is the best insurance that this knowledge is remembered and available for later use.

There also are times in which direct instruction strategies are inappropriate. When objectives other than learning facts, rules, and behavior sequences are desired, direct instruction strategies become clumsy, less efficient, and often far less effective than the inquiry or problem-solving strategies we will discuss in subsequent chapters. Teaching situations that need strategies other than direct instruction include (1) presenting complex material having objectives at the analysis, synthesis, and evaluation levels of the cognitive domain and (2) presenting content that must be learned gradually over a long period. Such material requires learner participation to heighten a commitment to the learning process and to create the intellectual framework necessary for learning concepts and recognizing patterns. You can attain this learner participation through carefully crafted classroom dialogue, which will be illustrated in Chapters 7 and 8.

Finally, when students are considerably above average in intelligence and achievement or are already well versed in the content, direct instruction strategies can be boring, inefficient, and ineffective forms of instruction.

AN EXAMPLE OF DIRECT INSTRUCTION

To see what direct instruction looks like in the classroom, consider the following dialogue in which the teacher begins a direct instruction lecture to teach the acquisition of facts, rules, and action sequences for forming and punctuating possessives. She begins with attention-getting examples of errors from the school newspaper. She opens by informing her students of the lesson's objective:

TEACHER: Today we will learn how to avoid embarrassing errors such as this when forming and punctuating possessives (circles an incorrectly punctuated possessive in a newspaper headline). At the end of the period I will give each of you several additional examples of errors taken from my collection of mistakes found in other newspapers and magazines. I'll ask you to make the proper corrections and report your changes to the class. Who knows what a possessive is?

BOBBY: It means you own something.

TEACHER: Yes, a possessive is a way of indicating ownership. It comes from the word *possession,* which means "*something owned*" or "*something possessed.*"

Forming possessives and punctuating them correctly can be difficult, as this newspaper example shows (points to paper again). Today I will give you two simple rules that will help you form possessives correctly.

But first, to show ownership or possession, we must know who or what is doing the possessing. Mary, can you recall the parts of speech from last week's lesson? (Mary hesitates, then nods.) What part of speech is most likely to own or possess something?

MARY: Well, umm ... I think ... I think a noun can own something.

TEACHER: Yes. A noun can own something. What is an example of a noun that owns something? Tommy.

TOMMY: I don't know.

TEACHER: Debbie.

DEBBIE: Not sure.

TEACHER: Ricky.

RICKY: A student can own a pencil. The word *student* is a noun.

TEACHER: Good. And who can remember our definition for a noun?

JIM: It's a person, place, or thing.

TEACHER: Good. Our first rule is: Use the possessive form whenever an *of* phrase can be substituted for a noun (teacher points to this rule written on board). Let's look at some phrases on the board to see when to apply this rule. Johnny, what does the first one say?

JOHNNY: The daughter of the policeman.

TEACHER: How else could we express the same idea of ownership?

MARY: We could say "the policeman's daughter."

TEACHER: And, we could say "the policeman's daughter" because I can substitute a phrase starting with *of* and ending with policeman for the noun *policeman*. Notice how easily I could switch the placement of *policeman* and *daughter* by using the connective word *of*. Whenever this can be done you can form a possessive by adding an *apostrophe s* to the noun following *of*.

Now we have the phrase (writes on board) *policeman's daughter* (points to the apostrophe). Betty, what about our next example, *holiday of three days* (pointing to board)?

BETTY: We could say "three days' holiday."

TEACHER: Come up and write that on the board just the way it should be printed in the school paper. (Mary writes *three day's holiday*.)

Would anyone want to change anything?

SUSAN: I'm not sure but I think I would put the apostrophe after the *s* in days.

TEACHER: You're right, which leads to our second rule: If the word for which we are denoting ownership already ends in an *s*, place the apostrophe after the *s*, not before it. This is an important rule to remember, because it accounts for many of the mistakes that are made in forming possessives. As I write this rule on the board, copy down these two rules for use later.

(Finishes writing second rule on board.) Now let's take a moment to convert each of the phrases on the overhead to the possessive form. Write down your answer to the first one. When I see all heads up again I will write the correct answer.

(All heads are up.) Good. Now watch how I change this first one to the possessive form; pay particular attention to where I place the apostrophe, then check your answer with mine. (Converts *delay of a month* to *month's delay*.) Any problems? (Pauses for any response.) OK, do the next one. (After all heads are up, teacher converts *home of Jenkins* to *Jenkins' home*.)

Any problems? (Johnny looks distressed.)

TEACHER: Johnny, what did you write?

JOHNNY: *J-E-N-K-I-N apostrophe S*.

TEACHER: What is the man's name, Johnny?

JOHNNY: Jenkins.

TEACHER: Look at what you wrote for the second rule. What does it say?

JOHNNY: Add the apostrophe after the *s* when the word already ends in an *s*. Oh, I get it. His name already has the *s*, so it would be *s apostrophe*. That's the mistake you showed us in the headline, isn't it?

TEACHER: Now you've got it. Let's continue. (Proceeds with the following in the same manner: *speech of the President* to *President's speech*, *the television set of Mr. Burns* to *Mr. Burns' television set*, *pastimes of boys* to *boys' pastimes*.)

Now open your workbooks to the exercise on page 87.

Starting with the first row, let's go around the room and hear your possessives for each of the sentences listed. Spell aloud the word indicating ownership, so we can tell if you've placed the apostrophe in the right place. Debbie ... (looking at "wings of geese")

DEBBIE: geeses wings ... spelled *W-I-N-G-S apostrophe*.

TEACHER: That's not correct. What word is doing the possessing?

DEBBIE: The geese, so it must be *G-E-E-S-E apostrophe S*.

TEACHER: Good. Next.

Now, let's look at our six direct instruction functions in Table 6.2 as they relate to the preceding dialogue.

DAILY REVIEW AND CHECKING THE PREVIOUS DAY'S WORK

This is the first ingredient in direct instruction (Table 6.2). Daily review and checking emphasizes the relationship between lessons so that students remember previous knowledge and see new knowledge as a logical extension of content already mastered. Notice that early in the example lesson the definition of a noun was brought into the presentation. This provided review of task-relevant prior knowledge needed for the day's lesson.

It also provided students with a sense of wholeness and continuity, assuring them that what was to follow was not a bit of isolated knowledge unrelated to past lessons. This is particularly important for securing the engagement of less-able students who often do not have appropriate levels of task-relevant prior knowledge or who may be overly anxious about having to master yet another piece of unfamiliar content.

Review and checking at the beginning of a lesson also is the most efficient and timely way of finding out if your students have mastered task-relevant prior knowledge sufficiently to begin a new lesson; if not, the missing content can be retaught.

You might think that beginning a lesson by checking previously learned task-relevant knowledge is a common practice. Yet, Good and Grouws (1979) found

A major purpose of daily review and checking is to emphasize the relationship between lessons and to provide students with a sense of wholeness and continuity, assuring them that what is to follow is a logical extension of content already mastered.

that only 50% of experienced teachers began a lesson in this fashion. This is unfortunate, because daily review and checking at the beginning of a lesson is easy to accomplish:

1. Have students correct each other's homework at the beginning of class.
2. Have students identify especially difficult homework problems in a question-and-answer format.
3. Sample the understanding of a few students who probably are good indicators of the range of knowledge possessed by the entire class.
4. Explicitly review the task-relevant information that is necessary for the day's lesson.

Dahllof and Lundgren (1970) have proposed the use of a *steering group* of low achievers as a particularly effective way of determining the extent to which review and reteaching may be needed. A somewhat expanded notion of the steering group is a small number of low, average, and high performers who can be queried at the start of class on the task-relevant prior knowledge needed for the day's lesson. When high performers miss a large proportion of answers, this warns you that extensive reteaching for the entire class is necessary. When high performers answer questions correctly but average performers do not, some reteaching should be undertaken before the start of the lesson. And, finally, if most of the high and average performers answer the questions correctly but most of the low performers do not, then you need to use individualized materials, extra reading and worksheets, or a tutorial arrangement for low performers. This ensures that large amounts of class time are not devoted to review and reteaching that may benefit only a small number of students.

Such strategies for daily review and checking, especially when used with a carefully selected steering group, are indispensable for warning you that previous instruction was over the heads of some or most of your students and, therefore, that additional review and reteaching is necessary.

PRESENTING AND STRUCTURING

Presenting new content is the second step in the direct instruction model (Table 6.2). One of the primary ingredients of the model is presenting material in small steps. Recall from Chapter 5 that lessons must be served up in small portions that are consistent with the previous knowledge, ability level, and interests of your students. Likewise, the content *within* the lessons must be partitioned and subdivided to organize it into small bits. No portion can be too large; if it is, you will lose your students' attention, which may lead to disruptive or distracting behaviors.

The key is to focus the material on one idea at a time and to present it so that one point is mastered before the next point is introduced. This is most easily accomplished by dividing a lesson into easily recognizable subparts, rules, or categories. It is no coincidence that the strategy of "divide and conquer" is as appropriate in the classroom as in military battles. Just like any great warrior, you can derive much benefit from it.

Remember that the subdivisions you use can be your own; they need not always follow those provided by the text, workbook, or curriculum guide. There is an important difference between content divisions used in books and content divisions needed in teaching: Content divisions in texts, workbooks, and curriculum guides generally are created for the purpose of communicating *content intended to be read,* not for the purpose of presenting *content that must be explained orally* to learners within the time frame of a specific lesson. Consequently, published divisions like chapter titles, subheadings, or Roman numerals in outlines sometimes are too broad to form bite-sized pieces that students can easily digest within a single lesson.

Unfortunately, many beginning teachers stick tenaciously to these formal headings without realizing either the volume of content that falls within them or the time it takes to orally explain, illustrate, and practice this content. The truth is that you are not discarding content by creating new organizational divisions; you only are breaking content into smaller steps suitable for presentation in a single period. You can create your own subdivisions consisting of rules ("here are some rules to fol-low"), steps ("we will do this, then that"), or practices ("here is the first of five things we will cover"). These subdivisions preorganize your instruction into bite-sized pieces and, most importantly, communicate this organization to your students.

In Chapter 3 several *learning structures* were provided for organizing con-tent in ways that are meaningful to students. Following is an elaboration of four additional ways of organizing content that are particularly relevant to direct instruc-tion. These are the part-whole, sequential, combinatorial, and comparative methods.

Part-Whole Relationships

A part-whole organizational format introduces the topic in its most general form ("What is a possessive?") and then divides the topic into easy-to-distinguish subdivi-sions ("Rule 1," "Rule 2"). This creates subdivisions that are easily digested and presents them in ways that always relate back to the whole. Students should always be aware of the part being covered at any particular time ("This is Rule 2") and its relationship to the whole ("This leads to our second rule for denoting ownership.") Use verbal markers to alert students that a transition is underway ("This is Rule 1," "Here is the first part," "This is the last example of this type; now let's move to the next type").

This type of organization creates bite-sized chunks; it helps students organize and see what is being taught and informs them of what portion they are on. Part-whole organization is illustrated in Figure 6.2a.

Sequential Relationships

Another way of structuring content is by sequential ordering; you teach the content according to the way in which the facts, rules, or sequences to be learned occur in the real world. Students may already have a feel for sequential ordering from practical experience.

In algebra, for example, equations are solved by first multiplying, then di-viding, then adding, and finally subtracting. This order of operations must occur for

FIGURE 6.2a
Structuring a lesson by
identifying part-whole
relationships

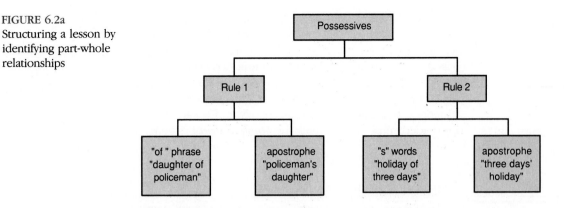

FIGURE 6.2a
Structuring a lesson by
identifying part-whole
relationships

any solution to be correct. A sequentially structured lesson, therefore, might introduce the manipulation of signed numbers in the order multiplication-division-addition-subtraction, which reinforces the way equations must actually be solved. In other words, all examples used in teaching signed-number multiplication would be completed before any examples about division would be introduced, thereby teaching the correct sequence as well as the intended content. Sequential ordering is illustrated in Figure 6.2b.

Combinatorial Relationships

A third way you can structure lesson content is to bring together in a single format various elements or dimensions that influence the use of facts, rules, and sequences. This allows an overall framework to direct the order of content by showing the logic of some combinations of facts, rules, and sequences and the illogic of other combinations.

FIGURE 6.2b
Structuring a lesson by
identifying sequential
relationships

$$y = a - b + \frac{cd}{e}$$

1. First, let's
   determine cd
   when

   $c = -1, \ d = 2$

   $c = 0, \ d = -4$

   $c = 2, \ d = -3$

3. Now, let's
   determine $b + \frac{cd}{e}$
   when

   $b = 1, \ \frac{cd}{e} = 1$

   $b = -3, \ \frac{cd}{e} = 0$

   $b = 2, \ \frac{cd}{e} = -1.5$

2. Next, let's
   determine $\frac{cd}{e}$
   when

   $cd = -2, \ e = -2$

   $cd = 0, \ e = 1$

   $cd = -6, \ e = 4$

4. Finally, let's
   determine $a - b + \frac{cd}{e}$
   when

   $a = 10, \ b + \frac{cd}{e} = 2$

   $a = 7, \ b + \frac{cd}{e} = -3$

   $a = 5, \ b + \frac{cd}{e} = .5$

For example, in teaching a direct instruction lesson in social studies, you might develop a scheme to reveal the relationship between marketable products and the various means of transporting them to market. You could draw an organizational chart (Figure 6.2c) to structure the content. You could show the chart to your students, and then teach all the relevant facts (e.g., relative weights of products), rules (the heavier the product, the more efficient the transportation system must be), and action sequences (first analyze the product's size and weight, then choose the best location). The shaded cells, then, identify the *combinations,* or dimensions of content, that are most relevant to the lesson objectives.

Comparative Relationships

In comparative structuring of content, you place different pieces of content side by side so that learners can compare and contrast them. Placing facts, rules, and sequences side by side across two or more categories lets students observe their similarities and differences. For example, you might want to compare and contrast governmental aspects of the United States and England. You could order the instruction according to the format in Figure 6.2d. Then you could teach the relevant facts (economic systems), politics (type of government), and source of laws (U.S. Constitution vs. legal codes) by moving first across the chart and then down. The chart structures content in advance, and students can easily see the structure and content to be covered.

Using the Methods

Whether you use one structuring method or a combination to organize a lesson, remember to divide the content into bite-sized pieces. To the extent that these structuring techniques divide larger units of content into smaller and more meaningful units, they will have served an important purpose.

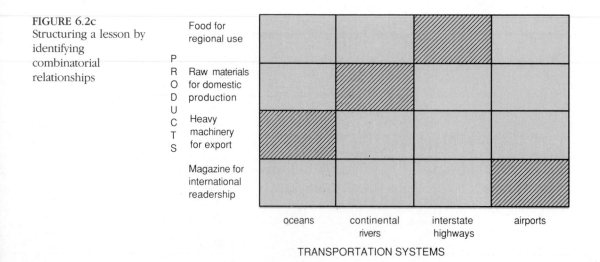

FIGURE 6.2c
Structuring a lesson by identifying combinatorial relationships

FIGURE 6.2d
Structuring a lesson by
identifying comparative
relationships

Points of Comparison	U.S.	England
Economics	capitalism	capitalism
Politics	representative democracy	parliamentary democracy
Source of laws	U.S. constitution	English legal codes
Representative body	congress	parliament

Finally, note how the teacher in our classroom dialogue combined rules and examples in organizing and presenting the content. She always presented the rule first and then followed with one or more examples. Note also that after some examples illustrating the rule, she repeated it—either by having students write the rule after seeing it on the board, or by having a student repeat it to the class. Learning a rule in one sensory modality (e.g., seeing it on the board) and then recreating it in a different sensory modality (e.g., writing or speaking it) generally promotes greater learning and retention than seeing the rule only once or reproducing it in the same modality in which it was learned.

Giving a rule, then an example of the rule, followed by repetition of the rule is called the rule-example-rule order. It generally is more effective than simply giving the rule and then an example (rule-example order), or giving an example followed by the rule (Hermann, 1971; Tomlinson & Hunt, 1971).

GUIDED STUDENT PRACTICE

This is the third step in the direct instruction model (Table 6.2). Recall from the structure of a lesson plan that presentation of stimulus material is followed by eliciting practice in the desired behavior. This section presents several ways of accomplishing this in the context of the direct instruction model. These elicitations are teacher guided, providing students with guided practice that you organize and direct.

Recall from Chapter 5 the important ingredients for eliciting a student response. One is to elicit the response in as nonevaluative an atmosphere as possible; this frees students to risk creating responses about which they may be unsure but from which they can begin to build a correct response. Any response, however crude or incorrect, can be the basis for learning if it is followed by proper feedback and correctives.

A second ingredient for eliciting a student response is the use of covert responses. This not only ensures a nonthreatening environment but also encourages student engagement in the learning task with the least expenditure of your time and effort. In the example, by having students privately write their responses before seeing the correct answers on the overhead, the teacher guided each student to formulate a response; it was not necessary to call on each of them. She guided the students into responding by encouraging, and later rewarding, their covert responses.

An equally important aspect of eliciting a desired response is to check for student understanding. When necessary, prompt to convert wrong answers to right ones. In the example, the teacher stopped after every item to see if there were problems, and prompted students to create correct answers when necessary. Prompting is an important part of eliciting the desired behavior, because it strengthens and builds the learners' confidence by encouraging them to use some aspects of the answer that have already been given in formulating the correct response (E. Gagné, 1985). In the example, Johnny was encouraged to *rethink* his response, to *focus* consciously on the specific part of the problem causing the error, and to *remember* the rule that will prevent such errors in the future.

You can check for understanding and prompt a correct response in several ways. The example showed one approach: all the students were asked to respond privately at the same time and then encouraged to ask for individual help ("Any problems?").

Another approach is to call on students whether or not their hands are raised, thereby seeking opportunities to prompt and correct wrong answers. One version of this is called *ordered turns,* in which you systematically go through the class and expect students to respond when their turn arrives. When groups are small, this approach is more effective in producing student achievement gains than randomly calling on students (Brophy & Evertson, 1976; Anderson, Evertson, & Brophy, 1982). But, generally, this method is less efficient than selecting students to respond during full-class instruction (Anderson et al., 1982).

Yet another approach is to have students write out answers to be checked and perhaps corrected by a classmate. Finally, you can develop questions beforehand to test for the most common errors. Check student responses for accuracy and prompt when necessary. This approach has the advantage of assuming that not everyone understands or has the correct answer when no responses are received. It has been found to be particularly effective in increasing student achievement (Singer & Donlon, 1982; McKenzie, 1979).

FEEDBACK AND CORRECTIVES

The next ingredient in the direct instruction model (Table 6.2) is provision of feedback and correctives. Simply put, you need strategies for handling right and wrong answers. Based upon several studies, Rosenshine (1983) identified four broad categories of student response: (1) correct, quick, and firm, (2) correct but hesitant, (3) incorrect due to carelessness, and (4) incorrect due to lack of knowledge. These are described in the following subsections, with some direct instruction strategies for handling them.

Correct, Quick, and Firm

The student response that teachers strive most to inspire is **correct, quick, and firm**. Such a response most frequently occurs during the latter stages of a lesson or unit, but it can occur almost anytime during a lesson or unit if you have divided the content into bite-sized portions. A moderate-to-high percentage of correct, quick, and firm responses is important if students are to become actively engaged in the learning process. Not every response from every student must be a correct one, but *for most learning that involves knowledge acquisition, make the steps between successive portions of your lesson small enough to produce approximately 60–80% correct answers in a practice and feedback session* (Bennett, Desforges, Cockburn, & Wilkinson, 1981; Brophy & Evertson, 1976).

This research suggests that your best response to a correct-quick-and-firm student response is to ask another question of the same student. This increases the potential for feedback or, if time does not permit, to move on quickly to another question and student. Keep the lesson moving quickly, involving as many students as possible in the practice exercise, and covering as many stimulus problems as possible. Once 60–80% right answers are produced, you will have created a rhythm and momentum that heightens student attention and engagement and provides for a high level of task orientation. The brisk pace of right answers also will help ensure that irrelevant student responses and classroom distractions are minimized.

Correct But Hesitant

The second student response is **correct but hesitant**. This type frequently occurs in a practice and feedback session at the beginning or middle of a lesson. Positive feedback to the student who supplies a correct-but-hesitant response is essential. The first feedback to provide in this instance is a positive, reinforcing statement, such as "good," or "that's correct," because the correct-but-hesitant response is more likely to be remembered when linked to a warm reply. This helps advance into the correct-quick-and-firm category the student's next response to the same type of problem.

Affirmative replies, however, seldom effect significant change on a subsequent problem of the same type unless the reasons behind the hesitant response are addressed. Although discovering the precise reason for a hesitant response is desirable, it takes time. A quick restatement of the facts, rules, or steps needed to obtain the right answer often accomplishes the same end more efficiently. This restatement not only aids the student who is giving the correct-but-hesitant response, but also helps reduce subsequent wrong answers or hesitant responses among other students who hear the restatement.

Incorrect Because of Carelessness

The third student response is **incorrect because of carelessness**. As many as 20% of student responses fall into this category, depending on the time of day and the students' level of fatigue and inattentiveness. When this occurs, and you feel that they really know the correct response, you may be tempted to scold, admonish, or even verbally punish students for responding thoughtlessly (e.g., "I'm ashamed of you," "That's a dumb mistake," "I thought you were brighter than that"). However, resist this temptation, no matter how justified it seems. Nothing is more frustrating than to repress genuine emotions, but researchers and experienced teachers agree that you do more harm than good if you react emotionally to this type of problem.

Verbal punishment rarely teaches students to avoid careless mistakes. Further, experience shows that the rhythm and momentum built and maintained through a brisk and lively pace can easily be broken by such off-task attention to an individual student. Emotional reaction rarely has a positive effect, so the best procedure is to acknowledge that the answer is wrong and to move immediately to the next student for the correct response. By doing so, you will make a point to the careless student that he or she lost the opportunity for a correct response and the praise that goes with it.

Incorrect Because of Lack of Knowledge

Perhaps the most challenging response is **incorrect because of a lack of knowledge**. Such errors typically occur, sometimes in large numbers, during the initial stages of a lesson or unit. It is better to provide hints, probe, or change the question or stimulus to a simpler one which engages the student in finding the correct response than to simply give the student the correct response. After all, the goal is not to get the correct answer from the student, but to *engage the learner in the process by which the right answer can be found*.

In the example, the teacher tried to focus Johnny on the *s* he had missed at the end of the proper noun *Jenkins* and to restate the rule concerning formation of possessives in words ending in *s*. Likewise, the teacher probed Debbie after her wrong answer by asking, "What word is doing the possessing?" Each of these instances led to the right answer without actually telling the student what the right answer was. When your strategy channels a student's thoughts to produce the right answer without actually giving it, you provide a framework for producing a correct response in all subsequent similar problems.

Strategies for Incorrect Responses

The most common strategies for incorrect responses are:

1. Reviewing key facts or rules needed for a correct solution.
2. Explaining the steps used to reach a correct solution.
3. Prompting with clues or hints representing a partially correct answer.
4. Taking a different but similar problem and guiding the student to the correct answer.

Such strategies used with one student benefit all the rest by clarifying information that they may have learned only partially. Because this type of corrective feedback is used with individual students, its effects on the entire class will be evidenced by an increasing percentage of correct responses. Reviewing, reexplaining, and prompting is effective until approximately 80% of the students respond correctly. After that point, make the correctives briefer, eventually guiding students who are making incorrect responses to helpful exercises in the text or to remedial exercises (Bennett et al., 1981).

Finally, note that when using the direct instruction model for teaching facts, rules, and sequences, an incorrect answer must never go undetected or uncorrected. Respond to every wrong answer with one or more of the preceding strategies. Leaving an answer uncorrected due to inattentiveness or distraction signals students who do know the answer that paying attention, responding correctly, and mastering the subject are not to be taken seriously.

INDEPENDENT PRACTICE

The fifth ingredient in direct instruction is the opportunity for independent practice (Table 6.2). Once you have successfully elicited the behavior, provided feedback, and administered correctives, students need the opportunity to practice the behavior independently. Often this is the time when facts and rules come together to form action sequences. For example, learning to drive a car requires a knowledge of terminology (gear shift, ignition, accelerator) and rules (signaling, what to do at stoplights, parking on hills). But until the knowledge and rules are put together, meaningful learning cannot occur.

Independent practice provides the opportunity in a carefully controlled and organized environment to make a meaningful whole out of the bits and pieces. Facts and rules must come together under your guidance and example in ways that (1) force simultaneous consideration of all the individual units of a problem and (2) connect the units into a single harmonious sequence of action. Learning theorists call these two processes **unitization** and **automaticity** (La Berge & Samuels, 1974).

Notice the manner in which these two processes were required in the example lesson. The individual "units" were the definition of a possessive (a fact) and two statements about forming possessives (Rules 1 and 2). The lesson connected these units into a single harmonious sequence of action in two ways. First was the exercise with which the example ends, in which the teacher directed students to a workbook to provide independent practice opportunity. The workbook sentences should contain possessives similar to those found in any newspaper, magazine, or school essay. Second was the teacher's intention to provide examples of real mistakes occurring in newspapers and magazines for additional practice at the end of the lesson. Table 6.3 traces the steps a student might take in combining the facts and rules into an action sequence for one sentence in the workbook.

In the preceding direct instruction dialogue, we saw that the meaningful *application* of knowledge requires knowledge that is highly familiar to the learner and rich in examples and associations (e.g, month's delay, Jenkins' home) learned from detailed and redundant practice. In this sense, less complex levels of behavior

TABLE 6.3
Steps involved in translating the sentence, "In Mrs. Jones paper there was an article about a friend of Robert" into correct possessive form

Step 1	Is ownership indicated in this sentence?
Step 2	If yes, where?
	the paper belongs to Mrs. Jones
	the friend belongs to Robert
Step 3	Has an *of* phrase been substituted for a noun (Rule 1)?
	If yes, where?
	friend of Robert has been substituted for Robert's friend
Step 4	Does any word denoting ownership end in *s*? (Rule 2)
	If yes, where?
	Jones paper should be written *Jones' paper*
Step 5	Therefore, the correct possessive form of this sentence is
	"In Mrs. Jones' paper there was an article about Robert's friend."

almost always are required for more complex forms of learning to occur. It is important that facts and rules not be left dangling but be practiced with detailed and redundant examples that create more complex forms of learning, such as action sequences.

Examples of errors from newspapers and magazines provided students an opportunity to form action sequences from the facts and rules they learned. These real-life examples further increased the meaningfulness of what was being learned. In your own classroom, make opportunities for practice increasingly resemble applications in the real world until the examples you provide are indistinguishable from those outside the classroom. Using clippings from actual newspapers and magazines was this teacher's way of doing so.

The purpose of providing opportunities for all types of independent practice is to develop automatic responses in students, so they no longer need to recall each individual unit of content but can use all the units simultaneously. Thus, the goal of the example lesson is "to write a sentence using possessives correctly," and not "to use Rule 1 and Rule 2." As we have seen, "automaticity" is reached through mastery of the units comprising a complete response and sufficient practice in composing these pieces into a complete action sequence. Your goal is to schedule sufficient opportunities for independent practice to allow individual responses to become "composed" and automatic (Samuels, 1981).

To ensure that students become actively engaged in the seatwork you provide, here are some recommendations:

1. Direct the class through the first independent practice item. This gives the scheduled seatwork a definite beginning, and students who are unclear about the assignment can ask questions without distracting others. This also provides a mental model for attaining a correct answer, which students can use in subsequent problems.

2. Schedule seatwork as soon as possible after the eliciting and feedback exercises. This helps students understand that independent practice is relevant to the guided practice provided earlier. If opportunities for independent practice are not provided immediately but on a later day, there likely will be a high number of requests for information; this will lead you inefficiently to repeat key portions of the previous day's lesson. As with all forms of learning, *practice should follow the time of learning as soon as possible* for maximum recall and understanding.

3. Circulate around the classroom while students are engaged in independent practice, to provide feedback, ask questions, and give brief explanations (Fisher et al., 1978). Spend circulation time equally across most of your students—don't concentrate on a small number of them. Try to average 30 seconds or less per student (if you average 30 seconds per student, and have 30 students, that consumes 15 minutes of class time). Minimize your scanning of written responses, prompting for alternative answers, or reminding students of facts and rules so as not to reduce your time available for monitoring the work of other students (Fisher et al., 1978; Scott and Bushell, 1974). Monitoring student responses during independent seatwork can be an important direct instruction function if you keep contacts short and focused upon specific issues for which a brief explanation is adequate.

WEEKLY AND MONTHLY REVIEWS

The sixth and final direct instruction function involves conducting weekly and monthly reviews (Table 6.2). Periodic review ensures that you have taught all task-relevant information needed for future lessons and that you have identified areas that require the reteaching of key facts, rules, and sequences. Without periodic review you have no way of knowing whether direct instruction has been successful in teaching the required facts, rules, and sequences.

Periodic review has long been a part of almost every instructional strategy. In the context of direct instruction, however, periodic review and the recycling of instruction take on added importance because of the brisk pace at which direct instruction is conducted. You usually establish the proper pace by noting the approximate percentage of errors occurring during guided practice and feedback; 60–80% correct responses indicates a satisfactory pace.

Weekly and monthly reviews also help determine whether the pace is right or whether to adjust it before too much content has been covered. When student responses in weekly and monthly reviews are correct, quick, and firm about 95% of the time, the pace is adequate (Bennett et al., 1981). Independent practice and homework should raise the percentage of correct responses from approximately 60–80% during guided practice and feedback to approximately 95% on weekly and monthly reviews. If results are below these levels—especially if they are substantially below—your pace

During independent practice, the teacher circulates around the classroom scanning written responses, prompting for alternative answers, and reminding students of necessary facts or rules, being careful to keep interchanges short so that the work of as many students as possible can be checked.

is too fast. Some recycling of facts, rules, and sequences is necessary, especially when they are prerequisites to later learning.

Another obvious advantage of weekly and monthly reviews is that they strengthen correct but hesitant responses. Reviewing facts, rules, and sequences that are the basis of task-relevant prior understandings for later lessons will give some learners a second chance to grasp material that they missed or only partially learned the first time around. These reviews often are welcomed by students; it is a chance to go over material that may have been missed, that was difficult to learn the first time through, and that may be covered on unit tests.

Finally, a regular weekly review (not a review every so often) is the key to performing this direct instruction function. The weekly review is intended to build momentum. Momentum results from gradually increasing the coverage and depth of the weekly reviews until it is time for a comprehensive monthly review (Posner, 1987). The objective is to create a review cycle that rises and falls in about a month. The low point of this cycle occurs at the start of a direct instruction unit, when only one week's material need be reviewed. The weekly reviews then become increasingly comprehensive until a major monthly review restates and checks for understanding all the previous month's learning. Momentum is built by targeting greater and greater amounts of instruction for review. This is done in gradual stages so that students are not overwhelmed with unfamiliar review content and so they always know what will be covered in the next review.

Table 6.4 presents the lesson plan for direct instruction based on the dialogue about possessives presented in this chapter.

OTHER FORMS OF DIRECT INSTRUCTION

So far direct instruction has been discussed as though it occurs only in a lecture format. This is perhaps the most popular format for direct instruction, but by no means the only one. Other ways of executing the direct instruction model (either independent of the lecture format or in association with it) include programmed instruction, computer-assisted instruction, peer and cross-age tutoring, various kinds of audiolingual devices (such as "speaking machines" for learning to read in the early grades), and single-concept films.

Some of these approaches have been creatively programmed to include all, or almost all, of the six direct instruction functions (daily review, new content, guided practice, feedback and correctives, independent practice, and periodic review). There is little question that some of these alternatives to lecture have been successful with certain types of content and with certain types of students (Slavin, Leavey, & Madden, 1982). However, because they are much less under your control than is the lecture format you create, you should carefully consider their applicability to your specific instructional goals and students. Although programmed texts, computer-assisted instructional software, and various drill and practice media often are associated with the direct instruction model, their treatment of the intended content may be far from direct. Therefore, whenever using these formats and associated "courseware," preview both method and content for close adherence to the six functions of the direct instruction model.

Finally, note that programmed texts, computer-assisted instruction software, specialized media, and audiolingual devices follow a direct instruction model most closely when they are programmed for remedial learning. This is where the direct instruction format is most effective in increasing student achievement (Slavin, 1980). At the same time, it can relieve you of the sometimes arduous chore of providing individualized remedial instruction to a small number of students. Building a library of remedial courseware is necessary in classes with less-able learners who can be served part of the time through individualized remedial instruction.

TABLE 6.4
Lesson Plan: Direct
Instruction

Unit Title: Punctuation
Lesson Title: Forming and punctuating possessives

1. Gaining attention	Display October school newspaper with punctuation error in headline. Point to error.
2. Informing the learner of the objective	At the end of the period students will be able to find mistakes in the newspapers (on file under "Punctuation") and make the necessary changes.
3. Stimulating recall of prerequisite learning	Review part of speech most likely to own or possess something by asking for the definition of a noun.
4. Presenting the stimulus material	Present two rules of possession: Rule 1. Use the possessive form whenever an *of* phrase can be substituted for a noun. Rule 2. For words ending in *s,* place the apostrophe after, not before, the *s.* Write rules on board.
5. Eliciting the desired behavior	Display the following examples on a transparency and ask students to convert them to the possessive form one at a time. On transparency: delay of a month home of Jenkins speech of the President the television set of Mr. Burns (See Smith, G. [1985]. *Understanding Grammar.* New York: City Press, pp. 101–103 for other examples.)
6 Providing feedback	Write the correct possessive form on the transparency as students finish each example. Wait for students to finish (all heads up) before providing the answer for the next example. Probe for complete understanding by asking for the rule.
7. Assessing the behavior	Use the exercise on page 87 of the workbook to assess student understanding and to provide additional practice. Use ordered recitation until about 90% correct responses are attained. Place 10 possessives on the unit test requiring the application of Rule 1 and Rule 2. Use examples in Smith (1985), pp. 101–103.

A FINAL WORD

This chapter has emphasized some of the direct, or more didactic, functions of teaching. As you have seen, these functions are particularly useful for teaching facts, rules, and action sequences, which tend to correspond to objectives at lower levels of behavioral complexity. When used in the proper sequence and with the behavioral objectives for which they are best suited, direct teaching functions can make teaching easier, more efficient, and more effective.

The next chapter discusses another and equally valuable model of instruction, emphasizing still other teaching strategies. This model not only complements a menu of direct instructional strategies with other varieties of instruction, but also is an approach that enables you to move your teaching to higher levels of behavioral complexity. As noted in Chapter 5, behaviors at these higher levels should comprise a significant portion of the outcomes planned at the unit level. Because these behaviors are among those most frequently required outside of the classroom, techniques through which your students can acquire them are indispensable additions to your teaching strategy menu.

SUMMING UP

This chapter introduced you to direct instruction strategies. Its main points were:

1. Two broad classifications of learning are facts, rules, and action sequences (Type 1) and concepts, patterns, and abstractions (Type 2).
2. Type 1 outcomes generally represent behaviors at the lower levels of complexity in the cognitive, affective, and psychomotor domains; Type 2 outcomes frequently represent behaviors at the higher levels of complexity in these domains.
3. Type 1 teaching activities require combining facts and rules at the knowledge and comprehension level into a sequence of actions that can be learned through observation, rote repetition, and practice. Type 1 outcomes have "right answers" that can be learned by memorization and practice.
4. Type 2 teaching activities go beyond facts, rules, and sequences to help the learner create, synthesize, identify, and recognize an answer that cannot be easily modeled or memorized. Type 2 outcomes may have many "right answers" that contain criterial attributes forming a concept or pattern.
5. The learning of facts, rules, and action sequences are most commonly taught with teaching strategies that emphasize knowledge acquisition; the learning of concepts, patterns, and abstractions are most commonly taught with teaching strategies that emphasize inquiry or problem solving.
6. The acquisition of facts, rules, and action sequences is most efficiently achieved through a process known as the *direct instruction model*. This model is primarily teacher-centered; facts, rules, and action sequences are passed on to students in a lecture format involving large amounts of teacher talk, questions and answers, review and practice, and the immediate correction of student errors.
7. The direct instruction model is characterized by full-class (as opposed to small-group) instruction; by the organization of learning based on questions posed by you; by the provision of detailed and redundant practice; by the presentation of material so that one new fact, rule, or sequence is mastered before the next is presented; and by the formal arrangement of the classroom to maximize drill and practice.
8. Direct instruction is most appropriate when content in texts and workbooks does not appear in appropriately sized pieces, when your active involvement in the teaching process is necessary to

arouse or heighten student interest, and when the content to be taught represents task-relevant prior knowledge for subsequent learning.

9. Some techniques for daily review and checking include:
   □ Have students identify difficult homework problems in a question-and-answer format.
   □ Sample the understanding of a few students who are likely to represent the class.
   □ Explicitly review task-relevant prior learning required for the day's lesson.

10. Some techniques for presenting and structuring new content include:
   □ Establish part-whole relationships.
   □ Identify sequential relationships.
   □ Find combinatorial relationships.
   □ Draw comparative relationships.

11. Some techniques for guiding student practice include:
   □ Ask students to respond privately and then be singled out for help.
   □ Call upon students to respond whether or not their hands are raised.
   □ Prepare questions beforehand and randomly ask students to respond.

12. Providing appropriate feedback and correctives involves knowing how to respond to answers that are (a) correct, quick, and firm, (b) correct but hesitant, (c) incorrect but careless, and (d) incorrect due to lack of knowledge.

13. For a correct, quick, and firm response, acknowledge the correct response and either ask another question of the same student or quickly move on to another student.

14. For a correct but hesitant response, provide a reinforcing statement and quickly restate the facts, rules, or steps needed for the right answer.

15. For a correct but careless response, indicate that the response is incorrect and quickly move to the next student without further comment.

16. For an incorrect response that is not due to carelessness but to a lack of knowledge, engage the student in finding the correct response with hints, probes, or a related but simpler question.

17. For most learning involving knowledge acquisition, the steps between successive portions of your lesson should be made small enough to produce approximately 60–80% correct answers in a practice and feedback session.

18. Reviewing, reexplaining, and prompting is effective until approximately 80% of your students respond correctly, after which correctives should be made briefer or students should be guided to individualized learning materials.

19. Design independent practice so that the learner puts together facts and rules to form action sequences that increasingly resemble applications in the real world. Make opportunities for independent practice as soon after the time of learning as possible.

20. Pace instruction so that student responses to questions posed in weekly and monthly reviews are correct, quick, and firm about 95% of the time.

21. Use independent practice and homework to raise the percentage of correct responses from approximately 60–80% during guided practice and feedback to approximately 95% on weekly and monthly reviews.

22. Other forms of direct instruction may include programmed texts, computer-assisted instruction software, peer and cross-age tutoring, audiolingual devices, and specialized media, such as single-concept films.

FOR DISCUSSION AND PRACTICE

*1. Identify the learning outcomes associated with Type 1 and Type 2 teaching strategies. To what levels of behavior in the cognitive domain does each type of learning apply?

*2. What type of learning outcomes are most commonly produced by instructional strategies that emphasize knowledge acquisition? What type of learning outcomes are most commonly produced by instructional strategies that emphasize inquiry or problem solving?

*3. Describe five instructional characteristics that define the direct instruction model.

*4. Give examples of action verbs that describe the type of outcomes expected by using the direct instruction model. Provide three examples each in the cognitive, affective, and psychomotor domains.

*5. Identify three areas of content in your teaching field in which the use of the direct instruction model would be especially appropriate.

*6. Identify four techniques for reviewing and checking the previous day's work.

*7. Identify and provide one original example of each of the four techniques for structuring content and presenting it in bite-sized portions.

*8. Identify the order in which rules and examples of the rules should be given to promote the greatest amount of comprehension and retention of content. Provide a real-life example of such a sequence.

*9. Explain why providing guided student practice in a nonevaluative atmosphere is important for learning to occur.

*10. How is prompting used to provide guided student practice, and for what purpose is it used?

*11. Name four different types of student responses that vary in their correctness and describe how you would respond to each.

12. The following second-grade student responses were received by a teacher after asking the question, "What does 5 plus 3 equal?"

MARY: I think it's 8.
TOMMY: 9.
BOB: 53.
BETTY: 8.

Role-play an appropriate teacher response to each of the answers.

13. The following tenth-grade student responses were received by a teacher who asked, "What was one of the underlying reasons for the Civil War?"

TIM: The South wanted the land owned by the North.
ROBERT: Religious persecution.
KEN: Well, let me think . . . it had something to do with slavery.
TRACY: The economic dependency of the South on slavery.

Role-play an appropriate teacher response to each of these answers.

*14. Identify four different strategies for responding to an incorrect response and give a real-life example of each.

*15. What approximate percentage of correct answers should you work toward in a practice and feedback session? Identify how you would change your instructional approach if only 30% of your student responses were correct in a practice and feedback session.

*16. What is the primary purpose of independent practice? How should the exercises used for independent practice change as additional time for practice becomes available?

*17. Identify two recommendations for being more effective in monitoring student work while you circulate around the classroom during independent practice.

*18. Approximately what percentage of student responses during weekly and monthly review sessions should be correct, quick, and firm?

*19. Explain how a review cycle could be planned to rise and fall in one-month cycles.

*20. What caution might you observe in choosing programmed texts, computer-assisted software, films, and other special types of media to provide direct instruction?

---

*Answers to asterisked questions (*) in this and the other chapters are in Appendix B.

SUGGESTED READINGS

Bennett, D. (1982). Should teachers be expected to learn and use direct instruction? *Association for Supervision and Curriculum Development Update, 24*(4), 5.

A statement on some of the uses of direct instruction and when it is most likely to be effective.

Berliner, D. (1982). Should teachers be expected to learn and use direct instruction? *Association for*

Supervision and Curriculum Development Update, 24(4), 5.

A critical statement on when and where direct instruction is most applicable.

Brophy, J. (1982). Successful teaching strategies for the inner-city child. *Phi Delta Kappan, 63,* 527–530.

A case for direct instruction employing recent research results confirming its positive effects on the achievement of inner-city students.

Fielding, G., Kameenui, E., & Gerstein, R. (1983). A comparison of an inquiry and a direct instruction approach to teaching legal concepts and applications to secondary school students. *Journal of Educational Research, 76,* 243–250.

A description of a research study investigating the pros and cons of the direct instruction model compared with an alternative approach (to be presented in Chapter 7).

Good, T., Grouws, D., & Ebmeier, H. (1983). *Active mathematics teaching.* New York: Longman.

An explanation of how best to apply direct instruction in mathematics.

Hunger, M., & Russel, D. (1981). Planning for effective instruction: Lesson design. In *Increasing your teaching effectiveness.* Palo Alto, CA: The Learning Institute.

A useful summary of how teachers can use the direct instruction model in preparing lesson plans.

Rosenshine, B. (1983). Teaching functions in instructional programs. *The Elementary School Journal, 83,* 335–351.

An oft-cited article that describes all of the functions of the direct instruction model as described in this chapter.

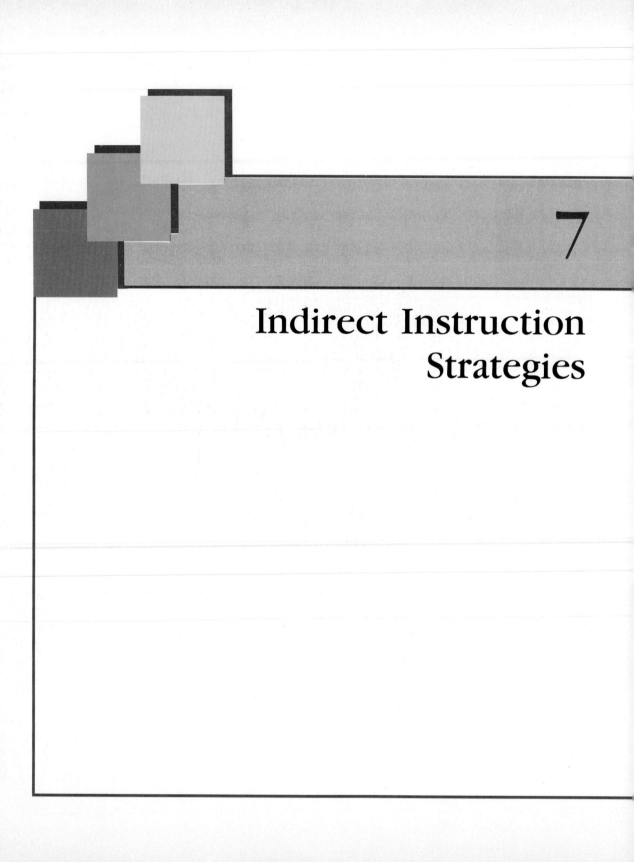

7

Indirect Instruction Strategies

The last chapter introduced you to direct instruction for teaching facts, rules, and action sequences. Now we will consider strategies of **indirect instruction** for teaching concepts, patterns, and abstractions. These behaviors most often are associated with the words *inquiry, problem solving,* or *discovery learning.*

Inquiry, problem solving, and discovery learning each are *different forms* of the more general concept of indirect instruction. Indirect instruction is an approach to teaching and learning in which:

> the learning process is *inquiry,*
>
> the result is *discovery,* and
>
> the learning context is a *problem.*

These three ideas—inquiry, discovery, and problem solving—are brought together in special ways in the indirect model of teaching and learning. This chapter presents instructional strategies you can use to compose your own indirect teaching approach. In subsequent chapters we expand upon these concepts to present other strategies, including self-directed and cooperative learning.

COMPARING DIRECT AND INDIRECT INSTRUCTION

Recall from the previous chapter the distinction between strategies for teaching facts, rules, and action sequences and strategies for teaching concepts, patterns, and abstractions (Table 6.1 summarized this). Because direct instruction strategies are best suited for the teaching of facts, rules, and action sequences, it should be no surprise to learn that indirect instruction strategies are best suited for teaching concepts, patterns, and abstractions.

When you present instructional stimuli to your learners in the form of content, materials, objects, and events and ask them to go beyond the information given to make conclusions and generalizations or find a pattern of relationships, you are using the indirect model of instruction. *Indirect* means that the learner acquires a behavior indirectly by transforming stimulus material into a response or behavior that differs from both (a) the stimulus used to present the learning and (b) any previous response given by the student. Because the learner can add to the stimulus material and rearrange it to be more meaningful, the elicited response or behavior can take many different forms. In contrast to direct instruction outcomes, there is rarely a single, best answer when the indirect model of instruction is used. Instead, the learner is guided to an answer that goes beyond the problem or stimulus material presented.

Indirect instruction is inefficient (even ineffective) for teaching many facts, rules, or action sequences because the desired response is almost identical to the learning stimulus. For example, rules for forming and punctuating possessives are most efficiently taught by giving students the rules and practice applying them, as was done in a previous example. In that example, knowledge acquisition and application were taught with a direct instruction strategy, because the stimulus material—written rules and examples—already contained the correct answers in desired form, and the purpose of the lesson was to apply the rules, not to discover them or to invent new ones.

You might wonder why, if direct instruction is so effective in these instances, it is not used all the time. The problem is that not all desired outcomes call for responses that resemble the stimulus material. Under the direct instruction model, very little conversion of, or change in, the stimulus material is required of the learner. Direct instruction is limited to (a) learning units of the stimulus material in some meaningful way so they can be remembered and (b) composing parts of the stimulus material into a whole, so a rapid and automatic response can occur. In the previous chapter these two cognitive processes were called *unitization* and *automaticity*.

Learning at the lower levels of the cognitive, affective, and psychomotor domains places heavy reliance on these two processes. Both can be placed efficiently into action by stimulus material that closely resembles the desired response (e.g., "Look at this word and then say it," "Watch me form a possessive and then you do the next one," "Read the instructions, then focus the microscope.") The desired response need not go much beyond what is provided. The task for the learner is simply to produce a response that mirrors the form and content of the stimulus. A great deal of instruction involves behavior that requires only unitization and automaticity. For this, the direct instruction model is most efficient and effective.

But not all learning is limited to the lower levels of behavioral complexity or requires only unitization and automaticity. In fact, if most lessons required only these two processes, students would not function successfully in subsequent grades or the world outside the classroom. This is because most jobs, responsibilities, and activities performed outside school require responses at higher levels of behavioral complexity.

Real-world activities often involve analysis, synthesis, and decision-making behaviors in the cognitive domain, organization and characterization behaviors in the affective domain, and articulation and naturalization behaviors in the psychomotor domain. This complicates instruction, because these behaviors are not learned in the same way as behaviors at lower levels of complexity. It is true that many lower-level behaviors are required to attain more complex behaviors, but much more is needed by both teacher and learners before these higher-level behaviors can be learned. As you will see in this chapter, the teaching of higher-level behaviors requires a different set of instructional strategies.

EXAMPLES OF CONCEPTS, PATTERNS, AND ABSTRACTIONS

Before describing the strategies that allow your learners to acquire these higher-level behaviors, let's consider some examples of topics that require complex behavior to master:

Concept of a quadratic equation (algebra).

Process of acculturation (social studies).

Meaning of *contact sports* (physical education).

Workings of a democracy (government).

Playing of a concerto (music).

Demonstration of photosynthesis (biology).

Understanding of the law of conservation of energy (general science).

Learning these topics requires not just facts, rules, and action sequences, but much more: *concepts, processes, meanings,* and *understandings*. If you teach just the facts, rules, and action sequences about quadratic equations—"Here is the *definition,*" "Here are the *rules* for solving them," or "Follow this *sequence* of steps"—your students may never learn the concept that binds together quadratic equations of different forms, or how to use these equations in a new or novel situation. Instead, your students must learn to add to, rearrange, and elaborate upon the stimulus material you present, using more-complex cognitive processes. Let's consider how this is done.

Recall from Table 6.1 the distinction between Type 1 and Type 2 behaviors. Type 1 behaviors become Type 2 behaviors by using facts, rules, and sequences to form concepts. Notice what would be required if students tried to learn the concept of a frog in the same way they acquired facts, rules, and action sequences about a frog.

First, they would have to commit to memory all possible instances of frogs (of which there may be hundreds). Trying to retain hundreds of frog images *in the same form they were presented* would quickly overburden their memories. Second, even after committing many types of frogs to memory, learners could confuse frogs with similar animals. This is because the memorization process does not include the characteristics that exclude other animals from being frogs (e.g., a hard shell, dry skin, color changes, tail).

The processes of generalization and discrimination, if planned for in the presentation of your lesson, can help students overcome both of these problems. *Generalization* helps them respond in a similar manner to stimuli that differ, thereby increasing the range of instances to which particular facts, rules, and sequences apply (e.g., to all types of frogs). In addition, *discrimination* selectively restricts this range by eliminating things that appear to match the student's concept (e.g., a chameleon) but that differ from it in critical dimensions (e.g., has a tail).

Generalization and discrimination help students classify visually different stimuli into the same category, based on *criterial attributes*. Criterial attributes act as magnets, drawing together all instances of the same type without requiring the learner to memorize (or even see) all possible instances. As a concept (frog) becomes combined with other concepts to form larger patterns (amphibians), patterns of increasing complexity are produced. Figure 7.1 shows a hierarchy of concepts, patterns, and abstractions typically found in a science curriculum.

It is apparent that both your role as teacher and your organization of stimulus material need to be different for the learning of concepts, patterns, and abstractions. For outcomes at higher levels of behavioral complexity, the stimulus material cannot contain all possible instances of the concept being learned. However, it must provide

FIGURE 7.1
A hierarchy of
abstraction representing
possible units of
instruction in a science
curriculum

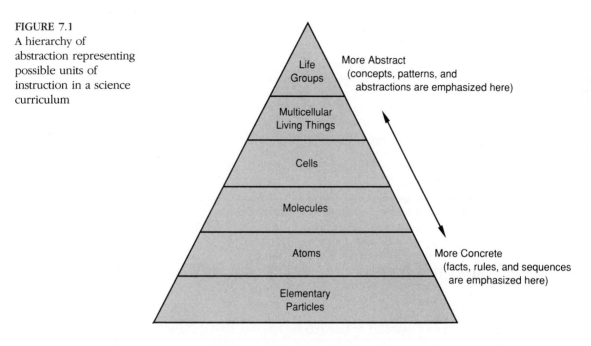

the appropriate associations or generalizations necessary to distinguish the most important dimensions—the criterial attributes—of the concept being learned. In this sense, there is less similarity between the stimulus material and the learner's written or oral response in the teaching of concepts, patterns, and abstractions than there is in the teaching of facts, rules, and action sequences.

The indirect instruction model uses instructional strategies that encourage the cognitive processes required to form concepts and to combine concepts into larger patterns and abstractions. Table 7.1 shows some of the functions performed by a teacher using the indirect instruction model.

You can see from Table 7.1 that indirect instruction is more complex than direct instruction in both teacher and student behavior. Classroom activities are less teacher centered. This brings student ideas and experiences into the lesson and lets students begin evaluating their own responses. Because the behaviors are more complex, so too are your teaching strategies. To build toward outcomes that may require either advance organization or inductive and/or deductive reasoning, extended forms of reasoning and questioning are required. A variety of examples and group discussions are used to accomplish this.

The indirect instruction functions in Table 7.1 and the teaching behaviors that comprise them are among the teaching functions having the highest correlation with positive student attitudes (Fielding, Kameenui, & Gerstein, 1983; Rosenshine, 1970b). These also are the teaching functions thought to be most useful in providing behaviors that students will use in their adult lives (Palincsar & Brown, 1989; Morine & Morine, 1973).

TABLE 7.1
Some indirect instruction functions

1. Provides a means of organizing content in advance
   Provides advance organizers and conceptual frameworks, which
      serve as "pegs" on which to hang key points that guide and channel thinking to the most
      productive areas
   Allows for concept expansion to higher levels of abstraction
2. Provides conceptual movement using inductive and deductive methods
   Focuses generalization to higher levels of abstraction by:
      Inductive methods (selected events used to establish concepts or patterns)
      Deductive methods (principles or generalizations applied to specific instances)
3. Uses examples and nonexamples:
   To define criterial attributes and promote accurate generalizations
   To gradually expand set of examples to reflect real world
   To enrich concept with noncriterial attributes
4. Uses questions to guide the search and discovery process
   Uses questions to: raise contradictions
                       probe for deeper level responses
                       extend the discussion
                       pass responsibility for learning to the individual learner.
5. Encourages students to use examples and references from their own experience, to seek clarification, and to
   draw parallels and associations that aid understanding and retention
   Relates ideas to past learning and to students' own sphere of interests, concerns, and problems
6. Allows students to evaluate the appropriateness of their own responses and then provides guidance as
   necessary
   Provides cues, questions, or hints as needed to call attention to inappropriate responses
7. Uses discussion to encourage critical thinking and help students to:
   Examine alternatives, judge solutions, make predictions, and discover generalizations
   Orient, provide new content, review and summarize, alter flow of information, and combine areas to
   promote the most productive discussion

AN EXAMPLE OF INDIRECT INSTRUCTION

Now let's examine a dialogue of indirect instruction and compare it to the dialogue of direct instruction in Chapter 6. The objective this time is Type 2 outcomes, not Type 1 outcomes. This dialogue reflects some facts, rules, and sequences that were taught previously, but the ultimate goal is the formation of concepts, patterns, and abstractions. This is a glimpse into a government class where a lesson on different economic systems is in progress. The teacher gets the students' attention by asking if anyone knows what system of government in the world is undergoing the most change. Marty raises his hand.

TEACHER: Marty.
MARTY: I think it's communism, because they've torn down the Berlin wall.
TEACHER: That's right. And because this change will probably affect all our lives in the years
         ahead, it may be a good idea to know what communism is and why those who live

under it want to change it. To get us started, let me ask if anyone knows where the phrase "government of the people, by the people, for the people" comes from. (Rena raises her hand.) Rena?

RENA: From Lincoln's Gettysburg Address...I think near the end.

TEACHER: That's right. Most nations have similar statements that express the basic principles on which their laws, customs, and economics are based. Today, we will study three systems by which nations can guide, control, and operate their economies. The three systems we will study are *capitalism, socialism,* and *communism.* They often are confused with the political systems that tend to be associated with them. A political system not only influences the economic system of a country but also guides individual behavior in many other areas, such as what is taught in schools, what the relationship is between church and state, how people get chosen for or elected to political office, what jobs people can have, and what newspapers can print.

For example, in the United States we have an economic system that is based on the principles of capitalism—or private ownership of capital—but a political system that is based on the principle of democracy—or rule by the people. These two sets of principles are not the same, and in the next few days you will see how they sometimes work in harmony and sometimes create contradictions that require changes in an economic system, like those occurring today in Eastern Europe.

Today we will cover only systems dealing with the ownership of goods and services in different countries—that is, just the economic systems. Later I will ask you to distinguish these from political systems. Who would like to start by telling us what the word *capitalism* means?

ROBERT: It means making money.

TEACHER: What else, Robert?

ROBERT: Owning land...I think.

TEACHER: Not only land, but...

ROBERT: Owning anything.

TEACHER: The word *capital* means tangible goods or possessions. Is a house tangible?

BETTY: Yes.

TEACHER: Is a friendship tangible?

BETTY: Yes.

TEACHER: What about that, Mark?

MARK: I don't think so.

TEACHER: Why?

MARK: You can't touch it.

TEACHER: Right. You can touch a person who is a friend but not the friendship. Besides, you can't own or possess a person....So, what would be a good definition of *tangible goods*?

BETTY: Something you own and can touch or see.

TEACHER: Not bad. Let me list some things on the board and you tell me whether they could be called capital. (Writes the list)

> car
> stocks and bonds
> religion
> information
> clothes
> vacation

OK. Who would like to say which of these are *capital?* (Ricky raises his hand.)

RICKY: Car and clothes are the only two I see.

BARBARA: I'd add stocks and bonds. They say you own a piece of something, although maybe not the whole thing.

TEACHER: Could you see or touch it?

BARBARA: Yes, if you went to see the place or thing you owned a part of.

TEACHER: Good. What about a vacation? Did that give anyone trouble?

MICKEY: Well, you can own it. . .I mean you pay for it, and you can see yourself having a good time. (The class laughs.)

TEACHER: That may be true, so let's add one last condition to our definition of capital. You must be able to own it, see or touch it, and it must be durable—or last for a reasonable period of time. So now, how would you define *capitalism?*

SUE: An economic system that allows you to have capital—or to own tangible goods that last for a reasonable period of time. And, I suppose, sell the goods, if you wanted.

TEACHER: Very good. Many different countries across the world have this form of economic system. Just to see if you've got the idea, who can name three countries, besides our own, that allow the ownership of tangible goods?

JOE: Japan, Germany, and Canada.

TEACHER: Good. In all these countries capital, in the form of tangible goods, can be owned by individuals.

            Now that we know a little about capitalism, let's look at another system by which a nation can manage its economy. Ralph, what does the word *socialism* mean to you?

RALPH: Well, it probably comes from the word *social.*

TEACHER: And what does the word *social* mean?

RALPH: People coming together, like at a party—or maybe a meeting.

TEACHER: And why do people usually come together at a party or a meeting?

RALPH: To have fun. (laughter)

TEACHER: And what about at a meeting?

RALPH: To conduct some business or make some decisions, maybe.

TEACHER: Yes, they come together for some common purpose and benefits. For example, they make decisions about the things they need to live and prosper. Does that sound like a basis for a kind of economic system? (no response from class) Suppose that a large number of individuals came together to decide what they needed to live and prosper? What types of things do you think they would consider?

BILLY: You mean like a car or a home of your own?

TEACHER: Yes, but let's say that the need for a car or a home of your own among individuals of the group is so very different that this group could never agree on the importance of these for everyone. What types of things could a group of people, say the size of a nation, agree on that would be absolutely essential for everyone's existence?

RONNIE: Food.

TEACHER: Good. What else?

BILLY: A hospital.

TEACHER: Very good.

SUE: Highways.

TEACHER: OK. Any others?

RICKY: If they couldn't agree on the importance of cars for everyone, then they would have to agree on some other form of transportation, like buses, trains, or planes.

TEACHER: Yes, they would, wouldn't they? These examples show one of the purposes of a *socialist* economic system—that is, to control and make available to everyone as many things as possible that (a) everyone values equally and (b) everyone needs for everyday existence.

SUE: You mean free, without paying?

TEACHER: Yes, or paying very little. In that way both rich and poor can use these services about equally.

SUE: But who pays?

TEACHER: Good question. Who pays for the services provided under a socialist system?

MARK: The government.

TEACHER: And who is the government?

MARK: Oh, I get it. The people pay taxes, just like us, and the government uses the taxes to provide the essential services.

SUE: So, how is that different from America?

TEACHER: Good question. Who can answer that one?

ROBERT: It's the same.

MARK: No, it's not. Our government doesn't own hospitals, farms, trains, and that kind of stuff.

TEACHER: Who owns Amtrak?

ROBERT: I think our government does.

TEACHER: It also, believe it or not, owns some hospitals; and at least some local governments, like ours, own their own bus lines. (The class looks bewildered.) So, if you looked at our country's economic system and compared it to that of a socialist country, you might not see such a big difference. But there *is* a difference. What might that difference be? Ralph, you began this discussion.

RALPH: I think it's a matter of degree. Almost all of the major things like hospitals and transportation systems that everyone needs are owned and run by the government under a socialist system, but only a few of these things are owned by the government in a capitalist system. On the other hand, there are things like highways, rivers, forests, and so on that are owned by the government under both systems.

TEACHER: And how would the amount of taxes you pay differ in these two systems?

RALPH: You'd pay more taxes under a socialist economy than under a capitalist economy, but some services would be free—or almost—in a socialist system. In a capitalist country like ours, we'd pay more for these services but we'd also have more money to spend for them after taxes.

TEACHER: That was a nice way of putting it. Now, what about our third economic system? What's a word similar to communism?

BILLY: Oh. . .*community?*

TEACHER: Yes. And who has ownership under communism?

ROBERT: The community.

TEACHER: . . .which is represented by?

ROBERT: The government.

TEACHER: Yes. Just a moment ago we discovered that much of the difference between capitalism and socialism, as economic systems, was a matter of degree. If this were also true of the difference between socialism and communism, how might you describe ownership under the communist economic system?

SUE: More is owned by the community—I mean by the government.

TEACHER: Ronnie, you mentioned food before. Do you think food—or the farms on which the food is grown—is owned by the government under communism?

RONNIE: I guess so. But, aren't they becoming more like us?

TEACHER: Yes, and that must mean . . . (nodding to Ronnie)

RONNIE: ... that it's harder or less efficient to grow food under the communist system.

TEACHER: So, you've given us one of the contradictions that may be making some countries that have a communist economic system to become more like us. Now, let's take some other examples. Billy, you mentioned hospitals; Sue, you mentioned highways; and Ricky, you mentioned planes. Who owns these in a communist economic system?

CLASS: The government.

TEACHER: OK. Now let's create a chart that shows some examples of things likely to be owned by the governments under all three of our economic systems, so that we can see them side by side and compare them. (Teacher writes chart on board)

Capitalism	*Socialism*	*Communism*
highways	highways	highways
rivers	rivers	rivers
forests	forests	forests
	hospitals	hospitals
	planes	planes
	buses	buses
	trains	trains
		food supply
		housing
		industries

Now, what kinds of things *don't* we find up here?

RICHARD: Personal things, like clothes, watches, and television sets.

TEACHER: Good. Ownership of these items cannot be used to distinguish economic systems. What can distinguish economic systems, however, is the *degree* to which the goods and services that affect large numbers of individuals are owned by the government: The most is owned by the government under communism, and the least is owned by the government under capitalism. As we have seen in the past few years the balance of goods and services owned by governments under communism is changing—with the responsibility for greater numbers of goods and services being turned over to individuals just like in our own economic system. Now, how do you think the amount of taxes paid by individuals living under these three systems would differ?

CLASS: Communism would have the highest, then socialism, then capitalism.

TEACHER: Good. And this is another point we will follow up. Tomorrow we will discuss other causes for some of the changes that have occurred in communism. Then we'll compare each of these three economic systems with the political systems that represent them. For tomorrow, look up in the encyclopedia the words *democracy* and *totalitarianism* and bring with you a one-page description of the major differences between these two political systems. Be prepared to know the differences between economic and political systems. Then, choose two countries that you think represent these different political systems, and we will discuss and study them further.

This dialogue illustrates one variation of the indirect model of instruction as it might be implemented in a high school government class. Table 7.1 summarizes some of the functions used in indirect instruction. Remembering these functions, consider the extent to which this example contains some of the key aspects of indirect instruction.

ADVANCE ORGANIZERS

Comparing the dialogues for direct and indirect instruction, what differences do you notice? Obviously they differ in length and complexity. This is not by chance, because teaching more complex behaviors takes more time and planning. The extensive planning needed for higher-order learning is one of the most overlooked aspects of indirect instruction. With more expansive and complex content, the lesson must be introduced with a framework or structure that organizes the content into meaningful parts *even before the content is presented*. This is the first element of planning for indirect instruction—organizing the content in advance (Table 7.1).

One way of providing this framework is to use advance organizers (Luiten, Ames, Aerson, 1980; Ausubel, 1968). An advance organizer gives learners a *conceptual preview* of what is to come and helps prepare them to store, label, and package the content for retention and later use. In a sense, an advance organizer is a treelike structure with main limbs that act as pegs, or place holders, for the branches that are yet to come. Without these limbs on which to hang content, important distinctions can easily become blurred or lost.

For example, the lesson dialogue began with an introduction about coverage of the day's lesson. To set the stage, the teacher introduced two abstractions (economic systems and political systems), each comprised of a complex network of concepts (taxes, ownership, goods, services, etc.). At the beginning of the lesson, he alerted students to the reason for drawing such an early distinction between a political and an economic system ("*capitalism, socialism,* and *communism* . . . often are confused with the political systems"; "Today we will cover only. . .*economic* systems. Later I will ask you to distinguish these from political systems.")

Note that the overall ideas for which students are responsible on homework assignments and in the following day's lesson require them to distinguish between these systems. The important role of advance organization was to channel or focus student thinking for today's lesson onto the economic system branch of the overall organizer, while putting in place another branch on which additional content (political systems) will soon be placed.

Advance organizers, especially at the higher levels of behavioral complexity, are rarely single words or phrases that enlighten students when merely uttered. Instead, they are concepts woven into the lesson fabric to provide an overview of the day's work *and all topics to which it will subsequently relate*. Advance organizers can be presented orally or as charts and diagrams. Here are examples of advance organizing activities provided at the beginning of a lesson:

- ☐ Showing a chart that illustrates the skeletal evolution of humans prior to explaining the skeletal relationships among forms of animal life (biology).
- ☐ Drawing examples of right, equilateral, and isosceles triangles before introducing the concept of a right triangle (plane geometry).
- ☐ Discussing origins of the Civil War before describing its major battles (American history).

☐ Describing what is meant by a *figure of speech* before introducing the concepts of *metaphor* and *simile* (English).

☐ Listening to examples of both vowels and consonants before teaching the vowel sounds (reading).

☐ Showing and explaining the origins of the periodic table of elements before introducing any of the individual elements (chemistry).

Notice that each of these examples presents a general concept into which fits the specific concept that is the subject of the day's lesson. This is not accomplished by reviewing earlier content, which often is confused with the idea of an advance organizer. Instead it is done by creating a conceptual structure—skeletal evolution, various triangular shapes, Civil War origins, figures of speech, the alphabet, an organized system of chemical elements—into which can be placed not only the content to be taught but also the content for related lessons.

Therefore, these advance organizers set the groundwork for focusing the lesson topic. They prevent every lesson from being seen as something entirely new. Finally, they integrate related concepts into larger and larger patterns and abstractions that later become unit outcomes (evolution of skeletal forms, triangular shapes, major battles of the Civil War, figures of speech). An advance organizer identifies the highest level of behavior resulting from a lesson sequence and to which the outcome of the present day's lesson will contribute. In the example, this higher-level outcome was to distinguish between economic and political systems, a distinction organized in advance by the teacher's introductory remarks.

Chapter 6 offered several suggestions for structuring content in ways particularly suited to direct instruction. You may recall that these were the part-whole, sequential, combinatorial, and comparative methods. This chapter adds several methods that are particularly suited for structuring content for indirect instruction. These methods are problem-centered, decision-making, and network approaches to organizing lesson content—and to composing advance organizers.

Problem-Centered

A problem-centered approach identifies and provides students in advance with all the steps required to solve a particular problem. This approach begins by observing a specific event and concludes with how or why it occurred. For example, you might begin a general science lesson by demonstrating that liquid cannot be removed through a straw from a tightly sealed bottle. The question, "Why does this happen?" establishes the problem. You then might give your students a problem-solving sequence like the one in Figure 7.2a. Such a chart and its sequence of events become the advance organizer for the lesson. Each of its steps provides an organizational branch for a particular part of the lesson.

Decision-Making

This same problem can also be organized hierarchically by showing the internal branching, or steps, that you must follow to arrive at a conclusion. While the

FIGURE 7.2a
Structuring a lesson
using a
problem-centered
approach

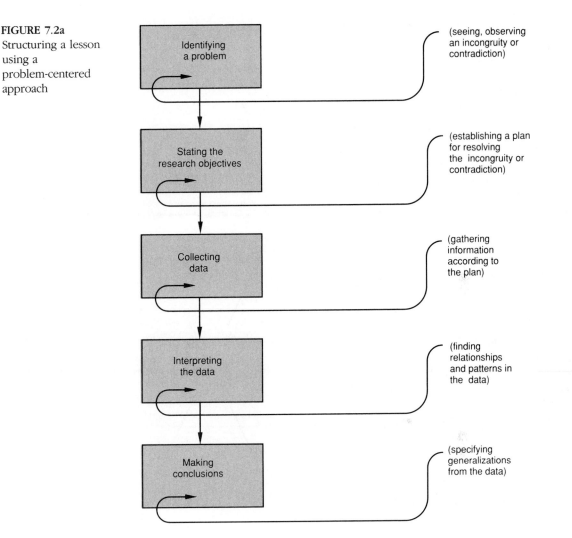

Identifying
a problem

(seeing, observing
an incongruity or
contradiction)

Stating the
research objectives

(establishing a plan
for resolving
the incongruity or
contradiction)

Collecting
data

(gathering
information
according to
the plan)

Interpreting
the data

(finding
relationships
and patterns in
the data)

Making
conclusions

(specifying
generalizations
from the data)

problem-centered approach establishes the steps to be followed, the decision-making approach focuses on *alternative paths* that might be followed—or decisions that must be made—in exploring and discovering new information about a topic.

Figure 7.2b shows how this can be applied to the science question posed in the preceding paragraph. Although the students don't know at what level of the hierarchy the experiment will end, they could be shown the entire list of possible alternatives. This form of advance organizer is a particularly effective attention-getter when you are asking students to contribute branches to the hierarchy and allowing them to trace the results of their inquiry as each decision point is reached (as indicated by the solid lines).

FIGURE 7.2b
Structuring a lesson
using a decision-making
approach

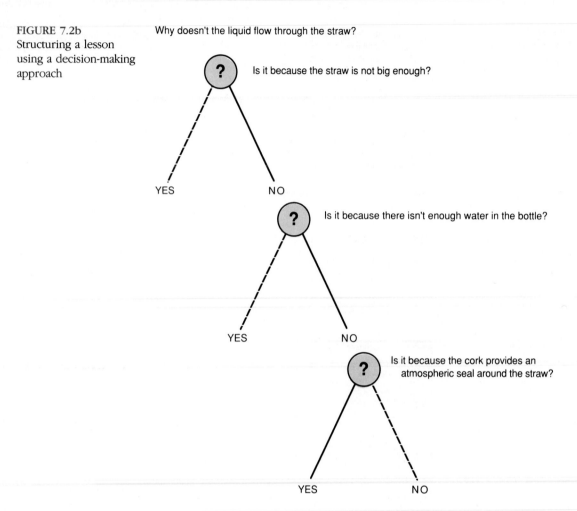

Networking

Networking is a third type of organization often helpful for organizing and communicating the structure of a lesson in advance. Networking illustrates relationships among the data, materials, objects, and events that students must consider to solve a problem. When different aspects of a problem are to be considered in relation to each other, as in Figure 7.2c, a picture of the network of relationships becomes the advance organizer. The triangular network in Figure 7.2c is particularly important to the goals of the example science lesson, because it is the *relationship among several events* that may provide the best solution to this problem.

Each of these structuring methods—problem-centered, decision-making, networking—is a useful advance organizer when you communicate it to students in advance and when you tie key steps, decisions, or relationships back to the advance organizer as they occur in the lesson. To the extent these structuring devices can

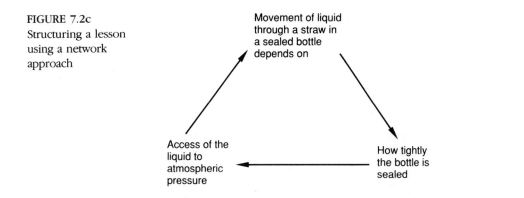

FIGURE 7.2c
Structuring a lesson
using a network
approach

provide the branches on which subsequent content can be placed, they serve a useful purpose as advance organizers. As we will see in Chapter 9, they also can become mental strategies by which students can learn similar subsequent content, independent of the teacher.

CONCEPTUAL MOVEMENT—INDUCTIVE AND DEDUCTIVE

This is the second element of planning for indirect instruction (Table 7.1). The words *inductive* and *deductive* refer to the way in which ideas flow. The following sections compare these methods.

Inductive Reasoning

Inductive reasoning is a thinking process used when a set of data is presented and students are asked to draw a conclusion, make a generalization, or develop a pattern of relationships from the data. It is a process in which students observe specific facts and then generalize them to other circumstances. Common sense tells us that much of our everyday thinking proceeds in this manner. For example:

1. We notice that rain-slick roads are causing accidents on the way to school, so we reduce speed at all subsequent intersections.
2. We get an unsatisfactory grade on a chemistry exam, so we study six extra hours a week for the rest of the semester in all our subjects.
3. We see a close friend suffer from the effects of drug abuse, so we volunteer to disseminate information about substance abuse to all our acquaintances.
4. We get a math teacher who is cold and unfriendly, so we decide never to enroll in a math course again.

What these instances have in common is that they started with a specific observation of a limited set of data and ended with a generalization in a much broader context. Between the beginning and end of each sequence was an interpretation of observed events and the projection of this interpretation to all similar circumstances. Simply put, when we think inductively we believe that what happens in one place (e.g., at this intersection), can happen wherever or whenever circumstances are similar (at all other rain-slick intersections).

Deductive Reasoning

Deductive reasoning, on the other hand, proceeds from principles or generalizations to their application in specific instances. Deductive thinking includes testing generalizations to see if they hold in specific cases. Typically, a laboratory experiment in the sciences (chemistry, physics, biology, psychology, mathematics, geology) follows the deductive method. In these fields the experimenter often begins with a theory or hypothesis about what should happen and then tests it with an experiment to see if it accurately predicts. If it does, the generalization with which the experiment began is true, at least under the conditions of the experiment. The steps frequently used in deductive thinking are:

1. Stating a theory or generalization to be tested.
2. Forming a hypothesis in the form of a prediction.
3. Observing or collecting data to test the hypothesis.
4. Analyzing and interpreting the data to determine if the prediction is true, at least some of the time.
5. Concluding whether or not the generalization held true in the specific context in which it was tested.

Deductive methods are familiar in everyday life. For example, consider the four examples of inductive thinking listed previously to see how much change is required for them to become examples of deductive thinking. Here are the examples again—this time illustrating deduction:

1. We believe that rain-slick roads are the prime contributor to traffic accidents at intersections. We make observations one rainy morning on the way to school and find that, indeed, more accidents have occurred at intersections than usual—our prediction that wet roads cause accidents at intersections is confirmed.
2. We believe that studying six extra hours a week will *not* substantially raise our grades. We study six extra hours and find that our grades have gone up—our prediction that extra studying will not influence our grades is *not* confirmed.
3. We believe that drug abuse can be detrimental to one's physical and emotional well being. We observe and find physical and emotional effects of drug abuse in everyone that has admitted to using them—our prediction that drug abuse and physical and emotional impairment are related has been confirmed.
4. We believe that we could never like a subject if it is taught by a cold and unfriendly teacher, regardless of how good we are in it. We think back and

Many forms of investigation and laboratory experiments follow the deductive method in which the student begins with a prediction about what should happen in a specific instance and then conducts an investigation to see if the prediction comes true.

remember that we had just such a teacher in high school, who taught math. We observe that we have always done everything possible to avoid a math course—our prediction that we could never like a subject taught by a cold and unfriendly teacher has been shown to be accurate.

These examples have in common the fact that they begin with a general statement of belief—a theory or hypothesis—and end with some conclusion based upon an observation that tested the truth of the initial statement. Of course, we could be wrong, even though in some instances the prediction *appeared* to be true (e.g., you might have no problem liking sports despite the fact that you once had a cold and unfriendly gym teacher). As you might expect, deductive logic has been most closely associated with the scientific method. In the social, behavioral, and physical sciences, it is known as the **hypothetico-deductive** method (Kaplan, 1964) to emphasize the close connection between forming hypotheses and making predictions deduced from general beliefs and theories.

Applying Induction and Deduction

Both induction and deduction are important methods for teaching concepts, patterns, and abstractions. One application for such teaching is to move into progressively deeper levels of subject complexity, using inductive and deductive methods and occasionally changing from one to the other:

> Greater levels of complexity are achieved using the *inductive* process when specific examples or events introduced earlier are later linked to other examples or events to create concepts and generalizations.

> Greater levels of complexity are achieved using the *deductive* process when generalizations and patterns introduced earlier in the lesson are later applied to specific instances, testing the adequacy of the generalizations.

In the earlier example of the government lesson about economic systems, consider how these two processes were employed. Using induction, the teacher built a definition of *tangible goods* beginning with a specific example: "Is a house tangible?" Notice how the examples increased not only in number, but also in abstraction (e.g., stocks and bonds). Also, he provided both examples and nonexamples to round out the definition of tangible goods in a capitalist system and to fine tune the concept. In other words, tangible goods could exist at different levels of abstraction, but some abstractions (e.g., friendships, vacation) could not qualify as tangible goods. This teacher skillfully used the inductive process, beginning with specific examples (making money and owning land) and increasingly broadening the examples to form a generalization (tangible goods that last for a reasonable length of time).

Also notice that a brief venture into deduction ended the teacher's introduction to capitalism. By asking students to name three countries that fit the concept of capitalism, he made them find specific instances that fit the general concept. He asked whether the general notion of ownership of tangible goods could be applied to the real world, and it could, of course, thereby testing the credibility of the more general statement.

Note that, although the concept of capitalism was understood by most students at the end of the first part of the lesson as "an economic system that allows the ownership of tangible goods that last," it was a rather crude interpretation that would fail many subsequent tests. For example, Soviet citizens own tangible goods that last a reasonable period of time (e.g., a wrist watch, a tie, a set of dinnerware). Recall that this crude version of the concept of capitalism emerged even after providing carefully planned examples and nonexamples. This means that the teacher's job was far from over at the end of the first part of the lesson. Further *conceptual movement* must be made to fine tune this concept, producing more accurate discriminations to be applied to the concept of capitalism.

This is precisely what occurs in subsequent portions of the lesson, in which the teacher can be seen moving students from the ownership of tangible goods as their working definition of an economic system to a definition that had the following five different elements:

TABLE 7.2
A comparison of steps in inductive versus deductive teaching

Teaching Inductively	Teaching Deductively
1. Teacher presents specific data from which a generalization is to be drawn.	1. Teacher introduces the generalization to be learned.
2. Each student is allowed uninterrupted time to observe or study the data that illustrates the generalization.	2. Teacher reviews the task-revelant prior facts, rules, and action sequences needed to form the generalization.
3. Students are shown additional examples and then nonexamples containing the generalization.	3. Students raise a question, pose an hypothesis, or make a prediction thought to be contained in the generalization.
4. Student attention is guided first to the criterial (relevant) aspects of the data containing the generalization and then to its noncriterial (irrelevant) aspects.	4. Data, events, materials, or objects are gathered and observed to test the prediction.
5. A generalization is made that can distinguish the examples from nonexamples.	5. Results of the test are analyzed and a conclusion is made as to whether the prediction is supported by the data, events, materials, or objects that were observed.
	6. The starting generalization is refined or revised in accordance with the observations.

1. The *degree* to which
2. goods and services
3. that all value
4. and see as essential for daily living
5. are owned by a government.

The teacher, using questions and examples, redefined the initial concept until it expanded to include a greater number of attributes, thereby making it more accurate. The teaching of concepts, patterns, and abstractions with the indirect instructional model is patterned around the inductive and deductive movement of concepts wherein you process initially crude and overly restrictive concepts into more expansive and accurate abstractions. Table 7.2 illustrates the different steps involved in inductive versus deductive teaching.

USING EXAMPLES AND NONEXAMPLES

Both inductive and deductive methods help in concept teaching. Recalling our previous examples, one generalization was made after seeing several accidents: "accidents tend to occur at intersections on rainy days." Is there a concept, pattern, or abstraction here? Are there also facts, rules, and sequences?

There is no question that facts had to be known to form this generalization—facts about cars, streets, rain, and intersections. Rules also had to be present, such as "don't accelerate quickly on wet pavement," "slow down at intersections," and "a red light means stop." And, of course, sequences of actions had to be understood, such as "watch for intersections—look for signs—slow down—brake gently."

However, the intended generalization cannot be derived from these facts, rules, and sequences alone. Why? Because they are not sufficiently separated from specific examples to be applied appropriately in all circumstances. For example, you may learn the rule "stop at red lights" to perfection, but until you have seen examples of when to modify the rule (e.g., when an emergency vehicle with flashing lights is behind you), you do not have the complete concept of a red light—only the rule.

Likewise, for other rules we formulated previously, you will acquire only facts, rules, and sequences unless you see both examples and nonexamples. Observing examples and nonexamples—when six extra hours of study pays off and when it does not, when disseminating drug abuse literature is likely to help and when it is not, when a cold and unfriendly teacher is likely to adversely affect your performance in a subject and when not—allows you to grasp *concepts*. Therefore, the third element for the teaching of concepts, patterns, and abstractions is the use of both examples and nonexamples that define the **criterial** and **noncriterial attributes** of a concept that are needed for producing accurate generalizations (Table 7.1).

As another example, consider the concept that private ownership of goods and services under socialism is more limited than under capitalism. How did this teacher develop this concept, moving from a definition of capitalism to a discussion of socialism? Recall that initially the concept was poorly understood by Billy, who concluded that "a car" and "a home of your own" were the types of capital that could become the basis for a socialist economic system. His response was reasonable, because both could be defined as tangible goods according to the discussion on capitalism.

However, this teacher would be in trouble and the outcome of the lesson would be in jeopardy if further concept expansion did not occur. The abstraction of an economic system at this point in the lesson was limited to one in which nearly all tangible goods could be privately owned. The teacher's job was to expand this initial version of the abstraction to include economic systems in which both goods and services are owned and to show that ownership extends to the government as well as to individuals.

Also, the teacher somehow had to make clear that ownership in the context of different economic systems is always a matter of degree. That is, the system determines not only *what* is owned by a government but *how much,* and therefore is unavailable for private ownership. Accordingly, the teacher arranged the next set of interchanges to bring out these specific points. Recall this exchange:

TEACHER: . . . What types of things could a group of people, say the size of a nation, agree on that would be absolutely essential for everyone's existence?
RONNIE: Food.
TEACHER: Good. What else?
BILLY: A hospital.

TEACHER: Very good.

SUE: Highways.

TEACHER: OK. Any others?

RICKY: If they couldn't agree on the importance of cars for everyone, then they would have to agree on some other form of transportation, like buses, trains, or planes.

TEACHER: Yes, they would, wouldn't they? These examples show one of the purposes of a socialist economic system—that is, to control and make available to everyone as many things as possible that (a) everyone values equally, and (b) everyone needs for everyday existence.

The teacher redirected the discussion by having students think about things that "a group of people, say the size of a nation, could agree on that would be absolutely essential for everyone's existence"—thereby encouraging them to broaden their earlier definitions. The question generated examples for discriminating between capitalism and socialism; some were useful (ownership of hospitals) and some were not (ownership of highways). Because some hospitals are owned by capitalist governments, these examples could be confusing; but Ralph makes the clarifying statement:

RALPH: I think it's a matter of degree. Almost all of the major things like hospitals and transportation systems that everyone needs are owned and run by the government under a socialist system, but only a few of these things are owned by the government in a capitalist system. On the other hand, there are things like highways, rivers, forests, and so on that are owned by the government under both systems.

The nonexample of *highways* clarifies the concept that neither socialism nor capitalism are mutually exclusive, all-or-none propositions. Some tangible things (highways and forests) are owned by both capitalist and socialist governments. Notice how this effective teacher used examples and nonexamples to expand the learners' concept of an economic system and to provide clear discrimination between capitalism and socialism.

These are not easy distinctions from a student's point of view. They were accomplished in this episode by:

1. Providing more than a single example.
2. Using examples that vary in ways that are unimportant to the concept being defined (e.g., house is tangible, stocks and bonds are abstract, but both are instances of "tangible goods").
3. Including nonexamples of the concept that nonetheless possess important dimensions of the concept (e.g., a vacation can be bought or "owned" but is not an example of a "tangible good").
4. Explaining why nonexamples are nonexamples, even though they may share some of the same characteristics as examples (e.g., a vacation is not durable).

THE USE OF QUESTIONS TO GUIDE SEARCH-AND-DISCOVERY

Guiding the search-and-discovery process with questions is the fourth indirect instruction function (Table 7.1).

One difference you may have noticed between the direct and indirect instruction dialogues is *the way* in which the teachers asked questions. In the direct dialogue, the questions were specific and to the point, aimed at eliciting a single right answer. But in the indirect dialogue, questions steered the students to seek and discover the answer with minimum assistance from the teacher. In direct instruction, answering questions is how students show what they know (expose their level of understanding) so that clues, hints, and probes may be provided. In indirect instruction, your questions guide students into discovering new dimensions of a problem or ways of resolving a dilemma. This important distinction among questioning strategies will be demonstrated repeatedly in the following chapters.

For now, notice that the indirect instruction dialogue included several questions that guided the search-and-discovery process. For example, several major twists and turns in the dialogue begin and end with questions for which there are no single right answers:

"Who would like to start by telling us what the word *capitalism* means?"

"What does the word *socialism* mean to you?"

"What's a word similar to *communism?*"

These questions did not ask for specific definitions of capitalism, socialism, or communism; few students would know these accurately at the start of the lesson. Rather, they were asked in such a way that students could search for and find an answer that would be at least partially correct. By inserting a phrase such as ". . . means to you" or ". . . similar to," this teacher encouraged a response from almost every student who has ever heard these words used.

Therefore, the purpose of the questions was not to quiz or even to teach, but to focus students' attention and to promote the widest possible discussion of the topic. In this manner the class begins with everyone equally able to participate, *regardless of their task-relevant prior knowledge*. By being able to accept almost any answer at the beginning, the teacher can use student responses to formulate subsequent questions, which begin to shape more accurate responses.

The point of using questioning strategies in indirect instruction, then, is not to arrive at the correct answer in the quickest and most efficient manner. The point is to *stimulate a process* that not only forms successively more correct answers, but also forms those answers using search and discovery. For example, the teacher follows up Robert's response that capitalism means "making money" with the phrase ". . . what else?" and, finally, follows Robert's next response ("owning land") with a leading response (". . . not only land but . . ."), encouraging Robert to broaden his answer.

By beginning with a broad question such as "What does the word capitalism mean to you?", this teacher could have been confronted just as easily with the task of narrowing, not broadening, Robert's first response. In the next interchange this problem actually occurs, because Robert replies that capitalism means "owning anything." Now the job is to narrow or limit his response, which is accomplished by presenting the first criterial attribute of the concept of capitalism, tangible goods.

You can see that a single guided question in the context of indirect instruction is seldom useful in itself. Questions must dovetail into other questions that continually refocus the response (e.g., broaden, then narrow, then broaden slightly again) and keep the search going. The process is much like focusing a camera, because rarely is the camera initially set at the right focus for the subject. Similarly, we could not expect Robert's first response to perfectly represent the concept of capitalism. Just as one begins focusing the camera in the appropriate direction, often passing the point at which the subject is in focus, so also the teacher's follow-up probe led Robert to overshoot the mark and respond with too broad a response (e.g., owning anything). The teacher acknowledged the error and slightly narrowed Robert's response by noting that "The word *capitalism* means tangible goods or possessions."

Questions also can be used in the search-and-discovery process to:

Present contradictions to be resolved—

"Who owns Amtrak?"

"But there is a difference. What might that difference be?"

Probe for deeper, more thorough responses—

"What does the word *social* mean?"

"Why do people usually come together at a party or a meeting?"

Extend the discussion to new areas—

"What things could a group of people, say the size of a nation, agree are absolutely essential for everyone's existence?"

"What types of things don't we find written here on the board?"

Pass responsibility back to the class—

"Good question. Who knows the answer to who pays for services provided under a socialist system?"

"Good question. Who can answer that one?"

Questions like these guide students to increasingly better responses through a search-and-discovery process. This process is one of the most useful for forming concepts and abstractions and for recognizing patterns. The back-and-forth focusing of student responses often is required to attain the appropriate level of generalization.

USE OF STUDENT IDEAS

The Changing View

Until recently the use of student ideas was considered the centerpiece of indirect instruction. Using student ideas meant incorporating student experiences, points of view, feelings, and problems into the lesson by making the student the primary point of reference. A completely student-oriented lesson might be initiated by asking students what problems they were having with the content; these problems would become the focus of the lesson. This approach was intended to heighten student interest, to organize subject content around student problems, to tailor feedback to individual students, and to encourage positive attitudes and feelings toward the subject. However, when a lesson attempts to accomplish only these objectives, it risks failing to achieve the most important objective of all: teaching students to reason, solve problems, and to think critically.

This is not to say that heightening student interest, focusing on student problems, providing individual feedback, and increasing positive attitudes are not important goals for the effective teacher. But these goals can and should be achieved *in the context of classroom dialogue that encourages students to think independently and assume responsibility for their own learning*.

This is where early attempts to use student ideas often went astray. The goals of incorporating student ideas, problems, feelings, and attitudes into the lesson in an open discussion format often became the end itself, rather than the means by which learning could be accomplished. Unfortunately, many forms of problem solving, inquiry, and discovery learning were thought to be synonymous with open, freewheeling discussions that began and ended with student-determined ideas and content. Also, some advocates believed such goals and approaches could be executed solely as processes, not requiring any of the formal structure or content of the traditional classroom. At least some of the curriculum reforms suggested by the national committees and reports reviewed in Chapter 3 were a response to just such misguided notions.

Where does this book stand on the matter? The position of this text, like that of recent research, is that while heightening student interest, selecting content based on student problems, providing individual feedback, and increasing affect are desirable goals, they can be achieved only in a carefully crafted teacher-student dialogue that promotes higher-order thinking. As we have seen earlier in the problem-centered, decision-making (hierarchical), and network approaches and in our example dialogue, even highly abstract content should be structured. Therefore, even in the indirect instruction model, which is designed to contribute to student-centered goals, these goals are only the means for achieving the essential outcomes of concepts, patterns, and abstractions. Thus, using student ideas is our fifth indirect instruction function (Table 7.1).

Productively Using Student-Centered Ideas

So, how can student-centered ideas be used productively in the context of indirect instruction? In this context, you can use student ideas by:

- ☐ Encouraging students to use *examples* and *references* from their own experience, from which they can construct their own meanings from text.
- ☐ Sharing of mental strategies by which the students can learn more easily and efficiently.

☐ Asking students to seek clarification of and to draw *parallels* to and *associations* from things they already know.

☐ Encouraging understanding and retention of ideas by relating them to the students' own sphere of *interests, concerns, and problems*.

For examples of these uses of student ideas, recall again the dialogue about economic systems. By asking students to name three other countries that follow a capitalistic economic system, or to name the things a nation could agree on that are absolutely essential for everyone's existence, the teacher elicited examples and references from the learners' experience.

Perhaps more important than the questions themselves was the way in which the teacher incorporated student responses into the lesson. In one instance, the response even partially directed lesson content. This followed a general question, "What things could a group of people . . . agree on that would be absolutely essential for everyone's existence?" Almost any equally general response could be used, as when students contributed the concepts of food, hospitals, and highways, all of which were within the overall framework of the lesson established by the teacher. This allowed students to contribute almost any response without letting the choice itself alter the lesson agenda.

Also, by asking what the word *capitalism* "means to you," this teacher was asking students to express themselves by using parallels and associations they already understood—perhaps by having a job, or by recalling a conversation about occupations, or by remembering television images of life in Eastern Europe. Parallels and associations such as these are likely to be vastly different among students. This is desirable, both for heightening student interest and involvement and for exposing the students to a variety of responses, many of which may be appropriate instances of the concept to be learned.

A third way to incorporate student ideas into your lesson is to allow students to respond using their own interests, concerns, and problems. An instance of this occurred when the teacher asked students to name two countries having different political systems. Presumably these countries would be referred to in the future, perhaps in individual reports or research papers, perhaps in library reading or in a class discussion; in all of these cases, the individuality of each student's choice could be examined. Student interests—and especially individual choices affecting future assignments—can be important motivators for ensuring active student involvement in subsequent assignments that may be lengthy and time consuming.

Finally, notice that even within the context of these examples the instruction remained *content centered*. It allowed students to participate in determining the *form* in which learning occurred, but not the *substance* of what was learned. This substance usually is determined by the curriculum guide and textbook. Our example dialogue, therefore, contrasts with what is called *student-centered learning*, which allows both the form and substance to be selected by the student. This is sometimes associated with *unguided discovery learning*, wherein the goal is to maintain high levels of student interest, accomplished largely by selecting content based on student problems or interests and by providing individually tailored feedback.

Sometimes unguided discovery learning is desired, in the context of independently conducted experiments, research projects, science fair projects, and demonstrations where the topic is independently selected by the student. However, even when unguided discovery learning is desired, the content still must fit within the confines of the prescribed curriculum. Therefore, whether your approach is the guided use of student ideas (as in this example) or unguided (as in research assignments), some preorganization and guidance always will be necessary prior to your soliciting and using student ideas. In the next two chapters, we will have more to say about using student ideas within the naturally occurring dialogue of the classroom.

STUDENT SELF-EVALUATION

The sixth ingredient of indirect instruction (Table 7.1) is to engage students in evaluating their own responses and thereby take responsibility for their own learning. Because there are many right answers when teaching concepts, patterns, and abstractions, it is virtually impossible for you to judge them all. In direct instruction, nearly all instances of the learned facts, rules, or action sequences likely to be encountered can be learned during guided and independent practice. But, because specifying all possible instances of a concept is neither possible nor efficient, you must use indirect instruction to have students look critically at their own responses.

You can encourage self-evaluation by explicitly giving control of the evaluation function to students and by letting them provide reasons for their answers so that you and other students can suggest needed changes. Recall that early in the dialogue, the teacher let the students know that some of the responsibility for determining appropriate answers would fall on them. After writing a list on the board, he said, "OK. Who would like to say which of these are *capital?*" The message is received when Ricky responds and Barbara modifies Ricky's response:

RICKY: Car and clothes are the only two I see.
BARBARA: I'd add stocks and bonds. They say you own a piece of something, although maybe not the whole thing.

Even after Barbara's efforts to correct Ricky's response, the teacher still does not supply an answer, but instead keeps the evaluation of the previous responses going by responding with "Could you see or touch it?"

The goal here was to create a student dialogue focused on the appropriateness of previous answers. The success of this self-evaluation strategy is most readily seen in the sequence of dialogue that occurs between students and teacher. This strategy promotes a student-to-student-back-to-teacher interchange, as opposed to the more familiar teacher-to-student-back-to-teacher interchange. The teacher's role is to maintain the momentum by offering hints or focusing statements that students can use to evaluate their previous responses.

An example of a student-to-student-to-teacher interchange took place when Sue, hearing that people in socialist countries pay taxes, asks, "So how is that different from America?"

TEACHER: Good question. Who can answer that one?
ROBERT: It's the same.
MARK: No, it's not. Our government doesn't own hospitals, farms, trains, and that kind of stuff.
TEACHER: Who owns Amtrak?

The answer obviously needs some evaluation, so the teacher simply keeps the ball rolling with, "Good question. Who can answer that one?" Robert responds with an incomplete answer and Mark quickly informs the class not only that the answer is wrong, but also why he thinks it is wrong. At that point the teacher retakes control and raises another question, suggesting that even Mark's response is not completely accurate.

In the process of these student-to-student-to-teacher exchanges, students learn the reasons for their answers in slow, measured steps. By allowing partially correct answers to become the bases for more accurate ones, this teacher is showing the class how to modify incorrect and partially correct answers into better ones. Especially for the learning of concepts, patterns, and abstractions that involve more than a single criterial attribute, these layers of refinement, gradually built up by student interchange, help the students develop a level of generalization.

Of course, there is no reason why such interchanges must be limited in size. Three, four, or even five successive exchanges among students before control returns to the teacher can work fine in circumstances that need less guidance and structuring. Classes of students who are more able or who have considerable knowledge of the content can sustain protracted exchanges without going so far astray that you need to restructure.

USE OF GROUP DISCUSSION

When student-to-student-to-teacher exchanges grow into long interactions among large numbers of students, a group discussion has begun. In these discussions, you may intervene only occasionally to review and summarize main points, or you may schedule periodic interaction to evaluate the group's progress and to redirect if necessary.

Group discussions can be useful for encouraging critical thinking, for engaging average and less-able learners in the learning process, and for promoting the "reasoning together" that is necessary in a democratic society (Gall & Gall, 1976). Because group discussion helps students think critically—i.e., examine alternatives, judge solutions, make predictions, and discover generalizations—it is yet another approach to teaching concepts, patterns, and abstractions. It is the seventh and last indirect instruction function in Table 7.1.

When your objective is to teach well-established concepts, patterns, or abstractions that already are structured in the text and workbook, a lecture is more efficient and effective than a discussion. Agreement among students about the topic may be so high that too little controversy exists to promote discussion. This might be the case with topics not requiring personal opinion and judgment, such as photosynthesis, General MacArthur, or the legislative branch of government.

But sometimes you may prefer a group discussion to a lecture. When concepts, patterns, and abstractions have a less formal structure and are treated minimally in the text or workbook, then the lack of consensus can make a discussion rewarding. Examples of such topics are: Would photosynthesis be useful in space? How much aggression do you think it takes to start a war? In what ways can the legislative branch of government be influenced by the executive branch? Topics that are not formally structured by the text and for which a high degree of consensus does not yet exist make good candidates for discussion sessions for building, expanding, and refining concepts, patterns, and abstractions.

During the discussion, you are the moderator. Your tasks include:

1. Orienting the students to the objective of the discussion:
   "Today we will discuss when a nation should decide to go to war. Specifically, we will discuss the meaning of the concept of aggression as it has occurred in history. In the context of wars between nations, your job at the end of the discussion will be to arrive at a generalization that could help a president decide if sufficient aggression has occurred to warrant going to war."

2. Providing new or more accurate information where needed:
   "It is not correct to assume that World War II started with the bombing of Pearl Harbor. Many events occurred earlier on the European continent that some nations considered to be aggression."

3. Reviewing, summarizing, or putting together opinions and facts into a meaningful relationship:
   "Bobby, Mary, and Billy, you seem to be arguing that the forcible entry of one nation into the territory of another nation constitutes aggression, while the rest of the class seems to be saying that undermining the economy of another nation also can constitute aggression."

4. Adjusting the flow of information and ideas to be most productive to the goals of the lesson:
   "Mark, you seem to have extended our definition of aggression to include criticizing the government of another nation through political means, such as shortwave media broadcasts, speeches at the U.N., and so forth. But that fits better the idea of a cold war, and we are trying to study some of the instances of aggression that might have started World War II."

5. Combining ideas and promoting compromise to arrive at an appropriate consensus:
   "We seem to have two definitions of aggression—one dealing with the forcible entry of one nation into the territory of another, and another that has to do with undermining a nation's economy. Could we combine these two ideas by saying that anything that threatens either a nation's people or its prosperity, or both, could be considered aggression?"

Group discussion can take several different forms. **Large group discussions** in which all members of the class participate are the most familiar. Large groups can be difficult to handle, because discipline and management problems occur easily when numerous learners are interacting in student exchanges that you interrupt only occasionally. The moderating functions just listed allow you to control and redirect the discussion as necessary without overly restricting the flow of ideas. During a large group discussion, you should frequently perform one or more of these moderating functions. The frequency will vary with the topic and students, but the greater the consensus, the fewer the students, and the higher their ability to grasp the concepts and abstractions to be learned, *the more you can relinquish authority to the group* (Slavin, 1983).

Small group discussions of five to ten students also are useful for teaching concepts, patterns, and abstractions. When multiple topics must be discussed within the same lesson and time does not permit full class discussion of the topics in sequential order, try using two, three, or four small groups simultaneously. You have three tasks here: to form groups whose members can work together, to spread troublesome students across groups, and to move among the groups as moderator. Stopping the groups periodically, either to inform the entire class of important insights discovered by a group or to apply moderating functions across groups, will help keep the groups reasonably close together and will help maintain your control and authority.

Another group format for indirect instruction is to have students work in **pairs or teams**. This can be effective when the discussion entails writing (e.g., for a summary report), looking up information (in the text, encyclopedia, etc.), or preparing materials (chart, diagram, graph, etc.) (Johnson & Johnson, 1987; Slavin, 1987). In the pair or team arrangement, your role as moderator increases in proportion to the number of pairs or teams, so only brief interchanges with each may be possible.

Small group discussions often require the teacher to become a moderator, visiting each group periodically to answer questions, review and summarize, redirect group work, provide new or more accurate information, and achieve consensus.

The pair-or-team approach works best when the task is highly structured, when a fair consensus about the topic already exists, and when the orienting instructions fully define each member's role (e.g., student A searches for the information, student B writes a summary description of what is found, and both students read the summary for final agreement). Pairs or teams frequently become highly task oriented, so pairing or teaming tends to be most productive when discussion objectives go beyond just an oral report and include a product to be delivered to the class.

Table 7.3 presents the lesson plan for this indirect instruction lesson, following the written format provided in Chapter 5.

TABLE 7.3
Lesson plan: Indirect instruction

Unit Plan: Economic Systems
Lesson Plan: Comparisons and contrasts among capitalist, socialist, and communist economies

1. Gaining attention	Ask if anyone knows where the phrase "government of the people, by the people, for the people" comes from, to establish the idea that the principles and rules by which a country is governed also influence its economic system.
2. Informing the learner of the objective	This session: To relate economic systems to the ownership of goods and services in different countries Next session: To be able to distinguish economic systems from political systems and to show why the communist economic system is changing
3. Stimulating recall of prerequisite learning	Ask for a definition of capitalism and then refine with questioning and probing of the definition given. Continue probing until a definition is arrived at that defines capitalism as "an economic system that allows the ownership of tangible goods that last for a reasonable period of time." Check understanding by asking for three countries (other than ours) that have capitalist economies.
4. Presenting the stimulus material	A. Ask what the word *socialism* means. Refine definition by questioning and probing until a definition is arrived at that defines socialism as "an economic system that allows the government to control and make available to everyone as many things as possible that (a) everyone values equally, and (b) are seen as essential for everyday existence." Have students compare capitalism and socialism by degree of ownership of public services and degree of taxes paid under each system. B. Ask what the word *communism* means and establish its relationship to the idea of *community*. Refine definition, using the concept of degree of ownership by questioning and probing until still more examples of things owned and controlled by the government under communism are arrived at by the students.

COMPARISON OF DIRECT AND INDIRECT INSTRUCTION

The direct and indirect instruction models were presented in separate chapters because each includes distinctive teaching strategies. As you have seen, the models have two different purposes:

> The direct model is best suited to the teaching of facts, rules, and action sequences, and provides six teaching functions for doing so—daily review and checking, presenting and structuring new content, guided student practice, feedback and correctives, independent practice, and weekly and monthly reviews.

TABLE 7.3

Unit Plan: Economic Systems
Lesson Plan: Comparisons and contrasts among capitalist, socialist, and communist economies

5. Eliciting the desired behavior	A. Use questions to encourage the identification of public services most commonly owned under socialism, for example, hospitals, trains, and communication systems. Some types of farms and industries will also be accepted when their relation to the public good is understood.
	B. Use questions to encourage the identification of those public services most commonly owned under communism, for example, food supply, housing, and industries. Emphasis will be placed on those services and goods that are different from those identified under socialism.
	C. Use questions to identify the amount and types of things owned by the government across the three systems, to establish the concept that differences among the systems are a matter of degree of ownership and degree of taxation.
6. Providing feedback	Questions will be posed in a manner that encourages the student to evaluate his or her own response and those of other students. Probes will be given until student responses approximate an acceptable answer. Placed side by side on the board will be those goods and services the students have identified as likely to be owned by the government in all three systems and those likely to be owned uniquely by any one or combination of systems. A distinction may be made between these and the personal items that may have been mentioned, such as clothes or household goods, but which cannot be used to distinguish economic systems.
7. Evaluating the behavior	After completion of a research paper describing three countries of the students' own choosing each of which represents a different economic system, students will be graded on their comprehension of the concepts of (a) degree of ownership, and (b) degree of taxation as discussed by L. Rutherford, (1986) *Economics in a Modern World,* Columbus, OH: Intex.

The indirect model is best suited for the teaching of concepts, patterns, and abstractions, and provides seven teaching functions for doing so—advance organization of content, inductive and deductive conceptual movement, use of examples and nonexamples, use of questions to guide search and discovery, use of student ideas, student self-evaluation, and group discussion.

Neither model should be used to the exclusion of the other. And, many times the two models can be effectively interwoven in a single lesson, as when a small number of facts, rules, or action sequences must be acquired prior to introducing a concept, pattern, or abstraction.

Let us now place the direct and indirect models of instruction side by side for comparison. Table 7.4 summarizes some teaching events you can employ using both models.

Under direct instruction, the objective is rapid attainment of facts, rules, and action sequences. Content is divided into small, easily learned steps through a lecture format involving brief explanations, examples, practice, and feedback. Both guided and independent practice, under tight control of the teacher, help ensure that students

TABLE 7.4
Some example events under the direct and indirect models of instruction

Direct Instruction	*Indirect Instruction*
Objective: To teach facts, rules, and action sequences	Objective: To teach concepts, patterns, and abstractions
Teacher begins the lesson with a review of the previous day's work.	Teacher begins the lesson with advance organizers that provide an overall picture and that allow for concept expansion.
Teacher presents new content in small steps with explanations and examples.	Teacher focuses student responses using induction and/or deduction to refine and focus generalizations.
Teacher provides an opportunity for guided practice on a small number of sample problems. Prompts and models when necessary to attain 60–80% accuracy.	Teacher presents examples and nonexamples of the generalization identifying criterial and noncriterial attributes.
Teacher provides feedback and corrections according to whether the answer was correct, quick, and firm; correct but hesitant; careless; or incorrect.	Teacher draws additional examples from students' own experiences, interests, and problems.
Teacher provides an opportunity for independent practice with seatwork. Strives for automatic responses that are 95% correct or higher.	Teacher uses questions to guide discovery and articulation of the generalization.
	Teacher involves students in evaluating their own responses.
Teacher provides weekly and monthly (accumulative) reviews and reteaches unlearned content.	Teacher promotes and moderates discussion to firm up and extend generalizations when necessary.

are actively engaged in the learning process at high rates of success. Everything that is not learned is revealed in weekly and monthly reviews and retaught as needed.

Under indirect instruction, the objective is to engage students in inquiry to eventually develop concepts in the form of patterns or abstractions. Here the teacher prepares for the complexity of the lesson by providing an overall framework into which the day's lesson is placed, allowing room for expansion of concepts. Initially crude and inaccurate responses are gradually refined through inductive and deductive movement, focusing the generalization to the desired degree. To do this, both examples and nonexamples (some drawn from the students' interests and experiences) are used to separate criterial from noncriterial attributes. Throughout, the teacher uses questions that guide students to discover the generalization and to evaluate their own responses. When the concepts are relatively unstructured and have moderate-to-low degrees of consensus, discussion groups may replace a more teacher-controlled format; in this case, the teacher becomes a moderator.

A FINAL WORD

This chapter and the preceding one presented a variety of teaching strategies. When used with the appropriate content and purpose, these strategies can significantly improve your teaching effectiveness. Although both the direct and indirect models of instruction are significant contributions to teaching and learning, neither should exclusively dominate your instructional style. It would be unfortunate if you exemplified only the direct model or the indirect model, because the original purpose of introducing these models was to *increase the variety* of instructional strategies at your disposal.

These models and their strategies provide a variety of instructional tools that you can mix in many combinations to match your particular objectives and students. Just as different entrées have prominent and equal places on a menu, so too do the direct and indirect models have prominent and equal places in your classroom.

The underlying point of these two chapters, then, is that you should alternately employ the direct and indirect models to create tantalizing combinations of "educational flavors" for your students. Your own objectives are the best guide to what combination from the menu you will serve on any given day. In the chapters ahead we will extend this basic menu to provide still greater variety in the teaching methods at your command.

SUMMING UP

This chapter introduced you to indirect instruction strategies. Its main points were:

1. Indirect instruction is an approach to teaching and learning in which the process of learning is *inquiry,* the result is *discovery,* and the learning context is a *problem*.

2. In indirect instruction, the learner acquires information by transforming stimulus material into a response that is different (a) from the stimulus used to present the learning and (b) from any previous response emitted by the student.

3. During indirect instruction, concepts, patterns, and abstractions are acquired through the processes of generalization and discrimination, which require the learner to rearrange and elaborate on the stimulus material.

4. The generalization process helps the learner respond in a similar manner to different stimuli, thereby increasing the range of instances to which particular facts, rules, and sequences apply.

5. The process of discrimination selectively restricts the acceptable range of instances by eliminating things that may look like the concept but that differ from it on critical dimensions.

6. The processes of generalization and discrimination together help students classify different-appearing stimuli into the same categories on the basis of criterial attributes. Criterial attributes act as magnets, drawing together all instances of a concept without the learner having to see or memorize all instances of it.

7. The indirect instruction model provides instructional strategies that encourage the processes of generalization and discrimination for the purpose of forming concepts, patterns, and abstractions.

8. The instructional functions of the indirect model are:
   □ use of advance organizers
   □ conceptual movement—inductive and deductive
   □ use of examples and nonexamples
   □ use of questions to guide search and discovery
   □ use of student ideas
   □ student self-evaluation
   □ use of group discussion

9. An advance organizer gives the learner a conceptual preview of what is to come and helps the learner store, label, and package content for retention and later use.

10. Three approaches to composing advance organizers are the problem-centered approach, the decision-making (hierarchical) approach, and the networking approach.

11. Induction starts with a specific observation of a limited set of data and ends with a generalization about a much broader context.

12. Deduction proceeds from principles or generalizations to their application in specific contexts. The testing of a generalization to see if it holds in specific instances is sometimes referred to as the hypothetico-deductive method.

13. Providing examples and nonexamples helps define the criterial and noncriterial attributes needed for making accurate generalizations.

14. Using examples and nonexamples correctly includes:
   □ providing more than a single example
   □ using examples that vary in ways that are irrelevant to the concept being defined
   □ using nonexamples that also include relevant dimensions of the concept
   □ explaining why nonexamples have some of the same characteristics as examples

15. In indirect instruction, the role of questions is to guide students into discovering new dimensions of a problem or new ways of resolving a dilemma.

16. Some uses of questions during indirect instruction include:
   □ refocusing
   □ presenting contradictions to be resolved
   □ probing for deeper, more thorough responses
   □ extending the discussion to new areas
   □ passing responsibility to the class

17. Student ideas can be used to heighten student interest, to organize subject content around student problems, to tailor feedback to fit individual students, and to encourage positive attitudes toward the subject. Because these goals should not become ends unto themselves, you must plan and structure the use of student ideas to promote reasoning, problem solving, and critical thinking.

18. Student-centered learning, sometimes called unguided discovery learning, allows the student to select both the form and substance of the learning experience. This is appropriate in the context of independently conducted experiments, research projects, science fair projects, and demonstrations. However, preorganization and guidance always are necessary to ensure that the use of student ideas fits within the prescribed curriculum.

19. Self-evaluation of student responses occurs during indirect instruction when students are given the opportunity to reason their answers so that you and other students can suggest needed changes. Self-evaluation is most easily conducted in the context of student-to-student-to-teacher exchanges, wherein you encourage students to comment on and consider the accuracy of their own and each others' responses.

20. A group discussion involves student exchanges with successive interactions among large num-

bers of students. During these exchanges, you may intervene only occasionally to review and summarize, or you may schedule periodic interaction to evaluate each group's progress and to redirect when necessary.

21. The best topics for discussion include those that are not formally structured by texts and workbooks and for which a high degree of consensus among your students does not yet exist.

22. Your monitoring functions during discussion include:
    □ orienting students to the objective of the discussion
    □ providing new or more accurate information that may be needed
    □ reviewing, summarizing, and relating opinions and facts
    □ redirecting the flow of information and ideas back to the objective of the discussion.

23. The greater the group consensus, the fewer the students in the group, and the higher their ability to grasp concepts and abstractions, then the more you can relinquish authority to the group.

24. Direct and indirect instruction generally are used together and you should not adopt one model to the exclusion of the other. Each contains a set of functions that can compose an efficient and effective method for the teaching of facts, rules, and sequences or concepts, patterns, and abstractions.

FOR DISCUSSION AND PRACTICE

*1. What three learning concepts are brought together in the indirect model of instruction?

*2. What types of behavioral outcomes are the direct and indirect instructional models most effective in achieving?

*3. Where does the word *indirect* come from in the *indirect instruction model*?

*4. Why can direct instruction not be used all the time?

*5. Explain in your own words what is meant by the words *unitization* and *automaticity* as applied to direct instruction. Give an example of a learning task in which only these two processes are required.

*6. Explain in your own words the meanings of *generalization* and *discrimination*. Give an example of a learning task in which both these processes are required.

*7. Identify which of the following learning tasks involve only facts, rules, or action sequences (Type 1) and which, in addition, involve concepts, patterns, and abstractions (Type 2).
    (1) naming the presidents
    (2) selecting the best speech
    (3) shifting the gearshift in a car
    (4) writing an essay
    (5) describing the main theme in George Orwell's *1984*
    (6) hitting a tennis ball
    (7) winning a tennis match

    (8) inventing a new soft drink
    (9) reciting the vowel sounds
    (10) becoming an effective teacher

*8. Describe two problems that would result if a concept or abstraction had to be learned using only the cognitive processes of unitization and automaticity by which facts, rules, and sequences are acquired.

9. Prepare a two-minute introduction to a lesson of your own choosing that provides your students with an advance organizer.

10. Provide one example of an advance organizer using the problem-centered, decision-making, and networking approaches.

*11. In your own words, define inductive and deductive reasoning. Give an example of each, using content from your preferred teaching area.

*12. Identify the five steps to deductive reasoning commonly applied in the laboratory.

13. For each of the following, show with specific examples how the concept might be taught both inductively and deductively. Pay particular attention to whether your instruction should begin or end with a generalization.
    democracy
    freedom
    education
    effective teaching
    parenting

*14. For the concept of effective teaching, give five criterial attributes and five noncriterial attributes.

*15. Identify four ways in which examples and non-examples should be used in the teaching of concepts.

*16. Distinguish the different purposes for asking questions in the direct and indirect models of instruction.

*17. Besides refocusing, what other types of questions can be used in the search-and-discovery process? Choose a lesson topic and provide an example of each of these.

*18. What type of learning might be represented by discussions that begin and end with student-determined ideas and content? How is this different from the use of student ideas in the context of the indirect instruction model?

*19. What are three ways student ideas might be incorporated into an indirect instruction lesson?

*20. Why is student self-evaluation more important in the indirect model of instruction than in the direct model of instruction?

*21. What are five monitoring responsibilities of the teacher during group discussion?

22. For which of the following teaching objectives might you use the direct model of instruction, and for which might you use the indirect model? Teaching your class to:

   (1) sing
   (2) use a microscope properly
   (3) appreciate Milton's *Paradise Lost*
   (4) become aware of the pollutants around us
   (5) solve an equation with two unknowns
   (6) read at grade level
   (7) type at the rate of 25 words per minute
   (8) write an original short story
   (9) build a winning science fair project
   (10) distinguish war from aggression

Are there any for which you might use both models?

---

*Answers to asterisked questions (*) in this and the other chapters are in Appendix B.

SUGGESTED READINGS

Gagné, R. M. (1971). The learning of concepts. In M. David Merrill (Ed.), *Instructional design: Readings*. Englewood Cliffs, NJ: Prentice-Hall.

An introduction to this important form of learning—with plenty of practical illustrations.

Gall, M., & Gall, J. (1976). The discussion method. In N. L. Gage (Ed.), *The psychology of teaching methods: The seventy-fifth yearbook of the national society for the study of education, part I*. Chicago: University of Chicago Press.

A discussion of the research and logic that underlie this popular method.

Giaconia, R. (1987). Open versus formal methods. In M. J. Dunkin (Ed.), *International encyclopedia of teaching and teacher education*. New York: Pergamon.

An introduction to some of the most important differences between the direct and indirect models.

Joyce, B., & Weils, M. (1986). *Models of teaching*. Englewood Cliffs, NJ: Prentice-Hall.

A review of many of our most popular styles of teaching—a good complement to the two models described in this chapter.

Maerhoff, G. (1983). Teaching to think: A new emphasis. *The New York Times*. January 9, Section 12, 1–37.

A current and thoughtful piece on how to teach thinking skills, using many of the functions of the indirect model.

Morine, H., & Morine G. (1973). *Discovery: A challenge to teachers*. Englewood Cliffs, NJ: Prentice-Hall.

A practical text about how to implement the indirect model in all of its many forms—with plenty of examples for lesson plans.

Shulman, L., & Keislar, E. (Eds.). (1966). *Learning by discovery: A critical appraisal*. Chicago: Rand McNally.

An authoritative book on discovery learning that identifies its weaknesses as well as its strengths.

Slavin, R. (1983). *Cooperative learning*. New York: Longman.

An extensive presentation on how to form different kinds of groups and use them productively in the classroom.

Slavin, R. (1987). Small group methods. In M. J. Dunkin (Ed.), *International encyclopedia of teaching and teacher education*. New York: Pergamon.
An overview of some ideas on how to use small groups to promote a cooperative classroom environment.

Withall, J. (1987). Teacher-centered and learner-centered teaching. In M. J. Dunkin (Ed.), *International encyclopedia of teaching and teacher education*. New York: Pergamon.
An introduction to the direct and indirect models of instruction from the point of view of the teacher and learner.

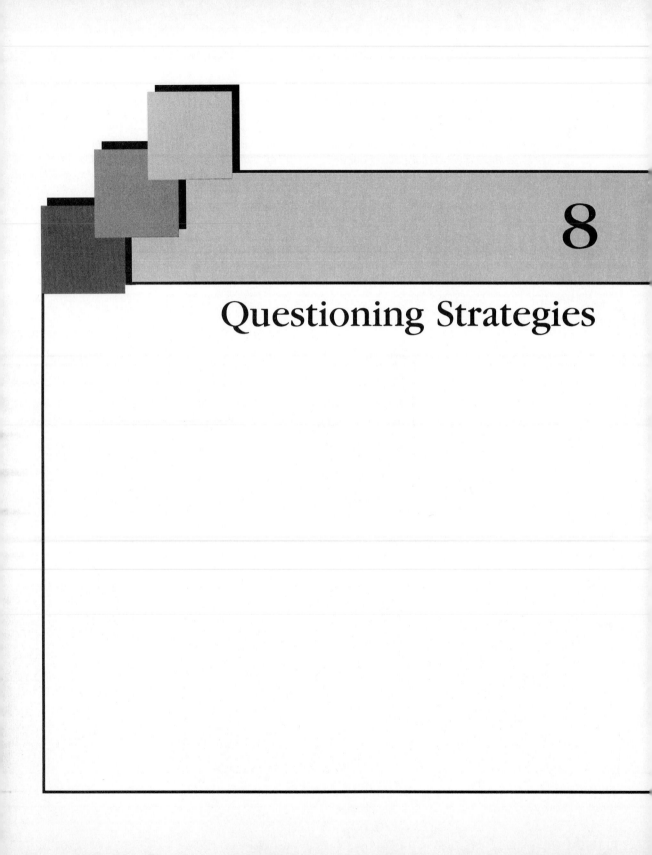

8

Questioning Strategies

In the classroom dialogues of previous chapters, you saw the important role of questions in the effective teacher's menu. This is no coincidence, for most exchanges between teachers and students involve questions in some form. This chapter explores the definition of a question, the varied ways questions can be asked, and the types of questions that you should ask more frequently than others.

Also discussed is the closely related topic of *probes*. Like questions, probes are effective catalysts for performing the five key behaviors of (a) lesson clarity, (b) instructional variety, (c) task orientation, (d) engagement in the learning process, and (e) student success. Subsequent chapters extend these questioning techniques, showing how you can use them to form other types of teaching strategies.

WHAT IS A QUESTION?

In the context of a lively and fast-paced exchange in a classroom, questions are not always obvious. As observed by Brown and Edmondson (1984), students routinely report difficulty in distinguishing some types of questions in the context of a classroom dialogue—and even whether a question has been asked. For example, imagine hearing these two questions:

Raise your hand if you know the answer.

Aren't you going to *answer the question?*

The first is expressed in command form (italics), yet it contains an implicit question. The second sounds like a question, yet contains an implicit command. Will your students perceive both of these statements as questions? Will they both evoke the same response?

Voice inflection is another source of confusion; it can indicate a question even when sentence syntax does not. For example, imagine hearing the following two sentences spoken with the emphasis shown:

You *said* the President can have two terms in office?

The President can have *two* terms in office?

The proper voice inflection can turn almost any sentence into a question, whether you intend it or not. In addition, a real question can be perceived as a rhetorical question because of inflection and word choice:

We all have done our homework today, *haven't we?*

Whether this is intended as a question or not, it is certain that all who failed to complete their homework will assume the question to be rhetorical.

Effective questions are ones for which students actively compose a response and thereby become engaged in the learning process. The previous examples show that effective questions depend on more than just words. Their effectiveness also depends on *voice inflection, word emphasis, word choice,* and the *context* in which the question is raised. Questions can be raised in many ways and each way can determine whether the question is perceived by your students, and how.

In this chapter any oral statement or gesture intended to evoke a student response is considered to be a question. And if it evokes a response that actively engages a student in the learning process, it is an *effective question*. With this distinction in mind, let us now explore many ways of asking questions that actively engage students in the learning process.

What Consumes 80% of Class Time?

In almost any classroom at any time you can observe a sequence of events in which the teacher structures the content to be discussed, solicits a student response, and then reacts to the response. These activities performed in sequence are the most common behaviors in any classroom. They were first described by Bellack, Kliebard, Hyman, and Smith (1966) as a chain of events in which:

1. The teacher provides structure, briefly formulating the topic or issue to be discussed.
2. The teacher solicits a response or asks a question of one or more students.
3. The student responds or answers the question.
4. The teacher reacts to the student's answer.

The teacher behaviors in this chain of events compose the activities of **structuring, soliciting, and reacting**. The previous two chapters discussed strategies you can use for structuring the content. This chapter focuses upon the soliciting and reacting elements in this chain of events.

At the heart of this chain is soliciting, or question-asking behavior. Questions are the tool for bridging the gap between your presentation of content and the student's understanding of it. Many bridging strategies were presented in the previous chapters: advance organizers, guided practice, feedback and correctives, inductive and deductive logic, self-evaluation, discussion, and so on. These strategies included all possible ingredients of both direct and indirect instruction, ingredients whose function is to promote and stimulate thinking.

Just as these ingredients actively engage learners in the learning process, so can questions perform this same function and add still more variety to a teaching menu. The purpose of using questions must not be lost among the many *forms* and *varieties* of questions presented in this chapter. Like all the ingredients of direct and indirect instruction, questions are tools to encourage students to think about and act upon the material you have structured.

Classrooms and content can become boring if a teacher fails to have students do something with the content *as quickly as possible after presenting it*. This is why the effective teacher intersperses questions throughout a lesson and wraps them around small bits of content, to actively engage the student and evoke a response (sometimes *any* response). Consequently, the cycle of structuring, soliciting, and reacting is the most frequently occurring chain of events in any classroom.

The centerpiece of this chain—soliciting or questioning—is so prevalent that an average of 100 to 150 questions per class hour are asked in the typical elementary and secondary classroom (Brown & Edmondson, 1984). Further, 80% of all school time is devoted to questions and answers (Gall, 1984). This enormous concentration on a single strategy attests both to its convenience and to its perceived effectiveness. But, as has been noted, not all questions are *effective* questions. That is, not all questions actively engage students in the learning process.

Are We Asking the Right Questions?

Some research data indeed show that not all questions actively engage students in the learning process. Early studies estimated that 70–80% of all questions require the simple recall of facts, while only 20–30% require the higher-level thought processes of clarifying, expanding, generalizing, and making inferences (Haynes, 1935; Corey, 1940). Evidently little has changed since these early studies. Recent work in the United States and England indicates that, of every five questions asked, three require data recall, one is managerial, and only one requires higher-level thought processes (Brown & Edmondson, 1984).

This lopsided proportion of recall questions to thought questions is alarming. Behaviors most frequently required in adult life, at work, and in advanced training— those at the higher levels of cognitive complexity involving analysis, synthesis, and evaluation—seem to be the least-emphasized behaviors in the classroom. As we have seen, there are good reasons for asking questions at the knowledge, comprehension, and application level. But there is little explanation for why such questions form so great a percentage, to the exclusion of higher-level thought questions. Higher-level thought questions not only develop the behaviors most frequently required outside the classroom but also are believed to more actively engage your students in the classroom.

WHAT ARE THE PURPOSES OF QUESTIONS?

It would be easy to classify all questions as either lower-order (requiring the recall of information) or higher-order (requiring clarification, expansion, generalization, and inference). But such a broad distinction would ignore the many specific purposes for which questions are used. Questions are asked:

- ☐ To arouse interest and curiosity.
- ☐ To focus attention on an issue.
- ☐ To stimulate learners to ask questions.
- ☐ To diagnose specific learning difficulties.
- ☐ To encourage reflection and self-evaluation.
- ☐ To promote thought and the understanding of ideas.
- ☐ To review content already learned.
- ☐ To help recall specific information.
- ☐ To reinforce recently learned material.
- ☐ To manage or remind students of a procedure.
- ☐ To teach via student answers.
- ☐ To probe deeper after an answer is given.

Even this substantial list does not cover all the reasons why questions are asked. Nevertheless, most reasons for asking questions can be classified into these general categories:

1. Interest-getting and attention-getting:
   "If you could go to the moon, what would be the first thing you would notice?"
2. Diagnosing and checking:
   "Does anyone know the meaning of the Latin word *via?*"
3. Recall of specific facts or information:
   "Who can name each of the main characters in *The Adventures of Huckleberry Finn?*"
4. Managerial:
   "Did you ask my permission?"
5. Encourage higher-level thought processes:
   "Putting together all that we learned, what household products exhibit characteristics associated with the element sodium?"
6. Structure and redirect learning:
   "Now that we've covered the narrative form, who can tell me what an expository sentence is?"
7. Allow expression of affect:
   "What did you like about *Of Mice and Men?*"

Most of the questions in these categories have the purpose of shaping or setting up the learner's response. In this sense, a well-formulated question serves as an advance organizer, providing the framework for the response that is to follow.

WHAT ARE CONVERGENT AND DIVERGENT QUESTIONS?

Questions can be narrow or broad, encouraging either a specific, limited response or a general, expansive one. A question that limits an answer to a single or small number of responses is called a **convergent**, **direct**, or **closed** question. For such questions, the learner has previously read or heard the answer, and so the learner has only to recall certain facts.

Convergent questions set up the learner to respond in a limited, restrictive manner: "Does anyone know the meaning of the Latin word *via?*" "Who can name the main characters in *The Adventures of Huckleberry Finn?*" The answers to these questions are easily judged right or wrong. Many convergent, or closed, questions are used in direct instruction. As mentioned, up to 80% of all questions may be of this type.

Another type of question encourages a general or open response. This is the **divergent**, or **indirect**, question. It has no single best answer, but it can have wrong answers. This is perhaps the most misunderstood aspect of a divergent question. Not just any answer will be correct, even in the case of divergent questions raised for the purpose of allowing students to express their feelings. If Johnny is asked what he liked about *Of Mice and Men* and says "Nothing," or "The happy ending," then either Johnny has not read the book or he needs help in better understanding the events that took place. A passive or accepting response on your part to answers like these is inappropriate, regardless of your intent to allow an open response.

Convergent and divergent questions, therefore, both have right and wrong answers. Divergent questions may have many right answers and therefore a much broader range of acceptable responses. But if you receive a wrong or meaningless response, or no response at all, you should guide the student to an appropriate response and have the student try again. You may need to hint, encourage, or probe further—"Now, why would you say death and tragedy make a happy ending?"

You can expect far more diverse responses from divergent questions than from convergent questions—which may explain why only 20% of all questions are divergent. It always will be easier to determine the right or wrong answer to a convergent question than it will be to sift through the range of acceptable responses to a divergent question. Even so, it is your responsibility to identify inappropriate responses, to follow them up, and to bring them back into the acceptable range. Thus, you often will need to follow up divergent questions with more detail, new information, or encouragement. In this sense, divergent questions become a rich source of lively, spontaneous follow-up material that can make your teaching fresh and interesting.

Note that the same question can be convergent under one set of circumstances and divergent under another. Suppose you ask a student to *decide* or *evaluate*, according to a set of criteria, which household products exhibit characteristics of the element sodium. If the student only recalls products from a previously memorized list, then the question is convergent. But if the student has never seen such a list, and must analyze the physical properties of products for the first time, then the question is divergent.

Convergent questions also can inadvertently turn into divergent questions. When the answer to a question thought to involve simple recall ("Does anyone know the meaning of the Latin word *via?*") has never been seen before, and the student arrives at the right answer through generalization and inductive reasoning (e.g., by thinking about the meaning of the English word *viaduct* or the phrase "via route 35"), then the question is divergent.

To complicate matters further, a convergent question in one context may be a divergent question in another, and vice versa. The question "What do you think of disarmament?" may require the use of evaluation skills by eighth graders but only the recall of facts by twelfth graders who have just finished memorizing the details of the Strategic Arms Limitation Treaty. Also, both of the questions "What do you think about disarmament?" and "What do you think about the Dallas Cowboys?" may require some analysis, synthesis, or decision making, but for most of your students disarmament will require a higher level of thought than will the Dallas Cowboys. As has been shown, effective questions depend on more than just words—they depend on the *context* of the discussion in which the question is raised, *voice inflection, word emphasis,* and *word choice.*

What Research Exists on Convergent vs. Divergent Questions?

Classroom researchers have studied the effects on student achievement of convergent and divergent questions (Redfield & Rousseau, 1981; Winne, 1979; Gall et al., 1978). Remember that far more convergent questions are raised in classrooms than divergent questions; the ratio is about 4:1. Most rationales for using higher-level, divergent-type questions include promotion of thinking, formation of concepts and abstractions, encouragement of analysis-synthesis-evaluation, and so on. But interestingly, research has not clearly substantiated that the use of higher-level questions is related to gains in student achievement—at least not as measured by tests of *standardized* achievement.

Although some studies report modest improvements in achievement scores with the use of divergent questioning strategies, others have not. Some studies even report larger achievement gains with convergent questioning than with divergent questioning strategies. Although these studies found a large imbalance in favor of convergent questions, four important factors must be considered when looking at their results:

1. Tests of achievement—and particularly tests of *standardized* achievement—employ multiple-choice items that generally test for behaviors at lower levels of cognitive complexity. Therefore, the achievement measures in these studies may have been unable to detect increases in behaviors at the higher levels of cognitive complexity, increases that might have resulted from the use of divergent questions.
2. The diversity of responses normally expected from divergent questions, and the added time needed to build upon and follow up on responses, may prohibit large amounts of class time from being devoted to higher-order questioning. Because less instructional time often is devoted to divergent questioning than to convergent questioning, some study results may simply reflect the imbalance in instructional time, not their relative effectiveness.
3. The content best suited for teaching more complex behaviors may constitute only a small amount of the content in existing texts, workbooks, and curriculum guides. Much of the typical curricula in math, science, English, and even the social sciences emphasizes facts and understandings at the knowledge and comprehension level. This may be because such achievements are the most easily measured and because needed improvements can be identified from standardized tests. Until larger portions of curricula are *written to encourage or require higher-level thought processes*, the time teachers actually devote to these behaviors probably will not increase.
4. Thinking and problem-solving behaviors most closely associated with divergent questions may take much longer to become noticeable in the behavior of learners than less-complex behaviors. Less-complex behaviors (learning to form possessives, memorizing Latin roots, knowing multiplication tables) are quickly elicited with convergent questioning strategies

and are readily detected with fill-in, matching, or multiple-choice exams at the end of a lesson or unit. But more complex behaviors (learning to distinguish economic systems from political systems, learning to analyze household products for their chemical components, recognizing forms of quadratic equations) may take a unit, a grading period, or even longer to build to a measurable outcome. This time span is beyond that of most, if not all, of the studies that have compared the effects of convergent and divergent strategies on school achievement.

Thus, the seeming imbalance in the use and effectiveness of divergent and convergent questioning strategies may have little to do with the strategies themselves. Because factual recall always will be required for higher-order thought processes, numerous convergent questions always will be a necessary precondition for achieving higher-level behaviors. Also, because more instructional time is needed for higher-order questioning to be used effectively, the consistent use of moderate amounts of divergent questions may be more effective than intense but brief episodes of divergent questioning. The most appropriate *convergent:divergent* question ratio may be about 70:30 in classrooms where lesson content emphasizes lower levels of behavioral complexity, to about 60:40 in classrooms where lesson content emphasizes higher levels.

It is important to note that many of the same studies that fail to link higher-order questioning with increases in school achievement indicate that higher-order questioning tends to encourage students to use higher thought processes in composing a response. Research discussed by Dunkin and Biddle (1974) and Martin (1979) indicates that teachers who ask questions requiring analysis, synthesis, and evaluation elicit these behaviors from students more frequently than teachers who use fewer higher-level questions.

Therefore, these higher-level thought processes seem desirable, regardless of whether their effects show up on immediate tests of achievement. The effects of higher-level questioning on the thinking process in itself may justify applying higher-level questions consistently at moderate rates over extended periods.

WHO ARE THE TARGETS OF QUESTIONS?

Research by Brown and Edmondson (1984) suggests that questions should be directed to students on the basis of *group size* and *group ability*. Questions can be directed to individuals, to groups, or to the entire class. Or, questions can be directed to more-able learners, average learners, less-able learners, and learners of mixed ability. Figure 8.1 combines both of the group-size and group-ability dimensions to show some of the targets at which your questions can be directed.

Although most questions are framed for a mixture of abilities and are directed to the entire class, not all questions need fit this format. To be an effective teacher, you should vary not only the targets for whom you compose questions (individuals, groups of various sizes, or full class), but also the level of the questions.

FIGURE 8.1

Some possible targets
and groups for framing
questions

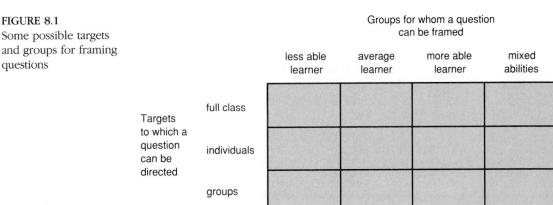

Questions specifically "framed" for low-ability and high-ability learners and targeted to individuals, sprinkled among questions framed for a mixture of abilities and directed to the entire class, will keep all students alert and engaged in the learning process.

In a heterogeneous class of mixed abilities, occasionally posing questions over the heads of less-able learners and under the heads of more-able students may be a necessary precondition for engaging the entire class in acting upon, thinking about, and using the content being presented. For example, a general question can be composed in one way for less-able learners and in another way for more-able learners by varying the kind and amount of advance organization with which the question is framed, as illustrated in these examples:

For the Less Able

"Tell me, Johnny, if you sat down to breakfast, what things at the breakfast table would most likely contain the element sodium?"

"After the death of Lenny in *Of Mice and Men*, what happens to the other main character?

"After thinking about the words *photo* and *synthesis*, who wants to guess what *photosynthesis* means?"

"Ted, if we have the equation $10 = \frac{2}{x}$, do we find x by multiplying or dividing?"

For the More Able

"Mary, what are some forms of the element sodium in our universe?"

"What would be an example of an anticlimax in *Of Mice and Men?*"

"Who can tell me how photosynthesis supports plant life?

"Rich, can you solve this problem for $x?$ $10 = \frac{2}{x}$."

Notice that these examples vary not only in cognitive complexity but also in how they are phrased. More advance organizers, hints, and clues are typical in questions directed to less-able learners—whether as individuals or in groups—than is appropriate for average or more-able learners.

Another way of framing questions for heterogeneous classes is to design them so different responses at various levels of complexity will be correct. You can accept less-complex responses from less-able learners as being just as correct as more-complex answers from more-able learners, if they match the level of the question being asked. Although a response from a less-able learner may not be as complete, you should evaluate the response in terms of the behavioral complexity required by the question and the student's ability to respond to it. Therefore, the elaboration given and depth of understanding required may be less for one type of learner than another.

Chapter 13 reviews specific instructional strategies for less-able and more-able learners. But for now, keep in mind that although most of your questions will be aimed at the average ability level in your class—or targeted for a mixture of abilities—you should specifically target some questions to both the less-able and the more-able learners and vary them among the full class, smaller groups, and individuals. Table 8.1 suggests some questioning strategies to use with less-able and more-able learners.

WHAT SEQUENCES OF QUESTIONS ARE USED?

Questions also can vary according to the type of sequence in which they are used. Recall that the most basic sequence involves structuring, soliciting, and reacting. However, many variations are possible. Studies by Brown and Edmondson (1984) and

TABLE 8.1 Some different questioning strategies for the less- and more-able learner	More Able	Less Able
	Use more open questions to make sure they can generalize the content to new problems.	Use more review questions to make sure they have not forgotten task-relevant prior content.
	Ask some questions that stymie, mystify, and challenge that only the more able could be expected to answer.	Use questions with specific and concrete examples, settings, and objects with which your students are familiar.
	Pose questions in the context of an investigation or problem that is broader than the question itself.	Use questions in a step-by-step approach, where each question is slightly broader or more complex than the preceding one.
	Ask students to go deeper, clarify, and provide additional justification or reasons for the answers they provide.	Use questions that rephrase or reiterate the answers to previous questions.
	Use more abstract concepts by asking students to see how their answers may apply across settings or objects.	Suggest one or two probable answers in your questions that lead students in the right direction.
	Use sequences of questions to build to higher and more complex concepts, patterns, and abstractions.	Use questions and answers as a game (e.g., 20 questions) with points and scores.

Smith and Meux (1970) note that one of the most popular sequences employs divergent questions that lead to convergent questions. They report that many teachers begin structuring-soliciting-reacting by starting with an open question that leads to further structuring, and then subsequent questions that involve recall or simple deduction.

This general-to-specific approach can take several twists and turns. For example, in the following dialogue, the teacher begins by encouraging speculative responses and then narrows to a question requiring simple deduction:

TEACHER: What do astronauts wear on the moon?
STUDENTS: Spacesuits.
TEACHER: So what element in our atmosphere must *not* be in the atmosphere on the moon?

It is the same approach when a teacher poses a problem, asks several simple recall questions, and then reformulates the question to narrow the problem still further:

TEACHER: If the Alaskan Eskimos originally came from Siberia on the Asian continent, how do you suppose they got to Alaska?
STUDENTS: (No response)
TEACHER: We studied the Bering Strait, which separates North America from Asia. How wide is the water between these two continents at their closest point?
STUDENT: About 60 miles. The Little and Big Diomede Islands are in between.
TEACHER: If this expanse of water were completely frozen, which some scientists believe it was years ago, how might Asians have come to the North American continent?

This type of funneling, adding conditions of increasing specificity to a question, was frequently employed by teachers in many studies reviewed by Redfield and Rousseau (1981). There is, however, no evidence that one sequencing strategy is any more effective in promoting student achievement than any other. The specific sequence chosen should depend on the behavioral objectives, the instructional content being taught, and the ability level of the students.

Some other types of questioning sequences that can be implemented in a cycle of structuring, soliciting, and reacting have been suggested by Brown and Edmondson (1984) and are illustrated in Table 8.2. With the appropriate objectives, content, and students, all offer useful additions to your teaching menu.

WHAT LEVELS OF QUESTIONS ARE USED?

As we have seen, as an effective teacher you must be able to formulate divergent and convergent questions, to target questions to specific types of learners, and to arrange questions in meaningful sequences. You also must be able to formulate questions at different levels of cognitive complexity. Recall from a previous illustration how important this is when classes are heterogeneously grouped with both less-able and more-able students.

TABLE 8.2
Some sequences of questions

Type		Description
Extending	———————	A string of questions of the same type and on the same topic
Extending and lifting		Initial questions request examples and instances of the same type, followed by a leap to a different type of question; a common sequence is likely to be recall, simple deduction and descriptions leading to reasons, hypothesis
Funneling		Begins with open question and proceeds to narrow down to simple deductions and recall or to reasons and problem solving
Sowing and reaping		Problem posed, open questions asked, followed by more specific questions and restatement of initial problem
Step-by-step up		A sequence of questions moving systematically from recall to problem solving, evaluation or open ended
Step-by-step down		Begins with evaluation questions and moves systematically through problem solving towards direct recall
Nose-dive		Begins with evaluation and problem solving and then moves straight to simple recall

From "Asking Questions" by G. Brown and R. Edmondson (pp. 97–119) in *Classroom Teaching Skills,* ed. E. Wragg. Copyright © 1984 by Nichols Publishing Company. Adapted by permission of Nichols Publishing Company.

One of the best-known systems for classifying questions according to cognitive complexity is the taxonomy of objectives in the cognitive domain that was presented in Chapter 4. This system has the advantage of going beyond the simple recall-versus-thought dichotomy frequently used in the research cited previously. Not all recall questions should deal with the lowest and most mundane forms of learning (e.g., recall of names, dates, facts), and not all thought questions should deal with the highest and most superlative forms of learning (e.g., discovery, insight, judgment). A continuum of question complexity that fills the space between these ends of the scale is a useful addition to the art of asking questions.

Recall that the cognitive-domain taxonomy contains these six levels of behavioral complexity:

Knowledge

Comprehension

Application

Analysis

Synthesis

Evaluation

Table 8.3 identifies the types of student behaviors associated with each level. Look at each level to get a feel for the question-asking strategies that go along with it.

TABLE 8.3
A question classification scheme

Level of Behavioral Complexity	Expected Student Behavior	Instructional Processes	Key Words
Knowledge (remembering)	Student is able to remember or recall information and recognize facts, terminology, and rules.	repetition memorization	define describe identify
Comprehension (understanding)	Student is able to change the form of a communication by translating and rephrasing what has been read or spoken.	explanation illustration	summarize paraphrase rephrase
Application (transferring)	Student is able to apply the information learned to a context different than the one in which it was learned.	practice transfer	apply use employ
Analysis (relating)	Student is able to break a problem down into its component parts and to draw relationships among the parts.	induction deduction	relate distinguish differentiate
Synthesis (creating)	Student is able to combine parts to form a unique or novel solution to a problem.	divergence generalization	formulate compose produce
Evaluation (judging)	Student is able to make decisions about the value or worth of methods, ideas, people, or products according to expressed criteria.	discrimination inference	appraise decide justify

Knowledge

Recall from Chapter 4 that knowledge objectives require the student to recall, describe, define, or recognize facts that already have been committed to memory. Some action verbs you can use to formulate questions at the knowledge level are:

define	list
describe	name
identify	recite

Some example questions are:

What is the definition of capitalism?

How many elements are in the periodic table?

Can you recite the first rule for forming possessives?

Can you give the equation for a straight line?

Notice that each of these questions can be answered correctly simply by recalling previously memorized facts. They do not require understanding of what was memorized or the ability to use the learned facts in a problem-solving context. Robert could parrot the definition of capitalism (as given in our dialogue in Chapter 7) without having the slightest notion of the differences between capitalism and other economic systems—or even that he is living in a capitalist system.

It is not unusual for meticulously memorized facts to be forgotten within days or weeks. You probably can cite a personal experience of doing well on fact-type quizzes during the semester, only to do poorly on the end-of-semester exam. In such cases, either your time spent memorizing the facts was wasted because it did not stick, or the instructor failed to relate those facts to the higher-level behaviors tested at the end of the course. (Your author vividly recalls his fifth-grade teacher, who spent nearly

Knowledge questions require recalling previously memorized facts. They do not require that the student understand what was memorized or be able to use the facts in a problem-solving context, for which higher-level questions will be needed.

every social studies lesson having the class memorize dates of major historical events and administering brief oral quizzes about them. Indelibly etched into your author's memory are hundreds of dates—but not one was ever comprehended, applied, analyzed, synthesized, or evaluated!)

When facts are linked to other forms of knowledge, such as those in subsequent lessons and units, they become steppingstones for gradually increasing the behavioral complexity of teaching outcomes. To avoid the overuse or disconnected use of questions at the knowledge level, ask yourself: Do the facts required by my questions represent task-relevant prior knowledge for subsequent learning?

If your answer is "No," you might consider assigning text, workbook, or supplemental material that contains the facts, instead of incorporating them into your question-asking behavior. If your answer is "Yes," then determine in what ways the facts will be used in subsequent lessons, and raise questions that eventually will help form more complex behaviors.

Your students may *not* need the ability to recite the names of the presidents, the Declaration of Independence, or the elements in the periodic table, because these facts may not be task-relevant prior knowledge for more complex behavioral outcomes. On the other hand, it is likely that your learners *will* need to recite the multiplication tables, the parts of speech, and the rules for adding, subtracting, multiplying, and dividing signed numbers, for these will be used countless times in completing exercises and solving problems at more complex behavioral levels. Always take time to ask yourself: Are the facts that I am about to teach task-relevant prior knowledge for subsequent lessons? By doing so, you will avoid knowledge questions that may be trivial or irrelevant.

Comprehension

Comprehension questions require some level of understanding of facts the student has committed to memory. Responses to these questions should show that the learner can explain, summarize, or elaborate upon the facts that have been learned. Some action verbs you can use in formulating questions at the comprehension level are:

convert	paraphrase
explain	rephrase
extend	summarize

Some example questions are:

Can you, in your own words, explain the concept of capitalism?

Who can summarize the main idea behind the periodic table of elements?

In converting a possessive back to the nonpossessive form, what must be rephrased so that the first rule applies?

What steps are required to solve an equation for a straight line?

In responding to each of these questions, the student acts upon previously learned material by changing it from the form in which it was first learned. For example, the teacher asks not for the definition of capitalism, but "in your own words, explain the concept of capitalism." This requires translation or conversion of the original definition (the teacher's) into another (the student's).

There is an important step in moving from knowledge-level questions to comprehension-level questions. Knowledge-level questions require no cognitive processing—thinking—at the time of response, but comprehension-level questions do. In the former case, the learner actually may think about the material only once, at the time it was originally learned. In the latter case the learner must actively think about the content twice: once when the facts are memorized and again when they must be composed into a response in a different form. Although fact questions must logically precede comprehension questions, comprehension questions are superior to knowledge questions for arousing the cognitive processes of the learner and thereby encouraging long-term retention, understanding, and eventual use of the learned material.

Application

Application questions extend facts and understanding to the next level of behavioral complexity. They go beyond memorization and translation of facts, requiring the student to use the previously acquired facts and understandings. Application questions require the student to apply facts to a problem, context, or environment that is different from the one in which the information was learned. Thus, the student can rely on neither the original context nor the original content to solve the problem.

Some action verbs you can use in formulating questions at the application level are:

apply	operate
demonstrate	solve
employ	use

Some example questions are:

What countries from among those listed do you believe have a capitalist economic system?

How is the periodic table of elements used to identify still-to-be-discovered elements?

Consider the first rule for forming possessives; who can apply it to the errors in the following newspaper article?

Who can solve for and plot the results of $Y = a + bX$, when $a = 1$, $b = 1.5$, $X_1 = 15$, $X_2 = 10$?

These questions ask the learner to use previously learned facts and under-standings to solve a problem. Your job in application questions is to present your learners with a context or problem different from that in which they learned the material. Application questions not only encourage the student to act upon learned material, thereby increasing engagement in the learning process, but also encourage the transfer of newly learned material to a new and different environment.

Application questions require two related cognitive processes: (a) the simultaneous recall and consideration of all the individual units (facts) pertaining to the question, and (b) the composing of units into a single harmonious sequence wherein the response becomes rapid and automatic. Recall that these two cognitive processes were introduced in Chapters 6 and 7 as unitization and automaticity. They are required for all Type 1 behaviors—that is, for acquiring facts, rules, and action sequences. It is through these two processes that action sequences are created from the application of previously learned facts and rules.

Application questions ask students to compose (put together) previously learned responses under conditions approximating some real-world problem, with the goal of making the correct response rapid and automatic. You can see that action sequences require two precedents: learned facts and understandings acquired via knowledge and comprehension questions *and* the use of previously learned facts and rules in new contexts. The number and quality of your application questions will determine how rapid and automatic your learners' action sequences become.

The number of application questions you ask may be less important than your *consistency* in asking them. Many beginning teachers inappropriately believe that application questions should be reserved for the end of a unit—or even worse, for the end of a grading period. But, as you have seen, they are essential any time a rapid, automatic response involving facts or rules is desired, or when an action sequence is the lesson goal.

The quality of your application questions will be determined largely by how much you change the problem, context, or environment in which the facts or rules were learned. If your change is too small, transfer of learning to an expanded context will not occur, and your "parrots" will recite facts and rules from the earlier context. On the other hand, if your change is too great, the new context may require a response beyond the grasp of most of your learners. The key is to raise application questions that require the transfer of learning to new problems or contexts only after all task-relevant facts and rules have been taught. The easiest way to accomplish this is to change the context only a bit at first, and then gradually shift to more unfamiliar contexts.

Analysis

Questions at the analysis level require the student to break a problem into its component parts and to draw relationships among the parts. Some purposes of questions at the analysis level are to identify logical errors; to differentiate among facts, opinions, and assumptions; to derive conclusions; and to find inferences or generalizations—in short, to discover the reasons behind the information given.

Some action verbs you can use in formulating questions at the analysis level are:

break down	point out
differentiate	relate
distinguish	support

Some example questions are:

What factors distinguish capitalism from socialism?

Where on the periodic table are the next new elements likely to be found?

In what ways can you differentiate Rule 1 possessive errors from Rule 2 possessive errors in the following essay?

Where are the mistakes, if any, in the following graphs, given their respective linear equations?

Analysis questions tend to promote Type 2 behaviors in the form of concepts, patterns, and abstractions. They generally are the most elementary form of the inquiry or problem-solving process, which is most closely associated with the functions of indirect instruction. In this respect, analysis questions are a movement away from the teaching of facts, rules, and action sequences and toward the more complex behavioral outcomes of concepts, patterns, and abstractions. You may consider analysis questions to be the start of the inquiry or problem-solving process, and the beginning of a change from direct to indirect instructional strategies.

Although not all Type 1 and Type 2 behaviors can be neatly divided between application and analysis, several important changes occur in the example questions at this level. Observe that the majority of the questions lack the single best answer so common in the teaching of facts, rules, and action sequences. Consequently, you will encounter and evaluate a much broader range of responses at the analysis level.

You may not anticipate all the varied responses you will receive (some in fact may be surprising). If you cannot prepare for all possible responses (which is very likely at the higher levels of behavioral complexity), then you should prepare yourself psychologically for the diverse responses that analysis questions generate. Preparing yourself psychologically may mean simply shifting your classroom to a less rigid, more deliberate, and slower-paced climate to give yourself some time to evaluate responses on the spot. It also may help to admit to yourself that some of the responses you hear may never have been heard before.

Synthesis

Questions at the synthesis level ask the student to produce something unique or original—to design a solution, compose a response, or predict an outcome to a problem for which the student has never before seen, read, or heard a response. This behavior level often is associated with *creativity*, which may be broader than what is intended here. The creativity sought at the synthesis level is not freewheeling ideas from out of the blue but *directed* creativity in which not all responses are equally acceptable. The facts, rules, action sequences, and any analysis questions that have gone before will define the limits and directions of the synthesis requested. Thus, the relationship of your synthesis questions to the Type 1 behaviors needed by students and the Type 2 behaviors you wish to create should be clear to your students.

Some action verbs you can use in formulating questions at the synthesis level are:

compare	formulate
create	predict
devise	produce

Some example questions are:

What would an economic system be like that combines the main features of capitalism and socialism?

By means other than the periodic table, how might we predict undiscovered elements?

How could a paragraph showing possession be written without using any possessives?

Given a general equation for a curved line, what additional information would you need to graph the curve?

This illustrates that even more diversity can be expected with synthesis questions than with analysis questions. This is due to the divergent nature of the questions used to teach Type 2 behaviors. Such openness is apparent at the analysis level, but it is even more pronounced at the synthesis level. Therefore, your preparation for diversity is critical to how your synthesis questions are received by your students.

A question asking for ways to identify undiscovered elements other than by using the periodic table opens up many possible responses. Some may not be acceptable ("consult an astrologer") but others will be ("analyze minerals from the moon and other planets"). Accept all reasonable answers, even though your own solutions may be limited to one or two efficient, practical, accurate solutions. Recognize that your question is sufficiently open that an acceptable answer need not be contingent on efficiency, practicality, or accuracy. Efficiency, practicality, and accuracy might be built from student responses, but you cannot initially expect it of them.

Another characteristic of higher-level questions is the multiple responses they are likely to generate. Multiple response questions are ones that actively encourage diverse responses and that are used to build increasingly more appropriate answers. Table 8.2 showed different types of questioning sequences, several of which are capable of molding student responses to be either more expansive or more restrictive than the original. You can use diverse responses to synthesis questions to draw out and direct creativity without restricting or narrowing the question itself, as this dialogue illustrates:

TEACHER: In what ways other than from the periodic table might we predict the undiscovered elements?

BOBBY: We could go to the moon and see if there are some elements there we don't have.

BETTY: We could dig down to the center of the earth and see if we find any of the missing elements.

RICKY: We could study debris from meteorites—if we can find any.

TEACHER: Those are all good answers. But what if those excursions to the moon, to the center of the earth, or to find meteorites were too costly and time consuming? How might we use the elements we already have here on earth to find some new ones?

BETTY: Oh! Maybe we could try experimenting with the elements we do have to see if we can make new ones out of them.

This simple exchange illustrates a funneling strategy: broad, expansive answers are accepted and then are followed up with a narrower question on the next round. In this manner, the diverse multiple responses that typically result from synthesis and other higher-level questions can be used to direct creative responses into gradually more structured avenues of inquiry, thereby contributing to critical thinking.

Evaluation

Questions at this highest level of behavioral complexity require the student to form judgments and make decisions using stated criteria. These criteria may be subjective (when a personal set of values is used in making a decision) or objective (when scientific evidence or procedures are used in evaluating something). In both cases, however, it is important that the criteria be expressed to be clearly understood—although not necessarily valued—by others.

Some action verbs you can use in formulating questions at the evaluation level are:

appraise	defend
assess	judge
decide	justify

Some example questions are:

Using evidence of your own choosing, do capitalist or socialist countries have a higher standard of living?

If accuracy were your sole criterion, how would you compare laboratory analysis of known elements with interplanetary surveys for discovering the missing elements in the periodic table?

Using Rules 1 and 2 for forming possessives and assigning one point for each correct usage, what grade would you give the following student essay?

Given these graphed curved lines, how accurately have the four equations been plotted?

Evaluation questions have the distinct quality of confronting the learner with problems much as they appear in the real world. In this sense, evaluation questions link the classroom to the world outside. Because decisions and judgments are prime ingredients of adult life, it is essential that classroom experiences start learners toward the world in which they will live, regardless of their age or maturity.

Unfortunately, evaluation questions often are reserved for the end of a unit, or even for the end of a larger block of instruction. Even more misguided is the notion that evaluation questions are more suited to junior high and high school than to elementary grades. Both misconceptions have reduced the impact of evaluation questions on learners and no doubt have contributed to the lower percentage of higher-order questions observed in classrooms. If learners are to cope with real-world problems, they must learn to do so starting at the earliest grades and throughout their schooling. Therefore, your ability to ask evaluation questions that can bring the world to your learners at their own level of knowledge and experience is one of the most valued abilities that you, the effective teacher, can have.

This ability, however, does not come easily. To be sure, all characteristics of the previously discussed higher-order questions—diversity of responses, opportunities for open-ended or divergent questioning, and multiple responses—are present in evaluation questions. But criteria must be applied to these in deciding the appropriateness of a solution. Notice in the preceding examples that the criteria (or their source) are identified: "using evidence of your own choosing," "if accuracy were your sole criterion," "using Rules 1 and 2," "given the graphs." The more specific your criteria, and the better your learners know them, the more actively engaged they will become in answering the question.

It is important to note that evaluation questions can be either convergent or divergent. When you ask "Is the equation $2 + 2 = 4$ correct?" you are asking an evaluation question for which only a single, narrow, correct response is possible. Here, the student's engagement in the learning process may be limited to simply conjuring up a memorized portion of the addition table. This evaluation question has far fewer implications for training learners to judge, to make decisions, and to think critically than one that asks, "What kinds of goods and services would be owned by a government under a socialist economic system that would not be owned by a government under a capitalist economic system?"

The first question is convergent, focusing on a single, best answer ("Yes, $2 + 2 = 4$ is correct."). The second question is divergent. It allows a range of responses, the acceptability of which could only be judged by applying a set of subjective or objective criteria. The criteria to apply in determining the appropriateness of the first question allow no room for judgment; the criteria to apply in the second question allow a great deal of judgment. Your fundamental criteria for evaluation questions are decisions and judgments as they are made in the real world.

SUMMARY OF QUESTION TYPES

You now know the levels of questions that can be asked of learners and some factors to consider in selecting the appropriate question type. To summarize:

☐ Type 1 behaviors (those calling for the acquisition of facts, rules, and action sequences) generally are most efficiently taught with convergent questions that have a single best answer (or a small number of easily definable answers). Type 1 behaviors are most effectively learned with a direct instruction model that focuses convergent questions at the knowledge, comprehension, and application levels of behavioral complexity.

□ Type 2 behaviors (those calling for the acquisition of concepts, patterns, and abstractions) generally are most efficiently taught with divergent questions, for which many different answers may be appropriate. Type 2 behaviors are most effectively learned with an indirect instruction model that poses divergent questions at the analysis, synthesis, and evaluation levels of behavioral complexity.

Now that you are acquainted with these broad distinctions among types of questions, we will turn to several specific techniques that can help you deliver these questions to your students with ease and perfection.

HOW ARE PROBES USED?

Recall from Chapter 1 the five catalytic or helping behaviors (use of student ideas and contributions, structuring, questioning, probing, teacher affect) that assist performance of the five key behaviors (lesson clarity, instructional variety, task orientation, engagement in the learning process, student success). In this section, we will look at one of the catalytic behaviors—probing—in the context of a questioning strategy.

A probe is a question that immediately follows a student's response to a question provided for the purpose of:

□ Eliciting clarification of the student's response.
□ Soliciting new information to extend or build upon the student's response.
□ Redirecting or restructuring the student's response in a more productive direction.

Use probes that **elicit clarification** to have students rephrase or reword a response so you can determine its appropriateness or correctness. These probes, such as "Could you say that in another way?" or "How would that answer apply in the case of _____?" induce learners to show more of what they know, thereby exposing exactly what they understand. The brief and vague responses often given in the context of a fast-paced and lively classroom discussion can mask partially correct answers or answers that are correct but for the wrong reason. When you are unsure how much understanding underlies a correct response, slow the pace with a probe for clarification.

Use probes that **solicit new information** to follow a response that is at least partially correct or that indicates an acceptable level of understanding. This time you are using the probe to push the learner's response to a more complex level (e.g., "Now that you've decided the laboratory is the best environment for discovering new elements, what kind of experiments would you conduct in this laboratory?" or "Now that you've taken the square root of that number, how could you use the same idea to take its cube root?").

This type of probe builds higher and higher plateaus of understanding by using the previous response as a steppingstone to greater expectations and more complete responses. This involves treating incomplete responses as part of the next

Probes follow questions and are used to clarify a student's response, solicit new information, or redirect a response in a more productive direction.

higher-level response—not as wrong answers. The key to probing for new information is to make your follow-up question only a small extension of your previous question; otherwise, the leap will be too great and the learner will be stymied by what appears to be an entirely new question. This type of probe, therefore, requires much the same process for finding the right answer as does the previously correct question, only this time applied to a different and more complex problem.

Use probes to **redirect the flow** of ideas instead of using awkward and often punishing responses such as "You're on the wrong track," "That's not relevant," or "You're not getting the idea." Probes for redirecting responses into a more productive area can accomplish the needed shift less abruptly and more positively, to avoid discouraging students from venturing another response. A probe that accomplishes this purpose moves the discussion sideways, setting a new condition for a subsequent response that does not negate a previous response.

For example, recall that, in our dialogue on socialism in Chapter 7, the teacher asked for "the kinds of things individuals would likely need to live and prosper." Ricky responded, "You mean like a car or a home of your own." But, because all individuals in a socialist economy might not agree on the value of these for everyone, the teacher had to redirect the discussion to objects more consistent with a socialist economy, without negating the value of the earlier response. She did this by stepping sideways and imposing two new conditions to get the discussion back on track: "What types of things could a *group of people,* say the size of a nation, agree on that would be *absolutely essential* for everyone's existence?" This probe successfully leaves behind objects such as cars and homes without negatively valuing Ricky's response.

Probing to redirect or restructure a discussion can be a smooth and effortless way of getting learners back on track. Notice in the following example how the teacher blends the use of all three types of probes in the context of a single discussion:

TEACHER: What do we call the grid system by which we can identify the location of any place on the globe? (To begin the questioning)

BOBBY: Latitude and longitude.

TEACHER: Good. What does longitude mean? (To solicit new information)

BOBBY: It's the grid lines on the globe that ... go up and down.

TEACHER: What do you mean by *up and down?* (To elicit clarification)

BOBBY: They extend north and south at equal intervals.

TEACHER: OK. Now tell me, where do they begin? (To solicit new information)

BOBBY: Well, I think they begin wherever it's midnight and end where it's almost midnight again.

TEACHER: Let's think about that for a minute. Wouldn't that mean the point of origin would always be changing according to where it happened to be midnight? (To redirect)

BOBBY: Yes, so the grids must start at some fixed point.

TEACHER: Anybody know where they begin? (To solicit new information)

SUE: Our book says the first one marked *0* starts at a place called Greenwich, England.

TEACHER: How can a grid that runs continuously north and south around the globe *start* any-place, Sue? (To elicit clarification)

SUE: I meant to say that it *runs through* Greenwich, England.

TEACHER: Good. Now let's return to Bobby's point about time. If we have a fixed line of longi-tude, marked *0,* how might we use it to establish time? (To solicit new information)

BOBBY: Now I remember. Midnight at the *0* longitude—or in Greenwich, England—is called *0* hours. Starting from there, there are timelines drawn around the world, so that when it's midnight at the first timeline, it will be one o'clock back at Greenwich, England; and when it's midnight at the next timeline, it will be two o'clock back at Greenwich, England, and so on.

TEACHER: What does that mean? (To elicit clarification)

BOBBY: Each line equals one hour—so ... so there must be 24 of them!

TEACHER: It should be no surprise to learn that time determined in reference to the *0* grid of longitude is called Greenwich Mean Time.

HOW SHOULD YOU USE WAIT TIME?

An important consideration during questioning and probing is how long to wait before initiating another question. Sometimes your "wait time" can be as effective in contributing to the desired response as the question or probe itself, especially when you give students time to thoughtfully compose their answers. Wait times that are either too short or too long can be detrimental, and when too long they also waste valuable instructional time. Obviously, wait time will be longer when students are weighing alternative responses (which often occurs during indirect instruction) than it will when their responses must be correct, quick, and firm (which often occurs during direct instruction).

Generally, you should wait *at least three seconds* before asking another question, or repeating the previous question, or calling on another student. During indirect instruction, where divergent questions may require thinking through and weighing alternatives, up to *15 seconds* of wait time may be appropriate. Rowe (1974), Tobin (1980), and Tobin and Capie (1982) suggest that when wait time is increased to three seconds or longer:

> length of responses increases,
>
> number of voluntary (unsolicited) responses increases,
>
> level of behavioral complexity of responses increases,
>
> students ask more questions,
>
> students show more confidence in the responses, and
>
> students' failure to respond decreases.

These research findings provide impressive testimony to the important role that wait time can have on learners' responses. If only a single piece of advice were given to beginning teachers such as yourself concerning wait time, it would be: *slow down and pause longer between questions and answers than what at first feels comfortable.*

WHAT ARE COMMON PROBLEMS IN USING QUESTIONS?

Based upon classroom observations of the question-asking behavior of beginning teachers, here are some of the most frequently observed problems to watch for, and suggested remedies.

Do You Use Complex, Ambiguous, or "Double" Questions?

One of the commonest question-asking problems of beginning teachers is the use of the complex, ambiguous, or "double" question. This is a question that is so long and complicated that students easily lose track of the main idea by the time it is completed. Sometimes, a teacher will unknowingly pack two (or even more) questions within its complicated structure.

Because such questions are delivered orally and are not written, students have no way of rereading the question to gain its full intent. It is unfortunate that these questions sometimes are so complicated that even the teacher cannot repeat the question precisely when requested, thus providing different versions of the same question. Consider the following three examples of needlessly complex questions and their simpler but equally effective revisions.

Example 1.

> *Complex Form:* "We all know what the three branches of government are, but where did they come from, how were they devised, and in what manner do they relate?"

This question is actually three questions in one, and requires too long a response if each point in the question were responded to individually. Besides, the first two questions may be redundant—or are they?—while the third is sufficiently vague to bewilder most students. Finally, what if some students do not know or cannot recall the three branches of government? For those students, everything that follows is irrelevant, opening the door to boredom and off-task behavior.

> *Simpler Form:* Recall that there are three branches of government: the executive, judicial, and legislative. What governmental functions are assigned to each by the Constitution?

Example 2.

> *Complex Form:* How do single-celled animals propagate themselves and divide up to create similar animal life that looks like themselves?

If you were to ask this question, you can be sure that some of your students would ask you to repeat the question, in which case you might not remember your own complex wording. This question fails to get to the point quickly and appears to ask the same thing three times: how do single-celled animals propagate . . . divide up . . . create similar animal life? This redundancy could easily be mistaken for three separate questions by students struggling to understand single-celled reproduction at an elementary level. State your questions only one way and rephrase later, if need be, when students know that it is the same question being rephrased.

> *Simpler Form:* By what process do single-celled animals reproduce?

Example 3.

> *Complex Form:* What do you think about the Civil War, or the Vietnam War, or war in general?

Depending on what part of this question a student wants to hear, you may get noticeably different answers. The intention was to raise a question that would provide enough options to get almost any student involved in composing a response; but, unless you intend only to start a controversy, the range of responses will probably be so broad that moving to the next substantive point may be impossible. This question may leave students arguing feverishly for the entire period without being able to focus on the real purpose for raising the question in the first place (e.g., as an introduction to the Civil War, or to unpopular wars, or to the concept of war). This question is too broad, too open, and too divergent to be of practical value for framing a day's lesson.

> *Simpler Form:* What are the factors that you believe would justify a war among groups within the same nation?

Here are basic rules for avoiding complex, ambiguous, or "double" questions:

1. Focus each question on only one idea.
2. State the main idea only once.
3. Use concrete language.
4. State the question in as few words as possible.

Do You Accept Only the Answers You Expect?

Another common mistake of beginning teachers is to rely almost exclusively on the answer they expect. Recall the discussion in Chapter 3 regarding the bias that teachers sometimes have about whom they call on and interact with in classroom exchanges. Biases can extend to favorite answers as well as to favorite students. When teaching new content, which frequently is the case during your first year, you naturally strive to become more secure and confident by limiting answers to those with which you are most familiar. Your first reaction will be to discourage responses at the edge of what you consider to be the appropriate range. This range is directly related to the openness of your questions. Open questions encourage diversity, and it is this diversity that often catches the beginning teacher off guard and forces an expansive question into a limited one. Note in the following dialogue how this teacher's posture is changed by the nature of the response.

TEACHER: OK, today we will study the European settlers who came to America, and why they came here. Why did they come to America?
STUDENT 1: To farm.
TEACHER: No, not to farm.
STUDENT 2: To build houses and churches.
TEACHER: No, that's not right either.

If this exchange were to continue for very long it no doubt would turn off many students, if only because they know that these responses cannot be entirely wrong even if they are not what the teacher wants. What does the teacher want? Probably, the desired answer is that the early Americans came because of religious persecution in their European communities. The last student's response, "to build houses and churches," was a perfect opportunity for a probe that simply asked "Why churches?" Unfortunately, this teacher missed that opportunity in favor of waiting for the exact response, because this teacher was unable or unwilling to build upon existing responses. This teacher may have a long wait, in which case valuable instructional time will be lost by calling on student after student in the hope that the only acceptable answer will eventually emerge.

Answers that are just what you are looking for are always desirable, but remember that partially correct answers and even unusual and unexpected ones can become effective additions to the discussion through the use of probes. The solution to this problem is to use probes and build gradually toward your targeted responses.

Why Are You Asking This Question?

Perhaps the most serious error of all in question-asking is not being certain of why you are asking a question. Remember, questions are tools that support the teaching and learning processes. Your first decision in using questions is to determine whether your lesson is teaching facts, rules, and action sequences or concepts, patterns, and abstractions. If the former is your goal, convergent questions at the knowledge, comprehension, or application levels probably are the ones to ask. If the latter is your goal, then divergent questions at the analysis, synthesis, or evaluation levels usually are the questions to ask. This decision strategy is summarized in Figure 8.2.

If you have not determined where you are on Figure 8.2, you are likely to ask the wrong type of question, and your questions will lack logical sequence. They may jump from convergent to divergent and move back and forth from simple recall of facts to the acquisition of concepts and patterns. Your students will find your questions disconcerting, because your ideas will not be linked by any common thread—at least not by one that they can follow—and you will be seen as vague or lacking the ability to connect content in meaningful ways. Therefore, it is important that you decide in advance where your questioning strategy is going and then move toward this goal by choosing appropriate questions and levels of behavioral complexity.

Finally, it is important to note that just because your goal may be Type 1 or Type 2 behaviors, this does not mean that you cannot vary your questioning strategy across the levels shown on Figure 8.2. Questions should vary within types of learning (e.g., from knowledge to application or from analysis to synthesis) and across types of learning (e.g., from application to analysis). It is important to keep in mind your ultimate goal for the lesson and to choose the best combination of questions to reach that goal.

Do You Answer the Question Yourself?

Another common problem with beginning teachers is posing a question, and then answering it yourself. Sometimes a student begins a response but is cut off, only to hear the remainder of the response supplied by the teacher:

TEACHER: So, who was the president who freed the slaves?
STUDENT: Abraham—
TEACHER: Lincoln! Yes, that's right.

FIGURE 8.2
A decision tree for deciding on the types of questions to ask

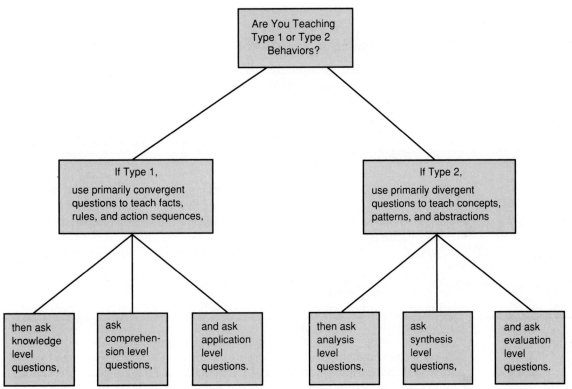

Sometimes the reverse occurs: a student begins a response that the teacher knows is wrong and then is cut off by the teacher, who gives the correct response:

TEACHER: So, who was the president who freed the slaves?
STUDENT: George—
TEACHER: No, no! It was Abraham Lincoln.

Needless to say, both outcomes demoralize the student, who either is deprived of the chance to completely give a right answer or is shown to have a response so incorrect that it is not even worth hearing in its entirety. Neither of these outcomes may be intended, but this is how your students will see it.

Your job is to use student responses to build to other more complex outcomes. Probes to elicit new information, to go beyond an already-correct answer, or to provide hints and clues after a wrong answer are particularly useful, because they extend to your students the right to give a full and deliberate response, right or wrong. Teachers who frequently interrupt student responses because of a desire for perfect answers, a dominant personality, or talkativeness, may ultimately produce frustrated learners who never learn to give full and thoughtful responses or to participate voluntarily.

Do You Use Questions as Punishment?

Our final problem, and perhaps the most difficult, is the use—or rather abuse—of questions to punish or to put a student on the defensive. Being asked a question can be a punishment as well as a reward. For example, here are some ways in which questions can be used as punishment:

1. A student who forgot to do the homework is deliberately asked a question from that homework.
2. A student who never volunteers is always asked a question.
3. A student gives a wrong response and then is asked an even harder question.
4. A student who disrupts the class is asked a question for which the answer cannot possibly be known.
5. A student who gives a careless response is asked four questions in a row.

Nearly every teacher has, at one time or another, used questions in one or more of these ways. Interestingly, some teachers do not always see these uses as punishment. Regardless of intent, however, such questions *are* punishment in that they (a) are unlikely to engage the student actively in meaningful learning, and (b) leave the student with a poorer self-image, less confidence, and more anxiety (perhaps anger) than was present before the question. These are behaviors that can only impede the learning process and which, therefore, have no place in your repertoire of questioning strategies. Each of the student-centered problems reflected in the preceding examples could have been handled more effectively, perhaps by:

1. Making a list of students who don't do homework.
2. Giving example questions beforehand to students who never volunteer.
3. Giving another try and providing hints and clues to students who give wrong responses until partially correct answers are received.
4. Giving disciplinary sanctions or reprimands to students who disrupt class.
5. Passing quickly to another student after receiving a careless answer.

Ample means are available for dealing with misbehavior and such means are far more effective than using questions. Questions are *academic tools* that should be prized and protected for their chosen purpose. To misuse them or to use them for any other purpose may affect how your questions will be perceived by your students (Did I get the hard question because she thinks I'm smart or because I'm being punished?). Such conflicts can drain students of the energy and concentration needed to answer your questions and may forever cast doubts on your motives.

The other side of questions is that they can be implicit rewards when used correctly. The opportunity to shine, to know and display the correct answer in front of others, and to be tested and get an approving grade are rewarding experiences for any learner. Consequently, every learner, regardless of ability level or knowledge of a correct response, should periodically experience these emotions.

Don't ignore students who are incapable of responding and don't accept wrong answers. Instead, occasionally try a broader criterion than correct/incorrect to help all students share in the emotional and intellectual rewards of answering questions. For example, try rewarding the most novel, most futuristic, most practical, and most thought-provoking answers along with the most accurate response. This will let every learner share in the challenge and excitement of questions.

A FINAL WORD

This chapter presented many aspects of the art of questioning. However, the most important lesson in this chapter is that questioning is a tool for actively engaging your learners in the learning process. All your teaching efforts will meet an untimely end unless you can get your learners to act upon, think about, or work on the content you present in ways that evoke the cognitive processes required by Type 1 and Type 2 learning. Guided practice, review, feedback and correctives, independent study, advance organizers, discussion, and so on are some approaches for setting in motion the cognitive processes necessary for meaningful learning to occur. Questions are another tool to add to your teaching menu. Because of their almost endless variety they may well be the most flexible tool on your menu.

SUMMING UP

This chapter introduced you to questioning strategies. Its main points were:

1. An effective question is one for which students actively compose a response and thereby become engaged in the learning process.

2. An effective question depends on voice inflection, word emphasis, word choice, and the context in which it is raised.

3. The three most commonly observed teacher behaviors in the classroom are structuring, soliciting, and reacting.

4. Soliciting—or question-asking behavior—encourages students to act upon and think about the structured material as quickly as possible after it has been presented.

5. It has been estimated that 70–80% of all questions require the simple recall of facts, but only 20–30% require clarifying, expanding, generalizing,

and the making of inferences. In other words, as few as one out of every five questions may require higher-level thought processes, even though behaviors at the higher levels of cognitive complexity are among those most frequently required in adult life, at work, and in advanced training.

6. Some of the most common purposes for asking questions include:
   □ getting interest and attention
   □ diagnosing and checking
   □ recalling specific facts or information
   □ managerial
   □ encouraging higher-level thought processes
   □ structuring and redirecting learning
   □ allowing expression of affect

7. A question that limits possible responses to one or a small number is called a convergent, direct, or closed question. This type of question teaches

the learner to respond in a limited, restrictive manner.

8. A question that has many right answers or a broad range of acceptable responses is called a divergent question. Divergent questions, however, can have wrong answers.

9. The same question can be convergent under one set of circumstances and divergent under another, as when so-called creative answers to a divergent question have been memorized from a list.

10. Research has not established that the use of higher-order questions is related to improved performance on standardized achievement tests. However, higher-order questions have been found to elicit analysis, synthesis, and evaluation skills, which are among the skills most sought in adult life.

11. Questions can be specifically worded for low-ability and mixed-ability learners as well as directed to individuals, groups, or the entire class.

12. Questions may be used in the context of many different sequences, such as funneling, where increasingly specific conditions are added to an original question, narrowing it to one requiring simple deduction.

13. In addition to being divergent, convergent, and targeted to specific types of learners, questions can be formulated at different levels of cognitive complexity that comprise the knowledge, comprehension, application, analysis, synthesis, and evaluation levels of the cognitive domain.

14. Knowledge questions ask the learner to recall, describe, define, or recognize facts that already have been committed to memory.

15. Comprehension questions ask the learner to explain, summarize, or elaborate upon facts that have been learned.

16. Application questions ask the learner to go beyond the memorization of facts and their translation and to use previously acquired facts and understandings in a new and different environment.

17. Analysis questions ask the learner to break a problem into its component parts and to draw relationships among the parts.

18. Synthesis questions ask the learner to design or produce a unique or unusual response to an unfamiliar problem.

19. Evaluation questions ask the learner to form judgments and make decisions, using stated criteria for determining the adequacy of the response.

20. A probe is a question that immediately follows a student's response to a question; its purpose is to elicit clarification, to solicit new information, or to redirect or restructure a student's response.

21. The key to probing for new information is to make the follow-up question only a small extension of the previous question.

22. The time you wait before initiating another question or turning to another student may be as important in actively engaging the learner in the learning process as the question itself. A wait time of at least three seconds should be observed before asking another question, repeating the previous question, or calling on another student.

23. Longer wait times have been associated with longer responses, greater numbers of voluntary responses, greater behavioral complexity of the response, greater frequency of student questions, and increased confidence in responding.

24. To avoid problems commonly observed in the question-asking behavior of beginning teachers:
    ☐ Do not raise overly complex or ambiguous questions that may require several different answers.
    ☐ Be prepared to expect correct but unusual answers, especially when raising divergent questions.
    ☐ Always establish beforehand why you are asking a particular question. Know the complexity of behavior you may expect as a result of the question.
    ☐ Never supply the correct answer to your own questions without first probing. Never prevent a student from completing a response to a question, even if incorrect. Use partially correct or wrong answers as a platform for eliciting clarification, soliciting new information, or redirecting.
    ☐ Never use questions as a form of embarrassment or punishment. Such misuse of questions rarely changes misbehavior, and questions are academic tools that should be prized and protected for their chosen purpose. To misuse them or to use them for any other purpose may affect how your questions will be perceived by your students.

FOR DISCUSSION AND PRACTICE

*1. What is the definition of an effective question as used in this chapter?

*2. Identify the chain of events that forms the most frequently observed cycle of teacher-student interaction.

*3. Approximately what percentage of all school time may be devoted to questions and answers?

*4. Approximately what percentage of questions asked require simple recall of facts, and approximately what percentage require clarifying, expanding, generalizing, and the making of inferences?

*5. Identify seven specific purposes for asking questions and give an example of each.

*6. In your own words, what is a convergent question and what is a divergent question? How do they differ with respect to right answers? How are they the same with respect to wrong answers?

7. Using the same question content, give an example of both a convergent and a divergent question.

*8. Under what circumstances might a divergent question such as "What propulsion systems might airplanes use in the year 2050?" actually function as a convergent question?

*9. Explain under what circumstances a convergent question such as, "What is 2 multiplied by 4?" might actually function as a divergent question.

*10. How does the asking of higher-order questions affect (a) a learner's standardized achievement score,

and (b) a learner's use of analysis, synthesis, and evaluation skills in thinking through a problem?

11. Compose a question to be directed to a less-able learner and another to be directed to a more-able learner. How do these two questions differ?

12. Write a brief dialogue, using realistic teacher and student responses, that illustrates a sequence of related questions that funnels student responses.

13. Using Table 8.2 as a guide, compose a sequence of related questions that extend and lift student responses.

14. Using the same content area as above, prepare one question that elicits the appropriate level of behavioral complexity at each level of the cognitive domain—knowledge, comprehension, application, analysis, synthesis, and evaluation.

15. In the context of a brief classroom dialogue, provide one example each of questions that (a) elicit clarification, (b) solicit new information, and (c) redirect or restructure a student's response.

*16. What is meant by the phrase *wait time?* Generally speaking, should beginning teachers work to increase or decrease their wait time?

*17. Identify and give an example of the five most troublesome question-asking problems for the beginning teacher.

---

*Answers to asterisked questions (*) in this and the other chapters are in Appendix B.

SUGGESTED READINGS

Doneau, S. (1987). Soliciting. In M. J. Dunkin (Ed.), *International encyclopedia of teaching and teacher education*. New York: Pergamon.
An overview of the many ways teachers can solicit responses from their students during a lesson.

Gall, M. D., Ward, B., Berliner, D., Cahen, I., Winne, P., Elashoff, J., & Stanton, G. (1978). Effects of questioning techniques and recitation on student learning. *American Educational Research Journal, 15,* 175–199.
Results of a research study on the effects of various styles and types of questioning on student behavior.

Hunkins, F. (1976). *Involving students in questioning.* Boston: Allyn & Bacon.
Covers the important aspects of getting students to ask questions and how to integrate student questions into the instructional dialogue of the classroom.

Martin, J. (1979). Effects of higher-order questions on student process and product variables in a single-classroom study. *Journal of Educational Research, 72,* 183–187.
An interesting study that confirms the value of asking higher-order (divergent) questions for engaging students in the learning process.

Redfield, D., & Rousseau, E. (1981). A meta-analysis of experimental research of teacher questioning behavior. *Review of Educational Research, 51,* 237–245.
A comprehensive review of research summarizing the most consistent findings on teacher questioning behavior.

Riegle, R. P. (1976). Classifying classroom questions. *Journal of Teacher Education, 27,* 156–161.
Reviews the many ways questions can be classified and shows examples of some important but less-used types of questions.

Ross, H. S., & Killey, J. C. (1977). The effect of questioning on retention. *Child Development, 48,* 312–314.
Results of a study confirming the close connection between questioning strategies and their effects on what is remembered.

Servey, R. (1974). *Teacher talk: The knack of asking questions.* Belmont, CA: Fearon.
This is a brief how-to-do-it book on asking different types of questions.

Tobin, K. (1980). The effect of an extended teacher wait-time on science achievement. *Journal of Research in Science Teaching, 17,* 469–475.
An interesting report of research that shows the influence that wait time can have on your students' behavior.

Self-Directed Learning

9

285

In this chapter on self-directed learning we will study an important method for engaging your students in the learning process. Recall that in Chapter 7 we studied indirect instruction, in which concepts, patterns, and abstractions are learned through the processes of generalization and discrimination. We used the word *indirect* to indicate that the learner acquires a behavior indirectly by transforming content (facts, rules, and action sequences) into a response that differs (a) from the original content presented and (b) from any previous responses made by the learner.

This chapter carries this approach one step further. Here we show you how to teach learners to go beyond the content given—to think critically, reason, and problem-solve—using a *self-directed* approach to learning. You will see how to use self-directed strategies to actively engage your students in the learning process and to help them acquire the reasoning, critical-thinking, and problem-solving skills required in today's complex society.

Much of today's classroom learning is focused upon activities by which the learner acquires facts, rules, and action sequences. The majority of lessons require outcomes only at the lower levels of behavioral complexity—knowledge, comprehension, and application (Gall, 1984). This may explain why the national studies cited in Chapter 3 found many students unable to think independently of the teacher or to go beyond the content in their texts and workbooks. The manner in which most schooling occurs may not be teaching students to become aware of their own learning and to derive their own patterns of thought and meaning from the content presented.

Self-directed learning is an approach to teaching *and* learning that actively engages students in the learning process to acquire outcomes at the higher levels of behavioral complexity. Self-directed learning helps students construct their own understanding and meaning from textual content, and helps them to reason, problem-solve, and think critically about the content.

Self-directed learning requires several unique teaching functions, in which you:

1. Provide information about when and how to use mental strategies for learning.
2. Explicitly illustrate how these strategies are to be used to think through solutions to real-world problems.
3. Encourage your learners to become actively involved in the subject matter by going beyond the information given, to restructure it in their own way of thinking and prior understanding.
4. Gradually shift the responsibility for learning to your students through practice exercises, question-and-answer dialogues, and/or discussions which engage them in increasingly complex thought patterns.
5. Monitor and correct student responses as needed.

Consider the following excerpt, which illustrates how some of these teaching functions might be accomplished in a typical lesson:

TEACHER: (A poem is written on the board; teacher reads it to class)

> Man is but a mortal fool
> When it's hot, he wants it cool
> When it's cool, he wants it hot
> He's always wanting what is not.

Today, I want to illustrate some ways to understand a poem like the one I've just read. This may seem like a simple poem, but its author put a lot of care and meaning into each one of its words. Now, let me give you an approach to studying poems like these and gaining from them the meaning intended by their authors. First, let's identify the key words in this poem. Bobby, what do you think are some of the most important ones?

BOBBY: Well, I'd say the word "man" because it's the first.

TEACHER: Any others? (still looking at Bobby)

BOBBY: Not that I can see.

TEACHER: Anita?

ANITA: The words "hot" and "cold" have to be important, because they appear twice and they rhyme with the last words of the first and last lines.

TEACHER: Any other key words? Rick?

RICK: Well, I think a "mortal fool" is supposed to be telling us something, but I don't know what.

TEACHER: Good. So, now we've identified some words we think are especially important for understanding this poem. Why don't we look up in the dictionary the meanings of any of these words we don't know or are unsure of. That will be our second step. Ted, look up the word "mortal" for us, while we begin work on our third step. The third step is to paraphrase what you think this author is saying. Susan, can you paraphrase what he is saying?

SUSAN: I think he's saying we're always changing our minds and that's why we look so stupid sometimes.

TEACHER: We are all human, so we certainly change our minds a lot, don't we? Rhonda looks like she wants to say something. Rhonda?

RHONDA: Well, I'd say it's not that we're stupid that we change our minds, but that it's just part of who we are—we can't help wanting what we can't have.

TEACHER: So, you've added a little something to Susan's interpretation. What do you think, Susan? Do you agree?

SUSAN: Yeah, we're not stupid; we're just mortals.

TEACHER: Chris, do you want to add anything?

CHRIS: I'd say that we're not stupid at all. That to really enjoy something, we must have experienced its opposite—otherwise we wouldn't know how good it is.

TEACHER: Now, that brings us to our fourth and last step. Let's try to relate what Chris just said to our own experience. Anyone ready? Bobby?

BOBBY: I agree with Chris, because I remember thinking how much I welcomed winter because of how hot it was last summer.

TEACHER: (Marcia is waving her hand) Marcia, what do you have to say about this?

MARCIA: But, now that it's winter, I can't wait for the cold weather to end, so I can go swimming again. (class nods in agreement)

TEACHER: It looks as though Chris was right. We sometimes have to see both sides of something—hot/cold, good/bad, light/dark—to fully appreciate it. Now, Ted, what did you find for "mortal" in the dictionary?

TED: It says "having caused or being about to cause death," "subject to death," and "marked by vulnerability."

TEACHER: Which of those do you think best fits the use of "mortal fool" in our poem?

TED: Well, hmm . . . the last one, because it kind of goes with what we have been saying about how we choose one thing and then another . . . like when we get too cold, dream of summer, and then when summer comes, think it's too hot.

TEACHER: I agree; it fits with what we all have experienced in our lives—and that means we are on the right track to the interpretation the author intended. Now, let's go one step further. Putting all of our ideas together, what is this poet saying? (nodding to Alex)

ALEX: Well, I'd say life's a kind of circle. We keep going around and around—back to where we've come, and then trying to escape to where we've been—maybe that's one kind of vulnerability—like it said in the dictionary.

TEACHER: That's good thinking, Alex. Bobby, because we began with you, I'll let you have the final word.

BOBBY: I think Alex got it, because now I understand why the author thinks we're all fools—we're like a dog going in circles chasing our tails, always wanting what we don't have. That explains the first and the last line, doesn't it? Because we are human, we are vulnerable to always ". . . wanting what is not." Yes, so we're "mortal fools." I get it.

TEACHER: Very good. Now, let's think for a moment about the four steps we just went through to understand this poem. I will repeat them slowly while you write them down. They will become your guide for reading the rest of the poems we study.

Notice how this teacher contributed something to each of the four components of self-directed learning (how to use mental strategies for learning, how to think through solutions to real-world problems, actively involving learners in the subject, and shifting responsibility for learning to the student).

First, she provided the learners with a mental strategy for learning—in this case a framework of four easy-to-follow steps for interpreting poetry. These steps were sufficiently familiar and practical enough to be followed by almost any student, regardless of ability or experience. Notice that they were not just divisions of the task, but steps that ultimately *force learners to go beyond the content presented* to find their own meaning and understanding, based on personal experience and individual thinking. In other words, there were no wrong answers with this strategy—only answers that could be improved to raise the learner onto the next rung of the learning ladder.

Second, the strategy provided wasn't just routinely given to the learners by listing its steps on the board; the steps were *illustrated in the context of a real problem*. The application was real world and typical of other examples to which they would be asked to apply the strategy.

Third, the learners were invited to become *participants in the learning*, not just passive listeners waiting to be told what to do. By using a question-and-answer dialogue to provide a structure for the learners' opinions and experiences, students became an active part of the process by which new knowledge was being generated. They were, in a sense, their own teachers without knowing it. This was made possible through the format of an unscripted discussion, which removed any fear of producing a wrong response that might have prevented some learners from participating.

And fourth, note that as the lesson evolved, more and more of the most important conclusions were provided by the students, not the teacher. The highest level of interpretation with which the lesson ended came almost entirely from the summarizing remarks of students. By the end of the lesson the teacher's role was more that of a monitor and codiscussant than of an information provider—that role having been assumed by the students themselves as they actively applied each of the steps given earlier in the lesson.

Now let's look more closely at some of the invisible mental strategies that actually can be used by learners to acquire meaning and understanding from text.

METACOGNITION

One invisible strategy for self-directed learning is metacognition. *Metacognition* refers to mental processes used by the learner to understand the content being taught. The prefix *meta* means *above* or *in front of,* and the word *cognitive* refers to the *thinking process.* Therefore, metacognition refers to the mental processes used by the learner to understand the content being taught. Metacognitive strategies assist learners in internalizing, understanding, and recalling the content which is to be learned. Metacognitive techniques often include thinking processes like self-interrogation, self-checking, self-monitoring, and analyzing, as well as memory aids (*mnemonics*) for classifying and recalling content.

Metacognitive strategies are most easily conveyed to learners through a process called mental modeling (Duffy, Roehler, & Herrmann, 1988). Mental modeling involves three important stages (Duffy & Roehler, 1989):

1. Showing students the reasoning involved.
2. Making students conscious of the reasoning involved.
3. Focusing students on applying the reasoning.

These steps usually are carried out through verbal statements that walk learners through the process of attaining a correct solution. They begin with *verbal markers* such as:

"Now, I will show you how to solve this problem by talking out loud as I go through it, identifying exactly what is going on in my mind."

"Think about each decision I make, where I stop to think and what alternatives I choose—as though you are making the same decisions in your own mind."

Notice that the teacher is not giving the learner the mechanics of getting a right answer—do step A, then B, then C—but, more importantly, is providing an actual "live" demonstration of the mental procedures that may lie behind the routine completion of a problem.

These mental procedures help students to internalize, recall, and then generalize problem solutions to different content at a later time. You do not just convey information according to the preceding steps, but actually demonstrate the decision-making process as it occurs within your own thoughts. By contrast, the mechanical memorization of steps rarely helps learners to solve similar problems in other contexts or allows content to be recalled when the present topic has lost its immediate importance (no exam in sight or homework due).

You then monitor the process as it occurs in the learner, provide feedback, and adjust the complexity and flow rate of content as needed. This leads to a second important concept for self-directed learning called mediation.

TEACHER MEDIATION

On-the-spot adjustments to content flow and complexity that you make to accommodate idiosyncratic learning needs are called *teacher mediation*. Your role during mediation is to adjust the instructional dialogue to help students restructure their learning and move them closer to the intended outcome. In other words, the interactive dialogue you provide helps learners construct their *own* meanings from the content. This aids retention and the generalization of the reasoning process to other contexts.

The knowledge or skills that learners are to acquire are not given to them in the form of end products. Instead, learners are provided the cognitive stimulation at just the proper times to acquire the end products through their own reasoning. The need for adjustment of flow and content seldom can be anticipated. It requires mediation—your on-the-spot judgment of what new information would bring a learner's response to the next level of refinement of which the learner is capable at that moment. This next level reflects the content difficulty and behavioral complexity from which the student can most benefit at that moment.

The Zone of Maximum Response Opportunity

This level of content difficulty and behavioral complexity is the learner's **zone of maximum response opportunity**.* It is the zone of behavior that, if stimulated by you, will bring a learner's response to the next level of refinement. Thus, your response directed at the zone of maximum response opportunity must be at or near the learner's current level of understanding, but also designed to lift the learner's following response to the next higher level. Your response directed to the zone of maximum response opportunity need not elicit the correct answer, because the learner at that precise moment may be incapable of benefiting from it. It should, however, encourage the learner to refine an initially crude response.

---

*The zone of maximum response opportunity is called the "zone of proximal development" by Vygotsky (1978).

Here are two classroom dialogues in which the first teacher hits the "zone of maximum response opportunity," but the second misses it:

TEACHER: When you see a proportion, such as 4/5 (writes it on board), think of the number on top as "what is" and the number on the bottom as "what could be." Think about a box of cereal that you make your breakfast from. If I wrote the proportion of cereal in the box as 3/4 (writes it on board), I would say to myself, the full box is equal to the number 4—that's the "could be" part. But this morning, after I fixed my breakfast, what's left is only the number 3, which is the "what is" part. That's how I can tell the box is still pretty full, because the number for "what is" is close to the number for "what could be."

Now, Johnny, explain to me what it means when it says on a label that the proportion of vitamin C for one 4-ounce glass of orange juice is ½ the minimum daily requirement.

JOHNNY: I'm not sure.

TEACHER: Okay, what words can we use to describe the number on top?

JOHNNY: You said it's "what is."

TEACHER: What does that mean?

JOHNNY: I guess it's how much vitamin C is really in the glass.

TEACHER: And, now for the bottom.

JOHNNY: You said the bottom is "what could be." Does that mean that it's all you need?

TEACHER: Yes, it does—good. Now, think of another example—one of your own—in which something was less than it could have been.

JOHNNY: Well, I finished Ms. Enro's social studies test before the end of the period.

TEACHER: And how long was the period?

JOHNNY: Umm, about 40 minutes, I guess.

TEACHER: Using our words, what would you call that part of the problem?

JOHNNY: "What could be." OK, I get it. Then, the time I actually took is what really happened? Yeah, I finished the test in about 20 minutes.

TEACHER: So, how would you express that proportion in numbers?

JOHNNY: It would be 20, for "what is," over 40, for "what could be." The top is half of the bottom, so I guess one glass of orange juice gives you half the vitamin C you need in a day.

TEACHER: Okay. Let's retrace the steps you just followed for another problem....

Now let's imagine that Johnny relives this episode in another classroom. After the same introductory remarks, Johnny is asked the identical question:

TEACHER: Now, Johnny, explain to me what it means when it says on a label that the proportion of vitamin C for one 4-ounce glass of orange juice is ½ the minimum daily requirement.

JOHNNY: I'm not sure.

TEACHER: Look, if the number 1 is on the top and the number 2 is on the bottom, it must mean the top is less than the bottom. Right?

JOHNNY: Right.

TEACHER: So, if the top number represents what is and the bottom number what could be, "what is" is one half less than "what could be." And, that can only mean the glass contains half of the minimum daily requirement of vitamin C. Got it?

JOHNNY: Yep.

Well, maybe he does and maybe he doesn't. Notice in the first example that, by retracing the mental steps for Johnny to recall, the teacher hit Johnny's "zone of maximum response opportunity" because his prior understanding and response were taken into account in moving the dialogue forward, closer to the intended goal of the lesson. It provided a peg with which Johnny lifted himself onto the next rung of the learning ladder.

The second teacher simply provided the right answer. This gave Johnny no opportunity to construct *his own* response by using the mental steps provided and thereby derive a process to use for independently arriving at other right answers in similar circumstances. The first teacher focused upon developing for the learner a process of reasoning—a "line of thinking"—that would give the content its own individual meaning and yet be consistent with the intended goal of the lesson.

Through classroom dialogues such as these, you can encourage your learners to construct their own meanings and interpretations, for example, to substitute their own unique constructions for "what is" and "what could be," and to share them with others through discussion and classroom dialogue. Such diversity among self-directed learners activates their unique learning histories, specialized abilities, and personal experiences, thus engaging them in the learning process.

Hitting the Zone of Maximum Response Opportunity

The "zone of maximum response opportunity" is particularly important in self-directed learning, because you can rarely provide the most appropriate response to each learner at all times. This is the key difference between individualized learning (e.g., programmed instruction) and self-directed learning. In individualized learning, the content writer anticipates the most probable errors and provides remedial or alternative learning routes (called branching) for all learners, regardless of their zones of maximum response opportunity. Because the instruction assumes that relatively homogeneous groups of "individual" learners will work through the content, the same types of errors must be anticipated for all learners. In some cases the remedial steps or alternative branching provided may fall within a learner's zone of development, but in some cases it may not.

Because self-directed learning almost always occurs during a student response–teacher reaction sequence, it affords the opportunity to more accurately aim your spoken or written reaction at the learner's zone of maximum response opportunity. However, there can be a variety of teacher reactions that fall within the learner's zone of maximum response opportunity with equal effect. After all, your target is not a point but a zone that in some instances may be as broad as the outfield in a major league ballpark.

In this broad field, a hit is a hit, whether it falls in left field, center field, or right field, as long as it is within the appointed zone. This is an important point, because aiming your reaction to a student response too sharply—to a fixed point like lower center field—may so restrict your response that it will exclude the learning history, specialized abilities, and personal experiences of the learner. And, it may not consider your own content knowledge, specialized abilities, and instructional style.

Diversity among self-directed learners can be activated by teacher interaction and the "gentle interplay" that taps the learner's zone of maximum response opportunity and provides appropriate steppingstones to higher levels of learning.

Thus, the concept of a zone affords both you and your students some latitude within which to construct and to create meanings and understandings that consider the unique needs of both. In this manner, self-directed learning promotes a "gentle interplay" between the minds of learner and teacher, pulling and pushing each other in a student response–teacher reaction sequence designed to help the learner climb to the next rung of the learning ladder.

FUNCTIONAL FAILURE (STUDENT ERRORS)

Another concept important to self-directed learning is *functional failure*. Student errors play an important role in the "gentle interplay" between learner and teacher. If your reaction promotes an inaccurate and meaningless response, the interplay may not be so gentle, at least not in the learner's mind. But, if your reaction creates (or even intentionally promotes) a student response that is inaccurate *but* meaningful, the play returns to a gentler state.

The latter condition describes a class of student errors called *functional* errors. Whether these errors are unexpected or are "planted" by you, they enhance the learner's understanding of content. Functional errors provide a logical stepping-stone for climbing onto the next rung of the ladder, which may eliminate an erroneous thought process from ever occurring again in the learner's mind. For example, such an error may be necessary so the student will not arrive at the right answer for the wrong reason, thereby compounding the mistake in other contexts.

Consider the following dialogue in which a student error becomes a functional steppingstone to the next level of understanding:

TEACHER: As you recall from yesterday, we were studying the reasons behind the Civil War. Does anyone recall under what president of the United States the Civil War began?

ALEXIS: Our book says Jefferson Davis.

TEACHER: Well, it so happens Jefferson Davis was a president at the time. But, that's not the right answer. Now, how do you think Jefferson Davis could be *a* president, but not *the* president of the United States at the time of the Civil War?

ALEXIS: Well, maybe at the start of the war there were two presidents, Jefferson Davis and someone else.

TEACHER: As a matter of fact, there were two presidents, but only one could be President of the United States.

ALEXIS: Well, if he wasn't President of the United States he must have been president of the other side.

TEACHER: But, do you recall the name of the government that represented the "other side?"

ALEXIS: Yeah, now I remember. It was the Confederacy. It was Lincoln who was the President of the North—which must have been called the United States—and Jefferson Davis, who must have been the President of the South, called the Confederacy. I guess I got confused with all the different names.

Even though the student response was incorrect, this teacher's reaction fell within the zone of maximum response opportunity, because from it directly followed a more correct response. Notice also how the teacher encouraged the learner to supply the answer, using her previous mistake as an aid to obtaining the correct answer. This strategy actually led to information that went beyond the question itself—to putting Jefferson Davis in geographic perspective and in correctly naming the governments representing both North and South.

But, what if this teacher had made a less thoughtful reaction, encouraging not only another inaccurate response but, worse, a blind alley not useful for refining or extending the student's initial response? What might such a reaction look like?

TEACHER: Does anyone recall under what President of the United States the Civil War began?

ALEXIS: Our book says Jefferson Davis.

TEACHER: I said President of the United States, not President of the Confederate States of America. See the difference?

ALEXIS: I guess so.

TEACHER: Well, OK. Then, let's go on to Mark.

The interplay here becomes considerably less gentle, as the specter of failure is left hanging over the learner and the teacher has no easy way out of this awkward ending.

Self-directed learning requires considerable *anticipatory teaching*. This means you respond to the learner at the learner's current level of understanding, to promote a student response, correct *or* incorrect, that is functional for moving to the next rung of understanding on the way to the intended goal of the lesson. This is why scripted approaches to instruction (like programmed instruction), although useful in certain contexts, cannot replace the gentle interplay between student response and teacher reaction, supported by the classroom dialogue and group discussion methods of self-directed learning.

RECIPROCAL TEACHING

One way you can apply self-directed learning in your classroom is with a strategy called **reciprocal teaching** (Palincsar, 1987). Reciprocal teaching provides opportunities to explore the content to be learned via classroom dialogue. At the center of reciprocal teaching are group discussions in which you and your students take turns as leader in discussing the text.

Gall (1984) observed that most classroom discussions amount to little more than recitation of facts by students with the aid of question-and-answer sequences in which all or most of the answers are known. This leaves little opportunity for students to construct their own meaning and content interpretation so they can attain higher levels of understanding. In practice, many classroom discussions promote little meaningful dialogue that actually helps students struggle with the adequacy of their ideas and opinions on their way to arriving at acceptable solutions. More often, these discussions are driven by text content, with rapid-fire questions that stay close to the facts as presented in the text.

Reciprocal teaching is a strategy to make such a typical discussion into a more productive and self-directed learning experience. It accomplishes this through four activities—predicting, questioning, summarizing, and clarifying. These unfold into the following sequence, described by Palincsar and Brown (1989):

- *Predicting*—discussion begins by generating predictions about the content to be learned from the text, based on:
  (a) its title or subheading in the text,
  (b) the group's prior knowledge or information pertaining to the topic, and
  (c) experience with similar kinds of information.
  Following the group's predictions about what they expect to learn from the text, the group reads and/or listens to a portion of it.
- *Questioning*—one individual is chosen to lead a discussion of each portion of the text that is read. Afterward, the discussion leader asks questions about the information. Students respond to the questions and raise additional questions.
- *Summarizing*—the discussion leader then summarizes the text and other students are invited to comment or elaborate on the summary.

> ☐ *Clarifying*—if points in the text were unclear (e.g., concepts or vocabulary), they are discussed until clarity is achieved. In this case, more predictions may be made and portions of the text reread for greater clarity.

The following is a dialogue (based on Palincsar & Brown, 1989) illustrating the four activities of predicting, questioning, summarizing, and clarifying that comprise reciprocal teaching:

TEACHER: (reading from text) "The pipefish change their color and movements to blend with their surroundings. For example, pipefish that live among green plants change their color to a shade of green to match the plants."

CLAIRE: (leading the discussion) One question that I had about this paragraph is: What is special about the way the pipefish looks?

TEACHER: (clarifying) Do you mean the way that it is green?

ANDY: (elaborating) It's not just that it's green, it's that it's the same color as the plants around it, all around it.

CLAIRE: (continuing) Yes, that's it. My summary of this part tells how the pipefish looks and that it looks like what is around it. My prediction is that this is about its enemies and how it protects itself and who the enemies are.

MONTY: (adding to the summary) They also talked about how the pipefish moves . . .

KEITH: (rejoining) It sways back and forth . . .

ANDY: (adding) . . . along with the other plants.

TEACHER: (questioning) What do we call it when something looks like and acts like something else? The way we saw the insect called a "walking stick" yesterday? We clarified this word when we talked about the walking stick.

ANGEL: Mimic.

TEACHER: That's right. We said we would say that the pipefish mimics the . . .

STUDENTS: (together) . . . plants.

TEACHER: OK! Let's see if Claire's predictions come true. (class turns to the text)

Notice in this discussion how the teacher supports student participation in the dialogue. The teacher's aim is to engage as many students as possible in the learning process by providing reactions to student responses that are in their zones of maximum response opportunity. This is accomplished by elaborating on student responses and allowing ample opportunity for students to participate in the dialogue, from their perspective. This gives the teacher ample data upon which to form a reaction that is within their zone of maximum response opportunity.

As the discussion continues, more responsibility for reading and developing the dialogue is given over to the students until, over time, the teacher becomes more of an advisor—or coach—who refines responses instead of providing them. At that point, more and more of the discussion represents the internalization of the text by the students, who now express it through their unique learning histories, specialized abilities, and experiences.

The ultimate goal of reciprocal teaching is to sufficiently engage students in the learning process so that they become conscious of their reasoning process. This occurs through their own modeling, other students' modeling, and the teacher's modeling of that process, and is refined in the context of classroom dialogues. This requires your continuous attention to the ongoing dialogue and to the meanings students are deriving from the text so you can continually adjust the instructional content to meet your learners' current level of understanding.

As students gradually accept the shift in responsibility from teacher to student, you reduce the amount of explaining, explicitness of cues, and prompting that may have marked the earlier part of the lesson. Figure 9.1 indicates some classroom activities that can guide the gradual shift of responsibility from teacher to learner during self-directed learning.

Palincsar and Brown (1989) summarize the teacher's role during reciprocal teaching on page 298.

FIGURE 9.1
Shifting responsibility from teacher to learners

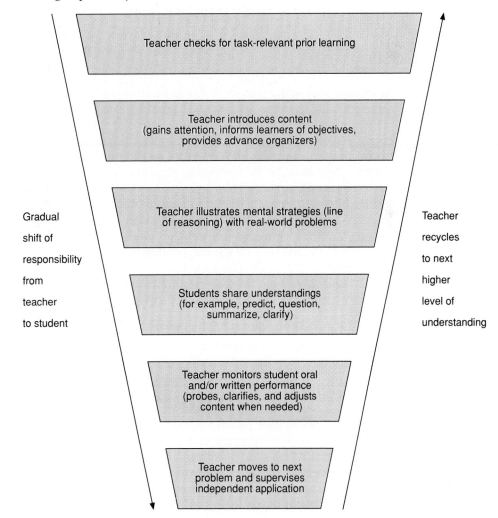

☐ The teacher and students share responsibility for acquiring the strategies employed in reciprocal teaching.

☐ The teacher initially assumes major responsibility for teaching these strategies ("thinks aloud" how to make a prediction, how to ask a question, how to summarize, how to clarify), but gradually transfers responsibility to the students for demonstrating use of the strategies.

☐ All students are expected to participate in the discussion and are given the opportunity to lead it. The teacher encourages participation by supporting students through prompting, providing additional information, or raising/lowering the demand on students so that responses meaningful to learners will be achieved.

☐ Throughout each self-directed lesson, the teacher consciously monitors the successfulness with which comprehension is occurring and adjusts the content as needed to the zone of maximum response opportunity.

SOCIAL DIALOGUE

As we have seen in the preceding dialogues, classroom conversation between teacher and students is central to self-directed learning. Verbal interactions within a classroom are vastly different from those occurring outside of it. In many classrooms, verbalizations are adult dominated, leaving students with little alternative but to responding to teacher requests for facts and information. These traditional teaching settings may offer few opportunities for students to elaborate or comment on the topic at hand.

However, self-directed learning strategies use classroom dialogue differently. Instead of verbalizations intended to confirm the teacher's authority, classroom dialogue is purposefully guided to gradually shift responsibility to the learner. The teacher "scaffolds," building the dialogue layer by layer, each time increasing the challenge to the learner to think independently of earlier constructions provided by the teacher.

Scaffolding must be done carefully to keep the challenge within the learner's zone of maximum response opportunity. This requires:

your close monitoring of the learner's response,

your awareness of the learner's current functioning level (for example, familiarity with the task), and

your awareness of the understanding level the learner can attain at the moment (based on, for example, past learning performance).

Attention to these details lets you scaffold the cognitive demands placed on the learner. You do so to increasingly shift the learner from responding to textual material to internalizing its meaning by elaborating, extending, and commenting upon it.

As we have seen, the strategy of reciprocal teaching uses group discussion and rotating discussion leaders to achieve this goal. It does so not just by getting students to talk, as do many traditional discussions, but by getting them to expose and elaborate the *processes* by which they are learning the content. The clear articulation and rehearsal of these mental strategies (1) guides the learner in subsequent performances and (2) helps you adjust the flow and level of prompts, cues, and questions to hit inside the zone of maximum response opportunity.

THE ROLE OF INNER SPEECH

As we have seen, an important aspect of classroom dialogue in self-directed learning is the increasing responsibility it places on the learner for creating original verbalizations in the form of comments, elaborations, and extensions. These verbalizations, if properly scaffolded, are believed to create an "inner speech" within the learner (Vygotsky, 1962). This inner speech ultimately leads to private internal dialogue that takes the place of the teacher's prompts and questions and self-guides the learner through similar problems.

As the responsibility for unique and original productions beyond the text gradually shifts to the learner, the learner increasingly acquires the ability to speak internally, modeling the same line of reasoning and mimicking the same types of questions, prompts, and cues used by the teacher at an earlier stage. In other words, the verbal interactions that were increasingly asked of the learner become internalized in a form of private speech used by the learner in the absence of direct teacher involvement.

It is at this point that the teacher's role turns to one of monitoring, prompting and cuing only when necessary to keep the learner on track. Ultimately, it is hoped that by internalizing the scaffold verbalizations of the teacher and recalling them at will in private dialogue, the learner becomes his or her own teacher, mimicking the logic and reasoning process modeled by the teacher. As we shall see in the following chapter (Cooperative Learning and the Collaborative Process), such self-direction can be stimulated by many different techniques in addition to reciprocal teaching, including many forms of cooperative and group learning.

The role of inner speech in guiding the behavior of both children and adults is central to self-directed learning strategies. The topic has long been a research interest and considerable evidence documents its usefulness in learning (Wiertsch, 1980; Bruner, 1978; Berk, 1990).

Although we adults seldom realize it, we often use inner speech to guide our actions. Most notably, when taking examinations, learners young and old verbally think through previously learned steps to obtain correct answers. During exams we talk to ourselves just as we talked ourselves through the same steps the night before, or were asked by our teacher to verbalize them before the class. These verbalizations gradually turn inward, from class discussions or recitations to private discussions with ourselves.

They become inner guideposts for thinking through and reasoning solutions to problems, using a process first modeled by a teacher and then gradually shifted to us through scaffolded verbalizations that "fade out" some portions of the model, requiring us to "pick them up" internally and to apply them on our own. This occurs

Outward verbalizations by the learner, if properly scaffolded, can be turned into inner speech that eventually replaces the teacher's prompts and self-guides the learner through similar problems.

most notably when the teacher no longer accepts regurgitations of the factual material in the text but begins to require their internalization through elaborations, comments, and extensions in our own unique constructions.

SOME EXAMPLE DIALOGUES OF SELF-DIRECTED LEARNING

Let's look at three classroom dialogues that exhibit characteristics of self-directed inquiry. In different teaching contexts, these dialogues illustrate:

☐ How a teacher models the process by which meaning and understanding can be derived from textual material.
☐ How questions, prompts, and cues can be used to scaffold responses, gradually shifting the responsibility for learning to the student.
☐ How the teacher thereafter can monitor student responses for continued understanding.

First, let's look at a fourth-grade classroom in which Ms. Koker is teaching reading. We'll observe how she models the process by which meaning and understanding can be derived from text. Our discussion begins with Ms. Koker reading an excerpt from a short story to the class from the daily reader:

Ms. Koker:	"Some of the coldest climate on earth occurs in the northern parts of Alaska. In this land, a small but hardy group of Native Americans lives and prospers in small villages where hunting and fishing is a way of life. This small group of villagers . . ."
Debbie:	(interrupting) Ms. Koker, I don't know what the word "hardy" means.
Ms. Koker:	What do you think it means, Debbie? (asking her to make a prediction)
Debbie:	Well, something that's hard—like, maybe, ice.
Ms. Koker:	Let's see if you are right. Let's think of some other words that might mean almost the same thing as "hard." (introducing the idea of synonyms)
Tim:	Something that's hard is strong.
Mickey:	Yeah, and it also lasts a long time.
Ann:	If you're strong, you can't be hurt.
Ms. Koker:	OK, now let's see if any of these ideas fit with the sentence, "In this land a small but hardy group of Native Americans lives and prospers in small villages where hunting and fishing is a way of life." What do you think, Tim? (encouraging the idea of fitting synonyms into the text to clarify meaning)
Tim:	Well, if we took the word "hardy" out and put in the word "strong," I think it would mean the same thing.
Ms. Koker:	What do you think, Barbara?
Barbara:	It makes sense, because when you're strong you can't be hurt—say by all the cold up north—and then you live a long time. (summarizing)
Mickey:	But, how do we know they live a long time, just because they're strong? (asking for clarification)
Ms. Koker:	That's a good point; we really don't know that yet, so what do you think? (calling for a prediction again)
Tina:	I think they won't live as long as us because of all the cold weather.
Ms. Koker:	So, how do you think they stay warm? Let's read on to see.

Notice that Ms. Koker was modeling a strategy for deriving meaning from text. To accomplish this, she introduced the idea of synonyms—by asking Debbie what she thought the word "hardy" meant and then by asking her students to insert the synonym into the text to check its appropriateness. Thus, she was conveying a model—a mental strategy—that can be used time and again by the students themselves, unaided by the teacher, whenever a word is unknown to them.

Next, let's observe Mr. Willis's junior high science class to see how he uses questions, prompts, and cues to encourage self-direction. In the following discussion, Mr. Willis is teaching a fundamental law of physics by providing questions and reactions that are scaffolded to his learners' zones of maximum response opportunity:

Mr. Willis:	Here you see a balloon, a punching bag, and a tire pump. Watch carefully as I let the air out of the balloon (lets air out), punch the bag (punches it), and press down on the pump handle (pushes handle). What did you notice about all three actions? Bobby?
Bobby:	You got tired. (class laughs)
Mr. Willis:	You're right, especially when I did the punching and pumping. (Then, reaching to Bobby's current level of understanding:) Yes, you saw a reaction in me; I got tired. What other action did you see?

Bobby:	The balloon flitted across the room.
Mr. Willis:	And, what else?
Bobby:	The punching bag moved forward—and, well the pump handle went down and then a little up.
Mr. Willis:	You saw several reactions, didn't you. What were they?
Bobby:	Something happened to the object you were playing with and . . . well . . . I guess something else was going on too.
Mr. Willis:	Anita, what did you see in all three cases?
Anita:	Movement in two directions, I think.
Mr. Willis:	What were the movements?
Anita:	Well, for the balloon, it went forward, but also it pushed the air backward . . . over your face. And, for the punching bag, it went forward . . . umph (mimics the sound) . . . and stopped. I don't know what other movement there was.
Mr. Willis:	(pushing to the next higher level of understanding now:) Think about what happened both after *and* before I punched the bag. To help you, write on the top of a piece of paper the words "before" and "after." Now, write down what you saw in each of these three instances—the balloon, the punching bag and the pump. Let's all take a minute to do this.
Anita:	(after about a minute) Now I remember. The punching bag came back to hit your hand again. That was the second movement.
Mr. Willis:	(checking for understanding among the others) And, what about the tire pump? Michael, you have your hand up.
Michael:	When you pushed the pump handle down to inflate the tire, it came back up a little.
Mr. Willis:	Yes, in each case there were two identifiable movements—which we will call an action and a reaction. Now, let's check to see if this is true for some other movements by identifying on your paper the action and reactions associated with the following. I'll say them slowly so you have time to write:
	The space shuttle taking off from Cape Canaveral.
	An automobile moving down the street.
	A gunshot.
	A football being kicked over a goalpost.

Notice how Mr. Willis used questions targeted to his students' current level of understanding. This allowed them to respond in some meaningful way, which gave him the opportunity to build upon an earlier incomplete response to reach the next higher level of understanding. For example, Bobby's first crude response, aided by the prompt "What other action did you see?" was used to introduce the concept of action followed by a reaction. Each time the questioning turned to a new student, Mr. Willis' question, prompt, or cue was targeted higher, but still within the learners' zone of maximum response opportunity.

Also, the idea of thinking through a solution on paper—called **think sheets**—kept students actively engaged in working through their responses. At the same time, it provided a strategy from which they might more easily derive actions and reactions for the new problems presented at the end of the dialogue. Mr. Willis' use of questions, prompts, and cues at various levels of difficulty kept this class moving through the lesson with increasingly more sophisticated responses.

Now, let's look in on a third classroom. Mrs. LeFluir is teaching Spanish to a high school class not just by altering the level of questioning, as did Mr. Willis, but by altering the tasks from which learners experience the application of content first hand. Without realizing it, Mrs. LeFluir's class is experiencing the difference between "propositional knowledge"—intended only for oral or verbal regurgitation—and "practical knowledge"—intended to be used in some problem-solving or decision-making task:

Mrs. LeFluir:	Today, we will study the gender of nouns. In Spanish all nouns are either masculine or feminine. Nouns ending in *o* are generally masculine, and those ending in *a* are generally feminine. Tisha, can you identify the following nouns as either masculine or feminine? (writes on board)
	libro
	pluma
	cuaderno
	gramática
Tisha:	(correctly identifies each)
Mrs. LeFluir:	Now, let's see how you identified each of the words and what each word means.
Tisha:	Well, I followed the rule that if it ends in an *o* it will be masculine but if it ends in an *a,* it will be feminine. I think the words are book, pen, notebook, and grammar.
Mrs. LeFluir:	Good. Now for the next step, you've all used indefinite articles *a* and *an* many times in your speaking and writing. In Spanish the word *un* is used for *a* or *an* before a masculine noun, and *una* is used for *a* or *an* before a feminine noun. In Spanish the article is repeated before each noun. Now, using the vocabulary words on the board, let's place the correct form of the indefinite article in front of each word. (shifting the task demand:) Why don't you take the first one, Ted?
Ted:	It would be *un libro.*
Mrs. LeFluir:	Mary.
Mary:	*Una pluma.*
Mrs. LeFluir:	Bob and Mike, take the next two.
Bob:	*Un cuaderno.*
Mike:	*Una gramática.*
Mrs. LeFluir:	OK. Now, we are ready to put our knowledge to work. I will give you a sentence in English and you translate it into Spanish, being sure to include the correct form of the indefinite article. (shifting the task demand again:) For this you will need to remember your vocabulary from last week. If you need to, look up the words you forgot. Mark, let's start with you. Come up to the board and write: Do you want a book?
Mark:	(writes on board) *Desea usted un libro?*
Mrs. LeFluir:	Good. And how did you decide to use *un* instead of *una?*
Mark:	The noun ended in *o.*
Mrs. LeFluir:	(Continues with three other examples)
	Do you need grammar?
	Do you want to study a language?
	Do you need a notebook?
	(After the students respond, she shifts the task demand again by moving to the following activity:) Now, read each sentence on the transparency and write down the correct form of the indefinite article that goes before the noun. (shows transparency)

Yo necesito _____ gramática.
Nosotros estudiamos _____ lengua.
Necesita Tomás _____ libro?
Es _____ pluma?
(After the students respond, she moves to a final activity and yet another task demand:) Now for the following sentences, I will speak in English, and I want you to repeat the same sentence entirely in Spanish. Be sure, once again, to include the correct form of the indefinite article. . . .

Notice in this episode the different activities required of the students and how they differed in cognitive complexity. Mrs. LeFluir gradually changed the demands being placed upon her learners by shifting the tasks to which they were to respond. Her lesson began by asking only for the simple regurgitation of rules (propositional knowledge), but ended by engaging students in oral delivery of the kind that might be required in ultimately having a conversation in Spanish (practical knowledge). She gradually shifted her tasks from propositional to application *in small enough degrees* to assure that all her students, or at least most of them, could follow.

This process also conveyed a language-learning model that will be helpful in subsequent contexts by providing a learning strategy that flows from memorization of rules and vocabulary, through completion and fill-in, to oral delivery. Notice that this sequence was completed even for this elementary lesson. This tells the learners that oral and written delivery, and not the regurgitation of rules, is the end goal to which all previous learning must contribute and toward which they must strive in their own individual learning and practice.

The systematic varying of task demands within a unit comprises an **activity structure**. Activity structures are most effective for self-directed learning when they vary the demands or problems being placed upon the learner in ways that gradually require the learner to assume responsibility for learning the content at a higher level of understanding.

Some steps you can follow in teaching self-directed inquiry to individual learners are:

☐ Provide a new learning task and observe how the student approaches it (for example, reading a short selection in a history text that will be the basis for an essay exam).

☐ Ask the student to explain how he or she approaches the task of learning the textual information—for example, in preparation for the exam. (This helps the student analyze his or her own cognitive approach.)

☐ Describe and model a more-effective procedure for organizing and accomplishing the task. For example, explain and demonstrate how to use the study questions at the end of the selection to help focus reading; highlight the main ideas in each paragraph of the selection with a fluorescent marker; write outline notes of key points on a separate sheet or on note cards as a study guide for later review. This gives the student new strategies for cognitively organizing the learning task.

- [ ] Provide the student with another, similar learning task for practicing the new cognitive strategies. Observe as the student proceeds with the task, giving reminders and corrective feedback.
- [ ] Model self-questioning behavior as you demonstrate analysis of a similar problem. For example, "What are the key questions you will need to answer?" "What is the main idea in this paragraph?" Write such questions on a small card for the student to use as a reminder.
- [ ] Provide another opportunity for the student to practice the skills using self-direction, decreasing your role as monitor.
- [ ] Check the result of the learning task by questioning for comprehension and asking the student to recall the specific learning strategies that were used.

OTHER COGNITIVE STRATEGIES

A number of cognitive strategies for organizing and remembering new material can be useful during self-directed learning. For example, Bradstad and Stumpf (1982) described four useful systems that can aid the mental organization of facts to increase recall—jingles or trigger sequences, narrative-chaining, number-rhyme or peg-word, and chunking. They are described in the following sections.

Jingles or Trigger Sentences

Jingles or trigger sentences can cue sequential letters, patterns, or special historical dates. For example, most music students learn some variation of the sentence, "Every Good Boy Does Fine," to recall the musical notes EGBDF on the lines of a music treble staff. "Spring forward, fall backward" helps one remember which way to adjust clocks at the spring and autumn time changes. And, many school children learn that, "In fourteen hundred and ninety-two, Columbus sailed the ocean blue." Such devices also can be used for recalling the steps of a mental strategy.

Narrative-Chaining

Narrative-chaining is the process of weaving a list of key words you wish to remember into a brief story. For example, if you need to memorize the life cycle of a butterfly in sequence, including the key stages of egg, larva, pupa, and adult, you could invent a narrative such as:

> This morning I cooked an *egg* for breakfast, but I heated it so
> long that it looked like molten *lava* from a volcano. A pupil from
> a nearby school stopped by, and when he saw my egg-turned-*lava*,
> he yelled, "I'm just a *pupil!* You're the *adult!* Couldn't you cook an
> egg better than that?"

In this case, *lava* and *pupil* sound enough like *larva* and *pupa* to trigger memory of the correct words in the life-cycle sequence.

Number-Rhyme or Peg-Word

A number-rhyme or peg-word mnemonic system uses words that rhyme with a sequence of numbers as a basis for developing odd, imaginative mental pictures that assist in memorizing a set of other, less-related words.

Using the life cycle of the butterfly as an example again, you might employ the number-rhyme system this way:

one-sun	Imagine a big, fried *egg* hanging in the sky overhead in place of a brightly shining sun.
two-stew	Imagine a bubbling stew erupting from a gigantic volcano under the fried egg, drying to form molten *lava*.
three-sea	Imagine a tiny, screaming *pupil* afloat on a swirling, angry sea where the hot lava sizzles as it meets the seawater.
four-door	Imagine a golden door in the side of the volcano that is opened by a gentle, helpful *adult* who reaches out to pull the pupil from the sea near the lava that was heated by the egglike sun.

Chunking

Chunking or grouping bits of information into sets of five to seven discrete pieces also can assist in memorization. If this is combined by chunking the data into logical categories, the information is then doubly processed in a mental framework for improved recall. A common example is memorizing a grocery list by splitting it into logical categories (dairy products, vegetables, beverages, etc.) of several items each. Teaching students to employ such mental organizers gives them creative alternatives by which to manipulate ideas and information, retain mental strategies for learning, and thus internally reinforce their own learning.

BEHAVIORAL SELF-CONTROL

Self-directed learning also has been applied to behavioral skills. For example, when a student demonstrates lack of self-control, several steps are recommended to help learners cope with frustration or anger. Kaplan (1982) suggests that self-control may be developed by teaching a student to:

- ☐ Recognize the environmental stimuli that precede or coincide with a feeling of anger.
- ☐ Recognize the earliest signs of physical feelings that coincide with anger (e.g., tightening of the stomach, clenched hands, rapid breathing, dry mouth, skin warmth, pounding heartbeat, tensed frown).

□ Relax in the presence of the environmental and physical stimuli by breathing deeply and slowly, using silent, calming self-talk, and consciously relaxing stomach, hand, and facial muscles.

□ Mentally review alternative responses to the external stimuli that are socially acceptable (e.g., walking away to "cool off"; asking a friend or adult for help; changing activities).

Socially acceptable behaviors may be provided in a written list of alternative responses, by explanation and demonstration, or by structuring an opportunity for the student to role-play preferred behavioral strategies.

As soon as the student uses a socially acceptable alternative in a real-life situation, give immediate praise and reinforcement. The goal of this type of instruction is to help the student self-monitor, and select appropriate strategies through self-talk, rather than relying on your external guidance to resolve the problem situation. As students learn to regulate their own problem-solving and social strategies effectively, they will be more able to profit from active exchanges with peers in a cooperative learning situation. It is to this important topic that we turn in the next chapter.

SUMMING UP

This chapter introduced you to strategies for self-directed learning. Its main points were:

1. Self-directed learning is an approach to teaching and learning that actively engages students in the learning process for the purpose of acquiring outcomes at higher levels of cognitive complexity.

2. Self-directed learning involves a sequence of activities that includes:

□ Providing information about when and how to use mental strategies for learning.

□ Illustrating how the strategies are to be used in the context of real problems.

□ Providing students the opportunity to restructure content in terms of their own ways of thinking and prior understandings.

□ Gradually shifting the responsibility for learning to students through activities (exercises, dialogues, discussions) that engage them in increasingly complex patterns of thought.

3. Metacognition is a strategy for self-directed learning that assists learners in internalizing, understanding, and recalling the content to be learned.

4. Metacognitive strategies include self-interrogation, self-checking, self-monitoring, and techniques for classifying and recalling content, called *mnemonics*.

5. Metacognitive strategies are taught through mental modeling in which learners are "walked through" the process of attaining a correct solution. Mental modeling includes:

□ Illustrating for students the reasoning involved.

□ Making them conscious of it.

□ Focusing learners on the application of the reasoning illustrated.

6. "Teacher mediation" is the teacher's on-the-spot adjustment of content flow rate and complexity to accommodate the individual learning needs of the student.

7. The role of teacher mediation is to adjust the instructional dialogue as needed to help the learner restructure what is being learned according to his or her unique abilities, learning history, and personal experiences.

8. A "zone of maximum response opportunity" represents the level of content difficulty and behavioral complexity from which the learner can most benefit at the moment a response is given.

9. The "zone of maximum response opportunity" is reached through a classroom dialogue in which the teacher provides reactions to student responses that activate the unique learning histories, specialized abilities, and personal experi-

ences of the learner from which individual meanings and interpretations of the content can be acquired.

10. Functional errors are incorrect or partially correct answers made by the learner that can enhance the meaning and understanding of content and provide a logical steppingstone for climbing onto the next rung of the learning ladder.

11. Reciprocal teaching provides opportunities to explore the content to be learned via group discussion.

12. Reciprocal teaching involves a type of classroom dialogue in which students are expected to make predictions, ask questions, summarize, and clarify when learning from text.

13. Reciprocal teaching involves a sequence of activities, which include:
    □ An initial class discussion that generates predictions about the content to be learned from text.
    □ Reading and/or listening to a portion of the text.
    □ Choosing a discussion leader who asks questions about the text of other students, who then respond with questions of their own.
    □ A summarization of the text by the discussion leader on which other students are invited to comment or elaborate.
    □ A clarification of any unresolved questions and a rereading of portions of text for greater clarity, if needed.

14. The teacher's role during reciprocal teaching is to gradually shift the responsibility for learning to the students by reducing the amount of explaining, explicitness of cues, and prompting that may have marked earlier portions of the lesson.

15. During reciprocal teaching the teacher's role is to:
    □ Jointly share the responsibility for learning with the students.
    □ Initially assume responsibility for modeling how to make a prediction, how to ask a question, how to summarize, and how to clarify, but then transfer responsibility to students for demonstrating use of these strategies.
    □ Encourage all students to participate in the classroom dialogue by prompting, providing additional information, and/or altering the response demand on students.
    □ Monitor student comprehension and adjust the rate and complexity of information as needed.

16. In self-directed learning, the teacher "scaffolds"—builds the dialogue within a discussion step by step—each time increasing the challenge to the learner to think independently of earlier constructions. Scaffolding must occur to the appropriate degree for each learner response to keep the challenge within the learner's zone of maximum response opportunity.

17. During self-directed learning, inner (private) speech helps the learner elaborate and extend the content in ways unique to the individual. As responsibility for learning beyond the text gradually shifts to the learner, the learner's inner-speech ability increases, modeling the same reasoning and using similar questions, prompts, and cues used by the teacher at an earlier stage.

18. Some steps for teaching self-directed inquiry to individual learners are:
    □ Provide a new learning task and observe how the student approaches it.
    □ Ask the student to explain how he or she would learn the content (e.g., preparing for an exam).
    □ Describe and model a more-effective procedure for organizing and learning the content (e.g., using study questions, notes, or highlighting key features in the text).
    □ Provide another, similar task on which the student can practice the strategies provided.
    □ Model self-questioning behavior during the task to ensure the learner follows the strategies correctly (e.g., "Did I underline the key words?").
    □ Provide other opportunities for the student to practice, decreasing your role as a monitor.
    □ Check the result by questioning for comprehension and use of the strategies taught.

19. Other cognitive strategies that can be helpful for organizing and remembering new material during self-directed learning include:
    □ Jingles or trigger sentences
    □ Narrative-chaining
    □ Number-rhyme or peg-word
    □ Chunking

20. Self-directed learning strategies also can be used to increase behavioral skills, self-control, and socially acceptable behavior.

FOR DISCUSSION AND PRACTICE

*1. Identify two purposes for engaging your students in self-directed learning.

*2. Identify four unique teaching functions associated with self-directed learning.

*3. What is "metacognition"? What do metacognitive strategies hope to accomplish?

*4. Identify the three stages of mental modeling.

5. Provide an example of a verbal marker in your content area that would alert learners that you are about to begin mental modeling.

*6. What specific outcomes can mental modeling help students acquire?

*7. What is the role of the teacher during "mediation"?

*8. Define "zone of maximum response opportunity" and give an example in the context of a classroom dialogue.

9. Give an example of a student response–teacher reaction that illustrates the concept of "functional failure."

*10. What is the purpose of reciprocal teaching?

*11. What is the sequence of activities comprising reciprocal teaching?

*12. What is the purpose of a classroom dialogue during self-directed learning?

*13. What is the role of inner (private) speech in self-directed learning?

14. Create a brief excerpt from a classroom dialogue to show what a scaffolded dialogue would be like in your teaching area.

*15. What is propositional knowledge as opposed to practical knowledge? Give an example of each.

16. Provide an example of an activity structure in your own subject area or grade level that varies task demand.

*17. Describe the steps you would take to teach self-directed learning to an individual learner.

18. Identify and give examples of each of four cognitive strategies for organizing and remembering new material.

_____

*Answers to asterisked questions (*) in this and the other chapters are in Appendix B.

SUGGESTED READINGS

Duffy, G., & Roehler, L. (1989). The tension between information-giving and mediation: Perspectives on instructional explanation and teacher change. In J. Brophy (Ed.), *Advances in Research on Teaching*, Vol. 1, 1–33. Greenwich, CT: JAI Press, Inc.
A review of research by the authors and others in which metacognitive strategies were effective in promoting learner comprehension.

Duffy, G., Roehler, L., & Herrmann, B. (1988). Modeling mental processes helps poor readers become strategic readers. *The Reading Teacher, 41*(8), 762–767.
A practical application of metacognitive strategies in an elementary classroom.

Meichenbaum, D. (1983). Teaching thinking: A cognitive-behavioral approach. In D. Carnine, D. Elking, A. Hendrickson, D. Meichenbaum, R. Sieben, & F. Smith (Eds.), *Interdisciplinary voices in learning disabilities and remedial education*, 127–142. Austin, TX: Pro-Ed Publishers.

A practical approach for teaching learners to think critically and independently of text and workbook.

Palincsar, A. (1986). The role of dialogue in providing scaffolded instruction. *Educational Psychologist, 21,* 73–98.
Some practical examples of the concept of "scaffolding," in which learners are moved toward increasingly complex patterns of thinking through classroom dialogue.

Palincsar, A., & Brown, A. (1989). Classroom dialogues to promote self-regulated comprehension. In J. Brophy (Ed.), *Advances in Research on Teaching*, Vol. 1, 35–71. Greenwich, CT: JAI Press, Inc.
The authors demonstrate how modeling and social dialogue in the classroom can contribute to student self-inquiry skills through reciprocal teaching.

Pressley, M., Borkowski, J., & Schneider, W. (1987). Good strategy users coordinate metacognition, strategy use, and knowledge. In R. Vasta & G. Whitehurst (Eds.), *Annals of Child Development* (Vol. 4, pp. 89–130). Greenwich, CT: JAI Press.

How metacognitive techniques can be combined with other effective teaching methods to increase independent thinking and problem solving.

Roehler, L., & Duffy, G. (1987). Why are some teachers better explainers than others? *Journal of Education for Teaching, 12*(3), 273–284.

Presents some techniques for achieving lesson clarity in which learners are encouraged to take responsibility for their own learning.

Rohrkemper, M., & Corno, L. (1988). Success and failure on classroom tasks: Adaptive learning and classroom teaching. *The Elementary School Journal, 88*(3), 298–312.

The authors discuss techniques by which learners can adapt classroom tasks to their individual learning styles to control their own learning.

Vygotsky, L. (1986). In A. Kozulin (Ed.), *Thought and language*. Cambridge, MA: Harvard University Press.

Introductions to the role of inner speech in learning and the concept of a zone of maximum response opportunity, by the author of these ideas.

10

Cooperative Learning and the Collaborative Process

What good are critical thinking, reasoning, and problem-solving skills if your learners cannot apply them in cooperative interaction with other people? In this chapter, you will learn ways to structure your students' learning goals cooperatively. This engages them in the learning process and promotes critical thinking, reasoning, and problem-solving skills, both inside and outside of your classroom.

In the previous chapter, you saw how self-directed learning could promote higher forms of thinking with the aid of metacognitive strategies. In this chapter, you will see how these same outcomes can be extended and reinforced through various forms of peer collaboration. You will learn how self-directed and cooperative learning share the complementary objectives of engaging students in the learning process and promoting higher patterns of thought (more complex behaviors) required in the world of work, family, and community.

The importance of cooperation among individuals is underscored by the many social problems we face. Few doubt that a greater understanding of others' viewpoints, and of the common good toward which every community and nation must strive, is important for reducing the sources of these problems. Not only must your learners know how to get along in a turbulent and ever-changing society, but they also must be prepared to contribute productively to it. Cooperative learning is a way your learners can build the skills they will need to reason and problem-solve in an adult world and to acquire the social skills that can make their reasoning and problem solving effective.

OUTCOMES OF COOPERATION

Cooperative learning activities instill in learners important behaviors that prepare them to reason and perform in an adult world. Let us consider a few of them.

Attitudes and Values

Adult learners form their attitudes and values from social interaction. Although we learn much about the world from books, magazines, newspapers, and audiovisual media, most of our attitudes and values are formed by discussing what we know or think with others. In this manner we exchange our information and knowledge with that of others who have acquired their knowledge in different ways. This exchange shapes our views and perspectives. It turns cold, lifeless facts into feelings, and then to attitudes and values that guide our behavior over longer periods of time.

These attitudes and values very often are left untaught in our schools. Many classrooms rely solely on formally acquired knowledge, with learners competing for grades and reinforcement. Yet, it is our attitudes and values that are one of the most important outcomes of schooling, because they alone provide the framework for guiding our actions outside the classroom, where there may be no formal sources of knowledge to fall back on. Cooperative learning is important in helping learners acquire from the curriculum the basic attitudes and values they need to think independently inside and outside of your classroom.

Prosocial Behavior

Models of acceptable behavior that contribute to the common good of family, friends, and community may not always be available in the home today. This is due in part to the dramatic increase in working couples, demanding occupations, and single-parent households. The "quality time" at home between adults and children is shrinking as our society becomes more technocratic, impersonal, and complex. For many, family burdens are heavy—driving long distances to and from work, finding appropriate and affordable after-school childcare, and grocery shopping and housekeeping forced into the evenings and weekends. This complexity often places stress upon family members that can make intimate and meaningful contact among family members difficult or even impossible.

It is during close and meaningful encounters among family members that models of "prosocial" behavior are communicated. Children learn right from wrong implicitly through their actions and the actions of others that come to the attention of adult family members. These adults are quick to point out the effects of these actions on family, friends, and the community.

With the decreasing presence of adults in the homes of many school-age learners, the classroom becomes an important vehicle for bolstering home and community values, or providing a substitute for them when none exist. Cooperative learning brings learners together in adultlike settings which, when carefully planned and executed, can provide appropriate models of social behavior.

Alternative Perspectives and Viewpoints

It is no secret that we form our attitudes and values by confronting viewpoints contrary to our own. Our likes and dislikes, the things we aspire to and avoid, come from our exposure to alternatives we could not have thought of on our own, given the limitations of our immediate context and experience. These alternatives—some of which we adopt, some we borrow from, and some we reject—are the raw material from which we form our own attitudes and values.

Confronted with these alternatives, we are forced into an objectivity necessary for thinking critically, reasoning, and problem solving. In other words, we become less self-centered. Depending on the merits of what we see and hear, we grow more open to exchanging our feelings and beliefs with those of others. It is this active exchange of viewpoints and the tension it sometimes creates within us that is the catalyst for our growth. Cooperative learning provides the context or "meeting ground" where many different viewpoints can be orchestrated, from which we form more articulate attitudes and values.

Integrated Identity

One of the most noticeable outcomes of social interaction is its effect on how we develop our personalities and learn who we are. Social interaction over long periods forces us to "see ourselves"—our attitudes, values, and abilities—in many different circumstances. The main result is that inconsistencies and contradictions in who we are—or think we are—cannot be hidden, as might be the case in a single interaction or small number of social interactions.

If we say and think one way in one situation, and say and think another way in another situation, we cannot help but notice our own inconsistency and wonder why it exists. We attempt to resolve such contradictions, to clarify what we really believe and to believe what we really say. Our personality (at least what we show to others) becomes more coherent and integrated and is perceived by others as a more forceful and confident projection of our thoughts and feelings. Over time, repeated social interactions reduce the contradictions until our views become singular and consistent.

Cooperative learning can be the start of stripping away the irrelevant, overly dramatic, and superficial appendages that mask our deepest thoughts and feelings. Thus we begin to gain an integrated sense of self—not coincidentally, one that we increasingly grow proud of.

Higher Thought Processes

If all of the preceding benefits of cooperative learning were not enough, the fact that it has been linked to increases in the use of higher thought processes in learners is another reason for its use (Slavin, 1987; Slavin et al., 1985; Johnson & Johnson, 1987). As noted, cooperative learning actively engages the student in the learning process and seeks to improve the critical thinking, reasoning, and problem-solving skills of the learner. Critical thinking, reasoning, and problem solving cannot occur outside a context of attitudes and values, prosocial behavior, alternative perspectives and viewpoints, and an integrated identity. Cooperative learning provides the ingredients for higher thought processes to occur and sets them to work on realistic and adultlike tasks.

These higher thought processes—required for analyzing, synthesizing, and decision making—are believed to be stimulated more by interaction with others (peers and adults) than by books and lectures, which typically are not interactive. Books and lectures may be useful for teaching knowledge, comprehension, and application, but they seldom are sufficient to bring about the private speech required for thinking critically, reasoning, and problem solving. These behaviors require interaction with others as well as oneself to "unleash" the motivation required for thinking and performing in complex ways.

The model of cooperative learning we have been discussing thus far is illustrated in Figure 10.1.

COMPONENTS OF A COOPERATIVE LEARNING ACTIVITY

In the rest of this chapter you will see how to organize your classroom for cooperative learning. In planning a cooperative learning activity, you need to decide the type of interactions you will have with your students, the type of interactions your students

FIGURE 10.1
Model of cooperative learning

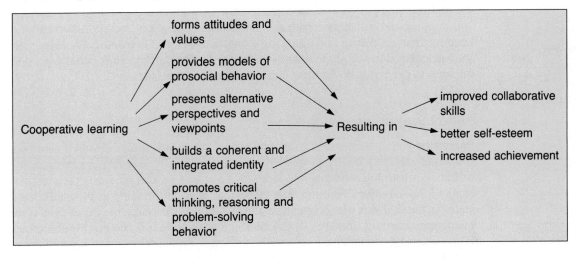

will have with one another, the task and materials you select, and the role expectations and responsibilities you will assign. These four aspects are discussed in the following sections.

Teacher-Student Interaction

One purpose of teacher-student interaction during cooperative learning is to promote independent thinking. Much like student response–teacher reaction sequences during self-directed inquiry, exchanges between your learners and yourself in the cooperative classroom focus on getting learners to think for themselves, independently of the text. To accomplish this goal, you model, intervene, and collaborate with learners in much the same way as in the self-directed classroom. This should come as no surprise, as the goals of cooperative and self-directed inquiry are complementary. This also is why you may develop self-directed inquiry skills in your students first, as an effective catalyst to cooperative learning.

However, the way you establish teacher-student interaction during cooperative learning is different from self-directed learning. In self-directed inquiry, the interaction usually is one-on-one, with verbal messages directed to individuals one at a time and adjusted to their zones of maximum response opportunity. On the other hand, cooperative learning occurs in groups that share a common purpose and task, so you must broaden interactions to fit the zone of maximum response opportunity that is common to most group members. And, instead of bringing individuals to a greater understanding and awareness of their own thinking, your goal now is to help the *group* become more self-reflective and aware of their own performance.

"Think about that some more," "Why not check with the reference at the learning center," and "Be sure you've followed the guidelines I've given you," are frequent expressions you will address to a group of four or five learners assigned a specific task. Your role is to intervene at critical junctures and then to retreat, allowing the group to grapple with the new perspective or information given. In this manner, you monitor and collaborate with the group during brief but focused interventions, keeping them on course and following a productive line of reasoning. Thus, teacher-student interactions take on an air of well-timed and brief intrusion into the group's thinking to periodically stimulate and stir a flurry of new ideas.

Student-Student Interaction

Interaction among students in cooperative learning groups is intense and prolonged. Unlike self-directed inquiry, in which the learner eventually takes responsibility for his or her own learning, students in cooperative learning groups gradually take responsibility for *each other's* learning. The effect may well be the same as in self-directed learning. Again, this is why cooperative and self-directed learning may be used as complementary learning strategies, with one reinforcing the skills acquired in the other.

During cooperative learning, the feedback, reinforcement, and support come from student peers in the group, as opposed to coming from you. Interactions among students constitute the majority of time and activity during cooperative learning, unlike the modest amount of direct student-to-student interaction that occurs in the self-directed classroom. Groups of four or five, working together in the physical closeness promoted by a common task, encourage collaboration, support, and feedback from the closest, most immediate source—one's peers. An essential ingredient of cooperative learning is the desire of each learner to facilitate the task performance of his or her fellow group members.

Task Specialization and Materials

Another component of cooperative learning is the task to be learned and the materials that comprise a cooperative learning activity structure. Cooperative learning tasks are preplanned activities; they are timed, completed in stages, and placed within the context of the work of others (for example, the tasks of other groups). This promotes the sharing of ideas and/or materials and the coordination of efforts among individuals. The choice of task and supporting materials is very important to promote meaningful student-student interaction.

Group discussion also may have considerable teacher-student and student-student interaction, but task specialization is what separates cooperative learning from group discussion.

Cooperative learning tasks typically use "division of labor" to break a larger task into smaller subparts on which separate groups (sometimes individuals) work. Eventually these efforts come together to create the whole, and thus each member of the class has contributed. Therefore, each group may be asked to specialize, focusing its efforts on a smaller yet meaningful part of some larger end product for which the entire class receives credit. Groups may even compete against one another with the idea of producing a better "part" or more quality "product" than other groups. However, the purpose is not the competition that produces the final product, but the *cooperation* within and between groups that the competition creates.

Cooperative task structures have the goal of dividing and specializing the efforts of small groups of individuals across a larger task whose outcome depends on the sharing, cooperation, and collaboration of individuals within groups.

Role Expectations and Responsibilities

Proper assignment of roles is important to the success of cooperative learning activities. In addition to groups being assigned specialized tasks, individuals often are assigned specialized roles to perform within their groups. Some roles that can be assigned to facilitate a group's work and to promote communication and sharing among its members are group leader, researcher, recorder, and summarizer.

The success of a cooperative learning activity depends upon your communication of role responsibilities and modeling them where necessary. This is another reason why cooperative learning has little resemblance to loosely formed discussion groups—not only must you divide labor among learners and specialized tasks, but you also must designate roles that foster the orderly completion of a task.

If someone's duties are unclear, or a group's assignment is ambiguous, cooperative learning quickly degenerates into undisciplined discussion, in which there may be numerous "uninvolved and passive participants." Uninvolved and passive participants are individuals who successfully "escape" sharing anything of themselves, choosing to rest within the confines of their own selfish behavior. This defeats the purpose of cooperative learning, for if a group produces an outstanding report but only a few students contributed to it, the group as a whole probably will have learned no more than if each member had completed the assignment alone. Worst of all, the critical thinking, reasoning, and problem solving that are so much a part of the shared effort of a cooperative learning activity will not have occurred.

ESTABLISHING A COOPERATIVE TASK STRUCTURE IN YOUR CLASSROOM

Now let us put to work in your classroom the four components of cooperative learning—teacher-student interaction, student-student interaction, task specialization and materials, and role expectations and responsibilities. Establishing a cooperative learning activity involves five specific steps:

1. Specifying the goal of the activity.
2. Structuring the task.
3. Teaching the collaborative process.
4. Monitoring group performance.
5. Debriefing.

1—Specifying the Goal

The goal of a cooperative learning activity specifies the product and/or behaviors that are expected at the end of the activity. The outcome can take different forms:

- ☐ Written group reports
- ☐ Higher individual achievement on an end-of-activity test
- ☐ Oral performance, articulating the group consensus
- ☐ Enumeration of critical issues
- ☐ Critique of an assigned reading
- ☐ List of bibliographic references

To assure the desired outcome, your job is to identify the outcome, check for understanding, and set a cooperative tone. Each of these steps is described in the following subsections.

Identify the Outcome.   The form of the final product or performance must be clearly articulated from the beginning. For each of the outcomes just listed, you would illustrate the style, format, and length of the product that will constitute acceptable group work. For a written report, you might write on the board the acceptable length and format and display a sample report to guide group efforts. Or, if the goal is to increase test performance, you would identify the amount of improvement expected for each group as a standard to guide their performance. For oral performances, you would identify the nature of their content, thoroughness of research, and completeness. In each case, you must give your students signs of acceptable progress or milestones to be achieved and, where possible, examples of a successfully completed final product.

Following clear specification of the goal, you must place it in the context of past and future learning. Organize the content so that students will attach meaning and significance to it and see it in terms of their own experience. Typically, statements like "Remember when we had trouble with . . ." or "Next week we will need these skills to . . ." sufficiently highlight the importance of the impending activity. They also separate it from a casual exercise that has no consequences for either good or poor performance.

Check for Understanding.   Next, check for understanding of the goal and your directions for achieving it. Using a few average and high performers as a "steering group," ask for an oral regurgitation of your goal and directions. The entire class can benefit from hearing them again and you can correct them if needed. Because so much effort typically is expended by groups during a cooperative learning activity, misinterpretation of the goal and your directions for attaining it can severely affect classroom morale.

In self-directed learning, one individual can be led astray by poorly understood directives. But in cooperative learning, entire groups, not just occasional individuals, can wander off the path, leaving a significant portion of your classroom working toward the wrong goal. Having one member of each group restate the goal and your directions for attaining it is time well spent.

Set a Cooperative Tone.   Your final task in introducing the goal of your cooperative learning activity is to set a tone of cooperation.

Students customarily begin cooperative learning activities as they have begun thousands of school activities before—as individuals competing against individuals. This competitive style has been ingrained in us from earliest childhood. It culminates in school with tests and grades that are placed on a "normal" or bell-shaped curve, which assures that for every test or graded performance there will be some winners and some losers. It may be difficult for some of your learners to get the competitive spirit out of their blood, because it has become so much a part of their schooling.

While competition has its place even within cooperative learning (for example, competing against other groups or one's own previous performance), effective group work depends on collaboration among its members, not competition. Therefore, your job at the start of a cooperative learning activity is to set the tone: "two heads are better than one." Other phrases such as "united we stand, divided we fall," or "work together or fail together," can remind groups of the cooperative nature of the enterprise. You could ask each group to choose or create a group motto (for example, "all for one and one for all") that provides a distinctive identity as well as reminding them that collaboration, not competition, is the goal.

As you will see shortly, your role also must be one of cooperation, and this too must be communicated at the outset. "I am here to help ... to answer your questions ... to be your assistant ... your consultant ... your information provider...." These reassuring comments can lift your classroom from the realm of competition and into the world of cooperation.

2 —Structuring the Task

As we saw earlier, the structure of the task is what separates just any group activity (like a discussion) from a cooperative learning activity. Group discussions have tasks, but they often are so generally defined (discuss the facts, raise issues, form a consensus) that they rarely allow for the division of labor, role responsibilities, collaborative efforts, and end products that so effectively promote critical thinking, reasoning, and problem solving in a cooperative learning activity.

In structuring a cooperative learning task, you must decide several factors in advance:

  □ How large will the groups be?
  □ How will group members be selected?
  □ How much time will be devoted to group work?
  □ What roles, if any, will be assigned to group members?
  □ What incentives/rewards will be provided for individual and group work?

Let's look at alternatives for each of these factors and how you can choose among them.

Group Size.   How many in the group? Group size is one of your most important decisions. Although influenced by the size of your class, the number of individual learners assigned to groups has far-reaching consequences for:

Division of labor, often overlooked when structuring tasks, is critical to the success of group learning. Allowing students to analyze the task and identify divisions of labor can foster metacognitive growth and higher-order thinking.

the range of abilities within a group,

the time required for a group to reach consensus,

the efficient sharing of materials within a group, and

the time needed to complete the end product.

Each of these factors—ability range, time to consensus, sharing of materials, and time to complete the end product—will be altered by the number of members assigned to groups. This is why, when subtasks are comparable, group sizes should be made approximately equal.

The most efficient group size for attaining a goal in the least time is 4 or 5 members (Slavin, 1987). Thus, in a class of 25 students, 5 or 6 groups can be formed. Smaller groups make monitoring of group performance more difficult, because the number of times you can interact with each group is reduced accordingly. On the other hand, groups of 7 or 8 generally argue more, reach consensus later, have more difficulty sharing limited materials (for example, a reference that must be shared), and take longer to complete the final product.

Thus, the rule of thumb is to compose groups of 4 or 5 members for single-period activities and slightly larger groups (5 or 6) when the activity stretches over more than a class period, requiring greater task complexity and role specialization. Keep in mind, however, that large groups—like large group discussions—often have more nonparticipants who more easily hide behind the work of others or find ways to maintain their anonymity in the context of a busy group.

Group Composition. Whom will you select for each group? Unless the task specifically calls for specialized abilities, you will form most groups heterogeneously, with a representative sample of all the learners in a class. Therefore, you will assign to groups a mix of higher/lower ability, more verbal/less verbal, and more task-oriented/less task-oriented learners. This diversity usually contributes to the collaborative process by creating a natural flow of information from those who have it to those who need it. Surprisingly, it also promotes the transmission of alternative perspectives and viewpoints that often reverses the flow of information in unexpected and desirable directions.

Groups within a classroom generally should reflect the composition of the community outside it. This composition confronts learners with differences as well as similarities to provide the motivation for dialogue, the need for sharing, and the natural division of interests and abilities needed to get the job done.

It also is important that groups not only represent a diversity of talents, interests, and abilities but that typically nonengaged students be represented across groups. Social scientists long have observed that the pressure from peers working together often "pulls in" even recalcitrant and passive learners, sweeping them up in the excitement of some larger goal. This is especially true if they are deprived of the support of other passive or inactive participants.

Johnson and Johnson (1987) provide several additional suggestions for forming groups:

1. Ask students to list three peers with whom they would like to work. Identify isolated students who are not chosen by any other classmates. Then, build a group of skillful and supportive students around each isolated learner.
2. Randomly assign students by having them count off; place the 1s together, the 2s together, and so forth. If groups of 5 are desired in a class of 30, have students count off by 6s.
3. To build constructive relationships between majority and minority students, between handicapped and nonhandicapped, and between male and female, use heterogeneous groups with students from each category.
4. Share with students the process of choosing group members. First, you select a member for a group, then that member selects another, and so on, alternating between your choice and students' choices until the group is complete.

One approach to drawing nonengaged learners into the cooperative activity is to structure the task so that success depends on the active involvement of all group members. This addresses the problems of active and passive uninvolvement. An example of active uninvolvement is when a group member talks about everything but the assigned goal of the group. Passive uninvolvement is when a student doesn't care and becomes a silent member of the group. Here are ways you can design a task to increase the likelihood that all group members will be actively involved:

☐ Request a product that requires a clearly defined division of labor to generate (e.g., looking up new words, writing a topic sentence, preparing a chart, finding examples, etc). Then assign specific individuals to each activity at the start of the session.

☐ Within groups, form pairs that are responsible for looking over and actually correcting each other's work/contribution.

☐ Chart the group's progress on individually assigned tasks and encourage poor or slow performers to work harder to improve the group's overall progress. (A wall chart may be all that is needed.)

☐ Purposefully limit the resources given to a group, so that individual members must remain in personal contact to share materials and complete their assigned tasks (e.g., one dictionary or hand calculator to share).

☐ Make one stage of the required product contingent on a previous stage that is the responsibility of another person. This way, pressure will be applied or help provided by group members to those not performing adequately, so that they can complete their contribution.

Time on Task.   How much time should you allot for group work? This obviously depends on task complexity (for example, single class period or multiple periods), but you must make some more refined estimates as well. You need to determine the time to devote to group work and the time to devote to all groups coming together to share their contributions. This latter time may be used for group reports, a whole-class discussion, debriefing to relate the work experiences of each group to the end product, or some combination.

Group work can easily get out of hand in the excitement, controversy, and natural dialogue that can come from passionate discussions. This requires you to place limits on each stage of the cooperative learning activity, so that one does not eclipse time from another and leave the task disjointed and incomplete in your learners' minds.

Most time naturally will be devoted to the work of individual groups, where the major portion of the end product is being completed. This normally will consume 60–80% of the time devoted to the cooperative learning activity. The remaining time must be divided among individual group presentations and/or whole-class discussion that places the group work into the perspective of a single end product.

If you plan both group reports and a whole-class discussion for the same day, be aware that the whole-class discussion probably will get squeezed into a fraction of the time required to make it meaningful. To avoid this, schedule group discussions or debriefings for the following class day, so that class members have ample time to reflect upon their group reports and to pull together their own thoughts about the collaborative process that may or may not have occurred as intended. Fifteen or twenty minutes at the beginning of class the next day usually provides students the proper distance to meaningfully reflect on their experiences the day before.

Role Assignment. What roles should you assign to group members? As you saw, division of labor both within and across groups is an important dimension of cooperative learning that is not shared by most group discussion methods. It is this task specialization, and the division of labor it often requires, that promotes the responsibility and idea-sharing that marks an effective cooperative learning activity. The acceptance of individual responsibility and idea-sharing in a cooperative learning experience is encouraged by role assignments within groups and sometimes task specialization across groups. These roles and responsibilities are used to complement group work and to interconnect the groups.

Some of the more popular role functions suggested by Johnson and Johnson (1987) that can be assigned within or across groups are:

1. *Summarizer*—paraphrases and plays back to the group major conclusions to see if the group agrees and to prepare for (rehearse) the group's contribution before the whole class.
2. *Checker*—checks controversial or debatable statements and conclusions for authenticity against text, workbook, or references. Assures that the group will not be using unsubstantiated facts, or be challenged by more accurate representations of other groups.
3. *Researcher*—reads reference documents and acquires background information when more data are needed (for example, may conduct an interview or seek a resource from the library). The researcher differs from a checker in that the researcher provides critical information for the group to complete its task, while the checker certifies the accuracy of the work in progress and/or after it has been completed.
4. *Runner*—acquires anything needed to complete the task—materials, equipment, reference works. Far from a subservient role, this requires creativity, shrewdness, and even cunning to find the necessary resources, which may also be diligently sought by other groups.
5. *Recorder*—commits to writing the major product of the group. The recorder may require individuals to write their own conclusions, in which case the recorder collates, synthesizes, and renders in coherent form the abbreviated work of individual group members.
6. *Supporter*—chosen for his or her upbeat, positive outlook, the supporter praises members when their individual assignments are completed and consoles them in times of discouragement (for example, if proper references can't be found). Keeps the group moving forward by recording major milestones achieved on a chart for all the class to see, identifying progress made, and encouraging efforts of individuals, particularly those who may have difficulty participating or completing their tasks.

7. *Observer/Troubleshooter*—takes notes and records information about the group process that may be useful during whole-class discussion or debriefing. Reports to a class leader or to you when problems appear insurmountable for a group or individual members.

Typically, any one of the preceding role functions also could serve as a group leader. However, because each of these roles entails some form of leadership, the formal designation of "leader" may not be necessary. This has the desirable effect of making all role functions more equal and eliminating an authority-based structure that can lead to arguments and disunity among members who may see themselves as more or less powerful than others.

In addition to these specific role functions assigned to individual group members, there are other roles and responsibilities for all group members to perform. You can write these on the board or provide a handout prior to the cooperative learning activity:

☐ Ask others to explain their points more clearly when one or more group members do not understand.
☐ Check your own answers and those of others against references or the text.
☐ Encourage others to go farther, expanding their points to surpass their previous standards and expectations.
☐ Let everyone finish what they have to say without interrupting, whether you agree or disagree.
☐ Do not be bullied into changing your mind, if you really don't want to.
☐ Criticize ideas but not individuals.

Providing Reinforcement and Rewards.   Besides deciding upon group composition, size, time, and the individual responsibilities of group members, you need to establish a system of reinforcement and reward to keep your learners on-task and working toward the goal. Among the reinforcement strategies that have been used effectively with cooperative learning activities are:

☐ Grades—individual and group
☐ Bonus points
☐ Social responsibilities
☐ Tokens or privileges
☐ Group contingencies

Grades—the familiar type used in competitive learning—can be used to reinforce and reward the behavior of individuals and groups during cooperative learning. However, use of individual grades in the context of cooperative learning should stress the importance of individual effort in achieving *the group goal*. For this reason, cooperative learning grades usually incorporate both individual performance (quality and/or extensiveness of work toward accomplishing the group goal) and the thoroughness, relevance, and accuracy of the group product. Each individual's grade can be in two separate parts or can be a composite grade that combines his or her own plus the group's effort.

For example, individuals can rate each other on a five-point scale measuring the active involvement of each teammate in the group process, the average of which could be a score for individual effort. Also, you can rate the end product produced by the group (or other groups and the average taken) on a five-point scale, providing two scores for each individual. These scores could be entered individually (e.g., individual effort = 4, group product = 5) or as a ratio (⅘ = .80). Ratios smaller than 1.0 indicate the group product exceeded this individual's contribution. Scores greater than 1.0 indicate the individual's contribution exceeded the group product. Each individual in a group would be given the same group score, either determined by the teacher or by averaging each group's evaluation of one another.

Other types of grades used as rewards include:

1. Averaging of individual scores to determine the group grade.
2. Assigning all group members the average of the highest (or lowest) half of the members' scores.
3. Averaging an individual's score with the group score (for example, averaging an individual score of 4 with a group score of 5: 4 + 5 = 9, ÷ 2 = 4.5).
4. Adding points to the group score for each active participant within the group (or subtracting points from the group score for each nonparticipant), to be determined by the teacher.

Another reinforcement technique you can use in partnership with grades is bonus points, earned on the basis of how many group members reach a preestablished level of performance by the end of their group's activity. You might devise a group quiz (or take it from the text or workbook) and then assign an expected score for each individual member, which could vary according to ability or task. Those obtaining or exceeding their expected score would earn their group a bonus point.

Another popular form of reinforcement during cooperative learning includes rewarding individual efforts with desirable social responsibilities, such as granting the high performer the first pick of group role next time (observer, supporter, checker, etc.). Also, you can employ tokens or privileges to motivate individuals and group members. The highest-performing group might receive independent study time, time out, trips to the learning center, or use of special materials and/or resources. High-performing individuals within groups could be accorded these same privileges where exemplary performance is noted.

Finally, group contingencies frequently have been used to motivate and reinforce members during cooperative learning. Johnson and Johnson (1987) describe three ways of rewarding the group based on the performance of its individuals:

1. Average-performance contingency, in which all members are graded or reinforced based on the average performance of all group members.
2. High-performance group contingency, in which the highest quarter of the group is the basis for grades, reinforcements, or privileges.
3. Low-performance group contingency, in which the lowest quarter of the group is the basis for individual grades or other forms of reinforcement.

3 — Teaching and Evaluating the Collaborative Process

Another responsibility you have during cooperative learning is teaching the collaborative process. Most learners lack the collaborative skills needed to benefit from many cooperative learning activities. Therefore, you need to identify collaborative behaviors, place them in proper sequence, and demonstrate them. Just as self-directed learning strategies must be modeled, so must collaborative behaviors.

At the heart of collaborative skills is the ability to exchange thoughts and feelings with others at the same conceptual level. Students need to feel comfortable in communicating their ideas, beliefs, and opinions to others in a timely and efficient manner. Some important "sending" skills suggested by Johnson and Johnson (1987, p. 126) and some of the ways you can encourage them are:

1. *Teach how to communicate one's own ideas and feelings.* Encourage use of *I* and *my* to let students know it is *their* ideas and feelings that make the collaborative process work. Let students know that their personal experiences—events observed, problems encountered, people met—are valued information they can use to justify their own ideas and feelings.

2. *Make messages complete and specific.* Indicate that, along with the message being sent, there should be a frame of reference, perspective, or experience that led to the content of the message. For example, "I got this idea while traveling through a Pueblo Indian reservation in southern Colorado during our vacation last summer." Or, "I heard the President speak and his main point reminded me of . . ." or, "I read this newspaper article and it led me to believe some things about. . . ."

3. *Make verbal and nonverbal messages congruent.* Establish a serious tone in which hidden meanings or snide remarks are not acceptable. Indicate that voice and body language always are to reinforce the message being conveyed and that communicating serious information comically or over-dramatizing will confuse both the message and the listener.

4. *Convey an atmosphere of respect and support.* Indicate that all students can contribute information, ideas, feelings, personal experiences, and reactions without fear of ridicule. Make clear that unsupportive behaviors ("You're crazy if you . . .") are not allowed. Make clear that cooperation rests upon sharing both emotional and physical resources, receiving help, dividing responsibility, and in looking out for one another's well being.

5. *Demonstrate how to assess whether the message was properly received.* Instruct your learners in how to ask for interpretive feedback from listeners. Ask them to use phrases such as "What do you think about what I said?" "Does what I said make sense?" "Can you see what I'm trying to say?" The more listeners are asked to paraphrase the message, the more the sender is sure the message has been received as intended.

6. *Teach how to paraphrase another's point of view.* Most learners will want to agree or disagree with the speaker without checking to see if they have the full intent of the message. Make it known that before one can be either critical or supportive of another's viewpoint, it must be paraphrased to the satisfaction of the sender. The rules of paraphrasing should include:

a. Restate the message in your own words—not those of the speaker.

b. Introduce your paraphrased remarks with phrases such as "It seems to me you're saying . . ."; "If I understand you, you believe that . . ."; "From what I heard you say, your position is. . . ."

c. During the paraphrasing, avoid any indication of approval or disapproval. For example, let it be known that responses such as "I disagree with you" or "I think you're right" should not be part of the paraphrased response, for its sole purpose is to determine whether the message has been accurately received.

7. *Demonstrate how to negotiate meanings and understandings.* Often one's understanding of a message must be corrected or fine tuned, because the message was ambiguous, incomplete, or misinterpreted. This means that paraphrases often must be recycled to a greater level of understanding, sometimes for the benefit of both sender and receiver. This requires tactful phrases from the sender such as "What I mean to say is . . ."; "What I forgot to add was . . ."; or "To clarify further. . . ." It also requires tactful phrases from the receiver, such as "What I don't understand is. . ."; "Can you say it some other way. . . ?" This approach is indispensable for refining the message and assuring more accurate interpretation. Sender and receiver each must provide a graceful means for the other to correct misperceptions of what was said or heard, without emotional injury to either.

8. *Teach participation and leadership.* Communicate the importance of:

   Mutual benefit—what benefits the group will benefit the individual.

   Common fate—each individual wins or loses on the basis of the overall performance of group members.

   Shared identity—everyone is a member of a group, emotionally as well as physically.

   Joint celebration—receiving satisfaction in the progress of individual group members.

   Mutual responsibility—being concerned for underperforming group members.

4—Monitoring Group Performance

To establish a cooperative learning structure you must observe and intervene as needed to assist your learners in acquiring their group's goal. Your most frequent monitoring functions will be telling students where to find needed information, repeating how to complete the task, exhibiting the form of the product to be produced (in whole or part), and/or modeling for a group the process to be used in achieving the group goal. Your role is critical in keeping each group on track. Thus, your constant vigilance of group performance is necessary to discover problems and trouble spots before they hamper group progress.

Via monitoring, you must identify when a group needs assistance. One common need will be to repeat or remind the group of its goal. Groups easily become disengaged, sidetracked, or will invent new and perhaps more interesting goals for themselves. Typically, you will move from group to group at least once at the begin-

A teacher's role as monitor during group work includes identifying when additional resources may be needed by a group, redirecting group work in more productive directions, and providing emotional support to encourage commitment to the task.

ning of a cooperative activity, repeating the task and the goal just to be certain it is understood by each group. You may have to return to a troubled group a second or even third time to repeat the goal. Some groups will require more vigilance than others.

A second form of intervention you will perform is to redirect groups that have discussed themselves into a blind alley. The heat of discussion and debate frequently distracts groups from productive thought, raising issues that may be only marginally relevant to accomplishing the group goal. Worse yet, group discussion can raise issues for which a consensus cannot be reached in reasonable time or for which resources or advanced knowledge are required that cannot be provided. When this happens, it is time for you to redirect the group's work and set them back on course.

Key to your monitoring is your ability to recognize when a group is at a difficult juncture. A group might pursue an avenue of fruitless discussion and waste valuable time, when a different avenue could set their course productively toward an attainable goal. Your close vigilance and direction of group work can make the difference between aimless talk and productive discussion.

A third monitoring function you will perform during cooperative learning is to provide emotional support and encouragement to overwhelmed and frustrated group members. Not all group members will gladly accept their individual assignments, nor will all groups accept their designated goal. Your encouragement and support can instill the confidence some will need to complete a task they may be unsure of and that may not be of their own choosing. In between your periodic restatement and redirection of group goals, you may need to visit selected individuals or groups to bestow confidence, support, and technical advice on how to get the job done. Your expression of confidence in individuals often is all that is needed to nudge an inactive group participant into actively pursuing the group's goals.

5 — Debriefing

Your feedback to the groups on how well they are collaborating is important to their progress in acquiring collaborative skills. You can accomplish debriefing and evaluation at the end of the collaborative activity by:

1. Openly talking about how the groups functioned—ask students for their opinions. What were the real issues that enhanced or impeded each group (a) in producing the product and (b) in completing the process?
2. Soliciting suggestions for improving the process and avoiding problems so that higher levels of collaboration can be reached.
3. Getting viewpoints of predesignated observers. You might assign one or two individuals to record instances of particularly effective and ineffective group collaboration and to report to the full class at the time of the debriefing.

Group members also can rate each other's collaborative skills during debriefing. Individual group members could receive their ratings privately while group averages could be discussed during the debriefing session to pinpoint strengths and deficiencies. Figure 10.2 is a scale for rating collaborative skills of group members. It can be used (a) by group members to rate each other, (b) by a group member (e.g., an observer) assigned the task of rating group members, or (c) by you, the teacher.

Use the scale as a checklist. On it, note the presence or absence of each skill for each group member by placing a checkmark in the appropriate box. Use *NA* (not applicable) for skills that do not apply for a given role or task. If you wish, instead of listing the names of group members, assign each member a number to keep the ratings anonymous. The whole group then could be assigned one point for each check placed on the scale and the "winning" group given a reward or special recognition.

Here is a summary of some obstacles to debriefing and how you can structure your cooperative learning activity to promote evaluation and feedback (based on Dishon and O'Leary, 1984):

1. *There is not enough time for debriefing.* For many reasons (announcements, assemblies, ensuing lessons), teachers often believe they do not have the time to evaluate and gather feedback about the cooperative activity. Try:

a. Doing quick debriefing by asking the class to tell how well their groups functioned. You can do this by asking a question, such as "Did each group have enough time?" Then, have students indicate agreement or disagreement by answering:

yes—hand in air,

don't know—arms folded, or

no—hands down.

Two or three questions can be asked and responded to in a minute or so.

b. Doing debriefing during the cooperative activity or having the class complete a questionnaire or checklist at home pertaining to how well their group functioned.

FIGURE 10.2
Collaborative rating scale

	Names of Group Members				
Collaborative Skills					
Provides knowledge and information to help group's progress					
Is open and candid to whole group with personal feelings					
Provides individual assistance support to group members who need it					
Evaluates contributions of others in a nonjudgmental, constructive manner					
Shares physical resources—books, handouts, written information—for group to use					
Accurately paraphrases or summarizes what other group members have said					
Gives recognition to other group members when key contributions are made					
Accepts and appreciates cultural, ethnic, and individual differences					

2. *Debriefing stays vague.* When students conclude, "We did OK," "We did a good job," or "Everyone was involved" several times, you know that the feedback is not specific enough. Try:

   a. Giving the group specific written questions to be answered about their group's functioning.
   b. Identifying key events or incidents that occurred during the collaborative process for which students must indicate their comfort or satisfaction.
   c. Using student observers so that specific events indicating effective and ineffective group functioning are recorded.

3. *Students stay uninvolved in debriefing.* Occasionally there are groups whose members consistently stay uninvolved in the debriefing process. Try:

   a. Asking for a written report from the group, reporting the strengths and weaknesses of their group's functioning.
   b. Using questionnaires that require completion by everyone.
   c. Assigning a student the job of debriefer for the group.
   d. Having each member sign a statement summarizing how their group functioned.
   e. Giving bonus points for good debriefing reports.

4. *Written debriefing reports are incomplete.* Some groups may hand in incomplete debriefing reports. Try:

   a. Having group members read and sign each other's debriefing reports to show that each has been checked for accuracy and completeness.
   b. Giving bonus points for completeness.

5. *Students use poor collaborative skills during debriefing.* When group members do not listen carefully to each other, when they are afraid to contribute to the debriefing process, or when the discussion becomes divisive, try:

   a. Assigning specific roles for the debriefing.
   b. Having one group observe the debriefing of another group and discuss the results.

TEAM-ORIENTED COOPERATIVE LEARNING ACTIVITIES

Recent research indicates that teams of heterogeneous learners can increase the collaborative skills, self-esteem, and achievement of individual learners when pursuing a cooperative learning activity (Slavin, 1983). Four team-oriented techniques have been particularly successful in bringing about these outcomes: Student Teams–Achievement Division (STAD), Teams-Games-Tournaments (TGT), Jigsaw II, and Team-Assisted Individualization (TAI). A brief summary of these follows, based on the work of Slavin (1983, 1987).

Student Teams–Achievement Division (STAD)

In STAD, students are assigned to four-or-five-member learning teams. Each team is made as heterogeneous as possible to represent the composition of the entire class (boys/girls, less-able/more-able, etc.).

Begin the cooperative learning activity by presenting new material via lecture or discussion and providing worksheets of problem sets, vocabulary words, questions, and such from which students can review the main points of the lecture or discussion. Team members then study the worksheets, quizzing each other. They work in pairs or as a group in which team members discuss the worksheet content, clarifying difficult or confusing questions or problems for others.

Give at least one team member the answers to all questions or problems on the worksheet and assign this member the task of checking the written or oral responses of others. Allow team members sufficient time for all of them to complete all problems or questions on the worksheet (make the worksheet concise to permit this). After the team practices with the worksheet and answer key, give them individual quizzes over the material (team members may not help one another during this activity).

Score the quizzes immediately and form individual scores into team scores (for example, by averaging all, top half, or bottom half). Determine the contribution of individual students by how much each student's quiz score exceeds his or her past quiz average—or a preset score based on each student's learning history. This way, while the entire group receives a score based on each individual member's performance, individual learners also receive an improvement score based on the extent to which their individual score exceeds past performance or a preestablished standard that recognizes their learning history.

During STAD, you act as a resource person and monitor group study activities to intervene when necessary to suggest better study techniques ("Why not choose partners now and quiz each other on the questions you've been discussing?").

Research shows that, during Student Teams–Achievement Divisions, learners gain a sense of camaraderie and helpfulness toward fellow team members, pursue self-directed learning and rehearsal strategies modeled by the teacher, and become self-motivated through having some control over their own learning.

Teams-Games-Tournaments (TGT)

A cooperative learning activity closely related to STAD is the use of Teams-Games-Tournaments. TGT uses the same general format as STAD (four-to-five-member groups studying worksheets). However, instead of individually administered quizzes at the end of a study period, students play academic games to show their mastery of the topic studied.

Have students play games (e.g., 20 Questions) as weekly tournaments in which teams that are matched by ability based on previous performance compete against one another until one emerges the winner. Make the teams as heterogeneous and as evenly matched as possible so that none has a preponderance of high or low achievers. This assures that the competition is always seen as fair by the learners and that all learners have an opportunity to contribute to a winning team. Because games and tournaments naturally interest class members, let the teams take on competitive names, such as The Warriors against The Miracle Workers, The Scholars against The Pragmatists, and so on, to enhance the excitement. Often change teams (monthly) to create different heterogeneous groupings from which new cooperative relationships can emerge.

As in STAD, you can assign team points based on the number of questions answered correctly, and accumulated over a period of about four tournaments (weeks). Then, before exchanging team members, announce the winner for that month, along with the number of points accumulated by each member of the winning team (for example, number of total questions answered correctly in the past four tournaments). Keep both team and individual member statistics to see if a team and individual members can exceed the scores accumulated during any preceding month. Have an official scorekeeper keep a history of team and individual scores and record them on a handout or wall chart.

Again, you can see that TGT uses much the same format as STAD, except that academic games are substituted for individually administered quizzes, adding more intensity and competition to increase interest, participation, and excitement.

Jigsaw II

In the cooperative learning activity called Jigsaw II, you assign students to four-to-six-member teams to work on an academic task that is broken into several subtasks, depending on the number of groups. You assign students to five-member teams and then assign a unique responsibility to each team member. Assign each student within each team a section of the text to read. Then, give each team member a special task with which to approach the reading. For example, assign one team member to write down and look up the meanings of any new vocabulary words. Assign another to summarize or outline the main points in the text. Assign another the job of identifying major and minor characters, and so on.

When all team members have their specific assignments, "break out" from their original group all team members having the same assignment (e.g., finding and defining new vocabulary words) to meet as "expert groups" to discuss their assignment and to share their conclusions and results. Once in an "expert group," members may assist each other by comparing notes (e.g., definitions) and identifying points overlooked by other group members. When all the expert groups have had the opportunity to share, discuss, and modify their conclusions, return them to their respective "home groups." Each member then takes turns teaching their teammates about their respective responsibility.

Jigsaw II heightens interest among group members because the only way other team members can learn about the topics to which they were not assigned is to listen to the teammate who received that assignment. After each "expert" makes his or her presentation to the team, attempting to teach the group what they learned from their expert group, give individual quizzes to assess how much they have learned. As in STAD, you can assign both an overall group score as well as individual improvement score based on past performance. These scores become the basis for team and individual rewards for the highest scorers.

Team-Assisted Individualization (TAI)

One of the newest cooperative learning activities is Team-Assisted Individualization, which combines some of the characteristics of individualized and cooperative learning. Although originally designed for elementary and middle school mathematics classes, TAI can be used with any subject matter and grade level for which some individualized learning materials are available (for example, programmed or self-paced texts). In TAI, you start each student working through the individualized materials at a point designated by a placement test or previous learning history. Thus, students may work at different levels depending on the heterogeneity of abilities in the classroom.

Give each student a specified amount of content to work through (e.g., pages, problem sets, questions and answers) at his or her own pace. Also, assign each learner to a team selected to represent all ability levels and, therefore, individuals who enter the individualized materials at different levels of complexity. Heterogeneity within the teams is important, because you then ask each team member to have their work checked by another teammate. "Checkers" are expected to have completed portions of the materials that are more advanced than others. Have as many group members as possible assume the role of checker. When necessary, give the checkers answer sheets.

Have student monitors give quizzes over each unit and score and record the results on a master score card. Base team scores on the average number of units completed each week by team members and their scores on the unit quizzes. Reward those teams that complete a preset number of units with a minimum average quiz score (e.g., with certificates, time outs, learning center privileges). Assign one student monitor—who is rotated frequently—to each team to manage the routine checking, distribution of the individualized materials, and administering and recording the quizzes.

Because TAI uses individualized materials, it is especially useful for teaching heterogeneous classes that afford you few opportunities for whole-class instruction and little time to instruct numerous small groups who may have diverse learning needs.

Overviewing Team-Oriented Cooperative Learning Activities

Similarities and differences among the four cooperative learning methods are summarized in Table 10.1.

Many different forms of cooperative learning have been successfully used in classrooms of all grade levels and subject matter. Some of the most successful cooperative learning activities, however, have come from the ingenuity and creativity of individual teachers who, with little formal preparation, devise a group activity to promote social interaction when cooperative outcomes are encouraged by the nature of the content being taught. Although many versions of cooperative learning can be

TABLE 10.1
Similarities and differences among four cooperative learning activities

Student Teams–Achievement Divisions (STAD)	Team-Games-Tournament (TGT)	Jigsaw (II)	Team-Assisted Individualization (TAI)
1. Teacher presents content in lecture or discussion	1. Teacher presents content in lecture or discussion	1. Students read section of text and are assigned unique topic	1. Students are given diagnostic test/exercise by student monitor to determine placement in materials
2. Teams work through problems/questions on worksheets	2. Teams work through problems/questions on worksheets	2. Students within teams with same topic meet in "expert groups"	2. Students work through assigned unit at their own pace
3. Teacher gives quiz over material studied	3. Teams play academic games against each other for points	3. Students return to "home" group to share knowledge of their topic with teammates	3. Teammate checks text against answers and student monitor gives quiz
4. Teacher determines team average and individual improvement scores	4. Teacher tallies team points over four-week period to determine best team and best individual scorers	4. Students take quiz over each topic discussed	4. Team quizzes are averaged and number of units completed are counted by monitor to create team scores
		5. Team Recognition—Individual quizzes are used to create team scores and individual improvement scores	

devised from the preceding four, as an effective teacher you should seize the opportunity to create a cooperative learning experience whenever content goals lend themselves to promoting collaborative skills. This, in turn, can increase your learners' self-esteem, critical thinking, and problem-solving abilities.

SUMMING UP

This chapter introduced you to strategies for cooperative learning. Its main points were:

1. Critical thinking, reasoning and problem-solving skills are of little use if they cannot be applied in cooperative interaction with others.

2. Self-directed and cooperative learning share the complementary objectives of engaging students in the learning process and promoting higher (more complex) patterns of behavior.

3. Cooperative learning activities can instill in your learners:
   □ Attitudes and values that guide the learner's behavior outside of the classroom.
   □ Acceptable forms of social behavior that may not be modeled in the home.
   □ Alternative perspectives and viewpoints with which to think objectively.
   □ An integrated identity that can reduce contradictory thoughts and actions.
   □ Higher thought processes.
4. Planning for cooperative learning requires decisions pertaining to:
   □ Teacher-student interaction
   □ Student-student interaction
   □ Task specialization and materials
   □ Role expectations and responsibilities
5. The primary goal of teacher-student interaction during cooperative learning is to promote independent thinking.
6. The primary goal of student-student interaction during cooperative learning is to encourage the active participation and interdependence of all members of the class.
7. The primary goal of task specialization and learning materials during cooperative learning is to create an activity structure whose end product depends on the sharing, cooperation, and collaboration of individuals within groups.
8. The primary goal of assigning roles and responsibilities during cooperative learning is to facilitate the work of the group and to promote communication and sharing among its members.
9. Establishing a cooperative task structure involves five steps:
   (1) Specifying the goal of the activity
   (2) Structuring the task
   (3) Teaching the collaborative process
   (4) Monitoring group performance
   (5) Debriefing
10. The goal of a cooperative activity may take different forms, such as:
    □ Written group reports
    □ Higher individual achievement
    □ An oral performance
    □ An enumeration or listing
    □ A critique
    □ Bibliographic research
11. Your responsibility in specifying the goal of a cooperative activity is to:

□ Illustrate the style, format, and length of the end product.
□ Place the goal in the context of past and future learning.
□ Check for understanding of the goal and directions given for achieving it.
□ Set a tone of cooperation, as opposed to competition.
12. Structuring the cooperative learning task involves decisions pertaining to:
    □ How large the groups will be.
    □ How group members will be selected.
    □ How much time will be devoted to group work.
    □ What roles group members will be assigned.
    □ What incentives will be provided for individual and group work.
13. Generally, the most efficient size for a group to reach the desired goal in the least amount of time is 4 or 5 members.
14. Unless a group task specifically calls for specialized abilities, groups should be formed heterogeneously—or with a representative sample of all learners in the class.
15. Methods for selecting group members include:
    (1) Asking students to list peers with whom they would like to work.
    (2) Randomly assigning students to groups.
    (3) Choosing matched opposites: minority/majority, male/female, handicapped/nonhandicapped, etc.
    (4) Sharing with students the process of choosing group members (for example, teacher selects first; then person selected chooses another; and so on).
16. An actively uninvolved group member is one who talks about everything but the assigned goal of the group; a passively uninvolved group member is one who doesn't care about the work of the group and becomes silent.
17. Methods for discouraging active and passive uninvolvement include:
    □ Requesting a product requiring division of labor.
    □ Forming pairs that oversee each other's work.
    □ Charting group progress on individually assigned tasks.
    □ Purposefully limiting group resources to promote sharing and personal contact.
    □ Requiring a product that is contingent on previous stages that are the work of others.

18. Group work should entail 60–80% of the time devoted to a cooperative activity, the remainder being devoted to whole-class discussion and debriefing.

19. Division of labor within a group can be accomplished with role assignments. Some of the most popular are:
    □ Summarizer
    □ Checker
    □ Researcher
    □ Runner
    □ Recorder
    □ Supporter
    □ Observer/Troubleshooter

20. Some of the types of reinforcement strategies that can be used with cooperative learning activities include:
    □ Individual and group grades
    □ Bonus points
    □ Social responsibilities
    □ Tokens or privileges
    □ Group contingencies

21. Teaching the collaborative process involves showing your learners how to:
    □ Communicate their own ideas and feelings.
    □ Make messages complete and specific.
    □ Make verbal and nonverbal messages congruent.
    □ Convey respect and support.
    □ Assess if the message was properly received.
    □ Paraphrase another's point of view.
    □ Negotiate meanings and understandings.
    □ Actively participate in a group and assume leadership.

22. During the monitoring of group performance, the teacher's role is to see that each group remains on track, to redirect group efforts when needed, and to provide emotional support and encouragement.

23. During debriefing, feedback about the collaborative process is gathered in a whole-class discussion by:
    □ Openly talking about how the groups functioned during the cooperative activity.
    □ Soliciting suggestions for how the process could be improved.
    □ Obtaining the viewpoints of predesignated observers.

24. Four popular team-oriented cooperative learning activities for which desirable outcomes have been documented are:
    □ Student Teams–Achievement Division (STAD)
    □ Teams-Games-Tournaments (TGT)
    □ Jigsaw II
    □ Team-Assisted Individualization (TAI)

FOR DISCUSSION AND PRACTICE

*1. What two complementary objectives do self-directed and cooperative learning share?

*2. Identify five specific outcomes that cooperative learning activities can instill in learners.

*3. What three general outcomes can result from these more specific outcomes?

*4. Identify the four most important components of a cooperative learning activity and one critical decision pertaining to each.

*5. What five specific steps are required for establishing a cooperative learning activity?

*6. List the forms of end products that a cooperative learning activity can take.

*7. Approximately how large should a cooperative learning group be to reach a specified goal in the least amount of time?

*8. Identify four methods for selecting group members.

*9. Identify three methods for minimizing passive and active uninvolvement in a cooperative learning activity.

*10. Name seven popular role functions that can be assigned to group members and briefly describe their responsibilities.

*11. Identify five types of reinforcement and reward that could be given to group members for appropriate performance. Create one specific example of each.

*12. Describe a procedure for combining individual and group work into a single score.

*13. Name the eight "sending" skills identified by Johnson and Johnson (1987) and give one specific example of how you would teach each.

*14. What three forms of intervention might you have to provide when monitoring group performance?

*15. Debriefing entails what three activities?

*16. Identify the five obstacles to debriefing identified by Dishon and O'Leary (1984) and one approach to dealing with each.

17. Describe four team-oriented cooperative learning activities with respect to the structure of the activity to be performed, the work of the teams, your role as teacher, and procedures for team scoring and recognition.

---

*Answers to asterisked questions (*) in this and the other chapters are in Appendix B.

SUGGESTED READINGS

Aronson, E., Blaney, N., Stephan, C., Sikes, J., & Snapp, M. (1978). *The jigsaw classroom*. Beverly Hills, CA: Sage.

A thorough introduction to one of the most popular and consistently used learning activities, from which the current version of Jigsaw II originated.

Dishon, D., & O'Leary, P. (1984). *A guidebook for cooperative learning*. Kalamazoo, MI: Learning Publications.

This practical introduction to cooperative learning provides countless ideas on how to get started teaching and reinforcing collaborative skills among all age groups.

Johnson, D. (1986). *Reaching out: Interpersonal effectiveness and self-actualization* (2nd ed.). Englewood Cliffs, NJ: Prentice-Hall.

Presents some of the reasons why cooperative learning is so important, based on practical research and experience.

Johnson, D., & Johnson, R. (1987). *Learning together and alone* (2nd ed.). Englewood Cliffs, NJ: Prentice-Hall.

One of the most popular and complete texts on cooperative learning, written especially for the beginning teacher.

Johnson, D., Johnson, R., Holubec, E., & Roy, P. (1984). *Circles of learning: Cooperation in the classroom*. Alexandria, VA: Association for Supervision and Curriculum Development.

More practical activities for cooperative learning that can be implemented in any subject and at any grade level.

Slavin, R. (1980). Cooperative learning. *Review of Educational Research, 50,* 315–342.

A review of the research that indicates the effects of cooperative learning on collaborative skills, self-esteem, and classroom achievement.

Slavin, R. (1987). *Cooperative learning: Student teams* (2nd ed.). Washington: National Educational Association.

A concise, practical description of how to implement four cooperative learning activities in the classroom STAD, TGT, Jigsaw II, and TAI.

Slavin, R., Sharan, S., Kagan, S., Hertz-Lazarowitz, R., Webb, C., & Schmuck, R. (1985). *Learning to cooperate, cooperating to learn*. New York: Plenum Press.

A book of 16 individually authored chapters on many of the most important dimensions of cooperative learning, including cooperative learning activities in mathematics and science and multiethnic classrooms.

Motivation and Classroom Management

For most teachers, confronting some sort of behavior problem is a daily occurrence. These problems may include simple infractions of school or classroom rules, or they can involve far more serious events, including disrespect, cheating, obscene words and gestures, and open display of hostility. This chapter and the next, "Classroom Order and Discipline," will explore the important related topics of classroom management and order.

This chapter presents strategies for motivating students and managing your classroom. These strategies assist in *preventing* classroom behavior problems and in *anticipating* problems that are about to occur. The following chapter presents strategies for maintaining classroom order, strategies that assist in *altering* or *stopping* disruptive behavior if it does occur.

The best way to deal with classroom behavior problems is to prevent them. "An ounce of prevention is worth a pound of cure" applies to your classroom as well as to your health. The "ounce of prevention" is presented in this chapter in the hope that you will never need the "pound of cure" to be presented in the next.

MOTIVATING STUDENTS

The first step in preventing classroom behavior problems is to keep students motivated and thereby engaged in the learning process. **Motivation** is a word used to describe what energizes or directs a learner's attention, emotions, and activity. It often can account for why one student uses free time to complete homework, while another goes out to play; or why one student spends class time writing a love note, while another eagerly attends to the lesson; or why one student picks a fight with another, but the second student declines the invitation. Sports, affections toward the opposite sex, or aggressive needs are just three of the many motivators that can energize and direct students in the wrong direction, away from the learning process. This chapter shows that other types of motivators, when properly applied, can just as easily energize and direct students toward the learning process.

Motivators are things that influence learners to choose one activity over another (e.g., homework vs. baseball, a love note vs. paying attention, fighting vs. studying). Motivators can be *internal,* coming from within the individual, such as a tendency to be aggressive. Motivators also are *external,* coming from the environment, such as the social pressure to be "tough" in the eyes of one's peers. Behavior often is the complex blending of these two sources of motivation. When both internal and external sources motivate in the same direction, they powerfully influence a learner's behavior both in and outside the classroom.

To motivate in positive ways, you must know your learners' internal motivators, such as their interests, attitudes, and aspirations. You also must know the external motivators in your classroom, such as peer-group influences, the physical arrangement of the classroom, and classroom rules. The key to motivating students is bringing these internal and external sources of motivation together to actively engage your students in learning. This chapter explores ways in which effective teachers use internal and external motivation to energize and engage their students in learning.

INTERESTS, NEEDS, AND ASPIRATIONS

Among the most important personal characteristics you can know about your learners are their interests, needs, and aspirations. When motivating learners, these **internal motivators** somehow must be linked to classroom activities: lessons must be directed at the learners' current level of experience and familiarity with the world around them.

Although it often is not recognized, textbooks and workbooks are written for the hypothetical average student who has no specific interests, needs, and aspirations. Therefore, such books seldom are motivators for energizing learners and engaging them in the learning process. You must blend what you know about your learners' interests, needs, and aspirations with the knowledge and facts in textbooks to produce a sufficient level of motivation.

Let us take a closer look at interests, needs, and aspirations and how you might put them to work in your classroom:

Interest: A focusing of attention on an object, event, or idea that is enjoyable (e.g., cars, football, the opposite sex—but also computers, "live" demonstrations, science fiction).

Need: A perceived lack of something that is important to one's well-being (e.g., a ride to the game, to be seen and noticed, a date for the dance—but also a good grade, recognition from adults, being liked by others).

Aspiration: A wish or longing for a certain kind of achievement (e.g., to be class president, an athlete, a fashion model—but also to be a good student, a scientist, a National Honor Society member).

These three characteristics can account for a learner's classroom performance when differences in intellectual ability seem inadequate to explain events (e.g., when an *A* student fails a test but a less-able learner does unexpectedly well). Regardless of learners' intellectual abilities, their interests, needs, and aspirations can either accentuate or dampen the effects of their abilities on tests of school achievement.

This is never more obvious than with an *underachiever* or *overachiever,* students whose ability level alone does not account for their performance on achievement tests. The designation *overachiever* may be given to an individual whose school achievement is greater than predicted by tests of intelligence or scholastic aptitude. The designation *underachiever* may be given to an individual whose school achievement is less than predicted. No strict rules govern use of these terms, and their use is sometimes controversial.

It is generally believed that interests, needs, and aspirations (or a lack of these) can cause individuals to perform above or below the level expected solely from their intelligence or aptitude test scores. If interests, needs, and aspirations can have that powerful an effect on school achievement, it will be worth your time to note them and, when possible, plan classroom instruction around them.

Calderhead (1983) reported that experienced teachers know at the beginning of the school year the home backgrounds of their students, the range of knowledge to expect, which children need special help, and the types of misbehavior and discipline problems likely to occur. They then plan their instruction around these characteristics.

Thus, planning instruction around your students' characteristics begins by actively soliciting your learners' interests, needs, and aspirations at the start of the school year. From the beginning, convey to your students that they are not destined to be passive participants in your classroom, but that their interests, needs, and aspirations will be the origin of at least some of the things that will be presented during the year. A feeling among your students that their interests, needs, and aspirations will have some influence in the classroom—which is both theirs and yours—is an important step toward activating their internal motivators, especially in the culturally diverse classroom (Hill, 1989).

It also is important for students to feel that they can make some choices or contributions in instructional materials (e.g., contributing readings to a class library), topics to be covered (e.g., choosing special interest areas), and learning methods (e.g., arranging for special investigations or independent projects). These choices can be conditional upon good behavior and satisfactory achievement in the regular curriculum. Of course, students cannot decide what and how you teach; but your decisions should, in part, be influenced by their interests, needs, and aspirations.

There is no better way to find out learners' interests, needs, and aspirations than to ask them. Figure 11.1 suggests questions you can use in a class discussion or brief questionnaire at the beginning of the school year.

SOME TECHNIQUES FOR MOTIVATING LEARNERS

Here are some ways you can organize instruction to motivate learners for active engagement in learning:

> Contracts
>
> Games and simulations
>
> Self-paced, programmed texts
>
> Grouping
>
> Volunteering
>
> Grades and tests.

Let us see how each of these might be used in the classroom.

Contracts

Contracts can apply either to the standard curriculum or to additional special-interest areas. In either case, students complete work in anticipation of an agreed-to reward. Contracts exchange work for a grade, extra credit, dropping the lowest test score, skipping an assignment, and so on. They may involve additional reading, writing, or research, or may simply state that the reward will be given when performance on regularly scheduled assignments exceeds what is expected from past performance.

FIGURE 11.1
Some questions for
determining the
interests, needs, and
aspirations of learners

Name _____   Class _____

1. What was the most interesting or exciting thing that you did this past
    summer?
    _____
    _____

2. What job would you like to have when you finish school?
    _____

3. What hobbies or interests do you like to spend time on after school?
    _____

4a. How difficult do you find   4b. How much do you enjoy
    school work?   coming to school?

    _____ very difficult   _____ very much
    _____ fairly difficult   _____ some
    _____ a little difficult   _____ a little
    _____ not difficult   _____ not at all

5. Name something you look forward to about this coming school year.
    _____

6. What worries you the most about this coming school year?
    _____

7a. What subjects do you like   7b. What subjects do you like
    the most?   the least?

    _____   _____
    _____   _____
    _____   _____
    _____   _____

To tap students' interests, needs, and aspirations, give them flexibility in writing their own contracts—for example, they might suggest what additional reading they would like to complete, or what will be written in what style or format, or what type of information would be collected. You might allow students to negotiate the achievement level they must attain, awarding points or a grade for both the quantity and the quality of work completed.

O'Banion & Whaley (1981) found that contracts are especially useful in two areas. Contracts encourage less-able learners in reviewing fundamental concepts by allowing them to choose materials and methods (e.g., reading popular magazines they find particularly interesting). Contracts also stimulate more-able learners to go beyond the standard curriculum to independently acquire inquiry and problem-solving behaviors (e.g., by conducting an investigation on their own for extra credit). But most importantly, contracts allow students to match their interests, needs, and aspirations to their own learning styles.

Games and Simulations

Games and simulations are other ways of engaging learners. With the large-scale availability of computers in schools, games and simulations have taken on added importance as an instructional technique. Because games and simulations usually allow a great deal of independent choice and judgment, they can become excellent motivators in the classroom. They typically provide pictures of real-life situations that promote the direct involvement of learners in the learning process.

Economic theories, forms of government, scientific investigation, and even musical scores have been simulated by computer software in gamelike settings. Spelling, punctuation, and word-choice games also are available at different grade levels to motivate learners during traditionally boring and repetitive tasks. Although games and simulations will make up only a small portion of your total instructional time, they are valuable assets when matched to your learners' interests, needs, and aspirations (Johnson & Johnson, 1987).

Self-Paced, Programmed Texts

Self-paced texts are perhaps the most popular motivators used in classrooms today. They break content into small pieces and present the learner with immediate feedback about the correctness of the response to each piece, which is called a *frame*.

Although more-able students sometimes find them boring due to their slow pace and repetitiveness, programmed texts often are successful in getting less-able learners to master basic facts and understandings they would not acquire through whole-class instruction (Bunderson & Faust, 1976). These materials can contribute to a high level of motivation by providing a nonthreatening, individualized context for learning. You can give less-able learners an assignment in a self-paced text while average and above-average students complete more advanced assignments.

Grouping

One of the most frequent comments of poorly motivated learners is "I can't do the work." Whether or not they can may be less important than *why* they do not try. Often, fear of failure is the reason. To avoid the embarrassment of failure, some students avoid even starting to work, sometimes in favor of off-task or disruptive behavior.

You can reduce fear of failure and get learners to start sampling the learning task by grouping them. Group learners by their abilities (less-able, average, more-able), interests (practical, academic), needs (facts, problem-solving skills), or tasks (cooperative, individualistic). If you properly compose groups of students who have complementary skills and abilities, and if the materials are appropriate to the group, students are likely to continue sampling until the task is completed (Slavin, 1987).

Thus, and as we saw in the previous chapter, cooperative groups can be an important motivator. When students are assigned to groups whose members have complementary skills or abilities, they generally work harder and are more attentive to the learning task (Sharan, 1980).

Volunteering

The use of volunteers has not always been recognized as a motivational strategy, but it sometimes works when nothing else does. As simple as this strategy seems, it has been known to energize even the most reluctant learners. The secret lies not in a simple call for volunteers but in the *design of the task* for which you ask students to volunteer.

By creating an appealing but instructive task at the current level of functioning of poorly motivated learners and asking for their assistance, you can instill a sense of pride and accomplishment that can pique a student's interest in a topic. For example, ask for volunteers to find elementary spelling and punctuation errors in other students' papers. Ask them to prepare a practical demonstration about something with which they are especially familiar. Ask them to tutor those who know less. Such tasks can provide a sense of immediacy and accomplishment that may motivate some learners who might otherwise be disinterested and inattentive.

Grades and Tests

We can include grades and tests as motivators, with the understanding that they must be used selectively. As you have seen, grades and tests serve many different purposes, such as checking progress, diagnosing weaknesses, evaluating performance, and reviewing content. To these can be added *motivating*, a use not entirely independent of these other purposes. However, tests become motivators only when their difficulty level allows for moderate-to-high rates of success. In other words, tests specifically prepared and administered to raise the motivation level of learners should be of minimal difficulty.

Grades and tests are double edged: they can be incentives to work harder, or to stop working altogether. Difficult tests, although sometimes needed and inevitable, may be a disincentive for some types of learners. Students associate grades with reinforcement, both internal (e.g., a sense of accomplishment) and external (e.g., praise from parents).

A poor test grade also can have a double edge. For some students it may be all the reason they need for giving up, while for others it may be all the reason they need for studying harder. Frequent tests having a difficulty level that allows for moderate-to-high success rates have been associated with better class attendance, more work being completed outside of class, and higher achievement on tests (Fitch, Drucker, & Norton, 1957). But frequent use of difficult tests that result in low success rates have been associated with high levels of student anxiety, more self-doubt, and greater uncertainty (Dowaliby & Schumer, 1973). Tests that work best as motivators tend to cover recently learned material for which most students have an adequate grasp. These progress checks or review quizzes provide a timely reward for staying on top of homework and class exercises as well as an incentive to continue to work hard to maintain an impressive string of good marks.

LESS FORMAL WAYS OF MOTIVATING LEARNERS

You have seen how to use contracts, games and simulations, self-paced texts, grouping, volunteering, and grades and tests to increase the attention and motivation of your learners. In addition, there are many less formal means. Here are some other ways of motivating learners that have proven effective.

Using Praise and Encouragement

The most efficient means for motivating and engaging students in the learning process is the use of praise and encouragement. But surprisingly, use of praise occupies relatively little class time for most teachers (Brophy & Good, 1986). Wragg and Wood (1984) report that an average of only about 2% of a teacher's day is devoted to any kind of praise. Simple phrases such as "Well done," "That was good," or "Good work; keep it up," can be particularly effective motivators when applied *consistently* and when they are *honest appraisals* of the learner's true achievement. These simple verbal responses tell the student that the reward is contingent upon appropriate performance. More importantly, praise tells the learner that by producing the correct response, he or she can control the flow of reward.

When consistently applied, the link between performance and reward can become strong enough that a *need to achieve* is created. This occurs when the link becomes so internalized that much of the learner's behavior is directed by the expectation of the next reward that comes from a correct or acceptable response. There is little doubt among behavioral psychologists that a reward contingent upon an appropriate behavior increases the frequency of that behavior.

Because the strategy of praise always is available to you, it can be one of the most effective means of motivating learners *if* it is applied consistently and immediately after an acceptable response.

Providing Explanations

Another effective device for motivating learners is to explain why you are giving a certain request or assignment. Learners who know the reasons behind your request or assignment are more likely to work on it earnestly and to complete it, even if they may not fully understand or agree with it. In a study reported by Wragg and Wood (1984), relatively few teachers explained why particular work assignments were given. But when they did explain, students appreciated the explanations and responded with renewed motivation.

When assignments are lengthy or particularly difficult, placing them in perspective can be an important external source of motivation. For example, you can say, "This assignment will help prepare you for the end-of-the-chapter test," or "We are doing this exercise to check on our basic skills so that we will not have difficulty with our next topic." Such simple, brief explanations send your learners an important message: you think highly of their abilities to reason and they are capable of understanding the reasons behind what you are doing.

These explanations also loosen the sometimes rigid teacher-student authority structure, against which some students naturally rebel. By treating your students much as you would adults, they will come to see your assignments as a means to an end and not as arbitrary orders that too often are misconstrued as punishment and control. When punishment or control is perceived to be your motivation, your learners probably will respond begrudgingly and with little motivation.

Offering to Help

Another way to motivate learners is through frequent offers of help. Not all students will require individual assistance, but all of them will appreciate knowing that assistance is available if needed.

Some students fail to start assignments or fail to take them seriously because they fear being unable to complete them. For these students, off-task or disruptive behavior may be far safer than losing self-respect or being ridiculed because they are not able to understand an assignment or to complete it correctly. Even when these students do begin the activity, their anxiety and self-doubt usually halt their engagement in the learning process at the slightest difficulty.

Whether many of your learners will actually need your assistance, or only a few, the warmth and support implied by your offer to help goes a long way toward getting all of them to start an assignment with equal and sufficient motivation. Keep your assistance to individual students brief and focused on the problem so that instructional time is not monopolized by only one student or a few.

Accepting Diversity

Your classroom is likely to be a microcosm of the world outside. The variety of people, ideas, needs, habits, and cultures in your community will not stop at your classroom door. Students might have similar ability levels, but they will be vastly different in other ways. Perhaps more devastating to students' motivation than anything else is a teacher's unwillingness to tolerate this natural diversity of interests, needs, and aspirations. Because your life experiences inevitably will be different from your students', you may be confronted with values, habits, dress, and lifestyles different from those to which you are accustomed.

Infractions of school rules and unacceptable dress and personal habits that impede learning should not be accepted, regardless of their origins. However, your ability to accept your learners for who and what they are, regardless of how different their experience is from yours, can be an important motivating factor. An intolerant attitude on your part, however subtle, will create an almost immediate sense of isolation among some of your learners. This may extend to their reluctance, resistance, or even refusal to complete assignments you give.

If an "I'm different from you" attitude becomes established in your classroom, experience shows that almost any overture you make to break the ice probably will fail. If students feel it is futile to gain your unconditional acceptance, they are unlikely to give you the respect you need to conduct your classroom in an orderly and efficient manner.

Your tolerance for the diverse lifestyles, attitudes, and values that likely will exist among your learners can be an important motivating force, but it also has another valuable function. Your tolerance also sets an example of how your students, who must one day live and work in a culturally diverse democratic society, should behave toward others.

Emphasizing Reward, Not Punishment

Finally, in motivating your learners, it is important to note the difference between the use of reinforcement (incentives) and the use of punishment (aversives). In a school setting, it often is natural to set an aversive tone—to say why we *should not* do something rather than why we *should*. Recall how frequently you have heard phrases like:

> If you don't study, you'll flunk the course.
>
> Failure to do the homework will mean five points off.
>
> Do it right the first time, or you'll have to do it over.
>
> If you fail to understand it today, you'll have to get it on your own later.
>
> If it's too difficult, you shouldn't be here.
>
> If you think I'm going too fast, you must not have studied.

In a superordinate-subordinate environment such as school, it is natural for those in authority to reinforce the existing structure with penalties. However, when this is the only incentive for good conduct, it can be detrimental to learners' motivation. Learners generally respond far better to rewards for acceptable behavior than to punishment for unacceptable behavior. Such a penalty-oriented structure may work well in the military, but it is not as effective as a reward-oriented structure in the classroom. Unless special circumstances prevail, rewards are more effective than punishment in getting individuals to behave appropriately.

Television advertisers learned this lesson early when they were surprised to discover that the rewards of having fresh, clean teeth persuaded more people to change brands of toothpaste than the negative consequences of ugly tooth decay. When negative consequences (penalties) provoke high levels of anxiety and fear of the consequences, they become dysfunctional in motivating behavior. The implications of advertising research should not be lost on educators: It is more effective to inform learners of the positive consequences of appropriate behavior than to enumerate the negative consequences of misbehavior.

Although both rewards and penalties are necessary, the emphasis on rewards (the positive consequences of the right behavior) always should outweigh the emphasis on penalties. Compare the following restated phrases, which now emphasize reward and not punishment:

- □ Let's not forget to do the studying. It will make the lessons a lot more meaningful.
- □ If you do all the homework, the tests will be easy. There will be a five-point penalty, however, for homework not turned in.
- □ Be careful to follow the directions carefully. Otherwise, you may have to do it over.
- □ Listen carefully today, because it will be easier to understand my explanation now than if you have to get it on your own.
- □ Tell me if this assignment is too difficult. That will help us decide on what to do next.
- □ I may be going too fast for some of you. If so, you may want to reexamine how much study time you should be devoting to this subject.
- □ Listen and study hard so that you know the material well. That way, we will not have to practice any more.

Table 11.1 summarizes the five informal motivational devices and provides some suggestions for their use.

TABLE 11.1
Some motivators and their appropriate uses

Motivator	Use phrases such as . . .	Avoid phrases such as . . .
Using praise and encouragement	You've got it.	That's a dumb answer.
	Good work.	You're being lazy again.
	Good try.	I can see you never study.
	That was quick.	You can never pay attention, can you?
Providing explanations	The reason this is so important is . . .	Today you will have to learn this, or else . . .
	We are doing this assignment because . . .	Complete this excercise; otherwise, there'll be trouble.
	This will be difficult, but it fits in with . . .	This is a long assignment, but you'll just have to do it.
	Experience has shown that without these facts the next unit will be very difficult.	We must cover this material, so let's get going.

TABLE 11.1
concluded

Motivator	Use phrases such as ...	Avoid phrases such as ...
Offering to help	Should you need help, I'll be here.	You should be able to do this on your own.
	Ask if you need help.	If you have to ask for help, you must not have studied.
	I'll be walking around; catch me if you have a problem.	Please don't ask a dumb question.
	Don't be afraid to ask a question if you're having trouble.	Raise your hand only if you're stuck on a difficult problem.
Accepting diversity	That's not the answer I expected, but I can see your point.	That's not the kind of answer we can accept around here.
	That's not how I see it, but I can understand how others might see it differently.	I've never heard that expression before—so let's not start something new.
	This is not something I'm familiar with. Where did you get that idea?	Please use ideas that fit in with what I say in class.
	That is not a word I've heard before. Tell us what it means.	Don't ever use foreign words in this class.
Emphasizing reinforcement and reward	All homework completed means five extra points.	Five points off for missing homework.
	If you get a *C* or better on all the tests, I'll drop the lowest grade.	If you have less than a *C* average on all your tests, you'll have to take an extra test.
	Those who complete all the exercises on time can go to the learning center.	If you don't complete the exercise on time, there can be no use of the learning center.
	If you have a *C* average, you get to choose any topic for your term paper.	If you don't have a *C* average, you must choose your term paper topic from a restricted list of difficult topics.

ESTABLISHING AN EFFECTIVE CLASSROOM CLIMATE

Classroom climate is the atmosphere or mood in which interactions between you and your students take place. Your classroom climate is created by the manner and degree to which you exercise authority, show warmth and support, encourage competitiveness or cooperation, and allow for independent judgment and choice. Although seldom recognized, the climate of your classroom is your choice, just as are your instructional methods.

Unfortunately, in many classrooms the climate is determined haphazardly. It is allowed to develop randomly, depending on what is occurring at the moment. This is not the case in a well-managed classroom. This section introduces two related aspects of an effective classroom climate: the **social environment**, meaning the interaction patterns you promote in the classroom, and the **organizational environment**, meaning your physical or visual arrangement of the classroom. Both are your choice, and you can alter them to create just the right climate for the proper objective.

The Social Environment

The social environment varies from **authoritarian**, in which you are the primary provider of information, opinions, and instruction, to **laissez faire**, in which the students become the primary providers of information, opinions, and instruction. Be-

One aspect of an effective learning climate is the physical or visual arrangement of the classroom. This arrangement is a matter of choice that can be altered to create just the right climate for your learning objectives.

tween these extremes lies the middle ground in which you and students **share responsibilities**: students are given freedom of choice and judgment under your direction. Although many variations are possible, the variation you choose will have pronounced effects on what can and cannot take place in your classroom.

For example, a group discussion might be a colossal failure in a rigid authoritarian climate, because the climate clues students that their opinions are less important than yours, that teacher talk and not student talk should take up most of the instructional time, and that the freedom to express oneself spontaneously is your right but not theirs. In a more open atmosphere this same attempt at discussion might well be a smashing success, because all the ingredients of a good discussion—freedom to express one's opinion, high degree of student talk, and spontaneity—have been provided by the classroom climate.

The social atmosphere you create, whether authoritarian, laissez faire, or somewhere between, is determined by how you see yourself: Are you a commander-in-chief who carefully controls and hones student behavior by organizing and providing all the learning stimuli? Or, are you a translator or summarizer of the ideas provided by students? Or, are you an equal partner with students in creating ideas and problem solutions? Consider the effects of each climate and how you can create it.

The effective teacher not only uses a variety of teaching strategies, but also can create a variety of classroom climates. However, your ability to create a certain climate always will be less important than your ability to *change* the climate when the objectives and the situation demand. Although early research in social psychology tried to identify the type of climate most conducive to individual behavior (Lewin, Lippitt, & White, 1939), the results suggest that each climate has both advantages and disadvantages, depending on the intended goals.

Because goals change from lesson to lesson and week to week, so too must your classroom climate that supports the goals. When the goals change but your classroom climate does not, the stage is set for off-task, disruptive, and even antagonistic behavior among your students.

Competitive, Cooperative, or Individualistic.   We have already examined several ways you can vary your authority, and that of your students, in accordance with your objectives. These variations correspond not only with how much you relinquish your authority and therefore your control of the learning process, but also how **competitive, cooperative,** or **individualistic** you wish the interactions among members of your class to be. These three conditions are illustrated in Table 11.2.

You can see in the table that, as you shift classroom climate from competitive, to cooperative, to individualistic, you relinquish control over the learning process until, in the individualistic mode, students have almost sole responsibility for judging their own work. Note also that an individualistic mode all but eliminates student expressions of opinion, student talk, and spontaneity of responses, all of which are encouraged and promoted in a cooperative climate.

Each of the three climates has characteristic activities: the competitive mode features drill and practice in which students respond to your questions; the cooperative mode has group discussions in which both you and your students pose questions

TABLE 11.2
Three types of classroom climate

Social climate	Definition	Example activity	Authority vested in students	Authority vested in teacher
Competitive	Students compete for right answers among themselves or with a standard established by the teacher. The teacher is the sole judge of the appropriateness of a response.	Drill and practice	None	To organize the instruction, present the stimulus material, and evaluate correctness of responses
Cooperative	Students engage in dialogue that is monitored by the teacher. The teacher systematically intervenes in the discussion to sharpen ideas and move the discussion to a higher level.	Small and large group discussion	To present opinions, to provide ideas, and to speak and discuss freely and spontaneously	To stimulate the discussion, arbitrate differences, organize and summarize student contributions
Individualistic	Students complete assignments monitored by the teacher. Students are encouraged to complete the assignment with the answers they think are best. Emphasis is on getting through and testing one's self.	Independent seatwork	To complete the assignment with the best possible responses	To assign the work and see that orderly progress is made toward its completion

and answers; and the individualistic mode uses detailed seatwork assignments in which students practice independently. Your control and authority and the behaviors you can expect from your students will differ among these social climates in ways indicated in Table 11.2.

Applying the Three Climates.   In addition to encouraging the proper climate for a given instructional activity (e.g., drill and practice, group discussion, or seatwork), you must decide to which segments of the class each climate applies. Figure 11.2 suggests that each climate can be applied to the full class, to groups, and to individuals with equal effectiveness. For example, it is not necessary that all group discussions be conducted in a cooperative climate.

You can form subgroups to compete against each other in a gamelike atmosphere (see Cell 21 in the figure), or individuals can work in a cooperative arrangement by exchanging papers and correcting each other's errors (Cell 32). Likewise, your entire class can perform seatwork in lockstep fashion as though the class were a single individual (Cell 13), and subgroups can be asked to work as independent teams (Cell 23), and individuals can be teamed in pairs to compete with each other (Cell 31).

Although some cells in Figure 11.2 may be more popular than others, various arrangements of students and climates are possible, depending on your instructional goals. Your job is to ensure that the degree of authority you impose matches your instructional goal (e.g., the expression of student opinion you allow, the amount of time you devote to student talk, and the spontaneity with which you want your students to respond).

The Organizational Environment

In addition to arranging the social climate of your classroom, you also must arrange the physical climate. It goes without saying that a classroom should be attractive, well-lighted, comfortable, and colorful. But, aside from a colorful bulletin board and neatness, you may have very little influence over the external features of your classroom (e.g., paint, lighting, windows, and even such things as the availability of bookshelves and a file cabinet). Attempts to improve these external conditions always are worth a try, but do not be surprised if your repeated requests are in vain. It is not unusual for teachers to bring their own essential items, such as a clock, bookcase, file cabinet, rug, or pedestal stool to the classroom at the beginning of the year and take them home again for the summer.

What may be more important than these items, however, is the way the internal features of your classroom (desks, chairs, tables) are arranged. Students quickly get used to and accept the external features of a classroom, good or bad. But the internal arrangement of the classroom will affect your students every day of the school year.

The most flexible furniture arrangement places your desk at the front of the room and aligns the student desks in rows. Although it may seem strange to associate this traditional format with flexibility, it is the most flexible arrangement because you

FIGURE 11.2
Targets for three types
of classroom climates

	Competitive	Cooperative	Individualistic
Full Class	Students compete with other students by having the correct answer when it's their turn. <div align="right">11</div>	Students are allowed to call out hints or clues when a student is having difficulty finding the right answer. <div align="right">12</div>	The entire class recites answers in unison. <div align="right">13</div>
Groups	Subgroups compete against each other as opposing teams. <div align="right">21</div>	Subgroups work on different but related aspects of a topic combining their results into a final report to the class. <div align="right">22</div>	Each subgroup completes its own assigned topic which is independent of the topics assigned the other subgroups. No shared report is given to the class. <div align="right">23</div>
Individual	Individuals compete with each other by having to respond to the same question. The quickest most accurate response "wins." <div align="right">31</div>	Pairs of individuals cooperate by exchanging papers, sharing responses, or correcting each other's errors. <div align="right">32</div>	Individuals complete seat work on their own without direct teacher involvement. <div align="right">33</div>

can use it to create competitive, cooperative, or individualistic environments, although not always with equal effectiveness. This fact, plus the difficulty of rearranging classroom furniture every time a change in social climate is desired, makes the traditional classroom arrangement almost as popular today as it was 50 years ago.

There are times, however, when you should change the arrangement to encourage a more cooperative, interactive, and group-sharing climate. Such a classroom arrangement has many variations that depend on the external features of the classroom and available furniture, but one such model is shown in Figure 11.3.

The important feature to note in this arrangement is the deliberate attempt to get people together. The barriers to interpersonal sharing and communication that sometimes result from the rigid alignment of desks are avoided in this setting by the more informal, but still systematic, furniture arrangement. As the internal features of the classroom turn from traditional to this less formal arrangement, so too will the social climate of the classroom change. Because this arrangement suggests that interpersonal communication and sharing is permitted, increased interpersonal communication and sharing will undoubtedly occur, whether you desire it or not.

From such an arrangement, expect more expression of student opinion, increased student talk, and greater spontaneity in student responses. This emphasizes

FIGURE 11.3

A classroom arrangement conducive to group work

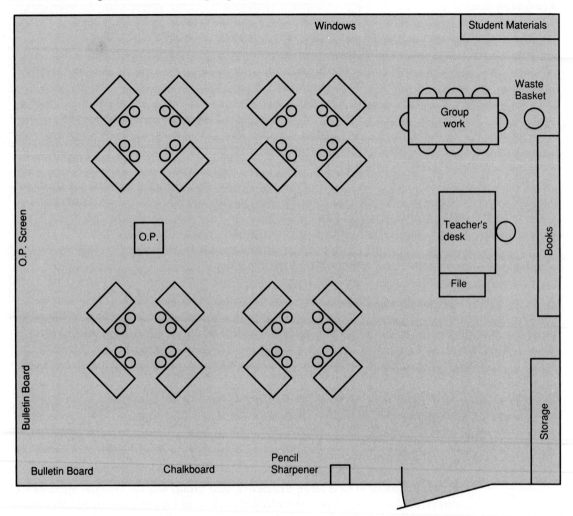

the important notion that *the social climate created by your words and deeds always should match the organizational climate created by the physical arrangement of your classroom*. It also explains why the traditional or formal classroom actually is quite flexible and has remained so popular. A cooperative climate (e.g., for conducting a group discussion) always can occur in a formal classroom, but a competitive climate (e.g., for drill and practice) becomes exceedingly difficult in a less formal arrangement. This is not a reason to abandon the appeal of a less rigid classroom arrangement, but only to use it with a firm grasp of the student behavior it is likely to promote.

Of course, it always is refreshing to change the internal arrangement of a classroom from time to time for the sake of variety. This can be an effective psychological boost for both teacher and students in the midst of a long and arduous school year. Keep in mind, however, that time and effort allow for only so much back-and-forth switching. You might compromise by maintaining the basic nature of the formal classroom but, space permitting, setting aside one or two less formal areas (e.g., a learning center or group discussion table) for times when instructional goals call for interpersonal communication and sharing.

ESTABLISHING RULES AND PROCEDURES

Establishing rules and procedures to reduce the occurrence of classroom discipline problems will be one of your most important classroom management activities (Emmer, Evertson, Sanford, Clements, & Worsham, 1989). These rules and procedures, which you should formulate prior to the first school day, are your commitment to providing the ounce of prevention to avoid having to provide a pound of cure.

Different types of rules and procedures are needed for effectively managing a classroom. Here are the categories:

Rules related to academic work.

Rules related to classroom conduct.

Rules that must be communicated your first teaching day.

Rules that can be communicated later.

Rules pertaining to 27 different areas of classroom management are handily summarized in Figure 11.4. About half of them need to be communicated on the first day of class or shortly thereafter. Of course, you need not tell your students the rules in each category all at the same time or in the same way. For example, some rules are best held until just the right opportunity presents itself to reinforce the rule (e.g., when a visitor comes to the door). Others should be communicated the first day of class (how to respond or speak out) or shortly thereafter (when to complete makeup work).

You can communicate rules orally, in a handout, on the bulletin board, or show them on an overhead projector. Regardless of how or when you communicate them, however, you need to consider the problem area and compose a rule for it *prior* to the first day of school.

The top half of Figure 11.4 identifies rules commonly needed the very first day of class, either because students will ask about them or because incidents are likely to arise requiring their use. Notice that these rules are divided into seven conduct rules and seven work rules. For the elementary grades, it is best that you present them orally, *and* provide a handout, *and* post them for later reference by the students. In the lower grades, learners can forget oral messages quickly—or choose to ignore them if there is no physical representation of the rule as a constant reminder. In the later elementary grades and junior high, your recital of the rules while students copy them into their notebooks may be sufficient. For high school students, simply hearing the rules may be sufficient, as long as they are posted for later reference.

Not all "first day" rules are equally important, and other rules may have to be added as special circumstances require. But rules about responding and speaking out,

FIGURE 11.4

Classroom rules related
to conduct and work

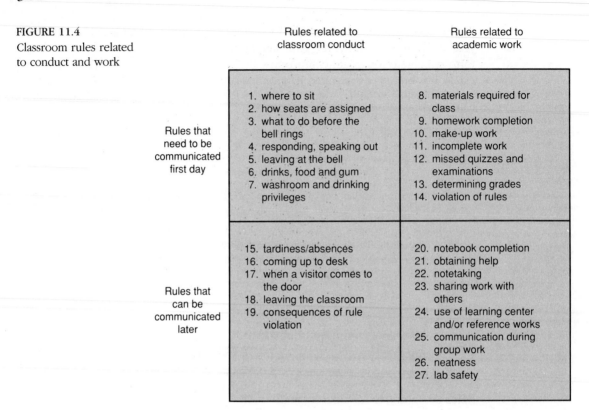

	Rules related to classroom conduct	Rules related to academic work
Rules that need to be communicated first day	1. where to sit 2. how seats are assigned 3. what to do before the bell rings 4. responding, speaking out 5. leaving at the bell 6. drinks, food and gum 7. washroom and drinking privileges	8. materials required for class 9. homework completion 10. make-up work 11. incomplete work 12. missed quizzes and examinations 13. determining grades 14. violation of rules
Rules that can be communicated later	15. tardiness/absences 16. coming up to desk 17. when a visitor comes to the door 18. leaving the classroom 19. consequences of rule violation	20. notebook completion 21. obtaining help 22. notetaking 23. sharing work with others 24. use of learning center and/or reference works 25. communication during group work 26. neatness 27. lab safety

making up work, determining grades, and violation of due dates are among the most
important. It is in these areas that confusion often occurs on the very first day. For
example, some of the issues you must consider in these four rule areas are:

Rule Area	*Issues*
Responding, speaking out	☐ Must hands be raised? ☐ Are other forms of acknowledgement acceptable (e.g., head nod)? ☐ What will happen if a student speaks when others are speaking? ☐ What will you do about shouting or using a loud voice?
Make up work	☐ Will makeup work be allowed? ☐ Will there be penalties for not completing it? ☐ Will it be graded? ☐ Whose responsibility is it to know the work is missing?
Determining grades	☐ What percentage will quizzes and tests contribute to the total grade? ☐ What percentage will class participation count? ☐ When will notification be given of failing performance? ☐ How much will homework count?

Violation of due dates	☐ What happens when repeated violations occur?
	☐ Where can a student learn the due dates if absent?
	☐ What penalties are there for copying another person's assignment?
	☐ Will makeup work be required when a due date is missed?

A few moments of thought before these issues are raised in class can avoid embarrassing pauses and an uncertain response when a student asks a question. You may want to identify alternative issues for the remaining rule areas in Figure 11.4 and to extend those just listed.

The bottom half of Figure 11.4 identifies areas for which rules can be communicated as the situation arises. Some are specific to a particular situation (e.g., safety during a lab experiment, notebook completion, obtaining help) and are best presented in the context to which they apply. They will be more meaningful and more easily remembered *when there is a circumstance or incident that applies to the rule and thus aids in its retention*. Many other rules in these areas, however, are likely to be needed in the first few days or weeks of school (e.g., tardiness/absences, leaving at the bell, notetaking). Even though you may not communicate these rules on the first day of school, they usually are required so soon afterward that you must compose a procedure for them prior to your first class day.

Some of the most troublesome behaviors in this category include students getting out of their seats, communicating during group work, completing in-class assignments early, and violating rules. Some issues to be considered for these behaviors are:

Behavior	*Issues*
Getting out of seat	☐ When is out-of-seat movement permissible?
	☐ When can a student come to the teacher's desk?
	☐ When can reference books or learning centers be visited?
	☐ What if a student visits another?
Communicating during group work	☐ Can a student leave an assigned seat?
	☐ How loudly should a student speak?
	☐ Who determines who can talk next?
	☐ Will there be a group leader?
Early completion of in-class assignments	☐ Can work for other classes or subjects be done?
	☐ Can a newspaper or magazine be read?
	☐ Can the next exercise or assignment be worked on?
	☐ Can students rest their heads on their desks?
Rule violation	☐ Will names be written on the board?
	☐ Will extra work penalties be assigned?
	☐ Will you have after-class detention?
	☐ When will a disciplinary referral be made?

It is a secure feeling when you know that you have created procedures for dealing with the many possible problem areas. However, unless you clearly communicate your rules and apply them consistently, all your work in making them will be meaningless. Consistency is a key reason why some rules are effective while others are not.

Your rules actually can become a double-edged sword: at one moment they can work to control and manage your classroom and at another they can show you in the poorest light. Rules that are not enforced or that are not applied evenly and consistently over time result in a loss of prestige and respect for the person who has created the rules and has the responsibility for carrying them out.

Among the many reasons why a particular rule is not applied consistently, the most frequent are (Emmer et al., 1989):

1. The rule is not workable or appropriate. It does not fit a particular context or is not reasonable, given the nature of the individuals to whom it applies.
2. The teacher fails to monitor students closely and consequently some individuals violating the rule are caught while others are not.
3. The teacher does not feel strongly enough about the rule to be persistent about its enforcement and thus makes many exceptions to the rule.

When you realize that any of the preceding conditions apply, think about changing the rule. One cannot state flatly that rules are made to be broken, but it is true that even good rules should be altered, changed, or even abandoned when circumstances change. If you allow a rule to be repeatedly ignored or broken, it will have the worst possible effect on your ability to manage your classroom effectively. On the other hand, rigidly clinging to a rule that obviously is not working or is not needed will have an equally detrimental effect.

When a rule is unworkable or inappropriate for particular students or a particular classroom situation, change it. Be sure, however, to give the rule a chance by keeping it in effect for a while after you first suspect it may not be working. Keep in mind that no one likes rules and that almost all of your students would prefer not having any—but that does not mean the rule is not working or not needed. *Inability to enforce a rule over a reasonable period of time is the best sign a change may be needed.*

If you cannot monitor a situation closely enough to enforce a rule, another kind of change may be necessary. When enough infractions go unnoticed so that your response becomes noticeably inconsistent, some change is in order. If you find yourself being inconsistent about a rule, be fair when you finally observe an infraction. Sometimes it is all too easy to purge your guilt for not catching past infractions by overreacting to the person finally caught. Overreacting in such cases can be as damaging to your respect as is missing the prior infractions.

Keep in mind that minor deviations in a rule may not be worth your effort to respond when (a) it would provide an untimely interruption to your lesson or (b) it is only momentary and not likely to recur. However, when problems in applying a rule persist over time, either increase your vigilance or adjust the rule to allow more flexibility in your response (e.g., coming up to the desk without permission for help may be acceptable, but coming up just to talk is not).

PROBLEM AREAS IN CLASSROOM MANAGEMENT

A primary purpose of effective classroom management is to keep learners actively engaged in the learning process. Active engagement means getting learners to work with and act upon the material presented, as evidenced by carefully attending to the material, progressing through seatwork at a steady pace, participating in class discussions, and being attentive when called upon. This section describes four events that are particularly crucial for keeping students actively engaged in the learning process: *monitoring students, making transitions, giving assignments,* and *bringing closure to lessons.* Following are some effective classroom management practices in each of these areas.

Monitoring Students

Monitoring is the process of observing, mentally recording, and, when necessary, redirecting or correcting students' behaviors. Monitoring occurs when you look for active, alert eyes during discussion sessions, faces down and directed at the book or assignment during seatwork, raised hands during a question-and-answer period, and, in general, signs that indicate the learner is participating in what is going on. These signs of engagement (or their absence) indicate when you need to change the pace of your delivery, the difficulty of the material, or even the activity itself.

Kounin (1970) used the word **withitness** to refer to a teacher's ability to keep track of many different signs of engagement at the same time. Kounin observed that one of the most important distinctions between effective and ineffective classroom managers is the degree to which they exhibit withitness. Effective classroom managers who exhibited withitness were aware of what was happening in all parts of the classroom and were able to see different things happening in different parts of the room at the same time. Furthermore, these effective classroom managers were able to *communicate this awareness to their students.*

Few of us are blessed with eyes in the backs of our heads—or are capable of detecting multiple behaviors even when they occur in front of our heads. But there are several simple ways to increase your withitness and the extent of your students' active engagement in the learning process.

One way is to increase your physical presence through eye contact. If your eye contact is limited to only a portion of the classroom, you effectively lose withitness for the rest of the classroom. It is surprising to note that a great many beginning teachers consistently:

> talk only to the middle-front rows,
>
> talk with their backs to the class when writing on the chalkboard,
>
> talk while looking toward the windows or ceiling, or
>
> talk while not being able to see all students due to other students blocking their view.

In each of these instances, you see only a portion of the classroom, and *the students know only a portion of the classroom is seen.* Your eye contact that covers all portions of the classroom is one of the most important ingredients in conveying a sense of withitness.

A second ingredient for improving withitness is learning to monitor more than one activity at a time. Here, the key not only is to change your eye contact to different parts of the room, but also to change your focus of attention. For example, progress on assigned seatwork might be the focus of your observations when scanning students in the front of the class, but potential behavior problems might be your focus when scanning students in the back of the class.

You should switch back and forth from conduct-related observations to work-related observations at the same time you change eye contact. However, a great impediment to such switching is a tendency to focus exclusively on one student who is having either conduct or work-related problems. Once other students realize you are preoccupied with one of their peers, problems with other students in other parts of the classroom may be inevitable.

Making Transitions

Another problem area is transitions. It is difficult to keep students' attention during a transition from one instructional activity to another. Switching from lecture to seatwork, from discussion to lecture, or from seatwork to discussion is a time for some students to misbehave. Moving the entire class from one activity to another in a timely and orderly manner can be a major undertaking. Problems in making these transitions often occur for two reasons: (a) learners are not ready to perform the next activity (or may not even know what it is), and (b) learners have unclear expectations about appropriate behavior during the transition.

When students are uncertain or unaware of what is coming next, they naturally become anxious about their ability to perform and make the transition. This is the time that transitions can get noisy, with some students feeling more comfortable clinging to the previous activity than changing to the next. The beginning of the school year is a time of noisy transitions as students fumble to find the proper materials (or guess which ones are needed) and to find out what is expected of them next. They will not rush headlong into a new activity, for fear they will not like it or will be unable to do well.

In this sense, transitions are as much psychological barriers as they are actual divisions between activities. Students must adjust their psychology for the next activity, just as they must adjust their books and papers. You can help in their adjustment by telling them the daily routine you expect of them. This routine becomes second nature after a few weeks, but it deserves special attention during the first days of school. This is the time for you to describe these daily activities and the order in which they will occur (e.g., 10 minutes of lecture, 15 minutes of questions and answers, 15 minutes of seatwork, and 10 minutes of checking and correcting).

Here are some suggestions for addressing the problems that occur during transitions:

Problems	*Solutions*
Students talk loudly at the beginning of transitions.	It is difficult to *allow* a small amount of talking and *obtain* a small amount. So, establish a no-talking rule during transitions.
Students socialize during the transition, delaying the start of the next activity.	Allow no more time than is necessary between activities (e.g., to close books, gather up materials, select new materials).

One approach to moving the entire class from one activity to another in a timely and orderly manner is to communicate clearly the actual divisions in time between activities.

Students complete assignments before the scheduled time for an activity to end.

Make assignments according to the time to be filled, not the exercises to be completed. Always assign more than enough exercises to fill the allotted time.

Students continue to work on the preceding activity after a change.

Give five-minute and two-minute warnings before the end of any activity and use verbal markers such as "Shortly we will end this work," and "Let's finish this up so that we can begin. . . ." Create definite beginning and end points to each activity, such as "OK, that's the end of this activity; now we will start . . ." or "Put your papers away and turn to. . . ."

Some students lag behind others in completing the previous activity.

Don't wait for stragglers. Begin new activities on time. When a natural break occurs, visit privately with students still working on previous tasks to tell them that they must stop and change. Be sure to note the reason they have not finished (e.g., material too hard, lack of motivation, off-task behavior).

You delay the beginning of the activity to find something (file cabinet keys, materials, roster, references, etc.).

Always be prepared—pure and simple!

Giving Assignments

Another crucial time for effective classroom management is when you are giving or explaining assignments. This can be a particularly troublesome time because it often means assigning work that at least some students will not be eager to complete. Grunts and groans are common student expressions of distaste for homework or other assignments that must be completed outside of the regular school day. At times like these outbursts of misbehavior are most likely to occur.

Evertson and Emmer (1982) found that one difference between effective and ineffective classroom managers was the manner in which they gave assignments, particularly homework. Giving assignments appeared almost effortless for the effective managers, while for the ineffective managers the normal classroom routine sometimes abruptly halted, noise level went up, and much commotion ensued. The difference was attributed to several simple procedures that were commonplace among experienced teachers but not among inexperienced teachers.

One procedure was to attach assignments directly to the end of an in-class activity. By doing so, the teacher avoided an awkward pause and even the need for a transition, because the assignment was seen as a logical extension of what already was taking place. The practice of giving the assignment immediately after the activity to which it most closely relates, as opposed to giving it at the end of class or the day, may be much like getting an injection while the physician is engaging you in a friendly conversation and looking at you with a smile: if the conversation is engaging enough, you might not feel the pain.

By contrast, imagine how you might feel being given an assignment under these conditions:

TEACHER A: I guess I'll have to assign some homework now, so do problems 1 through 10 on page 61.

TEACHER B: For homework do the problems under Exercise A and Exercise B—and be sure all of them are finished by tomorrow.

TEACHER C: We're out of time, so you'll have to finish these problems on your own.

In each of these assignments there is a subtle implication that the homework may not really be needed or that it is being given mechanically or as some sort of punishment. Why this homework is being assigned may be a complete mystery to most students, because none of the teachers mentioned either the in-class activities to which the homework presumably relates or the benefits that may accrue from the assignment. These explanations are important if you expect anything other than a mechanical or grudging response. Students expect and appreciate knowing why an assignment is made before they are expected to do it.

Now consider these assignments again, this time with some explanations added:

TEACHER A: Today we have talked a lot about the origins of the Civil War and some of the economic unrest that preceded it. But some other types of unrest also were responsible for the Civil War. These will be important for understanding the real causes behind this war. Problems 1 through 10 on page 61 will help you understand some of these other causes.

TEACHER B: We have all had a chance now to try our skill at forming possessives. As most of you have found out, it's a little harder than it looks. So let's try Exercises A and B for tonight, which should give you just the right amount of practice in forming possessives.

TEACHER C: Well, it looks like time has run out before we could complete all the problems. The next set of problems we will study requires a lot of what we have learned here today. Let's complete the rest of these for tonight to see if you've got the concept. This should make the next lesson go a lot smoother.

Keep in mind that effective classroom managers give assignments that (a) immediately follow the lesson or activities to which they relate, (b) explain which in-class lessons the assignment relates to, and (c) avoid any *unnecessary* negative connotations (e.g., "finish them all," "be sure they are correct," "complete it on time"), which may make your assignment sound more like a punishment than an instructional activity.

Finally, it always is a good idea to display prior assignments somewhere in your classroom so that students who have missed an assignment can conveniently look it up without requiring your time to remember or find an old assignment. A simple two-foot square sheet of art board, divided into days of the month and covered with plastic to write on, can be a convenient and reusable way of communicating past assignments on a monthly basis.

Bringing Closure

Another time for effective classroom management is when you are bringing a lesson to its end. Closure is as important as the attention-getting device with which the lesson began. Typically, beginning teachers pay little attention to closure, coming to abrupt endings such as:

Oops, there's the bell!

I guess we're out of time, so we'll have to stop.

That's all for today.

We'll have to finish tomorrow.

Our time is gone; let's move on.

Although phrases such as these end the lesson, they do little else. Recall from Chapter 5 that the attention-getting event can serve the double purpose of gaining students' attention and providing an advance organizer to mentally prepare students for the ensuing lesson. Closing comments also should serve a double purpose—not only ending the lesson but also reviewing, summarizing, or highlighting its most important points. If good attention-getting devices help organize a lesson in advance, then good closing comments help organize it in retrospect and provide students a mirror through which they can see the preceding events.

Closure, therefore, is more than simply calling attention to the end of a lesson. It means reorganizing the bits and pieces of what has gone before into some unified body of knowledge that can help students remember what has been taught.

Combining or Consolidating Key Points.   One way of accomplishing closure is by combining or consolidating key points into a single overall conclusion. Consider the following:

TEACHER: Today we have studied the economic systems of capitalism, socialism, and communism. We have found each of these to be similar in that some of the same goods and services are owned by the government. We have, however, found them different with respect to the *degree* to which various goods and services are owned by the government; the least number of goods and services are owned by a government under capitalism and the most goods and services are owned by a government under communism.

This teacher is drawing together and highlighting the single most important conclusion from the day's lesson. The teacher is doing so by expressing the highest-level generalization or conclusion from the lesson without reference to any of the details that were necessary to arrive at it. This teacher consolidated many different bits and pieces by going to the broadest, most sweeping conclusion that could be made, capturing the essence of all that went before.

Summarizing or Reviewing Key Content.   Another procedure for bringing closure to a lesson is by summarizing or reviewing the key content that has been presented. Here the teacher reviews the most important content to be sure everyone understands it. Obviously, not all of the content can be repeated in this manner, so some selecting is in order, as is illustrated by the following:

TEACHER: Before we end, let's look at our two rules once again. Rule 1: Use the possessive form whenever an *of* phrase can be substituted for a noun. Rule 2: If the word for which we are denoting ownership already ends in an *s*, place the apostrophe after, *not* before, the *s*. Remember, both these rules use the apostrophe.

Now the teacher is consolidating by summarizing, or touching on each of the key features of the lesson. The teacher's review is rapid and to the point, providing students with an opportunity to fill in any gaps about the main features of the lesson.

Providing a Structure.   Still another method for closing consists of providing learners with a structure by which key facts and ideas can be remembered without an actual review of them. With this procedure, facts and ideas are reorganized into a framework for easy recall, as indicated in this example:

TEACHER: Today we studied the formulation and punctuation of possessives. Recall that we used two rules—one for forming possessives wherever an *of* phrase can be substituted for a noun and another for forming possessives for words ending in *s*. From now on, let's call these rules the *of rule* and the *s rule,* keeping in mind that both rules use the apostrophe.

By giving students a framework for remembering the rules (the *of rule* and *s rule*), the teacher organizes the content and indicates how it should be stored and remembered. The key to this procedure is giving a code or symbol system whereby the lesson contents can more easily be stored and recalled for later use.

Notice that in each of the previous dialogues, closure was accomplished by looking back at the lesson and reinforcing its key components. In the first instance this was accomplished by restating the highest-level generalization that could be made; in the second by summarizing the content at the level at which it was taught; and in the third by helping students to remember the important categories of information by providing codes or symbols.

The most important point of these dialogues is that closure means more than just calling attention to the end of a lesson. Endings to good lessons are like endings to good stories: they leave listeners with a sense that they have understood the story and can remember it long after the action has ended.

PLANNING YOUR FIRST DAY

If your first class day is like that of most teachers, it will include some or all of these activities:

- ☐ Keeping order before the bell
- ☐ Introducing yourself
- ☐ Taking care of administrative business
- ☐ Presenting rules and expectations
- ☐ Introducing your subject
- ☐ Closing

Because your responses in these areas may set the tone in your classroom for the remainder of the year, consider them in more detail to see how you can prepare an effective first-day routine.

Before the Bell

As the sole person responsible for your classroom, your responsibility extends not just to when your classes are in session but to whenever school is in session. Consequently, you must be prepared to deal with students before your classes begin in the morning, between classes, and after your last class has ended—or anytime you are in your classroom. Your first class day is particularly critical in this regard, because your students' before-class peek at you will set in motion responses, feelings, and concerns that may affect them long after the bell has rung. Following are a few suggestions that can make these responses, feelings, and concerns positive ones.

To provide a sense of control and withitness, stand near the door as students enter your classroom. In this way you will come in direct contact with each student and be visible to them as they take their seats. Your presence at the doorway, where students must come in close contact with you, will encourage an orderly entrance (and exit) from the classroom. Remember, your class starts when the first student walks through your classroom door.

Another suggestion is to have approximately 8 to 12 rules, divided between conduct and work, clearly visible on the chalkboard, bulletin board, overhead, or in the form of a handout already placed on each student's desk. You may want to prepare rules for the areas in the upper half of Figure 11.4 that you feel will be most critical to your classes during the first few days of school. You can formally introduce these rules later, but they should be clearly visible as students enter your class the first day.

This communicates a sense of structure and organization which most students look for and expect, even on their very first day of school. It also occupies the attention of early arrivals, who otherwise may be inclined to talk loudly, move about the classroom, or talk with you, interfering with your ability to monitor students who are making the transition from hallway to classroom.

It is not unusual (considering the tension and anxiety associated with anyone's first day on the job) for you to be forgetful or to get sidetracked onto one activity (e.g., introducing yourself), leaving no time for other important business. Experience suggests that you may forget important business (e.g., reminding students of your classroom rules) or fall into a less logical order of activities if you do not use a reminder to keep yourself on track.

Therefore, it is important that you prepare a brief outline of your opening day's routine. This outline should list all the activities you plan to perform that day (or class period), in the order in which you will perform them. You can make a "cue card" for yourself—a simple 4" × 6" index card can be used to remind yourself to:

1. Greet students and introduce yourself (5 min.)
2. Take roll (5 min.)
3. Fill out forms (10 min.)
4. Assign books (15 min.)
5. Present rules (10 min.)
    a. Conduct rules
    b. Work rules
6. Introduce course content (0–10 min.)
7. Remind students to bring needed materials (2 min.)
8. Close (3 min.)

In the elementary grades, this schedule easily can be amended to include an introduction to the entire day.

Let us look briefly at several of these activities for your first day.

Introducing Yourself

Introduce yourself by giving your name, the subject or class you are teaching, your special areas of expertise, and so on. However, after this formal introduction, you need to break the ice by showing a part of your personality at the same time that you maintain your role as a teacher. Frankly, this is not always easy. Some beginning teachers ramble too much about themselves, trying to convince students they are "regular people." Others maintain a cold and stern aura to keep students disciplined and at a distance. Both approaches are extreme and often create more problems than they solve. In the first instance students may get too friendly too soon, forgetting the discipline and order that school requires; and in the second instance students may stay frightened of you for weeks or even months.

Your personality will, and should, unfold in small degrees during the first few weeks of school. There is no need to rush it. However, a small glimpse of the kind of person you are outside of the classroom often is a nice touch for students, who would like to see you as a friend as well as a teacher. A short comment about your interests, hobbies, or special experiences—even family or home life—often is appreciated by students, who at the end of this first day will be struggling to remember just who you are.

Administrative Business

Your first opportunity to meet your students up close will be while taking the roll. This is when you may want to turn the tables and have your students not only identify themselves but indicate some of their own interests, hobbies, or special experiences. Such introductions tend to be lengthier in the elementary grades than in junior high and high school, where time is more limited.

Also, in the higher grades, interests, hobbies, or special experiences can be more efficiently determined with a brief interest inventory of the type shown in Figure 11.1. The advantage of using this approach is that time can be set aside in the future for looking through the student responses to help in planning future projects and lessons that coincide with your learners' special interests.

Your other administrative duties at this time can be considerable, and in some cases can consume most of the remainder of the class period at the upper grades and a full hour or more in the lower grades. Filling out forms requested by the school and school district, checking course schedules, guiding lost students to their correct rooms, and accepting new students during the middle of the class will make this first class day seem long and disorderly.

Rules and Expectations

Regardless of how much time administrative tasks require during your first day, plan to devote some time to discussing your classroom rules and your overall expectations about both conduct and work. This is the time to remove student uncertainties and let them know what to expect. There is no better way to begin this process than by referring to the conduct and work rules that either have been posted for all to see or that you have handed out.

In addition to your rules, however, there will be related concerns to address. For example, for younger students you will want to reiterate certain important school rules (e.g., what to do in the event of sickness, consequences of repeated tardiness or absence, procedures for going to the cafeteria) in addition to your own classroom rules.

You also will want to set the tone for the rigor and fairness with which you will grade and for the level of effort you expect. These comments should tell your students that you will "be fair but tough," "expect a lot but will reward hard work," "give difficult tests but teach what is needed to get a good grade," and "expect a lot of work but that the work will be interesting." Each of these phrases communicates not only your high standards, but your understanding and fairness. This delicate balance is the most important impression with which you can leave your students on their first day.

Introducing Your Subject

Although time probably will not permit you to present much content on the first day, here are several tips for presenting content on the second or third days. First, begin your instruction to the whole class in a direct instruction format. This is a time when students will not be eager to participate in discussion, nor will they be relaxed enough to give meaningful contributions to inquiry or problem-solving questions. Effective indirect instruction formats depend on the trust and confidence that students have in their teacher, and this trust and confidence take time to develop. Therefore, use the direct instruction model, at least for the first week or so.

Second, during your first week choose simple content activities that everyone can successfully complete. This will go a long way toward building confidence and promoting enthusiasm for the work that lies ahead. Avoid especially difficult tasks that preclude high rates of success; otherwise, some of your students may experience a fear of failure that can suppress their true abilities long into the school year. Also, at this time you cannot yet know the difficulty level that is most appropriate for your learners. If you try to judge this prematurely, there may be unintended consequences (e.g., some students asking to change to another class).

Following are some examples of first-day activities that can give the flavor of a content area in which most students could demonstrate a high level of understanding and which could be used to begin to convey facts, rules, and action sequences:

- ☐ Conducting a brief experiment and explaining its consequences in real life (science).
- ☐ Reading a lively excerpt from a short story and providing an interpretation (English or reading).
- ☐ Demonstrating a concrete procedure and having students practice it, such as using a calculator, equipment, charts, or tables (math and the sciences).
- ☐ Describing a typical current event and explaining how it can affect their lives (social studies).
- ☐ Teaching a few words of conversation and having students try them out (foreign language).

Closure

Your final first-day activity will be to close on a positive, optimistic note. Have a definite procedure for closing in mind (e.g., a preview of things to come, instructions to follow for tomorrow's class, a reminder of things to bring to class). Begin closing a full three minutes before the bell is to ring. End with a note of encouragement that *all* of your students can do well in your grade or class.

SUMMING UP

This chapter introduced you to motivation and classroom management. Its main points were:

1. *Motivation* is a word used to describe what energizes or directs a learner's attention, emotions, and activity.

2. Motivators can be *internal,* coming from within the individual (e.g., aggressiveness), and *external,* coming from the environment (e.g., peer pressure).

3. You can use your knowledge of a learner's interests, needs, and aspirations to motivate and actively engage the learner in the learning process.

4. An overachiever is an individual whose school achievement is greater than predicted by tests of intelligence or scholastic aptitude. An underachiever is an individual whose achievement is less than predicted. Both underachievement and overachievement often can be attributed to a learner's motivation.

5. Some more formal ways in which instruction can be organized to motivate learners include performance contracts, games and simulations, programmed texts, grouping, volunteering, and grades and tests.

6. Some less formal ways of motivating learners include:
   - □ Using praise and encouragement
   - □ Providing explanations
   - □ Offering to help
   - □ Accepting diversity
   - □ Emphasizing reward, not punishment

7. Classroom climate refers to the atmosphere or mood in which interactions between you and your students take place. A classroom climate can be created by the social environment, which is related to the patterns of interaction you wish to promote in your classroom, and by the organizational environment, which is related to the physical or visual arrangement of the classroom.

8. The social climate of the classroom can extend from authoritarian (in which you are the primary provider of information, opinions, and instruction) to laissez faire (in which your students become the primary providers of information, opinions, and instruction).

9. Your role in establishing authority in the classroom and the social climate can vary. You can adopt different roles that may include:
   - □ Commander-in-chief, who carefully controls and hones student behavior by organizing and providing all the stimuli needed for learning to occur.
   - □ Translator or summarizer of ideas provided by students.
   - □ Equal partner with students in creating ideas and problem solutions.

10. The social climate of your classroom also can vary depending on how competitive, cooperative, or individualistic you wish the interactions among class members to be. Differences among these include extent of opportunities for students to express opinion, time devoted to student talk, and spontaneity with which your students are allowed to respond.

11. Organizational climate pertains to the physical or visual arrangement of the classroom and is determined by the positioning of desks, chairs, tables, and other internal features of a classroom.

12. The degree of competition, cooperation, and individuality in your classroom are a result of the social and organizational climate you create.

13. Rules can be divided into those that:
    - □ relate to academic work,
    - □ relate to classroom conduct,
    - □ must be communicated your first teaching day,
    - □ can be communicated later.

14. Rules can be communicated orally, on the board, on a transparency, or in a handout. Rules for the early elementary grades should be presented orally, provided as a handout, and posted for reference. Rules for the elementary grades and junior high school may be recited and copied by students. Rules for high school may be given orally and then posted.

15. Your inability to enforce a rule over a reasonable period of time is the best sign that you need to change the rule.

16. Monitoring students, making transitions, giving assignments, and bringing closure are four particularly troublesome areas of classroom management.

17. *Withitness* is a form of monitoring in which you are able to keep track of many different signs of student engagement at the same time.

18. Problems during transitions most frequently occur when learners are not ready to perform the
next activity and do not know what behavior is
appropriate during the transition.
19. Homework assignments should be given immediately following the lesson or activities to which
they relate and without negative connotations.

20. Closing statements should gradually bring a lesson to an end by combining or consolidating key
points into a single overall conclusion, by summarizing or reviewing key content, or by providing a symbol system whereby contents of the lesson can be easily stored and later recalled.

FOR DISCUSSION AND PRACTICE

1. Identify three motivators that could be considered internal and three motivators that could be
considered external.
2. Give one example each of an interest, a need,
and an aspiration that some of the students you
will be teaching are likely to have.
*3. Distinguish between an overachiever and an un-
derachiever, as these definitions might be used
in your classroom.
4. Ask a sample of schoolchildren that you are
observing (or that live near you) to complete
the questionnaire in Figure 11.1. If they are in
the early elementary grades, ask them the questions orally and then record their responses.
From the data provided, identify two curriculum
additions that would be responsive to the needs,
interests, and aspirations identified on the questionnaire.
5. Provide an example of a performance contract
for a poorly motivated learner in your teaching
area. Identify the content to be taught, the behavioral outcome to be achieved, the manner in
which it is to be obtained, the proficiency expected, and the reward provided if the contract is
met.
6. Devise a plan to engage poorly motivated students in the learning process by asking them to
help you perform some meaningful classroom
activity. Identify the task you are asking the students to perform and explain why they might
want to volunteer to do it.
*7. In addition to contracts and volunteering, iden-
tify four other techniques for engaging poorly
motivated students in the learning process.
*8. Identify five less formal ways of engaging poorly
motivated students in the learning process.

9. Give an example of how an assignment might
emphasize punishment and then rephrase your
example to emphasize reward.
*10. What are three roles that communicate different
levels of authority that you can assume in your
classroom? How will expression of student opinions, proportion of student talk to teacher talk,
and spontaneity of response change as a function
of each of these three roles?
*11. Provide example classroom activities that would
result in (a) a competitive, (b) a cooperative, and
(c) an individualistic classroom climate.
12. Draw three diagrams of the internal features of a
classroom, each illustrating how to promote one
of the three classroom climates in question 11.
13. Identify four academic rules and four conduct
rules (that must be communicated your first day
of class) that you believe are among the most
important. Write out a rule for each of these eight
areas, exactly as it might be shown to your students on a handout or transparency on the first
day of class.
*14. Identify two rules whose retention might be
aided if they were communicated in the context
of a circumstance or incident with which to associate the rule.
*15. Identify a practical criterion for deciding when a
rule should be revised or eliminated.
16. Explain in your own words what withitness
means. Give an example from your own experience of when you displayed withitness, and
when you did not but should have. What were
the consequences of each event?
*17. What are four teaching practices that can help
avoid misbehavior during a transition?

Anyone who reads the local newspaper, listens to candidates running for public office, attends school board meetings, or overhears conversations in a teachers' lounge quickly realizes that classroom order and discipline are among the topics most discussed. Inability to control a class is one of the most cited reasons for dismissing or "failing to reemploy" a teacher. Beginning teachers consistently rate classroom discipline among their most urgent concerns on the Teacher Concerns Checklist shown in Appendix A (Borich, 1992).

Problems in maintaining classroom order and discipline, however, can be exaggerated. The facts are that major disciplinary problems (vandalism, violent fighting, physical abuse toward teachers) rarely if ever occur in most schools. Unfortunately, these rare incidents attract media attention, and often are reported to the exclusion of the many positive events that may be happening within a school. Although this chapter addresses some of these major discipline problems, our primary focus is upon the many less-dramatic problems that can wear you down and divert attention from the teaching process.

The previous chapter discussed ways to anticipate problems before they occur and planning to avoid them. This chapter focuses upon developing systematic procedures for stopping or altering misbehavior that already has occurred. As noted in the previous chapter, anticipating discipline problems and planning to avoid them always is preferable to dealing with discipline problems once they have occurred. Nevertheless, not all misbehaviors can be anticipated and not all classroom management techniques for avoiding them work every time. Consequently, this chapter is devoted to techniques for dealing with misbehaviors such as:

talking out without raising hand

talking back

acting out

tardiness

showing hostility

disrupting others

moving about without permission

failing to complete assignments

ignoring rules

We also address more serious but less common problems:

cheating

vandalism

fighting

substance abuse.

TEACHER CHARACTERISTICS RELATED TO CLASSROOM MANAGEMENT

Most discipline problems are low intensity, continuous, and unconnected with any larger, more serious event. For example, Kounin (1970) analyzed classroom discipline problems and found that about 55% were related to talking and noise; 26% were related to lateness, incomplete homework, or moving about without permission; and 17% were related to off-task behavior, such as completing other assignments, reading without permission, or daydreaming.

Other researchers have attempted to identify teacher behaviors that might evoke or encourage such discipline problems. Insightful glimpses of how some teachers needlessly create disciplinary problems appear in several classroom studies (Emmer, Evertson, Sanford, Clement, & Worsham, 1989; Leinhardt, 1983; Emmer, Evertson, & Anderson, 1980). From these studies are emerging two behavioral profiles:

1. Teachers whose classrooms consistently exhibit discipline problems.
2. Teachers whose classrooms are relatively free of them.

The following sections present behavioral profiles of both.

Teachers Having Classrooms with Discipline Problems

In the studies cited, some teachers had classrooms in which a large percentage of students were off-task, talked without raising hands, talked back, moved about the room without permission, ignored rules, disrupted others, and failed to complete assignments. The teachers who had these classrooms exhibited at least some of the following characteristics:

- Extreme negativity
- Exclusive authoritarian climate
- Overreacting
- Mass punishment
- Blaming
- Lack of a clear instructional goal
- Repeating or reviewing thoroughly understood material
- Pauses and interruptions
- Dealing with a single student at length
- Lack of recognition of ability levels

In the following sections, we examine the detrimental effects each of these can have in your classroom.

Extreme Negativity.

Went out today to observe Mrs. _____'s first day of class. She spent the first 15 minutes of class reading the kids the "riot act." By that I mean she told them they had to overcome their poor study habits and laziness because this class would be tougher than all their others. "Tests will be hard, and some may not make it," she said. Class continued with a brief lesson in life science. Teacher seemed to focus on what the kids did not know but should know, using phrases such as, "You should have gotten this in other courses," or "Most everyone at this grade level already should know this." Kids' faces mostly were expressionless; they seemed to leave class wondering when the other shoe would drop.*

Teachers in classrooms having high levels of disciplinary problems placed students on the defensive from the start. These teachers used phrases such as: "If you disobey the rules in this classroom, and I know some of you will, you will be punished," or "Some of you should expect to get failing grades in here," or "Don't underestimate my ability to catch those of you who like to violate the rules." Instead of seeing the bright side of things—or at least hoping the bright side would occur— these teachers seemed determined to create an aura of punishment, difficulty, and failure in their classrooms.

It is unclear why they acted in such a manner. However, we can speculate that, by casting a scary light on things from the start, perhaps they hoped to prevent misbehavior. This seemed to correspond with the teachers' lack of confidence in their teaching skills. Perhaps by conveying the image of being stern disciplinarians and difficult teachers, they may have been trying to cover their lack of confidence. Whatever the reason for their negativity, it was not difficult for some students in these classrooms to conclude that, because they were so "bad," the teacher might be disappointed if they did not live up to expectations. *These teachers, therefore, may have created their own self-fulfilling prophecy*—one that students made sure would come true.

Exclusive Authoritarian Climate.

This is my third observation of _____ . Nothing much seems to have changed. Teacher reads from workbook and kids recite answers in unison. Some students, however, seem to purposely shout out wrong or silly answers. Think they may just be bored or are challenging the teacher to find out who they are. Because voices are in unison, teacher had difficulty spotting the culprits. Kids would "lay low" for a time and then shout out another wrong answer. Teacher noticeably was distraught at the disruption but proceeded by pretending not to have heard it. This provoked more kids to join in the game.

Closely associated with these teachers' negativity was the rigid, authoritarian climate that usually prevailed in their classrooms. Outward appearances indicated that these teachers valued being stern disciplinarians even more than being good teachers. Their

---

*This and subsequent excerpts are from the Evaluation of Teaching Project (NIE–C–74–0088, Research and Development Center for Teacher Education, The University of Texas at Austin), during which observers were asked to record at least one critical incident that characterized the classrooms they were observing.

authoritarian atmosphere took the form of excessive teacher talk, little or no acceptance or solicitation of student responses, and a virtual absence of spontaneity. The aim of these teachers seemed to be that they were to be in absolute command at all times and they were to be the only worthwhile source of anything to be discussed or learned.

Again, this rigid atmosphere appears to have been a cover for anxiety about the teachers' lack of control. Their solution was to arrange instruction in the most rigid format to prevent the slightest opportunity for misbehavior; thus there could be no potentially embarrassing moments when the teacher might lose absolute control. Although useful for the teacher, such extreme rigidity provoked rebelliousness in some learners.

This strategy might work in the military, but in the typical public school classroom a continually authoritarian climate invites students to test the teacher's authority. Because there is strength in numbers, more than one student soon challenged these teachers. Worse, the teachers' responses often induced an even greater challenge by the students, until a major confrontation arose to create disorder and confusion.

There is little doubt among experienced teachers that effective classroom order and discipline *depends as much on the voluntary cooperation of students as it does on a clear communication of rules and the ability to enforce them*. Remember that an overly rigid climate in your classroom—with little opportunity for student talk, student opinion, or spontaneity—may quickly create a warlike atmosphere.

Overreacting.

> I arrived at _____'s class all ready to give the math posttest. Earlier that morning I had given the Student Questionnaire, and everything had gone quite well—although I was a bit perturbed by the police whistle hanging from the substitute teacher's neck. As I was saying, I arrived for the math posttest and was greeted by thunderous applause which was turning into a standing ovation until the whistle went off and for one split second the room was quiet. It didn't take long for me to see what was happening—there was a contest of sorts going on to see who could make the distraught woman scream the loudest and blow her whistle the most. Kids were leaving their desks, well, not actually leaving, just climbing on top of them and jumping off.

This scenario portrays students testing the limits of an overly authoritarian teacher and the teacher fighting back, inevitably resulting in teacher overreaction. In the problem classrooms it was not unusual for teachers to have an emotional outburst in response to some misbehavior; the teacher's voice would increase in volume and pitch and a shouting match would ensue. More often than not, this resulted from a challenge to the teacher's authority, with students purposely taunting or provoking until the outburst rewarded them.

One misbehavior often led to another until a cycle began—teacher response to a problem, followed by a student challenge, followed by a more intense teacher response. The only effect of the teacher's emotional response, of course, was to escalate the problem.

An emotional outburst is among the strongest responses a teacher can make. When it fails to solve a problem, the teacher is left in the uncomfortable position of having few more intense responses. *Although emotional responses may be effective at times, frequent use diminishes their effectiveness at the time they may be needed most.* Because most of these teachers were extreme in their emotional reactions to problems, they were challenged more often. Thus, it was easy for students to manipulate them into increasing their responses to misbehavior.

Mass Punishment.

> Went to Mr. _____'s first class after lunch. Students complained about the long homework assignment they were given the previous night that, I take it, not many students finished. Teacher was upset at not everyone completing it, because today's class was to be devoted to students reading their answers to the assignment. Teacher seemed threatened by the apparently large number of students who had not completed the assignment and, so, gave another equally long assignment for tonight. The remainder of the class was devoted to students independently finishing last night's assignment and, if time permitted, beginning on the new assignment. But, because most students had difficulty with the assignment the night before, few students seemed to be concentrating. Others, who completed the assignments, seemed dismayed by being given another long assignment.

When a cycle of misbehavior involving large numbers of students started in these classrooms, a common teacher response was to assign punishment to the entire class. The most frequent punishment in the upper grades was extra homework. In the lower grades it was purposeless writing assignments (writing 25 times "I will always do my assignments," or "I will not talk in class").

These teachers' mass punishment for misbehavior made sure that every student who misbehaved was punished, along with the rest of the students who had not misbehaved. However, the students who had not misbehaved often felt such deep resentment that few had the enthusiasm to stay on task or to cooperate in the learning task the remainder of the period. Perhaps the teacher assumed that peer pressure from those who did behave would influence the others to conform to classroom rules and procedures. But if that was the logic, it has no merit in fact.

First, *students who obey often come from a different peer group than those who frequently disobey and, therefore, obedient students have little or no influence over misbehavers, either in or out of school.* Second, these peer groups often are so at odds with each other that the disobedient actually derive satisfaction from seeing the obedient wrongly punished along with themselves—and may even repeat the misbehavior to derive this same satisfaction again. These two social facts explain why mass punishment is seldom if ever a lasting solution for misbehavior. Like an emotional outburst, mass punishment escalates the teacher's response to one of its highest levels.

Blaming.

> Toward the end of class, Mr. _____ was writing on the chalkboard when an alarm to someone's wristwatch went off. He turned and asked whose it was and no one responded. One student looked suspicious but few actually knew whose it was. This student was given an extra set of homework assignments, but complained bitterly—and, so, was given another set of homework assignments. A shouting match of sorts erupted leading to the student being sent to the office. I honestly can't say whether it was this kid or not—but obviously someone was going to catch it.

Another behavior that was observed in these classrooms was the teachers' tendency to blame *someone* for every discipline problem that occurred. These teachers knew the troublemakers and blamed them repeatedly, even when the true source of the problem was in doubt. These students became scapegoats for discipline problems that could not be attributed clearly to an identifiable individual.

Phrases such as "You're at it again," or "You've created trouble in here since the beginning," or "You won't get away with it this time," often were used to identify the supposed culprit responsible for throwing paper, making a noise, or disrupting others behind the teacher's back. Sometimes the true source was a group of students, which often included the one singled out. But sometimes the true source was unidentifiable. In either case, because the teacher misjudged, the one being blamed quickly and loudly corrected the error by attributing blame to others. The troublemaker responded with "It's not me," or "It was those two over there," or "I wasn't the only one," engaging the teacher in a tug-of-war to see if the blame could be spread to others.

These teachers thus placed themselves in a win-or-lose conflict to prove that the one blamed actually was the one responsible. In the meantime, the class was disrupted by the teacher's preoccupation with a single individual's behavior.

At the root of this problem was the teacher's misguided notion that every misbehavior always must be attributed to someone, even at the expense of innocent parties whose prior history of misbehavior makes them the most likely culprits. In these teachers' minds there were only winners or losers—and they themselves intended never to be the losers, regardless of the cost to classroom morale and instructional time.

Lack of a Clear Instructional Goal.

> Was in Ms. _____'s class to observe. Lesson was about modern art, I think. Some students talked about the pictures in the text taken from the National Museum of Modern Art. Others talked about making art objects from old car parts—hubcaps, carburetors, that sort of thing. Everyone seemed to have a different idea as to what modern art was—but the teacher did not venture any rules or guidelines. She seemed to want the kids to find them for themselves. Finally, a shouting match erupted between the "old car parts" people and the "painting" people until each side could hardly hear the other. Much of the rest of the period was devoted to returning the classroom to order.

Another characteristic behavior in problem classrooms was the noticeable lack of an instructional goal—at least one that was discernible to the students. These were classrooms in which students often engaged in loosely structured discussions with no apparent direction, agenda, or expected results. Students drifted from one topic to the next without establishing meaningful connections or unifying concepts among topics. They meandered through so many different ideas that, while they appeared to cover extensive content, in reality each topic was touched upon so lightly that little of substance was ever said.

In essence, the discussion had no momentum, and student expectations were unclear about the kind or quality of contribution they should be making. The class became ripe for misbehavior, because little forward momentum existed to keep their attention on task and their energies directed toward an identifiable instructional goal. With no clear goal, some students drifted off the subject while others took the looseness of the discussion as a sign that they could turn discussion into argument.

It was not unusual during such sessions to find students arguing with each other or with the teacher, or trying to discuss a problem from incompatible points of view. Discipline problems were not unusual during such loosely organized sessions, including loud talking, clowning, moving out of seat, and interrupting. The message these teachers forgot, or never learned, is that *even the most indirect discussions must be crafted to communicate a structure, an end result, and clear expectations of student conduct.*

Repeating or Reviewing Thoroughly Understood Material.

> Just returned from class. They're still reviewing verb conjugations in the workbook. Noise level in classroom seems a bit high, as some students were "whispering" to their friends across the aisle and passing notes around. Seems as though some students are copying from others just so they won't have to complete another exercise. Teacher seems engrossed in paper grading—or doesn't much care.

Another time when discipline problems seemed to occur was when the class was expected to repeat or review material that already had been thoroughly learned. The name often given to such assignments is **busywork**. Busywork often is given students to keep them quiet while the teacher pursues some more important activity, but its actual effect can be just the opposite. There is nothing wrong with assigning busywork so that you can have a much-needed psychological break, prepare materials for another class, or get some grading finished, *as long as the busywork poses some challenge to your students.*

As noted in earlier chapters, assigning work for which students can achieve moderate-to-high levels of success is a prerequisite for actively engaging students in the learning process. However, assigning work for which learners uniformly achieve at high levels of success quickly becomes boring and repetitious. In these instances students often fail to complete the assignment, or may complete it so rapidly that plenty of time remains for off-task behavior.

In these classrooms, discipline problems frequently occurred during long assignments, which students quickly recognized as busywork. They responded subconsciously with "What's the point?" and, not being able to find one, shifted their attention to anything in the environment that was more exciting. These teachers failed to realize that *there always must be some mystery, challenge, or curiosity about what is to be learned*. But there is no mystery, challenge, or curiosity in long, easy assignments.

There always must be some uncertainty about the next question or item and whether it can be answered correctly. When all uncertainty is eliminated by a repetitively high success rate, the magnetism that focuses and directs a learner's attention also is eliminated. Off-task behavior, including behavior disruptive to others trying to complete the assignment, becomes a more desirable focus.

Pauses and Interruptions.

> Observed Mr. _____'s social studies lesson today. Lesson seemed to proceed smoothly until the teacher realized that the map he would be using was locked up in the map room. Teacher put a student in charge while he left the room to retrieve the map. Student went to the front of the room but as soon as the teacher left, a few students made fun of her for being "teacher's pet." She got upset and told everyone to "shut up." Noise level went up and commotion began. Teacher returned and spent the next five or so minutes inquiring what had happened and getting the class back to order. Teacher returned without the map—said another teacher must be using it.

Teachers in the problem classrooms paused or interrupted the flow of instruction more frequently than did teachers in classrooms with fewer discipline problems. Pauses to clean an overhead transparency, to round up graded assignments, to look for reference materials, and to write lengthy assignments on the board were not uncommon. These chores break the momentum of classroom activity, and once that momentum is broken, for whatever reason, it is exceedingly difficult to regain it without losing valuable class time.

Many pauses or interruptions are needless. They can be avoided by planning ahead—by arranging for needed materials before class, or by placing assignments on the board during a break or during seatwork, and so forth. The "withitness" of these teachers was lost during these pauses, and an open invitation was extended for misbehavior. Although not all students take advantage of such pauses, it takes only a few—sometimes only one—to place a classroom in disorder.

Awkward gaps, pauses, and interruptions in which you lose eye and visual contact almost always disengage your students from the learning process.

Two of the most frustrating sources of pauses in your instruction will be unexpected announcements over the public address system and unexpected visitors at your door (e.g., counselor, parent, teacher). In the problem classrooms, teachers seemed to lack procedures for handling these common occurrences. In the classrooms that had fewer disciplinary problems, teachers continued to move silently about the room during announcements to let their presence be known and asked unexpected visitors to return after class or to leave a message.

Dealing with a Single Student at Length.

> Completed my last observation in _____ class. Students seemed particularly anxious due to it being the next-to-the-last day before the holidays. Things seemed to go well, even given the high noise level, until one student turned to another with an obscene gesture. Both seemed to be about to start a fight so the teacher slammed the book down and lectured them on how their grade in the class would depend on their good conduct. This went into a discussion about today's changing morals and values, which some in the rest of the class thought was humorous. Some laughing and "snickering" could be heard and, finally, the teacher began handing out disciplinary referrals to whoever opened their mouth.

Another characteristic of the problem classrooms was the teacher's tendency to deal at length with a single troublesome student. The teacher would disrupt the instructional momentum to discipline a student after a breach of classroom rules (usually talking back, acting out, disrupting others, or fighting). The teacher used these incidents as opportunities not only to assign punishment to the offender, but also to lecture on the implications of the offense (for getting a good grade; for becoming a good citizen; for "making it in life").

During the teacher's preoccupation with the misbehaving student, other discipline problems often would arise. Sometimes 5 to 10 minutes of class time would elapse while the teacher questioned and lectured the offender on the implications of the misbehavior and arranged for some form of punishment. Because the teacher's eye contact and attention were on the misbehaving student, there were opportunities for mischief to occur elsewhere in the classroom.

In contrast, teachers in the classrooms with fewer discipline problems had established a set routine to handle the most common problems. They often would deal with a problem quickly by *deferring the lecture phase or punishment phase until after class or after school, taking time only to call out the student's name and the offense during class*. Some ways these teachers quickly dispensed with a misbehavior, and the approximate times expended, were:

- ☐ Silently writing the student's name on the board (5 sec.)
- ☐ Calling out the student's name and assigning a prearranged page number for an exercise (10 sec.)
- ☐ Pointing to the rear of the room and indicating the student must stand there (5 sec.)
- ☐ Moving the student's name from the "good behavior" to "poor behavior" side of the bulletin board (10 sec.)
- ☐ Calling out the student's name and writing a referral to a counselor, indicating the nature of the offense (30 sec.)

In each of these instances class disruption was only 5 to 30 seconds, with few words spoken. In these classrooms, students knew that when their names were called, a visit to the teacher after class or after school for their punishment was mandatory; disruption to the flow of instruction was minimized. This routine was explained during the first week of school, so all students knew exactly what to expect when their names were called for discipline.

Lack of Recognition of Ability Levels.

> Went to observe Ms. _____'s Spanish class. Teacher was using the direct instruction model. Students were expected to respond in Spanish using the correct verb form to her questions, given in Spanish. It was plain to see that when she came to students in the back of the room few, if any, could converse in sentences with the correct verb form—some didn't even try. It seemed as though whenever the action returned to the front of the room two or more students in the back would begin to "socialize" among themselves until the teacher would have to stop and ask them to "be quiet." Things would be quiet for a brief time and, then, the noise level would go up and the whole cycle would start over again. Some students seemed able to keep up but others were most certainly lost.

The teachers in these problem classrooms taught over the heads of some of their students, at least part of the time. Although these teachers may have known the ability levels of their students, they treated this information as irrelevant. They seemed to enjoy being thought of as tough or difficult, pouring on the homework and moving swiftly through material until a major test produced the inevitable poor grades—which they blamed on laziness, lack of interest, or insufficient study and homework.

As a result, some students in these classrooms all but gave up long before they were given any real test of their progress. Sometimes a quarter to a third of the class had trouble understanding the material and were a consistent group of troublemakers who often banded together in mischief, making harder the teacher's progress with the rest of the class.

These teachers rarely reviewed previously taught material or gave progress checks before major tests to determine specific weaknesses. They gave no consideration to *remedial activities or ability grouping, by which slow learners could catch up or pursue alternative paths*. Also, they seemed not to notice that they were teaching each day to a smaller and smaller percentage of the class—and that this created increasing pauses for disciplinary action.

Summary of Characteristics of Ineffective Classroom Managers.   Emerging from these classrooms is a profile of teaching practices that are associated with discipline problems. When several of these practices come together in a single classroom, discipline problems likely will follow, regardless of what good practices may be occurring in that classroom. Recall the main features of this profile:

> extreme negativity
>
> exclusive authoritarian climate
>
> overreacting
>
> mass punishment

blaming

lack of clear instructional goal

repeating or reviewing already learned material

pauses and interruptions

dealing with a single student at length

lack of recognition of ability levels.

Although few teachers can avoid all of these behaviors all of the time, the effective teacher knows their potentially damaging effects on classroom order and discipline. Being consciously aware of these characteristics is the first step toward avoiding them.

Teachers Having Classrooms with Fewer Discipline Problems

Now let us contrast the characteristics of problem classrooms against the characteristics of classrooms that had noticeably fewer discipline problems.

As you might expect, the teachers in these classrooms exhibited greater levels of withitness. They always placed themselves in the position of *seeing all aspects of the classroom at once* and avoided situations that cut them off from the rest of the class (such as dealing with a single student at length). These teachers also were able to perform *overlapping activities,* such as presenting content while at the same time being alert for misbehavior in the back of the classroom, and writing up a disciplinary referral for one student while keeping eye contact on the rest of the class.

They also were noticeably *less autocratic and authoritarian* than teachers in the problem classrooms. That is, they allowed more student talk, expression of opinion, and spontaneity, all of which made the students feel like participants in their own instruction. Therefore, the students became more willing to accept responsibility for their own learning.

These teachers also seemed to realize that no degree of attention to rules and violations can keep a classroom free of discipline problems unless the teacher first secures the cooperation and goodwill of the students. They accomplished this by being flexible and allowing *some freedom of student expression and spontaneity,* which promoted an *adultlike cooperative environment* rather than a militarylike autocratic environment.

Flexibility and freedom were not randomly dispensed but were given as good conduct rewards or were allowed under clearly established conduct guidelines. In addition to students being treated as partners in the learning process, they were given *clear rules and directions* on how to behave and what to expect if they failed to do so.

These classrooms also maintained a *balance between direct and indirect instruction, and between self-directed and cooperative learning.* When the more rigid formality of direct instruction began to affect the students' enthusiasm, the teacher would switch to the indirect instruction model, self-directed learning, or cooperative activities, and then later back again; this maintained instructional variety and interest.

These classrooms also maintained a *businesslike pace* that always kept learning stimuli before the students; there were no awkward pauses when students did not

Teacher "withitness" is the ability to identify potential management problems in all types of students—not just those who are among the more verbal and overt. It is easy to overlook the reluctant individual who may also present a management problem.

know what to do next. They were kept moving through the material from one activity to the next without hesitation, establishing a momentum that focused their attention on the learning task, and leaving little time or energy for misbehavior. Once misbehavior did occur, however, it was dealt with quickly. The *assignment of punishment was made later,* so the flow of an instructional activity was not interrupted.

Finally, when the pace was found to be too fast for some students, different paces were established through the *formation of ability or activity groups* or through the use of self-paced materials.

In summary, these classrooms could be distinguished from classrooms having noticeably more discipline problems by:

- ☐ Teacher withitness and ability to overlap activities.
- ☐ A less autocratic and authoritarian classroom climate.
- ☐ More freedom of student expression and spontaneity.
- ☐ Clear rules and directions.

- ☐ Balance between direct and indirect instruction.
- ☐ Businesslike pace.
- ☐ Deferred assignment of punishment.
- ☐ Use of ability or activity groups.

Now that you have seen teaching practices that can help avoid discipline problems, as well as those that cause them, let us consider more closely your role in solving discipline problems.

DEGREES OF TEACHER INVOLVEMENT IN SOLVING DISCIPLINE PROBLEMS

Table 12.1 lists some common discipline problems and teacher responses in the classroom. For your own classroom, you will need to prepare procedures for at least some of these. In some cases, school-wide rules and policies adequately address a problem (e.g., tardiness, cutting class, plagiarism). But in other cases, your classroom will be center stage for both the problem and its resolution.

How you handle these problems is as important as the problem itself. You must decide on how you will use your authority to bring about a resolution. At least three alternatives are available to you: (1) you alone decide the punishment, (2) you and the student participate in choosing the punishment, and (3) you choose punishment from student alternatives.

TABLE 12.1

Some common discipline problems and typical teacher responses

Problems	Typical Teacher Responses
Talking out	Mary, if you have something to say, raise your hand.
Acting out	Bobby, if you don't stop clowning around, you'll be punished.
Talking back	Joan, you know I dislike your talking back to me.
Getting out of seat	Mary, that's the last time I'm going to stand for you leaving your seat to visit.
Note passing	Let me have that.
Noncompliant	I told you three times to open your workbook.
Ignoring rules	You know that make-up assignments must be due the same week they are assigned.
Obscene words or gestures	If I see that again, you'll go straight to the office.
Fighting	Tom and Joe, stop it immediately or you're both in big trouble.
Cheating	Mark, I can see you have another piece of paper under your test.
Stealing	Karl, where did you get this stapler?
Vandalism	Who wrote their initials on this desk?
Substance abuse	Tom, do I smell alcohol on your breath?

You Alone Decide Punishment

You may decide that you are the ultimate authority. You will be the only judge of what occurred, you alone will decide the punishment, and you are the only one available or qualified to determine if the conditions of punishment are met. When a misbehaving student is unable to take responsibility for his or her own actions or to admit to the misbehavior, this approach is the most practical and effective. It may not, however, be the best approach to every situation.

You and Student Participate in Choosing Punishment

In some situations it may be desirable for you and the student to discuss and agree on the punishment. One approach is for *you to provide* some alternative forms of punishment from which the *student must choose,* thereby giving the student some choice in deciding his or her own fate. Providing students with an opportunity to participate in the punishment phase of the misbehavior sometimes can reduce both their hostility toward you for disciplining them and the likelihood that the infraction will occur again.

You Choose Punishment from Student Alternatives

A third alternative is to allow the students to participate in choosing their punishment by *having them provide alternatives from which you choose.* This can work well with students mature enough to judge the severity of the wrongdoing and to suggest punishments accordingly, but may be inappropriate for students who cannot take responsibility for their own actions and who may not even be willing to own up to having misbehaved. Contrary to what you might expect, experience reveals that when students pose alternatives for their own punishment, the punishments they suggest often are harsher than those assigned by teachers.

RESPONSES TO MISBEHAVIOR

There are many responses at your disposal for dealing with misbehavior. You may choose to ignore an infraction if it is momentary and not likely to recur (e.g., when students jump out of and back into their seats to stretch their legs after a long assignment). At the other extreme, you may call an administrator to help resolve the problem. Between these extremes are many alternatives; in order of increasing severity, they are:

- ☐ Looking at the student sternly
- ☐ Walking toward the student
- ☐ Calling on the student to provide the next response
- ☐ Asking the student to stop
- ☐ Discussing the problem with the student

□ Assigning the student to another seat
□ Assigning punishment, such as a writing assignment
□ Assigning the student to detention
□ Writing a note to the student's parents
□ Calling the student's parents

These alternatives vary in severity from simply giving the student a look of dissatis-faction to involving parents in resolving the problem. More important than the variety these alternatives offer, however, is your ability to *match the correct response to the type of misbehavior that has occurred*. One of the most difficult problems you will encounter in effectively maintaining classroom discipline will be deciding upon a response that is neither too mild nor too severe.

Although all rule violations consistently must receive some response, the severity of the punishment can and should vary according to the nature of the viola-tion and the frequency with which such a violation has occurred in the past. If you respond too mildly to a student who has violated a major rule many times before, nothing is likely to change. If you respond too severely to a student who commits a minor violation for the first time, you will be unfair. Flexibility is important in the resolution of different discipline problems and must take into account *both the con-text in which the violation occurs and the type of misbehavior that has occurred*.

Here is some general advice for dealing with mild, moderate, and severe misbehavior:

□ Mild misbehaviors like talking out, acting out, getting out of seat, disrupting others, and similar misbehaviors deserve a mild response, *at first*. But if they occur repeatedly, a moderate response may be appropriate. In un-usual cases, such as continual talking that disrupts the class, a severe re-sponse may be warranted.
□ Moderate misbehaviors like cutting class, abusive conduct toward others, fighting, and use of profanity deserve a moderate response, *at first*. But if these behaviors become frequent, a severe response may be warranted.
□ Severe misbehaviors like cheating, plagiarism, stealing, and vandalism de-serve a severe response. But don't try to handle major incidents of van-dalism, theft, incorrigible conduct, and substance abuse in your classroom. Immediately bring these to the attention of school administrators.

Table 12.2 presents responses you can make to mild, moderate, and severe misbe-havior.

REINFORCEMENT THEORY APPLIED IN THE CLASSROOM

Clearly there are multiple ways to use your authority in managing discipline problems (you alone decide the punishment; you have students share in the responsibility; you choose punishment from alternatives provided by the student) and multiple levels of response severity (from a stern glance to calling parents). But still more options exist

TABLE 12.2
Examples of mild, moderate, and severe misbehaviors and some alternative responses

Misbehaviors	*Alternative Responses*
Mild misbehaviors	**Mild responses**
Minor defacing of school property or property of others	Warning
Acting out (horseplaying or scuffling)	Feedback to student
Talking back	Time out
Talking without raising hand	Change of seat assignment
Getting out of seat	Withdrawal of privileges
Disrupting others	After-school detention
Sleeping in class	Telephone/note to parents
Tardiness	
Throwing objects	
Exhibiting inappropriate familiarity (kissing, hugging)	
Gambling	
Eating in class	
Moderate misbehaviors	**Moderate responses**
Unauthorized leaving of class	Detention
Abusive conduct towards others	Behavior contract
Noncompliant	Withdrawal of privileges
Smoking or using tobacco in class	Telephone/note to parents
Cutting class	Parent conference
Cheating, plagiarizing, or lying	In-school suspension
Using profanity, vulgar language, or obscene gestures	Restitution of damages
Fighting	Alternative school service (e.g., clean up, tutoring)
Severe misbehaviors	**Severe responses**
Defacing or damaging school property or property of others	Detention
Theft, possession, or sale of another's property	Telephone/note to parents
Truancy	Parent conference
Being under the influence of alcohol or narcotics	In-school suspension
Selling, giving, or delivering to another person alcohol, narcotics, or weapons	Removal from school or alternative school placement
Teacher assault or verbal abuse	
Incorrigible conduct, noncompliance	

for dealing with discipline problems. In this section you will learn basic principles of reinforcement theory. Reinforcement theory involves determining how learners respond to rewards and punishments, why they respond to them differently, and how you can use them effectively in your classroom.

Reinforcement theory states that behavior can be controlled by the consequences that immediately follow it. The word *controlled* means that the consequences of a particular behavior can change the likelihood that the behavior will recur. Consider the following:

Event	Consequence	Future Event
You start going to the library to study.	Your test grades go up.	You begin going to the library more often.
You go to a new restaurant.	You get lousy service.	You never go there again.
You give your boyfriend or girlfriend a word of encouragement before a big test.	He or she gives you a kiss and a hug.	You give a word of encouragement before every big test.

When the consequence following a behavior changes the probability of that behavior's occurrence (test grades go up; you don't go there again; you get more kisses and hugs), reinforcement has occurred.

In your classroom, many events and their consequences will demonstrate the effects of reinforcement—whether you intend it or not. You may be surprised to learn that you are unintentionally increasing the frequency of some misbehaviors in your classroom through reinforcement. How can this happen? Consider another sequence of behaviors that, unknown to you, may occur in your classroom:

Event	Consequence	Future Event
Johnny cheats on a test.	He gets a good grade.	Johnny plans to cheat again.
Mary passes a note to her boyfriend.	Her boyfriend is able to pass a note back.	Mary buys a special pad of perfumed paper for writing more notes in class.
Bobby skips school.	He earns five dollars helping a friend work on a car.	Bobby plans to skip again the next time his friend needs help.

In each instance an undesirable behavior was reinforced (with a good grade; a returned note; five dollars). In each case the probability of recurrence increased because the consequence was desirable. In these examples, there is nothing you could have done, because your vigilance cannot be perfect—you didn't know about the cheating, note, or that school was missed for the wrong reason. But here are some ways you may unwittingly reinforce undesirable behaviors, which you *can* do something about:

  □ A student complains incessantly that her essay was graded too harshly. To quiet her, you add a point to her score. Reinforced, she complains after every essay for the rest of the year.
  □ Parents complain to you about their child's poor class participation grade. You start calling on the student more often, probing and personally eliciting responses. Reinforced, the student believes she no longer needs to volunteer or raise her hand.
  □ A student talks back every time you call on him, so you stop calling on him. Reinforced, he does the same in his other classes, to be left alone.

In each of these cases, the link connecting the behavior, the consequence, and the students' perception of the consequence might not be immediately apparent to you. Nevertheless, reinforcement of an undesirable behavior occurred.

In the first instance, you might believe that the extra point could do no harm, because a single point would not change the end-of-term grade. However, the important link was not between your behavior (giving the point) and the student's behavior (quieting her), but between the student's behavior (complaining) and your behavior (giving the point).

The problem in each instance was that you chose to remove the misbehavior in a way that rewarded the student, thereby actually reinforcing the misbehavior. Notice that in each case you considered the consequence of your actions *only from your own point of view* (e.g., quieting an annoying student, preventing a parent from calling back, avoiding an ill-mannered student), without realizing that your actions *reinforced* the very behavior you wished to discourage.

Now that you see how reinforcement theory works, here are some guidelines for making it work not against you, but for you.

Rewards

Many reinforcers—or consequences—are available that can increase the probability of a desirable response:

- □ Verbal or written praise
- □ Smile, a head nod
- □ Special privileges (e.g., visit to the learning center, library, etc.)
- □ Time out of regular work to pursue a special project (e.g., lab experiment)
- □ Permission to choose a topic or assignment
- □ Getting to work in a group
- □ Extra points toward grade
- □ "Smiley face" stickers on assignments
- □ Note to parents on top of a test or paper
- □ Posting a good exam or homework for others to see
- □ Special recognitions and certificates (e.g., "most improved," "good conduct award," "neatest," "hardest worker," etc.)

Not all of these rewards may be equally reinforcing, however. Some learners may disdain verbal praise; others will have no desire to visit the library or learning center. Some students like to be called on; others may be too shy and dislike the added attention. A reinforcement to one student may be completely irrelevant to another.

Finding the right reinforcer for each student often requires trial and error; if one type of reward does not seem to increase the probability of a desirable behavior, try another. Knowing the interests, needs, and aspirations of your learners can save valuable time in finding the right mix of reinforcers. For example, students who are mechanically inclined might enjoy time out looking at issues of *Popular Mechanics* or

Rewards consistent with the goals of your classroom and matched to student interests keep learners engaged in the learning process and responding at high rates of success.

Model Airplaner, and those interested in fashion might like *Vogue* or *Mademoiselle* in a reading center.

You also can ask students for a menu of rewards (e.g., readings, music, magazines), that are in tune with their specific interests. You could compile this list from an interest survey of the type shown in Figure 11.1. Or, you could ask students to select rewards from a list you prepare, which ensures that what is chosen will be feasible and desirable for your classroom.

Punishments

Punishments also can be used to reinforce—or to change the probability or likelihood that a behavior will occur. For example, you can try to keep Johnny in his seat either (a) by giving him an extra assignment every time he is out of his seat, or (b) by giving him a trip to the reading center for every 30 minutes he stays in his seat. In the first instance you are giving Johnny a *punishment* to encourage him to do what's expected, and in the second you are giving him a *reward* to achieve this same end.

Punishment as well as rewards, therefore, can be used to increase the frequency of a desired behavior—to reinforce it. Punishment, sometimes called an *aversive,* can be given explicitly to increase the likelihood of a desired behavior. For example, when your car's buzzer reminds you to buckle up, you have been given an aversive (the buzzer) to increase the likelihood of a desired behavior (putting on your seat belt). An aversive creates an avoidance response to an undesirable behavior, thereby increasing the likelihood of a desired behavior. On the other hand, a reward encourages a desirable behavior to recur by dispensing something pleasant or rewarding immediately after the desirable behavior.

But rewards and punishments generally are not equally effective in promoting a desired behavior. Given two choices to keep Johnny in his seat—the punishment of extra homework, or reward of something interesting to work on—the reward usually will be more successful. Here are several reasons:

Punishment does not guarantee that the desired response will occur. The extra homework may indeed keep Johnny in his seat the next time he thinks of moving about, but it by no means ensures that he will pursue the truly desired behavior, which is to perform some meaningful instructional activity while he is there. Instead, he can daydream, write notes to friends, or even pull Mary's hair. All succeed in keeping him from being punished again for getting out of his seat. Punishment in the absence of rewards can create other undesired behaviors.

The effects of punishment usually are specific to a particular context and behavior. This means that extra homework is not likely to keep Johnny in his seat when a substitute teacher arrives, because it was not *that* teacher who assigned the punishment. Also, *that* punishment is not likely to deter Johnny from pulling Mary's hair, because the punishment was associated only with keeping him in his seat. Punishment rarely keeps one from misbehaving beyond the specific context and behavior to which it was most closely associated.

The effects of punishment can have undesirable side effects. If extra homework is truly an aversive reinforcer for Johnny—if it is a highly undesirable and painful consequence in his eyes—he may decide never to risk leaving his seat again, even to ask for your assistance or to use the rest room. Johnny may decide to take no chances about leaving his seat, and not even to trust his own judgment about when an exception to the rule may be appropriate.

Punishment sometimes elicits hostile and aggressive responses. Although any single punishment is unlikely to provoke an emotional response, students receive punishment in various forms all day long, both at school and at home. If your punishment is the "straw that breaks the camel's back," do not be surprised to observe an emotional outburst that is inconsistent with the amount of punishment rendered. This is not sufficient reason to avoid assigning punishment when it is needed, but it is reason to use it sparingly and in association with rewards.

The punishment can become associated with the punisher. If you use punishment consistently as a tool for increasing the likelihood that a desirable behavior will occur, you may lose the cooperation you must have for managing your classroom effectively. With this cooperation gone, you will find that the vital link for making management techniques work is gone. *Plan not to solve every discipline problem by using punishment;* otherwise, the punishment could become more strongly associated with you than the desired behavior you wish to encourage.

Punishment that is rendered to stop an undesired *behavior, but which is not immediately associated with the* desired *behavior, seldom has a lasting effect.* If the desired behavior is not clear to your students at the time punishment is administered, the punishment will be seen only as an attempt to hurt and not as an attempt to encourage the desired behavior.

At many times during the school day and for many different infractions of school rules, an aversive is the only logical choice to reinforce a desired behavior. For example, it would be extremely difficult or undesirable to deal with spontaneous infractions of school rules (e.g., cheating, vandalism, obscene language, theft) in any way other than to provide the appropriate punishment that has been determined for these offenses, as long as the desired behavior is made clear to the student at the time of the punishment.

Also, *punishment works best in conjunction with rewards,* as when Johnny is given an extra assignment for jumping out of his seat *and* is rewarded with a trip to the reading center for staying in his seat. Even relatively minor classroom misbehaviors (e.g., talking out, sleeping in class, eating in class, throwing objects) often must be followed with punishment, but their recurrence is less likely when the desired behavior is made known at the time of the punishment, and rewarded when it occurs. Table 12.3 offers guidelines for effectively using rewards and punishments.

WARNINGS

Warnings can prevent minor problems from intensifying to where punishment is the only recourse. For the misbehaviors listed as mild in Table 12.2, it is not unusual to provide several warnings before punishment is dispensed. However, *after two or three warnings you must assign a punishment,* because waiting any longer reinforces the student's belief that you are not serious about the punishment. This undermines the integrity of the rule being violated and your credibility as well.

Some moderate misbehaviors also may be given warnings. In the case of severe behaviors, however, warnings are rare. For these behaviors, the consequences of a recurrence are too damaging. Therefore, warnings and rewards are untimely and punishment must be rendered immediately, *along with a clear indication of the desired behavior.*

CORPORAL PUNISHMENT

Conspicuously absent from the common forms of punishment listed in Table 12.2 is any form of corporal punishment, such as paddling a student. Such punishment, although permissible in some school districts when administered by a specifically designated school authority, has not proven particularly effective in deterring misbehavior.

A reason is that the heightened emotion and anxiety on the part of the student (and the administrator) at the time of the punishment often prevents rational discus-

TABLE 12.3

Guidelines for using rewards and punishments

Rewards	Punishments
1. Give the reward immediately following the desired behavior. ☐ Good grade on paper—congratulatory note on top of paper. ☐ Insightful answer in class—verbal praise immediately afterward.	1. Let the student know exactly what behavior will be punished, before punishment is given. ☐ Rick, if you talk back again, I will assign you the optional exercises for tomorrow. ☐ Marty, if you throw a paper wad again, I will write a note home.
2. Be specific about what behavior is being rewarded. ☐ Johnny, I want you to stay in your seat the whole period—here is a reading assignment that fits your interests. ☐ Mary, I want you to try to read a little faster—let's not grade this one.	2. Give the punishment immediately following the undesired behavior. ☐ OK, that's the second time I saw you look at Sue's paper. That's an automatic five points off your test score. ☐ That's the second warning about throwing things, Carl. I will have to assign you an extra problem for homework.
3. Be sure the reward is meaningful to the student. ☐ Bob, there will be some mechanics magazines waiting at the Learning Center when you're finished. ☐ Betty, you can study for that test next period if you have no misspellings.	3. Use the punishment after *every* occurrence of the undesired behavior. ☐ Every time I see you sleeping, Bobby, I will assign extra work. ☐ For each time I catch you clowning around, you'll have to make up the work for homework.
4. Use a variety of reinforcers so that the reward is always fresh and new. ☐ Bob, last time you got to go to the Learning Center. This time you can go to the library. ☐ Tom, last week we put you on the all-star list. This week you can work on your term paper.	4. Use punishment only after rewards do not work or are impractical given the severity and spontaneity with which the undesired behavior occurs. ☐ I let you sit near your friends last week so you would not fight with Mark. This time I have to write up a referral. ☐ I let you go to your locker during class last week, but I'll have to report it as a missing assignment this week.
	5. Be explicit about the desired behavior you want to occur as a result of the punishment. ☐ I am giving you two extra homework problems because *I want you to turn in completed homework.* ☐ You must *always do your own work,* so I will have to give you a zero for this assignment.

sion of the appropriate behavior that the punishment is supposed to encourage. In addition, corporal punishment easily can provoke aggression and cause hostility in both students and parents. This can outweigh any immediate benefit that might accrue from the punishment.

Generally, you should not have physical contact with a student, because such contacts are easily misunderstood. This applies whether the contact is to administer punishment or, in the case of older students, is a reward (patting a student for doing a good job) or assistance (placing your arm around a student in times of high anxiety). Although your own judgment, the situation, and age of the student will be your best guides, the only clear exception is a situation where your assistance is needed immediately. Examples of such situations are breaking up a fight to prevent physical injury, curtailing the movement of a student who is hurting another, or restraining a student from self-injury. At such times, you should call an administrator as quickly as possible.

THE PARENT-TEACHER CONFERENCE

When a major infraction of a school or classroom rule has occurred, more effective than any form of corporal punishment is the parent-teacher conference. This is your opportunity to inform one or both parents of the severity of the misbehavior and for eliciting their active help in preventing it. Without the support of the student's family in providing the appropriate rewards and punishment at home, there is little chance that the relatively small interventions at school (including corporal punishment) will have a lasting effect in deterring the misbehavior (Rotter, Robinson, & Fey, 1987).

Being "grounded" for the week, having to be in at a certain time, completing extra study time in the quiet of one's bedroom, or performing extra chores around the house *always will have more impact than any aversive that can be administered during the school day,* as long as these family aversives are administered with a complete understanding of the desired behavior (Rich, 1987).

Notifying parents that a conference is desired usually is the responsibility of the principal or a counselor. However, because the request for a conference is the result of a specific problem in your classroom, you will be involved in preparing any formal notification telling the parents why a conference is being requested. This notification should consist of a letter sent through the mail containing:

1. Purpose of the conference, including a statement of the joint goal of supporting the student's success in school.
2. Statement pointing out the integral role of the parent in the discipline-management process (this may include a citation from any state or school policy regarding such matters).
3. Date, time, and location of conference.
4. A contact person (and phone number).
5. A response form for parents' reply, preferably with a self-addressed stamped envelope.

If the request for a conference is made to the student's parents by phone, these same points can be orally presented; it is important that the date, time, location, and contact person for the conference are recorded by the parent at the time of the call.

During the conference you should:

☐ Try to gain the parents' acknowledgment of the problem and their participation in the discipline-management process.
☐ Present a plan of action for addressing the problem at home and at school.
☐ Identify follow-up activities (e.g., note home each week indicating progress, immediate phone call if problem should recur, a review of the situation at the next parent-teacher night).
☐ Document what took place at the conference, including the agreements and disagreements.

THE INFLUENCE OF HOME AND FAMILY ON CLASSROOM BEHAVIOR PROBLEMS

Finally, it is important to note that some of the discipline problems you will face in your classroom have their origin at home. Living in a fast-paced, upwardly mobile society has created family stresses and strains that could not have been imagined by our grandparents. Their lives while growing up were not necessarily any easier than yours or your students', but they were most assuredly different, particularly in the intensity and rapidity with which children today experience developmental stages and life-cycle changes.

For example, by some estimates, boys and girls are maturing a full five years earlier than they did 50 years ago. This means that they come under the influence of the intense emotions of sex, aggression, love, affiliation, jealousy, and competitiveness far earlier than our own parents probably did. Teachers of the seventh and eighth grades no longer are surprised by the depth of understanding and ability of young students to emulate the media's attractively packaged images of adult behavior and lifestyles, especially as they relate to sex, clothes, relationships, and dominance.

Although not often recognized, these generational differences sometimes are even more difficult for parents to accept than for you, the teacher. This often leads to major conflicts at home that surface in your classroom as seemingly minor but persistent misbehaviors. You can have little influence over home conflicts, except to understand that they originate in the home and not in your classroom.

There will be times when no amount of reward or punishment will work, because the source of the problem is within the home and may be far more serious than you suppose—including marital discord, verbal or physical abuse, competition among brothers and sisters, financial distress, and divorce. You need to realize that one or more of these family disturbances easily could be occurring in the families of some of your students.

These are not trivial burdens for students, especially when combined with the social and academic demands of school, the uncertainties of a future job or education, and the tension that school-age children always feel between youth and adulthood. If a problem persists and your rewards and punishments are to no avail, you must consider the possibility that such a family problem may be occurring. Although there is no easy way to know what is happening in the lives of your students at home, many students welcome the opportunity to reveal the nature of these problems, *when they are asked*. For some it will be just the opportunity they have sought to shed some of the emotional burden these events are creating in their lives.

It is not your role to resolve such problems, but knowing the reason they are occurring may explain why your rewards and punishments may not be working. Knowing the reason also can help you decide whether to refer the problem to other professionals who are in a position to help (e.g., social worker, counselor, school psychologist).

SUMMING UP

This chapter introduced you to some concepts and techniques for maintaining classroom order and discipline. Its main points were:

1. Most classroom discipline problems are low intensity, continuous, and unconnected with any larger, more serious event.
2. Classrooms in which a large percentage of students are off-task, talk without raising hands, talk back, move about without permission, ignore rules, disrupt others, and/or fail to complete assignments are characterized by the following:
   □ Extreme negativity
   □ Exclusive authoritarian climate
   □ Overreacting
   □ Mass punishment
   □ Blaming
   □ Lack of clear instructional goals
   □ Repetition of already learned material
   □ Pausing and interruptions
   □ Dealing with a single student at length
   □ Lack of recognition of ability levels
3. Classroom order and discipline depends as much on the voluntary cooperation of students as it does on the clear communication of rules and the ability to enforce them.
4. Although emotional responses may be effective at times, their frequent use diminishes their effectiveness at the times they may be needed most.
5. Obedient students often come from a different peer group than those who frequently disobey and, therefore, the former have little or no influence over the latter, either in or out of school.

6. It is not essential that every misbehavior be attributed to someone, even if the most likely person actually is responsible.
7. Even the most indirect discussions must be crafted to communicate a structure, an end result, and a clear expectation of student conduct.
8. There always should be some mystery, challenge, or curiosity about what is to be learned. That is, there always should be some uncertainty as to what the next question or item will be and whether or not it can be answered correctly.
9. Awkward gaps, pauses, and interruptions in which you lose eye and visual contact almost always will disengage your students from the learning process.
10. The punishment phase of a disciplinary action should be left until after class or after school to cause the least disruption to the class.
11. Ability grouping can be used with remedial activities to help slow learners either catch up or pursue alternative instructional goals.
12. Some characteristics of effective classroom management include the following:
    □ Seeing all aspects of the classroom at once
    □ Overlapping activities
    □ Less autocratic and authoritarian
    □ Some freedom of student expression and spontaneity
    □ Adultlike cooperative environment
    □ Clear rules and directions
    □ Balance between direct and indirect instruction
    □ Businesslike pace

☐ Assignment of punishment later
☐ Formation of ability or activity groups.

13. Three ways to apply your authority in dealing with misbehavior are:
   ☐ You alone judge what occurred and what the punishment should be.
   ☐ You provide some alternative forms of punishment from which the student must choose.
   ☐ You select a punishment from alternatives that the students provide.

14. The level of severity with which you respond to a misbehavior should match the misbehavior that has occurred.

15. The idea behind reinforcement theory is that any behavior can be controlled by the consequences that immediately follow it. When the consequences that follow a behavior change the probability of the behavior's recurrence, reinforcement has occurred.

16. Some misbehaviors that occur in classrooms are unintentionally increased through reinforcement, in which case the probability of the misbehavior increases because a consequence that follows the misbehavior is perceived as desirable by the student.

17. Both rewards and punishment can increase the probability of a behavior, although punishment without reward is rarely effective.

18. A reward that is reinforcing to one student may be irrelevant to another.

19. Reinforcement is the use of a reward to increase the probability of a desired behavior. An aversive is the use of punishment to increase the probability of a desired behavior.

20. Punishment in the absence of rewards tends to be less effective in increasing the probability of a desired behavior because:
   ☐ Punishment does not guarantee that the desirable response will occur.
   ☐ The effects of punishment are specific to a particular context.
   ☐ The effects of punishment can spread to undesirable behavior.
   ☐ Punishment can create hostile and aggressive responses.
   ☐ Punishment can become associated with the punisher.

21. After two or three warnings a punishment should be assigned.

22. Corporal punishment is rarely effective in deterring misbehavior.

23. One feature of the parent-teacher conference that accounts for its effectiveness is the involvement of the parent in eliminating the misbehavior.

FOR DISCUSSION AND PRACTICE

*1. Identify the classroom characteristics most commonly associated with poor classroom managers.

2. Give an example of a teacher-student interaction that illustrates each of the characteristics identified in the preceding discussion topic.

*3. Why is obtaining the voluntary cooperation of students in obeying classroom rules important to becoming an effective classroom manager?

*4. Why would the use of repeated emotional responses in dealing with misbehavior diminish your effectiveness as a classroom manager?

*5. Why is mass punishment rarely effective in creating peer pressure that reduces misbehavior?

*6. What would be a reason for not insisting that every misbehavior must be attributed to someone?

*7. What would be some good advice to a fellow teacher who wants to conduct an open discussion in his or her class?

*8. Why does repetition of material that already has been learned at high rates of success often create misbehavior?

*9. What are two frequent sources of pauses and interruptions in classrooms? What strategies would you use to combat their effects on misbehavior?

*10. Identify three ways of dealing with misbehavior that defer the punishment phase to a later time.

*11. How can learners who lack the task-relevant prior knowledge to participate in class be given a chance to catch up or pursue alternative paths?

12. Using your own words, write a narrative profile of the kinds of behaviors and classroom activities that would be indicative of an effective classroom manager.

*13. Name three different ways you can use your authority to assign punishment.

14. Identify responses that reflect the severity of the offense for the following misbehaviors. Do not use the same response more than once.

Talking back

Cutting class

Eating in class

Jumping out of seat

Smoking in class

Sleeping in class

Acting out

Obscene gesturing

Selling drugs

Fighting

15. Give one reward and one aversive that might be used to get a student to:

Do homework

Stop talking

Stop talking back

Turn in assignments on time

Be on time for class

Remember to bring pen and pencil

Not talk without raising hand

*16. Identify five reasons why punishment is rarely effective in the absence of rewards.

*17. Under what two conditions is the use of punishment most effective?

*18. Identify two important objectives for having a parent-teacher conference.

---

*Answers to asterisked questions (*) in this and the other chapters are in Appendix B.

SUGGESTED READINGS

Brodinsky, B. (1980). *Student discipline: Problems and solutions*. Arlington, VA: American Association of School Administrators.
A practical handbook written from the perspective of a school administrator about what every teacher should know about classroom discipline.

Charles, C. M. (1981). *Building classroom discipline*. New York: Longman.
A useful book because of its many scenarios on how to handle classroom discipline and to be an effective classroom manager.

Clarizio, H. F. (1980). *Toward positive classroom discipline*. New York: Wiley.
Details the strategies currently most used for establishing a system for classroom order and discipline—very comprehensive.

Glickman, C., & Wolfgang, C. (1979). Dealing with student misbehavior: An eclectic review. *Journal of Teacher Education, 30*(3), 7–13.
An overview and philosophical background to some approaches to classroom discipline.

Kindsvatter, R. (1978). A new view of the dynamics of discipline. *Phi Delta Kappan, 70*, 322–325.
An analysis of some of the reasons behind classroom discipline problems and how they affect school performance.

Long, N. J., Morse, W. C., & Newman, R. G. (1980). *Conflict in the classroom*. Belmont, CA: Wadsworth.
Covers the theory and practice of classroom management with especially good illustrations of how effective classroom discipline can be achieved.

O'Banion, D. R., & Whaley, D. L. (1981). *Behavior contracting: Arranging contingencies of reinforcement*. New York: Springer.
An authoritative source on the ways to use rewards to create and maintain desirable student behavior.

Rich, D. (1987). *Teachers and parents: An adult-to-adult approach*. Washington: National Education Association.
An up-to-date resource on the changing role of the family and the responsibility of teachers in creating ties between home and school.

Rotter, J., Robinson, E., & Fey, M. (1987). *Parent-teaching conferencing*. Washington: National Educational Association.
An extensive guide to planning and conducting parent-teacher conferences.

Wolfgang, C. H., & Glickman, C. D. (1980). *Solving discipline problems: Strategies for classroom teachers*. Boston: Allyn & Bacon.
Down-to-earth treatment of classroom discipline; speaks to the most immediate and pressing classroom management needs of teachers.

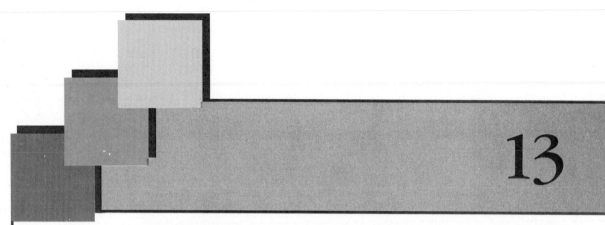

13

Teaching Special Learners in the Regular Classroom

This chapter presents a diverse, heterogeneous classroom that includes both average learners and some less-able, gifted, bilingual, and handicapped as well. Your classroom is unlikely to contain all of these learner types at once, but you are likely to teach some combination of them at almost any time. Because these special learners comprise a sizable percentage of our school-age population, you are likely to encounter them in any school.

Our pluralistic culture includes the physically strong and weak, the mentally able and less-able, native and nonnative speakers, rich and poor, and well-educated and undereducated. Unlike so many other cultures and educational systems throughout the world, we have welcomed this diversity in our communities and our schools, because this cultural mix is illustrative of a nation based on democratic principles. These principles give equal rights to all learners irrespective of race, creed, intellect, language, or any other physical, cultural, or mental characteristic, and these equal rights include the right to a free, public education. Our nation's principles also mandate an educational policy that extends educational opportunity to all individuals in the least restricted (least segregated) environment.

This policy and the federal and state laws that undergird it make this chapter important to you. As a regular classroom teacher, you may expect to have a teaching career devoted to educating the "average" student. However, in the American school system, "average" does not mean the absence of diversity; rather, it increasingly incorporates the diversity of people, cultures, and values represented in our communities and nation.

Less-able, gifted, bilingual, and handicapped learners are only a small part of this diversity, but they are a part that is rapidly redefining the composition and character of the "regular" classroom. This means you must be aware of the special learning needs of these students and be able to execute teaching strategies that meet their instructional needs. It also means you must be able to manage and teach in a classroom that is no less "average" than the community existing outside it.

Here are a couple of important observations concerning special learners. First, *special learner types are not necessarily independent of each other*. A slow, gifted, or handicapped learner also may be bilingual. A gifted learner also might be physically handicapped. A learner can be average in one subject and gifted in another. It is even conceivable that a learner could be both slow and gifted, when you consider his or her accomplishments in widely different areas of the curriculum, such as math versus art. Many combinations exist in our schools, found both in special instructional programs and mixed classrooms. Also, some learners may be ineligible or overlooked for membership in one group due to their membership in another group.

This leads to a second observation, that *any attempt to categorize or group students will be flawed*. This is so because, even when individuals are grouped by a common characteristic, they still differ in many other characteristics that also affect their behavior. Sometimes the variation in behavior *within* a group of learners may be greater than the variation found *between* groups.

So, why categorize learners at all? Because, once the flaws in categorizing systems are recognized and measures are taken to minimize the importance of category labels, the advantages outweigh the disadvantages. The advantages include the assistance that categorization provides in:

1. Dispensing state and federal funds that often are earmarked for specific types of learners.
2. Developing and organizing instructional materials, texts, and media appropriate for certain types of learners.
3. Training and assigning the most qualified instructional staff to teach certain types of learners.

Now, let us use what you have learned in earlier chapters to explore the similarities and differences among these four types of learners and to suggest teaching methods specific to their special learning needs.

THE SLOW LEARNER

Contrary to common belief, slow learners in the regular classroom are neither rare nor unique. Up to one-third of today's students will drop out of school before graduation (Borich, 1992), and of these, over half can be described as slow learners (Hodgkinson, 1986). Your overall effectiveness as a teacher, therefore, may well depend on your ability to recognize slow learners and to teach them appropriately. This section dispels common misconceptions about slow learners, explains who they really are, and suggests procedures for becoming aware of and instructing this special group.

One common misperception about slow learners is that they are mentally retarded, emotionally disturbed, or that they require continual disciplining. But "slow learner" refers to none of these characteristics. Nor does it refer to the student of average intelligence who may fail a subject due to difficulty with the language, lack of sufficient discipline to study, or a lack of interest in school. Although such groups may include slow learners, these are not defining characteristics.

The student commonly called a slow learner is one who cannot learn at an average rate from the instructional resources, texts, workbooks, and learning materials that are designated for the majority of students in the classroom (Bloom, 1982). These students need special instructional pacing, frequent feedback, corrective instruction, and/or modified materials, all administered under conditions sufficiently flexible for learning to occur.

Slow learners usually are taught in one of two possible instructional arrangements: (1.) a class composed mostly of average students, in which case up to 20% may be slow learners, or (2) a class specifically designated for slow learners. The latter classes sometimes are part of a *track system* in which different sections of math, English, science, and social studies are allocated for less-able, average, and more-able students. The desirability and fairness of various tracking systems has been debated, but we address them here because you may well teach in a system that uses them.

Eligibility for a track usually is determined by a student's percentile rank, which is derived from a score on a subscale of a standardized achievement test that represents the student's achievement in the subject. For example, a percentile rank of 30 on a subscale might be made the cutoff for admission to a track for less-able learners. This means that 30% of all the students from across the country who took the standardized test scored equal to or below those admitted to the track. Cutoff percentiles vary considerably across school districts and frequently are supplanted by parental wishes and by administrator and teacher recommendations, based upon a student's past performance.

Whether you meet slow learners in a regular class or a special class, you will immediately feel the challenge of meeting their learning needs. Their most obvious characteristic is a limited attention span compared to more-able students. To keep these learners actively engaged in the learning process requires more than the usual variation in presentation methods (e.g., direct, indirect), classroom climate (cooperative, competitive), and instructional materials (films, workbooks, cooperative games, simulations). If this variation is not part of your lessons, these students may well create their own variety in ways that disrupt your teaching.

Other immediately noticeable characteristics of slow learners are their deficiencies in basic skills (reading, writing, mathematics), their difficulty in comprehending abstract ideas, and most disconcerting, their sometimes unsystematic and careless work habits. These deficiencies often make instructional lessons that are geared to the average student too difficult for the slow learner. When presentation method and content organization do not accommodate their special characteristics, the result for slow learners often is a failing performance. A further result is continuation of a cycle of deficiencies that promotes poor self-concept, misbehavior, and disinterest in school—all of which have contributed to the particularly high dropout rate for this type of learner.

Compensatory and Remedial Teaching

An important aspect of teaching slow learners is knowing the difference between *compensatory* teaching and *remedial* teaching (recall the discussion of these two approaches to *adaptive teaching* in Chapter 2).

Compensatory Teaching.   The term compensatory teaching originally referred to preschool programs of the 1960s, which were designed to *compensate* for the cultural deprivation of disadvantaged children (Dembo, 1981). Compensatory programs are based on the premise that enriching a child's environment can influence intellectual and academic development.

Compensatory teaching is an instructional approach that *alters the presentation* of content to circumvent a student's fundamental weakness or deficiency. Compensatory teaching reorganizes content, transmits it through alternate modalities (e.g., pictures versus words), and supplements it with additional learning resources and activities (learning centers and simulations; group discussions and cooperative learning). This may involve modifying an instructional technique by including a visual representation of content, by using more flexible instructional presentations (e.g., films, pictures, illustrations), or by shifting to alternate instructional formats (e.g., self-paced texts, simulations, experience-oriented workbooks).

The objective of compensatory teaching is to deemphasize instructional stimuli that require the use of weaker learning modalities (e.g., verbal, conceptual) and to emphasize instructional stimuli and arrangements that require the use of stronger learning modalities (e.g., visual, tactile).

Remedial Teaching. This is an alternate approach for the regular classroom teacher in instructing the slow learner. **Remedial teaching** is the use of activities, techniques, and practices to *eliminate* weaknesses or deficiencies that the slow learner is known to have. For example, deficiencies in basic math skills are reduced or eliminated by *reteaching* the content that was not learned earlier. The instructional environment does not change, as in the compensatory approach. Conventional instructional techniques, such as drill and practice, might be employed.

Comparing Compensatory and Remedial Teaching. Important practical and philosophical differences exist between these strategies. Practically, the compensatory approach is favored because the remedial approach requires more instructional time to extensively reteach basic skills with no guarantee they will be learned. Because earlier attempts failed to teach these skills, subsequent efforts may meet the same fate. Also, the compensatory approach uses currently planned instruction, altering the instructional environment as needed so that basic deficiencies become less important in acquiring new content.

Philosophically, the compensatory approach represents a belief that many paths can be taken to acquire new knowledge. One path may emphasize one set of abilities, while another path may emphasize a different set. The teacher's role is to be flexible and seek a path to learning that works.

Some remediation always will be necessary with the slow learner. Some basic skills are so fundamental to subsequent learning that they must be acquired at almost any cost of instructional time. However, for the regular classroom teacher who must deal with students of all ability levels, the remediation of specific deficiencies may be secondary to the acquisition of new concepts and understandings using alternative instructional strategies.

It is interesting to note that tracked classes specifically devoted to the slow learner often represent an integration of both the remedial and the compensatory approaches. In these classes, deficiencies often are compensated for through the reorganization of subject matter. On the other hand, because these classes are devoted entirely to slow learners where traditional content coverage is abbreviated, more time is allowed for reteaching fundamental skills through drill and practice.

Instructional Strategies for Slow Learners

While no single technique or set of techniques is sufficient for teaching the slow learner, the suggestions that follow are a starting point for developing instructional strategies that specifically address the learning needs of the slow learner.

Develop Lessons Around Students' Interests, Needs, and Experiences. This helps address the short attention spans of slow learners. Also, these students should be made to feel that some of the instruction has been designed with their specific interests or experiences in mind. Oral or written autobiographies at the beginning of the year, or simple inventories in which students indicate their hobbies, jobs, and unusual trips or experiences can provide the structure for lesson plans, special projects, or extra-credit assignments later in the year.

Frequently Vary Your Instructional Technique.   Switching from lecture to discussion and then to seatwork provides the variety that slow learners need to stay engaged in the learning process. In addition to keeping their attention, variety in instructional technique offers them the opportunity to see the same content presented in different ways. This increases opportunities to accommodate the different learning styles that may exist among slow learners and provides some of the remediation that may be necessary.

Incorporate Individualized Learning Materials.   Slow learners respond favorably to frequent reinforcement of small segments of learning. Therefore, programmed texts and interactive computer instruction often are effective in remediation of basic skills for slow learners. In addition, an emphasis on frequent diagnostic assessment of the student's progress, paired with immediate corrective instruction, often is particularly effective.

Incorporate Audio and Visual Materials.   One common characteristic among slow learners is that they often learn better by seeing and hearing than by reading. This should be no surprise, because performance in the basic skill areas, including reading, usually is below grade level among slow learners. Incorporating films, videotapes, and audio into lessons helps accommodate the instruction to the strongest learning modalities among slow learners. Emphasizing concrete and visual forms of content also helps compensate for the general difficulty slow learners have in grasping abstract ideas and concepts.

Develop Your Own Worksheets and Exercises.   Textbooks and workbooks, when written for the average student, often exceed the functioning level of the slow learner and sometimes become more of a hindrance than an aid. When textbook materials are too difficult, or are too different from topics that capture your students' interests, develop your own. Sometimes only small changes in worksheets and exercises are needed to adapt the vocabulary or difficulty level (e.g., in the case of math problems) to the ability of your slow learners. Also, using textbooks and exercises intended for a lower grade can ease the burden of creating materials that are unavailable at your grade level.

Provide Peer Tutors for Students Needing Remediation.   Peer tutoring can be an effective ally to your teaching objectives, especially when tutors are assigned so that everyone being tutored also has responsibility for being a tutor. The learner needing help is not singled out and has a stake in making the idea work, because his or her pride is on the line, both as a learner and as a tutor.

Encourage Oral Expression Instead of Written Reports. For slow learners, many writing assignments go unattempted or are begun only half-heartedly because these learners recognize that their written product will not meet even minimal writing standards. A carefully organized taped response to an assignment might be considered; this has the advantage of avoiding spelling, syntax, and writing errors. Such errors can be so pervasive as to destroy slow learners' hopes that an acceptable level of performance can be obtained, no matter how good the content.

When Testing, Provide Study Aids. Study aids are advance organizers that alert students to the most important problems, content, or issues. They also eliminate irrelevant details that slow learners often laboriously study in the belief that they are important. The slow learner usually is unable to weigh the relative importance of competing instructional stimuli unless explicitly told or shown what is important and what is not. Example test questions or a list of topics from which questions may be chosen help focus student effort.

Increase Learning Skills. You can increase learning skills by teaching notetaking, outlining, and listening. These skills are acquired through observation by higher-ability students, but they must be specifically taught to slow learners.

All five key behaviors—lesson clarity, instructional variety, task orientation, engagement in the learning process, and student success—are relevant to the slow learner. But the most important for this special learner are instructional variety in your teaching method and student engagement at moderate-to-high rates of success. If you are unable to capture and maintain their attention with a flexible and variable instructional style, little else can be accomplished in your classroom.

Unless your slow learners are actively engaged in the learning process through interesting concrete visual stimuli, there will be little contact emotionally and intellectually with the content you are presenting. This contact can be attained most easily when you *vary your instructional material often and organize it into bits small enough to ensure moderate-to-high rates of success.*

THE GIFTED AND/OR TALENTED LEARNER

A student who reads rapidly, comprehends quickly, has an exceptional memory, is imaginative and creative, has a long attention span, and is comfortable with abstract ideas is described with words like *bright, exceptional, gifted,* and *talented.* Not all schools have programs for the learning needs of the gifted and talented. However, awareness is growing that gifted and talented students are an important natural resource that must be encouraged, activated, directed, and fully developed.

The size and scope of most specialized school programs, such as those for the handicapped or disadvantaged, make programs for the gifted look pale by comparison. But teaching the gifted remains an important objective of virtually every school. Because of their importance to your school's objectives and of the distribution of gifted and talented across every social class, community, and type of school, you should be aware of the learning needs of this special learner. This section explains characteristics that make students gifted and talented and some ways you can alter your teaching to meet their learning needs.

When Will You Teach Gifted Students?

If you were to observe gifted and talented programs in different school districts, you would quickly see that the word *gifted* has many meanings. These different definitions of giftedness have created considerable diversity among both the students called gifted and the instructional programs designed to meet their needs. Gifted students are a population every bit as diverse as the slow learners just described. You need to know how giftedness is determined and about the diversity of programs designed for them.

As with slow learners, you will meet the gifted in several instructional arrangements. One is a gifted class that is part of a districtwide gifted and talented program. Another is a tracked class specifically intended for the more-able student. Still another is a so-called "average" or regular class composed mostly of average learners but including some slow, more-able, and gifted learners.

The number of gifted learners you might have depends largely on factors beyond your control, such as the availability of a special gifted program in your school, the existence of a formal tracking system of more-able learners, and the proportion of gifted learners in the school community where you teach. The essential point is this: whether you teach a gifted class, a more-able class with some gifted learners, or a regular class with one or more gifted learners, you likely will be responsible for teaching the gifted *during your very first year of teaching*.

It is a mistaken notion that gifted learners, especially compared to slow learners, are easy to teach. As most experienced teachers of the gifted will attest, nothing could be further from the truth! It is sometimes the case that the experienced teacher who has taught the gifted will prefer *not* to do so again, due to the extra work (e.g., preparing intellectually challenging exams, grading extended essays, dealing with parents' expectations) and special demands (e.g., knowing how to use specialized library resources, supplemental materials, and equipment). Hence, the assignment may be given to a beginning teacher like yourself, who has no choice in the matter.

The truth is that the job of teaching the gifted is as difficult and as challenging as teaching any other type of learner. There are important differences among learning types, but these are differences in kind, not degree. For example, preparation for teaching the gifted is different, but not measurably less, than for a class of slow learners. Likewise, discipline problems encountered with the gifted are different, but not measurably less, than for other types of learners. The time you spend teaching mastery of a concept does not vary measurably among types of learners, because the difficulty level also must vary with types of learners.

Therefore, when you teach the gifted, whether as an intact class in junior and senior high or as individuals in an average or regular elementary class, approach the task free of any illusion that something less will be required of you. On the contrary, it is likely that something more will be required.

Defining Gifted

Because the words *gifted* and *talented* often include considerable diversity among these learners, you must be aware of the different ways in which gifted students are identified. The most important thing to realize is that no single standard or definition of giftedness has ever been agreed upon, or is likely to be. However, the *Congressional Record* of October 10, 1978, provides a broad definition of gifted and talented:

> Gifted and talented children means children, and whenever applicable youth, who are identified at the preschool, elementary, or secondary level as possessing demonstrated or potential abilities that give evidence of high performance capability in areas such as intellectual, creative, specific academics, or leadership abilities, or in the performing and visual arts, and who by reason thereof require services or activities not ordinarily provided by the school (H–12179).

While a consensus exists as to what general abilities and behaviors compose giftedness, there is considerable variation in how to measure both the degree of ability and the proper combination of sub-abilities that represent giftedness. The following are some of the most important behavioral ingredients from which an individual school district's definition of giftedness is likely to be composed.

Intelligence. Foremost among the characteristics of giftedness is general *intelligence*. We noted in Chapter 2 that aptitude in a specific area often is more predictive of future productivity and accomplishments (in that area) than is general intelligence, but nevertheless, most formulae for defining giftedness include general intelligence. This is particularly true in the elementary grades, where it is believed that learners are still developing their specialized intellectual capacities while their general intelligence was almost completely formed in the critical preschool years. The emphasis on general intelligence for aiding identification of giftedness at the elementary level also is a function of the difficulty of measuring specific aptitudes at that age, when many of the words and concepts required for accurately testing specific aptitudes have yet to be taught.

At the junior high and secondary levels, measures of specific intelligence are more likely to be substituted for general intelligence. The most common are verbal and mathematical aptitude, scores for which can be derived from most general IQ tests. For example, a sufficiently high score on verbal intelligence could qualify a learner for gifted English but not for gifted math, and vice versa; this gives greater flexibility to the definition of giftedness.

How high must a student score on tests of general or specific intelligence to be considered gifted? This depends upon the school district's criteria. However, it is known how intelligence is distributed among individuals in the entire population. Recall that intelligence is distributed in a bell-shaped curve, with most individuals scoring around the middle of the curve, which represents an IQ score of 100. From the shape of this curve, we also know that less than 1% of the population scores 145 or higher, about 2–3% scores 130 or higher, and approximately 16% scores 115 or higher.

Although these percentages vary slightly depending on the test used, they are a useful guideline for selecting gifted learners. An IQ score of about 130 or higher generally makes one eligible for gifted instruction (Dembo, 1981). However, in practice, because giftedness almost always is defined in conjunction with at least several other behaviors, admission to gifted programs and classes usually is far less restrictive. It is not uncommon to accept scores below 130 as eligible for gifted instruction (of course, this is highly variable among schools and states). Sometimes IQ is not considered at all in determining giftedness, in which case the learner must exhibit unusual ability in one or more other areas.

Because IQ tests rely greatly on standard language usage that predominates in the middle class, a school district with a high concentration of low-SES students may not require a high level of tested intelligence (at least not as measured by standardized tests). In most cases, intelligence is among several behaviors that constitute giftedness. Rarely is intelligence used as the only index of giftedness, nor should it be.

Achievement.   Among other behaviors frequently used to determine giftedness is the learner's *achievement,* usually in the areas for which gifted instruction is being considered. Achievement is measured by yearly standardized tests which cover areas such as math, social studies, reading comprehension, vocabulary, and science. Cutoff scores in the form of percentile ranks are determined in each subject area, with a percentile score of 90–95 representing a typical cutoff. Although cutoff percentiles differ among school districts, a cutoff percentile of 90 means that a learner is eligible for gifted instruction if his or her score on the appropriate subscale of a standardized achievement test is higher than the scores of 90% of all those who took the test.

Creativity.   In addition to intelligence and achievement, indices of *creativity* often are considered in selecting gifted learners. Inclusion of this behavioral dimension has broadened the definition of this type of learner to include both the gifted and the talented. The significance of this addition is that not all gifted learners are talented, nor are all talented learners gifted. The phrase "gifted and talented," which is widely used, can mean talented but not gifted, gifted but not talented, mostly talented with some giftedness, mostly gifted with some talent, or both gifted and talented.

These alternative categorizations are made possible by inclusion of creativity indices in the eligibility standards. Because creative behaviors generally are considered in selecting gifted students, this type of learner more appropriately might be called "gifted and/or talented." Some observable signs of creativity in a learner include:

- ☐ Applying abstract principles to the solution of problems
- ☐ Being curious and inquisitive
- ☐ Giving uncommon or unusual responses
- ☐ Showing imagination
- ☐ Posing original solutions to problems
- ☐ Discriminating between major and minor events
- ☐ Seeing relationships among dissimilar objects.

In identifying the gifted and talented learner, the creative component usually is composed of recommendations from teachers based upon these and other signs of creativity and any observable creative products (e.g., sculpture, painting, musical score, science fair project, short story). It is interesting to note that studies have shown only a modest relationship between intelligence and creativity, indicating that creativity is fairly independent of both IQ and achievement.

Task Persistence. A fourth behavior sometimes used in selecting gifted and talented learners involves recommendations from teachers and other knowledgeable sources concerning a learner's *task persistence*. This behavior is difficult to evaluate, but often is considered indispensable for satisfactory achievement in a gifted and talented program, because both the quantity and quality of the work are likely to be considerably above what is expected in the regular classroom. Obviously this trait alone would not be sufficient for qualifying a learner for gifted instruction, but if such instruction is indeed geared to the extremely able student, students will need unusual levels of task persistence to succeed. Behaviors teachers look for in determining task persistence include:

- Ability to devise organized approaches to learning
- Ability to concentrate on detail
- Self-imposed high standards
- Persistence in achieving personal goals
- Willing to evaluate own performance, and capable of doing so
- Sense of responsibility
- High level of energy, particularly in academic tasks.

It is in evaluating these behaviors that parents play the greatest role in influencing their child's eligibility for gifted instruction. By providing testimony to the school about the ability of their child to work hard, to accept additional responsibility, and to live with increased performance and grading expectations, parents may convince the school that the learner can indeed profit from gifted instruction. Because prestige accrues to both parent and student from being in a gifted class, you can expect considerable pressure from parents to consider students who may not meet the standards of intelligence, achievement, and creativity. In some cases, you may need to point out why a particular learner would not benefit from gifted instruction and to help secure an alternative placement.

Instructional Strategies for Gifted and Talented Learners

You may consider one of your students gifted as a result of previously being assigned to gifted classes, or you may arrive at this conclusion from an independent assessment of the student's intelligence, achievement, creativity, and task persistence. In either case, there are several methods for teaching the gifted who must be taught among regular students. The following suggestions are starting points for managing and teaching the gifted and talented learner.

Choose Learning Activities to Allow Freedom and Include Interests.   This encourages independent thinking, while at the same time giving the student the extra motivation often required to pursue a topic in much greater depth than would be expected of an average student. Because gifted learners tend to take greater responsibility for their own learning than do average students, self-directed learning methods (Chapter 9) often predominate among teachers of the gifted.

Along with this, let students know that you are giving them a unique opportunity to, in a sense, create their own curriculum. Some gifted students become disenchanted with school, feeling that nothing there is relevant to their interests at their intellectual level. By letting them pursue and investigate some topics of their own choosing and construct their own meanings and interpretations, you will be making them participants in the design of their own learning.

Occasionally Plan Instruction Involving Group Activities.   Gifted students are among those most capable of picking up ideas from others and creating from them new and unusual variations. Brainstorming sessions, group discussion, panels, peer interviews, teams, and debates are among the ways you can start interactions among students. When carefully organized, this can create a "snowballing" of ideas that can turn initially rough ideas about a problem into polished and elegant solutions.

Gifted learners require flexibility of responding and independence of thought. This is most easily accomplished through self-directed learning methods that are relevant to the learner's interests and specialized abilities.

Include Real-Life Problems that Require Problem Solving.   Let your gifted students become actual investigators in solving real-world dilemmas in your content area. This will force them to place newly acquired knowledge and understandings in a practical perspective and to increase the problem-solving challenge. Ask them pointed questions that do not have readily available answers: "How would you reduce world tensions among the superpowers?" "How would you eliminate acid rain?" "How could we harvest the seas?" "How could life be sustained on the moon?" "What would a school for the gifted look like?"

Be careful not to accept glib and superficial responses. Make clear that an inquiry must be conducted into the nature of the problem using methods of inquiry like those used by professionals—scientists, engineers, political scientists—in answering the question. Finally, require actual library or laboratory research that produces not just opinions, but objective evidence leading to a possible answer.

Pose Challenging Problems.   Perhaps more than any other learners, the gifted both are capable of and enjoy the freedom to independently explore issues and ideas that concern them. Give them this opportunity by posing a challenging problem and organizing data (e.g., references, materials, and documents) that they must screen for relevance. Focus the problem so the learner must make key decisions about what is important for a solution. This feeling of responsibility and control over the inquiry is essential if the learner is to see it as truly self-directed. Throughout the inquiry, students should feel your support, encouragement, and above all, availability to provide additional references and materials relevant to directions they wish to explore.

In Testing, Draw Out Knowledge and Understanding.   Because gifted students tend to be verbally fluent, it can be difficult to know whether an articulate response substitutes superficiality and glibness for an in-depth understanding. Fancy words at a high vocabulary level may hide a lack of hard work and investigation. Such responses may even be purposefully composed to intimidate the listener, whether teacher or classmate. Testing and questioning the gifted, therefore, should draw out the knowledge and understanding that lies within, to separate articulate superficiality from in-depth understanding.

Use tests and questions that make the student go beyond knowing and remembering facts. Asking your gifted students to explain, analyze, compare, contrast, hypothesize, infer, adopt, justify, judge, prove, criticize, and dispute are means of indicating that more than a verbally fluent response is required. Asking your students to explain the reasons behind their answers, to put together the known facts into something new, and to judge the outcome of their own inquiry are useful means of separating "slick" responses from meaningful answers.

THE BILINGUAL LEARNER

Approximately five million students—about 10% of the entire school-age population in this country—have a primary language other than English (Baca and Cervantes,

1984). Although their number varies with state and region, you can expect to meet some of them in your classroom. If you teach in some areas of the South, Southwest, and Northeast, as many as a third of your students may not speak English as their primary language.

Predominant among this group are Mexican-American, Puerto Rican, Cuban, Central American, and South American students. They generally are considered bilingual, which implies proficiency in both their native Spanish and adopted English. In reality, however, many have "limited English proficiency" (LEP). This means they may range from being unable to express themselves at all in English to being marginally proficient, either orally or in writing. The vast—and increasing—numbers of these students in our school population presents a challenge to develop instructional materials and use techniques that meet their special learning needs.

Because Hispanics are the largest language minority in the United States, Spanish is used as an example in this chapter, but the information provided applies to all non-English speakers.

Although initially a regional concern, bilingual education is now a national issue of considerable importance. Our society's great mobility, plentiful transportation, and rapidly changing employment opportunities have integrated the bilingual learner into the school-age population of almost every state. This has caused considerable financial and curriculum-development pressure on individual school districts where little if any planning existed for maximum development of the bilingual learner. The federal government and many state governments are providing funds for developing and operating bilingual programs. Although more than 30 states now make bilingual programs mandatory or encourage them through guidelines and statewide policies, only 29% of the bilingual programs use both native and English languages for instruction (Zakariya, 1987).

Laws and school district policies now require regular classroom teachers to assume some responsibility for teaching LEP bilingual students. Although special LEP programs exist in some areas, LEP students still spend at least part of their day *mainstreamed* in regular classrooms. This is in keeping with a general philosophy embodied in federal law that encourages use of the least restrictive instructional environment for a learner wherever it is deemed conducive to a child's education.

The more instruction that LEP students receive in a regular classroom, the less restrictive will be their instructional environment. This is because the regular classroom has a mix of learning types, personalities, and ethnicities that represents the community in which LEP students will live and work. Thus, many programs require LEP students to spend only part of the instructional day in a concentrated program of bilingual education and the remaining time in the regular classroom.

Bilingual education refers to a mix of instruction in two languages. This means teaching skills and words in English as well as in another language, which in the United States is predominately Spanish. The primary goal of bilingual education is not to teach English as a second language, but to teach concepts, knowledge, and skills through the language the learner knows best and then to reinforce this information through the second language (English), in which the learner is less proficient. This raises important related issues: Should the goal of bilingual education be to bring about a transition to the second language as quickly as possible? Or, should some emphasis be placed on maintaining and even improving the learner's proficiency in his or her native language?

Such issues arise from the observation that *bilingual* or even *limited English proficiency* do not in reality mean that learners are proficient in their native language; experience shows that this very often is not the case. Essential skills in vocabulary, syntax, and reading comprehension may be lacking in both languages. This not only complicates instruction but also raises the issue of whether the bilingual program and schools have responsibility for nurturing and improving the native language in addition to English. Not surprisingly, the linguistic and cultural goals of bilingual education often differ from program to program. They also differ among states, which fund the majority of bilingual programs.

Four Approaches to Bilingual Education

From the two basic philosophies—transition to a second language versus maintenance of the native language—four general approaches have emerged. These are defined by Baca and Cervantes (1984) as transition, maintenance, restoration, and enrichment.

Transition Approach. The **transition approach** uses learners' native language and culture only to the extent necessary for them to learn English. Learners are not taught reading or writing in their native language. In the transition approach, the regular classroom teacher should encourage and sometimes expect LEP learners to respond, read, and write in English. The teacher using the transition approach first discerns the level of English proficiency of the learner and then expects the learner to function in English at or slightly above this level.

Maintenance Approach. The **maintenance approach**, in addition to encouraging English language proficiency, endorses the idea that learners also should become proficient in their native language. The goal is to help learners become truly bilingual—to become fluent in both languages. Such learners have come to be called *balanced bilinguals* to emphasize that their proficiency is limited neither in English nor in Spanish.

Federal funding requirements favor transitional bilingual programs. But school districts, particularly in the South and Southwest where the Hispanic culture is most prominent, often supplement federal funds with local resources to meet the dual purposes of a maintenance approach. The implication for the regular classroom teacher is that alternative expressions in English and Spanish *must* be accepted as equally valid communication within the classroom.

That is not to say that a Spanish response can replace one in English, which clearly would be inappropriate if you are a non-Spanish-speaking teacher. It means that, if the learner wishes, both languages can be used in articulating the same expression. This can be an important aid to the LEP student because thoughts can be organized, formulated, and even expressed in the comfort of the native language and then safely translated into English.

Those who have had to express themselves in a foreign language can attest to the helpfulness of this strategy. If they were not proficient in the language and were as yet unable to think in it, they invariably composed what they wanted to say in English and then replaced the English formulation word-by-word with its counterpart in the other language.

Restoration Approach.   The **restoration approach** attempts to restore the native language and culture of the bilingual student to its purest and most original form. As other languages have been assimilated into standard American culture, they have developed abbreviated forms in which words and phrases that mix both languages often compose regional dialects. These are like separate languages unto themselves. Even native speakers from other regions sometimes have difficulty deciphering these nonstandard, subcultural expressions.

Restoration's goal is to replace these nonstandard dialects with the original form of the language. From this perspective, the classroom teacher should discourage mixing Spanish and English phrases when they occur in the context of expressing the same idea or thought. In other words, expressions that are expressed alternatively and fully in both English and Spanish may be encouraged, but expressions that are half English and half Spanish are to be discouraged.

Enrichment Approach.   The fourth perspective is popularly called the **enrichment approach**. Like the transition approach, the goal of enrichment is movement from Spanish to English competence in the shortest time possible. However, in addition to this goal, Spanish culture and heritage also are emphasized. Avoided is any direct responsibility for maintaining and improving Spanish language proficiency.

The rationale for this approach comes from a desire to follow federal guidelines for the funding of bilingual education (they favor the transition approach) while maintaining a positive attitude and self-concept of the bilingual learner toward his or her native culture. Some argue that native language proficiency must be part of any such attempt, and so this approach sometimes is considered as giving only "lip service" to bilingual education. Regardless of this, it nevertheless strives, through classroom films, publications, clubs, and local cultural events, to create a warm and nurturing atmosphere that conveys acceptance of any minority culture in the school.

The implications for the regular classroom teacher following this approach are to convey respect for the cultural heritage of the bilingual student through the arrangement of bulletin boards, transmission of information about cultural events, and the teacher's own attitude.

Names of Bilingual Programs

A recent report by the U.S. General Accounting Office (1987) included a definition of the many different terms used to describe bilingual programs. This report categorized bilingual programs as shown in Table 13.1.

	Program Name	Description
TABLE 13.1 Names of bilingual programs	English as a second language	Programs of bilingual education; instruction is based on a special curriculum typically involving little or no use of the native language and usually is taught only during certain periods of the school day. For the rest of the school day, the student may be placed in regular (or submersion) instruction or a bilingual program.
	Immersion	General term for an approach to bilingual instruction not involving the child's native language. Two specific variations are *structured immersion* and *submersion*.
	Structured immersion	Programs of bilingual education; taught in English, but (a) the teacher understands the native language and students may speak it to the teacher (although the teacher generally answers only in English) and (b) no knowledge of English is assumed and the curriculum vocabulary and pacing are modified so the content will be understood. Some programs include some language-arts teaching in the native language.
	Submersion	Programs in which students having limited English proficiency are placed in ordinary classrooms where English is the language of instruction. Students receive no special program to overcome language problems, and their native language is not used in the classroom; also called "sink or swim." The Supreme Court found this type of submersion unconstitutional (Lau vs. Nichols, 414 U.S. 463 [1974])
	Sheltered English	Programs which use a simplified vocabulary and sentence structure to teach school subjects to students who lack sufficient English-language skills to understand the regular curriculum.
	Transitional bilingual	Programs of bilingual education with emphasis on developing English-language skills to enable students having limited English proficiency to shift to an all-English program of instruction. Some programs include English as a second language.

Instructional Strategies for Bilingual Learners

Because many regular classroom teachers will encounter bilingual learners either as fulltime students or as part of a "pull-out" program in which part of the student's time is spent in the regular classroom, techniques for teaching bilingual learners can be an important adjunct to your list of teaching strategies. The suggestions that follow are starting points for developing instructional strategies for bilingual learners.

If You Don't Speak Spanish, Emphasize Other Communication.   Other forms of communication include the visual, kinesthetic, and tactile modalities. You have seen the importance of the *visual mode* in teaching the slow learner, and it is no less important with the bilingual learner. Use pictures, graphs, and illustrations to supplement your teaching objectives wherever possible. Pictures cannot take the place of auditory cues, but they can place these cues in context, making them easier to recognize in relation to an illustration or picture.

Infrequently used but equally important are the kinesthetic and tactile modes of communication. The *kinesthetic mode* adds movement to the learning process by pointing or tracing so that the learner can feel the motion required to create a particular form, such as a word or letter. The *tactile mode* appeals to the sense of touch; in conjunction with auditory cues, it can be used to remember concepts and objects when some physical representation of them is available.

Thus, a multisensory approach is most appropriate for bilingual learners, using visual, kinesthetic, and tactile modalities wherever possible to reinforce and expand upon auditory communication.

Learning materials that emphasize the visual, kinesthetic, and tactile modalities are often necessary for instructing the nonnative speaker. Supplement your teaching objectives with pictures, graphs, and illustrations when bilingual learners are present.

Use Direct Instruction.   Most bilingual learners learn best from, and are most accustomed to, the direct presentation of instructional material. For example, the "look and say" approach to reading is more effective than the phonetic approach during the initial stages of reading instruction. Especially for those lacking almost any proficiency in English, repetition of material (particularly drill and practice) generally is superior to more conceptual presentations that emphasize perspective, justification, and rationale.

Conceptual presentations are subtleties that quickly become lost in translation. Your first step should be to foster acquisition of facts and their retention in the most visual, concrete way possible to provide building blocks for later conceptual presentations. You will find that Hispanic learners initially respond better to direct instruction than indirect instruction or independent seatwork for acquiring basic skills; the structure and organization of the former supersede any advantages of the latter.

Be Alert to Cultural Differences.   Your awareness of cultural differences can be extremely important to successful communication. There is no substitute for understanding the culture of students you are teaching, even if you have little understanding of their language. For example, several cultural preferences have been noted among bilingual Hispanic learners. They appreciate the cooperation of group achievement more than the competitive aspects of individual achievement. This means that group work, sharing of assignments, and working as a team potentially are useful instructional strategies for Hispanic students. This in turn suggests the value of a cooperative classroom climate (Chapter 10).

Also, the acceptance, warmth, and nurturing of Hispanic culture are aspects you should not lose in the classroom. Frequent praise and encouragement can set the stage for learning more efficiently than the repeated recitation of conduct rules and warnings. As mentioned, bilingual Hispanic learners learn best when physical demonstrations and experience activities supplement verbal presentations. This supports the multisensory approach that conveys information using various modalities, creating both alternate paths for learning and needed redundancy.

Carefully Evaluate Reading Level and Format of Materials.   When selecting or adapting materials, you may find a Spanish version of comparable content, but the reading level and format may not benefit your learners. If you are not fluent in Spanish, have someone who is fluent evaluate the difficulty level of the material. It is not unusual to initially select verbal material several grades below the level you are teaching. After a suitable trial, evaluate the materials again and adjust the reading level accordingly.

The format of materials is important, too. Material with illustrations and pictures is better than concentrated prose. Notice whether the objects pictured will be familiar to the learners or whether they are specific to the Anglo audience for whom the materials may have been written.

Know Your Learners' Language Ability and Achievement Levels.   From school records or your school administrator, find out for each learner:

- □ Dominant language in the receptive mode (e.g., listening, reading).
- □ Dominant language in the expressive mode (e.g., talking, writing).
- □ Proficiency level in the dominant language.
- □ Past achievement levels in the areas relevant to your instruction.

This information is invaluable in selecting special materials and determining the best level and manner to begin instruction. For example, it is not unusual to find bilingual learners who choose Spanish as their dominant means of speaking but English as their dominant means of listening. Knowing this allows you to speak and be understood in English even though at least some of the learners' communications to you might be in Spanish. In this case, little adjustment is needed to your regular instructional plan, compared to what you would have to do if the opposite were true. Knowing your learners' ability and achievement levels makes your initial instructional contact far more effective, potentially avoiding weeks and even months of failing to communicate—and not knowing it!

THE HANDICAPPED LEARNER

The 1950s and 1960s saw considerable litigation concerning the educational rights of handicapped children. In response, Congress established a coherent national legislative program for directing their education: Public Law 94–142, titled The Education for All Handicapped Children Act of 1975. It mandates a free, appropriate program of public school education for all handicapped children in the nation.

This section reviews that law and its implications for the regular classroom teacher and alerts you to important issues you must consider as a member of an interdisciplinary team responsible for the educational progress of handicapped learners.

Since the enactment of PL 94–142, "public education for all" has come to mean that every school-age child has the basic constitutional right to be educated with programs and services appropriate to his or her educational needs. Further, PL 94–142 ensures that handicapped children receive education in the *least restrictive environment* compatible with their educational needs. The special-education profession and the public schools have interpreted this law as a mandate to provide minimally restrictive educational and supportive services to the handicapped, whenever possible, *in the context of the regular school program*. The significance of this law for the regular classroom teacher is that, for some types of handicapping conditions and for some instructional objectives, the regular classroom is the least restrictive alternative for meeting the educational needs of the handicapped.

Over the past few decades handicapped students have been classified and defined in a number of ways and new definitions continue to evolve as more becomes known about these special learners. Before the significance of a handicapping condition for public school instruction can be discussed, we must determine the kind of handicap. To do so, several categories of handicapping conditions have been identified to indicate the types of special services and instruction most appropriate. These categories usually include the physically handicapped, auditorially handicapped, vi-

Public Law 94–142 states that "Schools have the responsibility to provide every child of school age with instruction in the least restricted environment compatible with his or her educational needs." In many instances, the regular classroom will be the least restricted learning environment for the handicapped learner.

sually handicapped, mentally retarded, emotionally disturbed, learning-disabled, speech handicapped, autistic, and multiply handicapped, all described in Table 13.2.

The purpose of these categories is not to label the handicapped child but to identify specific students whose physical, emotional, and/or cognitive functions are so impaired from any cause that they can be educated adequately and safely only with the provision of special services. These special services are the direct responsibility of the special-education program within a school. However, the regular classroom teacher is expected to help provide these services by assisting in child identification, individual assessment, Individual Education Plan (IEP) development, individualized instruction, and review of the IEP. Let us consider what the provision of each of these services means for you.

Child Identification

Child identification consists of a school's or district's procedures for identifying handicapped children who need special education. Students needing such services may

TABLE 13.2
Categories of
handicapping conditions

Physically Handicapped	Students whose body functions or members are impaired by congenital anomaly and disease, or students with limited strength, vitality, or alertness due to chronic or acute health problems.
Auditorially Handicapped	Students who are hearing impaired (hard of hearing) or deaf.
Visually Handicapped	Students who, after medical treatment and use of optical aids, remain legally blind or otherwise exhibit loss of critical sight functions.
Mentally Retarded	Students with significantly subaverage general intellectual functioning existing concurrently with deficiences in adaptive behavior. Severity of retardation is sometimes indicated with the terms profound, trainable, and educable. Not all of the students who are educable are placed in the regular classroom.
Emotionally Disturbed	Students who demonstrate an inability to build or maintain satisfactory interpersonal relationships, develop physical symptoms or fears associated with personal or school problems, exhibit a pervasive mood of unhappiness under normal circumstances, or show inappropriate types of behavior under normal circumstances.
Learning Disabled	Students who demonstrate a significant discrepancy, which is not the result of some other handicap, between academic achievement and intellectual abilities in one or more of the areas of oral expression, listening comprehension, written expression, basic reading skills, reading comprehension, mathematical calculation, mathematics reasoning, or spelling.
Speech Handicapped	Students whose speech is impaired to the extent that it limits the communicative functions.
Autistic	Students with severe disturbances of speech and language, relatedness, perception, developmental rate, or motion.
Multiply Handicapped	Students who have any two or more of the handicapping conditions described above.

never have entered school or could be among those who are attending school but who have not been identified as handicapped. The regular classroom teacher may be expected to play an important role in identifying these students.

One stage of this identification is the referral process by which a child comes to be recommended for special services. Although referrals may be made by parents, physicians, community agencies, and school administrators as a result of districtwide testing or screening, you also may recommend students for special services. For students currently enrolled in regular education, you are the individual most likely to identify those needing special services. In such cases you will become a liaison between the child and the school's special education staff. In such a capacity you will be responsible for reporting data that accurately portray:

1. The student's current educational status, including attendance records, grades, achievement data, and written accounts of classroom observation.
2. Previous instructional efforts and strategies provided the student and the result of those efforts.
3. Data about the learner reported or provided to you by parents.

You need to distinguish between the learning-disabled and the slow learner. Learning-disabled is a classification under PL 94–142 and describes a student who does not achieve on a level commensurate with his or her age and ability levels. This designation is used when a lack of achievement is found in oral expression, listening comprehension, written comprehension, basic reading skills, reading comprehension, mathematics calculation, mathematics reasoning, and/or spelling. On the other hand, slow learners are not considered for special education services under PL 94–142, but instead may be recommended for other remedial programs.

A discrepancy between intellectual ability and academic achievement usually is severe enough to qualify a student as learning-disabled if:

1. The student's assessed *intellectual functioning* is above the mentally retarded range, but is significantly below the mean (usually one standard deviation) for the school district in one or more areas, or
2. The student's assessed *educational functioning* is significantly below his or her intellectual functioning (usually one standard deviation).

When achievement level is below the mean of the district but is consistent with the student's intellectual functioning, he or she usually is not classified as learning-disabled. Many measurement decisions are required in assigning such a designation for a learner. Although this designation is made cooperatively by a multidisciplinary team of regular teachers, special educators, school administrators, parents, and special service staff such as counselors, psychologists, and diagnosticians, the regular classroom teacher is expected to be sufficiently knowledgeable about the learner so that discrepancies between achievement and academic aptitude can be accurately assessed.

Individual Child Assessment

A second process to which you may contribute is individual child assessment. This is the collecting and analyzing of information about a student to identify an educational need in terms of:

1. The presence or absence of a physical, mental, or emotional disability.
2. The presence or absence of a significant educational need.

3. Identification of the student's specific learning competencies together with specific instructional or related services that could improve and maintain the student's competencies.

Although evaluation of a child's capabilities is the responsibility of certified professionals who assess the handicapped, you may be expected to corroborate the findings of these professionals with performance data from the classroom. Foremost among these data are formal and informal indications from workbooks, homework assignments, weekly and unit tests, and classroom observation of the student's language dominance and proficiency in both the expressive and receptive domains. Often, your observation and recording of these data will suggest that special educators evaluate the validity of any standardized tests the student took and whether they were in the child's dominant language.

Corroborative data on the student's physical attributes also can be recorded. You may be the only one to observe daily the learner's ability to manipulate objects necessary for learning, ability to remain alert and attentive during instruction, and ability to control bodily functions in a manner conducive to instruction. In some instances, you may provide the only available data source about the ability of the learner to benefit from regular class instruction.

You may be expected to provide data about sociological and environmental influences on the learner that might influence his or her classroom behavior. Such data often are obtained through communication with the family and knowledge of the circumstances leading to and/or contributing to the student's intellectual and emotional behavior. The extent to which the child's home life and out-of-school support and services contribute to the educative function can provide an important adjunct to in-school data.

Finally, there is the student's intellectual functioning, as demonstrated by both verbal and nonverbal performance. Although these behaviors usually are assessed by professionals certified in special education, you may be asked to provide corroborating data on the child's adaptive behavior, which indicates the degree to which the student meets standards of personal independence and social responsibility expected of his or her age and cultural group. Within the context of the regular classroom, you will have many opportunities to observe the social functioning of the child and to gain insights into the appropriateness of this functioning.

Individual Educational Plan (IEP)

A third stage in which you may become involved in the implementation of PL 94–142 is in helping to develop an individual educational plan (IEP) for a handicapped student in your classroom. A student receives special-education services only after the multidisciplinary team mentioned previously has reviewed data from the comprehensive assessment. Data from this assessment are expected to address the language, physical, emotional/behavioral, sociological, and intellectual functioning of the child. If this assessment determines that the student has a physical, mental, or emotional disability that establishes his or her eligibility to receive special-education services, an

IEP is written to state short-term and long-term objectives for instructional services and to specify the least restrictive environment where the instruction can occur.

The IEP developed for each student by the multidisciplinary team considers a statement of the student's present competencies taken from the overall assessment data, and includes:

1. Long-term (annual) and short-term (weekly, monthly) instructional objectives.
2. The specific educational services to be provided the student within the least restrictive environment designated.
3. The dates for the initiation of the services, the approximate amount of time to be spent providing each service, and a justification for the services and settings in which they will be provided.
4. The criterion for and time of evaluating each long-term and short-term objective.

Figure 13.1 illustrates the composition of a typical IEP.

Individualized Instruction

A fourth stage in which you may become involved in implementing PL 94–142 is in providing individualized instruction to the handicapped student. This is the day-to-day instruction provided according to the objectives set forth in the student's IEP. This program should be consistent with the student's needs and with your curriculum. Your activities may include providing any or all of the following:

☐ Specific instructional objectives, based on student needs as stated in the IEP.
☐ Learning activities appropriate to each student's learning style, presented as specifically and sequentially as needed for the student to progress toward attainment of each instructional objective.
☐ Instructional media and materials used for each learning activity, selected on the basis of the student's learning style.
☐ An instructional setting that provides multiple arrangements for learning.
☐ A schedule of teaching time ensuring the provision of instruction to each handicapped student in individual or group arrangements.
☐ Procedures by which the teacher measures, records, and reports each handicapped student's progress.

You also may be responsible for writing specific instructional objectives in accord with the student's IEP, and you may prepare and administer tests to record the student's progress toward these objectives.

Review of IEP

A fifth activity in which you may become involved is a review of the IEP. School districts usually have procedures or a system for reviewing each handicapped stu-

FIGURE 13.1 Example Individual Educational Plan (IEP)

INDIVIDUAL EDUCATIONAL PLAN

Student's Name: _Bob Miller_   School: _Oak Hill Elem._   Grade: _4_   Date of Meeting: _2-25-87_

Date of Birth: _12-18-78_   Parent/Guardian: _Tom + Ann Miller_   Address: _25 Ruth Drive_   Phone: _443-2187_

COMMITTEE MEMBERS PRESENT:

Name: _Paula Scott_ Position: _Principal_
Name: _Mary White_ Position: _Spec. Ed. Teacher_
Name: _Ann Miller_ Position: _Parent_
Name: _Terry Hull, Ph.D._ Position: _Psychologist_
Name: _Jackie Morgan_ Position: _Teacher_
Name: _Suzanne Martin_ Position: _Speech Therapist_

	Present Levels of Performance	Learning Strengths	Learning Weaknesses
Word Recognition	1.5	Good auditory learning skill	Short attention span in visual presentations & handwriting tasks
Reading Comprehension	2.0	Know all basic computation facts	
Spelling	1.9	Positive social interaction	Articulation
Math	3.5		
Social Adaptation	4th		
Other(s) – _Speech below age level_			

From a review of pertinent data, the committee determined that this student (DOES) / DOES NOT meet eligibility criteria for: _Learning Disabled, Speech Handicapped_

Recommended Placement: _2_ hrs. per day/(week) Special Education; _4_ hrs. per day/(week) Regular Education; _1_ hrs. per day/(week) Related Services

ANNUAL GOALS	SHORT TERM OBJECTIVES	EVALUATION CRITERIA	SPECIFIC SERVICES	DATE SERVICES BEGIN/END	SUGGESTED MATERIALS	STAFF RESPONSIBLE NAME	POSITION
Increase word recognition to 3.0	Complete Word Drill on Dolch Lists 1 and 2	Brigance Word Recognition Lists 2nd grade level completion	1/2 hr. instruct in resource room	2/26/87 5/29/87	Dolch word Cards Computer game "Word Review"	Mary White	Resource Teacher
Increase reading comprehension to 2.5	Complete SRA series 2nd level	Woodcock Johnson perform at 2nd grade level	1 hr. instruct in resource room	2/26/87 5/29/87	SRA Series Scholastic Scope Magazine	Mary White	Resource Teacher
Increase spelling skill to 2.5	Complete 2nd level of "Spelling Sounds"	T.O.W.L. spell at 2.5 level on the spelling section	1/2 hr. instruct in resource room	2/26/87 5/29/87	Speak – White Spell Kit	Mary White	Resource Teacher
Articulate r-blends correctly	Articulate /Ar/ and /Gr/ correctly	Therapist and teacher observation of daily speech	1 hr./wk. speech therapy	2/26/87 5/29/87		Suzanne Martin	Speech therapist

dent's progress compared to the IEP objectives. This review determines not only the student's progress toward objectives, but also the need for modifying the plan and supplying further special services. A critical aspect of this review is documenting either the movement of a student to a more or less restrictive environment or the student's release from all special educational services.

Recommendations for major changes in the IEP, including placement (for example, to a more or less restrictive environment), is the multidisciplinary team's responsibility. However, all those involved in implementing the student's IEP are likely to be involved in this review. For example, among the many pieces of information that must be gathered prior to a major change in a student's placement are:

☐ The number of instructional options that have been attempted, including those within the regular classroom.
☐ The appropriateness of the long-term and short-range educational objectives, including those written by the regular classroom teacher.
☐ The reliability, validity, and accuracy of the testing that led or contributed to a review of the student's current placement, including testing completed within the regular classroom.

In each of these areas, data contributed by you may be critical, because you may be in the most advantageous position to assess the student's everyday performance. Here, as elsewhere in implementing PL 94–142, your data will directly reflect your effectiveness in the regular classroom.

Instructional Strategies for Handicapped Learners

Several of the previously described service responsibilities required by PL 94–142 (e.g., implementation of the IEP and provisions of individualized instruction) involve the direct instruction of the handicapped learner in the regular classroom. Many approaches to such instruction have been and currently are being used. The following suggestions have been found particularly useful by regular classroom teachers.

Encourage Self-Management Skills. One of the first things you will notice about some handicapped learners is their lack of self-management skills. Many low-achieving students consistently use poor organizational strategies: they may work impulsively, hurriedly, and fail to accurately perceive and gauge time, and they may not adequately judge and search for needed information. Part of your role as teacher of the handicapped in the regular classroom is to encourage self-management skills that can lead to greater independence and task completion. This can be accomplished through one or more of the following:

1. The use of study guides that present to the handicapped learner your instructional objectives, the specific assignment you want accomplished, and timelines for completion.
2. Topical outlines that show the learner the sequence in which you will cover content in the workbook or class presentation.

3. Technical vocabularies and glossaries that provide definitions for the more difficult words and concepts to be used.
4. Brief summaries of the lesson that emphasize its most important points.

Each of these teaching aids can assist the learner to better manage the learning task, making task completion more likely.

Use Peer Tutoring. This approach often is indispensable for teaching the handicapped learner in the regular classroom because your time may not permit dealing directly with the handicapped learner without neglecting other students. Of course, this does not mean that peer tutoring can be used to avoid the responsibility for teaching the handicapped. But if you prepare precise instructional objectives, if you carefully select and train tutors from among your regular students, and if you choose the tutors for compatibility and knowledge level, this practice can be an important adjunct to other strategies for teaching the handicapped. It can be especially effective when you have a master list on which specific target skills are identified and from which the tutor works in a detailed and systematic manner. However, it is important to select tutors not only for their knowledge of the material to be covered and ability to communicate, but also for their sincerity and commitment toward helping the handicapped learner.

Have Handicapped and Nonhandicapped Learn from Each Other. A primary purpose of PL 94–142 is to bring handicapped and nonhandicapped students together so they can learn from each other. The nonhandicapped learner may discover just how "average" a handicapped learner is, and the handicapped learner may derive benefits from listening to and learning from someone having different experiences and perspectives.

These benefits are never more obvious than when heterogeneous groups of handicapped and nonhandicapped learners are formed explicitly on the basis of their *differences* in skill and ability level. These heterogeneous groups can lead to the more-able students spontaneously taking responsibility for checking the work of the handicapped learners, correcting their errors, reviewing key concepts, and probing for additional responses. They also can provide the social and intellectual interaction conducive to cooperative learning.

Use Learning Centers. Sometimes abused and misunderstood, learning centers function much like peer tutoring and heterogeneous groupings when they are carefully thought out and made relevant to your instructional objectives. That is, they can provide valuable instruction to the handicapped learner without your having to neglect the more-able learners in the classroom. Centers of instructional resources that include books, audiovisual aids, arts and crafts, graphic illustrations, exercises, study guides, topical outlines, and vocabulary lists allow students to work independently and at their own pace. These tools also give learners an opportunity to learn through different modalities (visual, auditory, tactile), and can be planned in ways that provide immediate feedback. These are all key elements to successfully teaching the handicapped.

Use a Less Formal Classroom Arrangement. The arrangement of the classroom itself is an important aspect of teaching handicapped learners. Engagement in the learning process, one of the key teaching behaviors, can be either promoted or restricted by classroom arrangement and organization. Traditional arrangements place the teacher's desk at the front of the classroom and student desks in formal rows extending outward. This arrangement conveys a teacher-centered classroom in which lectures, supervision, control, and tests are the most predominant student expectations.

Unfortunately, this arrangement also suggests that all of your students will learn in the same way. When more than a few of your learners are handicapped or depart from the norm in your classroom in any other way (e.g., are gifted or LEP), a more flexible use of classroom space may be called for. A less formal arrangement allows more freedom of movement for those who may wish to benefit from a learning center, independent study carrel, computer terminal, or audiovisual library. It also can more readily accommodate group projects, a heterogeneous grouping of students, and peer tutoring. However, because a less structured classroom arrangement can create more noise and movement, try making only one or two areas of the classroom into a less structured format as an initial first step or a necessary compromise.

Use Microcomputer Software. By some estimates, well over a million microcomputers are used in classrooms today, and this number is increasing each year. The microcomputer's capacity not only to ease your administrative burden but also to actually teach parts of the curriculum has been well demonstrated. To lessen the demands on you, particularly in teaching the handicapped, considerable microcomputer software has been developed for individualized instruction, developing IEPs, testing, and reporting the performance of the handicapped learner.

Use of the computer in the regular classroom can substantially lessen the sometimes overwhelming paperwork entailed in teaching heterogeneous ability groups. You may want to use the computer to provide remediation in critical skill areas, because this is where much of the available computer software is focused. There are programs that instruct in remedial mathematics and spelling, that teach verbs and how to use them in sentences, that correct misspelled words, and that even provide an analysis of common writing errors. You can become familiar with the most current versions of these and other software programs through your school's special education coordinator.

SUMMING UP

This chapter introduced you to slow, gifted and talented, bilingual, and handicapped learners. Its main points were:

1. The advantages of categorizing learners include the assistance they provide for:
   - Dispensing state and federal funds that often are earmarked for specific types of learners.

- Developing and organizing instructional materials, texts, and media appropriate for certain types of learners.
- Training and assigning the most qualified instructional staff to teach certain types of learners.

2. The disadvantages of categorizing learners include the fact that variation within learner catego-

ries can exceed variation between categories, and learners may be ineligible for membership in one group due to their membership in another group.

3. A slow learner is a student who cannot learn at the same pace as the majority when using instructional resources, texts, workbooks, and learning materials that have been designated for the majority of students in your classroom.

4. It has been estimated that up to 20% of all students attending school today are slow learners in one subject or another.

5. Slow learners require more than the usual variation in pacing, presentation method, classroom climate, and instructional materials to keep engaged in the learning process.

6. Slow learners usually have deficiencies in the basic skills of reading, writing, and mathematics, difficulty in comprehending abstract ideas, and unsystematic work habits. These deficiencies make instructional lessons that are geared to the average student too difficult for the slow learner.

7. Compensatory teaching is an instructional approach that alters the presentation of content by reorganizing it, transmitting it by way of alternate modalities, and supplementing it with additional learning resources, with the aim of circumventing a student's fundamental weakness or deficiency.

8. Remedial teaching is an instructional approach that uses techniques and practices specifically chosen to eliminate known deficiencies or weaknesses.

9. Some instructional strategies for addressing the learning needs of the slow learner are:
   □ Developing lessons around the interests, needs, and experiences of the student.
   □ Frequently varying instructional techniques (e.g., switching from lecture to discussion to seatwork).
   □ Incorporating audio and visual materials into lessons that match the strongest learning modalities of your learners.
   □ Developing original worksheets and exercises when existing materials are too difficult or uninteresting to the slow learner.
   □ Modifying the pace of instruction to meet the optimal learning rate of the individual student.
   □ Making peer tutors available for students who need remediation.

   □ Encouraging oral expression, especially for those limited in writing ability.
   □ Providing study aids and advance organizers to alert students to important content or issues.
   □ Teaching notetaking, outlining, and listening.

10. The preparation and time required to teach the gifted may not be measurably less than for teaching any other type of learner—and may be more.

11. Among the behavioral characteristics for defining giftedness are intelligence, achievement, creativity, and task persistence.

12. Variations in the use of these behavioral characteristics to define giftedness have created considerable diversity, both among the types of students classified as gifted and in the instructional programs designed to meet their needs.

13. Some instructional strategies for addressing the learning needs of the gifted learner are to:
   □ Allow students to investigate some topics of their own choosing, making them participants in the design of their own learning.
   □ Plan instructional activities that involve group work, such as brainstorming sessions, group discussions, panels, peer interviews, and debates.
   □ Plan instructional lessons that include individual and small group investigations of real-life problems.
   □ Pose challenging problems that allow the learner to make key decisions about what is important for a solution.
   □ Test and question in a manner that draws out knowledge and understanding and requires more than a verbally fluent response.

14. Approximately five million students—about 10% of the entire school-age population in this country—have a primary language other than English.

15. Bilingual education refers to a mix of instruction through the medium of two languages. Although the word *bilingual* implies proficiency in two languages, it more often applies to students with limited English proficiency (LEP), who range between an inability to express themselves at all in English (either orally or in writing) to marginal proficiency in English.

16. Different approaches to bilingual education include:
   □ The transition approach, which uses the native language and culture of the learner only to the extent necessary to learn English.

☐ The maintenance approach, which in addition to encouraging English language proficiency endorses the idea that the learner should become proficient in his or her native language as well.

☐ The restoration approach, which attempts to restore the native language and culture of the bilingual student to its purest and most original form.

☐ The enrichment approach, which not only moves from Spanish to English competence in the shortest possible time but also emphasizes Spanish culture and heritage.

17. Some instructional strategies for addressing the learning needs of the bilingual learner in the regular classroom are:

☐ Emphasize forms of communication that use pictures, graphs, and illustrations to supplement teaching objectives.

☐ Emphasize the acquisition of facts and their retention in visual, concrete ways.

☐ Emphasize group achievement more than the competitive aspects of individual achievement.

☐ Adapt instructional materials to the teaching level of your students.

☐ Know the language ability level and achievement level of your learners and select special materials accordingly.

☐ Understand and use cultural differences to enhance the overall learning environment and educational experience.

18. Some of the special education functions mandated by PL 94–142 that may involve the regular classroom teacher include child identification, individual child assessment, development of the individual educational plan (IEP), individualized instruction, and a review of the IEP.

19. Some instructional strategies for addressing the learning needs of the handicapped child in the regular classroom include:

☐ Teaching of self-management skills that can increase the student's ability to learn independently.

☐ Use of peer tutoring to teach a specific list of targeted skills.

☐ Use of heterogeneous groups composed of both handicapped and nonhandicapped students to provide the social and intellectual instruction conducive to cooperative learning.

☐ Use of instructional resource (learning) centers to allow students to work independently at their own pace.

☐ Use of a less structured classroom arrangement to promote group projects, heterogeneous grouping, and peer tutoring.

☐ Use of the microcomputer to teach basic skills and content.

FOR DISCUSSION AND PRACTICE

1. Explain in your own words what is meant by the phrase "variation in behavior occurring within a category of learners may be greater than the variation found between categories of learners." Using the IQ categories of *average* and *more-able,* give an example illustrating your answer.

*2. Give three advantages of categorizing students by learning type.

*3. In your own words, give a practical, working definition of a slow learner in your classroom.

4. What is one source of data a school district probably would use to assign a student to a class of less-able learners?

*5. Identify the difference between compensatory and remedial teaching and give an example of each, using content from your teaching area.

*6. What are the four behaviors from which giftedness is most likely to be determined?

*7. What would be one argument against the exclusive use of IQ in selecting students for a gifted program?

*8. Give four different signs of creativity that might be used in determining a student's eligibility for a gifted and talented program.

*9. Give four different signs of task persistence that might be used in determining a student's eligibility for a gifted and talented program.

*10. Describe the language proficiency of a learner who has limited English proficiency (LEP).

*11. What is a balanced bilingual?

*12. Contrast the structured immersion method with the transitional method for teaching the bilingual student.

*13. In your own words, how do the requirements contained within PL 94–142 affect the regular classroom teacher?

*14. Identify nine categories of handicapping conditions which make a student eligible for special education services.

*15. Describe the difference between a slow learner and a learning-disabled learner.

———————

*Answers to asterisked questions (*) in this and the other chapters are in Appendix B.

SUGGESTED READINGS

Algozzine, B., & Ysseldyke, J. E. (1982). *Critical issues in special and remedial education.* Boston: Houghton Mifflin.
Based on a large body of research, this book explores a number of key concerns to educators who work with students who exhibit learning problems.

Baca, L. M., & Cervantes, H. T. (1984). *The bilingual special education interface.* Santa Clara, CA: Times Mirror/Mosby.
An orientation to the historical background, legal basis, and practical implementation of bilingual services and bilingual special education.

Bloom, B. S. (1982). *Human interactions and school learning.* New York: McGraw-Hill.
The author explores the notion that slow learners have a learning capacity commensurate with that of average learners if only they are instructed at the appropriate pace using mastery learning techniques.

Coleman, M. C. (1986). *Behavior disorder: Theory and practice.* Englewood Cliffs, NJ: Prentice-Hall.
An introductory text on behavior disorders that presents a combination of theory and practical guidelines for classroom teachers.

Dembo, M. H. (1981). *Teaching for learning: Applying educational psychology in the classroom* (2nd ed.). Glenview, IL: Scott, Foresman.
A comprehensive and practical overview of educational theory which provides a basis for understanding educational adaptations for special learners.

Gearheart, B. R., & Weishahn, M. W. (1984). *The exceptional student in the regular classroom.* Santa Clara, CA: Times Mirror/Mosby.
Overviews the legal basis for special services and programming strategies for mainstreamed exceptional students.

Torrance, E. (1981). Predicting the creativity of elementary schoolchildren and the teacher who "made a difference." *Gifted Child Quarterly, 25,* 55–62.
The role of creativity in the performance of the gifted and how instructional strategies can promote creative behavior.

Wang, M. C., & Walberg, H. J. (Eds.). (1985). *Adapting instruction to individual differences.* Berkeley, CA: McCutchan.
A collection of readings that covers the many unintended problems associated with categorizing and separating students into a variety of programs.

14

Evaluating Student Achievement

Some of your strongest childhood and adolescent memories probably include taking tests in school. For that matter, test-taking probably is among the strong impressions from your college experience. If you are like most people who have spent many years in school, you have strong or mixed feelings about tests. In this chapter we will try to dispel some of the discomfort you might feel about them and show how they can be effective tools in your classroom.

Previous chapters focused upon effectively bringing your learners to a greater understanding and comprehension of the material you teach. But how do you know whether you have been effective? You will find out by constructing tests that yield reliable measures of how well your students learn. You need to know how to use test results to measure your learners' attitudes and social behavior and evaluate their products and performance.

In this chapter we introduce key decisions you must make to evaluate and diagnose your learners' achievements. You will need to read more than this intro-ductory chapter to evaluate your students, so Kubiszyn and Borich (1990) is recom-mended for more information on measuring the attitudes and social behavior of your learners and evaluating their products and performance.

NORM-REFERENCED AND CRITERION-REFERENCED TESTS

To evaluate your learners' progress, what type of information do you need? That de-pends on your purpose. Testing can provide two types of information:

1. A student's place or rank compared to other students is revealed by a **norm-referenced test (NRT)**, so named because it compares a student's performance to that of a "norm group" (a large, representative sample of learners). Such information is useful when you need to compare a learn-er's performance to that of others at the same age or grade level.
2. A student's level of proficiency in or mastery of a skill or set of skills is revealed by a **criterion-referenced test (CRT)**, so named because it com-pares student performance with an absolute standard called a *criterion* (such as "75% correct"). Such information helps you decide whether a student needs more instruction to acquire a skill or set of skills.

Figure 14.1 illustrates when to use NRTs and CRTs. As the figure indicates, you always must identify the type of information needed *before* selecting a particular test.

Unfortunately, some teachers know little more about a student after testing than they did before. In our technically oriented society, test scores sometimes have become ends in themselves, without the interpretation of them that is essential for improvement of the learner. In such cases teachers, parents, and others may be quick to denounce a test, often suggesting that such abuse of testing "proves" that test data are useless. In reality, it may only indicate that the teacher who selected the test either failed to identify the specific information needed *before* administering the test or failed to carefully match the test to this purpose.

FIGURE 14.1
Relationships among the purpose of testing, information desired, and the type of test required

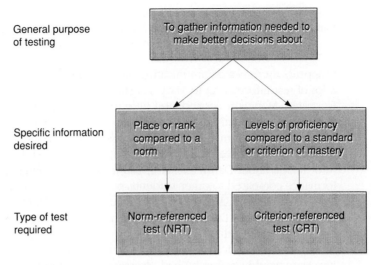

General purpose of testing

Specific information desired

Type of test required

A similar situation can occur when existing test data are inappropriately used or interpreted. An example is this situation, in which counselor John is checking his records when sixth-grade teacher Mary taps on his door:

MARY: I just stopped by to see you about Danny. He's been in remedial classes for the last five years, and now he'll be in my class this year. Mrs. Rodrigues had him last year, and she said you have all the test information on him.

JOHN: Yeah. In fact, I was just reviewing his folder. Danny's Math Cluster score on the Woodstock-Johnson is at the sixth percentile, and his Reading Cluster is at the first percentile. Good luck with him!

MARY: Boy, he sure is low. I guess that's why he's been in the remedial classroom for so long.

JOHN: You've got it!

MARY: Well, really that's about what I was expecting. What about his skill levels?

JOHN: What do you mean?

MARY: You know, his academic skill levels.

JOHN: Oh, his grade levels! Umm, let's see . . . his math grade equivalent is 2.6, and his reading grade equivalent is even lower, 1.7.

MARY: Well . . . that's not really what I need to know. I know he's way below grade level, but I'm wondering about his skills—specific skills, that is. You know, like what words he can read, what phonetic skills he has, if he can subtract two-digit numbers with regrouping . . . things like that.

JOHN: (becoming a bit irritated) Mary, what more do you need than what I've given you? Don't you know how to interpret these scores? Perhaps you should have learned about tests in college.

MARY: (stung and frustrated) John, I *did* learn about tests and I *do* know what those scores mean, but they only compare Danny to other students. I'm not interested in that. I want to know what he *can* and *can't* do, so I can begin teaching him at the proper skill level.

JOHN: (shaking his head) Look, he's at first-grade level in reading and second-grade level in math. Isn't that enough?

MARY: But, what level of mastery has he demonstrated?
JOHN: Mastery? He's years behind! He has mastered very little of anything.
MARY: This has been a very enlightening conversation. Thank you for your time.

It appears there is a communication gap between Mary and John. John has conveyed a lot of test information to Mary, yet she doesn't seem to get much out of it. John is frustrated, Mary is frustrated, and little that will help Danny has been accomplished. What is the problem?

The problem appears to be John's. Mary's questions refer to competencies or mastery of skills. Referring to Figure 14.1, we can conclude that she was interested in information about Danny's *level of proficiency*. But John's answers refer to test performance compared to other students, which means information about Danny's *rank compared to others*. Answers to Mary's questions can come only from a test designed to indicate whether Danny exceeded some standard of performance taken to indicate mastery of some skill.

If a test indicated that Danny could subtract two-digit numbers with regrouping, Mary would say that he had "mastered" this skill if, for example, "80% or more correct" was the criterion for mastery. In other words, he would have exceeded the standard of "80% mastery of subtraction of two-digit numbers with regrouping." Recall that a criterion-referenced test is designed to measure whether a student has mastered a skill, where the definition of mastery depends on an established level or criterion of performance.

But the information John provided was normative or comparative. Danny's grade-equivalent scores allow decisions only involving comparisons between his performance and that of the typical or average performance of learners in a "norm" group. Danny's grade-equivalent score of 1.7 in reading indicates that his reading ability equals that of the average first-grader after seven months in the first grade. It says nothing about which words he knows, nor does it give any information about the process he uses to read new words or how long it takes him to comprehend what he reads or learn the meaning of new words. All this score indicates is that his ability to read is well below that of the average fifth-grader and equivalent to that of an average first-grader after seven months of school.

In short, grade-equivalent scores and other scores obtained from standardized, norm-referenced tests allow only general, comparative decisions, not decisions about mastery of specific skills.

Comparing Norm-Referenced and Criterion-Referenced Tests

As you may have guessed, criterion-referenced tests must be specific to yield information about individual skills. This is both an advantage and a disadvantage. With a specific test of individual skills you can be relatively certain that your students have either mastered or failed to master the skill in question. However, the major disadvantage is that many CRTs would be necessary to make decisions about the multitude of skills taught in the average classroom.

The appropriateness of a given type of test depends on the purpose of testing.
Criterion-referenced tests (CRTs) measure specific skills related to lesson objectives or
unit content, while norm-referenced tests (NRTs) measure skills related to general
categories of achievement and aptitude.

The norm-referenced test, on the other hand, tends to be general. It measures a variety of specific and general skills at once, but cannot measure them thoroughly. Thus, with NRT results, you are not as sure as you would be with CRT results that your students have mastered the individual skills in question. On the other hand, NRT results give you an estimate of ability in a variety of skills much faster than you could achieve with a large number of CRTs. Because of this trade-off in the uses of criterion-referenced and norm-referenced measures, there are situations in which each is appropriate. Determining the appropriateness of a given type of test depends on your purpose in testing.

THE TEST BLUEPRINT

In Chapter 4 we discussed writing and analyzing instructional objectives, including the technique we call a *content-by-behavior blueprint* for writing objectives at different levels of behavioral complexity. In this chapter, we will use an extended version of this same technique (called a test blueprint) for matching test items to your objectives.

The test blueprint ensures that you do not overlook details essential to a good test. More specifically, it ensures that a test will sample learning across the range of (1) content areas covered by your instruction and (2) the cognitive and/or affective processes you consider important. It ensures that your test will include a variety of items that tap different levels of cognitive complexity. Figure 14.2 illustrates a test blueprint for a unit on elementary school mathematics.

A test blueprint is constructed according to the following procedure:

1. Determine the classification of each instructional objective from the categories in Chapter 4.
2. Record the number of items to be constructed for the objective in the cell corresponding to its category.

FIGURE 14.2
Test blueprint for a unit on subtraction without borrowing

Content Outline	Knowledge	Comprehension	Application	Total	Percent
1. The student will discriminate the subtraction sign from the addition sign.	1			1	4%
2. The student will discriminate addition problems from subtraction problems.	2			2	8%
3. The student will discriminate correctly solved subtraction problems from incorrectly solved subtraction problems.		4		4	16%
4. The student will solve correctly single-digit subtraction problems.			6	6	24%
5. The student will solve correctly subtraction problems with double-digit numerators and single-digit denominators.			6	6	24%
6. The student will solve correctly double-digit subtraction problems.			6	6	24%
Total	3	4	18	25	
Percent	12%	16%	72%		100%

3. Repeat steps 1 and 2 for each objective in the outline.
4. Total the items for the instructional objective, and record the number in the *Total* row.
5. Repeat steps 1 through 4 for each topic.
6. Total the number of items falling into each category and record the number at the bottom of the table.
7. Compute the column and row percentages by dividing each total by the number of items in the test.

Constructing a test blueprint before preparing a test ensures that you have adequately sampled the content area and have accurately matched test items to your instructional objectives.

OBJECTIVE TEST ITEMS

Your test blueprint may call for objective test items. Objective test items have one of four formats: true-false, matching, multiple-choice, and completion (short-answer). In this section we will consider some characteristics of each that can make your objective test items more effective.

Your first decision after completing the test blueprint will be to choose a format, or a combination of formats, for your test. The way you wrote the objectives may have predetermined the format, but in many instances you will have a choice among several item formats. For example, consider the following objectives and item formats.

True-False Items

True-false items are popular because they are quick and easy to write, or at least they seem to be. True-false items really do take less time to write than good objective items of any other format, but *good* true-false items are not so easy to prepare.

As you know from your own experience, every true-false item, regardless of how well or poorly written, gives the student a 50% chance of guessing correctly, even without reading the item! In other words, on a 50-item true-false test, we would expect individuals who were totally unfamiliar with the content being tested to answer about 25 items correctly. Fortunately, ways exist to reduce the effects of guessing. Some of these are:

1. Encourage *all* students to guess when they do not know the correct answer. Because it is virtually impossible to prevent certain students from guessing, encouraging all students to guess should equalize the effects of guessing. The test scores will then reflect a more or less equal "guessing factor" *plus* the actual level of each student's knowledge. This also will prevent test-wise students from having an unfair advantage over nontest-wise students.

2. Require revision of statements that are false. In this approach, provide space at the end of the item for students to alter false items to make them true. Usually the student first is asked to underline or circle the false part of the item and then to add the correct wording, as in these examples:

T (F)   High-IQ children <u>always get</u> high grades in school.
          tend to

T (F)   Panama is <u>north</u> of Cuba.
          south

T (F)   <u>September</u> has an extra day during leap year.
          February

With this strategy, full credit is awarded only if the revision is correct. The disadvantage of such an approach is that more test time is required for the same number of items and scoring time is increased.

Here are some suggestions to keep in mind when writing true-false test items:

1. Tell students clearly how to mark *true* or *false* (for example, circle or underline the T or F) before they begin the test. Write this instruction at the top of the test, too.
2. Construct statements that are definitely true or definitely false, without qualifications. If the item is true or false based on someone's opinion, then identify the opinion's source as part of the item—for example, "According to the head of the AFL-CIO, workers' compensation is below desired standards."
3. Keep true and false statements at approximately the same length, and be sure that there are approximately equal numbers of true and false items.
4. Avoid using double-negative statements. They take extra time to decipher and are difficult to interpret. For example, avoid statements, such as "It is not true that addition cannot precede subtraction in algebraic operations."
5. Avoid terms denoting indefinite degree (for example, *large, long time, regularly*), or absolutes (*never, only, always*).
6. Avoid placing items in a systematic pattern that some students might detect (for example, True-True-False-False, TFTF, and so on).
7. Don't take statements directly from the text without first making sure that you are not taking them out of context.

Matching Items

Like true-false, matching items are a popular and convenient testing format. Just like good true-false items, however, good matching items are not easy to write. Imagine you are back in your ninth-grade American history class and the following matching item shows up on your test:

DIRECTIONS: Match A and B

A	B
1. Lincoln	a. President during the twentieth century
2. Nixon	b. Invented the telephone
3. Whitney	c. Delivered the Emancipation Proclamation
4. Ford	d. Only president to resign from office
5. Bell	e. Black civil-rights leader
6. King	f. Invented the cotton gin
7. Washington	g. Our first president
8. Roosevelt	h. Only president elected for more than two terms

See any problems? Compare the problems you identify with the descriptions of faults that follow.

Homogeneity.   The lists are not homogeneous. Column A contains names of presidents, inventors, and a civil-rights leader. Unless specifically taught as a set of related men or ideas, this is too wide a variety for a matching exercise.

Order of Lists.   The lists are reversed—column A should be in place of column B, and column B should be in place of column A. As the exercise is now written, the student reads a name and then has to read through all or many of the more lengthy descriptions to find the answer, a much more time-consuming process. It also is a good idea to introduce some sort of order—chronological, numerical, or alphabetical—to your list of options. This saves the student time.

Easy Guessing.   Notice that there are equal numbers of options and descriptions. This increases the chances of guessing correctly through elimination. If there are at least three more options than descriptions, the chance of guessing correctly is reduced to one in four.

Poor Directions.   The instructions are much too brief. Matching directions should specify the basis for matching:

> Column A contains brief descriptions of historical events. Column B contains the names of U.S. presidents. Indicate who was president when the historical event took place by placing the appropriate letter to the left of the number in column A.

Multiple Correct Responses.   The description "president during the twentieth century" has three defensible answers: Nixon, Ford, and Roosevelt. And, did you mean Henry Ford, inventor of the Model T automobile, or Gerald Ford? Always include first and last names to avoid ambiguities. Here is a corrected version of these matching items:

DIRECTIONS: Column A describes events associated with United States presidents. Indicate which name in Column B matches each event by placing the appropriate letter to the left of the number of column A. Each name may be used only once.

Column A	Column B
_____ 1. Only president not elected to office.	a. Abraham Lincoln
_____ 2. Delivered the Emancipation Proclamation.	b. Richard Nixon
_____ 3. Only president to resign from office.	c. Gerald Ford
_____ 4. Only president elected for more than two terms.	d. George Washington
_____ 5. Our first president.	e. Franklin Roosevelt
	f. Theodore Roosevelt
	g. Thomas Jefferson
	h. Woodrow Wilson

Notice that we now have complete directions, more options than descriptions, homogeneous lists (all items in Column A are about U.S. presidents and all the items in Column B are names of presidents), and we have made the alternatives unambiguous.

Suggestions for Writing Matching Items.

1. Keep short and homogeneous both the descriptions list and the options list—they should fit together on the same page. Title the lists to ensure homogeneity (e.g., Column A, Column B) and arrange the descriptions and options in some logical order.
2. Make sure that all the options are plausible "distractors" (wrong answer choices) for each description to ensure homogeneity of lists.
3. The descriptions list should contain the longer phrases or statements, while the options should consist of short phrases, words, or symbols.
4. Number each description (1, 2, 3, etc.) and letter each option (a, b, c, etc.).
5. Include more options than descriptions, or some that match more than one, or both.
6. In the directions, specify the basis for matching and whether options can be used more than once.

Multiple-Choice Items

Another popular item format is the multiple-choice question. Multiple-choice tests are more common in high school and college than in elementary school. Multiple-choice items are unique among objective test items because they enable you to measure higher-level cognitive objectives. When writing multiple-choice items, be careful not to give away answers by inadvertently providing students with clues in the following ways.

Stem Clue. The statement portion of a multiple-choice item is called the *stem*, and the answer choices are called *options* or *response alternatives*. A stem clue occurs when the same word or a close derivative occurs in both the stem and an option, thereby cluing the test taker to the correct answer. For example:

The free-floating structures within the cell that synthesize protein are called _____ .

a. chromosomes

b. lysosomes

c. mitochondria

d. free ribosomes

In this item the word *free* in the option is identical to *free* in the stem. Thus, the wise test taker has a good chance of answering the item correctly without mastery of the content being measured.

Grammatical Clue.   Consider this item:

U.S. Grant was an _____ .

a. president

b. man

c. alcoholic

d. general

Most students would pick up on the easy grammatical clue in the stem. The article *an* eliminates options a, b, and d, because *"an* man," *"an* president," or *"an* general" are ungrammatical. Option c is the only one that forms a grammatical sentence. A way to eliminate the grammatical clue is to replace *an* with *a/an*. Similar examples are *is/are, was/were, his/her,* and so on. Alternatively, place the article (or verb, or pronoun) in the options list:

Christopher Columbus came to America in _____ .

a. a car

b. a boat

c. an airplane

d. a balloon

Redundant Words/Unequal Length.   Two very common faults in multiple-choice construction are illustrated in this item:

When 53 Americans were held hostage in Iran, _____ .

a. the United States did nothing to free them

b. the United States declared war on Iran

c. the United States first attempted to free them by diplomatic means and later attempted a rescue

d. the United States expelled all Iranian students

The phrase "the United States" is included in each option. To save space and time, add it to the stem: "When 53 Americans were held hostage in Iran, the United States _____ ." Second, the length of options could be a giveaway. Multiple-choice item writers have a tendency to include more information in the correct option than in the incorrect options. Test-wise students know that the longer option is the correct one more often than not. Avoid making correct answers more than one and a half times the length of incorrect options.

All of the Above/None of the Above.   In general, use "none of the above" sparingly. Some item writers use "none of the above" only when there is no clearly correct option presented. However, students catch on to this practice and guess that "none of the above" is the correct answer without knowledge of the content being measured. Also, at times it may be justified to use multiple correct answers, such as "both a and c" or "both b and c." Again, use such options sparingly, because inconsistencies can easily exist among alternatives that logically eliminate some from consideration. Avoid using "all of the above," because test items should *encourage* discrimination, not discourage it.

Higher-Level Multiple-Choice Questions

A good multiple-choice item is the most time-consuming type of objective test item to write. Unfortunately, most multiple-choice items also are written at the knowledge level in the taxonomy of educational objectives. As a new item writer, you will tend to write items at this level, but you need to write some multiple-choice items to measure *higher*-level cognitive objectives as well.

First, write some of your *objectives* to measure comprehension, application, analysis, or evaluation. This ensures that your items will be at the higher-than-knowledge level. Following are some suggestions to make your higher-level multiple-choice questions more effective.

Use Pictorial, Graphical, or Tabular Stimuli.   Pictures, drawings, graphs, and tables require the student to think at least at the application level in the taxonomy of educational objectives and may involve even higher cognitive processes. Also, such stimuli often can generate several higher-level multiple-choice items rather than just one.

Use Analogies to Show Relationships Among Terms.   To answer analogies correctly, students must not only be familiar with the terms, but be able to *understand* how the terms relate to each other. For example:

Physician is to humans as veterinarian is to _____ .

a. fruits

b. animals

c. minerals

d. vegetables

Require Application of Principles or Procedures. To test whether students comprehend the implications of a procedure or principle, have them use the principle or procedure with new information, or in a novel way. This requires them to do more than just follow the steps in solving a problem. It has them demonstrate an ability to go beyond the context within which they originally learned a principle or procedure. Consider this example, from a division lesson that relied on computation of grade-point averages as examples:

> After filling his car's tank with 18 gallons of gasoline, Mr. Watts said to his son, "We've come 450 miles since the last fill-up. What kind of gas mileage are we getting?" Which of the following is the best answer?
>
> a. 4 miles per gallon
>
> b. 25 miles per gallon
>
> c. Between 30 and 35 miles per gallon
>
> d. It can't be determined from the information given.

Suggestions for Writing Multiple-Choice Items.

1. Be sure that there is one and only one correct or clearly best answer.
2. Be sure all wrong answer choices ("distractors") are plausible. Eliminate unintentional grammatical clues, and keep the length and form of all the answer choices equal. Rotate the position of the correct answer from item to item randomly.
3. Use negative questions or statements only if the knowledge being tested requires it. In most cases it is more important for the student to know what the correct answer *is* rather than what it is not.
4. Include three to five options (two to four distractors plus one correct answer) to optimize testing for knowledge rather than encouraging guessing. It is not necessary to provide additional distractors for an item simply to maintain the same number of distractors for each item.
5. Use the option "none of the above" sparingly and only when all the answers can be classified unequivocally as wrong.
6. Avoid using "all of the above." It usually is the correct answer and makes the item too easy for students who have only partial information.

Completion Items

Like true-false items, completion items are relatively easy to write. The first tests constructed by classroom teachers and taken by students often are completion tests. Like items of all other formats, there are good and poor completion items. Here are some suggestions for completion items:

1. Require a single-word answer or a brief, definite statement. Avoid items so indefinite that they may be logically answered by several terms:
   Poor Item: World War II ended in _____ .
   Better Item: World War II ended in the year _____ .

TABLE 14.1
Advantages and disadvantages of various objective-item formats

True-False Tests	
Advantages	*Disadvantages*
Tend to be short, so more material can be covered than with any other item format; thus, use T–F items when extensive content has been covered.	Tend to emphasize rote memorization of knowledge (although complex questions sometimes can be asked using T–F items).
Faster to construct (but avoid creating an item by taking statements out of context or slightly modifying them).	They assume an unequivocally true or false answer (it is unfair to make students guess at your criteria for evaluating the truth of a statement).
Scoring is easier (tip: provide a "T" and "F" for them to circle, because a student's handwritten "T" or "F" can be hard to decipher).	Allow and may even encourage a high degree of guessing (generally, longer examinations compensate for this).

Matching Tests	
Advantages	*Disadvantages*
Simple to construct and score.	Tend to ask trivial information.
Ideal for measuring associations between facts.	Emphasize memorization.
Can be more efficient than multiple-choice questions because they avoid repetition of options in measuring association.	Most commercial answer sheets can accommodate only five options, thus limiting the size of a matching item.
Reduce the effects of guessing.	

2. Be sure the item poses a problem. A direct question often is better than an incomplete statement because it provides more structure for an answer:
   Poor Item: What do you think about a main character in the story "Lilies of the Field?"
   Better Item: The main character in the story "Lilies of the Field" was
   _____ .

3. Be sure the answer is factually correct. Precisely word the question in relation to the concept or fact being tested. For example, can the answer be found in the text, workbook, or class notes taken by students?

4. Omit only key words; don't eliminate so many elements that the sense of the content is impaired:
   Poor Item: The _____ type of test item usually is graded _____ than the _____ type.
   Better Item: The multiple-choice type of test item usually is graded more objectively that the _____ type.

5. Word the statement so the blank is near the end. This prevents awkward sentences.

6. If the problem requires a numerical answer, indicate the units in which it is to be expressed (for example, pounds, ounces, minutes).

TABLE 14.1 *continued*

Multiple-Choice Tests	
Advantages	*Disadvantages*
Versatile in measuring objectives, from the knowledge level to the evaluation level.	Time consuming to write.
Since writing is minimal, considerable course material can be sampled quickly.	If not carefully written, can have more than one defensible correct answer.
Scoring is highly objective, requiring only a count of correct responses.	
Can be written so students must discriminate among options varying in correctness, avoiding the absolute judgments of T–F tests.	
Reduce effects of guessing.	
Amenable to statistical analysis, so you can determine which items are ambiguous or too difficult (see Kubiszyn and Borich, 1990, Chapter 8.)	

Completion Tests	
Advantages	*Disadvantages*
Question construction is relatively easy.	Encourage a low level of response complexity.
Guessing is reduced because the question requires a specific response.	Can be difficult to score (the stem must be general enough to not communicate the answer, leading unintentionally to multiple defensible answers).
Less time is needed to complete than multiple-choice items, so more content can be covered.	Very short answers tend to measure recall of specific facts, names, places, and events instead of more complex behaviors.

Advantages and Disadvantages of Objective-Item Formats

Table 14.1 summarizes the advantages and disadvantages of each of the preceding objective item formats.

ESSAY TEST ITEMS

In this section, we will explain what an essay item is, describe the two major types, and provide suggestions for writing them. In essay items, the student supplies, rather than selects, the correct answer. It demands that the student compose a response, often extensive, to a question for which no *single* response or pattern of responses can be cited as correct to the exclusion of all others. The accuracy and quality of such a response often can be judged only by a person skilled in the subject area.

Like objective test items, essay items may be well constructed or poorly constructed. The well-constructed essay item tests complex cognitive skills by requiring the student to organize, integrate, and synthesize knowledge, to use information to solve novel problems, or to be original and innovative in problem solving. The poorly constructed essay item may require the student to do no more than recall information as it was presented in the textbook or lecture. Worse, the poorly constructed essay item may not inform the learner what is required for a satisfactory response.

Extended-Response Items

An essay item that allows the student to determine the length and complexity of a response is called an *extended-response* essay item. This type of essay is most useful at the analysis, synthesis, or evaluation levels of cognitive complexity. Because of the length of this type of item and the time required to organize and express the response, the extended-response item is sometimes better as a term-paper assignment or take-home test. The extended-response essay often is of value more in assessing communication ability than in assessing achievement. For example:

> Compare and contrast the presidential administrations of George Bush and Ronald Reagan. Consider economic, social, and military policies. Avoid taking a position in support of either president. Your response will be graded on objectivity, accuracy, organization, and clarity.

Restricted-Response Items

An essay item that poses a specific problem for which the student must recall proper information, organize it in a suitable manner, derive a defensible conclusion, and express it within the limits of the posed problem is called a *restricted-response* essay item. The statement of the problem specifies response limitations to guide the student in responding and to provide evaluation criteria for scoring. For example:

> List the major similarities and differences between U.S. participation in the Korean War and World War II, being sure to consider political, military, economic, and social factors. Limit your answer to one page. Your score will depend on accuracy, organization, and conciseness.

When Should Essay Questions Be Used?

Although each situation must be considered individually, some lend themselves to essay items. For example:

1. The instructional objectives specify high-level cognitive processes—they require supplying information rather than simply recognizing information. These processes often cannot be measured with objective items.

2. Only a few tests or items need to be graded. If you have 30 students and design a test with six extended-response essays, you will spend a great deal of time scoring. Use essays when class size is small, or use only one or two essays in conjunction with objective items.

3. Test security is a consideration. If you are afraid test items will be passed on to future students, it is better to use an essay test. In general, a good essay test takes less time to construct than a good objective test.

Here are some learning outcomes for which essay items may be used:

Analyze relationships

Arrange items in sequence

Compare positions

State necessary assumptions

Identify appropriate conclusions

Explain cause-and-effect relations

Formulate hypotheses

Organize data to support a viewpoint

Point out strengths and weaknesses

Produce a solution to a problem

Integrate data from several sources

Evaluate the quality or worth of an item, product, or action

Create an original solution, arrangement, or procedure.

Suggestions for Writing and Using Essay Items

1. Have clearly in mind what mental processes you want the student to use before starting to write the question. Refer to the mental processes required at the various levels in the taxonomy of educational objectives for the cognitive domain (for example, compare and contrast, create alternatives, make choices among). If you want students to analyze, judge, or think critically, determine what mental processes involve analysis, judgment, or critical thinking.

Poor item: Criticize the following speech by our President.

Better Item: Consider the following presidential speech. Focus on the section dealing with economic policy and discriminate between factual statements and opinion. List these statements separately, label them, and indicate whether each statement is or is not consistent with the President's overall economic policy.

2. Write the question to clearly and unambiguously define the task to the student. Tasks should be explained (a) in the overall instructions preceding the test items and/or (b) in the test items themselves. Include instruc-

tions for the type of writing style desired (for example, scientific vs. prose), whether spelling and grammar will be counted, and whether organization of the response will be an important scoring element. Also, indicate the level of detail and supporting data required.

Poor Item: Discuss the value of behavioral objectives.

Better Item: Behavioral objectives have enjoyed increased popularity in education over the years. In your text and in class the advantages and disadvantages of behavioral objectives have been discussed. Take a position for or against the use of behavioral objectives in education and support your position with at least three of the arguments covered in class or in the text.

3. Start essay questions with such words or phrases as *compare, contrast, give reasons for, give original examples of, predict what would happen if,* and so on. Do not begin with such words as *what, who, when,* and *list,* because these words generally lead to tasks that require only recall of information.

Poor Item: List three reasons behind America's withdrawal from Vietnam.

Better Item: After more than 10 years of involvement, the United States withdrew from Vietnam in 1975. Speculate on what would have happened if America had *not* withdrawn at that time and had *not* increased significantly its military presence above 1972 levels.

4. A question dealing with a controversial issue should ask for, and be evaluated in terms of, the presentation of evidence for a position, rather than the position taken. It is not defensible to demand that a student accept a specific conclusion or solution, but it is reasonable to appraise how well he or she has learned to use the evidence upon which a specific conclusion is based.

Poor Item: What laws should Congress pass to improve the medical care of all citizens in the United States?

Better Item: Some feel that the cost of all medical care should be borne by the federal government. Do you agree or disagree? Support your position with at least three logical arguments.

5. Avoid using optional items. That is, require all students to complete the same items. Allowing students to select 3 of 5, 4 of 7, and so forth decreases the uniformity of the test across all students, which will decrease your basis for comparison among students.

6. Establish reasonable time and/or page limits for each essay item to help the student complete the entire test and to indicate the level of detail you have in mind. Indicate such limits either in the statement of the problem or close to the number of the question.

7. Restrict the use of essays to those learning outcomes that cannot be satisfactorily measured by objective items.

8. Be sure each question relates to an instructional objective. Check your test blueprint to see if the content of the essay item is represented.

Advantages and Disadvantages of the Essay Item

Here are several advantages:

☐ To the extent that instructional objectives require the student to organize information to solve a problem, analyze and evaluate information, or perform other high-level cognitive skills, the essay test is an appropriate assessment tool.

☐ Although essay tests are relatively easy to construct, do not construct the items haphazardly. Consult your behavioral objectives blueprint, identify only the topics and objectives that can best be assessed by essays, and build items around those—and only those.

☐ If developing communication skills is an instructional objective, you can test it with an essay item. However, this assumes that you have spent time teaching communication pertinent to the course area, including special vocabulary and writing styles, as well as providing practice with arguments for and against controversial points.

☐ Because no options are provided, the student must supply rather than select the proper response, reducing guessing.

Here are several disadvantages:

☐ It is tedious for you to wade through pages and pages of student handwriting. Also, it is difficult not to let spelling and grammatical mistakes influence grading or to let superior communication abilities cover up for incomplete comprehension of facts.

☐ It is difficult to maintain a common set of criteria for all students. Two persons may disagree on the correct answer for any essay item; even the same person will disagree on the correctness of one answer read on two separate occasions.

☐ Fewer essay items can be attempted than with objective items. Also, students become fatigued faster with essay items than with objective items.

☐ It is no secret that longer essays tend to be graded higher than short essays, regardless of content! As a result, students may bluff.

The first two limitations—time required for grading and maintaining consistent objectivity—are serious disadvantages. Fortunately, there are some ways to make the task of scoring essays more manageable and reliable.

Scoring Essays

As mentioned, essays are difficult to score consistently across individuals. That is, the *same* essay answer may be given an A by one scorer and a B or C by another scorer. Or, the same answer may be graded A on one occasion, but B or C on another occasion by the *same* scorer! As disturbing and surprising as this may seem, these conclusions are supported by research findings (Coffman, 1971). What can you do to avoid such scoring problems?

Write Good Essay Items.   Poorly written questions are one source of scorer inconsistency. Questions that do not specify response length are another. In general, long (for example, three-page) essay responses are more difficult to score consistently than restricted essay responses (say, one page). This is due to student fatigue and subsequent clerical errors, as well as a tendency for grading criteria to vary from response to response, or for that matter, from page to page, or even paragraph to paragraph within the same response.

Use Several Restricted-Response Items.   Rather than a single extended-response item, use several restricted-response items. Writing good items and using restricted-response essays will help improve essay scoring. However, as mentioned, extended-response essays sometimes are desirable or necessary. When they are, use a predetermined scoring scheme.

Use a Predetermined Scoring Scheme.   All too often essays are graded without the scorer having specified in advance what he or she is looking for in a "good" answer. If you do not specify the criteria beforehand, your scoring consistency will be greatly reduced. If these criteria are not readily available (written down) for scoring each question, the criteria themselves may change (you may grade harder or easier after a number of papers, even if the answers do not change). Or, your ability to keep these criteria in mind will be influenced by fatigue, distractions, frame of mind, and so on. Because we all are human, we all are subject to these factors.

Some Criteria for Scoring Higher-Level Essay Items

Following are several criteria that are useful in scoring higher-level essay items.

Content.   Although essays are used less to measure factual knowledge than thinking processes, the content of an essay can and should be scored specifically for its prevision and accuracy, in addition to its organization and use (and tell your students if you are doing so).

Organization.   Does the essay have an introduction, body, and conclusion? If you are looking for these characteristics, let the students know that you will be scoring for organization. Beyond these three general organizational criteria, you may want to develop specific criteria for your class. For example: Are recommendations, inferences, and hypotheses supported? Is it apparent which supporting statements go with which recommendation? Do progressions and sequences follow a logical or chronological development? You also should decide on a spelling and grammar policy and develop these criteria, alerting the students *before* they take the test.

Process.   If your essay item tests at the application level or above, the most important criteria for scoring are those that reflect the extent to which the process has been carried out. Each process (application, analysis, synthesis, and evaluation) results in a solution, recommendation, or decision, or some reasons to justify or support the final decision, and so on. Thus, the process criteria should assess both the adequacy of the solution or decision and the reasons behind it.

Accuracy/Reasonableness. Will it work? Have the correct analytical dimensions been identified? You ultimately must decide what is accurate, but be prepared for unexpected, yet accurate, responses.

Completeness/Internal Consistency. Does the essay deal adequately with the problem presented? Again, your judgment will weigh heavily, but points should be logically related and cover the topics as fully as required.

Originality/Creativity. Again, it is up to you to recognize the unexpected and give credit for it. That is, expect some students to develop new ways of conceptualizing questions, and award credit for such conceptualizations when appropriate.

Tell students about any or all of the preceding criteria. Once they know how you are going to score the test, they can prepare better and more defensible responses.

PACKAGING THE TEST

After all the care and work you put into developing good test items, follow through and package the test properly for the sake of your learners and your own professionalism. As you study the following guidelines, you probably will recall seeing every one of them violated at some time on tests you have taken. Start off right by attending to these details.

Guidelines for Packaging

Here are guidelines for packaging your test:

- ☐ Group together items of similar format.
- ☐ Arrange test items from easy to hard.
- ☐ Properly space items.
- ☐ Keep items and options on the same page.
- ☐ Place illustrations near the descriptive material.
- ☐ Check for randomness in the answer key.
- ☐ Decide how students will record their answers.
- ☐ Provide space for the test taker's name and the date.
- ☐ Check test directions for clarity.
- ☐ Proofread the test.

Let us now briefly consider each of these.

Group Together All Items of Similar Format. If you have all true-false items grouped together, all completion items together, and so on, then students will not have to "shift gears" and adjust to new formats. This enables them to cover more items than if item formats were mixed throughout the test. Also, by grouping items of a given format together, only one set of directions is necessary for each type of format—another time-saver.

Arrange Test Items from Easy to Hard.   Arranging test items according to level of difficulty will enable more students to answer the first few items correctly, thereby building confidence and hopefully reducing test anxiety.

Space the Items for Easy Reading.   Provide enough blank space between items so that each is distinctly separate from others. When items are crowded together, students may inadvertently perceive a word, phrase, or line from an adjacent item as being part of the item they are focused upon.

Keep Items and Options on the Same Page.   Few things aggravate a test taker more than having to turn the page to read the options for multiple-choice or matching items, or to complete reading a true-false or completion item. To avoid this, do not begin an item at the bottom of the page unless you will have at least an inch left *after completing* the item. Not only does this eliminate carrying over items onto the next page, it also minimizes the likelihood that the last line or two of the item will be cut off when you photocopy the test.

Position Illustrations Near Descriptions.   Place diagrams, maps, or other supporting material immediately above the item or items to which they refer. In other words, if items 9, 10, and 11 refer to a map of South America, locate the map above items 9, 10, and 11 —not between 9 and 10 or between 10 and 11 and not below them. Also, if possible, keep any such stimuli and related questions on the same page to save the test taker time.

Check Your Answer Key for Randomness.   Be sure the correct answers follow a random pattern. Avoid true-false patterns such as TFTF or TTFF and multiple-choice patterns such as DCBADCBA. At the same time, see that your correct answers are distributed about equally between true and false and among multiple-choice options.

Determine How Students Record Answers.   Decide whether your students will record their answers on the test paper or on a separate answer sheet. In the lower elementary grades, it is best for students to record answers on the test papers. In the upper elementary and secondary grades, separate answer sheets can be used to facilitate scoring accuracy and to reduce scoring time. Also, in the upper grades, learning to complete separate answer sheets familiarizes students with the process they will use when taking standardized tests.

Provide Space for Name and Date.   Be sure to include a blank on your test booklet and/or answer sheet for the student's name and the date. If you think this is unnecessary, you have never graded a pile of unsigned papers from young children, wondering who they belong to! It is *not* always evident to a nervous test taker that a name

FIGURE 14.3
Test assembly checklist

	Test Assembly Checklist	Yes	No
	Check each statement to see that it applies to your test.		
1.	Are items of similar format grouped together?	☐	☐
2.	Are items arranged in order of difficulty from easy to hard?	☐	☐
3.	Are items properly spaced?	☐	☐
4.	Are items and options on the same page?	☐	☐
5.	Are diagrams, maps, and supporting material above designated items and on the same page with items?	☐	☐
6.	Are answers random?	☐	☐
7.	Have you decided whether an answer sheet will be used?	☐	☐
8.	Are blanks for name and date included?	☐	☐
9.	Have you checked the directions for clarity and completeness?	☐	☐
10.	Have you proofread the test for errors?	☐	☐

should be included on the test. Students are much more likely to put their names on tests if space is provided.

Check Test Directions. Check your directions for each item format to be sure they are clear. Directions should specify:

1. The numbers of the items to which the directions apply.
2. How to record answers.
3. The basis on which to select answers.
4. Criteria for scoring.

Proofread the Test. Proofread for typographical and grammatical errors and correct them before reproducing the test. Having to announce corrections to the class just before or during the test wastes time and will disturb the test takers' concentration.

Before reproducing the test, it's a good idea to check off these steps. The checklist in Figure 14.3 can be used for this purpose.

VALIDITY, RELIABILITY, AND ACCURACY

Test results are useful only if they are valid, reliable, and accurate. These terms are defined as follows:

1. *Validity*—does the test measure what it is supposed to?
2. *Reliability*—does the test yield the same or similar scores consistently?

3. *Accuracy*—does the test approximate an individual's true level of knowledge, skill, or ability?

Types of Validity

A test is valid if it measures what it says it is supposed to measure. For instance, if it is supposed to be a test of third-grade arithmetic ability, it should measure third-grade arithmetic skills, not fifth-grade arithmetic skills and not reading ability. If it is supposed to be a measure of ability to write behavioral objectives, it should measure that ability, not the ability to recognize poor objectives.

Clearly, if test results will be used to make any kind of decision and if the test information is to be useful, it is essential that the test be valid. There are several ways of deciding whether a test is sufficiently valid to be useful. The three methods most often used are *content validity, concurrent validity,* and *predictive validity.*

Content Validity.   The content validity of a test is established by examining its contents. Test questions are inspected to see whether they correspond to what the teacher feels should be covered. This is easiest when the test is measuring achievement, where it may be fairly easy to specify what to include. It is more difficult if the concept being tested is a personality or aptitude trait, because it can be difficult to specify beforehand what a relevant question would look like.

A test sometimes can look valid but measure something different from what is intended, such as guessing ability, reading level, or skills that may have been acquired before the instruction. Content validity is, therefore, a minimum requirement for a useful test but not a guarantee of a valid test.

Concurrent Validity.   A second form of validity is concurrent validity. Concurrent validity requires that an established test be administered at the same time as the new test you have designed. Unlike content validity, concurrent validity yields a numerical value in the form of a correlation coefficient, called a validity coefficient (see Kubiszyn and Borich, 1990, Chapter 14).

The concurrent validity of a test is determined by administering both the new test and the established test to a group of students and then finding the relationship— the correlation—between the two sets of test scores. If there exists an established test (criterion) with which the new test can be compared and in which people have confidence, concurrent validity provides a good method of estimating the validity of a test.

Predictive Validity.   A third form of validity is predictive validity. Predictive validity refers to how well the test predicts some future behavior of the examinee that is representative of the test's content. This form of validity is particularly useful for aptitude tests, which attempt to predict how well the test taker will do in some future setting. Predictive validity also yields a numerical index, also in the form of a correlation coefficient. This time, however, it is the relationship between the test and some future behavior that is being measured.

All three methods for determining validity—content, concurrent and predictive—assume that some criterion exists external to the test that can be used to anchor or validate it. In the case of content validity, it is the instructional objectives that provide the anchor or point of reference; in the case of concurrent validity, it is another well-accepted test measuring the same thing; and in the case of predictive validity, it is some future behavior or condition that we are attempting to predict.

Types of Reliability

The reliability of a test refers to the consistency with which it yields the same rank or score for an individual taking the test several times. In other words, a test is reliable if it consistently yields the same, or nearly the same, ranks among all individuals over repeated administrations during which we would not expect the trait being measured to have changed.

There are several ways to estimate the reliability of a test. The three basic methods most often used are called *test-retest, alternative form,* and *internal consistency.*

Test-Retest. Test-retest is a method of estimating reliability that is exactly what its name implies. The test is given twice to the same individuals and the relationship—or correlation—between the first set of scores and the second set of scores is determined.

Alternate Forms. If there are two equivalent forms of a test, both can be used to estimate the reliability of the test. Both are administered to a group of students, and the relationship—or correlation—between the two sets of scores is determined. Because the two forms have different items but equivalent content, this estimate eliminates the problems of memory and practice involved in test-retest estimates of reliability. Large differences in a student's score on two forms of a test which supposedly measures the same behavior would indicate an unreliable test. To use this method of estimating reliability, there must be two equivalent forms of the test available, and they must be administered under conditions as nearly equivalent as possible and at approximately the same time.

Internal Consistency. If the test measures a single basic concept, then it is reasonable to assume that people who get one item right will more likely get other, similar items right. In other words, items ought to be related or correlated with each other, and the test ought to be internally consistent. If this is the case, then the reliability of the test can be estimated by the internal-consistency method. (Specific numerical procedures for determining the internal consistency of a test and other methods of measuring reliability are in Kubiszyn and Borich, 1990).

Here are some tips and cautions about interpreting reliability coefficients:

- ☐ Higher coefficients will result from heterogeneous groups than from homogeneous groups. Groups comprised of very different types of individuals (for example, slow and fast, older and younger, motivated and unmotivated learners) will result in higher reliabilities than more homogeneous groups.

☐ Scoring reliability limits test reliability. If tests are scored unreliably, error is introduced that will limit the reliability of the test. A test cannot have reliability higher than the reliability of the scoring.

☐ All other factors being equal, the more items included in a test, the higher the test's reliability.

☐ Reliability tends to decrease as tests become too easy or too difficult.

Typically, validity coefficients for a test are lower than reliability coefficients. Acceptable validity coefficients for a test generally range between .60 and .80 or higher, while acceptable reliability coefficients generally range from .80 to .90 or higher. 1.0 is the maximum coefficient obtainable for either validity or reliability.

Marks and Marking Systems

After you have administered your test, you will have to score it and assign marks. Often the type of symbol a teacher uses to represent a mark is determined at the school or district level—for example: A–F, E–G–S–P–U (Excellent–Good–Satisfactory–Poor–Unsatisfactory), or a numerical marking system. However, the classroom teacher often has considerable flexibility in determining how to assign these marks to learners. You may have considerable control over *how* you decide who gets an A or B or 75 or 80. Marks are based on comparisons, usually comparisons of students with:

☐ Other students
☐ Established standards
☐ Aptitude
☐ Actual vs. potential effort
☐ Actual vs. potential improvement

Comparison with Other Students. The expression "grading on the curve" means that your grade or mark depends on how your achievement compares with the achievement of other students in your class. Sometimes districts or schools encourage grading on the curve by specifying the percentages of students who will be assigned various grades.

The main advantage of such a system is that it simplifies marking decisions. Either the student is in the top 10%, or he or she doesn't get an A. There is no deliberation or agonizing over what cutoff scores should determine whether students get this grade or that. However, this type of marking system fails to consider differences in the overall ability level of the class. Regardless of achievement, in such a system some students always will get As, and some always will get Fs.

Comparison with Established Standards. In this marking system, it is possible for any student to get an A or F or any grade between. Achievements of individual students are unrelated to other individual students. All that is relevant is whether a student attains a defined standard of achievement or performance. We labeled this approach

Comparisons with other students, established standards, aptitude, effort, and improvement all can be the basis for assigning grades. Ultimately, you must decide the balance of approaches to use that best fits the goals of the classroom and school.

criterion-referenced earlier in this chapter. In such a system, letter grades may be assigned, based on the percentage of test items answered correctly, as this distribution illustrates:

Grade	Percentage of Items Answered Correctly
A	85
B	75
C	65
D	55
F	less than 55

In theory, this system makes it possible for all students to obtain high grades if they put forth sufficient effort (assuming that the percentage cutoffs are not unreasonably high). Also, grade assignment is simplified; a student either has correctly answered 75% of the items or has not. As with the comparison with other students method, there is no deliberating or agonizing over assigning grades. Also, teachers who work to improve their teaching effectiveness can observe improvement in grades with the passage of time.

As you might expect, such a system also has its drawbacks. Establishing a standard for each grade attained is no small task, and what is reasonable for an A may vary from school to school and from time to time, as a result of ability levels, the content being taught, and curriculum changes.

Comparison with Aptitude. Aptitude is another name for potential or ability. In such systems students are compared neither to other students nor to established standards. Instead, they are compared to themselves. That is, marks are assigned depending on how closely to their potential they are achieving. Thus, students with high aptitude or potential who are achieving at high levels would get high grades, because they would be achieving at their potential. Those with high aptitude and average achievement would get lower grades, because they would be achieving below their potential.

But students with average aptitude and average achievement also would get high grades, because they would be considered to be achieving at their potential. Thus, the same grade could mean very different things in terms of absolute achievement.

Comparison of Achievement with Effort. Systems that compare achievement with effort are similar to those that compare achievement with aptitude. Students who get average test scores but have to work hard to get them are given high marks. Students who get average scores but do not have to work hard to get them are given lower grades. The advantage cited for grading on effort is that it motivates slower or turned-off students. However, it also may turn off brighter students, who quickly see such a system as unfair.

Comparison of Achievement with Improvement. Such systems compare the amount of improvement between the beginning and end of instruction. Students who show the most progress get the highest grades. An obvious problem occurs for the student who does well on a test at the beginning of the instruction, called the *pretest,* because improvement for this student is likely to be less than for a student who does poorly on the pretest.

Which marking system should you choose? Most now agree that comparisons with established standards would best suit the primary function of marking, which is to provide feedback about academic achievement. Once standards are established, comparisons among schools and students may be more easily made. In reality, many schools and districts have adopted multiple marking systems, such as assigning separate grades for achievement and effort or achievement, effort, and improvement. As long as the achievement portion of the grade reflects *only* achievement, such systems are appropriate.

STANDARDIZED TESTS

So far, we have limited our discussion to teacher-constructed tests. However, many teachers also are required at least once a year to administer *standardized* tests, evaluate their results, and interpret them to curious and sometimes concerned parents.

Standardized tests are developed by test-construction specialists, usually with the assistance of curriculum experts, teachers, and school administrators, to determine a student's performance level relative to others of similar age and grade. These

TABLE 14.2
A comparison of standardized and teacher-made achievement tests

	Standardized Achievement Tests	Teacher-Made Achievement Tests
Learning outcomes and content measured	Measures general outcomes and content appropriate to the majority of U.S. schools. These tests of general skills and understanding tend not to reflect specific or unique emphases of local curricula.	Well-adapted to the specific and unique outcomes and content of a local curriculum; adaptable to various sizes of work units, but tend to neglect complex learning outcomes.
Quality of test items	Quality of items generally is high. Items are written by specialists, pretested, and selected on the basis of results from quantitative item analysis.	Quality of items is often unknown. Quality is typically lower than standardized tests due to limited time available to the teacher.
Reliability	Reliability is high, commonly between .80 and .95, and frequently above .90 (highest possible is 1.0).	Reliability is usually unknown, but can be high if items are carefully constructed.
Administration and scoring	Procedures are standardized; specific instructions are provided.	Uniform procedures are possible, but usually are flexible and unwritten.
Interpretation of scores	Scores can be compared to norm groups. Test manual and other guides aid interpretation and use.	Score comparisons and interpretation are limited to local class or school situation. Few if any guidelines are available for interpretation and use.

tests are *standardized* because they are administered and scored according to *specific* and *uniform* (standard) procedures.

When standardized tests are employed, test results from different students, classes, schools, and districts can be more easily and confidently *compared* than is the case with different teacher-made tests. For the most part, standardized tests are used for comparative purposes. This is quite different from the purposes of teacher-made tests, which are to determine pupil mastery or skill levels, to assign grades, and to provide specific feedback to students and parents. Table 14.2 compares standardized and teacher-made tests on several important dimensions.

The results of standardized tests are reported as percentile ranks. Percentile ranks enable you to determine how a student's performance compares with others of the same grade or age. Two points to keep in mind when interpreting percentile ranks are:

1. Percentile ranks often are confused with *percentage correct*. In using percentile ranks, be sure you communicate that a percentile rank of 62 (for

example) means that the individual's score was *higher* than 62% of all the people who took the test (called the *norming sample*). Or, you can say that 62% of those who took the test scored *lower* than this individual. (Commonly, a score at the 62nd percentile is misinterpreted to mean that the student answered only 62% of the items correctly. But realize that a score at the 62nd percentile might be equivalent to a B or a C, whereas a score of 62% likely would be an F.)

2. Equal differences between percentile ranks do *not* necessarily indicate equal differences in achievement. In a grade of 100 pupils, the difference *in achievement* between the 2nd percentile and 5th percentile is substantial, whereas the difference between the 47th and 50th percentile is negligible. Interpretation of percentile ranks must take into consideration that percentiles toward the extreme or end points of the distribution tend to be spread out (like a rubber band), while percentiles toward the center tend to be compressed.

SUMMING UP

This chapter introduced you to some techniques for evaluating student learning. Its main points were:

1. A test that determines a student's place or rank among other students is called norm-referenced. This type of test conveys information about how a student performed compared to a large sample of pupils at the same age or grade.

2. A test that compares a student's performance to a standard of mastery is called criterion-referenced. This type of test conveys information about whether a student needs additional instruction on some skill or set of skills.

3. The major advantage of a norm-referenced test is that it covers many different content areas in a single test; its major disadvantage is that it is too general to be useful in identifying specific strengths and weaknesses tied to individual texts or workbooks.

4. The major advantage of a criterion-referenced test is that it can yield highly specific information about individual skills or behaviors. Its major disadvantage is that many such tests would be needed to make decisions about the many skills or behaviors typically taught in school.

5. A test blueprint is a graphic device that matches the test items to be written with the content areas and levels of behavioral complexity taught. The test blueprint helps to ensure that a test samples learning across (a) the range of content areas cov-

ered and (b) the cognitive and/or affective processes considered important.

6. Objective test item formats include:
   - □ True-false
   - □ Matching
   - □ Multiple choice
   - □ Completion or short answer

7. Two methods for reducing the effects of guessing in true-false items are to (a) encourage all students to guess when they do not know the answer and (b) require revision of statements that are false.

8. In constructing matching items:
   - □ Make lists homogeneous, representing the same kind of events, people, or circumstances.
   - □ Place the shorter list first and list options in chronological, numbered, or alphabetical order.
   - □ Provide approximately three more options than descriptions to reduce the chance of guessing correctly.
   - □ Write directions to identify what the lists contain, and specify the basis for matching.
   - □ Closely check the options for multiple correct answers.

9. Some flaws to avoid in writing multiple-choice items are:
   - □ Stem clues in which the same word or a close derivative appears in both the stem and an option.

☐ Grammatical clues in which an article, verb, or pronoun eliminates one or more options from being grammatically correct.

☐ Same words are repeated across options that could have been provided only once in the stem.

☐ Response options are of unequal length, indicating that the longer option may be correct.

☐ Use of "all of the above," which discourages response discrimination, or "none of the above," which encourages guessing.

10. Suggestions for writing higher-level multiple-choice items include use of:

☐ Pictorial, graphical, or tabular stimuli.

☐ Analogies that demonstrate relationships among items.

☐ Previously learned principles or procedures.

11. Some suggestions for writing completion items are:

☐ Require a single-word answer.

☐ Pose the question or problem in a brief, definite statement.

☐ Check to be sure that an accurate response can be found in the text, workbook, or class notes.

☐ Omit only one or two key words.

☐ Word the statement so the blank is near the end.

☐ If the question requires a numerical answer, indicate the units in which the answer is to be expressed.

12. An *extended-response* essay item allows the student to determine the length and complexity of a response.

13. A *restricted-response* essay item poses a specific problem for which the student must recall and organize the proper information, derive a defensible conclusion, and express it within a stated time or length.

14. Essay items are most appropriate when (a) the instructional objectives specify high-level cognitive processes, (b) relatively few test items (students) need to be graded, and (c) test security is a consideration.

15. Suggestions for writing essay items include:

☐ Identify beforehand the mental processes that you want to measure (for example, application, analysis, decision-making).

☐ Identify clearly and unambiguously the task to be accomplished by the student.

☐ Begin the essay question with key words, such as *compare, give reasons for, predict.*

☐ Require presentation of evidence for controversial questions.

☐ Avoid optional items.

☐ Establish reasonable time and/or page limits.

☐ Restrict the use of essay items to those that cannot easily be measured by multiple-choice items.

☐ Relate each essay question to an objective on the test blueprint.

16. Suggestions for increasing the consistency and accuracy of scoring essay items include:

☐ Specifying the response length.

☐ Use several restricted-response essay items instead of one extended-response item.

☐ Prepare a scoring scheme in which all ingredients necessary to achieve each of the grades that could be assigned are specified beforehand.

17. Some suggestions for packaging the test are:

☐ Group together all items of similar format.

☐ Arrange test items from easy to hard.

☐ Space items for easy reading.

☐ Keep items and options on the same page.

☐ Position illustrations near descriptions.

☐ Check the answer key.

☐ Determine beforehand how students are to record the answers.

☐ Provide space for name and date.

☐ Check test directions for clarity.

☐ Proofread the test.

18. Validity refers to whether a test measures what it says it measures. Three types of validity are content, concurrent, and predictive.

19. *Content* validity is established by examining a test's contents. *Concurrent* validity is established by correlating the scores on a new test with the scores on an established test given to the same set of individuals. *Predictive* validity is established by correlating the scores on a new test with some future behavior of the examinee that is representative of the test's content.

20. Reliability refers to whether a test yields the same or similar scores consistently. Three types of reliability are test-retest, alternative form, and internal consistency.

21. *Test-retest* reliability is established by giving the test twice to the same individuals and correlating the first set of scores with the second. *Alternative form* reliability is established by giving two parallel but different forms of the test to the same in-

dividuals and correlating the two sets of scores. *Internal consistency* reliability is established by determining the extent to which the test measures a single basic concept.

22. Accuracy refers to whether a test approximates an individual's true level of knowledge, skill, or ability.

23. Marks are based on comparisons, usually comparisons of students with:
   □ Other students

□ Established standards
□ Aptitude
□ Actual versus potential effort
□ Actual versus potential improvement.

24. Standardized tests are developed by test-construction specialists to determine a student's performance level relative to others of similar age and grade. They are *standardized* because they are administered and scored according to specific and uniform procedures.

FOR DISCUSSION AND PRACTICE

*1. Identify the characteristics of a norm-referenced and criterion-referenced test and the decisions for which each is best suited.

*2. What two instructional dimensions are measured by a test blueprint?

*3. Identify four formats for objective test items and give two advantages and two disadvantages of each.

*4. Identify four impediments to writing good multiple-choice test items.

*5. What three devices may be used to prepare multiple-choice questions at higher levels of cognitive complexity?

*6. Contrast the characteristics of extended-response and restricted-response essay items. Prepare an example of each in your teaching field.

*7. Identify three reasons for preparing an essay as opposed to objective test.

*8. Describe three advantages and three disadvantages of essay items.

*9. What is a "scoring scheme" for an essay item? Construct a scoring scheme for the essay item you prepared in question 6.

*10. Identify six possible criteria for scoring higher-level essay items.

*11. Identify ten guidelines for packaging a test.

*12. Define the concepts of validity, reliability, and accuracy.

*13. What three methods may be used to determine the validity of a test? Give an example of what information each would provide for a test given in your classroom.

*14. What three methods may be used for determining the reliability of a test? Give an example of what information each would provide for a test given in your classroom.

*15. Provide an approximate range for an acceptable validity and acceptable reliability coefficient. What is the maximum possible size of a validity or reliability coefficient?

*16. Identify five procedures for assigning marks and one advantage and one disadvantage of each.

*17. What is a standardized test?

*18. What does a percentile rank indicate for a given individual? What two points should be kept in mind in interpreting a percentile rank?

---

*Answers to asterisked questions (*) in this and the other chapters are in Appendix B.

SUGGESTED READINGS

Borich, G., & Madden, S. (1977). *Evaluating classroom instruction: A sourcebook of instruments.* Reading, MA: Addison-Wesley.
   A source book of over 100 instruments for evaluating the noncognitive outcomes of classroom instruction.

Coker, D., et al. (1988). Improving essay tests: Structuring the items and scoring responses. *Clearing House, 61*(6), 253–255.
   Some well-proven tips for writing effective essay items.

Dreher, M., & Singer, H. (1984). Making standardized tests work for you. *Principal, 63*(4), 20–24.
A brief nontechnical introduction to the practical side of standardized tests.

Gronlund, N. (1980). *How to construct achievement tests* (4th ed.). Englewood Cliffs, NJ: Prentice-Hall.
A comprehensive guide for constructing classroom tests, including extensive coverage of both multiple-choice and essay items.

Kubiszyn, T., & Borich, G. (1990). *Educational testing and measurement: Classroom applications and practice* (3rd ed.). New York: Harper Collins.
A practical introductory text on testing and measurement in the classroom prepared especially for the beginning teacher.

Linn, R. (1983). Testing and instruction: Links and distinction. *Journal of Educational Measurement, 20*(2), 179–189.
Shows the important role of tests in bridging the gap between teaching and the improvement of instruction.

Lyman, H. (1986). *Test scores and what they mean.* Englewood Cliffs, NJ: Prentice-Hall.
Emphasizes the practical use and interpretation of test scores from the teacher's perspective.

McKillip, W. (1979). Teacher-made tests: Development and use. *Arithmetic Teacher, 27*(3), 38–43.
Some useful tips from a teacher for constructing your own tests.

Mehrens, W., & Lehmann, I. (1987). *Using standardized tests in education* (4th ed.). New York: Holt, Rinehart & Winston.
Covers the basic issues of proper use and interpretation of standardized tests that are of primary concern to teachers, parents, and administrators.

Popham, W. (1981). *Modern educational measurement.* Englewood Cliffs, NJ: Prentice-Hall.
A thorough discussion of criterion-referenced tests and how to use them in your classroom.

Woodrow, J. (1986). Using the Apple Macintosh and MULTIPLAN spreadsheet to analyze tests. *Journal of Computers in Mathematics and Science Teaching, 5*(3), 34–44.
How to use your Macintosh to construct and improve classroom tests.

15

Effective Teaching
in the Classroom

For the past semester or quarter you have traveled through this book. It has been a long journey and perhaps at times a difficult one. Now we are near the end, and, as with any good journey, it is important to look back at the sights encountered along the way. Some of these sights appeared as the five key behaviors: *lesson clarity, instructional variety, task orientation, engagement in learning,* and *student success.* This final chapter revisits the key behaviors and their catalysts from the perspective of a practicing teacher.

This is your opportunity to see what an *effective* teacher does with these behaviors and, just as importantly, what an *ineffective* teacher does with them. To provide a picture of these two types of teachers, this chapter presents both positive and negative indicators of effective teaching as they pertain to the key behaviors. Throughout the discussion there will be references about how the helping behaviors (structuring, questioning, probing, use of student ideas, and teacher affect) can be used to achieve the key behaviors. Procedures for observing and recording each of the key and helping behaviors discussed in this chapter are provided in the companion volume to this text, *Observation Skills for Effective Teaching* (Borich, 1990).

CLARITY IN THE CLASSROOM

Being clear means being understood by your learners. Table 15.1 presents seven behaviors that relate to lesson clarity. The first column lists indicators of lesson clarity observed among effective teachers. The second column lists indicators of poor clarity observed among ineffective teachers. For a teacher who exhibits any of the behaviors of poor clarity, the third column suggests ways to improve.

The following sections review each of these behaviors.

Clarity at the Beginning of the Lesson

Being clear depends as much on what you do *prior* to teaching a lesson as on what you do *during* the lesson. Of the seven behaviors important to clarity, three need to occur at the beginning of a lesson:

1. Informing learners of the objective.
2. Providing learners with an advance organizer.
3. Checking for task-relevant prior learning and reteaching, if necessary.

These preinstructional activities establish a **learning set** that focuses your learners' attention. Without this focusing, they may not notice or grasp what comes after. Let's review how this might be done in your classroom.

Informing Learners of the Objective.   At the start of a lesson, most students will not know what behaviors, skills, or concepts you expect them to learn, or how you expect them to perform. Therefore, at the beginning of a lesson, tell them how you expect them to show their understanding of the subject matter. This can replace their unrealistic fears and uncertainty with realistic expectations.

TABLE 15.1
Indicators for clarity

	Being Clear (an effective teacher . . .)	Poor Clarity (an ineffective teacher . . .)	Solutions
1.	Informs learners of the lesson objective (e.g., describes what behaviors will be tested or required on future assignments as a result of the lesson)	Fails to link lesson content to how and at what level of complexity the content will be used	Prepare a behavioral objective for the lesson at the desired level of complexity (e.g., knowledge, comprehension, etc.). Indicate to the learners at the start of the lesson in what ways the behavior will be used in the future.
2.	Provides learners with an advance organizer (e.g., places lesson in perspective of past and/or future lessons)	Starts presenting content without first introducing the subject with respect to some broader context	Consult or prepare a unit plan to determine what task-relevant prior learning is required for this lesson and what task-relevant prior learning this lesson represents for future lessons. Begin the lesson by informing the learner that the content to be taught is part of this larger context.
3.	Checks for task-relevant prior learning at beginning of the lesson (e.g., determines level of understanding of prerequisite facts or concepts and reteaches, if necessary)	Moves to new content without checking for the facts, concepts, or skills needed to acquire the new learning	Ask questions of students at the beginning of a lesson or check assignments regularly to determine if task-relevant prior knowledge has been acquired.
4.	Gives directives slowly and distinctly (e.g., repeats directives when needed or divides them into smaller pieces)	Presents too much clerical, managerial, or technical information at once, too quickly	Organize procedures for lengthy assignments in step-by-step order and give as handout as well as orally.
5.	Knows ability levels and teaches at or slightly above learners' current level of functioning (e.g., knows learners' attention spans)	Fails to know that instruction is under or over heads of students. Seems not to know when most learners have "tuned out"	Determine ability level from standardized tests, previous assignments, and interests and retarget instruction accordingly.
6.	Uses examples, illustrations, and demonstrations to explain and clarify (e.g., uses visuals to help interpret and reinforce main points)	Restricts presentation to routine verbal reproduction of text or workbook	Restate main points in at least one modality other than the one in which they were initially taught (e.g., visual vs. auditory).
7.	Provides review or summary at end of each lesson	Ends lesson abruptly without "repackaging" key points	Use key abstractions, repetition, or symbols to help students efficiently store and later recall content.

You can do this most easily by translating the expected outcome of a lesson into some ways it might be used in an assignment, on a test, in a class discussion, or in a question-and-answer period. For example, you might write examples of expected proficiencies on the blackboard at the beginning of a unit, or state what tasks you expect them to complete by lesson's end.

Such simple techniques help learners organize and focus attention on the essential ingredients of the day's lesson. If they know what they are expected to recall at the end of a lesson, they are more likely to focus their search, retrieval, and retention processes on the outcomes expected. In Chapters 5 and 7 you saw how to accomplish this (a) by translating expected lesson outcomes into ways they might be used on an exercise or assignment, and (b) by using verbal markers to focus learner attention on the key ingredients in a lesson.

Providing Advance Organization.   Another behavior for achieving lesson clarity is to use advance organizers. Recall from Chapter 7 that advance organizers focus learners' thinking in advance of the lesson by providing mental "hooks" on which to hang key aspects. Advance organizers are concepts presented orally or visually (e.g., charts and diagrams) to overview the day's work and all topics to which it will subsequently relate. Advance organizers give learners a conceptual preview and prepare them to store, label, and package the content for retention and later use.

An advance organizer is a general concept; the specific content of the day's lesson fits into it, as well as the content for all related lessons. Thus advance organizers lay the groundwork for expanding the present lesson topic, thereby preventing every lesson from being seen as something entirely new. They also create a framework for integrating related concepts into ever-larger patterns and abstractions that later become unit outcomes. An advance organizer indicates the highest behavior level expected from a lesson sequence, to which the outcome of the day's lesson will contribute.

Checking for Task-Relevant Learning.   The third preinstructional activity for achieving lesson clarity needs little introduction, for it has been an important concept throughout this text. Without the mastery of task-relevant prior learning, a lesson may be incomprehensible to your learners. Checking for task-relevant learning is a behavior often neglected by both beginning and experienced teachers. Your lesson can have clarity only to the extent that your students exhibit the facts, skills, or concepts required to understand it. To achieve this, you must find out before the lesson whether your learners actually can exhibit the prerequisite behaviors.

Helping students retrieve previously acquired information requires condensing key aspects of prior learning into a brief, easily understood format. You cannot realistically summarize all that has gone before in a few minutes of preparatory comments, so you need thought-provoking and stimulating techniques to help them quickly recall sizable amounts of prior learning. Many options are available, from informal questions asked randomly of a few students to a formal check of workbooks and a review of a previous assignment.

Strategies for checking task-relevant prior learning, especially when used with a carefully selected **steering group**, are indispensable for informing you that previous instruction has been too advanced for some students and, therefore, that additional review and reteaching may be necessary before starting the day's lesson. If you discover extensive deficiencies in task-relevant prior learning, reteaching old but prerequisite content may be more important than teaching the new content you had scheduled.

Clarity During the Lesson

Of the seven behaviors important to lesson clarity, the remaining four should occur during the lesson:

4. Giving directives slowly and distinctly.
5. Knowing the ability levels of your learners and teaching to those levels.
6. Using examples, illustrations, and demonstrations to explain and clarify text and workbook content.
7. Providing a review or summary at the end of each lesson.

These behaviors differ from the first three because they pertain to the actual presentation of lesson content. (Of course, you'll still prepare for them in advance of your lesson.) These practices also are ways of establishing a clear dialogue with your students that not only will help them understand what you are saying, but retain it long afterward. Let's review how this might be done in your classroom.

Giving Directions.   One of the commonest criticisms of beginning teachers from students is "we weren't told (or didn't understand) what to do." Students often won't admit that they could not follow the directions given, either because they could not remember all that was said or that it was said so quickly and matter-of-factly that "things just whizzed by." These complaints illustrate that directives pertaining to completing workbook exercises, reading assignments, homework, and drill and practice need to be communicated with the *same deliberateness as the lesson content*.

It is common for beginning teachers to speed up and speak less distinctly when giving directives about what to do, how to proceed, and what rules to follow, and then slow down again when actually teaching the lesson to which the directives pertain. When students cannot follow your directions about how you want them to become engaged in the learning process, they usually will silently proceed on their own, sometimes missing the intent of the assignment.

Slow down when conveying instructions. Divide the directives into steps. Be sure each step is understood. (The three preceding sentences illustrate how presenting directions in short, specific steps improves comprehension.) Recall from Chapter 11 that effective classroom managers (a) give assignments immediately following the lessons or activities to which they relate, (b) provide reasons the assignment is of value, and (c) avoid unnecessary negative connotations of assignments.

Knowing Student Abilities.   The next behavior, knowing your students' ability levels and teaching material appropriate to them, is one of the most difficult to achieve. Several levels of ability likely will exist in your class (e.g., less-able, average, more-able). You may become frustrated by an inability to teach some students. Nevertheless, your clarity will depend in part upon packaging instructional stimuli in the form of oral presentations, visual messages, exercises, and reading assignments that are at the current level of functioning of all of your students.

To accomplish this, you may need to provide a *range of instructional stimuli* that intentionally hits some students and misses others. Learning centers, reference libraries, different types of pictorial displays, and even alternate texts and exercises that tap into abilities slightly above and below the average learner will be needed to provide a range of instructional stimuli that spans the current level of functioning of every student.

Using Examples, Illustrations, and Demonstrations.   Oral examples, visual illustrations, and practical demonstrations can measurably increase the clarity of your lesson—*if they are different from those in the text*. Repackaging content can add clarity to a lesson, giving students with diverse backgrounds or learning styles the opportunity to relate it to their own levels of experience and understanding. Content comes alive when communicated in different forms that highlight its most important features. Audiovisual media, worksheets, problem sets, and study aids can create a structure of activity that make textbook content meaningful to the learner, especially in group activities, discussions, and question-and-answer sessions.

Reviewing and Summarizing.   Reviews and summaries at the end of a lesson, or interspersed throughout, can have much the same effect as examples, illustrations, and demonstrations. Recall from Chapter 11 that a review or summary need not be an abbreviated parroting of what was taught. Instead, an effective review or summary often recasts content into a form slightly different from the original presentation, thereby elaborating upon and organizing earlier content differently for efficient storage and retrieval. This provides learners the opportunity to plug into the content at a different time and in a different manner. Content unlearned or misunderstood during the lesson can become learned and clarified during summaries and reviews that *go beyond simply repeating the content by repackaging it for retention and later retrieval*.

The last two behaviors for achieving lesson clarity—using examples, illustrations, and demonstrations and reviewing and summarizing—have aspects in common. Both occur far into the lesson. Both expand and clarify content in the text or workbook, which generally will not be understood completely or uniformly unless you elaborate upon it. This means you must make this content come alive for your students by putting it into different forms to highlight its most important features.

VARIETY IN THE CLASSROOM

Table 15.2 summarizes behaviors related to instructional variety:

☐ Using attention-gaining devices
☐ Showing enthusiasm
☐ Varying instructional activities

TABLE 15.2
Indicators for variety

	Using Variety (an effective teacher . . .)	Poor Variety (an ineffective teacher . . .)	Solutions
1.	Uses attention-gaining devices (e.g., begins with a challenging question, visual, or example)	Begins lesson without full attention of most learners	Begin lesson with an activity in a modality that is different from last lesson or activity (e.g., change from listening to seeing).
2.	Shows enthusiasm and animation through variation in eye contact, voice, and gestures (e.g., changes pitch and volume, moves about during transitions to new activity)	Speaks in monotone, devoid of external signs of emotion; stays fixed in place entire period or rarely moves body	Change position at regular intervals (e.g., every 10 minutes). Change speed or volume to indicate that a change in content or activity has occurred.
3.	Varies mode of presentation, (e.g., lectures, asks questions, then provides for independent practice [daily])	Lectures or assigns unmonitored seatwork for the entire period; rarely alters modality through which instructional stimuli are received (e.g., seeing, listening, doing)	Preestablish an order of daily activities that rotates cycles of seeing, listening, and doing.
4.	Uses a mix of rewards and reinforcers (e.g., extra credit, verbal praise, independent study, etc. [weekly, monthly])	Rarely praises or tends to use same words to convey praise every time	Establish lists of rewards and expressions of verbal praise and choose among them randomly. Provide reasons for praise along with the expression of praise.
5.	Incorporates student ideas or participation in some aspects of the instruction (e.g., uses indirect instruction or divergent questioning [weekly, monthly])	Assumes the role of sole authority and provider of information; ignores student opinion	Occasionally plan instruction in which student opinions are used to begin the lesson (e.g., "what would you do if . . .").
6.	Varies types of questions (e.g., divergent, convergent, [weekly]) and probes (e.g., to clarify, to solicit, to redirect [daily])	Always asks divergent, opinion questions (e.g., What do you think about . . .?) without follow up; or overuses convergent, fact questions	Match questions to the behavior and complexity of the lesson objective. Vary complexity of lesson objectives in accord with the unit plan.

☐ Mixing rewards and reinforcements
☐ Using student ideas.
☐ Varying types of questions and probes.

Let us review how each of these behaviors can contribute to the effective use of variety.

Gaining Attention

Using attention-gaining devices is the first ingredient of a good lesson plan, as described in Chapter 5. Recall that attention-gaining devices include visuals, audio/video media, demonstrations, and experiments, or less-spectacular strategies like posing a challenging question, presenting a dilemma or bewildering situation, or displaying an interesting wall chart (which brings about an attention-gaining silence). Beginning a lesson in this manner stimulates learners differently from their previous activity.

Don't try to present the spectacular all the time (although this always is fun when the opportunity arises). The goal is to present instructional stimuli that are different from what learners had grown accustomed to in the previous activity. This not only awakens the receptive modalities of sight and sound, but just as importantly stimulates the cognitive processes associated with them. Without this awakening and conscious change from the mood and tempo of an earlier activity, your learners' attention may never be fully on either you or the lesson.

Attention-gaining devices, therefore, help create natural cycles of highs and lows that make classroom life more interesting and less regimented. Although high points of curiosity, interest, and visual impact cannot be sustained, without them there can be no anticipation and excitement of waiting for the next peak to occur. This is good reason for spreading attention-gaining devices throughout your lesson and not limiting this important behavior to the beginning.

Showing Enthusiasm

One of the easiest ways to maintain the momentum of interest, curiosity, and excitement in your classroom is to vary your voice, eye contact, and gestures. When interest is waning in your class and no attention-getting device is readily available to engage your learners' attention, these techniques often do the job. You can learn much from the methods of dramatics. Lessons, like plays, need opening and closing acts, with occasional climaxes and anticlimaxes to keep the audience's attention. How well you plan your script (lesson) has much to do with its attention-getting quality. There is natural variety in the topics and instructional activities that your lesson contains, and you can enhance that variety by accentuating its high points and bolstering its low points with changes in your voice, eye movement, and body movement.

Therefore, frequently change your voice inflection, eye contact, and physical position in the classroom, especially during the high points (e.g., lively group discussion) and low points (e.g., rote recitation from the workbook). Raising the volume of your voice slightly, changing from scanning the front of the class to the back, and repositioning yourself in the classroom during these times will add to the instructional variety you bring to your learners. Students will sense your enthusiasm from these simple signs of *your* engagement in the learning process, and thus engage *them* in the learning process.

Varying Instructional Activities

Researchers and experienced teachers agree that effective teaching involves varied classroom activities. A teacher who lectures for an entire period, who engages students in prolonged seatwork, or who uses nothing but attention-gaining devices will have difficulty achieving unit outcomes, especially at the higher levels of behavioral complexity. This is not to say that you can't emphasize a single activity from time to time, but in most classes you should offer varied activities to present instructional stimuli. For example, you can mix lecture with questions and answers (which may include work at the board), followed by guided practice in which you have learners make their first attempts at responding appropriately in a nonthreatening atmosphere.

These instructional routines, when thought out in advance and well executed, form an **activity structure**. You can use an activity structure to vary the cognitive demands on your learners and to give them some responsibility for controlling their own learning. In this sense, the variety provided by different instructional activities is not so much to gain students' attention (although we hope it does) as it is to allow them to cognitively process the material in varied ways—by listening (lectures), seeing (texts), and doing (workbooks). Different modalities (hearing, seeing, doing) provide the redundancy often needed for mastery learning. They also present the stimulus material in different contexts which emphasize the different cognitive abilities that different learners may have to varying degrees.

Therefore, a lesson plan that includes some combination of lecture, discussion, question and answer, guided practice, and independent seatwork generally is preferable to one that exclusively emphasizes only one instructional alternative. Varying your instructional routine across two or more of these (but seldom all of them) and varying the combinations chosen from day to day will add the important dimension of variety to your teaching.

Mixing Rewards and Reinforcements

Perhaps because everyone seeks rewards in their daily lives, the most noticeable interchanges between teachers and students concern reward and punishment. As we saw in Chapter 11, verbal praise is the most frequently used reward in the classroom. However, the reinforcing effect of verbal praise depends on its variety and its association with other types of rewards. Nothing is less reinforcing than the phrase "that's good" or "that's correct" repeated in the same tone hundreds of times. The phrase becomes meaningless and loses any ability to reinforce behavior.

Thus you should not only vary the type, amount, and intensity of your verbal praise, but also experiment with other rewards. What is rewarding to one student may not be rewarding to another. Try using one student's correct answer as a model for the next problem, or have the student retrace for the class how the correct answer was obtained, or have peers comment on the correctness of a student's answer. These are some ways you can mix verbal expressions and reinforcements to make the reward more meaningful.

Using Student Ideas

Use of student ideas is closely related to divergent types of questions that have more than one correct answer and the self-directed learning strategies considered in Chapter 9. Because each student is unique, the diversity of student responses can be amazing; proper use of this diversity (variety) can add an important dimension to your teaching.

As noted in Chapter 8, this diversity also can be a problem, because unexpected or difficult-to-evaluate responses can put you on the defensive. To end the awkward pause that frequently follows an unusual and unexpected answer, a common response among beginning teachers is to invent a correct answer. This is not a proper

The use of student ideas promotes student behaviors at the analysis, synthesis, and decision-making level, and increases participation in the learning process. It also encourages self-direction in which the student increasingly takes responsibility for his or her own learning.

use of divergent questioning, because one purpose of divergent questions is to incorporate student ideas and participation into your lesson.

The example dialogue in Chapter 7 showed how almost any student answer can be worked into the lesson, pending later clarification and correction. A single question ("list some goods and services that a large number of individuals might agree were essential for them to live and prosper") brought many correct answers, although not all were equally useful for making important distinctions later in the lesson. The key to eliciting student ideas and opinions is to make the ideas and opinions useful to the goals of the lesson.

As we saw in Chapter 9, soliciting student ideas and opinions seldom can provide the necessary variety in a lesson, if they are not used to create greater understanding and targeted to your learners' *zones of maximum response opportunity*. Using this source of variety effectively means taking the contributions of individual students and building from them the more general concepts, patterns, and abstractions that are relevant to your lesson's goals.

Varying Questions and Probes

The art of questioning and probing is a popular topic for inservice teacher training and is one of your most important skills as an effective teacher. The variety you convey to your students will be determined in large measure by your flexible use of questioning and probing. The purpose of these related techniques is to draw out of the student a response, sometimes *any* response, that then can be refined and developed into a better or more complete one.

Examples in Chapters 6, 7, 8, and 9 showed that questions are rarely ends in themselves, but are beginnings. They are a means of engaging students in the learning process by getting them to act on, work through, or think about the material presented previously. To be effective, question types must be varied. Often, they must be followed up with probes or other questions to pierce through initial responses that sometimes are glib, superficial, or inadequate. Probes are questions that follow questions and are crafted to deepen, enrich, and extend an earlier response.

As you saw in Chapter 8, probes can be used to *elicit* a clarifying response to an earlier question, to *solicit* new information related to an earlier question, or to *redirect* the learner into a more productive area. Each of these uses can add variety and momentum to your questioning behavior. For example, your solicitation for new information can be followed by a request for clarification, which can be followed by a redirection. You can execute these cycles of probes in waves that return again and again, forcing learners to act upon and reshape their responses—and, most important, their thinking.

Your questions should be varied, alternating between convergent and divergent (but not necessarily in equal amounts). Convergent questions (which usually have a single right answer) are usually associated with direct instruction; divergent questions (which may have many right answers) are usually associated with indirect instruction. However, use of these two question types has less to do with the instructional model being used than with their capacity for eliciting lower or higher levels of behavioral complexity. Recall that *convergent* questioning often is best for eliciting behavior at the knowledge, comprehension, and application levels and *divergent* questioning often is best for the analysis, synthesis, and evaluation levels.

TASK ORIENTATION IN THE CLASSROOM

Table 15.3 summarizes behaviors related to task orientation:

☐ Developing unit and lesson plans that reflect the curriculum.
☐ Handling administrative and clerical interruptions efficiently.
☐ Stopping or preventing misbehavior with a minimum of class disruption.
☐ Selecting the most appropriate instructional model for the objectives being taught.
☐ Building to unit outcomes by establishing cycles of review, feedback, and testing.

Developing Unit and Lesson Plans

Effective task orientation begins with your certainty that what you are teaching coincides with the school's curriculum. The single most effective way of assuring this is to base your lessons on the curriculum guide or adopted text for your subject or grade. Although this may seem obvious, a surprising number of teachers stray from them. Without unit and lesson plans, you may be tempted to replace adopted curriculum and textbook content with topics of personal interest about which you may be knowledgeable, or which your students appear more eager to study.

However, you do have the latitude to reorganize topics within your curriculum guide into an **activity structure** that is based upon your learners' current level of understanding. You saw in Chapters 6 and 7 several ways of organizing content into an activity structure for direct and indirect instruction. Accenting adopted curriculum topics with personal experiences, examples, and illustrations from outside the text or curriculum often is the mark of effective teaching. But failing to relate these experiences, examples, and illustrations to the adopted curriculum will orient your students away from unit goals and make them harder to achieve.

Managing Interruptions

Managing administrative and clerical interruptions is an essential behavior for establishing effective task orientation. An extensive study of more-effective and less-effective classroom managers at elementary and secondary levels found this behavior to be among the most important to a teacher's task orientation over an entire class period (Emmer, Evertson, Sanford, Clements, and Worsham, 1989).

This should be no surprise, because it is difficult to return to an instructional task (e.g., group recitation) from a noninstructional one (e.g., passing out materials, checking for supplies). Not only have you spent time on the noninstructional activity,

TABLE 15.3
Indicators for task orientation

	Being Task Oriented (an effective teacher . . .)	Poor Task Orientation (an ineffective teacher . . .)	Solutions
1.	Develops unit and lesson plans that reflect the most relevant features of the curriculum guide or adopted text (e.g., each unit and lesson objective can be referenced back to curriculum guide or text)	Develops lessons almost exclusively from personal or student interests. Breadth and depth of lesson content fails to distinguish between primary and secondary content in the curriculum guide and text	Key each lesson to a unit plan, the curriculum guide, and the text to test its relevance. Confer with other teachers concerning the most relevant portions of the text and curriculum guide.
2.	Handles administrative and clerical interruptions efficiently (e.g., visitors, announcements, collection of money, dispensing of materials and supplies) by anticipating and preorganizing some tasks and deferring others to noninstructional time	Attends to every administrative and clerical task in detail during the time normally devoted to instruction	Establish a five-to-ten minute restriction on how much time per every hour of instruction you will devote to noninstructional tasks. Defer all other tasks to before or after the lesson.
3.	Stops or prevents misbehavior with a minimum of class disruption (e.g., has preestablished academic and work rules to "protect" intrusions into instructional time)	Attends at length to specific misbehavior; singles out individual students for punishment and lectures on the offense during instructional time	Establish punishments for the most common misbehaviors and post them conspicuously. Identify only the offender and offense during instructional time, deferring punishment to later.
4.	Selects the most appropriate instructional model for the objectives being taught (e.g., primarily uses direct instruction for Type 1 behaviors and indirect instruction for Type 2 behaviors)	Uses inefficient instructional methods for achieving lesson objectives (e.g., frequently attempts to teach facts, rules, and action sequences through discussion or concepts, patterns, and abstractions through drill and practice)	Using your unit plan, curriculum guide, or adopted text, divide the content to be taught into "candidates" for Type 1 and Type 2 objectives. Generally, plan to use direct instruction for the Type 1 content and indirect instruction for Type 2 content.
5.	Builds to unit outcomes with clearly definable events (e.g., weekly and monthly review, feedback, and testing sessions)	Has no systematic milestones toward which to work (e.g., tests on Fridays, major review every fourth Monday) which keep the class on schedule and moving toward a clearly defined goal	Establish a schedule in which major classroom activities begin and end with clearly visible events (e.g., minor and major tests, and review and feedback sessions).

but you may spend just as much time returning learners' attention to the instructional activity. Some learners use such pauses or lengthy transitions to disengage from the learning task. Chapter 11 discussed ways to make smooth and efficient transitions.

Also, you will need to preorganize clerical tasks, completing as many as possible before class begins. Taking time to collate, staple, and distribute a handout in the middle of an instructional activity wastes valuable instructional time on activities that should be completed before class by you or an early arriving student. Also, placing supplies and handouts on the students' desks before class (or having a student do so) is better than breaking the flow of your teaching and your learners' attention, even though the task is brief. Remember, a few seconds can turn into several minutes when you include the time it takes the learners to settle back into a concentrated instructional routine.

You cannot avoid unexpected interruptions, such as a messenger at your door or an unscheduled public-address announcement, but you can plan for them. Establish rules beforehand for what you and your students will do. You can maintain control by receiving messages, but responding to them after class. You can maintain engagement during unexpected announcements by continuing to move about the classroom silently, in a tasklike fashion. The less-effective classroom managers in the studies by Emmer et al. (1989) and Evertson et al. (1989) often spent large amounts of time returning a class to normal after interruptions, because they were caught off guard and had not planned for such events.

Preventing Misbehavior

Maintaining effective task orientation also involves preventing or stopping misbehavior with minimum class disruption. The intrusion of misbehavior into your teaching time can be devastating, for two reasons. First, you lose instructional time in administering warnings or punishments and maintaining classroom control. Second, dealing with misbehavior can so drain you of emotional energy that, when the disruption is over, you lack the stamina and enthusiasm to resume at full pace.

You can expect to deal with misconduct at every grade level, and how you handle it makes the difference between a classroom that is task oriented and one that is not. When misbehavior occurs, don't ignore it or treat it whimsically or halfheartedly. You must *deflect its consequences away from your teaching activity at the time it occurs*. This means that you must be prepared to deal with the misbehavior at a later, noninstructional time—a time and setting *chosen by you, not the student*. Being prepared to handle misbehavior this way wrests control of the consequences from the student and lets you promptly return to the teaching task.

Of course it is easier to give this advice than to do it, but there are methods for making it work in your classroom:

☐ Post and announce academic and work rules to set a climate of classroom organization that will deter much misbehavior. Having procedures concerning misbehavior and communicating them to students beforehand lets you return to task with minimal disruption when misbehavior occurs.

□ Deal quickly with any misbehavior that does occur and return to the flow of instruction, picking up exactly where you stopped at the time of the misbehavior.

□ Establish an efficient system for *deferring the punishment phase of the misbehavior to noninstructional time*, when your attention will be undivided and the time and arena will be your choice. For example, numbering your rules and associating a broken rule with the name of a misbehaving student can signal the student to see you after class.

Selecting Instruction Models

Maintaining effective task orientation requires efficient use of instructional time. Inefficient instructional strategies waste instructional time, just as do administrative chores and misbehavior, but are far more subtly draining. Inefficient strategies can especially damage your instructional goals, because efficient and inefficient strategies often look the same. Unless you give considerable thought to matching your objectives and the instructional activities you are using to promote them, it is not difficult to be fooled into thinking that great things are happening.

Chapters 6 and 7 devoted considerable attention to two frequently used instruction models. Although rarely implemented in their pure forms, the *direct* and *indirect* approaches and their respective functions have contributed the means to efficiently teach Type 1 and Type 2 behaviors. These two types of behaviors, representing the acquisition of facts, rules, and action sequences and the learning of concepts, patterns, and abstractions, represent the range of behavioral complexity and types of outcomes found at every grade level and subject.

However, it is not uncommon for beginning teachers (and some experienced ones) to teach concepts in the context of drill and practice and to teach facts in the context of an inquiry discussion. Although both outcomes could eventually be achieved in either context, the teaching of concepts by rehearsing facts is very inefficient. Teaching facts rarely allows for the generalizations and discriminations required for concepts to be acquired, and teaching concepts fails to emphasize the *unitization* (learning the parts) and *automaticity* (putting the parts together) required for fact acquisition. Therefore, matching the type of learning outcome you wish to achieve with the instructional model which most efficiently can accomplish your outcome is an important behavior for establishing an effective task orientation.

Establishing Cycles of Review, Testing, and Feedback

The final behavior for task orientation builds to unit outcomes by establishing cycles of weekly and monthly review and testing, built around clearly definable goals (e.g., a test at the end of the month, a review session next week, a demonstration or experiment at the end of the unit). These goals are the types of products that should be visible to your students and toward which your classroom activities must gradually build with increasing intensity, enthusiasm, and expectation.

Such end products create natural cycles of rising and falling intensity, enthusiasm, and expectation, with the high point of the cycle just before the expected event and the low point immediately afterward, marking the beginning of a new cycle. In the upper grades, several different cycles can proceed concurrently. For example, some classroom activities might prepare students to complete a term paper next week, while other classroom activities might prepare students for a test at month's end. Thus, different cycles may be put in place for tests, assignments, and major projects, and may be staggered so that one cycle is near its highest point when another is near its lowest. This will ensure that a high level of intensity, enthusiasm, and expectation pertaining to one or another clearly defined goal always is present in your classroom.

A brisk instructional pace is important to accentuating the intensity, enthusiasm, and expectation as the time for an event arrives. After a major assignment has been completed, such as a term paper or test, slow the instructional pace noticeably. This establishes the cycle and makes both cycle and goal more apparent to your learners. No one can sustain a high level of intensity, enthusiasm, or expectation for very long, so the low point of the cycle serves a desirable function: to regroup, to reflect on past performances, to think about changing study habits, and to place content in a broader perspective. Conversely, a brisker instructional style cues your learners that their performance should begin to change accordingly.

These pulses of energy help maintain a classroom rhythm that will keep your students interested and working with you toward your chosen goals. It also provides the instructional variety and gentle tension that keep both students and teachers task oriented.

ENGAGEMENT IN THE CLASSROOM

Table 15.4 summarizes behaviors related to engagement:

- ☐ Eliciting the desired behavior.
- ☐ Providing opportunities for feedback in a nonevaluative atmosphere.
- ☐ Using groups and individual activities as motivational aids, such as teams, performance contracts, programmed texts, games and simulations, and learning centers.
- ☐ Using meaningful verbal praise.
- ☐ Monitoring seatwork and checking for progress.

Eliciting Behavior

Engagement in the learning process begins when you provide stimulus material to learners with which they can practice using facts, action sequences, or concepts you have taught. Without practice, learning rarely occurs. It is unfortunate that some teachers teach as they themselves were taught in the college classroom, forgetting that vast developmental differences lie between the adult and the elementary or secondary school learner.

TABLE 15.4
Indicators for engaging students in the learning process

	Engaging Students Effectively in the Learning Process (an effective teacher ...)	Engaging Students Ineffectively in the Learning Process (an ineffective teacher ...)	Solutions
1.	Elicits the desired behavior immediately after the instructional stimuli (e.g., provides exercise or workbook problems with which the desired behavior can be practiced)	Fails to ask learners to attempt the desired behavior	Schedule practice exercises or questions to immediately follow each set of instructional stimuli.
2.	Provides opportunities for feedback in a nonevaluative atmosphere (e.g., asks students to respond as a group or covertly the first time through)	Formally evaluates the initial practice (e.g., individually calls on students to give correct answer in ways that could be threatening or embarrassing)	Require covert responding or nonevaluative (e.g., group) feedback at the start of a guided practice session.
3.	Uses individual and group activities (e.g., performance contracts, programmed texts, games and simulations, and learning centers as motivational aids) when needed	Fails to match instructional methods to the learning needs of special students (e.g., slow or bilingual learners)	Have individualized instructional materials available (e.g., remedial exercises or texts) for those who may need them.
4.	Uses meaningful verbal praise to get and keep students actively participating in the learning process	Fails to provide rewards and reinforcers that are timely and meaningful to the student (e.g., never says why something is "good")	Maintain a warm and nurturing atmosphere by providing verbal praise and encouragement that is meaningful (e.g., explain why the answer was correct). Praise partially correct answers, with qualification.
5.	Monitors seatwork and frequently checks progress during independent practice	Does not monitor student progress during seatwork evenly (e.g., spends too much time with some students, failing to observe work of other students)	Limit contact with individual students during seatwork to about 30 seconds each, providing instructionally relevant answers. Circulate among entire class.

As a college student, you are accustomed to hour-long lectures, during which no opportunity may be provided to apply what is being taught. At the college level, where considerable independence and motivation are expected, the instructor appropriately assumes that engagement in the learning process will take place at your convenience and initiative as you work through the lecture material on your own.

This must *not* be your assumption, however, at the elementary and secondary school level. At this level, if learning is to occur, lecture and practice often must go hand in hand, separated by minutes rather than days. Levels of development, independence, and motivation are vastly different for the elementary and secondary school learner than for the college student. Engagement in the learning process for learners at these ages must be part of your instruction, because young learners generally cannot leap from lecture to practice without your guidance.

In Chapter 5 we called this process "eliciting the desired behavior" and identified it as an important event within the lesson plan. In Chapter 9, we suggested oral questions, workbook exercises, and specially prepared "think sheets" and model answers, used under your step-by-step guidance, as ways to encourage students to think about, work through, or practice the material being presented. You should provide such practice closely in time to the related instruction and, for complex material, intersperse it throughout the classroom, creating cycles of presentation and practice.

Providing Feedback

In addition to eliciting the desired behavior through guided practice, you need to provide feedback about the correctness of the elicited response. At this point in the learning process, your feedback must be given in as nonevaluative a manner as possible to encourage repeated responses and, therefore, engagement in the learning process. A cold "that's wrong" at this stage in the learning process may be just the excuse a student needs to stop responding to your guided practice. A full-scale evaluation of your learners' performance can come later; for now, it is important to keep the learners responding to questions, workbook exercises, or handout problems.

At this stage of learning, crude and often inadequate responses are formed into slightly less crude and more adequate responses. These in turn are the basis for eventually producing finely tuned responses at a high level of accuracy. If behaviors related to acquiring knowledge are sought, this is the time when the processes of unitization and automaticity will be operating. If behaviors related to inquiry or problem solving are sought, the processes of **generalization** (learning to go beyond the examples given) and **discrimination** (learning to separate nonexamples from examples) will be operating.

In either case, your feedback must unambiguously tell learners whether their responses are adequate and must do so in a manner that will not embarrass or humiliate them or lower their expectations. Because initial responses to a guided practice exercise may be crude, even funny, and occasionally illogical (in your eyes), the potential for emotional harm is greatest during this phase of learning.

Computers are rapidly becoming one of the most widely used instructional tools for eliciting desired responses through guided practice and providing feedback in a nonevaluative context. More than five million computers are used for instruction in schools today.

Your job is not to pass judgment but to provide feedback so learners can judge their own work. You can accomplish this by having students respond in unison, by showing answers on a transparency after each problem, or simply by supplying the answer at the end of the designated work time. However, it is a good idea to request (and occasionally check) that students write out their responses. Then you can be certain that they are engaging in the problem solution and not simply waiting for the answer to be given.

Your knowledge of motivation (Chapter 11) also is important for engaging students in the learning process. For some students, guided practice and nonevaluative feedback are not enough to engage them in the learning process. These learners need additional motivators to become sufficiently energized or excited about learning so that they attempt a first crude response to the practice opportunities you provide. Motivational devices such as performance contracts, programmed learning materials, games and simulations, cooperative groups or teams, peer tutoring, volunteering, and learning centers may be useful in engaging these students, who may represent a sizeable portion of your class.

Using Individualized and Cooperative Activities

Most teachers do not have the time or flexibility to apply different instructional methods to different types of learners, and yet teaching one or two groups of problem learners in addition to your regular class may be required of you. Curriculum demands that often are prescribed by the curriculum guide or text make all such dual teaching responsibilities nearly impossible in today's busy classrooms. However, a library of individualized remedial materials can allow for different learning needs to be met in the midst of a heterogeneous class of learners, without interrupting regularly scheduled instruction.

When performance contracts, programmed texts, games and simulations, and learning centers are individualized, some students can be directed to work independently according to their own (often special) learning needs, while others work on other activities. A teacher who effectively engages students in the learning process will establish a resource library of individualized materials for use with special or poorly motivated learners. However, these libraries do not spring up overnight, nor are they likely to be provided entirely by your department or school. Instead, as an effective teacher, you will need to accumulate them over time, beginning on your first day of teaching.

You saw in Chapter 10 how cooperative group activities could be used to engage students in the learning process. Team activities that rely on division of labor, structured tasks, and individual role functions provide a ready learning context for independent inquiry and the communication and collaborative skills needed for adult life outside the classroom. Cooperative groups have been known to engage even the most passive learners by allowing them to become decision makers in their own classroom and to assume some responsibility for their own learning.

Giving Praise

An important motivation device that works for all students is verbal praise, provided after a correct or partially correct answer. There are pitfalls in praising: verbal praise in the absence of genuine accomplishment is obviously phony; a glib response like "correct," "OK," or "yep," may be too weak to be effective, and overly emotional responses like "that's wonderful," "beautiful," or "brilliant" may strain credibility. But between these extremes lies a range of verbal rewards that the student will receive sincerely and without embarrassment.

Your verbal responses should link a student's response with the exact *level of accomplishment attained*. For example, instead of simply saying that the response is correct, tell the learner "your response was correct because _____" (e.g., the directions were followed carefully, the correct sequence of events was chosen, care was taken to consult a reference book, etc.). Or, instead of praising a learner's response as brilliant, explain the higher-level thought processes that were used to produce such a response (e.g., "your answer shows you know how to find relationships among content learned in different chapters").

In each of these cases, the emotional impact on the student and the desire to keep engaged in the learning process is greater when verbal praise is in the context of the operation successfully accomplished by the student. In such cases, glib phrases like "correct," "good," and "OK" are never worn out, because they are associated with a unique production by the learner.

In Chapter 6, you saw the special importance of verbal praise in the case of partially correct or correct-but-hesitant responses. Here, your praise must be tempered with a sign that a better or less-hesitant response is desired. To ignore the inadequacy or hesitation in favor of a simple "OK" signals others that they, too, can provide a less-than-adequate response. In these cases, praise must be proportional to the adequacy of the response: "That's partly correct; now let's see if you can put it all together," or "Good try; now change one thing and you'll have it." These examples point up subtle differences between a partially correct answer and a wrong answer, a discrimination that you must judge. You will promote engagement in the learning process more by telling learners that the glass is half full rather than half empty.

Finally, avoid "meaningful verbal punishment" (e.g., scolding a learner for a careless response). Phrases that ridicule, demean, or draw the class's attention to a learner's ineptitude rarely, if ever, change the behavior that led to the learner's careless or incorrect response. (This is not to be confused with reminders to study harder, pay greater attention, think some more, or go over mistakes, which often are desirable stimulants to learning.) In these instances, your best approach is to avoid an emotional response and provide constructive tips for finding the right answer, or to solicit the answer from another.

Monitoring and Checking

The last behavior for effectively engaging students in the learning process involves monitoring and checking. These two processes go hand in hand, because one without the other cannot be effective. Monitoring involves **withitness**—systematically observing all aspects of your classroom. It also involves being able to perform overlapping activities in which your learners are actively being observed while you do other things. To assure your students that you have withitness, such monitoring should occur during both instructional and noninstructional activities.

During instructional activities such as guided practice and independent seatwork, monitor within a systematic routine of checking. Rather than visually scanning parts of the classroom, circulate among students and check their responses in workbooks or exercises. Be certain that your learners see your circulating behavior as not evaluative, but rather as a helpful response to their work. A casual glance at one paper and then another until you have covered the entire room is more constructive than long interactions with individual students. Limit interactions with individual students to brief interchanges of about 30 seconds and limit responses to address a particular problem a student is having. You can repeat this cycle many times, looking closer on subsequent rounds.

Monitoring and checking for progress, especially during guided and independent practice, are two of the most important tools you can have for effectively engaging your students in the learning process.

STUDENT SUCCESS

Table 15.5 summarizes behaviors related to student success. Engaging learners in the learning process at moderate-to-high rates of success involves:

- ☐ Establishing unit and lesson content that reflects prior learning.
- ☐ Correcting partially correct, correct-but-hesitant, and incorrect answers.
- ☐ Dividing instructional stimuli into bite-size pieces at the learners' current level of functioning.
- ☐ Changing instructional stimuli gradually.
- ☐ Varying the instructional tempo or pace to create momentum.

Establishing Content That Reflects Prior Learning

The first behavior for obtaining a moderate-to-high success rate takes place during unit planning, when you identify unit outcomes and choose a logical lesson sequence to achieve them. Surprising as it may be, many units are planned with little or no consideration of sequencing. Recall from Chapter 5 that, although some of your unit outcomes may be achieved by presenting content in any order, the cost in instructional time with such a haphazard approach can be considerable. The result of such planning, or lack of it, often is expressed as "I've run out of time," or "I couldn't get to topic X," or "I have too many interruptions this semester to finish the text."

Depending on the circumstances, these statements may or may not result from poor unit planning, but more often than not they could be avoided with good unit planning. Good unit planning means arranging lessons in a sequence that works for you, not against you. You may not realize that a minor change in the order in which you teach content can create major savings in instructional time by making each new lesson relate to the previous lesson. This means that task-relevant prior knowledge taught earlier is placed to immediately precede the lesson in which it will be needed (or as close in time as possible). The time savings results because you do not have to reteach the task-relevant prior learning, or because you do not have to reteach that day's lesson after you discover that the task-relevant information needed for it had not been learned.

You can consume considerable instructional time in backtracking to remove deficiencies in fact, skill, or concept that could have been avoided with better unit-level planning. Effective unit planning means making each lesson work for you by arranging an instruction sequence that builds logically and systematically to your unit outcomes. This emphasizes the importance of establishing unit plans in the first place, because without them you run the risk of randomly throwing content at learners. Some of them may be struggling to make the transition from earlier lessons and, finding no transition, will simply give up or tune out. Make each new lesson a logical extension of the previous lesson to secure moderate-to-high success rates during guided and independent practice.

TABLE 15.5
Indicators for student success

	Moderate-to-High Rates of Success (an effective teacher . . .)	Poor Rates of Success (an ineffective teacher . . .)	Solutions
1.	Establishes unit and lesson content that reflects prior learning (e.g., planning lesson sequences that consider task-relevant prior information)	Fails to sequence learning in advance to ensure that all task-relevant prior knowledge has been taught before moving to next lesson	Create a top-down unit plan in which all the lesson outcomes at the bottom of the hierarchy needed to achieve unit outcomes at the top of the hierarchy are identified. Arrange lessons in an order most logical to achieving unit outcomes.
2.	Administers correctives immediately after initial response (e.g., shows model of correct answer and how to attain it after first crude response is given)	Leaves students to practice and learn independently immediately after presenting instructional stimuli; waits until next day to show correct responses	Provide for guided practice prior to independent practice and provide means of self-checking (e.g., handout with correct answers) at intervals of practice.
3.	Divides instructional stimuli into small chunks (e.g., establishes bite-size lessons that can be easily digested by learners at their current level of functioning)	Packages instruction in chunks that are too large or small (e.g., teaches too complex of a lesson too early in an instructional sequence)	Break lessons at "bottom" of unit plan into smaller pieces. Use original "lessons" as units or divisions within units.
4.	Plans transitions to new material in easy to grasp steps (e.g., changes instructional stimuli according to a preestablished thematic pattern so that each new lesson is seen as an extension of previous lessons)	Abruptly changes instructional topics and perspectives from one lesson to another without themes and interconnections	Extend unit-plan hierarchy downward to more specific lessons that are tied together above with a single unit theme and outcome. Use the part-whole, sequential, combinatorial, comparative, or the problem centered, hierarchical, or networking approaches for organizing content.
5.	Varies the pace at which stimuli are presented and continually builds toward a climax or key event	Maintains same pace for too long a time, leading to a monotonous and static level of intensity and expectation	Use review, feedback, and testing sessions to form intervals of increasing and decreasing intensity and expectation.

Correcting Answers

Another essential behavior for securing moderate-to-high success rates is timely feed-back. During guided practice, in which you elicit the desired behavior for the first time, give correctives immediately after the learner's initial response.

The time between practice and feedback long has been considered by edu-cational psychologists as one of the most important elements of learning. The longer feedback is delayed, the less likely it is to influence the learner's performance on subsequent attempts to produce the behavior. The reasons are complex, but essen-tially the learner must hold a mental image of the first crude response in memory for the feedback to be effective. Unfortunately, mental images fade quickly, especially in young learners, so the effectiveness of the feedback deteriorates rapidly with any delay. For the learner to link your feedback to his or her image of the response, the corrective must immediately follow.

Chapters 6, 7, and 8 discussed several practices for accomplishing this, such as calling out the right answer after each practice item has been completed, displaying a model on a transparency that illustrates how to attain a right answer, or having students check the responses of other students according to some standard provided by you or the text. Note also that feedback using these and related procedures should be administered in a nonevaluative atmosphere. Both immediacy and a nonevaluative atmosphere must be present for the feedback to have its greatest effect on revising and refining the response.

To achieve moderate-to-high rates of success, provide feedback for every item during guided practice. A missed opportunity to correct a wrong, partially wrong, or even correct-but-hesitant response (which may be correct for the wrong reason) during this critical time can affect success rates during later independent practice (sustained seatwork, workbook exercises, or homework).

During direct instruction, continue guided practice until a success rate of approximately 60–80% is achieved. Generally, this will be possible only if the correct responses and the reasons for them are provided after every trial response. This paves the way for a still higher success rate at the end of independent practice, at which time you should expect about 90–95% correct answers. However, this higher success rate rarely can be achieved without first establishing the 60–80% success rate during guided practice. Then, feedback during independent practice may be delayed with no ill effect on success rate, such as when correct answers are given at the end of the period, or when homework is graded the next day.

Sizing Instructional Content

Our next behavior for establishing moderate-to-high success rates involves sizing unit and lesson plans to fit your learners. Of course, you should choose units to reflect some "whole" that is comprehensible to your learners. But units also must be sized so that, when broader concepts and abstractions are taught at the end of the unit, learners still remember specifics taught at the beginning of the unit.

For example, units that ramble through many historical periods, physical laws, mathematical operations, social issues, or elements of composition will prevent your learners from gaining a sense of direction and from connecting facts, rules, and sequences with the concepts, patterns, and abstractions to which they belong. This is true no matter how related the periods, laws, operations, issues, or elements may be. Experience teaches that, when in doubt, make units less encompassing than originally desired, simply because the depth and breadth of content that is comprehensible to you will rarely be comprehensible at the same depth and breadth to your learners.

Sizing mistakes at the unit level will return to haunt you at the lesson level. For instance, if your unit topic is too broad and encompassing, you will be forced to make the component lessons broad and encompassing to cover the unit content in the specified period of time. This is where considerable difficulty can occur at the lesson level in establishing moderate-to-high success rates. As lesson content becomes broader, it necessarily becomes less detailed, which often leaves less time for adequate periods of guided and independent practice. There will be a rush to cover the content, and adequate coverage may be compromised.

Also, behaviors at higher levels of complexity may be taught without adequate attention to the task-relevant prior facts, rules, and sequences needed to attain these outcomes. You may be tempted to walk across mountain tops without realizing that some valleys must be crossed as well. The indirect instruction model is valuable in covering concepts, patterns, and abstractions quickly and efficiently, but an entire unit planned around the indirect instruction model is a sign that too broad a content area is envisioned at the unit level and that some retrenchment may be necessary.

Finally, note that any individual piece of content chosen must be at your learners' current level of functioning if moderate-to-high success rates are to be achieved. When lengthy guided practice sessions or group discussion sessions do not provide 60–80% correct responses during direct instruction, lesson content may be both too broad and too complex for your learners. This is a sign that your pieces of content may not be bite-size and that you may have to divide a lesson into several smaller lessons before it can be digested by your learners. Keep in mind that unfinished lessons should be continued as subsequent lessons and not relegated to the excuse that "time ran out." This always is true when the unfinished content represents task-relevant learning for subsequent lessons.

Establishing Transition

The fourth behavior for obtaining moderate-to-high success rates employs transitions within and between lesson content. Although planning lesson content in bite-sized pieces helps learners make transitions between old and new content, this alone cannot ensure moderate-to-high success rates. In addition, you need to organize unit and lesson content to establish overarching themes that interconnect parts of a unit or an extended lesson.

In Chapters 6 and 7 you saw methods for organizing content to establish connections across different lessons or parts of a lesson. For direct instruction these were the part-whole, sequential, combinatorial, and comparative approaches to organizing content, and for indirect instruction they were the problem-centered, hierarchical, and networking approaches (these are not mutually exclusive).

Each approach is a means for organizing lessons, and content within lessons, to emphasize relationships among parts of a topic. Some link content procedurally, as in the sequential or problem-centered approaches; others link content by emphasizing themes in the content itself, as in the comparative and networking approaches. With either type the effect upon the learner is to make transitions more comprehensible. This organization helps the learner see how material being taught is a part of what has gone before and what will follow.

This is a valuable outcome for establishing moderate-to-high rates of success because the learner is able to build an understanding gradually and in measured steps, as opposed to cramming all the bits and pieces together at review and test time. Increasing one's understanding in a stairstep fashion is only possible when a direction and continuity link all the steps. Without direction and continuity, one quickly loses the underlying theme or connection between the pieces and learning is reduced to memorizing them and hoping they come together.

Unless your lessons are organized to come together from the very start, it is unlikely they will do so in your learners' minds. These organizational approaches make the transitions between lesson topics accessible to every student, even when lessons are disproportional in breadth and complexity. Easy and hard lessons may be inevitable, but the transition between them always will be more comprehensible when you explain to your learners the common structure of which they are a part.

Varying the Instructional Tempo

The final behavior for establishing moderate-to-high success rates has been mentioned in our discussion of several other effective teaching behaviors. It deserves special mention again, however, with respect to the concept of **momentum**. This last teaching-effectiveness indicator adds a subtle but important feature to establishing cycles of weekly and monthly review and testing.

Teaching in some ways is like conducting a symphony orchestra. These two occupations may have more in common than either the theatergoer or the student realizes. The thread that binds them is not their content, of course, but rather that both the maestro and the teacher must direct a melody that will be understood by their respective audiences even if it has never been heard before. This is quite a feat for both conductor and teacher, and perhaps it is why each has an extremely challenging profession. How can students be made to understand in a 45-minute lesson something they knew nothing about before, and how can the conductor make an abstract and perhaps heretofore unheard concerto recognizable to the audience?

The secret is in how the notes or individual pieces of lesson content are put together. How the notes are played against one another is reflected in the tune's melody, and how the individual pieces of content are related to one another is reflected in the lesson's momentum. Both teacher and maestro play a melody by putting together familiar notes or familiar facts and concepts in ways that make sense, even though that exact combination of notes or combination of facts and concepts has not been heard before.

Obviously, notes cannot be just thrown together to make a symphony, any more than facts and concepts can be thrown together to make a lesson. Instead, rules must be followed, discovered over years of painstaking inquiry, that put things together in ways understandable to *any* audience. This book has introduced you to the many and varied rules for effective teaching in the form of techniques (e.g., questioning/probing), strategies (e.g., drill and practice/cooperative learning), and methods (e.g., direct/indirect). However, to make your lesson concerto meaningful you will have to blend these in ways interpretable by your audience. One of the most important ingredients for ensuring that your melody will be listened to and understood is momentum.

Momentum is as important to you as to the symphony conductor. You establish momentum by varying the pace at which stimuli are presented during the process of reaching a climax or key event. In teaching, you accomplish this first by establishing cycles of weekly and monthly review, feedback, and testing and then by gradually increasing pace and intensity as the time for the major event draws near. Playing the same instructional note—or keeping the same monotonous pace—too long may be as boring as listening to a drab and lifeless musical score. Consequently, you must establish rising and falling action to move the instruction toward a discernable end. You can establish this by scheduling cycles of review, feedback, and testing and by gradually increasing the pace or tempo within cycles in ways that are visible to your learners.

FORMATIVE OBSERVATION OF EFFECTIVE TEACHING PRACTICES

This chapter has discussed many different indicators of effective teaching—28 in all. With the aid of the observation tips and recording forms provided in the companion volume to this text, *Observation Skills for Effective Teaching* (Borich, 1990), you now are ready to observe these key and helping behaviors for effective teaching in the classroom.

To help you get started, at the beginning of Appendix C you will find these 28 behaviors in the Formative Observation of Effective Teaching Practices Instrument, on which you can place a checkmark when one of these behaviors is observed. To provide practice in observing some of these effectiveness indicators, several classroom dialogues are provided in the appendix. Read these carefully, looking for signs of effectiveness and ineffectiveness pertaining to the five key behaviors, and record your results on the observation instrument.

Additional practice dialogues and other types of recording devices for each of the effective teaching behaviors discussed in this book are provided in the companion text, *Observation Skills for Effective Teaching*. This book will be a useful resource for your preteaching observations and student teaching experience.

A FINAL WORD

It is important to say that you will have second thoughts (maybe often) about becoming a teacher. The job may be as complex and challenging as that of a symphony conductor but, as we both know, the pay and working conditions are hardly the same—nor, probably, will they ever be. Rather, it is those indefinable qualities of teaching that draw us to it. Being around the youth and vitality that we will never again have, being able to lead and guide during the critical developing years of our learners' lives, and being able to instill and share an excitement and understanding for a subject we have come to respect and appreciate are all part of the best reasons to teach.

But even these may miss the most important reason of all for becoming a teacher: perhaps nowhere else on earth can we be so close to life with all of its excitement, exhilaration, and adversity. The casual traveler, as well as the anthropologist, travels far and wide looking for different cultures, new experiences, novelties, oddities, beauty, strange customs, excitement, and even love and compassion. But there is nowhere that all of these things are woven into such a rich tapestry of life than in the American classroom. The price for a front row seat indeed may be high. But for countless thousands of us, being able to observe, participate in, and most important, to work at improving this tapestry, always will be worth the cost. Be sure to open your heart and mind to this side of teaching, for which many travel far and wide but often fail to see. And good luck!

SUMMING UP

This chapter summarized how the effective teacher employs the five key behaviors of lesson clarity, instructional variety, task orientation, engagement in the learning process, and student success. Its main points were:

1. To be clear in the classroom, the effective teacher:
   - ☐ Informs learners of the objective.
   - ☐ Provides learners with advance organizers.
   - ☐ Checks for task-relevant prior learning and reteaches if necessary.
   - ☐ Gives directions slowly and distinctly.
   - ☐ Knows the ability level of learners and teaches to those levels.
   - ☐ Uses examples, illustrations, and demonstrations to explain and clarify text and workbook content.
   - ☐ Provides a review or summary at the end of each lesson.
2. To have instructional variety in the classroom, the effective teacher:
   - ☐ Uses attention-gaining devices.
   - ☐ Shows enthusiasm.
   - ☐ Varies mode of presentation.
   - ☐ Mixes rewards and reinforcers.
   - ☐ Uses student ideas.
   - ☐ Varies types of questions and probes.
3. To be task-oriented in the classroom, the effective teacher:
   - ☐ Develops unit and lesson plans that reflect the curriculum.
   - ☐ Handles administrative and clerical interruptions efficiently.
   - ☐ Stops or prevents misbehavior with a minimum of class disruption.
   - ☐ Selects the most appropriate instructional model for the objectives being taught.
   - ☐ Establishes cycles of review, feedback, and testing.
4. To engage students in the learning process, the effective teacher:
   - ☐ Elicits the desired behavior.
   - ☐ Provides opportunities for feedback in a non-evaluative atmosphere.
   - ☐ Uses group and individual activities as motivational aids when necessary.

☐ Uses meaningful praise.

☐ Monitors seatwork and checks for practice.

5. To establish moderate-to-high rates of success in the classroom, the effective teacher:

☐ Establishes unit and lesson content that reflects prior learning.

☐ Corrects partially correct, correct but hesitant, and incorrect answers.

☐ Divides instructional stimuli into bite-sized pieces that are at the learners' current level of functioning.

☐ Changes instructional stimuli gradually.

☐ Varies the instructional pace or tempo to create momentum.

FOR DISCUSSION AND PRACTICE

1. Identify the seven different signs of effectiveness pertaining to the key behavior of lesson clarity. Indicate which, in your opinion, are the most important.

2. Identify the six different signs of effectiveness pertaining to the key behavior of instructional variety. Which, in your opinion, should occur daily, which weekly, and which only monthly?

3. Identify the five different signs of effectiveness pertaining to the key behavior of task orientation. What curriculum resources, in your opinion, should be available during lesson planning to ensure task orientation?

4. Identify the five different signs of effectiveness pertaining to the key behavior of engagement in the learning process. Explain in your own words how engagement in the learning process differs from, but also is related to, task orientation.

5. Identify the five different signs of effectiveness pertaining to the key behavior of success rate. Approximately what percentage of correct responses should be achieved during guided practice, and what percentage during independent practice?

6. Identify one sign of ineffectiveness for each of the five key behaviors that, in your opinion, is the most serious for preventing effective teaching.

7. For each of the five key behaviors, identify the single helping behavior that would be most useful in executing that key behavior. The helping behaviors are structuring, questioning, probing, use of student ideas, and teacher affect.

8. Using the Formative Observation of Effective Teaching Practices Instrument in Appendix C as your guide, indicate which—of the 28 signs of effectiveness would be—for you personally—(a) the most difficult to achieve and (b) the easiest to achieve. For each of your (a) choices, explain why you think the behavior would be difficult to achieve. What resources, aids, and instructional devices, if available to you, would make these behaviors easier to achieve?

9. Apply the Formative Observation of Effective Teaching Practices Instrument to the three classroom dialogues in Appendix C. Compare the results, noting differences in the effectiveness profiles of the three teachers. Share your results in a group session, discussing any differences in profiles with members of your group or class.

10. Observe one or more classrooms and place checkmarks on the Formative Observation of Effective Teaching Practices Instrument (Appendix C) whenever a sign of effectiveness or ineffectiveness is noticed. At the end of your observation(s), sum the checkmarks within categories to create frequencies for each of the 28 signs. Now, construct two bar graphs indicating the relative frequencies with which the (a) effectiveness and (b) ineffectiveness indicators were observed.

SUGGESTED READINGS

Biddle, B. (1987). Effects of teaching. In M. J. Dunkin (Ed.), *International encyclopedia of teaching and teacher education*. New York: Pergamon.

An overview of the systematic positive influences on learners that teachers can have in the classroom.

Borich, G. (1990). *Observation skills for effective teaching*. Columbus: Macmillan.

A companion volume to this text—a practical guide to procedures and instruments for observing in classrooms with classroom dialogues and case examples.

Borich, G. (1992). *Clearly outstanding: Making each day count in your classroom*. Boston: Allyn and Bacon.

A self-improvement guide for the beginning teacher, extending to the in-service arena many of the ideas in this text.

Borich, G., & Nance, D. (1990). *The effective teacher program*. Professional Teachers' Library, 1009 Harwood Pl., Austin, TX 78704.

Twenty-seven activity booklets for the beginning teacher, containing extensive examples, entertaining classroom dialogues, and practical observation instruments for effective teaching, keyed to this and its companion volume.

Doyle, W. (1990). Classroom knowledge as a foundation for teaching. *Teachers College Record, 3*, 348–360.

A framework for creating teaching practices grounded in the realities of school settings.

Elliot, J. (1987). Teachers as researchers. In M. J. Dunkin (Ed.), *International encyclopedia of teaching and teacher education*. New York: Pergamon.

How the classroom teacher can contribute to modern definitions of effective teaching through careful observation and reflection.

Fogarty, J. E., Wang, M. C., & Creek, R. (1983). A descriptive study of experienced and novice teachers' interactive instructional thoughts and actions. *Journal of Educational Research, 77*, 22–32.

A contrast between experienced and novice teachers showing how the planning and instructional decision-making of experienced teachers differs from inexperienced teachers—and the potential effects on learners.

Huberman, M. (1989). The professional life cycle of teachers. *Teachers College Record, 91,* 31–57.

An informative account of the phases of a teacher's career and professional development.

Peterson, P. L., & Clark, C. M. (1978). Teachers' reports of their cognitive processes during teaching. *American Educational Research Journal, 15,* 555–565.

A comprehensive review of what teachers think about during teaching and how they choose some key behaviors for implementation.

Rohrkemper, M. (1987). Proactive teaching. In M. J. Dunkin (Ed.), *International encyclopedia of teaching and teacher education*. New York: Pergamon.

Summarizes the most important features of the direct instruction model.

Rohrkemper, M. (1987). Reactive teaching. In M. J. Dunkin (Ed.), *International encyclopedia of teaching and teacher education*. New York: Pergamon.

Summarizes the most important features of the indirect instruction model.

Winne, P., & Marx, R. (1982). Students' and teachers' views of thinking processes for classroom learning. *The Elementary School Journal, 82,* 493–518.

A report of the retrospective thoughts and concerns of both students and teachers during instruction—with implications for the use of key and catalytic behaviors.

APPENDIX A

Teacher Concerns Checklist

Francis F. Fuller   Gary D. Borich
The University of Texas at Austin

(See description of this questionnaire in the section "A Hierarchy of Planning Needs" in Chapter 3.)

DIRECTIONS: This checklist explores what teachers are concerned about at different stages of their careers. There are no right or wrong answers, because each teacher has his or her own concerns.

On the following page are statements of concerns you might have. Read each statement and ask yourself: WHEN I THINK ABOUT TEACHING, AM I CONCERNED ABOUT THIS?

☐ If you are *not concerned,* or the statement does not apply, write *1* in the box.
☐ If you are *a little concerned,* write *2* in the box.
☐ If you are *moderately concerned,* write *3* in the box.
☐ If you are *very concerned,* write *4* in the box.
☐ And if you are *totally preoccupied* with the concern, write *5* in the box.

Be sure to answer every item. Begin by completing the following:

1. Name _____ Male _____ Female _____ Age _____
   Date _____
2. Circle the number of the statement that best describes your teaching experience:
   (1) No education courses and no formal classroom observation or teaching experience.
   (2) Education courses but no formal observation or teaching experience.
   (3) Education courses and observation experience but no teaching.
   (4) Presently student teaching.
   (5) Presently an inservice teacher.
3. If you are a student: Freshman _____ Sophomore _____ Junior _____
   Senior _____ Graduate _____
4. The grade level you plan to teach (if student) or are now teaching (if inservice):
   Preschool _____ Elementary _____ Junior High _____
   Senior High _____ College _____ Other _____
5. Years of teaching experience (if inservice) _____

For each statement below, decide which of the five responses best applies to you now. Place the number of the answer in the box at the left of the statement. Please be as accurate as you can.

[1] Not concerned   [2] A little concerned   [3] Moderately concerned

[4] Very concerned   [5] Totally preoccupied

1. Insufficient clerical help for teachers.
2. Whether the students respect me.
3. Too many extra duties and responsibilities.
4. Doing well when I'm observed.
5. Helping students to value learning.
6. Insufficient time for rest and class preparation.
7. Not enough assistance from specialized teachers.
8. Managing my time efficiently.
9. Losing the respect of my peers.
10. Not enough time for grading and testing.
11. The inflexibility of the curriculum.
12. Too many standards and regulations set for teachers.
13. My ability to prepare adequate lesson plans.
14. Having my inadequacies become known to other teachers.
15. Increasing students' feelings of accomplishment.
16. The rigid instructional routine.
17. Diagnosing student learning problems.
18. What the principal may think if there is too much noise in my classroom.
19. Whether each student is reaching his or her potential.
20. Obtaining a favorable evaluation of my teaching.
21. Having too many students in a class.
22. Recognizing the social and emotional needs of students.
23. Challenging unmotivated students.
24. Losing the respect of my students.
25. Lack of public support for schools.
26. My ability to maintain the appropriate degree of class control.

27. Not having sufficient time to plan.
28. Getting students to behave.
29. Understanding why certain students make slow progress.
30. Having an embarrassing incident occur in my classroom for which I might be judged responsible.
31. Not being able to cope with troublemakers in my classes.
32. That my peers may think I'm not doing an adequate job.
33. My ability to work with disruptive students.
34. Understanding ways in which student health and nutrition problems can affect learning.
35. Appearing competent to parents.
36. Meeting the needs of different kinds of students.
37. Seeking alternative ways to ensure that students learn the subject matter.
38. Understanding the psychological and cultural differences that can affect my students' behavior.
39. Adapting myself to the needs of different students.
40. The large number of administrative interruptions.
41. Guiding students toward intellectual and emotional growth.
42. Working with too many students each day.
43. Whether students can apply what they learn.
44. Teaching effectively when another teacher is present.
45. Understanding what factors motivate students to learn.

Teacher Concerns Checklist by Francis F. Fuller and Gary D. Borich, The University of Texas at Austin, from Gary D. Borich, *Effective Teaching Methods* (2nd ed.), Merrill/MacMillan. This instrument was revised with the assistance of John Rogan, Western Montana University.

The following items on the Teacher Concerns Checklist represent the dimensions of Self, Task, and Impact:

Self	Task	Impact
2	1	5
4	3	15
8	6	17
9	7	19
13	10	22
14	11	23
18	12	29
20	16	34
24	21	36
26	25	37
28	27	38
30	31	39
32	33	41
35	40	43
44	42	45

REFERENCES

Borich, G. (1990). *Observation skills for effective teaching.* Columbus: Merrill/Macmillan (Chapter 4).

Borich, G. (1992). *Clearly outstanding: Making each day count in your classroom.* Boston: Allyn and Bacon (Chapter 8).

Fuller, F. F. (1969). Concerns of teachers: A developmental conceptualization. *American Educational Research Journal, 6,* 207–226.

Fuller, F., Brown, O., & Peck, R. (1966). *Creating climates for growth.* Austin: University of Texas, Research and Development Center for Teacher Education. ERIC Document Reproduction Service, ED 013 989.

Fuller, F., Pilgrim, G., & Freeland, A. (1967). *Intensive individualization of teacher preparation.* Austin: University of Texas, Research and Development Center for Teacher Education. ERIC Document Reproduction Service, ED 011 603.

Hall, G. E., & Hord, S. M. (1987). *Change in schools: Facilitating the process.* Ithaca: State University of New York Press.

Hord, S. M., Rutherford, W. L., Huling-Austin, L., & Hall, G. E. (1987). *Taking charge of change.* Alexandria: Association for Supervision and Curriculum Development.

Rutherford, W. L., & Hall, G. E. (1990). *Concerns of teachers: Revisiting the original theory after twenty years.* Paper presented at the annual meeting of the American Educational Research Association, Boston. (Available from W. Rutherford, College of Education, The University of Texas at Austin, Austin, TX 78712.)

APPENDIX B

Answers to Chapter Questions

These are answers to questions marked (*) in the "For Discussion and Practice" sections of the text chapters. Answers are not supplied for questions that lack the asterisk.

CHAPTER 1

1. 1, 2, 1 (or 2), 1 (or 2), 2, 3, 2, 3, 2 (or 1), 3, 2, 3, 3.

3.

Behavior	High SES	Low SES
Individualization	Ask difficult questions	Supplement standard curriculum with individualized materials
Teacher affect	Correct poor answers immediately when student fails to perform	Be warm and encouraging
Overteaching/overlearning	Assign homework	Present materials in small pieces
Classroom interaction	Engage students in questions and answers	Help students immediately when help is needed

CHAPTER 2

1. a. Match instructional methods to individual learning needs.
   b. Understand the reasons behind the school performance of individual learners.
2. ☐ High state anxiety: place value of specific assignment in perspective with other assignments.

☐ Low auditory ability: use visual forms of instruction.
☐ Gifted: encourage independent thinking.
☐ Low SES: make available popular reading sources and supplementary learning materials (e.g., visual aids).
☐ Poor self-concept: reflect back to students the value of their unique talents.

511

☐ High trait anxiety: create a range of acceptable alternatives for a given assignment.

☐ Unassertive, overassertive, or aggressive: encourage a broad list of occupations for both sexes, avoid sexual stereotypes, organize problem-solving activities that define the limits of independent and creative behavior.

☐ Disruptive peer group: break into more heterogeneous groups for learning exercises.

9. Get students to talk about themselves; reward unique talents.

10. a. state
    b. trait

c. trait
d. trait
e. state
f. trait
g. trait
h. state but also trait
i. trait
j. trait but also state

11. Self-concept is related to engagement in the learning process and success in an occupation.

12. Exchange some troublesome students with other classes. Form heterogeneous groups composed of members of different peer groups.

CHAPTER 3

1. a, g, a, g, a, g, a, g, g, g.

5. (1) Strengthening of the curriculum in the areas of math, science, English, foreign language, and social studies.

   (2) Renewed effort to teach higher-order thinking skills.

   (3) Raising school grading standards.

   (4) Raising college admission standards.

   (5) More work in core subjects.

6. To teach students how to think.

9. (1) Aims and goals (texts, curriculum guides, policy reports).

   (2) Learner needs (student achievement, workbook exercises, class performance).

   (3) Knowledge of academic discipline (subject matter texts).

   (4) Knowledge of teaching methods (key and catalytic behaviors).

   (5) Tacitly acquired knowledge from day-to-day experience in the classroom.

13. ☐ Front half/back half
    ☐ Girls/boys
    ☐ More-able/less-able
    ☐ Nonminority/minority

14. ☐ Spreading interactions across categories of students.
    ☐ Selecting students randomly.
    ☐ Pairing students.
    ☐ Coding class notes.

15. Self, task, impact.

17. First teacher has profile B, second teacher has profile A, third teacher has profile C, fourth teacher has profile D.

CHAPTER 4

1. a. To tie general aims and goals to specific classroom strategies that will achieve those aims and goals.

   b. To express teaching strategies in a format that allows you to measure their effects upon your learners.

2. The behavior is observable, it is measurable, and it occurs in a specifiable period of time.

3. The observable behavior, conditions under which it is to be observed, and level of proficiency at which it is to be displayed.

4. Teachers tended to focus their concerns on self and task, sometimes to the exclusion of their impact on students.

5. Because action verbs truly point toward the goal of achieving the desired behavior and observing its attainment.
6. A, O, A, A, A, O, O, O.
7. The circumstances under which the behavior is to be displayed.
8. By establishing the setting under which the behavior will be tested, which guides them in how and what to study.
9. The extent to which the conditions are similar to those under which the behavior will have to be performed in the real world.

10. The level of proficiency at which the behavior must be displayed.
12. (1) b
    (2) a
    (3) b
    (4) e
    (5) f

CHAPTER 5

1. Knowledge of aims and goals, knowledge of learners, knowledge of subject matter content and organization, knowledge of teaching methods, and tacit knowledge.
2. By the way in which individual lessons are sequenced and build upon one another to produce a unified whole.
3. □ Hierarchy helps us see the relationship between individual lesson outcomes and the unit outcome. It also helps us identify lessons that are not too big or too small, but that are just right.
   □ Task-relevant prior learning is used to identify the proper sequence of lessons needed to teach the unit outcome.
4. Both help us picture the flow and sequence of a lesson plan.
5. □ Cognitive: analysis, synthesis, evaluation
   □ Affective: valuing, organization, characterization
   □ Psychomotor: precision, articulation, naturalization

6. They represent smaller, more detailed portions of content.
8. It would take more intermediate levels to arrive at content suitably sized for a lesson.
9. Ability grouping, peer tutoring, learning centers, review, and follow-up materials.
10. Mastery learning is when each student displays a high level, if not complete proficiency, of each intended outcome.
11. Gaining attention, informing the learner of the objective, stimulating recall of prerequisite learning, presenting the stimulus material, eliciting the desired behavior, providing feedback, assessing the behavior.
12. Presenting the stimulus material.
13. Assessing the behavior.
14. Eliciting the desired behavior.
15. Providing feedback: immediate and nonevaluative Assessing the behavior: delayed and evaluative.

CHAPTER 6

1. □ Type 1: facts, rules, action sequences.
   □ Type 2: concepts, patterns, abstractions.
   □ Type 1 outcomes generally apply to the knowledge, comprehension, and application levels, while Type 2 outcomes generally apply to the analysis, synthesis, and evaluation levels.
2. □ Knowledge acquisition: facts, rules, action sequences.

   □ Inquiry or problem solving: concepts, patterns, and abstractions.
3. Full class instruction; questions posed by the teacher; detailed and redundant practice; one new fact, rule, or sequence mastered before the next is presented; arrangement of classroom to maximize drill and practice.
4. □ Cognitive: to recall, to describe, to list.

- ☐ Affective: to listen, to attend, to be aware.
- ☐ Psychomotor: to repeat, to follow, to place.
5. (1) To disseminate information that is not readily available from texts or workbooks in appropriately sized pieces.
  (2) To arouse or heighten student interest.
  (3) To achieve content mastery.
6. (1) Having students correct each other's work.
  (2) Having students identify difficult homework problems.
  (3) Sampling the understanding of a few students who represent the range of students in the class.
  (4) Explicitly reviewing the task-relevant information necessary for the day's lesson.
7. Part-whole, sequential, combinatorial, comparative.
8. Rule–Example–Rule.
9. To create a response, however crude, that can become the basis for learning.
10. It is used to help convert wrong or partially correct answers to right answers by encouraging the student to use some aspects of the answer given in formulating the correct response.
11. (1) Correct, quick, and firm: acknowledge correctness and either ask another question or move on.

(2) Correct but hesitant: acknowledge correctness and review steps for attaining correct answer.
(3) Incorrect but careless: acknowledge incorrectness and immediately move on.
(4) Incorrect due to lack of knowledge: acknowledge incorrectness and then, without actually giving the student the answer, channel student's thoughts in ways that result in a correct answer.
14. Review key facts, explain steps required, prompt with clues or hints, walk student through a similar problem.
15. 60–80%. Reduce content coverage, increase opportunities for practice and feedback.
16. To form action sequences. They should increasingly resemble applications in the real world.
17. Keep contacts to a minimum, on the average of 30 seconds; spread contacts across most students, avoiding concentrating on a few students.
18. About 95%.
19. Gradually increase the coverage and depth of weekly reviews until time for a comprehensive monthly review arrives.
20. Preview them carefully to ascertain their adherence to the six functions of direct instruction.

CHAPTER 7

1. Inquiry, discovery, and a problem.
2. ☐ Type 1: facts, rules and action sequences.
  ☐ Type 2: concepts, patterns, and abstractions.
3. The learner indirectly acquires a behavior by transforming stimulus material into a response or behavior that differs (a) from the stimulus used to present the learning and (b) from any previous response emitted by the learner.
4. It is not generally efficient or effective for attaining outcomes at the higher levels of complexity involving concepts, patterns, and abstractions.
5. ☐ Unitization: the learning of individual facts or rules.
  ☐ Automaticity: putting the facts or rules together in an action sequence and being able to execute the sequence rapidly and automatically.
  ☐ Example: learning to read.
6. ☐ Generalization: classifying apparently different stimuli into the same category on the basis of criterial attributes.

☐ Discrimination: distinguishing examples of a concept from nonexamples.
☐ Example: learning the meaning of *democracy*.
7. (1) 1
  (2) 2
  (3) 1
  (4) 2
  (5) 2
  (6) 1
  (7) 2
  (8) 2
  (9) 1
  (10) 2
8. Our memories would become overburdened trying to remember all possible instances of the concept; also, instances of the concept could easily be confused with noninstances.

11. ☐ Induction: the process of thinking in which a set of specific data is presented or observed and a generalization or unifying pattern is drawn from the data.

☐ Deduction: the process of thinking in which the truth or validity of a theory is tested in a specific instance.

12. Stating a theory, forming a hypothesis, observing or collecting data, analyzing and interpreting the data, making a conclusion.

14. ☐ Criterial: lesson clarity, instructional variety, task orientation, engagement in the learning process, moderate-to-high success rate.

☐ Noncriterial: number of credit hours attained, degree held, number of inservice workshops attended, college grades, years of teaching experience.

15. (1) Provide more than a single example.
(2) Use examples that vary in ways that are unimportant to the concept.
(3) Include nonexamples of the concept that also include important dimensions of the concept.
(4) Explain why nonexamples are nonexamples, even though they have some of the same characteristics as examples.

16. ☐ Direct instruction: to elicit a single right answer or reveal level of understanding.

☐ Indirect instruction: to help the student search for and discover an appropriate answer with a minimum of assistance.

17. Questions that present contradictions, probe for deeper responses, extend the discussion, and pass responsibility back to the class.

18. Student-centered or unguided discovery learning. In indirect instruction, student ideas are used as means of accomplishing the goals of the prescribed curriculum.

19. (1) Encouraging students to use examples and references from their experience; (2) asking students to draw parallels and associations from things they already know; (3) relating ideas to students' interests, concerns, and problems.

20. In direct instruction, nearly all instances of the facts, rules, and sequences are likely to be encountered during instruction. This is not true during indirect instruction, so student self-evaluation is essential.

21. Orienting students, providing new or more accurate information, reviewing and summarizing, adjusting the flow of information to more productive areas, and combining ideas and promoting compromise.

22. (1) direct
(2) direct
(3) indirect
(4) indirect
(5) direct
(6) direct
(7) direct
(8) indirect
(9) indirect
(10) indirect
Both models might be used for topics 3, 4, 8, and 10.

CHAPTER 8

1. A question that actively engages a student in the learning process.

2. Structuring, soliciting, reacting.

3. 80%.

4. As high as 80%; as low as 20%.

5. Interest- and attention-getting, diagnosing and checking, recall of specific facts or information, managerial, encourage higher-level thought processes, structure and redirect learning, allow expression of affect.

6. ☐ A convergent question has only a single or small number of correct responses.

☐ A divergent question has no single best answer and generally has multiple answers; however, divergent questions can have wrong answers.

8. If the learner previously has seen and memorized an answer to this question.

9. If the learner arrived at the solution by other than simple recall and memorization, perhaps by reasoning $2 + 2 + 2 + 2 = 8$, which is the same as 2 multiplied by 4.

10. Such questions are unlikely to affect standardized achievement but are likely to increase the learner's analysis, synthesis, and evaluation skills.

16. The time the teacher waits for a student to respond to a question. Generally, beginning teachers should work to increase their wait time.
17. Raising overly complex questions, not being prepared for unusual answers, not knowing the behavioral complexity of the response desired from a question, providing answers to questions before students can respond, using questions as a form of punishment.

CHAPTER 9

1. (1) To actively engage them in the learning process.
   (2) To help them acquire reasoning, critical thinking, and problem-solving skills.
2. (1) Providing when and how to use mental strategies.
   (2) Illustrating how the strategies are to be used.
   (3) Encouraging learners to go beyond the information given.
   (4) Gradually shifting the responsibility for learning to the student.
3. Metacognition refers to the mental processes used by the learner to understand the content being taught. Metacognitive strategies are procedures that assist learners in internalizing, understanding, and recalling the content to be learned.
4. (1) Illustrating the reasoning involved.
   (2) Making students conscious of it.
   (3) Focusing learners on the application of the reasoning illustrated.
6. Mental modeling can help students internalize, recall, and generalize problem solutions to different content at a later time.
7. During mediation, the teacher helps students restructure what they are learning to move them closer to the intended outcome.
8. The "zone of maximum response opportunity" is the content difficulty and behavioral complexity from which the student can most benefit at the moment.
10. Reciprocal teaching provides opportunities to explore the content to be learned via group discussion.
11. □ Asking what students think they will learn from the text.
    □ Reading from text.
    □ Choosing a discussion leader to ask questions regarding text.
    □ Asking the discussion leader to summarize text, and invite comments.
    □ Discussing points that remain unclear, inviting more predictions, and rereading text if needed.
12. To gradually shift the responsibility for learning to the student through scaffolded discussion.
13. To model the same line of reasoning and the same types of questions, prompts, and cues used by the teacher at an earlier stage.
15. Propositional knowledge is intended only for oral and verbal regurgitation. Practical knowledge is used in some problem-solving or decision-making task.
17. □ Provide a new learning task.
    □ Ask the student to explain how he or she will complete the task (for example, learn the content).
    □ Provide another learning task on which the student can try out the new approach.
    □ Model self-questioning behavior for the student as the new material is being learned.
    □ Provide a third opportunity for practice, decreasing your role as monitor.
    □ Check the result by questioning for comprehension.
18. (1) Jingles or trigger sentences
    (2) Narrative-chaining
    (3) Number-rhyme or peg-word
    (4) Chunking

CHAPTER 10

1. (1) Engaging students in the learning process.
   (2) Promoting higher—more complex—patterns of thought.
2. (1) Attitudes and values.
   (2) Prosocial behavior.
   (3) Alternative perspectives and viewpoints.

(4) Integrated identity.

(5) Higher thought processes.

3. (1) Improved collaborative skills.

(2) Better self-esteem.

(3) Increased achievement.

4. (1) Teacher-student interaction.

(2) Student-student interaction.

(3) Task specialization and materials.

(4) Role expectations and responsibilities.

5. (1) Specifying the goal.

(2) Structuring the task.

(3) Teaching the collaborative process.

(4) Monitoring group performance.

(5) Debriefing.

6. ☐ Written group reports

☐ Test achievement

☐ Oral performance

☐ Enumeration of issues

☐ Critique

☐ Reference list

7. 4 or 5 members.

8. (1) Ask students to list peers.

(2) Randomly assign students.

(3) Purposefully form groups heterogeneously.

(4) Share with students the selection process.

9. (1) Request a product that requires a clearly defined division of labor.

(2) Form pairs within groups which have the responsibility of looking over and correcting each other's work.

(3) Visually chart group's progress on individually assigned tasks.

10. (1) Summarizer

(2) Checker

(3) Researcher

(4) Runner

(5) Recorder

(6) Supporter

(7) Observer/Troubleshooter.

11. (1) Grades—individual and group

(2) Bonus points

(3) Social responsibilities

(4) Tokens or privileges

(5) Group contingencies

12. Forming a ratio, with a score for individual effort on top and a score for the group to which the individual belongs on the bottom.

13. (1) Communicating one's own ideas and feelings.

(2) Making messages complete and specific.

(3) Making verbal and nonverbal messages congruent.

(4) Conveying an atmosphere of respect and support.

(5) Assessing if the message was properly received.

(6) Paraphrasing another's point of view.

(7) Negotiating meanings and understandings.

(8) Participating and leading.

14. (1) Repeat or remind group of its assigned role.

(2) Redirect group's effort to more productive area.

(3) Provide emotional support and encouragement.

15. (1) Openly talking about how the groups functioned.

(2) Soliciting suggestions for how the process could be improved.

(3) Getting viewpoints of predesignated observers.

16. (1) Not enough time for group debriefing.

(2) Debriefing stays vague.

(3) Students stay uninvolved.

(4) Written reports are incomplete or messy.

(5) Students exhibit poor collaborative skills.

CHAPTER 11

3. An overachiever is an individual whose school achievement is greater than predicted by a test of intelligence or scholastic aptitude. An underachiever is an individual whose school achievement is less than predicted.

7. Games and simulations, programmed texts, grouping, grades and tests.

8. Use of praise and encouragement, providing explanations, offering to help, accepting diversity, emphasizing reward rather than punishment.

10. Sole provider of information (commander-in-chief), translator or summarizer of student ideas, and equal partner with students in creating ideas and problem solutions; student opinion, student

talk, and spontaneity will increase from the former to the latter.

11 (a) drill and practice
    (b) group discussion
    (c) seatwork

14. Visitor at the door; safety concerning equipment.

15. When the rule cannot be consistently reinforced over a reasonable period of time.

17. (1) Allow no talking.
    (2) Allow no more time than is absolutely necessary.

(3) Make arrangements according to time to be spent, not exercises to be completed.

(4) Give a five-minute and a two-minute warning.

18. Give reasons for the assignment and give assignment immediately following the content presentation to which it is related.

19. (1) Restating highest-level generalization.
    (2) Summarizing key aspects of content taught.
    (3) Providing codes or symbols for remembering the content.

CHAPTER 12

1. Extreme negativity, exclusive authoritarian climate, overreacting, mass punishment, blaming, lack of clear instructional goal, repetition of already learned material, pausing and interruptions, dealing with a single student at length, and lack of recognition of ability levels.

3. Classroom rules cannot effectively deal with all potential misbehaviors.

4. The consistent use of an emotional response diminishes its effectiveness at the time it may be needed most.

5. Those who misbehave seldom belong to the same peer groups as those who behave.

6. Sometimes the exact source of a misbehavior cannot be known with certainty. Blaming the wrong person tends to create long class disruptions during which the wrongly accused student fights back.

7. Open discussions must be crafted to communicate a structure, an end result, and clear expectations of student conduct.

8. There is no mystery, challenge, or curiosity about what is to be learned, and therefore nothing to focus the learners' attention and keep them from more exciting off-task behavior.

9. Visitors at the door and unexpected public address announcements.

10. Silently writing the student's name on the board, calling out the student's name and assigning a pre-

arranged punishment, and pointing to the rear of the room and indicating the student must stand there.

11. By assigning individuals to ability groups and pursuing remedial activities, such as those provided by programmed materials.

13. (1) You alone can be the judge of what occurred, what the proper punishment is, and whether the punishment has been met.
    (2) You provide alternative forms of punishment from which the student must choose.
    (3) You select a punishment from alternatives provided by the students.

16. Punishment does not guarantee that the desirable behavior will occur; the effects of punishment are specific to a particular context and behavior; the effects of punishment can spread to desirable behaviors; punishment can elicit hostile and aggressive responses; punishment can become associated with the punisher.

17. When the desired behavior is made clear at the time of the punishment and when used in conjunction with rewards.

18. (1) To gain support of the parent for assuming some of the responsibility for the discipline-management process.
    (2) To design a plan of action for addressing the problem at home and at school.

CHAPTER 13

2. (1) Dispensing state and federal funds.
   (2) Efficient development and organization of instructional materials, texts, and media.

(3) Training and assignment of instructional staff.

3. A student who cannot learn from the instructional resources designated for the majority of students.

5. ☐ Compensatory: transmitting content by way of alternate modalities to circumvent a fundamental weakness.

   ☐ Remedial: using conventional techniques and practices to repeat instruction to eliminate the weakness.

6. Intelligence, achievement, creativity, and task persistence.

7. It might eliminate gifted students whose tested IQs may not reflect their true intelligence.

8. Applying abstract principles, being curious, giving uncommon responses, showing imagination.

9. Ability to devise organizational approaches; ability to concentrate on detail; self-imposed high standards; persistence in achieving personal goals.

10. Anywhere from being unable to express themselves in English to being marginally proficient in English.

11. A learner who is equally proficient in two languages.

12. Structured immersion allows the student to respond in his or her native language, whereas the transitional method encourages the student to shift to English as soon as possible.

13. Because of the requirement that the handicapped child be educated in the least restrictive environment, some handicapped learners must be taught in the regular classroom, at least part of the time.

14. Physically handicapped, auditorially handicapped, visually handicapped, mentally retarded, emotionally disturbed, learning disabled, speech handicapped, autistic, multiply handicapped.

15. The learning-disabled individual is one who is not achieving commensurately with his or her age and ability levels. A slow learner is one who cannot learn from the instructional resources designated for the average learner.

CHAPTER 14

1. ☐ NRTs compare a student's performance to the performance of a large sample of pupils (called the norm group) representative of those being tested. It is useful when you need to compare a learner's performance to that of others of the same age or grade level.

   ☐ CRTs compare a student's performance to a standard of mastery called a criterion. It is useful when we wish to decide if a student needs more instruction in a certain skill or area of content.

2. (1) Level of cognitive complexity
   (2) Area of instructional content

3. (1) True-False
   (2) Matching
   (3) Multiple-choice
   (4) Completion or short answer

4. (1) Stem clues.
   (2) Grammatical clues.
   (3) Redundant words/unequal response length.
   (4) Use of "all of the above"/"none of the above."

5. (1) Pictorial, graphical, or tabular stimuli.
   (2) Analogues that demonstrate relationships among terms.
   (3) Application of previously learned principles or procedures.

6. ☐ Extended-response: Allows student to determine the length and complexity of a response. It is most useful when the problem provides little or no structure and outcomes at the synthesis and evaluation levels are desired.

   ☐ Restricted response: poses a specific problem for which the student must recall proper information, organize it, derive a defensible conclusion, and express it within the limits of the problem. It is most useful when the problem posed is structured and outcomes at the application and analysis levels are desired.

7. (1) Higher-level cognitive processes have been taught and are to be tested.
   (2) Only a few tests need be graded.
   (3) Test security is a consideration.

8. ☐ Advantages: they require students to utilize higher-level cognitive processes, some topics and objectives are best suited for them, and they can measure communication skills pertinent to a subject area.

   ☐ Disadvantages: they are tedious to read and score, may be influenced by communication skills of the learner, and may involve some degree of subjectivity on the part of the scorer.

9. A guide written in advance, indicating the criteria or components of an acceptable answer.

10. (1) Content
    (2) Organization
    (3) Process
    (4) Accuracy/reasonableness
    (5) Completeness/internal consistency
    (6) Originality/creativity

11. (1) Group similar items together.
    (2) Arrange items from easy to hard.
    (3) Properly space items.
    (4) Keep items and options on same page.
    (5) Place illustrations near descriptive material.
    (6) Check for randomness.
    (7) Decide how students will record answers.
    (8) Provide space for name.
    (9) Check directions for clarity.
    (10) Proofread the test.

12. ☐Validity—does the test measure what it is supposed to measure?
    ☐Reliability—does the test yield the same or similar scores consistently?
    ☐Accuracy—does the test approximate an individual's true level of knowledge, skill, or ability?

13. (1) Content
    (2) Concurrent
    (3) Predictive

14. (1) Test-retest
    (2) Alternate form
    (3) Internal consistency

15. ☐Validity, approximately .60–.80 or higher
    ☐Reliability, approximately .80–.90 or higher
    ☐1.0

16. Comparisons with:
    (1) Other students
    (2) Established standards
    (3) Aptitude
    (4) Actual versus potential effort
    (5) Actual versus potential improvement

17. A test constructed by specialists to determine a student's level of performance relative to other students of similar age and grade.

18. That the student's score associated with the percentile rank was higher than the scores of that percentage of individuals in the norming sample—or that in the norming sample the percent indicated scored lower than this individual.
    (1) It is not the percent of correct answers.
    (2) The extreme or end points of a percentile distribution tend to be spread out, while percentiles toward the center tend to be compressed, making comparisons between the same number of points at different portions of the scale difficult.

APPENDIX C

Formative Observation of Effective Teaching Practices Instrument

---

(See reference to this instrument in the section "Formative Observation of Effective Teaching Practices" in Chapter 15.)

The instrument (Figure C.1) contains 28 behaviors alongside which you can place a checkmark when you observe a particular effectiveness or ineffectiveness indicator. Your observations may lead you to check an *ineffective* practice, an *effective* practice, or *both*, in which case a teacher may have exhibited behaviors associated with both effective *and* ineffective teaching. When the lesson does not provide the opportunity to observe a particular teaching effectiveness indicator, write the code "N/A" for not applicable beside it.

The purpose of observing and recording your observations is to reflect upon what you see for *your own self-improvement*. (The purpose is not to make conclusions about individual teachers, for which your brief period and frequency of observation would be inadequate.) We call this a "formative" observation instrument to underscore its use in helping to *form* or mold effective teaching behaviors instead of to grade, test, or evaluate.

Following are three classroom dialogues with which you can practice "seeing" some of the behaviors identified on the instrument and discussed in Chapter 15. Additional practice dialogues and observation instruments appear in the companion text to this volume, *Observation Skills for Effective Teaching* (Borich, 1990).

DIALOGUE 1

The scene is a hard-to-handle lower-track junior high life science class in which the teacher is presenting a lesson on reproductive systems. Her goal is to teach the biological foundations of sexual reproduction required by the curriculum guide. This class is designed as an introduction to a unit on sex education to be taught the following semester. The teacher has taught for a year and a half and is certified in social studies (major) and biology (minor). The dialogue begins on page 524.

FIGURE C.1

Formative Observation of Effective Teaching Practices Instrument

Key Behavior	Indicators of Effectiveness	Observed* (√)	Observed* (√)	Indicators of Lack of Effectiveness
Clarity	1. Informs learners of skills or understandings expected at end of lesson			Fails to link lesson content to how and at what level of complexity the content will be used
	2. Provides learners with an advance organizer with which to place lesson content in perspective			Starts presenting content without first introducing the topic in some larger context
	3. Checks for task-relevant prior learning at beginning of lesson and reteaches when necessary			Moves to new content without checking understanding of prerequisite facts or concepts
	4. Gives directives slowly and distinctly; checks for understanding along the way			Presents too many directives at once or too quickly
	5. Knows learners' ability levels and teaches at or slightly above their current level of functioning			Fails to recognize that the instruction is under or over the heads of students
	6. Uses examples, illustrations, or demonstrations to explain and to clarify content in text and workbooks			Restricts presentation to oral reproduction of text or workbook
	7. Ends lesson with review or summary			Fails to restate or review main ideas at the end of the lesson
Variety	8. Uses attention-gaining devices			Begins lesson without full attention of most learners
	9. Shows enthusiasm and animation through variation in eye contact, voice, and gestures			Speaks in monotone and/or is motionless; lacks external signs of emotion
	10. Varies activities with which the instructional stimuli are presented (e.g., lecturing, questioning, discussion, practice [daily])			Uses single instructional activity for long periods at a time and/or infrequently alters the modality through which learning is to occur (seeing, listening, doing)
	11. Uses a mix of rewards and reinforcers (weekly, monthly)			Fails to provide rewards and reinforcements that are timely and meaningful to the student

522

Key Behavior	Indicators of Effectiveness		Observed* (√)	Observed* (√)	Indicators of Lack of Effectiveness
Variety (cont'd)	12. Uses student ideas and participation to foster lesson objectives when appropriate (weekly)				Assumes role of sole authority and provider of information; ignores student input
	13. Varies types of questions and probes	Q convergent / divergent			Repeatedly uses only one type of question or probe
		P to clarify / to solicit / to redirect			
Task Orientation	14. Develops unit and lesson plans in accordance with text and curriculum guide				Teaches topics tangential to curriculum guide and adopted text; easily gets side-tracked by student or personal interests
	15. Handles administrative and clerical interruptions efficiently				Uses large amounts of instructional time to complete administrative and clerical tasks
	16. Stops misbehavior with a minimum of disruption to the class				Focuses at length on individual instances of misbehavior during instructional time
	17. Generally, uses direct instruction strategies for teaching Type 1 behaviors and indirect instruction strategies for teaching Type 2 behaviors				Uses inefficient instructional methods for achieving lesson objectives (e.g., confuses drill and practice content with group discussion content)
	18. Establishes end products (e.g., reviews, tests) that are clearly visible to students				Fails to establish clearly identifiable weekly and monthly milestones (e.g., tests and reviews toward which the class works)
Engagement	19. Provides for guided practice				Fails to ask learners to attempt the desired behavior or skill after instruction has been given
	20. Provides correctives for guided practice in a nonevaluative atmosphere				Calls attention to the inadequacy of initial responses
	21. Uses individualized or attention-getting strategies to promote interest among special types of learners when appropriate				Does not attempt to match instructional methods to the learning needs of special students

FIGURE C.1, *concluded*

Key Behavior	Indicators of Effectiveness	Observed* (√)	Observed* (√)	Indicators of Lack of Effectiveness
Engagement *con't*	22. Uses meaningful verbal praise			Always uses same verbal clichés, (e.g., "OK"?) or fails to praise when opportunity occurs
	23. Monitors seatwork by circulating and frequently checking progress			Fails to monitor seatwork or monitors unevenly
Moderate-to-high success rates	24. Unit and lesson organization reflects task-relevant prior learning			Fails to sequence lessons based on task-revelant prior learning
	25. Administers correctives immediately after initial response			Delays in checking and correcting wrong responses after initial practice is completed
	26. Divides lessons into small, easily digestible pieces			Prepares lessons with more content or complexity than can be taught in the allotted time
	27. Plans transitions to new content in small, easy-to-grasp steps			Makes abrupt changes between lesson topics; no sign of "dovetailing"
	28. Establishes momentum (e.g., pacing and intensity gradually build toward major milestones)			Lessons lack changes in pacing (e.g., slower pace after a major event building to a faster pace just before a major event); intensity and tempo **are** static

*Checkmarks may be tallied over repeated observations to accumulate frequencies. Use the code "N/A" for not applicable where appropriate.

TEACHER:	I know everyone will be attentive to today's lesson, because it's about the reproductive cycle. (Some snickering can be heard in the back of the room.) Now this is serious stuff, and I don't want any laughing or fooling around. Who knows some ways by which lower forms of animal life reproduce?
TIM:	Well, one way we studied last year is by dividing in half.
TEACHER:	OK. That is reproduction by fission, in which the parent organism splits into two or more organisms, thereby losing its original identity. It is the way most single-celled animals reproduce. Can anyone think of any other means of reproduction?
TRACY:	Sometimes an egg—or something like an egg—gets fertilized.
TEACHER:	We're just talking about *lower* forms of animal life.
BILL:	Isn't there a way that new life can be created by parts of other things coming together?
TEACHER:	Good. You must be talking about the process called conjugation. This occurs when two similar organisms fuse, exchange nuclear material, and

	then break apart, taking on two different identities. This is the most primitive method of reproduction. Does anyone know of any other ways in which animal life can reproduce?
RICK:	You mean like dogs and cats?
TEACHER:	No! We're not at that point yet. Well, there is one other—and you should know this, because it's in the text. Many multicellular animals reproduce by having male and female reproductive cells, which unite to form a single cell called a zygote—which then divides to form a new organism. The word that describes the union of male and female cells is *fertilization*. In this form of reproduction, half the genes in the zygote come from one parent and half from the other.
MARK:	That's what sex is all about.
TEACHER:	OK . . . speaking out without raising your hand means an extra assignment for tonight. If it happens again, you will have one day in detention. If that doesn't cure you, we will make it two days. Answer all the questions under A, B, and C at the end of Chapter 7. Have you learned your lesson?
MARK:	I suppose so.
TEACHER:	Now, where were we?
BARBARA:	We were talking about zions.
TEACHER:	They're called zygotes. Now in higher animals—including humans—single species are either male or female, according to whether they produce male reproductive cells or female reproductive cells. Somewhere there's a picture of this in your text. The typical male reproductive cell is a sperm, and the typical female reproductive cell is an egg or ovum.
UNIDENTIFIED STUDENT:	We know all that!
TEACHER:	That's enough! I don't want to hear anyone . . .
PRINCIPAL:	(Breaking in over the P.A. system) Teachers, I'm sorry to interrupt, but I have an important announcement. Orders for individual and class pictures must be in no later than 3:00 P.M. today. Failure to place your order by that time means you will not receive pictures for this year. While I have your attention, I would like to tell students to remind their parents that tonight is parent-teacher night, and we would like a good turnout, so be sure to remind mom and dad. Thank you. (During the announcement, some students begin leaving their seats and talking with their neighbors.)
TEACHER:	Class isn't over yet, so be quiet and let's get back to work. Open your books to the questions at the end of Chapter 7. Mark, you take the first one. What is reproduction by fission?
MARK:	Fission. Well . . . I'm not sure.
TEACHER:	But I just told you. How could you forget so soon? Debbie?
DEBBIE:	It's reproducing by cellular division or the splitting of an organism into two parts.
TEACHER:	Next, Robert. What's reproduction by fusion?
ROBERT:	It's . . . it's when things come together.
TEACHER:	Mary, could you give us a better answer?
MARY:	It's when two similar organisms fuse, exchange nuclear material, and then divide again, producing new identities.
TEACHER:	That's a perfect answer. OK, class, now let's change our focus to how plant life reproduces, because that's in Chapter 7 too. Does anyone know how plant reproduction differs from animal reproduction? (There is silence for a few seconds.) OK, then, I'll tell you.

DIALOGUE 2

For this example we observe the beginning of an elementary school lesson in arithmetic. Today's lesson is about ratios and proportions and is taught by a teacher who has been at this school for two years and at another school in the same district for three years before that. Math ability does not seem high for most class members, and they have been noticeably anxious about an upcoming unit test. Moreover, some may not have grasped all that they should from earlier lessons in this unit.

TEACHER: Today our goal will be to study ratios and proportions, but using more real-life problems than in previous lessons. Some of you have had trouble learning how to calculate a ratio, so let's back up and review our skills in division. Who can tell me why division is so important in computing a ratio?

MARC: It's because ratios are nothing but division problems.

TEACHER: Yes, that's right, in the sense that ratios can be expressed as one number over another, like this (writes $\frac{4}{8}$ on board). Now, let's look at this cereal box I have here. Sue, take the box in your hands and tell me how full it is.

SUE: Well, I don't exactly know. It feels pretty heavy—I mean it's kind of full.

TEACHER: What if I asked you to tell me how much *kind of full* is?

SUE: I'd say *kind of* means almost full—well, maybe a little less than almost full (class laughs).

TEACHER: I think the class may have thought your answer was humorous because they would like to know what "a little less than almost full" means. Now, because this is a very typical problem—like the kind people face every day at home and at work—it would be nice to express some things more accurately without the use of words, which tend to be very imprecise when used to describe amounts of things. How might we be more precise, John?

JOHN: Let's form a ratio.

TEACHER: OK. But how do we go about forming a ratio to describe the amount of cereal in this box? Can you tell us some more?

JOHN: Well, we need to know how much the box holds.

TEACHER: That's right. You've got the first step. Now, Tim, what's the next step?

TIM: I don't know.

TEACHER: Mary?

MARY: (silence)

TEACHER: Betty? (after 10 seconds)

BETTY: (silence)

TEACHER: Come on, class. You were all doing so well. Somebody make a guess.

BETTY: (without raising her hand) I think we should compare how much the box holds to how much it has in it.

TEACHER: Never speak out without raising your hand, Betty. So, our second step, Betty, is . . .

BETTY: To measure how much is in the box.

TEACHER: That's right. You have just given us the form of a ratio, maybe without even knowing it. That form is (writes on board):

$$\frac{\text{what is}}{\text{what could be}} = \frac{\text{a little less than half full}}{\text{full}}$$

Now comes the hard part. How will we find numbers to put in the top and the bottom of this division problem? Any suggestions?

DANNY: I have an idea. Let's see how many glasses of water the box holds and then see how many glasses of water it takes to fill the box to where the cereal is.

TEACHER: That's a pretty clever idea, but it may have a few problems as well. Bobby, you have your hand up.

BOBBY: The box isn't going to hold water long enough to do the counting.

TEACHER: Right. And what if the box doesn't fill up exactly at a full glass? We'd have to measure in parts or fractions of glasses, and we haven't come to that yet. Let's look on the box and read how the manufacturer measured what's inside (hands box to Terri).

TERRI: It says, "This box contains six 8-ounce servings measured by volume."

TEACHER: So how many ounces does the whole box contain? Let's review (writes on board). You supply the answers as I go down the list.

$$1 \times 8 = 8$$
$$2 \times 8 = 16$$
$$3 \times 8 = 24$$
$$4 \times 8 = 32$$
$$5 \times 8 = 40$$
$$6 \times 8 = 48$$

So 48 ounces is our total. Now, let's go back to Danny's original idea with the water, but let's measure the contents of the box using ounces. I happen to have an 8-ounce measuring cup. Marc, you pour while the rest of us count.

CLASS: One.

MARC: Where do I empty it?

TEACHER: Let's put it here in the shoe box.

CLASS: Two . . . three . . . four . . . five

MARC: The sixth one's not full.

TEACHER: OK. Read on the side of the cup how full it is.

MARC: It's right at 2 on the cup.

TEACHER: That means 2 ounces. Let's do a little arithmetic. What's our total? Now, who wants to do this problem? (Mary raises her hand)

MARY: Well, we had five full cups, so that's $8 + 8 = 16 + 8 = 24 + 8 = 32$.

CLASS: One more.

MARY: Yea, I guess that's only four, so $32 + 8 = 40$ and then the 2 at the end makes 42.

TEACHER: OK. Now we have all that we need to create a ratio to describe exactly how full the box was. What does this ratio look like, class?

CLASS: 42 over 48 (teacher writes):

$$\frac{42}{48} = \frac{\text{what is}}{\text{what could be}}$$

TEACHER: Because you've learned this so well, we will move on to our next topic. But first, I need to get some overheads from my drawer. No talking, except in a soft voice.

DIALOGUE 3

This dialogue is from a high school English class for which the curriculum guide specifies a unit on poetry appreciation. Because the curriculum guide is vague about how to achieve this outcome, the teacher decides the best way to appreciate poetry is first to learn its fundamentals. To accomplish this he decides to introduce the unit with a lesson on poetic meter. This teacher has taught 11 years but has been at this school only one year after being transferred from another school to fill a midyear vacancy.

TEACHER: I want you to listen to a brief excerpt of two popular songs being played on the radio. I think you'll recognize them. Here they are—listen carefully. (Turns tape recorder on until about half of each song is played.) How many like the first song better than the second? (counts 12 hands) Now, how many like the second better? (counts 18 hands) Who can tell me what they like about the first song?

DIANA: I like the beat . . . I guess it's the rhythm.

TEACHER: Anyone care to say why they like the second song?

TOM: Well, I like its beat . . . the way it gets you stirred up inside . . . maybe its rhythm . . . just what Diana said, I guess.

TEACHER: I chose these two songs not only because they are both very popular right now and I knew you would recognize them, but because they have two very different beats or tempos. Because a good number of you chose each one, both tempos seemed to work—but in very different ways. Now: If you were to exchange the words of these two songs but keep the original tempos, do you think the songs would still be as popular as they are? Joan, you have your hand up.

JOAN: It just wouldn't work. The songs would sound silly. The words wouldn't match the rhythm, in my opinion.

TEACHER: Well, I think there would be quite a few who might agree with you. These songwriters had to find the right beat to match the words. Although today we will be talking about poetry and not your favorite songs (class groans in jest), the two have much in common. Poets, like songwriters, must find the right rhythm to match the words. In poetry, concepts such as *beat, tempo,* and *rhythm* are represented by a poem's meter.

To appreciate a poem—and especially to gain the full emotional impact intended by its author—you must be able to recognize its meter, or rhythm. Today I will describe the different meters used by poets. Listen carefully, because toward the end of the period we're going to have a little fun. Because you all groaned, and I knew you would, I plan to play parts of some of the other popular songs—some of your favorites—and then ask if you see any resemblance between their rhythms and the four types of poetic meter I will now describe. Let's begin by examining what meter is. Anyone care to venture a guess? (Debby raises her hand)

DEBBY: Well, meter is a form of measurement, like in millimeter or kilometer.

TEACHER: That's a good beginning. You've gone right to the root of the word itself. And, surprising to some people, it also is a form of measurement in poetry. So we're off to a good start. Because I don't think anyone would be interested in the length and width of a poem, how is meter used in poetry?

RUTH: Well, could it be to measure its rhythm, or what Diana meant when she used the word *beat?*

TEACHER: Correct. You've made the transfer from measuring something physical with the concept of meter to measuring what we will call *verse.* But maybe we should define verse. Any ideas?

ROLAND: It's like the lyrics in a song . . . the words, kind of . . . but they wouldn't look right if you saw them written out, only if they're sung or read out loud.

TEACHER: Yes. The lyrics in a song have much in common with verse in a poem, because both are the vehicles that convey the author's message. Now, *how* a poet communicates his or her message is just as important as *what* is communicated—just as you pointed out in the two songs I played, when you said the words wouldn't work if sung to the other song's rhythm. The poet has to get the rhythm right, otherwise the words—or verse— might not convey the message. To do this, the poet must choose an appropriate meter, which requires making a number of decisions; it's not as simple as it looks.

Today we will look at just one of these, called the *foot*. In the next few lessons we will cover the others, which will lead us to an appreciation of how the poet arranges the number of syllables to a line, creates a pattern among various lines by the use of rhyme, and forms groups of two or sometimes three lines, which are called *stanzas*. So—what's a foot?

RICH: It's what you put your socks over (class snickers).

TEACHER: No talking out without raising your hand. This is a warning, Richard. A foot is the way in which syllables in a line of poetry are accented. A foot consists of one accented syllable accompanied by one or two unaccented syllables. The accented syllable may precede or follow either one or two unaccented syllables in a regularly recurring sequence throughout the line. Let's look at this line on the transparency to actually see what I mean (switches on overhead).

Bŭt tár/riĕs yét / thĕ caúse / fŏr whích / hĕ díed.

(writing on board) This symbol "ˇ" means an unaccented syllable and this "´" means an accented syllable. What kind of consistent pattern do you see and hear? (reads line)

TOBY: Well, it's kind of singsong.

TEACHER: What do you mean by singsong?

TOBY: One unaccented syllable always precedes one accented syllable.

TEACHER: That's right. And, in fact, the poet wanted this line to vary, just as you said, in a down-up or singsong-type pattern, because that's the rhythm he felt would best convey his message. We will look at the rest of the lines of this poem later to get its full meaning, but for now you've gotten the idea of a foot and of meter. By the way, how many feet are in this line, Toby?

TOBY: Four.

TEACHER: No! You're not being careful. Mary, how many are there?

MARY: Five.

TEACHER: Very good. The pattern repeats itself five times. This type of pattern is called an *iamb* or an *iambic foot*. It is only the first of four different ways of accenting syllables that we will study. Before looking at some examples of these, let's practice recognizing the iambic foot. On the next four lines of poetry, place the accents where you think they should go to create an iambic foot. When you're finished, look up and I'll give you my answers. Oops, someone's at the door. Sue, would you take a message.

SUE: (whispering) It's a counselor.

TEACHER: When you've finished with these four, go on to the iambic exercise marked *D* at the end of Chapter 11. Check your work with the answer key in the appendix. I'll give bonus discussion points for those who get them all right. (Goes to door.)

References

American Association of School Administrators. (1988). *Teenage pregnancy: Developing life options*. Arlington, VA: Author.

Anderson, J. R. (1980). *Cognitive psychology and its implications*. San Francisco: W. H. Freeman.

Anderson, L., & Block, J. (1987). Mastery learning models. In M. J. Dunkin (Ed.), *International encyclopedia of teaching and teacher education* (pp. 58–67). New York: Pergamon.

Anderson, L., Evertson, C., & Brophy, J. (1982). *Principles of small group instruction in elementary reading*. East Lansing: Michigan State University, Institute for Research on Teaching.

Anderson, L., Stevens, D., Prawat, R., & Nickerson, J. (1988). Classroom task environments and students' task-related beliefs. *The Elementary School Journal, 88,* 181–296.

Armento, B. (1977). Teacher behaviors related to student achievement on a social science test. *Journal of Teacher Education, 28,* 46–52.

Ausubel, D. (1968). *Educational psychology: A cognitive view*. New York: Holt, Rinehart & Winston.

Baca, L., & Cervantes, H. (1984). *The bilingual special education interface*. Santa Clara, CA: Times Mirror/Mosby.

Barnes, J. (1987). Teaching experience. In M. J. Dunkin (Ed.), *International encyclopedia of teaching and teacher education* (pp. 608–611). New York: Pergamon.

Becker, W. (1977). Teaching reading and language to the disadvantaged—what we have learned from field research. *Harvard Educational Review, 47,* 518–543.

Bellack, A., Kliebard, H., Hyman, R., & Smith, F. (1966). *The language of the classroom*. New York: Teachers College Press.

Bennett, N., & Desforges, C. (1988). Matching classroom tasks to students' attainments. *The Elementary School Journal, 88,* 221–224.

Bennett, N., Desforges, C., Cockburn, A., & Wilkinson, B. (1981). *The quality of pupil learning experiences: Interim report*. Lancaster, England: University of Lancaster, Centre for Educational Research and Development.

Berk, L. (1990). Relationship of elementary school children's private speech to behavioral accompaniment to task, attention and task performance. *Developmental Psychology, 26.*

Berliner, D. (1970). Tempus educare. In P. Peterson and H. Walberg (Eds.), *Research on teaching: Concepts, findings and implications* (pp. 120–135). Berkeley, CA: McCutchan.

Bettencourt, E., Gillett, M., Gall, M., & Hull, R. (1983). Effects of teacher enthusiasm training on student on-task behavior and achievement. *American Educational Research Journal, 20,* 435–450.

Block, J. (1987). Mastery learning models. In M. J. Dunkin (Ed.), *International encyclopedia of teaching and teaching education*. New York: Pergamon.

Bloom, B. (1981). *All our children learning*. New York: McGraw-Hill.

Bloom, B. (1982). *Human interactions and school learning*. New York: McGraw-Hill.

Bloom, B., Englehart, M., Hill, W., Furst, E., & Krathwohl, D. (1956). *Taxonomy of educational objectives: The classification of educational goals.*

Handbook I: Cognitive domain. New York: Longman Green.

Bodwin, F. (1957). *The relationship between immature self-concept and certain educational disabilities.* Unpublished doctoral dissertation, Michigan State University, East Lansing.

Borich, G. (1990). *Observation skills for effective teaching.* Columbus, OH: Merrill/Macmillan.

Borich, G. (1992). *Clearly outstanding: Making each day count in your classroom.* Boston: Allyn & Bacon.

Borich, G., & Fuller, F. (1974). *Manual for teacher concerns checklist: An instrument for measuring concerns for self, task and impact.* Austin, TX: College of Education, 518, University of Texas at Austin.

Borich, G., & Nance, D. (1990). *The effective teacher program.* Professional Teachers' Library, 1009 Harwood Pl., Austin, TX 78704.

Bradstad, B., & Stumph, S. (1982). *A guidebook for teaching study skills and motivation.* Boston: Allyn & Bacon.

Brookover, W., Paterson, A., & Thomas, S. (1962). *Self-concept of ability and school achievement. Final report of Cooperative Research Project No. 845.* (Contract with U.S. Department of Health, Education and Welfare, Office of Education.) East Lansing: Michigan State University.

Brophy, J. (1981). Teacher praise: A functional analysis. *Review of Educational Research, 51,* 5–32.

Brophy, J. (Ed.). (1989). *Advances in research on teaching* (Vol. 1). Greenwich, CT: JAI Press.

Brophy, J., & Evertson, C. (1976). *Process-product correlations in the Texas Teacher Effectiveness Study: Final Report* (Research Report 74–4). Austin: University of Texas, Research and Development Center for Teacher Education. (ERIC Document Reproduction Service No. ED 091 094)

Brophy, J., & Evertson, C. (1976). *Learning from teaching: A developmental perspective.* Boston: Allyn & Bacon.

Brophy, J., & Good, T. (1974). *Teacher-student relationships: causes and consequences.* New York: Holt, Rinehart & Winston.

Brophy, J., & Good, T. (1986). Teacher behavior and student achievement. In M. C. Wittrock (Ed.), *Handbook of research on teaching* (3rd ed.) (pp. 328–375). New York: Macmillan.

Brown, G., & Edmondson, R. (1984). Asking questions. In E. Wragg (Ed.), *Classroom teaching skills* (pp. 97–119). New York: Nichols.

Bruner, J. (1978). The role of dialogue in language acquisition. In A. Sinclair, R. Jarvella, & W. Levelt (Eds.), *The child's conception of language* (pp. 241–256). New York: Springer-Verlag.

Bunderson, V., & Faust, G. (1976). Programmed and computer-assisted instruction. In N. L. Gage, *The psychology of teaching methods: The seventy-fifth yearbook of the National Society for the Study of Evaluation* (Part I) (pp. 44–90). Chicago: University of Chicago Press.

Calderhead, J. (1983). *Research into teachers' and student teachers' cognitions: Exploring the nature of classroom practice.* Paper presented at the annual meeting of the American Educational Research Association, Montreal, Canada.

Children's Defense Fund. (1986). *Adolescent pregnancy: Whose problem is it?* Washington: Author.

Children's Defense Fund. (1988). *Teenage pregnancy: An advocate's guide to the numbers.* Washington: Author.

Civil Rights Commission. (1973). *Teachers and students. Report V: Differences in teacher intervention with Mexican-American and Anglo students.* Washington: U.S. Government Printing Office.

Clark, C., & Elmore, J. L. (1981). *Transforming curriculum in mathematics, science, and writing: A case study of teacher yearly planning* (Research Series No. 99). East Lansing: Michigan State University, Institute for Research on Teaching.

Clark, C., & Peterson, P. (1986). Teachers' thought processes. In M. C. Wittrock (Ed.), *Handbook of research on teaching* (3rd ed.) (pp. 255–296). New York: Macmillan.

Clark, C., & Yinger, R. (1979). *Three studies of teacher planning* (Research Series No. 55). East Lansing: Michigan State University, Institute for Research on Teaching.

Coffman, W. (1971). Essay examinations. In R. Thorndike (Ed.). *Educational measurement* (2nd ed.). Washington: American Council on Education.

Congressional Record. 89th Cong., 2nd sess., 1978. P. H–12179.

Corey, S. (1940). The teachers out-talk the pupils. *School Review, 48,* 745–752.

Corno, L., & Snow, R. (1986). Adapting teaching to individual differences among learners. In M. C. Wittrock (Ed.), *Handbook of research on teaching* (3rd ed.) (pp. 605–629). New York: Macmillan.

Crawford, J., Gage, N. L., Corno, L., Stayrouk, N., Mitman, A., Schunk, D., & Stallings, J. (1978). *An experiment on teacher effectiveness and parent-assisted instruction in the third grade* (three vols.). Stanford, CA: Center for Educational Research, Stanford University.

Cronbach, L., & Snow, R. (1977). *Aptitudes and instructional methods*. New York: Irvington/Naiburg.

Dahllof, U., & Lundgren, U. P. (1970). *Macro- and micro approaches combined for curriculum process analysis: A Swedish educational field project*. Göteborg, Sweden: University of Göteborg, Institute of Education.

Davis, O., & Tinsley, D. (1967). Cognitive objectives revealed by classroom questions asked by social studies teachers and their pupils. *Peabody Journal of Education*, July, 21–26.

Dembo, M. (1981). *Teaching for learning: Applying educational psychology in the classroom* (2nd ed.). Glenview, IL: Scott, Foresman.

Dishon, D., & O'Leary, P. (1984). *A guidebook for cooperative learning*. Kalamazoo, MI: Learning Publications.

Doneau, S. (1987). Structuring. In M. J. Dunkin (Ed.), *International encyclopedia of teaching and teacher education* (pp. 398–406). New York: Pergamon.

Dowaliby, F., & Schumer, H. (1973). Teacher-centered versus student-centered mode of college classroom instruction as related to manifest anxiety. *Journal of Educational Psychology, 64*, 125–132.

Doyle, W. (1983). Academic work. *Review of Educational Research, 53*, 159–200.

Duffy, G., & Roehler, L. (1989). The tension between information-giving and medication: Perspectives on instructional explanation and teacher change. In J. Brophy (Ed.), *Advances in research on teaching* (Vol. 1, pp. 1–33). Greenwich, CT: JAI Press, Inc.

Duffy, G., Roehler, L., & Herrmann, B. (1988). Modeling mental processes helps poor readers become strategic readers. *The Reading Teacher, 41*(8), 762–767.

Dunkin, M., & Biddle, B. (1974). *The study of teaching*. New York: Holt, Rinehart & Winston.

Eisner, E. (1969). Instructional and expressive educational objectives: Their formulation and use in curriculum. In W. Popham, E. Eisner, H. Sullivan, & L. Tyler, *Instructional objectives. AERA Monograph Series on Curriculum Evaluation, No. 3* (pp. 1–18). Chicago: Rand McNally.

Elbaz, F. (1981). The teacher's "practical knowledge": Report of a case study. *Curriculum Inquiry, 11*, 43–71.

Emmer, E., Evertson, C., & Anderson, L. (1980). Effective classroom management at the beginning of the school year. *The Elementary School Journal, 80*(5), 219–231.

Emmer, E., Evertson, C., Sanford, J., Clements, B., & Worsham, M. (1989). *Classroom management for secondary teachers*. Englewood Cliffs, NJ: Prentice-Hall.

Epstein, J., & Karweit, N. (Eds.). (1983). *Friendships in school*. New York: Academic Press.

Erikson, E. (1968). *Identity, youth and crises*. New York: W. W. Norton.

Evertson, C., & Emmer, E. (1982). Effective management at the beginning of the school year in junior high classes. *Journal of Educational Psychology, 74*, 485–498.

Evertson, C., Emmer, E., Sanford, J., Clements, B., & Worsham, M. (1989). *Classroom management for elementary teachers*. Englewood Cliffs, NJ: Prentice-Hall.

Fielding, G., Kameenui, E., & Gerstein, R. (1983). A comparison of an inquiry and a direct instruction approach to teaching legal concepts and applications to secondary school students. *Journal of Educational Research, 76*, 243–250.

Fisher, C., Berliner, D., Filby, N., Marliave, R., Cahen, L., & Dishaw, M. (1980). Teaching behaviors, academic learning time and student achievement: An overview. In C. Denham and A. Lieberman (Eds.), *Time to learn*. Washington: National Institute of Education.

Fisher, C., Filby, N., Marliave, R., Cahen, L., Dishaw, M., More, J., & Berliner, D. (1978). *Teaching behaviors, academic learning time and student achievement. Final Report of Phase III–B, Beginning Teacher Evaluation Study* (Tech. Rep. No. V–1). San Francisco: Far West Laboratory for Educational Research and Development.

Fisher, C., et al. (1978). *Teaching and learning in the elementary school: A summary of the Beginning Teacher Education Study*. (Beginning Teacher Evaluation Study Report VII–I). San Francisco: Far West Laboratory for Educational Research and Development.

Fitch, M., Drucker, A., & Norton, J. (1957). Frequent testing as a motivating factor in large lecture classes. *Journal of Educational Psychology, 42,* 1–20.

Flanders, N. (1970). Analyzing teacher behavior. Reading, MA: Addison-Wesley.

Fuller, F. (1969). Concerns of teachers: A developmental conceptualization. *American Educational Research Journal, 6,* 207–226.

Fuller, F., & Borich, G. (1974). *Teacher concerns checklist: An instrument for measuring concerns for self, task and impact*. Austin, TX: Research and Development Center for Teacher Education, The University of Texas at Austin.

Gage, N. (1976). A factorially designed experiment on teacher structuring, soliciting and reacting. *Journal of Teacher Education, 16,* 35–38.

Gage, N., & Berliner, D. (1984). *Educational psychology* (3rd ed.). Chicago: Rand McNally.

Gagné, E. (1985). *The cognitive psychology of school learning*. Boston: Little, Brown.

Gagné, R. M. (1977). *The conditions of learning* (3rd ed.). New York: Holt, Rinehart & Winston.

Gagné, R., & Briggs, L. (1979). *Principles of instructional design*. New York: Holt, Rinehart & Winston.

Gall, M. (1970). The use of questions in teaching. *Review of Educational Research, 40,* 707–721.

Gall, M. (1984). Synthesis of research on questioning in recitation. *Educational Leadership, 42* (3), 40–49.

Gall, M., & Gall, J. (1976). The discussion method. In N. L. Gage (Ed.), *The psychology of teaching methods: The seventy-fifth yearbook of the national society for the study of education* (Part I, pp. 166–216). Chicago: University of Chicago Press.

Gall, M., Ward, B., Berliner, D., Cahen, I., Winne, P., Elashoff, J., & Stanton, G. (1978). Effects of questioning techniques and recitation on student learning. *American Educational Research Journal, 15,* 175–199.

Gallup, A., and Elam, S. (1988). The 20th annual Gallup poll. *Phi Delta Kappan, 70* (1), 34–46.

Good, T. (1979). Teacher effectiveness in the elementary school. *Journal of Teacher Education, 30,* 52–64.

Good, T., & Brophy, J. (1987). *Looking in classrooms* (4th ed.). New York: Harper & Row.

Good T., Ebmeier, H., & Beckerman, T. (1978). Teaching mathematics in high and low SES classrooms: An empirical comparison. *Journal of Teacher Education, 29,* 85–90.

Good, T., & Grouws, D. (1979). Teaching effects: A process-product study in fourth grade mathematics classrooms. *Journal of Teacher Education, 28,* 49–54.

Good, T., & Stipek, D. (1983). Individual differences in the classroom: A psychological perspective. In G. D. Fenstermacher & J. I. Goodlad (Eds.), *Individual differences and the common curriculum* (82nd yearbook of the National Society for the Study of Education, Part 2, pp. 9–43). Chicago: University of Chicago Press.

Goodlau, J. (1984). *A place called school*. New York: McGraw-Hill.

Green, J. (1983). Research on teaching as a linguistic process: A state of the art. In E. W. Godon (Ed.), *Review of research in education 10* (pp. 151–252). Washington: American Educational Research Association.

Hansford, B., & Hattie, J. (1982). The relationship between self and achievement/performance measures. *Review of Educational Research, 52,* 123–142.

Harris, L. and Associates. (1986). *American teens speak: Sex, myths, TV, and birth control—The Planned Parenthood poll*. New York, NY: Planned Parenthood Federation of America.

Harrow, A. (1969). *A taxonomy of the psychomotor domain: A guide for developing behavioral objectives*. New York: David McKay.

Hawking, S. (1988). *A brief history of time*. New York: Bantam Books.

Haynes, H. (1935). *The relation of teacher intelligence, teacher experience and type of school to type of questions*. Unpublished doctoral dissertation, George Peabody College for Teachers, Nashville, TN.

Hermann, G. (1971). Egrule vs. ruleg teaching methods: Grade, intelligence and category of learning. *Journal of Experimental Education, 39* (3), 22–33.

Hill, H. (1989). *Effective strategies for teaching minority students*. Bloomington, IN: National Educational Service.

Hodgkinson, H. (1986). Today's numbers, tomorrow's nation. *Education Week,* May 14, 14–15.

Hodgkinson, H. (1988). *All one system: Demographics of education, kindergarten through graduate school*. Washington: The Institute for Educational Leadership.

Hunt, G. (1979). Psychological development: early experience. *Annual Review of Psychology,* 103–143.

Hunter, M. (1982). *Mastery teaching*. El Segundo, CA: Instructional Dynamics, Inc.

Jackson, P. (1968). *Life in classrooms*. New York: Holt, Rinehart & Winston.

Jensen, A. (1969). How much can we boost IQ and scholastic achievement? *Harvard Educational Review, 39* (1), 1–123.

Johnson, D., & Johnson, R. (1987). *Learning together and alone* (2nd ed.). Englewood Cliffs, NJ: Prentice-Hall, Inc.

Joyce, B. (1978–1979). Toward a theory of information processing in teaching. *Educational Research Quarterly, 3* (4), 66–77.

Kaplan, A. (1964). *The conduct of inquiry*. San Francisco: Chandler Publishing.

Kaplan, J. (1982). *Beyond behavioral modification: A cognitive-behavioral approach to behavior management in the school*. Portland, OR: ASTEP Education Company.

Kash, M., & Borich, G. (1978). *Teacher behavior and pupil self-concept*. Reading, MA: Addison-Wesley.

Kim, E., & Kellough, R. (1978). *A resource guide for secondary teaching* (2nd ed.). New York: Macmillan.

Kounin, J. (1970). *Discipline and group management in the classroom*. New York: Holt, Rinehart & Winston.

Krathwohl, D., Bloom, B., & Masia, B. (1964). *Taxonomy of educational objectives. The classification of educational goals. Handbook II: Affective domain*. New York: David McKay.

Kubiszyn, T., & Borich, G. (1990). *Educational testing and measurement: Classroom application and practice* (3rd ed.). Glenview, IL: Scott, Foresman.

La Berge, D., & Samuels, S. (1974). Toward a theory of automatic information processing in reading. *Cognitive Psychology, 6,* 293–323.

Land, M. L. (1987). Vagueness and clarity. In M. J. Dunkin (Ed.), *Encyclopedia of teaching and teacher education* (pp. 292–397). New York: Pergamon.

Land, M., & Smith L. (1979). The effect of low inference teacher clarity inhibitors on student achievement. *Journal of Teacher Education, 31,* 55–57.

Leinhardt, G. (1983). *Overview of a program of research on teachers' and students' routines, thoughts and execution of plans*. Paper presented at the annual meeting of the American Educational Research Association, Montreal.

Levin, H. (1986). *Educational reform for disadvantaged students: An emerging crisis*. Washington: National Education Association.

Levine, D. (1979). Concentrated poverty and reading achievement in seven big cities. *The Urban Review,* Summer, 63–80.

Levine, D., & Havinghurst, R. (1984). *Society and education* (6th ed.). Boston: Allyn & Bacon.

Levis, D. S. (1987). Teachers' personality. In M. J. Dunkin (Ed.), *Encyclopedia of teaching and teacher education* (pp. 585–588). New York: Pergamon.

Lewin, K., Lippitt, Z., & White, R. (1939). Patterns of aggressive behavior in experimentally created social climates. *Journal of Social Psychology, 10,* 271–299.

Lightfoot, S. (1983). *The good high school*. New York: Basic Books.

Luiten, J., Ames, W., & Aerson, G. (1980). A meta-analysis of advance organizers on learning and retention. *American Educational Research Journal, 17,* 211–218.

Lysakowski, R., & Walberg, H. (1981). Classroom reinforcement and learning: A quantitative synthesis. *Journal of Educational Research, 75,* 69–77.

Martin, J. (1979). Effects of teacher higher-order questions on student process and product variables in a single classroom study. *Journal of Educational Research, 72,* 183–187.

Marx, R., & Peterson, P. (1981). The nature of teacher decision-making. In B. Joyce, C. Brown, & L. Peck (Eds.), *Flexibility in teaching: An excursion into the nature of teaching and training*. New York: Longman.

Marx, R., & Walsh, J. (1988). Learning from academic tasks. *The Elementary School Journal, 88* (3), 207–219.

McDonald, F., Elias, P., Stone, M., Wheeler, P., & Lambert, M. (1975). *Final report on Phase II Beginning Teacher Evaluation Study*. Prepared for the California Commission on Teacher Preparation and Licensing, Sacramento, CA. Princeton, NJ: Educational Testing Service.

McKenzie, R. (1979). Effects of questions and testlike events on achievement and on-task behavior in a classroom concept learning presentation. *Journal of Educational Research, 72*, 348–350.

McNair, K. (1978–1979). Capturing inflight decisions. *Educational Research Quarterly, 3*(4), 26–42.

Melton, R. (1978). Resolution of conflicting claims concerning the effect of behavioral objectives on student learning. *Review of Educational Research, 48*, 291–302.

Morine, G. (1973). Planning skills: Paradoxical parodies. *Journal of Teacher Education, 24*, 135–143.

Morine-Dershimer, G. (1977). *What's in a plan? Stated and unstated plans for lessons*. Paper presented at the annual meeting of the American Educational Research Association, New York.

Morine, H., & Morine, G. (1973). *Discovery: A challenge to teachers*. Englewood Cliffs, NJ: Prentice-Hall.

Moskowitz, G., & Hayman, J. (1976). Success strategies of inner-city teachers: A year-long study. *Journal of Educational Research, 69*, 283–289.

National Center for Education Statistics. (1980). *High school and beyond study*. Washington: Author.

National Research Council. (1987). Risking the future: *Adolescent sexuality, pregnancy, and childbearing*. Washington: Author.

Newson, J., & Newson, E. (1976). *Seven years old in the home environment*. London: Allen & Unwin.

O'Banion, D., & Whaley, D. (1981). *Behavior contracting: Arranging contingencies of reinforcement*. New York: Springer.

Palincsar, A. (1987). *Discourse for learning about comprehending text*. Paper presented at the National Reading Conference, St. Petersburg Beach, FL.

Palincsar, A., & Brown, A. (1989). Classroom dialogues to promote self-regulated comprehension. In J. Brophy (Ed.), *Advances in research on teaching* (Vol. 1, pp. 35–71). Greenwich, CT: JAI Press, Inc.

Polanyi, M. (1958). *Personal knowledge*. Chicago: University of Chicago Press.

Posner, G. (1987). Pacing and sequencing. In M. J. Dunkin (Ed.), *Encyclopedia of teaching and teacher education* (pp. 266–271). New York: Pergamon.

Public Law 94–142, The Education for All Handicapped Children Act, 20 U.S.C. 1401 et seq., 89 Stat. 773 (November 29, 1975).

Redfield, D., & Rousseau, E. (1981). A meta-analysis of experimental research on teacher questioning behavior. *Review of Educational Research, 51*, 237–245.

Reigeluth, C. (1983). In C. M. Reigeluth (Ed.), *Instructional-design theories and models: An overview of their current status*. Hillsdale, NJ: Erlbaum.

Rich, D. (1987). *Teachers and parents: An adult-to-adult approach*. Washington: National Education Association.

Rist, R. (1970). Student social class and teaching expectations: The self-fulfilling prophecy in ghetto education. *Harvard Educational Review, 40*, 411–451.

Rohrkemper, M., & Corno, L. (1988). Success and failure on classroom tasks: Adaptive learning and classroom teaching. *The Elementary School Journal, 88*(3), 298–312.

Rosenshine, B. (1970a). Enthusiastic teaching: A research review. *School Review, 78*, 499–514.

Rosenshine, B. (1970b). Experimental classroom studies of indirect teaching. *Classroom Interaction Newsletter, 5*(2), 7–11.

Rosenshine, B. (1971a). Objectively measured behavioral predictors of effectiveness in explaining. In I. D. Westbury & A. A. Bellock (Eds.), *Research into classroom processes* (pp. 51–100). New York: Teachers College Press.

Rosenshine, B. (1971b). *Teaching behaviors and student achievement*. London: National Foundation for Educational Research in England and Wales.

Rosenshine, B., (1983). Teaching functions in instructional programs. *The Elementary School Journal, 83*, 335–351.

Rosenshine, B., & Stevens, R. (1986). Teaching functions. In M. C. Wittrock (Ed.), *Handbook of research on teaching* (3rd ed., pp. 376–391). New York: Macmillan.

Rotter, J., Robinson, E., & Fey, M. (1987). *Parent-teaching conferencing*. Washington: National Educational Association.

Rowe, M. B. (1974). Wait-time and rewards as instructional variables, their influence on language, logic, and fate control: Part one—wait-time. *Journal of Research in Science Teaching, 11,* 81–94

Rutherford, L. (1986). *Economics in a modern world.* Columbus: Intex.

Ryan, F. (1973). Differentiated effects of levels of questioning on student achievement. *The Elementary School Journal, 41,* 63–67.

Samuels, S. (1981). Some essentials of decoding. *Exceptional Education Quarterly, 2,* 11–25.

Scott, J., & Bushell, D. (1974). The length of teacher contacts and students' off task behavior. *Journal of Applied Behavior Analysis, 7,* 39–44.

Sharan, S. (1980). Cooperative learning in small groups. *Review of Educational Research, 50,* 241–271.

Singer, H., & Donlon, D. (1982). Active comprehension problem-solving schema with question generation for comprehension of complex short stories. *Reading Research Quarterly, 17,* 116–186.

Slavin, R. (1980). Effects of student teams and peer tutoring on academic achievement and time on task. *Journal of Experimental Education, 48,* 252–257.

Slavin, R. (1981). Student team learning. *The Elementary School Journal, 82,* 5–17.

Slavin, R. (1983). *Cooperative learning.* New York: Longman.

Slavin, R. (1987). *Cooperative learning: Student teams* (2nd ed.). Washington: National Education Association.

Slavin, R., Leavey, M., & Madden, N. (1982). *Combining cooperative learning and individualized instruction: Effects on student mathematics achievement, attitudes and behaviors.* Baltimore: Johns Hopkins University, Center for Social Organization of Schools.

Slavin, R., Sharan, S., Kagan, S., Hertz-Lazarowitz, R., Webb, C., & Schmuck, R. (1985). *Learning to cooperate, cooperating to learn.* New York: Plenum Press.

Sleeter, C., & Grant, C. (1986). Success of all students. *Phi Delta Kappan, 68,* 298.

Smilansky, M. (1979). *Priorities in education: Preschool, evidence and conclusions.* Washington: World Bank.

Smith, B., & Meux, M. (1970). *A study of the logic of teaching.* Champaign: University of Illinois.

Smith, E., & Sendelback, N. (1979). *Teacher intentions for science instruction and their antecedents in program materials.* Paper presented at the annual meeting of the American Educational Research Association, San Francisco.

Smith, G. (1985). *Understanding grammar* (pp. 101–103). New York: City Press.

Smith, L., & Land, M. (1981). Low inference verbal behaviors related to teacher clarity. *Journal of Classroom Interaction, 17,* 37–42.

Soar, R., & Soar, C. (1973). *Follow through classroom process measurement and pupil growth (1970–1971, Final Report).* Gainesville: University of Florida, Institute for Development of Human Resources (ERIC Document Reproduction Service No. ED 106 297).

Spielberger, C. (Ed.) (1966). *Anxiety and behavior.* New York: Academic Press.

Stallings, J., & Kaskowitz, D. (1974). *Follow through classroom observation evaluation* (SRI Project URU–7370). Stanford, CA: Stanford Research Institute.

Stallings, J., & Keepes, B. (1970). *Student aptitudes and methods for teaching beginning reading: A predictive instrument for determining interaction patterns. Final report* (Project No. 9–1–099, Report OEG–9–70–0005). Washington: U.S. Department of Health, Education and Welfare, Office of Education, Bureau of Research.

Sternberg, R. (1986). *Intelligence applied.* New York: Harcourt Brace Jovanovich.

The Alan Guttmacher Institute. (1986). *Teenage pregnancy in industrialized countries.* New York: Author.

Thurstone, L. (1947). *Primary mental abilities, Form AH.* Chicago: Science Research Associates.

Tobin, K. (1980). The effect of an extended teacher wait-time on science achievement. *Journal of Research in Science Teaching, 17,* 469–475.

Tobin, K., & Capie, W. (1982). Relationships between classroom process variables and middle-school science achievement. *Journal of Educational Psychology, 74,* 441–454.

Tomlinson, P., & Hunt, D. (1971). Differential effects of rule-example order as a function of learner conceptual level. *Canadian Journal of Behavioral Science, 3,* 237–245.

Tyler, R. (1934). *Constructing achievement tests.* Columbus: Ohio State University Press.

U.S. Department of Education. (1986). *What works: Schools without drugs*. Washington: Author.

U.S. General Accounting Office (1987). *Bilingual education: A new look at the research evidence* (GAO/PEMD–87–12BR). Gaithersburg, MD: Author.

Vygotsky, L. (1962). *Thought and language*. Cambridge, MA: MIT Press.

Vygotsky, L. (1978). In M. Cole, et al. (Ed.). *Mind in society: The development of higher psychological processes*. Cambridge, MA: Harvard University Press.

Walberg, H. (1986). Syntheses of research on teaching. In M. C. Wittrock (Ed.), *Handbook of research on teaching* (3rd ed., pp. 214–229). New York: Macmillan.

Wang, M., & Lindvall, C. (1984). Individual differences and school learning environments. *Review of Research in Education, 11,* 161–225.

Weiner, B. (1972). *Theories of motivation: From mechanism to cognition*. Chicago: Markham.

Wiertsch, J. (1980). The significance of dialogue in Vygotsky's account of social, egocentric, and inner speech. *Contemporary Educational Psychology, 5,* 150–162.

Winne, R. (1979). Experiments relating teachers' use of high cognitive questions to student achievement. *Review of Educational Research, 49,* 13–50.

Wragg, E., & Wood, E. (1984). Teachers' first encounters with their classes. In E. Wragg (Ed.), *Classroom teaching skills* (pp. 47–78). New York: Nichols.

Wyne, M., & Stuck, G. (1982). Time and learning: Implications for the classroom teacher. *The Elementary School Journal, 83,* 67–75.

Zahorik, J. (1987). Reacting. In M. J. Dunkin (Ed.), *Encyclopedia of teaching and teacher education* (pp. 416–423). New York: Pergamon.

Zakariya, S. (1987). How to keep your balance when it comes to bilingual education. *The American School Board Journal, 6,* 21–26.

Zenger, W., & Zenger, S. (1982). *Curriculum planning: A ten-step process*. Palo Alto, CA: R and E Research Associates.

AUTHOR INDEX

ABOUT THE AUTHOR

Gary Borich grew up on the south side of Chicago, where he attended Mendel High School and later taught in the Chicago school system of Niles, Illinois. He received his Ph.D. from Indiana University, where he was director of evaluation at the Institute for Child Study under Nicholas J. Anastasiow. Dr. Borich presently is a member of the College of Education faculty at the University of Texas at Austin and a member of the Board of Examiners of the National Council for the Accreditation of Teacher Education.

Dr. Borich's other books include *Clearly Outstanding: Making Each Day Count in Your Classroom, Observation Skills for Effective Teaching, Educational Testing and Measurement* (with T. Kubiszyn), and *The Effective Teacher Program* (with D. Nance; an in-service mentoring curriculum for beginning teachers).

Dr. Borich lives in Austin, Texas with his wife, Kathy (a school teacher) and his two children, Brandy and Damon. His interests include training and riding Arabian horses, and pre-Columbian pottery.